Communicating Personal Information (continued)

SKILL BUILDERS ● Constructively Criticizing

SKILL	USE	PROCEDURE	EXAMPLE
Diplomatically describing the specific negative behaviors or actions of another and the their effects on others	To help people see themselves as others see them	1. Begin by asking permission to disclose negative personal feedback. 2. Whenever possible, preface negative statements with positive ones. 3. Describe the person's behavior or action. 4. Be as specific as possible. 5. When appropriate, suggest how the person can change the behavior or action.	Carol says, "Bob, I've noticed something about your behavior with Jenny. Would you like to hear it?" After Bob assures her that he would, Carol continues: "Although you seem really supportive of Jenny, there are times when Jenny starts to relate an experience and you interrupt her and finish telling the story. You did this a few times while Jenny was trying to talk about her trip to Colorado, and she looked a little hurt. She's pretty sensitive about being interrupted, so you might want to try to let her finish her stories the rest of this evening or she might get upset."

Using Interpersonal Influence

SKILL BUILDERS ● Complaining

SKILL	USE	PROCEDURE	EXAMPLE
"Sending" or "communicating" messages that tell someone that you find what is or has occurred unacceptable because it has violated your rights or expectations	To assert your rights and expectations when they have been violated	1. Begin by doing facework. 2. Describe what has happened that you believe violates your rights or expectations. 3. Explain why what has happened violates your rights or expectations. 4. Describe how you feel about what has happened. 5. Ask the person to comment on or paraphrase what you have said.	Colin ordered his food over twenty minutes ago. The people at two tables seated after him have eaten and left. Colin decides to complain, saying "Excuse me. I can see that things are really busy, but I ordered my food about twenty minutes ago, and two tables of people who ordered after me have come and gone. I expected that our food would be served in order. I'm really annoyed. Do you understand my position?"

SKILL BUILDERS ● Making a Personal Request

SKILL	USE	PROCEDURE	EXAMPLE
"Sending" or "communicating" messages that teach people how to treat you by directing them how to behave	To direct others to change their behavior because they are violating your rights or expectations	1. Politely but directly describe what you want the other person to do. 2. Do facework. 3. Describe how the behavior violates your rights or expectations. 4. When possible, offer an alternative to your partners' unacceptable behavior, which meets their needs while not violating your rights and expectations. 5. Assume that your partners will comply with the personal request and thank them.	"Rahm, don't criticize me in front of your children. If you don't agree with what I am doing, please tell me later when we can talk it out. I know you don't mean to undermine my authority, but when you interrupt me and contradict what I have said, that's what happens. It's hard to be a stepparent, but I think it's important for both sets of kids to see us as a team. I know you understand. Thanks, honey."

Listening Effectively (continued)

SKILL BUILDERS ● Paraphrasing

SKILL	USE	PROCEDURE	EXAMPLE
Verifying one's understanding of a message by putting it in one's own words and sharing it with the speaker	To increase listening efficiency; to avoid message confusion; to discover the speaker's motivation	1. Listen carefully to the message. 2. Notice what ideas and feelings seem to be contained in the message. 3. Determine what the message means to you. 4. Create a message in your own words that conveys these ideas and/or feelings.	Grace says, "At two minutes to five, the boss gave me three letters that had to be in the mail that evening!" Bonita replies, "I understand; you were really resentful that your boss dumped important work on you right before quitting time, when she knows that you have to pick up the baby at daycare."

Holding Effective Conversations

SKILL BUILDERS ● Turn-Taking

SKILL	USE	PROCEDURE	EXAMPLE
Engaging in appropriate turn-taking	Determining when a speaker is at a place where another person may talk if he or she wants	1. Take your share of turns. 2. Gear the length of turns to the behavior of partners. 3. Give and watch for turn-taking and turn-exchanging cues. Avoid giving inadvertent turn-taking cues. 4. Observe and use conversation-directing behavior. 5. Limit interruptions.	When John lowers his voice as he says, "I really thought they were going to go ahead during those last few seconds," Melissa, noticing that he appears to be finished, says, "I did, too. But did you notice …"

SKILL BUILDERS ● Initiating Conversation

SKILL	USE	PROCEDURE	EXAMPLE
Initiating conversation with a stranger	To start an interaction with someone you don't know	Do one or more of the following: 1. Make a comment about the situation, the other person, or yourself. 2. Ask a ritual question. 3. Introduce yourself.	Jenna is waiting in line at the grocery store. The woman in front of her is looking at the candy bars. Jenna says "Don't those look good? I always seem to end up at the store when I'm hungry."

SKILL BUILDERS ● Sustaining Conversation

SKILL	USE	PROCEDURE	EXAMPLE
Sustaining conversation	To sustain a first-time conversation, pass time enjoyably, and get to know someone	Do the following throughout the conversation: 1. Use and provide free information. 2. Ask closed-ended and open-ended questions. 3. Seek high-interest topics. 4. Make appropriate self-disclosures. 5. Listen actively.	Roger and Eduardo are chatting while waiting for treadmills to become available at the gym. Roger says, "Man, I wish this place had more treadmills. I really need to step up my workouts." Eduardo replies, "Are you training for something in particular?" "Yes," says Roger. "I've signed up for a half-marathon in a couple of months." "Phew," Eduardo comments. "That's a lot of miles. What got you into running races?"

Supporting Others (continued)

SKILL BUILDERS ● Giving Advice

SKILL	USE	PROCEDURE	EXAMPLE
Presenting suggestions and proposals a partner could use to satisfactorily resolve a situation	To comfort our partners after a supportive climate has been established and our partners are unable to find their own solutions	1. Ask for permission to give advice. 2. Word the message as one of many suggestions that the recipient can consider. 3. Present any potential risks or costs associated with following the advice. 4. Indicate that you will not be offended should your partner choose to ignore your recommendation or look for another alternative.	After a friend has explained a difficult situation she faces, Felicia might say, "I have a suggestion if you'd like to hear it. As I see it, one way you could handle this is to talk to your co-worker about this issue. This is just one idea—you may come up with a different solution that's just as good. So think this one over, and do what you believe is best for you."

Communicating Personal Information

SKILL BUILDERS ● Owning

SKILL	USE	PROCEDURE	EXAMPLE
Making an "I" statement rather than a generalization to identify yourself as the source of an idea or feeling	To help others understand that the feeling or opinion is yours	When an idea, opinion, or feeling is yours, say so.	Instead of saying, "Maury's is the best restaurant in town," say, "I believe Maury's is the best restaurant in town."

SKILL BUILDERS ● Describing Behavior

SKILL	USE	PROCEDURE	EXAMPLE
Accurately recounting the specific behaviors without drawing conclusions about those behaviors	To increase the accuracy of your self-disclosures and to provide descriptive rather than evaluative feedback to your partners	1. Identify the overall impression you are experiencing. 2. Recall the specific behaviors that led you to this impression. 3. Form a message in which you report only what you did, saw, heard, or experienced without drawing an evaluative conclusion about these behaviors.	Instead of saying, "She is such a snob," say, "She has walked by us three times now without speaking."

SKILL BUILDERS ● Describing Feelings

SKILL	USE	PROCEDURE	EXAMPLE
Owning and explaining the precise emotions one is feeling or felt	To honestly self-disclose your emotions rather than displaying or masking them	1. Identify what has triggered the feeling. 2. Identify what you are feeling—think specifically. Am I feeling amused? pleased? happy? ecstatic? 3. Own the feeling by using an "I feel" statement followed by naming the specific feelings.	"Because I didn't get the job, I feel depressed and discouraged." "The way you stood up for me when I was being put down by Leah makes me feel very warm and loving toward you."

Communicating Personal Information (continued)

SKILL BUILDERS ● Communicating a Personal Boundary

SKILL	USE	PROCEDURE	EXAMPLE
Politely tell someone your policy regarding disclosing a particular type of information or engaging in a particular behavior	To help others understand your policy about the privacy of certain information	1. Recognize why you are choosing not to share the information. 2. Identify your privacy policy that guides your decision. 3. Preface your boundary statement with an apology or some other statement that helps your partner save face. 4. Form a brief "I" message that diplomatically informs the person that you wish to keep that information private.	"Paul, I know that you are curious about how much money I make. And a lot of people are comfortable sharing that information, so forgive me, but I'm not. Don't take it personally. It's not you—I don't tell anyone what I make. That's just me. I hope you understand and are OK with it."

SKILL BUILDERS ● Asking for Feedback

SKILL	USE	PROCEDURE	EXAMPLE
Asking others for their reaction to you or to your behavior	Helping you understand yourself and your effect on others	1. Specify the kind of personal feedback you are seeking. 2. Ask neutral questions. 3. Try to avoid negative verbal or nonverbal reactions to the feedback. 4. Paraphrase what you hear. 5. Show gratitude for the feedback you receive.	Lucy asks, "Tim, when I talk with the boss, do I sound defensive?" Tim replies, "I think so—your voice gets sharp and you lose eye contact, which makes you look nervous." "So you think that the tone of my voice and my eye contact make the boss perceive me as defensive?" "Yes." "Thanks, Tim. I've really got to work on this."

SKILL BUILDERS ● Praising

SKILL	USE	PROCEDURE	EXAMPLE
Sincerely describing the specific positive behaviors or accomplishments of another and their positive effects on others	To help people see themselves positively	1. Make note of the specific behavior or accomplishment that you want to reinforce. 2. Describe the specific behavior or accomplishment. 3. Describe the positive feelings or outcomes that you or others experience as a result of the behavior or accomplishment. 4. Phrase your response so that the level of praise appropriately reflects the significance of the behavior or accomplishment.	"Marge, that was an excellent writing job on the Miller story. Your descriptions were particularly vivid."

Using Interpersonal Influence (continued)

SKILL BUILDERS ● Refusing a Personal Request

SKILL	USE	PROCEDURE	EXAMPLE
Messages that decline to act or believe as others would like you to	To inform others that we don't want to do or think what they want us to	1. When appropriate, thank people for what they are asking you to do. 2. Directly own that you are not willing to agree to the request. 3. State a generalized reason for your refusal, but don't feel obligated to disclose something that you wish to keep private. 4. When possible, identify an alternative to the request that you could agree to.	"Would you take my shift next Friday? I'd really appreciate it." "Thanks for offering it to me, but sorry, I already have plans. Check with Heather, though, when she comes in. I think she was interested in picking up a shift."

Managing Conflict

SKILL BUILDERS ● Behavior, Consequences, and Feelings (b-c-f) Sequence

SKILL	USE	PROCEDURE	EXAMPLE
Describing a conflict in terms of behavior, consequences, and feelings (b-c-f)	To help the other person understand the problem completely	1. Own the message, using "I" statements. 2. Describe the behavior that you see or hear. 3. Describe the consequences that result from the behavior. 4. Describe your feelings that result from the behavior.	Jason says, "I have a problem that I need your help with. When I tell you what I'm thinking and you don't respond (b), I start to think you don't care about me or what I think (c), and this causes me to get angry with you (f)."

SKILL BUILDERS ● Apologizing

SKILL	USE	PROCEDURE	EXAMPLE
A direct request for forgiveness	To repair a relationship that your behavior has damaged	1. Directly acknowledge your transgression by owning what you did. 2. Express regret or remorse for your behavior and its effect on your partner. 3. Directly request that your partner forgive you.	"I did lie about where I was Friday night. I was out with another girl. I am so sorry that I lied, and I'm really sorry that I hurt you and destroyed your trust in me. Can you forgive me?"

Forming and Using Social Perceptions

SKILL BUILDERS ● Perception Checking

SKILL	USE	PROCEDURE	EXAMPLE
A statement that expresses the meaning you perceive from the behavior of another	To clarify the accuracy of our perceptions of another person's behavior	1. Watch the behavior of another. 2. Ask yourself, "What does that behavior mean to me?" 3. Describe the behavior (to yourself or aloud) and put your interpretation of the nonverbal behavior into words to verify your perception.	As Dale frowns while reading Paul's first draft of a memo, Paul says, "From the way you're frowning, I take it that you're not too pleased with the way I phrased the memo."

Verbal Messages

SKILL BUILDERS ● Dating Information

SKILL	USE	PROCEDURE	EXAMPLE
Including a specific time referent to clarify a message	To avoid the pitfalls of language that allow you to speak of a dynamic world in static terms	1. Before you make a statement, consider or find out when the information was true. 2. If not based on present information, verbally acknowledge when the statement was true.	When Jake says, "How good a hitter is Steve?," Mark replies by dating his evaluation: "When I worked with him two years ago, he couldn't hit the curve ball."

SKILL BUILDERS ● Indexing Generalizations

SKILL	USE	PROCEDURE	EXAMPLE
Mentally or verbally accounting for individual differences when generalizing	To avoid "allness" in speaking	1. Before you make a statement, consider whether it pertains to a specific object, person, or place. 2. If you use a generalization, inform the listener that it does not necessarily apply in the situation being discussed.	"He's a politician and I don't trust him, although he may be different from most politicians I know."

Listening Effectively

SKILL BUILDERS ● Questioning

SKILL	USE	PROCEDURE	EXAMPLE
Phrasing a response designed to get further information or to remove uncertainty from information already received	To help get a more complete picture before making other comments; to help a shy person open up; to clarify meaning	1. Be specific about the kind of information you need to increase your understanding of the message. 2. Deliver questions in a sincere tone of voice. 3. Limit questions or explain that you need to ask multiple questions. 4. Put the burden of ignorance on your own shoulders.	When Connie says, "Well, it would be better if she weren't so sedentary," Jeff replies, "I'm not sure I understand what you mean by 'sedentary'—would you explain?"

Inter-Act

Inter-Act

Interpersonal Communication Concepts, Skills, and Contexts

Thirteenth Edition

Kathleen S. Verderber
Northern Kentucky University

Rudolph F. Verderber
University of Cincinnati

with

Brant Burleson, Purdue University, content consultant

Erina MacGeorge, Purdue University, content consultant
and co-author, Chapters 8 & 13

Joseph P. Mazer, Clemson University, social media consultant and
co-author, Social Media Factor

New York   Oxford
OXFORD UNIVERSITY PRESS

Oxford University Press, Inc., publishes works that further Oxford University's
objective of excellence in research, scholarship, and education.

Oxford   New York
Auckland   Cape Town   Dar es Salaam   Hong Kong   Karachi
Kuala Lumpur   Madrid   Melbourne   Mexico City   Nairobi
New Delhi   Shanghai   Taipei   Toronto

With offices in
Argentina   Austria   Brazil   Chile   Czech   Republic   France   Greece
Guatemala   Hungary   Italy   Japan   Poland   Portugal   Singapore
South Korea   Switzerland   Thailand   Turkey   Ukraine   Vietnam

Published by Oxford University Press, Inc.
198 Madison Avenue, New York, New York 10016
http://www.oup.com

For titles covered by Section 112 of the US Higher Education
Opportunity Act, please visit www.oup.com/us/he for the
latest information about pricing and alternative formats.

Library of Congress Cataloging-in-Publication Data
Verderber, Kathleen S., 1949–
    Inter-act: interpersonal communication concepts, skills, and contexts/
Kathleen S. Verderber, Northern Kentucky University, Rudolph F. Verderber,
University of Cincinnati.—Thirteenth Edition.
        pages cm
    ISBN 978-0-19-983688-8
    1. Interpersonal communication.   2. Interpersonal relations.
I. Verderber, Rudolph F.   II. Title.   III. Title: Interact.
    BF637.C45V47 2012
    158.2—dc23   2012006978

Printing number: 9 8 7 6 5 4 3 2 1

Printed in the United States of America on acid-free paper.

BRIEF CONTENTS

CONTENTS

CHAPTER 2 ● Forming and Using Social Perceptions 37

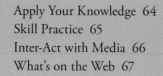

CHAPTER 3 ● Intercultural Communication **69**

CHAPTER 6 ●   Communication in the Life Cycle of Relationships **159**

PART 2 DEVELOPING INTERPERSONAL COMMUNICATION SKILLS

CHAPTER 7 ● Listening Effectively 195

CHAPTER 8 ● Holding Effective Conversations **225**

CHAPTER 9 ● Supporting Others **257**

CHAPTER 11 ● Using Interpersonal Influence 325

CHAPTER 12 ● Managing Conflict **357**

PART 3 USING COMMUNICATION SKILLS TO IMPROVE RELATIONSHIPS

CHAPTER 13 ● Communicating in Intimate Relationships: Families, Friendships, Marriages, and Other Life Partnerships **395**

CHAPTER 14 ● Communicating in the Workplace **429**

Preface

Welcome to the Thirteenth Edition of *InterAct*!

To Students Who Are About to Use This Text:

Few courses you take in college can have as profound an impact on your life as a course in interpersonal communication. You are embarking on a course of study that will help you be a better friend, family member, lover, partner, employee, manager, coworker, and leader. *Inter-Act* does this by empowering you with specific skills that can be used to improve communication and relationships with other people. Each chapter explores concepts and valid theories that explain how interpersonal communication processes work to define, develop, and sustain relationships. You will also be encouraged to practice, refine, and adopt specific interpersonal communication skills that can increase your interpersonal competence and ability to form healthy relationships. These skills cover the whole spectrum of human interaction, from developing messages to communicate your meaning, understanding the nonverbal behavior of others, listening effectively, managing conversations with strangers and acquaintances, providing support and comfort to others, maintaining your privacy, dealing with conflict, and simply finding the most effective way to speak up for yourself. You will also practice more complex skills to develop and sustain intimate relationships with family members, close friends, intimate partners, and people in your workplace. You will learn how cultural practices influence the effectiveness of communication. Finally you will study how practices in digital communication and social networking affect our relationships and learn techniques that can help you be effective as you "talk" with others via technology.

Goals of *Inter-Act*

As with previous editions, *Inter-Act,* thirteenth edition, meets six specific goals that are essential to a basic course in interpersonal communication.

1. Explain important communication concepts, frameworks, and theories that have been consistently supported by careful research so that you can understand the conceptual foundations of interpersonal communication.
2. Teach specific communication skills that research has shown facilitate effective relationships.
3. Present ethical frameworks you can use to be a moral communicator in your relationships.

4. Sensitize you as to how communication needs, rules, and processes differ among diverse people.
5. Challenge you to think critically and creatively about the concepts and skills you learn.
6. Provide abundant skills and practice activities that significantly enhance your learning.

To Instructors Who Have Selected This Text:

The skills-based approach that has made *Inter-Act* so popular over the years has been significantly expanded and reinforced with this new edition. Many of these changes are based on our desire to ground the book squarely within the message-centered approach to interpersonal communication (see Burleson, 2010). A message-centered approach allows us to explore how people form relationships and applies current theories and concepts as a framework for understanding interpersonal communication. The message-centered approach is consistent with the premise that there are basic universal message skills and guidelines that improve the likelihood of successful human interaction. *Inter-Act* has always taken a skills-based approach to teaching interpersonal communication. This edition introduces the concepts of canned plans and communication scripts as a way of understanding the mental processes involved in message preparation. Understanding these processes enables students to incorporate new skills into their behavioral repertoire and improve relationships. With this overview in mind, let's take a closer look at what is new in this edition.

New to This Edition

- **Emphasis on Social Media.** The book has been strengthened by expanded discussions of social media and its associated theories, skills, and applications in the realm of interpersonal communication. Ten chapters include new sections called The Social Media Factor that discuss the latest theories, practices, and guidelines for using social media within the context of each chapter. Every chapter includes new marginal activities called Inter-Act with Social Media. Many chapters are further enhanced by the addition of new summary questions and review activities specifically related to digital communication. This balanced approach to the topic was designed to complement the book's existing emphasis on understanding, developing, and using interpersonal communication skills.
- **Updated discussions on theories and concepts.** A key goal for this edition was to reflect changes to interpersonal concepts found in contemporary research. This is evidenced by many new discussions in the body of the text. Examples include an emphasis on a message-centered approach (Chapter 1), the dual processes of social perception (Chapter 2), intercultural communication competence (Chapter 3), the instrumental, constitutive, and indexical functions of communications

in relationships (Chapter 6), personal and cultural differences in listening (Chapter 7), new guidelines for improving conversational skills (Chapter 8), new suggestions for improving one's ability to empathize (Chapter 9), discussion of how to effectively ask for feedback (Chapter 10), the use of power to influence others (Chapter 11), face-to-face conflict management versus the use of digital communications (Chapter 12), new and expanded discussions of managing destructive conflict patterns and forgiveness (Chapter 12), skill clusters that are important to sustaining communications in friendships (Chapter 13), guidelines for maintaining a positive climate in intimate relationships (Chapter 13), and new discussions on hiring practices and co-worker relationships (Chapter 14).

- **Expanded suite of Skill Practice activities.** Skill Practice exercises at the end of every chapter reinforce *Inter-Act's* stature as a highly skills-based text. Dozens of new exercises have been added to this edition, providing the student with one or more activities for every skill discussed in the text.
- **Chapter 3, "Intercultural Communication."** This has been moved forward in response to instructor feedback, re-titled from the last edition, and revised to discuss the relationships between concepts.
- **Chapter 7, "Listening Effectively."** This has been moved forward in response to instructor feedback and now is placed before the chapter on conversation.

Hallmark Features of *Inter-Act*— Strengthened and Revised

- **Chapter openers.** Each chapter opens with a practical set of goals for the student and a sample conversation to set the scene for key ideas to be discussed. These fictional opening conversations have been reconceived for this edition and rewritten for all of the chapters. The conversations revolve around a recurring set of college-age students. What unifies this diverse group is that they are all taking the same interpersonal communication course.
- **Running chapter features.** Each chapter includes several unobtrusive features that reinforce learning by engaging the student. *Key Terms* and definitions are highlighted in the margins. *Observe and Analyze* activities ask students to observe common communication situations and analyze them using the concepts and theories that have just been presented in the text. New *Inter-Act with Social Media* activities direct students to think about how basic interpersonal processes are affected when we use social or electronic media. Instructors can assign these activities as graded exercises or as prompts for journal entries.
- **Chapter Box features.** A variety of special boxes highlight other perspectives on interpersonal communication. *Diverse Voices* include

excerpts of previously published articles that shed light on the communication experiences of people from a wide range of backgrounds and cultures. *A Question of Ethics: What Would You Do?* is a box that outlines ethical challenges and requires students to think critically about a variety of ethical dilemmas faced by communicators. Each of these kinds of boxes now features a set of critical thinking questions to help the student apply what they've read. Many chapters feature a self-administered poll called *Learn About Yourself,* an opportunity for the student to assess their own communication skills within the context of the chapter. Instructors may choose to assign these optional boxes for extra credit or use them to launch class discussion.

- **Spotlight on Scholars.** Once a box in the chapters, *Spotlight on Scholars* has been updated and moved to the book's companion Web site. These short essays highlight the interested work of leading scholars in the field. These are of particular interest to individuals who are considering a career in communication research. The student is reminded of these Web entries by a marginal note in associated chapters.

- **Skill Builders.** These entries, found in the many chapters, underscore the skills-based emphasis of *Inter-Act.* Each *Skill Builders* entry highlights a specific definition of a skill, provides a brief description of its use, explains the steps for enacting the skill, and includes an example to illustrate its use.

- **Inter-Action Dialogues and Analyses.** Found at the conclusion of Chapters 7 through 12, *Inter-Action Dialogues and Analyses* are a special interactive feature with a video component. Each chapter features a dialogue to illustrate specific skills presented in the chapter. Transcriptions of the conversations are printed in the chapter. The book's companion Web site, at www.oup.com/us/verderber, includes the associated video footage of the conversations as well as a worksheet for the student to record their analysis. One of the analyses is provided on the Web site. The resulting worksheet may be e-mailed to the instructor for assessment. These conversations can be used for class discussion or as analytical assignments.

- **End-of-chapter resources.** These begin with a Summary of key takeaway concepts from the chapter and bullet points indicating what the student should be able to *explain* and *do* after reading the chapter. A list of *Key Words* and page numbers enables the student to quickly scan the chapter for key concepts. This is followed by two sets of activities. Apply Your Knowledge includes activities that challenge students to apply the concepts, theories, and skills that they have used to understand or improve a communication situation. As part of this, Chapters 7–12 each include the transcript of an *Interaction Dialogue* that students can use to identify and diagnose what is happening in a conversation. At the book's companion website, at www.oup.com/us/verderber, students will find an associated video clip of the conversations as well as a worksheet they can use to record their analysis. The resulting worksheet may be emailed to the instructor for assessment or these activities may be assigned as homework and used as the basis for class discussion. At the website students will also find an example of completed analysis. Skill Practice activities are short drills that students may complete as they work to increase their ability to use the specific communication skills presented in the chapter. There is one of these activities for every skill discussed in the text. These may be assigned as written activities or used as part of in-class practice. A Communication Improvement Plan for each chapter helps students set a goal for improving some aspect of their communication. The companion website includes a handy form that can be downloaded to record a plan. Inter-Act with Media provides additional reinforcement for chapter concepts by using television programs and movies as content-related examples. Instructors might assign one of these to the class and use it as the basis for a class discussion or assessment activity.

- **Skill Builders Chart.** As an additional convenience for the reader, we provide a tear-out chart at the beginning of the book including all of the book's *Skill Builders* entries.

Significant Content Updates

In addition to new and enhanced features, every chapter has been revised to reflect current theory, scholarship, and ways that social and technological change are affecting our communication and relationships.

Chapter 1: "An Orientation to Interpersonal Communication," has been reorganized and significantly revised to reflect a message-centered philosophy of interpersonal communication. The chapter begins by defining interpersonal communication and uses the parts of that definition as the framework for organizing the chapter. The chapter includes a new **Social Media Factor** section: Understanding Social Media and Interpersonal Communication. New figures include Figure 1.1, A Model of Communication Between Two Individuals, Figure 1.2, Understanding Dark Side Messages, Figure 1.5, The Evolution of Social Networking Technology, and Figure 1.6, A Continuum of Media Richness.

Chapter 2: "Forming and Using Social Perception," has been streamlined and reorganized into three main points: The Perception Process, Perceiving Others, and Self-Perception: Self-Concept and Self-Esteem. Information on self-presentation has been moved to Chapter 8 "Holding Effective Conversations." The chapter includes a new **Social Media Factor** section: Human Factors in Using Social Media.

Chapter 3: "Intercultural Communication," has been moved forward, re-titled from the previous edition, and has been revised to clarify the relationships between concepts. A new section on intercultural communication competence has been added. The chapter includes the new Figure 3.2, The Pyramid Model of Intercultural Competence.

Chapter 4: "Verbal Messages," is major revision. This chapter introduces students to linguistics and the different ways the verbal parts of messages may be effective or ineffective. The chapter includes new and revised figures for Figure 4.1, Improving Message Semantics through Clear and Specific Language, Figure 4.2, Improving Semantic Accuracy by Dating Messages, and Figure 4.3, Improving Semantic Accuracy by Indexing Messages.

Chapter 5: "Nonverbal Messages," has been revised and updated to reflect new scholarship.

Chapter 6: "Communication in the Life-Cycle of Relationships," has a new title that reflects the major revisions to what was previously Chapter 3. The chapter begins with a new discussion of how communication functions in a relationship: instrumental, constitutive, and indexical. Next the types of relationships are described, categorized, and the dimensions of relationships are discussed. The life cycle of relationships is explained beginning with a discussion on how relationships changes happen: incrementally and suddenly. The chapter includes a new **Social Media Factor** section: Social Media and Relationship Closeness.

Chapter 7: "Listening Effectively," has been moved forward and is placed before the chapter on conversation. The chapter begins with a discussion of the dual approaches that we take when listening: reflexive or active listening. The chapter includes a new **Social Media Factor** section: Digital Listening Skills.

Chapter 8: "Holding Effective Conversations," has been substantially revised. The chapter begins with an overview of conversations including a definition, discussion of the characteristics of a conversation, and description of the types of conversations. Much of the chapter focuses on specific guidelines that can improve our general conversational skills. The chapter includes a new **Social Media Factor** section: Digital Conversation Skills. There is a new Figure 8.1, Twenty-Nine Types of Conversation.

Chapter 9: "Supporting Others," has been updated and undergone some organizational changes. Added to the discussion of empathy are specific guidelines for improving our ability to empathize. The chapter includes a new **Social Media Factor** section: Using Social Media to Offer Empathy and Support. There is a new Figure 9.1, Types of Social Support Messages.

Chapter 10: "Communicating Personal Information: Disclosure and Privacy," has been updated and the section on Asking for Feedback has been substantially revised. The chapter includes a new **Social Media Factor** section: Digitally Managing Your Personal Information. There is a new Figure 10.1, Risk and Benefits of Disclosure and Maintaining Privacy.

Chapter 11: "Using Interpersonal Influence," has been substantially revised. The discussion of power now includes references to how we can use each source of power directly or indirectly as we seek to influence others. The discussion of interpersonal influence begins by using the Elaboration Likelihood Model of Persuasion to explain that we can process influence attempts automatically or consciously. We then discuss the heuristics (compliance gaining strategies) in messages that appeal to automatic processors and the ways that extensive processors evaluate persuasive messages (quality of the reasoning, credibility of the speaker, and appropriateness of emotional appeals). The section on Assertiveness has been substantially revised.

Chapter 12: "Managing Conflict," has been revised to highlight different cultural approaches to disagreement. A new discussion addresses the role that face negotiation plays in conflict including cultural differences in the meaning of face and uses face negotiation theory to explain how culture and co-culture influence our personal conflict style preferences. New guidelines are provided for breaking destructive conflict patterns, and an expanded section on forgiveness offers specific guidelines and skills that can help repair the damage done to a relationship. The chapter includes a new **Social Media Factor** section: Managing the Dark Side of Digital Communication.

Chapter 13: "Communicating in Intimate Relationships," has been refocused to emphasize how communication patterns and skills affect intimate relationships. The chapter concludes with new material on the "dark side" of intimacy (relational uncertainty and possessiveness) and presents how effective communication can overcome these dark side tendencies. The chapter includes a new **Social Media Factor** section: Using Digital Communication Skills to Improve Relationships. There is a revised Figure 13.1, Common Family Structures.

Chapter 14: "Communicating in the Workplace," has been revised with new discussions. The section on the hiring process has been updated to reflect current practice that uses online job postings, company research, and application processes. The section on co-worker relationship has new content on the types of co-worker relationships and the communication patterns in each type. The chapter concludes with new material on the "dark side" of workplace relationships including aggression and sexual harassment. The chapter includes a new **Social Media Factor** section: Digital Communication Skills in Professional Relationships. New and revised figures for Figure 14.1, Sample Chronological Resume, Figure 14.2, Sample Functional Résumé, Figure 14.3, Sample Cover Letter E-mail, and Figure 14.4, Commonly Asked Interview Questions.

Supplementary Materials

As a reader of this text, you also have access to supplementary materials for both student and faculty.

Student Materials

- The *Student Success Manual,* written by Leah Bryant of DePaul University, is a printed supplement that will help students master the course material. It features study tips, chapter outlines and summaries, review questions and answers, key terms, and critical thinking exercises. The companion Web site, www.oup.com/us/verderber, offers a wealth of resources for both students and instructors, including online self-testing and other study aids, links to a variety of communication-related Web sites, and "Now Playing," reviews of recent films (see print version below).
- ***Now Playing: Learning Communication through Film,*** available as an optional printed product, looks at more than 60 contemporary and classic feature films through the lens of communication principles. Developed by Russell F. Proctor II and revised by Darin Garard of Santa Barbara City College, *Now Playing* illustrates a variety of both individual scenes and full-length films, highlighting concepts and offering discussion questions for a mass medium that is interactive, familiar, and easily accessible.

Faculty Materials

- The *Instructor's Manual* is available in print and is also included on the accompanying *Instructor's Resource CD* provided to adopters of the text. Revised by Jennifer Pitts of Volunteer State Community College, it provides teaching tips, exercises, and test questions that will prove useful to both new and veteran instructors. The *Instructor's Manual* includes pedagogical suggestions, sample syllabi, content outlines, discussion questions, chapter activities, simulations, and journal assignments. The comprehensive Test Bank offers approximately 400 exam questions in multiple-choice, true/false, and essay formats.
- The *Instructor's Resource CD with Computerized Test Bank,* available to adopters, includes an electronic copy of the *Instructor's Manual,* a computerized test bank, and newly revised PowerPoint®-based lecture slides by Jennifer Pitts of Volunteer State Community College.
- The Instructor's Companion Website at www.oup.com/us/verderber is a password-protected site featuring the *Instructor's Manual,* PowerPoint®-based lecture slides, and links to supplemental materials and films.
- *Now Playing: Instructor's Edition,* an instructor-only print supplement, includes an introduction on how to incorporate film examples in class, more sample responses to the numerous discussion questions in the student edition of *Now Playing,* viewing guides, additional films, and references.

- Course cartridges for a variety of e-learning environments allow instructors to create their own course Web sites with the interactive material from the instructor and student companion Web sites. Contact your Oxford University Press representative for access.

Acknowledgments

I was very fortunate to have the late Brant Burleson and Erina MacGeorge of Purdue work with me as content consultants in planning this edition. I have admired both of their scholarship and was honored to spend precious time with them during the summer of 2010 planning this edition. Their helpful guidance about content greatly informed my writing for this extensive revision. I am also indebted to Professor MacGeorge for her work revising both Chapter 8 on Conversational Basics and most of Chapter 13 on Intimate Relationships. Joseph Mazer of Clemson University, whose scholarship includes original research on social media and digital communication, drafted the new Social Media Factor sections found in most chapters, provided the Inter-Act with Social Media activities found in the margins, and revised the Inter-Act with Media exercises at the end of each chapter. Joe is gifted at translating the research in this area and making it accessible to students. It was a pleasure to learn from and work with him.

While writing can be a solitary activity, I am blessed to have worked with an outstanding team of professionals at Oxford University Press. I was delighted to have the opportunity to work with John Challice, who is the publisher for Higher Education at Oxford, USA, in planning this edition. His wisdom and viewpoint helped me to identify new themes that have been woven into this new edition. Thom Holmes, Development Manager, was the development editor for this project. His calm persona and editing expertise, as well as his project management skills, were deeply appreciated. Mary-Ann McHugh provided additional development editing and her expertise was greatly appreciated. As I was preparing this edition, Mark T. Haynes became the Communication and Journalism editor. His work in launching this edition has been invaluable. Assistant editor Caitlin Kaufman and editorial assistant Kate McClaskey were instrumental in making the photo program a success and in obtaining permissions. I am also grateful for the fine job of the production group: our managing editor, Lisa Grzan; project manager, Kate Scully; art director, Michele Laseau, and copyeditor Deanna Hegle.

In addition I'd like to thank others who helped in preparing the learning materials that accompany this edition including Leah Bryant, Jennifer Pitts, and Ellen Bremen. I am also grateful to the following colleagues across the discipline who reviewed the twelfth edition and provided me with useful suggestions about how to improve this edition:

Ken Bush, Norwich University
Sakile Camara, California State University at Northridge
Anita Chirco, Keuka College

Katie Dunleavy, La Salle University
Katrina Eicher, Elizabethtown Community and Technical College
Gail Hankins, Wake Technical Community College
Daniel Hebert, Springfield Technical Community College
Carlton Hughes, Southeast Kentucky Community/Technical College
Kelly Jones, Pitt Community College
David Majewski, Richard Bland College
Stan McKinney, Campbellsville University
Timothy Moreland, Catawba College
Paul Sanders, West Valley College
Julie Simanski, Des Moines Area Community College
Cynthia Stevens, Georgia Perimeter College
Renee Strom, St. Cloud State University
Dennis Sutton, Grand Rapids Community College
Kathie Wilcox, Lewis-Clark State College–Coeur d'Alene
Alesia Woszidlo, University of Kansas
Henry Young, Cuyahoga Community College

I would like to thank the various members of our family who have always supported Rudy and me in this work. Their love and encouragement has sustained us.

This edition is dedicated to my husband, Rudy, who is no longer able to actively author, but whose imprint on this book and on all basic textbooks in our field will be felt for many years to come.

Kathleen S. Verderber

Inter-Act

1

An Orientation to Interpersonal Communication

"Good afternoon class," began Professor Green. "Let's get started. I've had a chance to read your self-introduction e-mails, and I was surprised to find that several of you already know each other. Let's see if I can remember. Louisa and Amber, you're roommates, right?"

"Right," Amber and Louisa replied in unison, then looked at each other and laughed. They had only known each other for one term but had become close friends and often found themselves finishing each other's sentences.

"And Amber, isn't Brian, my graduate research assistant, your brother? He's a really excellent student. And you and Kai also know each other, right?"

"Um, yeah," Amber, obviously embarrassed, mumbled.

"How did you two meet?" Professor Green queried.

"We were doubles partners in high school," Kai answered.

"But I wasn't very good," Amber volunteered softly. "Kai was great, though. In fact, she's here at school on a tennis scholarship."

3

"Let's see, Terrell, you and Benjamin are also roommates, right?"

"Oh yeah. The 'great roommate god' has a twisted sense of humor," Terrell replied while glaring at Ben."

"And Ben, you're not only going to school full time but working full time as well? That's quite a load," said Professor Green.

"Yeah, it's rough, but my goal is to finish school with no debt, so ya gotta do what ya gotta do," replied Ben.

"Maria," said Professor Green, "you also have what must be a busy schedule. You told me that you're a full-time student and a widow with two preschoolers. And you're looking for a part-time job. Wow, that's a lot."

"Well, I don't play tennis, and they've cut my Pell Grant money. But I'm not giving up now. So, Ben's right, 'you do. . . .' I just wish someone would hire me. I've got bills, you know."

"I sure do," replied Professor Green. "OK. We'll do more to get acquainted later, but right now I want to change our focus. So you took this course because it meets a requirement, but besides the credit, why study interpersonal communication?"

What you should be able to explain after you have studied this chapter:

- The definition of interpersonal communication
- How messages are formed and meaning shared
- The three processes that comprise interpersonal communication
- The relationship between personal identity and interpersonal communication
- The purposes of interpersonal communication
- Ethical standards of interpersonal communication
- Dark-side messages
- Interpersonal communication competence and what it takes to be competent
- The foundational concepts affecting digital communication via social media

What you should be able to do after you have studied this chapter:

- Write a Communication Improvement Plan (CIP)

Why, indeed? You may be like Amber, Louisa, Kai, Ben, Terrell, and Maria. You're taking this course to meet a requirement of your program, and while it sounds somewhat interesting, you probably think that you have more important courses to spend your time on. Nothing could be further from the truth. Although you have been communicating with others since you were a toddler, you have probably never formally studied interpersonal communication. You may think of it as something basic and automatic like breathing. At times, we all interact this way. But whether we are on "automatic pilot" or being thoughtful about what we are saying, talking is not like breathing. We *learned* how to talk. As infants and children, we learned by observing and imitating the communication behaviors of those around us. And these people may or may not have been good communication role models. Think about it. How much of your interaction is patterned on what you learned in your home or through your experiences with friends? How often do you find yourself mouthing a script that could have come from your mother or brother? Have you accidently blown up a romantic relationship or hurt a close friend by inappropriate comments whose power you didn't recognize? Throughout our lives we have acquired scripts that we draw on in talking with others. We have developed our own informal theories of interpersonal communication to explain to ourselves what is happening when we communicate with others. If our personal theories are correct, we interact effectively with others, but when our theories are incorrect or incomplete, we create misunderstanding and harm our relationships.

What you will learn in this book can help you to become a more effective interpersonal communicator. The theories you will learn are based on research. Some will confirm your own theories, but some will provide a more accurate understanding of what happens when two people talk. Better understanding of interpersonal communication is an important goal, yet this book goes one step further. We want you not only to gain a richer understanding of how your interpersonal communication affects your relationships but also to develop new scripts so that you become more skillful when you create messages. These skills may not be second nature to you because they are not part of the automatic scripts you have learned through modeling other people in your life. In this course, you will have the opportunity to practice a variety of communication skills in a safe classroom setting before trying them out in your relationships with your family, friends, partners, coworkers, acquaintances, and others. So, let's get started.

> **Interpersonal communication is the complex process through which people express, interpret, and coordinate messages to create shared meaning, meet social goals, manage personal identity, and carry out their relationships.**

After studying this first chapter, you will understand each part of our definition of interpersonal communication. You will know the characteristics of interpersonal communication. You will have learned the ethical standards that we expect in our own and others' interpersonal communication. We realize that we can fall short of these standards, however, so you will have been introduced to both the bright and dark sides of interpersonal communication. Finally, you will recognize interpersonal communication competence, the types of skills that can help you become more competent, and the steps in learning new interpersonal communication skills.

Interpersonal Communication Messages

At the center of interpersonal communication is the exchange of messages. A **message** is a performance that uses words, sentences, and/or nonverbal behaviors to convey the thoughts, feelings, and intentions of the speaker. The process of choosing the words, sentences, and nonverbal behaviors to form a message is called **encoding**, while **decoding** is the process of interpreting the messages we receive from others. So when the toddler points to her bottle and cries out "ba-ba," her message, comprised of a nonverbal gesture and a word, "ba-ba," expresses her desire to have her father hand her the bottle of milk on the table out of her reach. How the father responds to this message depends on how he decodes it. He might respond by handing her the bottle. He might respond by saying, "Sorry, cutie, the bottle is empty," or he may just look at her with a puzzled expression on his face. Whatever his response, it too will be a message. **Feedback** is a message in response to a previous message, indicating whether and how the original message was understood.

Message—a performance that uses words, sentences, and/or nonverbal behaviors to convey the thoughts, feelings, and intentions of the speaker.

Encoding—the process of choosing the words, sentences, and nonverbal behaviors to form a message.

Decoding—the process of interpreting the messages we receive from others.

Feedback—a message in response to a previous message indicating whether and how the original message was understood.

Canned Plans and Message Scripts

How do we form and interpret messages? Each message you construct is unique to the particular situation, but it is also based on your memory of previous experiences. A **canned plan** is your mental library of scripts you draw on when you create certain types of messages and that you use to understand what others say to you. Canned-plan scripts include those that you have used effectively, or that you have heard used numerous times in similar situations, or that you have mentally rehearsed (Berger, 1997). A **script** is the text that instructs you what to say and do in a specific situation. Suppose you spot a good friend you haven't seen for a while sitting at a table across the room from you at a restaurant. What do you do? If you answered this question, it is because you have a canned greeting plan. When you have more than one script in that library, the one you select to be your template for a specific situation depends on whom you are greeting and the situation in which the greeting occurs. Greeting your friend when he comes to your door will probably be different from greeting a stranger at a club. The aptly named "pick-up line" you use in the club is most likely not appropriate for your friend. We have canned plans and scripts for a wide variety of our typical interactions, such as greeting people, making small talk, flirting, giving advice, complimenting, criticizing, persuading, etc.

We develop canned plans and learn scripts from our own previous experiences, from observation of what works for real or fictitious others, and from formal learning. Can you remember the first time you asked someone out on a date? How nervous were you? Did you mentally practice what you would say? How many different ways did you imagine bringing up the subject? Where did your ideas come from? In all likelihood they came from your canned ask-for-a-date scripts based on successful lines you had heard other people use. Although you will draw on scripts as you form a message, you customize what you say to fit the particular person and the situation. By now you may have a well-honed script for asking someone out, but you will modify it to use the right person's name, mention the activity to which you are inviting the person, etc.

Occasionally, we need to form a message for which we don't have a good script. In such situations we mentally search our library of canned plans for ones similar in some way to the situation we are facing and try to use these scripts to patch together an appropriate message. For example, I have never met a celebrity, so while I have many greeting scripts, I don't have one that fits this exact situation. Suppose that I am washing my hands in a restaurant restroom and look up to find a smiling Taylor Swift reflected in the mirror. What would I say? "Hi, Taylor?" "Hi, Ms. Swift?" "Omigod, are you really Taylor Swift?" Or something else? "Hi, Taylor" is drawn from my greet-a-friend/peer script. "Hi, Ms. Swift" is drawn from my show-respect script. And "Omigod . . ." is from my I-can't-believe-it script.

The point is that when we need to form a message, we don't usually start from scratch. Instead, we recognize what type of message we want to form, search

Canned plan—your mental library of scripts that you draw on when you create certain types of messages and that informs how you understand what others say to you.

Script—the text that instructs you what to say and do in a specific situation.

Canned Plans and Scripts

Describe a time when you met someone who was grieving the death of a close friend or family member. What did you do and say to express your sympathy? Recreate a script of the conversation as best you can recall it. How comfortable were you during this conversation? How did you know what to say? Would knowing or not knowing the deceased affect how you approached the conversation? Would it have mattered if the person who died was young or old? Died suddenly or after a long illness? Do you think you were effective and appropriate in what you said and did? How skillful were you in this encounter? What if anything would you do differently the next time you face this situation?

Process—a systematic series of actions that leads to an outcome.

Message production—the actions that you perform when you send a message.

Message interpretation—the activities that those listening to the message perform to understand what the speaker intends.

the canned plan for an appropriate script, and then customize it to fit the unique parts of the current situation. All this mental choosing happens in nanoseconds and often occurs somewhat automatically. In other words, we aren't really aware of how we are coming up with what we are saying. Nevertheless, if you reflect on what you have said in a certain situation, you will likely find it similar to something you have said or have heard said in the past.

We also use our canned plans and scripts to interpret the messages of others. When we receive a message, we try to match it with scripts in our library. Based on our understanding, we respond. When we can't find a good match, we may be confused or respond inappropriately.

Obviously, the larger your canned-plan library and the greater the number of scripts within each canned plan, the more likely you are to be able to form appropriate and effective messages as well as to understand and appropriately respond to the messages of others. One of the benefits of this course is that it enables you to enlarge your canned-plan library with scripts based on research and to improve or replace scripts that don't work well.

Interpersonal Communication Is a Complex Process

Our definition of interpersonal communication begins by describing it as a complex process. A **process** is a systematic series of actions that leads to an outcome. In interpersonal communication the actions are the exchanges of messages that lead to shared meaning. Interpersonal communication is complex because three different yet interrelated processes occur during a conversation (Burleson, 2010).

First, **message production** refers to the actions you perform when you send a message. It includes what you do when you encode. You begin by forming goals for the conversation based on your understanding of the situation and your values, ethics, and needs. Based on these goals, you recall a canned plan that was effective in achieving similar goals. From the canned plan, you select and adapt a script to the current conversation. You use this as a blueprint for building your message, choosing words and behaviors that correspond to that script. If you can't recall an appropriate canned plan, then you will need to construct one by drawing on other related plans and scripts. You perform your message. Finally, you monitor the impact of your message on those who are trying to interpret it so that you can repeat, modify, or clarify your message as necessary.

A second process in interpersonal communication, **message interpretation**, refers to the activities those listening to the message perform to understand what the speaker intends. It is what you do when you decode and provide feedback. The process begins when you notice that someone is trying to communicate with you. You listen to the words and observe the nonverbal behavior of the message. From these signals, you make inferences about what the sender means by comparing the sender's message to the canned-plan scripts you remember that are similar to this message. With your remembered script as a frame of reference, you evaluate the truthfulness, appropriateness, and sincerity of the message. Finally, based on this understanding and evaluation of the message, you prepare a feedback message.

Interaction coordination, the third process, refers to the activities participants perform to adjust their behavior to that of their partner. Interaction coordination is like a dance where each person's moves anticipate the other's (Burgoon, 1998). Sometimes you adjust your messages to mirror your partner's signaling. At other times you adjust your messages to display your differences. While talking with someone, you anticipate how he or she is likely to act and to respond. Then you adjust how you act and what you say depending on how your partner's actual messages and behavior match your expectations. If your partner's messages are more positive than you expected, you adjust your behavior by mirroring that positive behavior. If your partner's message or behavior is more negative than you expected, then you are likely to behave in a more positive way that encourages your partner to reciprocate. The goal of interaction coordination is to adjust your behavior so that your partner's behavior more closely matches what you would like it to be. At times you will adjust your behavior to match or mirror that of your partner to show similarity or unity. At other times you may act or say things in a way that signals your individuality or distinctiveness from your partner. And your partner will make similar adjustments.

> **Interaction coordination**—the activity participants in a conversation perform to adjust their behavior to that of their partner.

Let's look at an example of interaction coordination. Suppose that you see your instructor to discuss a paper on which you received a lower grade than you thought the paper deserved. You might begin with a very assertive statement, such as "I didn't deserve a C− on this paper." Your instructor may then respond, "Well, I could have made a mistake. Let's talk about what you thought I missed." His openness to your point of view would likely be more positive than what you expected, which would lead you to adjust what you were saying to accommodate or match his tone. On the other hand, suppose your instructor mirrors your assertiveness with a more negative response than you expected, replying, "Well, you're not the one giving the grade, are you?" You may try to encourage a more cooperative stance by becoming less assertive and more accommodating, responding, "I'm sorry. I didn't mean to question your authority, but I don't understand what I did wrong." In so doing, you are inviting your instructor to match your conciliatory message with his own.

How does it feel when you know that someone is really understanding what you're saying?

During any conversation, we juggle these three processes. We produce and interpret messages while constantly adjusting and coordinating our messages with those of our partner, who is juggling the same processes. This is what makes the interpersonal communication process so complex.

The Purposes of Interpersonal Communication

We exchange messages to (1) share meaning, (2) meet social goals, (3) manage our personal identity, and (4) conduct our relationships. Let's look at each of these.

We Share Meaning

Meaning—the significance that the sender (speaker) and the receiver (listener) each attach to a message.

Shared meaning—when the receiver's interpretation of the message is similar to what the speaker thought, felt, and intended.

Meaning is the significance that the **sender** (speaker) and the **receiver** (listener) each attach to a message. **Shared meaning** occurs when the receiver's interpretation of the message is similar to what the speaker thought, felt, and intended. We can usually gauge the extent to which meaning has been shared by the sender's response to the feedback message. In other words, both people in the exchange determine shared meaning. For example, Sarah says to Nick, "I dropped my phone, and it broke." Nick replies, "Cool, now you can get a Droid™." Sarah responds, "No, you don't understand. I can't afford to buy a new phone." It is Sarah's response to Nick's feedback message that lets Nick know he has misunderstood what she meant. The extent to which we are able to share meaning is affected by the communication situation and noise.

The Communication Setting

Communication setting—the background conditions surrounding an interaction including the physical, social, historical, psychological, and cultural contexts that influence the understandings in a communication encounter.

Physical context—the place where the participants exchange messages.

The situation in which an interaction occurs influences how accurately meaning is shared. The **communication setting** refers to the background conditions surrounding an interaction. Several environmental or contextual factors affect the meaning shared in an interaction. The communication setting includes the physical, social, historical, psychological, and cultural contexts that influence understanding in a communication encounter.

The **physical context** of a communication episode is the place where the participants exchange messages. In many communication situations, the participants are located in the same physical space. In these cases, the environmental conditions (e.g., temperature, lighting, noise level) and the physical proximity of participants to each other can affect how well meaning is shared. Increasingly, however, interpersonal exchanges do not occur face-to-face. And while mediated communication enables us to interact at a distance, the media we use may have an impact on our ability to share meaning. For instance, when you call someone on the phone you lose some nonverbal cues that are part of a face-to-face message, such as posture, gestures, eye contact, and facial expressions. Without these cues, you have less information on which to base your interpretation of the message. E-mail messages and text messages are missing even more of the nonverbal cues that help us accurately interpret a message.

Social context—the type of relationship that may already exist between the participants.

Historical context—the background provided by previous communication episodes between the participants.

The **social context** is the type of relationship that may already exist between the participants. The better you know someone and the better your relationship, the more likely you are to accurately interpret what your partner says.

The **historical context** is the background provided by previous communication episodes between the participants. For instance, suppose one morning Eduardo tells Anna that in the afternoon he will pick up the draft of the report they had left for their manager to read. As Anna enters the office that afternoon, she sees Eduardo and asks, "Did you get it?" Another person listening to the conversation would have no idea what the "it" is to which Anna is referring. Yet Eduardo may well reply, "It's on my desk." Anna and Eduardo understand one another because of the earlier exchange.

The **psychological context** includes the moods and feelings each person brings to the interpersonal encounter. For instance, suppose Corinne is under a great deal of stress. While she is studying for an exam, her friend Julia stops by and pleads with her to take a break and go to the gym with her. Corinne, normally good-natured, may respond in an irritated tone of voice that Julia may incorrectly interpret to mean that Corinne is mad at her.

The **cultural context** is the set of beliefs, values, and attitudes common to the specific cultures of each participant that influence understanding in an interpersonal encounter. Everyone is a part of one or more cultural groups (e.g., racial, ethnic, and religious cultures, or cultures defined by other characteristics such as region or country of birth, gender, sexual orientation, physical ability, etc.). Although we may differ in how much we identify with our cultures, culture penetrates every aspect of our lives, affecting how we think, behave, and communicate. When two people from different cultures interact, misunderstandings may occur because of their cultural variation.

Noise

Noise is any stimulus that interferes with shared meaning. Noises can be external, internal, or semantic. **External noises** are sights, sounds, and other stimuli that draw people's attention away from the message. For instance, a pop-up advertisement may limit your ability to read a Web page or blog. Static or service interruptions can play havoc in cell phone conversations. The sound of a fire engine may distract you from a professor's lecture, or the smell of donuts may disrupt your train of thought during a conversation with a friend. **Internal noises** are thoughts and feelings that interfere with interpreting meaning. If you lose track of the message you are communicating because you tune into a daydream or a past conversation, you are experiencing internal noise. Similarly, if you have a distracting emotional reaction to what someone is saying, you are experiencing internal noise. **Semantic noises** are distractions aroused by the speaker's words that interfere with meaning. For instance, if a co-worker describes a thirty-year-old administrative assistant as "the girl in the office," and you think "girl" a condescending term for a thirty-year-old woman, you might not even hear the rest of what this person has to say. Whenever we react emotionally to a word or a behavior, we are experiencing semantic noise, and when speakers misuse vocabulary in other ways or unclearly express themselves, they are producing semantic noise.

A Model of the Interpersonal Communication Process

A graphic model of the interpersonal communication process is helpful in putting this discussion of setting and noise in perspective. Figure 1.1 illustrates a message exchange between two people. The process begins when one person, whom we will call Andy, is motivated to share his thoughts with another person,

Psychological context—the moods and feelings each person brings to an interpersonal encounter.

Cultural context—the set of beliefs, values, and attitudes common to the specific cultures of each participant that influence the understandings in a communication encounter.

Noise—any stimulus that interferes with shared meaning.

External noises—sights, sounds, and other stimuli that draw people's attention away from intended meaning.

Internal noises—thoughts and feelings that interfere with interpreting meaning.

Semantic noises—distractions aroused by the speaker's words that interfere with meaning.

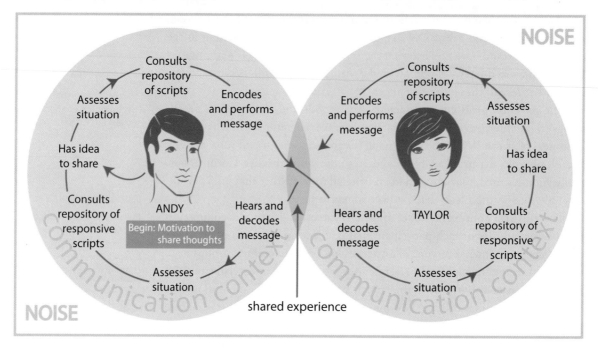

FIGURE 1.1 A Model of Communication between Two Individuals

Taylor. Andy reviews the communication situation including the communication context and sorts through the scripts in his canned-plan library to find one that he thinks will be appropriate and effectively convey his meaning. Based on this script, he encodes a customized message that includes verbal and nonverbal parts. Andy then performs this message using sensory channels like sound. The message may be distorted by physical noise during transmission. Assuming that Taylor hears the message, she will decode it, using her understanding of the situation and matching the message to scripts in her canned-plan library. Andy's intended meaning may be distorted during Taylor's decoding because of internal or semantic noise. It may also be distorted because Taylor's scripts don't match Andy's. But based on Taylor's interpretation of Andy's message, she will encode a feedback message, again using a script from her mental library as a guide. She will perform her message. Then Andy will decode Taylor's feedback. If Andy finds that Taylor understood what he was saying, he will extend the conversation building on what has been said. But if Andy believes that Taylor misunderstood his meaning, he will try to correct that with a new message on the same topic.

We Meet Social Goals

When people communicate with one another, they have one or more reasons for doing so. Or, as Charles Berger (2002), a leading communication scholar, observes: "Social interaction is a goal-directed activity." The goals that each person has for a particular conversation may be serious or trivial. Conversational goals include passing time; getting information about the other person or about something that they know; trying to influence the other person to think a certain way, accept your point of view, or do something; and talking about the relationship. The conversational goals may have important consequences to you or your partner. Then again, they may be trivial. Sometimes our conversational goals are simply to pleasantly pass time or to flirt with an attractive coworker.

An important way to evaluate the success of an interaction is to ask whether it has achieved its goals. When Shandi calls Sofia to ask if she'd like to join her for lunch to discuss a project they are working on, her goals may be to resolve a misunderstanding, to encourage Sofia to work more closely with her, and to explore if they have enough in common to become friends. For her part, Sofia may want to tell Shandi that she doesn't like the topic they have chosen and that she wants to get Shandi to agree to a change. If Shandi and Sofia have a good conversation, Shandi will listen to Sofia and agree to change the topic so that Sofia can be more excited about working on the project. If they are able to quickly agree on a new topic, they may have enough time left while they eat to get to know each other a bit better.

People may not always be aware of their goals when they communicate. For instance, when Jamal passes Tony on the street and asks casually, "Tony, what's happening?," Jamal probably doesn't consciously think, "Tony is an acquaintance, and I want him to understand that I see him and consider him worth recognizing." In this case, Jamal's social obligation to recognize Tony is met spontaneously with the first acceptable expression that comes into Jamal's mind. Regardless of whether Jamal consciously thinks about his goal, it still motivates his behavior. Jamal will have achieved his goal if Tony responds with an equally informal greeting.

We Manage Our Personal Identity

Your **personal identity** is comprised of the traits and characteristics that taken as a whole distinguish you from other people. Personal identity has three facets: (1) who you think you are, (2) who you want others to think you are, and (3) who others think you are.

We learn who we are and how to be who we are through our interactions with others. Parents begin this when they interact with their infants, and the process continues throughout childhood and adulthood. As a child you may have had a teacher who told you that you were smart. If you thought "smart" was a good thing to be, you incorporated "smart" into who you thought you were. Because of this, you may have behaved in ways that demonstrated you were smart so that other teachers would also believe this of you. You may even know that you are smart and love learning. But if your peers make fun of people who are smart, you may limit your vocabulary and what you say when you are with them so that they don't realize how smart you are and tease you.

Because we are social animals, one purpose we have when we communicate is to manage our personal identity to encourage others to think of us in favorable terms and as we would like them to. Sometimes your messages

Personal identity—the traits and characteristics that taken as a whole distinguish you from other people.

OBSERVE AND ANALYZE

Managing Your Personal Identity

Recall a time when you were with someone you knew really well who chose to present himself or herself as someone who you knew the person was not. Describe the circumstances. What do you suppose was this person's motivation? Did it work? Did you ever confront this person about how he or she acted? If so, what happened? Did this incident alter how you viewed this person? If so, how?

reflect who you know yourself to be. At other times, how you want to be seen by your conversational partner is not who you are. So you consciously choose scripts that portray yourself to be other than you are to gain the favor or avoid the ridicule of your conversational partner.

We Conduct Our Relationships

Relationship—a set of expectations that two people have for their behavior with respect to the other, based on the pattern of interaction between them.

Through interpersonal communication, we create and manage our relationships. A **relationship** is a set of expectations that two people have for their behavior with respect to the other based on the pattern of interaction between them (Littlejohn & Foss, 2008). Our interactions define the nature of the relationship between us as well as what that relationship will become. Is the relationship more personal or impersonal, closer or more distant, romantic or platonic, healthy or unhealthy, dependent or interdependent? The answers to these questions depend on how the people in the relationship talk to and behave toward each other. Think about this for a minute. You call someone your friend, romantic partner, or enemy because of the interactions you have had with that person. As we communicate, we "do" our relationships. Without communication, our relationships cannot exist. Some people have close relationships with their parents, while other people are estranged. Some people have a romantic relationship that is close and loving, while other romantic relationships are fraught with quarrels, verbal, and even physical abuse. In each of these cases, the partners come to expect certain behaviors from the other based on the previous interactions that they have had.

Interpersonal communication helps us initiate, develop, maintain, repair, and end our relationships. When Mateo drops down into the chair in class, noticing an attractive woman sitting next to him, he will have to say or do something to begin a relationship. After class he may ask her if she wants to get a cup of coffee at Starbucks. If they find that they enjoy some of the same things and the conversation they have when they are together, they may become friends. If they continue to enjoy each other, they may become a couple. When they have their first fight, or when Mateo becomes jealous of the time she is spending with Josh, they will repair their relationship by talking. And if one of them eventually wants to end the relationship, this will be done through communication as well.

Characteristics of Interpersonal Communication

Now that we have explored the definition of interpersonal communication, let's look at five characteristics (or essential qualities) that describe interpersonal communication.

Interpersonal Communication Is Continuous

Whenever we are in and aware of the presence of other people, consciously or subconsciously, we are constantly sending and receiving messages. These messages may be verbal, but in many cases, they are not. For instance, when you are in a room with someone else and you are silent, the other person may interpret your silence as a message and infer meaning based on your facial expressions and your body movements. Are you frowning, smiling, or looking anxious? Are you shaking, fidgeting, or stretching out in relaxation? So, it's useful to remember that whether you intend to or not, your behavior sends messages.

Interpersonal Communication Is Transactional

In a business or consumer transaction, each person or entity involved in the transaction gives and gets something. This is also true in an interpersonal communication episode where each person involved in the interaction gives and receives messages, gives and receives feedback, gets his or her goals met and helps others fulfill goals, and gives and receives information. It is impossible for only one of the parties to gain something from an interpersonal communication episode. Both parties get something, even if there are differences in what each person gets or how much information, feedback, or goal fulfillment each person receives. For instance, even in a seemingly one-sided communication in which Greg's landlord angrily tells him that he must pay his rent on time or face eviction, and Greg merely responds, "Yes, I promise," Greg and his landlord both gain from the transaction. Greg and his landlord both receive messages and feedback, both give and receive information, and both fulfill goals. Greg's landlord may appear to be the only one in the exchange to fulfill his goal (getting Greg to pay rent on time), but Greg also fulfills a relationship goal (reacting positively and assuaging the situation).

Interpersonal Communication Is Irreversible

Once an interpersonal exchange has taken place, we can never ignore it, take it back, or pretend it did not occur. In other words, although we can wish we hadn't said something, we can never go back in time and reverse the communication. We might be able to repair any damage we have done, but the message has been communicated. When you participate in an online discussion or leave a post on a blog, you are leaving an electronic "footprint" that others can follow and read. E-mails, instant messages (IMs), and text messages are not private, either. Once you push the "send" button, you lose control of that message. Not only can you not take it back, you can no longer direct where it goes.

Ashton Kutcher REPLY
How do you fire Jo Pa? #insult #noclass as a hawkeye fan I find it in poor taste
Updated about 10 hours ago via Twitter for iPhone Permalink

Interpersonal Communication Is Situated

When we say that interpersonal communication is situated, we mean that it occurs within a specific communication setting that affects how the messages are produced, interpreted, and coordinated. Interpersonal communication doesn't occur in the abstract but always in a specific concrete situation (Burleson, 2010). Do you swear or use profanities when you talk? For most of us, the answer is "it depends." While we may swear and make gross comments when we are with friends or peers, many of us wouldn't consider swearing in front of our grandmothers or minister, rabbi, imam, or other religious leader. Similarly, the interpretation of

INTER-ACT WITH SOCIAL MEDIA

Think for a moment about the different types of social media that you use on a daily basis—Facebooking, tweeting, texting, talking on your cell phone, accessing the Internet through your smartphone, listening to podcasts, etc. How do you use each form of social media to maintain your interpersonal relationships? Do you tend to favor one form of social media over another? What types of social media could you live without for 24 hours? Why is this the case?

the statement "I love you" varies with the setting. If made during a candlelit dinner shared by a couple who have been seeing each other since they were freshmen in college, it may be interpreted as a statement of romantic feelings. If made by a mother as she greets her daughter who has come home for Thanksgiving, it can be interpreted as a confirmation of motherly love and approval. If made in response to a joke at a gathering of friends to watch football, it will probably be interpreted as a compliment for being clever. Clearly, what is said and what that means depend on the situation.

Interpersonal Communication Is Indexical

The way in which we communicate is an index or measure of the emotional temperature of our relationship at a particular point in time. If, for instance, when getting in the car to leave for a holiday, Laura says to Darryl, "I've remembered to bring the map," she is not just reporting information. Through her tone of voice and the psychological and historical context in which she speaks, she is also communicating something about the relationship, whether that be "you can always depend on me" or "you never remember to think of these things."

Three aspects of a relationship can be indexed during a message exchange: (1) signaling the level of trust, (2) indicating who has control, or (3) revealing the degree of intimacy in the relationship (Millar & Rogers, 1984).

Trust is the extent to which partners in a relationship rely on, depend on, and have faith that their partner will not intentionally do anything to harm them. Part of our message shares how we are feeling about the relationship at that moment. When Mark says, "I'll pay the bills," to which Sandy replies, "Never mind, I'll pay the bills myself so they won't be late," her statement implies that she doesn't trust Mark to get them paid on time.

Control is the extent to which each person has power or is "in charge" in the relationship. When Tom says to Sue, "I know you're concerned about the budget, but I'll see to it that we have money to cover everything," through his words, tone of voice, and nonverbal behavior, he says that he is "in charge" of finances, that he is in control. In turn, Sue may respond by either verbally or subtly showing that she agrees with his being in control or by challenging him and asserting her desire to control the budget. In other words, the control aspect of the relationship is communicated with either a complimentary or a symmetrical behavior. If Sue says, "Great, I'm glad you're looking after it," her behavior compliments his. He asserts control, and she accepts it. But if Sue responds, "Wait a minute, you're the one who overdrew our checking account last month," she is challenging his control with this symmetrical response.

Relational control is not negotiated in a single exchange. Rather, it is determined through many message exchanges over time. There may or may not be one type of exchange that most characterizes a relationship. For instance, two people may typically engage in complimentary exchanges, or they may have mostly complimentary exchanges regarding social aspects of the relationship but symmetrical exchanges regarding the child-rearing aspects of their relationship. Regardless, the control in the relationship is negotiated in their messages.

Trust—the extent to which partners in a relationship rely on, depend on, and have faith that their partner will not intentionally do anything to harm them.

Control—the extent to which each person has power or is "in charge" in the relationship.

Intimacy is the degree of emotional closeness, acceptance, and disclosure in a relationship. When Cody asks Madison what she is thinking about, and Madison begins to pour out her problems, she is revealing the degree of intimacy she feels in the relationship. Likewise, should she reply, "Oh I'm not really thinking about anything important. Did you hear the news this morning about . . .," her changing the subject indicates that she does not view the relationship as intimate enough to share her problems.

Intimacy—the degree of emotional closeness, acceptance, and disclosure in a relationship.

Ethics and Interpersonal Communication

Can people depend on you to tell the truth? Do you do what you say you will do? Can people count on you to be respectful? In any encounter, we choose whether we will behave in a way that others view as ethical. **Ethics** is a set of moral principles that may be held by a society, a group, or an individual. Ethical standards, commonly held by a society or group, provide general guidelines for behavior and are open to some interpretation and gradual change. So an ethical standard does not tell us exactly what to do in any given situation, only what general principles to consider when deciding how to behave. Ethics directs your attention to the reasons behind the rightness or wrongness of any act and helps you to make a decision recognizing how others may view you and your behavior. Your personal ethic reflects your acceptance of the societal standards you consider to be good. When we behave ethically, we voluntarily act in a manner that complies with societal standards. However, we interpret these societal standards in a way that serves not only the greater good but also our own personal beliefs.

Ethics—a set of moral principles that may be held by a society, a group, or an individual.

Every field of activity—from psychology and biology to sociology and history—also has its own general ethical principles designed to guide the practice of that field. Interpersonal communication is no exception. Every time we communicate, we make choices with ethical implications, and those choices must fulfill both the greater good and our own personal interpretations of them. The general principles that guide ethical interpersonal communication include the following:

1. Ethical communicators are truthful and honest. "An honest person is widely regarded as a moral person, and honesty is a central concept to ethics as the foundation for a moral life" (Terkel & Duval, 1999, p. 122). The fundamental requirement of this standard is that we should not intentionally deceive, or try to deceive, others.

2. Ethical communicators act with integrity. Integrity is maintaining consistency between what we say we believe and what we do. The person who says, "Do what I say, not what I do," lacks integrity, while the person who "practices what he or she preaches" acts with integrity. Integrity, then, is the opposite of hypocrisy.

3. Ethical communicators behave fairly. A fair person is impartial and not biased. To be fair to someone is to gather all the relevant facts, consider only

OBSERVE AND ANALYZE

Indexing a Relationship through Communication

Record one episode of a television series that you aren't familiar with. Watch the episode and identify one relationship in the episode where the characters have a significant conversation. Then watch that portion of the episode again. This time, focus on what you can tell about how much each character trusts the other, who is in control, and how intimate the characters are. Write a short paragraph describing your conclusions and what you observed in the messages that led to your assessment.

circumstances relevant to the decision at hand, and not be swayed by prejudice or irrelevancies. For example, if two of her children are fighting, a mother exercises fairness if she allows both children to explain their side before she decides what to do.

4. Ethical communicators demonstrate respect. Respect is showing regard or consideration for someone else, that person's point of view, and that person's rights. We demonstrate respect through listening and understanding others' positions, even when they are vastly different from our own.

5. Ethical communicators are responsible. We act responsibly when we hold ourselves accountable for our actions. Responsible communicators recognize the power of words. Our messages can hurt others and their reputations. So we act responsibly when we refrain from gossiping, spreading rumors, bullying, etc. And if we unintentionally injure another, then this ethical standard compels us to attempt to repair the damage.

6. Ethical communicators are empathetic. This ethical standard calls on us to acknowledge and honor the feelings of others when we communicate. When Tomas has to turn down Julian's request for vacation the week of Christmas, his communication is ethical if he conveys his understanding of how disappointing this is to Tomas.

In our daily lives, we often face ethical dilemmas and must sort out what is more or less right or wrong. As we make these decisions, we reveal our personal ethical standards. But many times, the ethical response is not clear-cut, and we face an ethical situation that requires us to make hard choices. The end of each chapter features "A Question of Ethics," a short case presenting an ethical dilemma related to the material in that chapter. Your instructor may use these as a vehicle for class discussion, or you may be asked to prepare a written report.

The Dark Side of Interpersonal Communication

The dark side is a metaphor for inappropriate and/or unethical interpersonal communication (Spitzberg & Cupach, 2007). Hence, **dark-side messages** are those that fail to meet standards for ethical and/or appropriate behavior.

Dark-side messages—messages that are not ethical and/or appropriate.

Figure 1.2 illustrates four different types of messages based on the dimensions of ethicalness and appropriateness.

When Liz, who just spent a fortune having her hair cut and colored, asks, "Do you like my new hairstyle?," how do you respond if you think it is awful? The bright-side answer would be one that is both ethical (honest, respectful, empathetic, etc.) and appropriate (sensitive to Liz's feelings and to maintaining a good relationship). The hard dark-side answer would be ethical but inappropriate in that it is likely to hurt Liz and damage your relationship. The easy dark side would be unethical but would be appropriate in that it will spare Liz's feelings and not damage your relationship. The evil dark

	Appropriate ◄──► Inappropriate	
Ethical	Bright Side	Hard Dark Side
Unethical	Easy Dark Side	Evil Dark Side

FIGURE 1.2 Understanding Dark-Side Messages

side would be both unethical and inappropriate. Let's look at how someone might respond to Liz:

> **Bright-side response:** "Liz, it doesn't matter what I think. I can see that you really like how it looks, and that makes me happy."
>
> **Hard dark-side response:** "Wow, Liz, it's a dramatic change. I liked your hair long, and I'd always admired the red highlights you had. But I'm sure it will grow on me."
>
> **Easy dark-side response:** "It looks great."
>
> **Evil dark-side response:** "It doesn't matter what you do to your hair, you're still fat and ugly."

As you can see from these examples, relationships may benefit from bright-side, hard dark-side, and easy dark-side responses, depending on the situation. But evil dark-side responses damage people and their relationships. In various places in this book, we will look at relevant dark-side issues.

Diversity and Interpersonal Communication

Diversity, the variations between and among people, affects nearly every aspect of the interpersonal communication process we have just discussed. Whether we understand each other depends as much on who we are as it does on the words we use. The United States is one of the most multicultural nations in the world. We have succeeded in making the diversity of our people the strength of the nation. Individuals are free to observe a variety of customs, traditions, religious practices, and holy days. Respecting diversity while learning from one another

INTER-ACT WITH SOCIAL MEDIA

Pick up your cell phone and scan your history of sent and received text messages. Are any dark-side messages reflected in these past text messages? How might you categorize them in Figure 1.2? Can they be categorized into the blocks in Figure 1.2? Why did you send these messages to the people you did? How did these messages affect your relationships with these people?

Diversity—variations between and among people.

The marriage between sixteen-year-old Courtney Stodden and fifty-year-old Doug Hutchison caused controversy in the press. What kinds of communication problems might the difference in their ages create, and how might that affect the relationship?

Lessons from American Experience

by Harland Cleveland

Harland Cleveland was a distinguished diplomat and educator. A Medal of Freedom winner, he was president of the University of Hawaii and the World Academy of Art and Science. Cleveland died in 2008 but left behind a legacy of books and articles. In this selection, Cleveland explains how Hawaii, the most diverse of our 50 states, is a model for managing diversity.

We Americans have learned, in our short but intensive 200-plus years of history as a nation, a first lesson about diversity: that it cannot be governed by drowning it in "integration."

I came face-to-face with this truth when I became president of the University of Hawaii. Everyone who lives in Hawaii, or even visits there, is impressed by its residents' comparative tolerance toward each other. On closer inspection, paradise seems based on paradox: Everybody's a minority. The tolerance is not despite the diversity but because of it.

It is not through the disappearance of ethnic distinctions that the people of Hawaii achieved a level of racial peace that has few parallels around our discriminatory globe. Quite the contrary, the glory is that Hawaii's main ethnic groups managed to establish the right to be separate. The group separateness, in turn, helped establish the rights of individuals in each group to equality with individuals of different racial aspect, ethnic origin, and cultural heritage.

Hawaii's experience is not so foreign to the transatlantic migrations of the various more-or-less white Caucasians. On arrival in New York (passing that inscription on the Statue of Liberty, "Send these, the homeless, tempest-tossed, to me"), the European immigrants did not melt into the open arms of the white Anglo-Saxon Protestants who preceded them. The reverse was true. The new arrivals stayed close to their own kind; shared religion, language, humor, and discriminatory treatment with their soul brothers and sisters; and gravitated at first into occupations that did not too seriously threaten the earlier arrivals.

has made our nation vibrant. Nevertheless, when we interact with others, how we form our own messages and how we interpret the messages of others, as well as how we coordinate our interactions, depend on our cultural orientation. Intercultural communication scholar Peter Andersen asserts, "every communicator is a product of his or her culture" (Andersen, 2000, p. 260). Thus, as we become an increasingly diverse nation, the study of intercultural communication is more important than ever. Because culture permeates our interpersonal communication, each chapter of this book will discuss the ways that culture impacts how people act in communication situations. In addition, the "Diverse Voices" articles provide opportunities for you to empathize with the communication experiences of a variety of individuals. In the Diverse Voice article above, Harland Cleveland describes how diverse people in the United States have learned to live together.

The waves of new Americans learned to tolerate each other—first as groups, only thereafter as individuals. Rubbing up against each other in an urbanizing America, they discovered not just the old Christian lesson that all men are brothers, but the hard, new, multicultural lesson that all brothers are different. Equality is not the product of similarity; it is the cheerful acknowledgement of difference.

What's so special about our experience is the assumption that people of many kinds and colors can together govern themselves without deciding in advance which kinds of people (male or female, black, brown, yellow, red, white, or any mix of these) may hold any particular public office in the pantheon of political power.

For the twenty-first century, this "cheerful acknowledgement of difference" is the alternative to a global spread of ethnic cleansing and religious rivalry. The challenge is great, for ethnic cleansing and religious rivalry are traditions as contemporary as Bosnia and Rwanda in the 1990s and as ancient as the Assyrians.

In too many countries, there is still a basic (if often unspoken) assumption that one kind of people is anointed to be in general charge. Try to imagine a Turkish chancellor of Germany, a Christian president of Egypt, an Arab prime minister of Israel, a Tibetan ruler of Beijing, anyone but a Japanese in power in Tokyo. Yet in the United States during the twentieth century, we have already elected an Irish Catholic as president, chosen several Jewish Supreme Court justices, and racially integrated the armed forces right up to the chairman of the Joint Chiefs of Staff....

I wouldn't dream of arguing that we Americans have found the Holy Grail of cultural diversity when, in fact, we're still searching for it. We have to think hard about our growing pluralism. It's useful, I believe, to dissect in the open our thinking about it, to see whether the lessons we are trying to learn might stimulate some useful thinking elsewhere. We still do not quite know how to create "wholeness incorporating diversity," but we owe it to the world, as well as to ourselves, to keep trying.

Excerpted from Cleveland, H. (2006). The Limits to Cultural Diversity. In L. A. Samovar, R. E. Porter, and E. R. McDaniel (Eds.), *Intercultural Communication: A Reader* (11th ed., pp. 405–408). Belmont, CA: Wadsworth. Reprinted by permission of the World Future Society.

For Consideration:

1. Does Cleveland's analysis about how new immigrants become "Americanized" hold true today?
2. How does interpersonal communication facilitate the manner in which America deals with the cultural differences between people?
3. Recall one of your first encounters with someone who was culturally distinct from you. Think about the interaction you had. How did this first interaction affect subsequent ones with people who were different from you?

Interpersonal Communication Competence and You

Communication competence is another person's perception that your messages are both effective and appropriate in a given relationship (Spitzberg, 2000). **Effective messages** achieve the goals that you and your partner have for the interaction. **Appropriate messages** conform to the social, relational, and ethical expectations of the situation. Notice that the definition of competent communication is based on how your communication is seen by someone else. According to Brian Spitzberg (2000), who studies interpersonal communication competence, your ability to send, interpret, and coordinate your messages competently depends on three things: your personal knowledge of how interpersonal communication works, your skills, and your motivation. In other words, to be competent

Communication competence— another person's perception that your messages are both effective and appropriate in a given relationship.

Effective messages—messages that achieve the goals you and your partner have for the interaction.

Appropriate messages—messages that conform to the social, relational, and ethical expectations of the situation.

Spotlight on Scholars

Read about the communication competence research of Brian Spitzberg at www.oup.com/us/verderber.

communicators, we have to (1) know what to say and do (knowledge), (2) know how to say and do it (skills), and (3) have a desire to apply our knowledge and skills (motivation).

Acquire Interpersonal Communication Knowledge

First, we need knowledge about the communication process. The more you understand how to behave in a given situation, the more likely you are to be perceived as competent. You can gain knowledge about how to interact by observing what others do, by asking others how you should behave, by learning through trial and error, and by studying theories of interpersonal communication that have been research tested. For instance, if Emmie wants her manager to view her as competent during their conversation about increasing her responsibilities, she must know how to present her request in a way that her manager will find acceptable and persuasive. She may learn this by observing her manager's behavior in similar situations, asking coworkers how best to approach the situation, analyzing how similar communications with her boss went in the past, or researching persuasion and different approaches to influencing.

Second, competent interpersonal communicators must have not only theoretical and factual knowledge of the communication process and situation at hand but also knowledge about the emotional factors involved. **Emotional intelligence** is the ability to monitor your own and others' emotions and to use this information to guide your communications (Salovey & Mayer, 1990). People differ in the degree to which they are able to identify their own emotions and detect and interpret the emotions of others. In addition, people vary in their abilities to understand slight variations in emotion and to use these variations in communications. No one is born with emotional intelligence, but it can be learned and developed over time.

Emotional intelligence—the ability to monitor your own and others' emotions and to use this information to guide your communications.

Increase Interpersonal Communication Skill

Knowledge is not enough. Competent communicators are also skilled. **Communication skills** are generic message scripts that are appropriate in a particular situation and effective at meeting the goals of the interaction. A large communication skill library increases the likelihood that others will view you as competent because you will have flexibility in how you act. While Emmie can read about persuasion and understand it, this knowledge will be of little help if she doesn't have persuasive skill scripts that she can perform when she meets with her manager.

Communication skills—generic message scripts that are situationally appropriate and effective at meeting the goals of the interaction.

You will learn about two broad categories of interpersonal communication skills in this book. **Micro communication skills** are learned message templates with a specific interaction purpose. They include active listening, making a request, asking a clarifying question, praising, paraphrasing, perception checking, describing feelings, describing behavior, and others. In this course you will want to assess how proficient you are at each of the micro skills. When you identify one that is new to you or difficult for you, focus on mastering it. Micro skills are "lines" that form the foundation on which skill scripts are built. **Communication skill scripts** are mental texts that include micro communication skills and usually require a series of messages to reach the communication goal. These

Micro communication skills—learned message templates that have a specific interaction purpose.

Communication skill scripts—mental texts that include micro communication skills and usually require a series of messages to reach the communication goal.

include scripts for connecting with others in conversation, creating and managing close relationships, supporting others, managing difficulties with others, influencing others, etc. In many of the chapters in this book we provide "guidelines" that can help you build communication skill scripts.

Do you skateboard? Ski? Drive a car? Think about how you mastered these skills. Unless you were a natural talent, it probably took a lot of time and practice. Mastering communication skills is no different than mastering any other skill. Figure 1.3 enumerates the steps for developing interpersonal communication skills and identifies the activities in this book that you can use as you work through each step.

Improving communication skills is like learning a new hobby or sport. If you are learning to play basketball, for instance, you will need to learn techniques that feel uncomfortable at first. You will find it difficult to determine what skills to use when and how to use those skills smoothly and effortlessly. Because some communication skills may not be in your repertoire now, as you work on them you are likely to feel awkward and to see these skills creating unrealistic or phony-sounding messages. Communication skills must be practiced until they feel comfortable and automatic. The more you practice, the easier it will become to use a skill smoothly and with little conscious effort.

Be Motivated to Demonstrate Competence

You need two kinds of motivation if you are going to be a competent communicator. First, you need to be motivated to unlearn your old ineffective scripts and do the hard work required to replace them with better scripts. This means faithfully

1. Identify the situations in which the skill is useful.	**1. Chapter content** discussing interpersonal communication concepts, theory, and frameworks.
2. Learn the steps in executing the skill.	**2.** Skill steps presented in text and in **Skill Builder Boxes**.
3. Observe examples of both effective and ineffective skill use.	**3.** In text examples, **Observe & Analyze Exercises, Conversation and Analysis videos and transcripts**.
4. Practice writing and verbalizing your own messages using the steps.	**4.** End of Chapter **Skill Practice Activities**.
5. Critique your attempts and make appropriate repairs.	**5.** Self, peer, and/or instructor critique of End of Chapter **Skill Practice Activities**.
6. Create a canned plan for the skill by imagining different scenarios in which you might use the skills.	**6.** Canned Plans Journal Activity.
7. Practice using the skill during a conversation in a safe environment.	**7.** In-class skill practice dialogue exercises.
8. Seek and accept feedback on your skill performance and use it to guide further practice.	**8.** Feedback opportunities from peers and instructor followed by **Communication Improvement Plan**.
9. Repeat process.	**9.** Implement **Personal Improvement Plan**.

FIGURE 1.3 Interpersonal Communication Skill Acquisition Steps and Text Activities

working on the skill learning process that we just discussed. Second, you need to be motivated during an interaction to behave in a competent way. Being motivated during a conversation means saying "yes" to three questions: Do I want be perceived as competent? Do I know what will be considered competent in this situation? Have I mastered the skills I need to be competent? You are likely to answer "yes" to the first question if you think you will gain by being perceived as competent. If Emmie thinks that talking with her manager will result in more challenging job responsibilities, then she will be motivated to have the conversation. Emmie also needs to understand how her manager will view her in this particular situation. If Emmie knows her manager well or has seen how others have successfully dealt with this situation, she will answer the second question "yes." Finally, Emmie will be motivated if she can answer "yes" to the third question, confident in her mastery of the skills she will need to assertively influence her manager.

Develop Behavioral Flexibility

Because people, relationships, and conversations are unique, simple rote learning of scripts will not enable you to behave competently. Gaining knowledge and skill, however, will allow you to adapt to a unique situation and respond in more than one way. **Behavioral flexibility** is the capacity to react in a variety of ways to the same or similar situations. Let's look at a concrete example of behavioral flexibility. As her friend Grace is about to leave to go to the library, Tasha starts to emotionally recount a long list of problems to her. Grace must make many decisions and think about the various contexts in which the conversation is taking place. She may recall whether the historical context of their relationship suggests that this is really a serious situation or whether Tasha is just acting like her drama queen self. She may think about the social context and whether their relationship warrants her changing her study plans. She also may think about whether their location is the best physical context for this conversation and whether the psychological context leads her to feel that she is in the best psychological state to help Tasha at this time.

Suppose Grace decides to stay and talk with Tasha. If she is behaviorally flexible, she has many choices about what to say and how to behave. Grace can begin by listening actively. Later, after deciding that emotional support would be appropriate, she may form messages using her comforting skills. Then when she thinks Tasha is ready to hear her, she may give Tasha advice. With each new interpersonal skill she tries, Grace must analyze whether that skill is effective while adapting to what the situation requires, within the bounds of appropriateness and her own needs.

Develop Interpersonal Communication Improvement Plans

Improving your communication practice is a lifelong journey. Realistically, during this course you are not going to master all the skills described in this book, yet study in this area will help you understand how interpersonal communication works and identify a few areas in which skill development

Behavioral flexibility—the capacity to react in a variety of ways to the same or similar situations.

What problems do you personally experience when interacting in social networks like Facebook? Do you regularly misinterpret the messages you receive from friends? Are you nervous about sharing your personal information on Facebook? Do you tend to use Facebook to connect only with a small group of friends (yet you have hundreds of friends)? Using the examples provided in Figure 1.4, develop a Communication Improvement Plan specific to your use of Facebook or other social networks. Clearly state the problem you experience, develop a goal, outline your plan for improvement, and build a plan that will indicate when you have reached your goal.

STEP	DESCRIPTION	EXAMPLE
1. State the problem	Start by writing down a specific communication problem that you have. This problem may affect only one relationship or it may be more general.	Even though my manager consistently overlooks me for interesting projects, leaving me with boring repetitive work that is not preparing me for promotion, I haven't spoken up because I'm not very good at standing up for myself.
2. State the specific goal.	A goal is specific if it is measurable and you know when you have achieved it.	To use assertiveness skills in a conversation with my boss so that she understands that I would like to be assigned interesting projects.
3. Outline a specific plan for reaching the goal.	Identify the skills you need. Adapt them to your situation. Mentally rehearse what you will say. Identify alternative responses. Practice role playing with a friend.	I will need to competently make a complaint, make a request, and use persuasion. I need to practice how to make a complaint both by myself and with someone who can give me feedback. When my partner gives me only positive feedback and I am confident that I can appropriately and effectively make this complaint, I will schedule a meeting with my manager.
4. Identify how you will know you have reached your goal.	Since a good goal can be measured, state how you will determine if you have achieved your goal.	Goal Test: I will know I have achieved my goal when I have finished the conversation with my manager, when my manager has paraphrased what I have said to my satisfaction, and when my manager has agreed to consider me for the next interesting project.

FIGURE 1.4 Writing a Communication Improvement Plan

would benefit you the most. Concentrate on systematically applying the skill learning process to these skill areas during this term. Then as a lifelong learner, you can take what you have learned in this course and continue to develop your skills. During this term and in the years to come, you are more likely to improve your skills if you write formal communication improvement plans. Figure 1.4 describes and provides an example of the contents of a good plan.

At the end of each chapter of this book in which we introduce skills, you will be encouraged to form a communication improvement plan. Once you have written your plan, it will be helpful for you to have another person as a consultant and coach—someone who will provide support and hold you accountable. During this term, you can partner with a classmate, with each of you serving as witness and consultant for the other. You should plan to meet with this person periodically to assess your progress, troubleshoot problems, and develop additional procedures for reaching your goal.

THE SOCIAL MEDIA FACTOR

Understanding Social Media and Interpersonal Communication

Can you remember a time when you did not rely on some form of technology to communicate? Your answer to this question is probably a definite "no." Even if you go back to when you were an infant, your parents probably placed

Social media—highly accessible technologies that facilitate communication and interaction.

Digital communication—we use social media to express, interpret, and coordinate messages to create shared meaning, meet social goals, manage personal identity, and carry out our relationships.

Social network—a group of individuals who are connected by friendship, family ties, common interests, beliefs, or knowledge.

a two-way baby monitor by your crib to alert them when you started crying. That two-way monitor was probably your first interaction with the rapidly developing world of digital communication. Today, the baby monitor may be gone, but you rely on a host of technological tools to remain connected with the people in your life. We use **social media**—technologies that facilitate communication and interaction—to practice **digital communication**: the electronic transmission of digitally encoded information. This includes the use of social media to express, interpret, and coordinate messages to create shared meaning, meet social goals, manage personal identity, and carry out our relationships. From cell phones and YouTube to Facebook and Twitter, an endless list of social media all help us remain connected to others and the world in which we live. We use social media to remain connected with others in our **social network**— a digital web of people who are friends or share careers, organizations, family connections, and common interests. Our social networks are larger now than ever before. This is due primarily to the evolution of technology that connects us to others. Figure 1.5 depicts the evolution of social networking technology. In the mid-1800s to mid-1900s, people likely had simple social networks made up of close friends and family whom they saw on a regular basis and others with whom they connected via postal mail or maybe an occasional telephone call. When the first telephone call was made in the late 1800s, families and friends were probably quite excited because they were now better able to remain connected with others. But long-distance calling was expensive even into the second half of the twentieth century, so it was not a frequently used means of communication for most people. Notice the large gaps between the important points on the first half of the continuum. Technology was evolving but at a slow rate. Now, look at the points on the right half of the continuum. Since the first communication satellite (Telstar 1) was launched in 1962 and the first cell phone call was made in 1973, social media technology has evolved at a rapid rate. In the span of a few short years, the first text message was sent, Google launched, and Facebook, MySpace, YouTube, and Twitter took off. Today's social networks are significantly more complex than those of our ancestors.

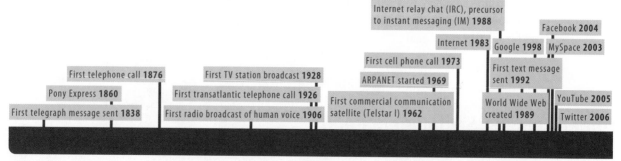

FIGURE 1.5 The Evolution of Social Networking Technology

This is because of the global connectedness, portability, and instantaneous access provided by social media. No matter where we are, we are *plugged in* to our social networks and what is happening in the world. Using social media effectively, however, presents both challenges and opportunities when it comes to interpersonal communication.

Traits of Social Media Technology

The technology of social media has evolved so quickly that we barely give a second thought to using it in place of face-to-face communication. Yet, we should consider the consequences because social media interactions are clearly different from face-to-face communication. These differences may even vary from one form of social media to another. Nancy Baym, a scholar in the emerging field of digital communication theory, identifies seven concepts that allow us to compare different types of social media to one another and to face-to-face communication: interactivity, temporal structure, social cues, replicability, storage, reach, and mobility (Baym, 2010).

Interactivity refers to the ability of a communication tool to facilitate social interaction between groups or individuals through its inherent attributes that foster two-way communication or the capacity to "talk back." Like face-to-face communication, many forms of social media are highly interactive. Because social media allow for interactivity across distances, we can remain connected and engaged with people who live in different cities, states, and countries.

Temporal structure refers to the time that it takes to send and receive messages or the time that elapses during a communication interaction. Communication tools have varying lag times between the sending and receiving of messages. Face-to-face conversations, phone calls, and other exchanges that occur in real time are called **synchronous** forms of communication. In synchronous communication, participants simultaneously act as senders and receivers. E-mail and voice mail are **asynchronous** methods of communication because sending and receiving messages do not happen at the same time; one action begins upon receipt of another. In practice, this means that asynchronous communication features conversational delays because each person must take turns serving as sender or receiver of a message. Sometimes the delay between sending and receiving messages is so short that one may perceive these actions as occurring simultaneously; instant messaging and texting often create this impression.

Social cues are the verbal and nonverbal aspects of a message that offer more information about the context, meaning, and identities of the involved parties. In face-to-face communication, social cues may take the form of facial expression, tone of voice, eye contact, inflection, and hand gestures. Many of the challenges we experience with social media stem from a lack of social cues. Media richness theory can help us better understand the social cues that accompany forms of social media. **Media richness theory** suggests that certain media are better suited than others for some types of messages because social media vary in how well

Interactivity—the ability of a communication tool to facilitate social interaction between groups or individuals.

Temporal structure—the time it takes to send and receive messages or the time that elapses during a communication interaction.

Synchronous—communication that occurs in real time; each interactant is simultaneously a sender and a receiver.

Asynchronous—delays that occur in communication; each interactant must take turns being the sender and receiver of a message.

Social cues—verbal and nonverbal features of a message that offer more information about the context, meaning, and the identities of the involved parties.

Media richness theory—describes communication channels by the amount of verbal and nonverbal information that can be exchanged through a particular channel.

Richness continuum

LEAN   **RICH**

| Bulk letters, posters | Letters, e-mail, texting | Facebook/ MySpace | Telephone | Skype | Face-to-face |

FIGURE 1.6 A Continuum of Media Richness

they reproduce the intended meaning (Daft & Lengel, 1984). Accordingly, some media are inherently richer in their social cues than others. Figure 1.6, displays common forms of social media by degrees of richness. You will note the position of face-to-face communication along the right side of the figure. As you scan further and further to the left, you will see how social media can become leaner (convey less of the message meaning) as the presence of rich social cues diminishes. Face-to-face is the richest form of communication. Bulk mail is a lean form of communication, while a handwritten note or e-mail are more robust and allow the sender to personalize a message for a specific receiver.

The richer the media, the more context cues are provided. For example, when you call a friend's cell phone, what is one of the first things you say after your friend answers the phone? More than likely, you will quickly say something to the effect of, "Hey, where are you?" You do this because the two of you are not sharing a physical context that can help you interpret your partner's social cues. When on the phone, you are unaware of these cues unless you ask. Social cues are even more limited in text-based social media. The more social cues available in a message, the more readily the receiver can understand the sender's intended meaning. The richness of a given medium directly affects the degree to which social cues are available.

Storage and *replicability* refer to the fact that some digital communication transpires in an environment that saves messages and provides continued electronic access, making it possible to view, copy, and redistribute past messages. In contrast, how many times have you recorded a face-to-face conversation or even a telephone call? Probably rarely or never. Generally speaking, face-to-face conversations are gone forever once they are completed. Text-based social media, on the other hand, automatically record interactions and create a permanent storage space for digital communication. You should assume that every one of your text-based social media interactions—including e-mail messages, posts to Facebook, photos that you upload, and tweets—are probably stored on a server somewhere and accessible to other people. Unlike voiced interactions like face-to-face and telephone conversations, text-based social media interactions can be accessed, replicated, and distributed at a later time. This gives text-based interactions a permanence in cyberspace that distinguishes them from the more transitive record of our voiced interactions.

Face-to-face communication is limited to people who can fit in one particular space. Social media has tremendous reach, the ability to connect with people in distant places. The messages we send through social media travel quickly and widely. With a single keystroke or tap of a Blackberry key, a message can be sent to thousands and maybe millions of people. When a message "**goes viral**," it reaches a level of replicability never intended, and certainly never imagined, by its original sender. Viral messages reach or "infect" enormous audiences. Different types of social media vary in their **mobility**, the extent to which they are portable. Some social media have limited mobility. A landline telephone or desktop computer is not mobile. Laptop computers

"Go viral"—messages that reach enormous audiences by "infecting" viewers and users with the message.

Mobility—extent to which social media are portable or stationary.

A QUESTION OF ETHICS ● What Would You Do?

Alisha and Rachelle became friends during high school and now live together in an off-campus apartment. Alisha, an only child, is a high-strung, anxious, and emotional person, while Rachelle, the oldest of six children, is easygoing and calm. Alisha depends on Rachelle to listen to her problems and to comfort and advise her; usually she is a good friend and supports Rachelle as well.

Currently, at work and at school, Alisha is under a lot of stress. Because of that, she hasn't had time to talk with Rachelle about what is going on in Rachelle's life. When they talk, the conversation is always about Alisha. Even when Rachelle tries to talk about what is happening to her, Alisha is distracted and manages to redirect the conversation back to her own problems. In the last two weeks, Alisha forgot that they had made plans to have dinner together, and another time she canceled their plans at the last minute.

This morning, Alisha told Rachelle, "I don't have time to pick up my prescription at the drugstore so you will have to do it, and my project group from biology is coming over to work this evening so I need you to straighten up this place. I don't have time to vacuum or dust, but I know that you have a break between classes and when you have to leave for work. Oh, and I'm really stuck in my Soc class. You know how slammed I am for time, and I have a one-page position paper due

tomorrow. I know that you aced Soc last semester, so it would be great if you would do a first draft for me. The assignment directions are on my desk." Before Rachelle could respond, Alisha continued, "Well, I've got to run. See you tonight."

After Alisha left, Rachelle plopped down in the chair and tried to sort out her feelings. As she talked to herself, she realized that while she was deeply concerned for Alisha, who seemed to be spinning out of control, she also believed that Alisha was taking advantage of her. It appeared to Rachelle that the relationship had become one-sided, with Alisha expecting Rachelle to serve her. Rachelle felt sad and abandoned as she recognized that Alisha had quit even trying to meet Rachelle's needs. "How," she asked herself, "has this happened?"

For Consideration:

1. How do the functions of interpersonal communication help you to understand what is happening to Rachelle and Alisha?
2. How do the elements of the communication setting (the social, historical, psychological, and cultural contexts) help you to understand?
3. Describe the levels of trust, control, and intimacy in the relationship. Be specific about what led you to your conclusions.
4. What ethical principles are involved in this case? Which principles does each woman violate?
5. What should Rachelle do now?

and electronic tablets are mobile, but smartphones are the most portable of all social media devices. The portability of some social media devices enables us to remain connected with friends and family no matter where we are. Social media mobility also comes with certain obligations. The downside to increased portability is that others expect us to be connected at all times and some people become annoyed if we are not instantly responsive to their messages. So with portability can come the troubling expectation that we are accountable to others at all times.

These seven concepts that characterize social media provide the playing field on which to practice our interpersonal communication skills in a digital world. Understanding the inherent properties that separate social media technology from face-to-face communication is critical to developing successful digital communication practices. In the following chapters, we'll build on this foundation by considering how personal communication habits, attitudes, and style influence how we use social media.

Summary

We have defined interpersonal communication as the complex process through which people express, interpret, and coordinate messages to create shared meaning, meet social goals, manage personal identity, and carry out relationships. Messages are performances that use words, sentences, and/or nonverbal behaviors to convey the thoughts, feelings, and intentions of the speaker. A canned plan is a library of scripts that you can draw from to create a message for the type of situation you are experiencing. A script is a mental message or series of messages acquired from previous experience, vicarious experiences, or formal learning. During a conversation you identify canned plans that you judge to be appropriate and select specific scripts as the template for the messages you perform and how you interpret the messages of others. The message production process consists of the activities that you undertake to encode and express a message. The message interpretation process consists of the activities you undertake to decode a message and provide feedback about it. Feedback messages tell others how the original message was interpreted. The interaction coordination process consists of the activities that you and your conversation partner use to adjust your messages to each other. Meaning is the significance that the sender and the receiver each attach to a specific message. Shared meaning occurs when the receiver's interpretation of the message is similar to what the speaker intended. Through interpersonal communication we meet our social goals, conduct our relationships, and manage our personal identity. Interpersonal communication is continuous, transactional, irreversible, situated, and indexical. Ethics is a set of moral principles that may be held by a society, a group, or an individual. When we communicate, we make choices with ethical implications involving truthfulness and honesty, integrity, fairness, respect, responsibility, and empathy. The dark side of communication is a metaphor used to describe messages that are unethical and/or inappropriate. Diversity, variations between and among people, affects nearly every aspect of the communication process. Communication competence is the impression that messages are both appropriate and effective in a given relationship. It involves increasing knowledge, skills, and motivation. Behavioral flexibility is the capacity to adapt messages to the same or similar situations. You can become a more competent communicator by studying interpersonal communication concepts, theories, and frameworks; by working to acquire new and improve existing interpersonal communication skills; and by desiring to communicate in ways that are effective and appropriate to the situation.

Interpersonal communication also encompasses the use of social media. The rapid evolution of social media technology has been widely adopted but poses special challenges to effective communication. The media richness of a given digital channel affects the robustness of possible communication. Various digital communication media may be compared by analyzing seven factors found in all types of social media: interactivity, temporal structure, social cues, replicability, storage, reach, and mobility.

Chapter Resources

What You Should Be Able *to Explain:*

- The definition of interpersonal communication
- The three processes that comprise interpersonal communication
- How messages are formed and meaning shared
- The purposes of interpersonal communication
- The characteristics of interpersonal communication
- The ethical standards of interpersonal communication
- The types of messages described as the dark side of interpersonal communication
- The definition and components of interpersonal communication competence
- The two kinds of interpersonal communication skills
- The concepts that allow us to compare different types of social media to one another and to face-to-face communication

What You Should Be Able *to Do:*

- Write a Communication Improvement Plan (CIP)

Self-test questions based on these concepts are available on the companion Web site (www.oup.com/us/verderber) as part of Chapter 1 resources.

Key Words

Flashcards for all of these key terms are available on the *Inter-Act* Web site.

Appropriate messages p. 21
Asynchronous, p. 27
Behavioral flexibility, p. 24
Canned plan, p. 7
Communication competence,
    p. 21
Communication setting, p. 10
Communication skill scripts, p. 22
Communication skills p. 22
Control, p. 16
Cultural context, p. 11
Dark-side messages, p. 18
Decoding, p. 6
Digital communication, p. 26
Diversity, p. 19
Effective messages, p. 21
Emotional intelligence, p. 22

Encoding, p. 6
Ethics, p. 17
External noises, p. 11
Feedback, p. 6
Go viral, p. 29
Historical context, p. 11
Interaction coordination, p. 9
Interactivity, p. 27
Internal noises, p. 11
Interpersonal communication, p. 6
Intimacy, p. 17
Meaning, p. 10
Media richness theory, p. 27
Message, p. 6
Message interpretation, p. 8
Message production, p. 8
Micro communication skills, p. 22

Mobility, p. 29
Noise, p. 11
Personal identity, p. 13
Physical context, p. 10
Process, p. 8
Psychological context, p. 11
Relationship, p. 14
Script, p. 7
Semantic noises, p. 11
Shared meaning, p. 10
Social context, p. 11
Social cues, p. 27
Social media, p. 26
Social network, p. 26
Synchronous, p. 27
Temporal structure, p. 27
Trust, p. 16

Apply Your Knowledge

The following questions challenge you to demonstrate your mastery of the concepts, theories, and frameworks in this chapter by using them to explain what is happening in a specific situation.

Interpersonal Communication Concepts

Rita and her daughter Jessica are shopping. As they walk through an elegant boutique, Jessica, who is feeling particularly happy, sees a blouse she wants. With a look of great anticipation and excitement, she exclaims, "Look at this, Mom—it's beautiful. Can I try it on?" Worried about the cost, Rita frowns, shrugs her shoulders, and replies hesitantly, "Well, yes, I guess so." Jessica, noticing her mother's hesitation, continues, "And it's marked down to twenty-seven dollars!" Rita relaxes, smiles, and says, "Yes, it is attractive—try it on. If it fits, let's buy it."

1.1   Use the definition of interpersonal communication to explain what is happening in this brief conversation between a mother and daughter.

1.2   How is each of the characteristics of interpersonal communication demonstrated in the conversation between Jessica and Rita?

1.3   Did Rita violate any ethical principle when she hesitantly responded, "Well, yes, I guess so." Was this a dark-side response? Explain your answer.

THE SOCIAL MEDIA FACTOR

Scott and Lynn have been dating for almost a year. As they approach their one-year anniversary, they begin drifting further and further apart. Right before their anniversary, Lynn finds out that Scott is cheating on her with one of her best friends. Lynn is furious. She immediately calls Scott and, in her rage, tells him that their relationship is over. After she hangs up on Scott, she texts her best friend and warns her to be on the lookout for revenge. Lynn then changes her relationship status on Facebook from "In a Relationship" to "Single." She tweets the following: "Scott is a huge jerk! And a certain girl better watch her back!!!"

1.4   Use the concepts that let us compare different types of social media to one another and to face-to-face communication to explain what is happening in this situation.

Skill Practice

Skill practice activities give you the chance to rehearse a new skill by responding to hypothetical or real situations. Additional skill practice activities are available on the companion Web site.

Communication Improvement Plan: Verbal Communication

1.5   Write a Communication Improvement Plan whose goal is to perfect scripts for turning down a date when you have a previous commitment but would like to see the person at some other time. As part of this activity, create at least three different response messages that meet your goal. You can download a Communication Improvement Plan form at the *Inter-Act* Web site.

State the problem: _____

State the Goal:_____

Procedure: _____

Goal Assessment Method: _____

Inter-Act with Media

Television

Family Guy, episode: "Peter, Peter, Caviar Eater" (1999).

In an episode of *FOX* television's, *Family Guy,* Marguerite Pewterschmidt, Lois Griffin's rich aunt, visits and dies as soon as she enters Lois' home. As Lois and her family scramble to coordinate the funeral arrangements, the attorney handling Aunt Marguerite's estate shows Lois and her husband, Peter, a prerecorded videotaped message from Aunt Marguerite. Aunt Marguerite tells Lois that she will become the owner of her lavish Cherrywood Manor estate in Newport, Rhode Island. Later in the episode, Lois and Peter Griffin arrive at Cherrywood Manor, where they are greeted with a musical welcome by the maids, butlers, and other staff. As Lois and Peter settle into their new life on the glamorous estate, Peter struggles to fit in with the family's new upper-class neighbors. During a dinner outing at the local yacht club, Peter sickens the neighbors by recounting a story about an ugly rat on a yacht. He continues to tell other inappropriate stories, making a dinner guest ill. Peter and his family are eventually thrown out of the yacht club.

IPC Concepts: Communication setting, communication competence, appropriate messages.

To the Point:

> How might Peter's behavior have influenced perceptions of his communication competence?
> Have you ever experienced a similar situation with a friend who acted out of turn at a formal function?

Cinema

Erin Brockovich (2000). Steven Soderbergh (director). Julia Roberts, Albert Finney, Aaron Eckhart.

Based on a true story, this film dramatizes the story of Erin Brockovich's legal battle against the Pacific Gas and Electric Company (PG&E). As an unemployed single mom with three children, Brockovich (Roberts) loses a personal injury lawsuit and subsequently asks her lawyer, Edward Masry (Finney), for assistance to find her a job to compensate for the loss. Ed hires her as a file clerk in his law office. In her new job, she runs across some files on a case involving medical records and the notation that PG&E offered to purchase the home of Donna Jensen in the town of Hinkley, California. After uncovering details surrounding the case, Erin is convinced that there are factual inconsistencies and conducts additional research. Her research reveals that Hinkley's water supply was poisoned. The health of the entire community is now compromised. Through her investigation, Erin found that PG&E should be held accountable for the serious illnesses that plagued Hinkley residents. Later in the film, Erin met a gentleman who reported that he destroyed important PG&E files. She uncovered a 1966 document that linked communication from a PG&E executive to the Hinkley station. This document revealed that officials knew that the water was contaminated. Advised to cover up the issue and not inform the Hinkley citizens, officials took no action to address this major problem. Erin tenaciously pursued justice for the Hinkley citizens and illustrated how important effective and appropriate messages are to communication competence.

IPC Concepts: Communication competence, effective messages, appropriate messages.

To the Point:

> How might Erin's persistence in this situation affect perceptions of her effectiveness as a communicator?

How might her persistence contribute to and/or detract from her effectiveness as a communicator?

How might this persistence affect her relationships with others?

What's on the Web

Find links and additional material, including self-quizzes, on the companion Web site at www.oup.com/us/verderber.

2

Forming and Using Social Perceptions

As they left class, Louisa turned to Amber and Kai and said, "Wow, Professor Green is a great lecturer. This is going to be my favorite course." "Mine too," Amber replied. Kai chimed in, "You know I hate to spoil the party, but a guy on the tennis team with me had Professor Green last semester, and he told me that Green's midterm test was really awful, and it took him forever to get them back to the class. It was past the final drop date when he finally figured out how he was doing in the class. Green's reputation is that he sucks you in and then kills your grade point average. You can have this guy. I wish there was another section."

What you should be able to explain after you have studied this chapter:

- The definition of perception and social perception
- How the mind selects, organizes, and interprets information
- The goal in forming perceptions of others
- The ways we form perceptions of others

- How we predict what others are likely to do and why they do it
- Why we sometimes misperceive others
- How we can improve the accuracy of our perceptions of others
- What self-perceptions, self-concept, and self-esteem are and how they are formed
- How culture dictates types of self-perceptions

- How we can improve our self-perceptions
- The way that our attitude about digital communication affects our use of social media

What you should be able to do after you have studied this chapter:

- Conduct a perception check
- Improve the accuracy of your social perception

Social perception—the set of processes by which people perceive themselves and others.

Three different women, with different views of the same man—how come? Who is right? Is Professor Green a great lecturer or a diabolical GPA breaker, or both? How could three women walk away from the same class with different ideas of who Dr. Green was? **Social perception** is the set of processes by which we comprehend who we believe others and ourselves to be. Our social perceptions influence how we communicate. How you view your conversational partner will impact what you say and how you say it. Likewise, what you think of yourself will also influence how you talk with others. Understanding these processes, then, provides a foundation for your study of interpersonal communication.

We begin this chapter by describing the process whereby we perceive anything. Next we explain how and why we perceive others as we do. We then discuss why our perceptions of others may be inaccurate and provide several guidelines for overcoming perceptual biases. In the latter part of this chapter, we explore how our social perception helps to determine our self-concept and self-esteem. We will see that these self-perceptions are dictated by our culture and greatly influence our interpersonal interactions. Finally, we discuss how we can improve your self-perceptions.

The Perception Process

Perception—the process of attending to, organizing, and interpreting the information that we receive through our senses.

Every second, your senses are bombarded with more stimuli than your mind can process. Consequently, you pay attention to some and ignore others. **Perception** is the process of attending to, organizing, and interpreting the information that we receive through our senses. Our perceptions form our understanding of what for us is real and true. Sometimes our perception of something agrees with that of others. Sometimes it does not. Another person who has the same sensory input may perceive the same situation entirely differently and regard this perception as real and true. When our perceptions are different from those with whom we interact, sharing meaning becomes more challenging. To get a better idea of the process of perceiving, let's explore each of the three stages. First, your brain attends to and selects the information or stimuli that it receives from your senses; then it organizes the stimuli; and then it interprets the stimuli, integrating the new information with previous learning.

Attention and Selection

Although we are subject to a constant barrage of sensory stimuli, we can focus our attention on relatively little of it. We choose or select the stimuli that matter to us based in part on our needs, interests, and expectations.

Needs are those things we consciously or unconsciously feel we require to sustain us biologically or psychologically. We are likely to pay attention to those things that meet these biological and psychological needs and filter out those things that don't. When you are hungry, you are more likely to notice the aroma wafting from the nearby Dunkin' Donuts shop than when you have just finished eating. How closely you pay attention in class is likely to depend on whether you believe the information will be on the test.

Needs—things we consciously or unconsciously feel we require to sustain us biologically or psychologically.

In contrast to needs, **interests** are those things that prompt our curiosity but are not essential to sustain us biologically or psychologically. In addition to what we need, we are likely to pay attention to information that pertains to our interests and filter out that which does not. For instance, you may not even notice that music is playing in the background until you realize that it's your favorite group. Similarly, when you are really interested in a person, you are more likely to pay attention to what that person is saying.

Interests—things that prompt our curiosity but are not essential to sustain us biologically or psychologically.

Expectations are those things we notice because we are accustomed to noticing them. We tend to see what we expect to see and to ignore information that defies our expectations. For example, take a quick look at the phrases in the triangles in Figure 2.1. OK, now that you've looked, did you notice anything unusual about the wording? If you have never seen this example before,

Expectations—things we notice because we are accustomed to noticing them.

FIGURE 2.1 A Sensory Test of Expectation

you probably read "Paris in the springtime" in the first triangle, "Once in a lifetime" in the second triangle, and "Bird in the hand" in the third triangle. But if you glance at the words from bottom to top, you will see that what you perceived was not exactly what is written. Do you now see the repeated words? If you missed them the first time, it's because we don't *expect* to see duplicate words in a sentence. In interpersonal situations, we may not notice when people change their behavior because we expect them to behave as they always have. So if Karen doesn't usually thank Chris for walking the dog, Chris may not even notice when she does.

Organization

Through the process of attention and selection, we reduce the number of stimuli our brains must process. Still, the number of stimuli we attend to at any moment is substantial. Our brains arrange these stimuli to make sense, using the organizing principles of simplicity and pattern.

Simplicity reduces very complex stimuli to easily recognizable forms. For instance, if you see a picture of a woman you don't know, you may notice what she is wearing, her posture, the expression on her face, and her surroundings. You might simplify them and conclude that she's a successful businesswoman, or a flight attendant, or a grandmother. When we receive complex messages, we also simplify these. For example, as Tony leaves an hour-long meeting with his student loan officer, he simplifies the many options discussed into one sentence: "I can't get enough grant aid to pay all of my tuition, so I'll go part time and look for a job."

Pattern recognition is the organization of stimuli into easily recognizable patterns or systems of interrelated parts. It occurs when the brain identifies that the complex stimuli it is sensing are similar to or fit something it already recognizes or knows. For example, when you see several people in the same uniform playing instruments instead of seeing each person, you may detect a pattern and organize what you are seeing into a trumpet section, trombone section, tuba section, drummers, etc. In our interactions with others, we use patterns to interpret messages and conversations. Suppose, for example, you are walking across campus and spy a friend hurrying toward you who says "Hi" as she passes without breaking stride. You recognize that this pattern of communication signals that she wants to acknowledge that she has seen you but doesn't want to engage in a real conversation.

Interpretation

As your brain attends to, selects, and organizes the stimuli it receives from the senses, it also interprets this information by assigning meaning to it. Look at the following three sets of numbers. What are they?

    A. 781 631 7348
    B. 285 37 5632
    C. 4632 7364 2596 2174

Simplicity—the reduction of very complex stimuli to easily recognizable forms.

Pattern recognition—the organization of stimuli into easily recognizable patterns or systems of interrelated parts.

As your brain looks at these patterns, it tries to interpret what they mean. If you are used to seeing similar sets of numbers every day, you probably interpreted A as a telephone number, B as a Social Security number, and C as a credit card number. But your ability to interpret these numbers depends on your familiarity with the patterns. A French person may not recognize 781 631 7348 as a phone number since the pattern for phone numbers in France is 0x xx xx xx xx.

Similarly, the way we interpret messages and conversational situations affects how we interact. Suppose, for example, that one evening Miguel sees a woman at a club looking across the room at him. As he notices her, she continues to maintain eye contact, slowly turns to directly face him, and begins to smile at him while flipping back her hair. Based on his previous experience, he may interpret her behavior as flirting. Not all people will interpret the same behavior the same way, though. Suppose, for instance, Sal and Daniel pass Tito on the way to eat lunch. Even though they both greet him, Tito walks past without saying a word. Sal notices that Tito looks troubled, is walking quickly, and is carrying a load of books. Daniel notices that Tito glanced at them quickly, grimaced, and then averted his eyes. "Boy," says Sal, "I guess Tito must really be worried about the history paper." "You think so?" Daniel replies, "I'd say that he's still mad at me for hitting on Carmen."

Dual Processing in Perception

You may be thinking, "Hey, I don't go through all of these steps. I just automatically 'understand' what's going on." You are right. Because humans are limited in their capacity to take in and process information, their minds have developed a dual approach to handling a wide variety of cognitive tasks (Baumeister, 2005). Most perceptual processing happens in our subconscious mind. This **automatic processing** is a fast, top-down, subconscious approach to perceiving that draws on previous experience to make sense out of what we are now encountering. This "mindless" approach to perception processing is our default mode. When the brain works in this manner, it is using shortcuts called **heuristics**, rules of thumb for how something is to be viewed based on our past experience with similar stimuli. If you have been driving a car for some time, you don't really think about the situations you encounter. When the light turns green, you "go." You don't consciously think about taking your foot off the brake and applying it to the gas pedal. When you see your mother, you know what to do. You don't consciously think about it. You just go up and give her a quick kiss on the cheek.

But what happens when you encounter things beyond the realm of your normal experience or when you think something important may be happening? Then you exert a conscious effort to perceive what is going on. **Conscious processing** is a slow, deliberative approach to perceiving during which we examine and think about the stimuli. Remember when you were first learning to drive? It took intense concentration to figure out what was happening on the road and

Automatic processing—a fast, top-down, subconscious approach to perceiving that draws on previous experience to make sense out of what we are now encountering.

Heuristics—rules of thumb for how something is to be viewed based on our past experience with similar stimuli.

Conscious processing—a slow, deliberative approach to perceiving during which we examine and think about the stimuli.

how you were supposed to react to it. While you might automatically greet your mother with a kiss, it probably takes much more conscious processing for you to accurately perceive when the situation is right for you to kiss the person you have just begun to date. As your study of interpersonal communication continues, you will see that dual process thinking influences other parts of our communication behavior.

Perceiving Others

Now that you have a basic understanding of how perception works, let's look at how that process works when we perceive other people. When you meet others for the first time, you are faced with two main questions: What is this person like, and what is this person likely to do and why? When we perceive others, we do so with the goal of reducing our uncertainty about them. As we get to know people, we get better at predicting their behavior, but some uncertainty remains.

Reducing Uncertainty

Uncertainty reduction theory—a way to explain how individuals monitor their social environments to know more about themselves and others.

Because uncertainty in social situations is uncomfortable, we naturally try to alleviate it by quickly finding answers to questions about other people. Charles Berger and James Bradac (1982) proposed **uncertainty reduction theory** as a way to explain how individuals monitor their social environments to know more about themselves and others (Littlejohn & Foss, 2005). In other words, when people interact they look for information about their partner to understand who their partner is and predict what their partner is likely to do. When we have reduced our uncertainty, we are more comfortable in our communications (Guerrero, Andersen, & Afifi, 2007). As we interact, we form impressions of others and make judgments about why they behave as they do.

We seek information about others because if we are uncertain about what they are like, we will have a difficult time predicting their behaviors and the outcome of our interactions with them, and this leads to discomfort. When we experience uncertainty we work to reduce it based on our knowledge. We use the cultural, sociological, and psychological information we have available to aid us in perceiving others and in reducing our uncertainty about them (Miller & Steinberg, 1975).

When we first meet someone, we don't have much available information to help us make predictions about him or her. So we tend to make so-called cultural-level predictions about the person based on what we can see. We make such predictions based on stereotypes of race, sex, age, and appearance. Because these predictions are broad generalizations based on very abstract and general information, they frequently tend to be inaccurate, so we need to interact with the person further to move to a greater level of certainty that is not based on stereotypes.

As we do so, we tend to ask questions about the groups to which the person belongs. Getting-to-know-you conversations often involve a series of questions about occupations, education, places of residence, hobbies, and interests. This questioning allows us to make less stereotypical and more sociological-level predictions based on the other person's membership groups. Answers to these questions allow us to discover common ground, thus easing our discomfort and allowing us to make more accurate predictions about how the other is likely to act. Increasingly, people are using the Internet as a way of getting to know others at a sociological level. It's not uncommon today for people to research new acquaintances by searching the web using Google or other search engines. It's even socially acceptable to admit that we've been researching our acquaintances, classmates, and potential romantic partners (Engdahl, 2007).

Sociological-level knowledge of others is still limited and based on stereotypes, however, so over time, as we come to know another person better, we refine our predictions based on the unique experiences and qualities of that person, rather than on appearance or group memberships. Eventually, we come to know with a great deal of accuracy, though never with total accuracy, how this unique person may respond in a situation. This last level of prediction is called the psychological level, and because it is based on individual differences among people rather than generalizations across large groups of people, it is the most accurate level of prediction. When we reach this level with a person, we feel closer to and more comfortable with that person.

Let's look at how we form impressions and how we make judgments about what causes others to act as they do.

Impression Formation

We form our perceptions about who others are in a variety of ways. But three of the most important ways are based on their physical appearance, the implicit theories we form about their personalities, and their assumed similarity to us.

Physical Appearance

The first thing we notice about other people is how they look. While it may seem a superficial way to judge others, if we don't know them, we have to use the information that is available, which is often their appearance. We notice their skin color, facial features, physique, clothing, and personal grooming. We form impressions based on physical appearance very quickly. In fact, one study found that we can assess how attractive, likeable, trustworthy, competent, and aggressive we think people are after looking at their faces for only 100 milliseconds (Willis & Todorov, 2006). Unfortunately, many African American men have experienced a DWB (driving while black)—the infuriating experience of being stopped by the police while lawfully driving a car simply because of race and sex. Clearly, our interpretation of physical appearance has far-reaching consequences for what we think of and how we interact with someone.

What are the individuals in this photograph communicating through their physical appearance, dress, and behavior?

Implicit Personality Theory

The second way we form impressions is by applying our implicit personality theories. **Implicit personality theory** is the belief that two or more personal traits or characteristics go together. Using implicit personality theory, if we see people displaying one trait, we assume that they have the others that we associate with it. For example, if you meet someone who is multilingual, you may expect her or him to be intelligent. Or if you meet someone volunteering at a homeless shelter, you may expect this person to be compassionate.

Implicit personality theory—a belief that two or more personal traits or characteristics go together.

Assumed Similarity

A third way you form initial impressions about others is by thinking that others who share one characteristic with you also share others. You will act on this belief until you have evidence that they are different. Suppose that both Mason and Sam belong to Christian Fellowship. Mason may not only assume that Sam's religious beliefs are similar to his but also believe that Sam is like him in other ways as well. For instance, because Mason is honest and does not cheat on exams, he may consider Sam to be the same. We continue to assume that others are like us until we get information that contradicts our impression.

Making Attributions

At the center of our quest to reduce uncertainty is our need to be able to predict how others behave. By its nature, predicting something depends on understanding the cause-and-effect relationship between things. When we see someone acting a certain way, we try to figure out what is causing the behavior. Once we have an explanation, we use it to predict how that person will act in similar situations in the future. **Attributions** are reasons we give for others' and our own behavior. For instance, suppose a co-worker with whom you had a noon lunch date has not arrived by 12:30. How do you explain her tardiness? One way might be to find a reason beyond your friend's control. A **situational attribution** is the perception that the cause of the behavior is some situation outside the control of the person. So you might assume that your co-worker must have received an important phone call at the last minute, needed to finish a task before lunch, or had an accident on the way to the restaurant. On the other hand, you may have made a **dispositional attribution**, attributing behavior to some cause that is under the control of the person. For example, you may perceive that your co-worker is forgetful, self-absorbed, or insensitive to others. In either case, your attribution has answered the question, "Why is my co-worker late?"

The attributions you make reduce your uncertainty about other people's behavior in two ways. First, when you make an attribution, identifying a cause for the specific behavior you see in the immediate situation, you have a better idea about how to respond. So when your co-worker arrives, if you made a situational attribution, you may ask, "Is everything alright?" Whereas if you made a dispositional attribution, your first comment to your co-worker might be, "I guess you

Attributions—reasons we give for others' and our own behavior.

Situational attribution—the perception that the cause of the behavior is some situation outside the control of the person.

Dispositional attribution—attributing behavior to some cause that is under the control of the person.

almost forgot to come." Second, the attributions we make about people's behavior in the current interaction will inform how we expect them to behave in the future. If your co-worker confirmed that she was late because she was called into her manager's office for a meeting, you will expect her to be prompt the next time. Likewise, if your co-worker confirmed your hunch that she had forgotten your lunch date, the next time you have plans, you might send a text to remind her.

Understanding and Overcoming Person-Perception Biases

As we have said, people are limited in their ability to accurately process all the information available to help them. When we first meet someone, we tend to make quick assumptions to answer such questions as "What is this person like?" and "What is this person likely to do?" These shortcuts we take can lead us to form inaccurate impressions of others and to make incorrect attributions and predictions about their behavior. Selective perception, stereotyping, halo effects, forced consistency, projection, and the fundamental attribution error are among the most common person-perception biases that result from these perceptual shortcuts. Let's briefly explore each of these and then consider ways that we can make our perceptions of others more accurate.

Selective Perception

Have you ever watched a friend's girlfriend at a party flirting outrageously with someone else in front of your friend while he seemed oblivious to it? Maybe you tried to point out to your friend what his girlfriend was doing, and he denied it or provided a different spin on her behavior. **Selective perception** is distortion that arises from paying attention only to what we expect to see or hear and from ignoring what we don't expect. Your friend didn't expect to see his girlfriend flirting, so he didn't notice it, or he attributed her behavior to some other cause. If you confronted him, he might have replied, "I didn't see that," or "She wasn't flirting, she's just really friendly."

Stereotyping

Stereotyping is applying the beliefs you have about the characteristics of a group to an individual whom you identify as a member of that group. There are at least two problems with stereotyping. First, the characteristics that your stereotype assigns to group members may be inaccurate for most members of the group. For example, while there are terrorists who are Muslims, the vast majority of Muslims are not jihadists bent on the destruction of Western civilization. Yet some people stereotype all Muslims in this way. Second, the individual you are stereotyping may not have the characteristics that you accurately associate with this group. Many—but not all—evangelical Christians are political conservatives. But there are evangelicals with liberal economic and environmental beliefs who would not fit the stereotype.

Stereotyping a person based on the characteristics of a group to which the person belongs without regard to how the person may vary from the group

---

Social Perception of Others

Go to a public place, like a mall, student union, or park. One at a time, identify three individuals whom you don't know and who seem different from you and different from each other.

After watching each person for at least 3 minutes, write a short paragraph describing that person. Begin by describing the physical person, then answer the question, "What do you think this person is like?"

Now compare your paragraphs. How are they similar and different? For example, are some of your descriptions more positive or flattering? Are some descriptions more specific than others? Beside considering their physical characteristics, how did you arrive at your conclusions?

Selective perception—distortion that arises from paying attention only to what we expect to see or hear and from ignoring what we don't expect.

Stereotyping—applying the beliefs you have about the characteristics of a group to an individual whom you identify as a member of that group.

Prejudice—stereotyping a person based on the characteristics of a group to which the person belongs without regard to how the person may vary from the group characteristics.

Discrimination—acting differently toward a person based on prejudice.

Spotlight on Scholars

Read about the cultural identity research of Ronald L. Jackson at www.oup.com/us/verderber.

Halo effect—a perceptual bias that occurs when we misperceive that a person has a whole set of related personality traits when only one trait has actually been observed.

characteristics is called **prejudice** (Jones, 2002). Prejudice often leads to **discrimination**, or acting differently toward a person based on prejudice (Jones, 2002). Prejudice results in inaccurate perception and attitudes, whereas discrimination is action based. For instance, when Laura meets Wasif and learns that he is Afghani, she may let what she has learned from the media about how men treat women in Afghanistan inform her perception of Wasif and conclude that he is a chauvinist without really talking to him. This is prejudice. If based on this prejudice, she refuses to be in a class project group with him, she would be discriminating. Laura's use of the perceptual shortcut may prevent her from getting to know Wasif for the person he really is, and she may have cost herself the opportunity of working with the best student in class.

Racism, ethnocentrism, sexism, heterosexism, ageism, and ableism are various forms of prejudice in which members of one group believe that the behaviors and characteristics of their group are inherently superior to those of another group. All people can be prejudiced and act on their prejudices by discriminating against others. Nevertheless, "prejudices of groups with power are farther reaching in their consequences than others" (Sampson, 1999, p. 131). Because such attitudes can be deeply ingrained and are often subtle, it is easy to overlook behaviors we engage in that in some way meet this definition. Prejudicial perceptions may be unintentional, or they may seem insignificant or innocuous, but even seemingly unimportant prejudices rob others of their humanity and severely impede accurate communication.

Halo Effects

The **halo effect** is a perceptual bias that occurs when we misperceive that a person has a whole set of related personality traits when only one trait has actually been observed. This biasing stems from our use of implicit personality theory. For instance, Heather sees Martina personally greeting and welcoming every person who arrives at a meeting. Heather views this behavior as a sign of warmth. She further associates warmth with generosity and generosity with honesty. As a result, she perceives that Martina is warm, generous, and honest.

In reality, Martina has demonstrated only the trait of warmth. Martina has not demonstrated whether she is the slightest bit generous or honest. She may be both of these things, but there is no evidence of this. This example demonstrates a "positive halo" (Heather assigned Martina a string of positive traits based on witnessing only one trait). We also attribute negative traits to people based on witnessing a single trait. For example, Megan notices Hannah sneaking a cigarette in the restroom prior to class. Since it's illegal to smoke on campus, Megan sees this behavior as dishonest. Associating dishonesty with untrustworthiness, disloyalty, and undependability, she equates these traits with dishonesty. As negative information more strongly influences our impressions of others than positive information (Hollman, 1972), we are more likely to give others negative halos than positive halos.

Halo effects seem to occur most frequently under one or more of three conditions: (1) when we are judging traits with which we have limited experience, (2) when the traits have strong moral overtones, and (3) when the perception is of a person we think we know well.

Forced Consistency

Our tendency to see what we expect to see and to find patterns in what we perceive can bias our perception of others. **Forced consistency** is the perceptual bias in which we inaccurately interpret different perceptions of another person so that our interpretation of what we see remains consistent. Imagine that Leah does not like Jill, the office assistant at the car dealership where they both work. If Jill supplies some missing information on a form that Leah has given her to process, Leah is likely to perceive Jill's behavior as interference, even if Jill's intention was to be helpful. If Leah likes Jill, however, she would likely perceive the very same behavior as helpful. In each case, the perception of "supplying missing information" is interpreted to agree with a preexisting perception of the person. It is consistent to regard someone we like as doing favors for us. It is inconsistent to regard people we don't like as doing favors for us. However, consistent perceptions of others are not necessarily accurate.

Forced consistency—the perceptual bias in which we inaccurately interpret different perceptions of another person so that our interpretation of what we see remains consistent.

Projection

Our tendency to assume that others are similar to us can create inaccurate perceptions. **Projection** is the perceptual bias that occurs when we incorrectly think that someone who is like us in one respect will share other characteristics and attitudes. For example, if you "meet" someone while playing Black Ops online and your avatars look similar, you may assume that since your online partner looks similar to you, she enjoys other activities that you enjoy. We are most likely to suffer from projection bias when we know someone well and are emotionally involved with something. Then we are likely to mistakenly believe that this person will feel the same way (Niedenthal, Halberstadt, Margolin, & Innes-Ker, 2000). For example, Steve, a rabid Cleveland Cavaliers fan, is furious that LeBron James is playing for the Miami Heat. Since his brother is also a Cavs' fan, Steve may project his own anger and assume that his brother is also angry. But his brother, who never really liked James, is actually indifferent to this development.

Projection—the perceptual bias that occurs when we incorrectly think someone who is like us in one respect will share other characteristics and attitudes.

Fundamental attribution error— the tendency to overattribute others' negative behavior to their disposition and overattribute our own negative behavior to the situation.

Fundamental Attribution Error

You will recall that to interpret other people's behaviors, we make judgments about whether their behavior is dispositional or situational. The **fundamental attribution error** is the tendency to attach reasons to others' negative behavior by believing that they could have acted differently while explaining away our own negative behavior by viewing it as the result of a situation over which we had no control. For example, suppose that you go to the drugstore to pick up a prescription, and the pharmacy tech waiting on people is frowning and very abrupt when interacting. You may explain this person to yourself by reasoning that he is by nature unhappy and rude. But just suppose that the tech is normally happy and polite to his customers but has just learned that his mother has been diagnosed with kidney cancer and his manager refused his request to leave work early to be with his mom. Your tendency to look for dispositional causes internal to the person will have biased your interpretation of his behavior. Because we like to think well of ourselves, we usually interpret our own bad behavior in light of the situation. For example, have you ever been cut off by another car in traffic? Did you yell and scream at the person and maybe even gesture rudely? How come? Well, you would probably not say, "Because I'm really a hot-headed jerk." Instead, you are likely to interpret your behavior as being caused by the situation, explaining, "Well, I'm not normally like that, but I was really in a hurry, and this guy just cut me off. I couldn't help it. I mean I almost got killed."

Since we often respond to others based on how we interpret their behavior, the fundamental attribution error can wreak havoc with our relationships. When Cassie doesn't call her mother for several days, her mother's attribution will drive the conversation with her daughter. Her opening line might be, "Well, I can see that the only one you ever think about is yourself. Otherwise, you would have called." Or it might be, "Honey, is everything OK? I was really concerned that something must have happened to you." Which of these responses is most likely to lead to a satisfying conversation that helps maintain a healthy relationship?

Improving Social Perceptions

Improving our social perceptions is an important first step in becoming a competent communicator. The following guidelines can aid you in constructing a more realistic impression of others, as well as in assessing the validity of your own perceptions.

1. Question the accuracy of your perceptions. Questioning accuracy begins by saying, "I know what I think I saw, heard, tasted, smelled, or felt, but I could be wrong. What other information should I be aware of?" By accepting the possibility that you have overlooked something, you will stop automatic processing and begin to consciously search out information that should increase your accuracy. In situations where accurate perception is important, take a few seconds to become conscious of what is happening. It will be worth the effort.

2. Seek more information to verify perceptions. If you are working with only one or two pieces of information, try to collect further information to better ground your perceptions. The best way to get additional information about people is to talk with them. It's OK to be unsure about how to treat someone you don't know well. But rather than letting your uncertainty cause you to make mistakes while talking with a person, ask for the information you need to become more comfortable.

3. Choose to use conscious processing as you get to know people. When you mindfully pay attention to someone, you are more likely to understand the uniqueness of this individual, and this will decrease uncertainty by increasing the accuracy of your predictions.

4. Realize that your perceptions of a person will change over time. People often base their behavior on perceptions that are old, out of date, or derived from incomplete information. When you encounter someone you haven't seen for a while, you will want to become reacquainted and let the person's current behavior rather than past actions or reputation inform your perceptions. A former classmate who was "wild" in high school may well have changed and become a mature, responsible adult.

5. Use the skill of perception checking to verify your impressions. A **perception check** (the first of the micro skills you will learn in this course), is sharing your perception of another's behavior to see if your interpretation is accurate. It is a process of describing what you have seen and heard and asking for feedback from the other person. By doing a perception check, you can verify or adjust the predictions you make about others. Perception checking calls for you to observe the behavior of the other person and ask yourself, "What does that behavior mean to me?" Then you are ready to describe the behavior and put your interpretation into words to verify your perception.

The following examples illustrate the use of perception checking. In each of the examples, the final spoken sentence is a perception check. Notice that body language sometimes provides the perceptual information that needs to be

Perception check—sharing your perception of another's behavior to see if your interpretation is accurate.

SKILL BUILDERS ● Perception Checking

SKILL	USE	PROCEDURE	EXAMPLE
A statement that expresses the meaning you perceive from the behavior of another	To clarify the accuracy of our perceptions of another person's behavior	1. Watch the behavior of another. 2. Ask yourself, "What does that behavior mean to me?" 3. Describe the behavior (to yourself or aloud) and put your interpretation of the nonverbal behavior into words to verify your perception.	As Dale frowns while reading Paul's first draft of a memo, Paul says, "From the way you're frowning, I take it that you're not too pleased with the way I phrased the memo."

checked, whereas at other times tone of voice provides this information. Also notice that the perception-checking statements do not express approval or disapproval but are purely descriptive statements of the perceptions.

> Valerie walks into the room with a completely blank expression. She neither speaks to Ann nor acknowledges that Ann is even in the room. Valerie sits down on the edge of the bed and stares into space. Ann inquires, "Valerie, did something happen? You look like you're in a state of shock. Am I right? Is there something I can do?"

> While Marsha is telling Jenny about the difficulty of her midterm chemistry exam, she notices Jenny smiling. She says to Jenny, "You're smiling. I'm not sure how to interpret that. What's up?" Jenny may respond that she's smiling because the story reminded her of something funny or because she had the same chemistry teacher last year, who purposely gave an extremely difficult midterm to motivate students but then graded them on a favorable curve.

> Cesar, speaking in short, precise sentences with a sharp tone of voice, gives Bill his day's assignment. Bill responds, "From the sound of your voice, Cesar, I get the impression that you're upset with me. Are you?"

When we use the skill of perception checking, we encode the meaning we have perceived from someone's behavior and feed it back for verification or correction. For instance, when Bill says, "I get the impression that you're upset with me. Are you?" Cesar may say, (1) "No. Whatever gave you that impression?," in which case Bill can further describe the cues that he received; (2) "Yes, I am," in which case Bill can get Cesar to specify what has caused the feelings; or (3) "No, it's not you; it's just that three of my team members didn't show up for this shift." If Cesar is not upset with him, Bill can examine what caused him to misinterpret Cesar's feelings; if Cesar is upset with him, Bill has the opportunity to change the behavior that bothered Cesar. Suppose that in place of the descriptive perception check, Bill had said to Cesar, "Why are you so upset with me?" Rather than describing his perception, Bill has made a judgment based on it. Replying as if his perception were "obviously" accurate would have amounted to mind reading.

You should check your perceptions whenever the accuracy of your understanding is important (1) to your current communication, (2) to the relationship you have with the other person, or (3) to the conclusions you draw about that person. Perception checking is especially important in new relationships or when you haven't communicated with someone for a long time.

Self-Perception: Self-Concept and Self-Esteem

Self-perception—the overall view people have of themselves.

Self-concept—your perception of your competencies and personality traits.

Self-esteem—your evaluation of your perceived competence and personal worthiness.

We also use social perception when we think about ourselves. **Self-perception** is the overall view people have of themselves. Your self-perception includes your self-concept and self-esteem. **Self-concept** is your perception of your competencies and personality traits (Baron & Byrne, 2003). **Self-esteem** is your evaluation of your perceived competence and personal worthiness (based on Mruk, 2006). In this section we explain how self-concept, self-esteem, and overall self-perception are formed. We also discuss how your culture affects the types of self-perceptions you develop. You will see that interpersonal communication plays a primary role in these processes. We conclude by describing how you can improve your self-perceptions.

Self-Concept

How do we learn what our skills, abilities, and personalities are? Your self-concept comes from the unique interpretations you make about yourself based on your experience and from the ways that others react and respond to you.

Your experiences are critical to forming your self-concept. You cannot know if you are competent at certain things until you have experience trying them, and you cannot find out what your personality traits are until you uncover them through experience. This is why the first experiences we have with particular situations are so important (Centi, 1981). For instance, someone who has been rejected in his first attempt at dating may perceive himself to be unattractive to others. If additional experiences in the same situation produce results similar to the first experience, this initial perception will be strengthened. But even when the first experience is not repeated, more than one contradictory additional experience will likely be required to change the original perception. On the other hand, when we have a positive first experience, we are likely to believe that we innately possess the competencies and personality traits we associate with that experience. If Sonya, for example, discovers at an early age that she is good at math and absorbs mathematical concepts easier than other children, she is likely to incorporate "competent mathematician" into her self-concept. If she continues to excel at math throughout her life, that self-concept will be reinforced and maintained.

In addition to being formed and maintained by our experiences, our self-concept is shaped by how others react and respond to us (Rayner, 2001). First, we use other people's comments as a check on our descriptions of ourselves. These comments serve to validate, reinforce, or alter our perceptions of who and what we think we are. For example, if during a brainstorming session, one of your co-workers tells you, "You're really a creative thinker," you may decide that this comment fits your image of who you are, thus reinforcing your self-concept as someone with a competent sense of creativity.

The feedback we receive from others may also reveal abilities and personality characteristics we had never associated with ourselves. On the way back to their apartment after volunteering at the local Head Start Center, Janet commented to her friend Madison, "Gee, you're a natural with kids. They just flock around you." Madison, who had been struggling to find a career direction, thought about Janet's comment and others like it that she had received over the years and decided to explore careers in early childhood education.

Not all reactions and responses we receive have the same effect on our self-concept. Reactions and responses are likely to be more powerful when you respect the person making the comment (Rayner, 2001) or when you are close to the person (Aron, Mashek, & Aron, 2004). This is especially important in families. Since your self-concept begins to form early in life, information you receive from your family deeply shapes your self-concept (Demo, 1987). One of the major responsibilities of family members, therefore, is to notice and comment on traits and abilities, a practice that encourages the development of accurate and strong self-concepts in other family members.

Self-Esteem

Self-concept and self-esteem are two different but related components of self-perception. Self-concept is our description of our competencies and personality traits, while self-esteem is our positive or negative evaluation of our self-concept. Our evaluation of our personal worthiness is rooted in our values and develops over time as a result of our experiences. Self-esteem is not just how well or poorly we do things (self-concept) but the importance or value we place on what we do well or poorly (Mruk, 2006). For instance, as part of Chad's self-concept, he sees himself as an excellent piano player, a thoughtful person, and a faithful friend. But if Chad doesn't believe that these or other competencies and personality traits he possesses are worthwhile or valuable, then his self-esteem will not be high. It takes both the perception of having a competency or personality trait and a personal belief that the competency or personality trait is of positive value to produce high self-esteem (Mruk, 2006). When we successfully use our competencies and personality traits in worthwhile endeavors, we raise our self-esteem. When we are unsuccessful in doing so and/or when we use them in unworthy endeavors, we lower our self-esteem.

Self-esteem depends not only on what each individual views as worthwhile but also on the ideas, morals, and values of the family, group, and culture to which the individual belongs. We all have talents and positive personality characteristics, but how we see them is strongly influenced by the group and society to which we belong. If Chad comes from a family where athletic success is valued but not artistic talent, if he hangs out with friends who laugh at his piano playing, and if he lives in a society where rock guitarists, not piano players, are the superstars, then he is unlikely to be proud of his piano-playing ability.

We noted that families are critically important to developing self-concepts, but they are even more central to helping family members develop positive self-esteem. For example, when his mother notes, "Rob, your room is always so neat. You are very organized," or when her brother observes, "Kisha, lending Tomika five dollars really helped her out. You are very generous," they are helping Rob and Kisha understand that they each have a positively valued personal characteristic. Unfortunately, some families frequently send negative messages that lower self-esteem. Communicating blame, calling names, and repeatedly pointing out another's shortcomings are particularly harmful to self-esteem, and some people never fully overcome the damage done to them by members of their families.

Bullying and cyber bullying, aggressive behaviors designed to intimidate others, are often accomplished through interpersonal communication messages. Bullying damages the self-esteem of another. Children who are just forming their self-concepts and self-esteem and adolescents whose self-images are in transition are particularly sensitive to bullying messages. Bullying can have long-lasting effects on people's self esteem. Years later people may still have inaccurate self-perceptions based on bullying incidents that occurred during childhood (Hinduja & Patchin, 2009).

LEARN ABOUT YOURSELF ●

Take this short survey to learn something about yourself. Act on your first response. There are no right or wrong answers. Just be honest in reporting what is true for you. For each question select one of the numbers to the right that best describes how much you feel the statement describes you.

0 = Strongly Disagree
1 = Disagree
2 = Agree
4 = Strongly Agree

_____ 1. I act the same way no matter who I am with.

_____ 2. It is important for me to maintain harmony within my group.

_____ 3. I enjoy being unique and different from others in many respects.

_____ 4. I often feel that my relationships with others are more important than my own accomplishments.

_____ 5. I am comfortable being singled out for praise or rewards.

_____ 6. I would stay in a group if they needed me even if I were not happy with the group.

_____ 7. I'd rather say "no" directly than risk being misunderstood.

_____ 8. My happiness depends on the happiness of those around me.

_____ 9. My personal identity as independent of others is very important to me.

_____10. It is important to me to respect decisions made by the group.

_____11. I prefer to be direct and forthright when dealing with people I have just met.

_____12. I will sacrifice my self-interest for the benefit of the group I am in.

Scoring the Survey: This survey measures the extent to which your self-perceptions are primarily independent or interdependent. To get your independent score, add your answers to the odd-numbered questions (1,3,5,7,9,11). To get your interdependent score, add your answers to the even-numbered questions (2,4,6,8,10,12). Which of the two scores is higher? The higher of the two scores indicates your cultural orientation to your self-perceptions.

Adapted from Fernández, I., Paez, D., & González, J. L. (2005). Independent and Interdependent Self-Construl and Culture. *Revue Internationale de Psychologie Sociale / International Review of Social Psychology,* 18(1), 35–63.

Culture and Self-Perceptions

As we have stated, how you think about yourself is a function of your culture (Chen & Starosta, 1998). In some cultures, like that of the United States, people form independent self-perceptions; whereas in other cultures, like that of Japan and China, people's self-perceptions are interdependent (Markus & Kitayama, 1991). So far, we have been describing the process by which people form independent self-concepts and self-esteem. People with **independent self-perception** view their traits and abilities as internal and universally applicable to all situations. The goal of those with independent self-perceptions is to demonstrate their abilities, characteristics, and personality during interaction with others. If you have an independent self-concept, you may believe that being persuasive is one of your abilities and a skill you can use in any situation. You gain self-esteem by demonstrating your powers of persuasion, convincing others, and having others praise you for it.

But in other cultures, people's sense of self depends on the situation and how they perceive themselves in relation to particular others. People with **interdependent self-perception** perceive their traits, abilities, and personality within the context of their relationships, with self-perception varying with the situation. Their goal is to maintain or enhance their relationship by using the appropriate abilities and by demonstrating the appropriate personality characteristics for the situation. People with interdependent self-perceptions don't think, "I am really persuasive," but rather, "When I am with my friends, I am able to convince them to do what is good for all of us. When I am with my father, I do what he believes is best for the good of our family." Self-esteem is gained through behaviors that advance the interests of the relationship or group.

Independent self-perception—self-perception in which people view their traits and abilities as internal and universally applicable to all situations.

Interdependent self-perception—self-perception in which people perceive their traits, abilities, and personality within the context of their relationships.

Self-fulfilling prophecies—events that happen as the result of being foretold, expected, or talked about.

Some people are closely involved with more than one culture. If one of the cultures encourages interdependent self-perceptions while the other encourages independent self-perceptions, these bicultural people may develop both types of self-perception. They can switch "cultural frames" and draw on self-perceptions appropriate to the situation. They are more likely to do this well when they have been able to integrate their bicultural identity by seeing themselves as part of both cultures and appreciating the strengths of both cultures (Benet-Martínez & Haritatos, 2005). For example, Nori, a fourth-generation Japanese American enjoys being both Japanese and American. When he is with his non-Asian American school friends, he enjoys showing off his quick wit and keen sense of humor by teasing others in the group and is praised for his cleverness. But when Nori attends the numerous extended family get-togethers at his very traditional grandparents' home in the Japantown section of San Francisco, he is careful to show his relatives, whom he would never consider teasing, deference and respect.

How do we affect the self-esteem of our partner who is physically present when we ignore her to answer a text message or email?

In the Diverse Voices selection in this chapter, Dolores V. Tanno describes the different labels that she and others use to describe her and how these reflect her sense of self.

Accuracy of Self-Concept and Self-Esteem

The accuracy of our self-concept and self-esteem depends on the accuracy of our own perceptions and how we process the reactions and responses of others. All of us experience success and failure, and all of us hear praise and criticism. If we are overly attentive to successful experiences and positive responses, our self-concept may become overdeveloped and our self-esteem inflated. If, however, we perceive and dwell on our failures while disregarding or devaluing our successes, or if we remember only the criticism we receive, our self-concept may be underdeveloped and our self-esteem low.

In either case, self-concept and self-esteem may suffer from incongruence, a situation in which there is a gap between self-perception and reality. Incongruence is a problem because our perceptions of self are more likely than our true abilities to influence our behaviors (Weiten, 2002). For example, Sean may actually possess all of the competencies and personality traits needed for effective leadership, but if he doesn't perceive that he has these talents and characteristics, he won't step forward in a situation where leadership is needed.

Likewise, Yuri, who believes she is too assertive at work, is reluctant to voice her opinion even about a problem in her area of expertise. Individuals tend to reinforce their self-perceptions by adjusting their behaviors to conform to them rather than attempting to break free from them. That is, people with high self-esteem behave in ways that lead to more affirmation, whereas people with low self-esteem tend to act in ways that confirm their self-perception. Two important ways in which people rationalize their inaccurate self-perceptions are engaging in self-fulfilling prophecies and filtering messages.

Self-Fulfilling Prophecies

Self-fulfilling prophecies are events that happen as the result of being foretold, expected, or talked about. They may be self-created or other-imposed. Self-created, self-fulfilling prophecies result from "talking ourselves into" success or failure. For example, research has found that people who expect rejection are more likely to behave in ways that lead others to reject them (Downey, Freitas, Michaelis, & Khouri, 2004, p. 437). Self-esteem has an important effect on our prophecies. People with high self-esteem view success positively and confidently predict that they can repeat successes; people with low self-esteem attribute their success to luck and so predict that they will not repeat their successes (Hattie, 1992, p. 253). For instance, if Aaron perceives himself as unskilled in establishing new relationships, he may say to himself, "I bet I'll know hardly anyone at the party—I'm going to have a miserable time." Because Aaron fears encountering strangers and sees himself as incompetent in this area, he is likely

Independent and Interdependent Self-Perceptions

Identify someone you know who is bicultural, with at least one of this person's cultures differing from your own. The two cultures that she or he experiences should have different approaches to self-perception. Make a date for an interview. Begin by sharing what you have learned about independent and interdependent self-perceptions. Then ask for a description of how your interviewee experiences self-perception and handles being part of two cultures with different approaches to self-perception. Write a short essay in which you present what you have learned, comparing and contrasting it with your own experience.

Do you know someone who's tendency is to dwell on their failures? How does that affect their self-esteem?

I Am . . .

by Dolores V. Tanno

Delores V. Tanno, University of Nevada Las Vegas, describes how her self-concept and self-esteem are shaped by labels others use to describe her and the multiple roles she plays related to gender and culture.

Over the course of my life one question has been consistently asked of me: *"What are you?"* I used to reply that I was American, but it quickly became clear this was unacceptable because what came next was, "No, really what are you?" In my more perverse moments I responded, "I am human." I stopped when I realized that people's feelings were hurt. Ironic? Yes, but the motive behind the question often justified hurt feelings. I became aware of this only after asking a question of my own: "Why do you ask?"

Confronting the motives of people has forced me to examine who I am. In the process I have had to critically examine my own choices, in different times and contexts, of the names by which I am placed in society. The names are "Spanish," "Mexican American," "Latina," and "Chicana."

"I am Spanish." Behind this label is the story of my childhood in northern New Mexico. New Mexico was the first permanent Spanish settlement in the Southwest, and New Mexicans have characterized themselves as Spanish for centuries. My parents, grandparents, and great-grandparents consider themselves Spanish; wrongly or rightly they attribute their customs, habits, and language to their Spanish heritage, and I followed suit. In my young mind, the story of being Spanish did not include concepts of racial purity or assimilation; what it did do was allow me to begin my life with a clearly defined identity and a place in the world. For me, the story of being Spanish incorporates into its plot the innocence of youth, before the reality of discrimination became an inherent part of the knowledge of who I am.

"I am Mexican American." When I left New Mexico, my sense of belonging did not follow me across the state border. When I responded to the question, "What are you?" by saying, "I am Spanish," people corrected me: "You mean Mexican, don't you?" My initial reaction was anger; how could they know better than I who I was? But soon my reaction was one of puzzlement, and I wondered just why there was such insistence that I be Mexican. Reading and studying led me to understand that the difference between Spanish and Mexican could be found in the legacy of colonization. Thus behind the name "Mexican American" is the story of classic colonization that allows for prior existence and that also communicates duality. As Richard A. Garcia argues, "Mexican in culture and social activity, American in philosophy and politics." As native-born Mexican Americans we also have dual visions: the achievement of the American Dream and the preservation of cultural identity.

"I am Latina." If the story behind the name Mexican American is grounded in duality, the story behind the

to feel awkward about introducing himself to anyone at the party and, just as he predicted, is likely to spend much of his time standing around alone thinking about when he can leave.

The prophecies or predictions others make about you also affect your behavior and your self-esteem. For example, if the soccer coach tells Javier, a talented fullback who is struggling to learn the skills of a forward, "I don't think you have the scoring abilities to play first string," Javier is likely to accept this assessment,

name "Latina" is grounded in cultural connectedness. The Spaniards proclaimed vast territories of North and South American [*sic*] as their own. They intermarried in all the regions in which they settled. These marriages yielded offspring who named themselves variously as Cubans, Puerto Ricans, Colombians, Mexicans, and so forth, but they connect culturally with one another when they name each other Latinas. To use the name *Latina* is to communicate acceptance and belonging in a broad cultural community.

"I am Chicana." This name suggests a smaller community, a special kind of Mexican American awareness that does not involve others (Cubans, Puerto Ricans, etc.). The name was the primary political as well as rhetorical strategy of the Chicano movement of the 1960s. Mirande and Enriquez argue that the dominant characteristic of the name *Chicana* is that it admits a "sense of marginality." There is a political tone and character to "Chicana" that signifies a story of self-determination and empowerment. As such, the name denotes a kind of political becoming. As the same time, however, the name communicates the idea of being American, not in a "melting pot" sense that presupposes assimilation, but rather in a pluralistic sense that acknowledges the inalienable right of existence for different peoples.

What, then, am I? The truth is I am all of these. Each name reveals a different facet of identity that allows symbolic, historical, cultural, and political connectedness. These names are no different than other multiple labels we take on. For example, to be mother, wife, sister, and daughter is to admit to the complexity of being female. Each name implies a narrative of experiences gained in responding to circumstances, time, and place and motivated by a need to belong.

In my case, I resort to being Spanish and all it implies whenever I return to my birthplace, in much the same way that we often resort to being children again in the presence of our parents. But I am also Mexican American when I balance the two important cultures that define me; Latina when I wish to emphasize cultural and historical connectedness with others; and Chicana whenever opportunities arise to promote political empowerment and assert political pride.

It is sometimes difficult for people to understand the "both/and" mentality that results from this simultaneity of existence. We are indeed enriched by belonging to two cultures. We are made richer still by having at our disposal several names by which to identify ourselves. Singly the names Spanish, Mexican American, Latina, and Chicana communicate a part of a life story. Together they weave a rhetorically powerful narrative of ethnic identity that combines biographical, historical, cultural, and political experiences.

For Consideration:

1. Does this author's use of these various identifiers parallel how you have heard them used in your community? If not, what is different?
2. How does a person's choice of ethnic or racial identifiers affect your perception of them?
3. Do you use ethnic or racial identifiers when you describe or think about yourself? If so, how are they similar or different from the ones used by other members of your family or peer group? If you don't use ethnic or racial identifiers is this a conscious decision? Why do you think you choose not to use them?

stop working on his scoring skills, and consequently continue to play in ways consistent with the coach's prediction. Other-created prophecies also have a powerful way of changing our self-concepts. For example, when a child hears, "Jump, I know you can do this," the child is likely to try to jump off the side of the pool and, because of the positive prediction, may succeed. But if a child hears, "Be careful. It's dangerous. You could drown," the child will probably not jump and may develop a fear of water that makes it difficult to learn to swim.

Filtering messages—the tendency to attend to messages that reinforce what we already think of ourselves and to downplay or not register messages that contradict this image.

OBSERVE AND ANALYZE

Reflecting on "At Seventeen"

Use the Internet to access and listen to "At Seventeen" by Janis Ian. Then download a copy of the lyrics to this song. Write a short essay in which you use the concepts in this chapter to explain the lyrics.

Filtering Messages

A second way that our self-perceptions can become distorted is through **filtering messages**, the tendency to attend to messages that reinforce what we already think of ourselves and to downplay or not register messages that contradict this image. People with low self-esteem may filter out positive messages. For example, suppose you have prepared a fundraising plan for your service organization and someone comments that you're a good organizer. If you have low self-esteem, you may not really hear the remark, ignore it, or discount it by replying, "Anyone could have done that—it was nothing special." Your response may encourage the sender to reevaluate and to agree with you. If, however, you have high self-esteem and see yourself as a good organizer, you are more likely to pay attention to the compliment and may even reinforce it by responding, "Thanks, I've had a lot of experience with organizing fundraising campaigns and I really enjoy doing it."

Improving Self-Perception

Self-concept and self-esteem are enduring characteristics of self-perception, but they can be changed. At times, comments that contradict self-fulfilling prophecies will get past the filter and begin to transform your self-perceptions. Then these new self-perceptions begin to filter other comments and become the basis of new self-fulfilling prophecies. Over the course of your life, your self-concept and self-esteem may change.

Certain situations seem to expedite this process. When experiencing profound changes in their social environments, people are likely to drop their filters and absorb information that they would have otherwise filtered out. During life transitions we become more susceptible to dropping our filters, such as when children begin school, when teens begin the independence process, or when young adults leave home. Starting a new job or college, falling in love, committing to or dissolving a relationship, becoming a parent, retiring, and grieving the death of a loved one can also make us more likely to attend to messages at odds with our current self-perception. As a result of these new experiences, people change their picture of who they are and begin to predict new things for themselves.

The use of therapy and self-help techniques can assist in the goal of changing self-concept and improving self-esteem. Numerous research studies have shown that self-esteem is increased through hard work and practice (Mruk, 2006). So why is it important to work on improving the accuracy of your self-concept and raising your self-esteem? Because an accurate self-concept allows you to really

"As near as I can understand it, they're my real Mom and Dad."

know who you are and what you have to offer others with whom you form relationships. Your self-esteem also influences your choice of relationship. Research has reported that "people with high self-esteem are more committed to partners who perceive them very favorably, while people with low self-esteem are more committed to partners who perceive them less favorably" (Leary, 2002, p. 130). Imagine how difficult it is for two low self-esteem individuals to maintain a healthy and satisfying relationship.

The Effects of Self-Perception on Communication

Your self-perception shapes your communication in a variety of ways. It informs how you talk to yourself, how you talk about yourself with others, how you talk about others to yourself, and how you communicate with others.

Self-Perception Influences How You Talk to Yourself

Self-talk is communicating with yourself through your thoughts. For example, when you think to yourself, "I handled that situation well," you are self-talking. If we feel good about ourselves, that is, if we have positive self-esteem, then our self-talk is likely to be more accurate. If we have negative self-esteem, then our self-talk is likely to be distorted and negative. In addition, people with positive self-esteem are generally better able to monitor accurately how they come across in a situation. They can be more realistic about what they are doing well and about what they are not doing well. People with negative self-esteem often overemphasize negative self-talk or, ironically, may inflate their sense of self. In other words, to compensate for a sense of insecurity, they may tell themselves they are good at everything they do, a tendency that may actually stem from an inability to talk to themselves accurately.

Self-talk—communicating with yourself through your thoughts.

Self-Perception Influences How You Talk about Yourself with Others

Just as our self-perception influences how we talk to ourselves, it also affects how we talk about ourselves with others. If we have positive self-perception, we are likely to communicate that we like ourselves and take credit for our successes. If we feel bad about ourselves or have negative self-perception, we are likely to communicate negatively by downplaying our accomplishments. Why do some people put themselves down regardless of what they have done? People who have low self-esteem are likely to be unsure of the value of their contributions and to expect others to view them negatively. Perhaps, people with a poor self-concept or low self-esteem find it less painful to put themselves down than to hear the criticism of others. Thus, to preempt others commenting on their unworthiness, they do it first.

Some research suggests that the Internet can influence how we communicate about ourselves with others in unique ways. Some Internet discussion groups, for example, are designed to be shared online journals in which the user engages in reflection and introspection. These users are actually communicating with themselves while imagining a reader. On the Internet, people can be more aware of themselves and less aware of the people whom they are addressing (Shedletsky & Aitken, 2004, p. 132). Such pervasive opportunities to engage in self-perception influence how we communicate with others.

Self-Perception Affects How You Talk about Others with Yourself

Self-concept and self-esteem are important not only because they moderate our self-talk but also because they affect how we talk about others with ourselves. First, the more accurate our self-perception, the more accurately we are likely to perceive others. Both self-perception and perception of others start with our ability to process data accurately. Second, the higher our self-esteem, the more likely we are to see others favorably. Studies have shown that people who accept themselves as they are tend to be more accepting of others; those with low self-esteem are more likely to find fault in others. Third, our own personal characteristics influence the types of characteristics we are likely to perceive in others. For example, people who are secure tend to see others as equally secure. You'll recall that we respond to the world as we perceive it to be and not necessarily as it is, so you can see that low self-esteem can account for misunderstandings and communication breakdowns.

Self-Perception Influences How You Talk to Others

Research demonstrates that we communicate our self-concept and self-esteem when we interact with others (Campbell, 1990, p. 538). Not only will our self-perception influence what we say about ourselves, but it will also affect whether and how we offer our opinions and how vigorously we defend our positions when they conflict with the positions of others. People with rich self-concepts are more likely to share their ideas in areas in which they believe they have competence. People with high self-esteem are likely to defend their positions during conflict since they value themselves and expect others to value them as well. People with impoverished self-concepts are less likely to share their ideas since they can't be sure that their ideas are good ones. People with low self-esteem are less likely to engage in behaviors that will lead to successful conflict resolution.

THE SOCIAL MEDIA FACTOR

Human Factors in Using Social Media

The way in which we form and apply social perceptions also affects our use of social media technology. In the previous chapter, we discussed the inherent attributes of social media that influence its use for interpersonal communication. The other half of the digital communication equation is the human factor. Our *attitude* toward online communication is another important element in the use of social media. Attitude shapes how we interact with other people and how we present ourselves through social media. This orientation toward social media, our **online communication attitude**, influences our media choices. Researchers have identified five concerns that influence our attitudes toward online communication and shape how we approach or avoid opportunities to communicate through social media. These are digital self-disclosure, digital social connection, convenience, digital apprehension, and miscommunication (Ledbetter, 2009). As you read about these concerns, think about how you view each.

Online communication attitude—a collection of cognitive and affective orientations that may foster or inhibit a person's tendency to engage in digital communication.

Digital Self-Disclosure

Digital self-disclosure is the degree to which individuals self-regulate what they reveal about themselves using social media. People using social media vary widely in this regard. The range of these tendencies can be easily observed by just looking at sample Facebook pages. Some people reveal nothing more than their name and location. Others use Facebook to display their personal philosophy, sexual orientation, interests, and other personal details. Others go further yet by posting photos of everything from pets to the latest party they attended to pictures of themselves in compromising situations. Interestingly, research has found that many people who share extensive personal information through social media are less likely to do so in face-to-face interactions with their friends. In some cases, these individuals come to depend on social media as an important outlet for sharing important details in their life.

Digital Social Connection

Those who use social media generally consider these effective forums for connecting with their social network. The belief that electronic communication enables social contact is known as **digital social connection**. Older generations relied on other means, such as the mail and telephone, to stay in touch with friends and family. Research indicates that a person's communication competence is positively associated with his or her attitude toward digital social connection (Ledbetter, 2009). This means that users can be motivated to more competently use online communication to socially connect with others.

Convenience

Another concern that influences our online communication attitude is the ease with which we engage in digital communication. As you might expect, the longer we use a particular form of digital communication technology, the more convenient we perceive it to be. When you are learning to use your new smartphone, you may find it less convenient than the phone you had before. Newcomers naturally feel more apprehensive and less competent than longtime users. The convenient nature of social media has implications for how you present yourself to others. You can easily snap a picture with your smartphone at a party and immediately post it to your Facebook page and tag your friends. Within seconds, you alter not only your online image but also that of your friends. The convenience of social media is compelling, but not without consequences that can quickly affect how others perceive your interpersonal communication competence.

Digital Apprehension

Digital communication apprehension involves the anxiety and nervousness associated with communicating through social media. Individuals who are nervous about the opportunities and challenges associated with social media often have negative attitudes toward online communication in

Digital self-disclosure—a tendency to reveal and conceal private information in digital settings versus other contexts.

Digital social connection—a tendency to use social media to maintain connection with others.

Digital communication apprehension—nervousness associated with communicating through social media.

THE SOCIAL MEDIA FACTOR

OBSERVE AND ANALYZE

Assessing Digital Self-Disclosure and Social Connection through Facebook

Go to your Facebook page. Spend some time looking through and reflecting on the information that you (or others) posted to your profile. Think about the amount of digital self-disclosure that is there. Look at your friends list. How many Facebook friends do you have? How many of these people do you communicate with on a regular basis? Think about the relationships that you maintain through Facebook. Write a short paragraph describing your assessment of your digital self-disclosure and digital social connection via Facebook.

general. Digital apprehension may stem from being unfamiliar with digital technology, or it may be limited to certain communication contexts. For example, your grandmother may avoid using her cell phone because she doesn't understand how to find the phone numbers or get her messages. But your brother who uses social media with his friends may avoid using it at work. What can be perceived as sharing good fun between friends can damage your professional self-image when the same pictures are viewed by co-workers or managers.

Miscommunication

Miscommunication—
misinterpretations associated with
deriving meaning from a digital
message.

Another factor that influences your attitude toward online communication is the fear of **miscommunication** or misinterpretations that may arise when deriving meaning from digital communication. The sources of miscommunication in social media are many and varied, from sending messages with misspellings or

---

A QUESTION OF ETHICS ● What Would You Do?

Rustown is a small Midwestern factory town. Over the years the white, middle-class citizens have formed a close-knit community that prides itself on its unity. Corpex, a large out-of-town corporation, which had just bought out the town's major factory, recently decided to move its headquarters there and to expand the current plant, creating hundreds of new jobs. This expansion meant that the new people coming into Rustown to manage and work in the factory would spend money and build homes, but it also meant that the composition of the small community would change.

Rustown inhabitants had mixed reactions to this takeover. The expectation of increased business excited owners of land and shops, but most Rustown residents who had been born and raised there were pretty much alike—and liked it that way. They knew that many of the new factory managers as well as some of the new employees were African and Hispanic Americans. Rustown had never had a black or Latino family, and some of the townspeople openly worried about the effects the newcomers would have on their community.

Otis Carr, a Corpex manager, had agreed to move to Rustown because of the opportunities that appeared to await him and his family, even though he recognized

that as a black man he might experience resentment. At work on the first day, Otis noticed that the workers seemed very leery of him, yet by the end of the first week, the plant was running smoothly, and Otis was feeling the first signs of acceptance. On Monday morning of the next week, however, he accidentally overheard a group of workers chatting on their break, trading stereotypes about African Americans and Latinos and using vulgarities and racist slurs to describe specific new co-workers.

Shaken, Otis returned to his office. He had faced racism before, but this time it was different. This time he had the power and the responsibility to make a difference. He wanted to change his workers' attitudes and behavior for the sake of the company, the town, and other minority group members who would be coming to Rustown. Although he knew he had to do something, he realized that brute managerial force would get him nowhere. He was familiar with the prejudices but not with ethical ways to change them.

For Consideration:
1. What are the ethical issues in this case?
2. What advice would you offer Otis if he asked you how he can ethically change the perceptions that must underlie the comments that he overheard?

unintended emotional implications to wondering why a friend didn't get back to you as quickly as you got back to him or her. Experienced users learn to anticipate miscommunication and manage ways to prevent it. You can improve your digital interpersonal communication competence by assuming that digital communication limits shared understanding and taking steps to minimize that possibility.

Summary

Social perception is a set of processes by which people perceive themselves and others. Perception is the process of selectively attending to information that we receive through our senses and assigning meaning to it. Our perceptions are a result of our selection, organization, and interpretation of stimuli. We use a dual-processing approach to perception. Most of the time our perceptions are automatic, but at other times we exert a very conscious effort to make sense of the stimuli we are receiving.

In perceiving others, we uncover information about them so we can reduce uncertainty. To do this, we form impressions and make attributions. We develop impressions based on physical appearances, using implicit personality theory and assuming that others are similar to us. We also tend to succumb to the fundamental attribution error by ascribing others' negative behavior to their dispositions while ascribing our negative behavior to the situation. Our perceptions of others can be biased due to selective perception, stereotyping, halo effects, forced consistency, projection, and the fundamental attribution error. You can learn to improve social perception if you question the accuracy of your perceptions, seek more information to verify perceptions, choose conscious processing as you get to know others, realize that perceptions of people will change over time, and use the skill of perception checking to verify your impressions. Self-perception is the overall view people have of themselves and consists of self-concept and self-esteem. Self-concept is our description of our competencies and personality traits. Self-esteem is our evaluation of our competence and personal worthiness. Self-concepts are interpretations of self based on our experience and the reactions and responses of others to us. Self-esteem develops in the same way, but it is also based on the worth an individual places on self-concepts. Our culture determines our type of self-perception. In some cultures, our self-perceptions are independent; in others, they are interdependent. Self-fulfilling prophecies and filtering messages can affect our self-concept and self-esteem. Self-perception influences communication. It affects how we talk to ourselves, how we talk about ourselves to others, how we talk about others to ourselves, and how we talk with others.

Self-perception also shapes how we interact with other people and how we present ourselves through social media. Our choice of media is influenced by our attitude toward using online communication. This attitude is formed by a combination of factors including concerns toward digital self-disclosure, digital social connection, media convenience, digital apprehension, and the potential for miscommunication.

Chapter Resources

What You Should Be Able *to Explain:*

- The definition of perception and social perception
- How the mind selects, organizes, and interprets information
- The dual processes in processing information
- The goal in forming perceptions of others
- The ways we form perceptions of others
- How we predict what others are likely to do and why they do it
- Why we sometimes misperceive others
- The types of mistakes in perceiving others
- How we can improve the accuracy of our perceptions of others
- What self-perceptions, self-concept, and self-esteem are and how they are formed
- How we can improve our self-perceptions
- How attitudes toward using social media are formed

What You Should Be Able *to Do:*

- Conduct a perception check
- Improve the accuracy of your social perception

Self-test questions based on these concepts are available on the companion Web site (www.oup.com/us/verderber) as part of Chapter 2 resources.

Key Words

Flashcards for all of these key terms are available on the *Inter-Act* Web site.

Attributions, p. 44
Automatic processing, p. 41
Conscious processing, p. 41
Digital communication apprehension, p. 61
Digital self-disclosure, p. 61
Digital social connection, p. 61
Discrimination, p. 46
Dispositional attribution, p. 44
Expectations, p. 39
Filtering messages, p. 58
Forced consistency, p. 47
Fundamental attribution error, p. 48

Halo effect, p. 46
Heuristics, p. 41
Implicit personality theory, p. 44
Independent self-perception, p. 54
Interdependent self-perception, p. 54
Interests, p. 39
Miscommunication, p. 62
Needs, p. 39
Online communication attitude, p. 60
Pattern recognition, p. 40
Perception check p. 49
Perception, p. 38

Prejudice, p. 46
Projection, p. 47
Selective perception, p. 45
Self-concept, p. 50
Self-esteem, p. 50
Self-fulfilling prophecies, p. 54
Self-perception, p. 50
Self-talk, p. 59
Simplicity, p. 40
Situational attribution, p. 44
Social perception, p. 38
Stereotyping, p. 45
Uncertainty reduction theory, p. 42

Apply Your Knowledge

The following questions challenge you to demonstrate your mastery of the concepts, theories, and frameworks in this chapter by using them to explain what is happening in a specific situation.

Identifying the Causes of Misperceptions of Others

2.1   What factors contribute to the misperception in this incident?

Amanda was depressed. Her daughter was having problems in school. She had just been informed that her work hours were being cut back, and her mother who had Alzheimer's was becoming more difficult to handle and was refusing to give up her own home. On her way home from work, she stopped to pick up her laundry at the dry cleaners, where a new man was working the counter. From looking at him, Amanda could tell he was quite old. She thought to herself that he could be a problem. When she requested her laundry, he asked to see her claim check. Because no one had ever asked her for this before, Amanda explained to him that she had started throwing these away. "Well," the man firmly replied, "I'm not able to give you clothes without a claim check. It's store policy, and if you think I'm going to jeopardize my job because you don't have a claim check, you're mistaken." After hotly demanding to see the manager and being told that he had left for the day, Amanda stormed out of the store. "I don't understand why old people have to be so difficult. Just wait until I get a hold of the manager. That old geezer will wish he had never fooled with me!"

Who Am I?

2.2   Write a short essay on the subject "Who am I?" To begin this task, list all of the competencies and personality traits that you believe describe you. Try completing the following sentences: I am skilled at . . . ; I have the ability to . . . ; I know things about . . . ; I am competent at doing . . . ; One part of my personality is that I am. . . . Do this over and over again. List as many characteristics in each category as you can think of.

Then develop a second list, only this time completing the following statements: Other people believe that I am skilled at . . . ; Other people believe that I have the ability to . . . ; Other people believe that I know things about . . . ; Other people believe that I am competent at doing . . . ; One part of my personality is that other people believe that I am. . . . Again, complete these statements over and over as many times as you can.

Compare your lists of self-perceptions and others' perceptions. How are they similar? Where are they different? Do you understand why they differ? Are your lists long or short? Why do you suppose that is? Reflect on how your own interpretations of your experiences and what others have told you about you have influenced your self-concept. Now organize the lists you have created, perhaps finding a way to group characteristics. Use this information to write an essay titled "Who I Am, and How I Know This."

Skill Practice

Skill Practice activities give you the chance to rehearse a new skill by responding to hypothetical or real situations. Additional skill practice activities are available at the companion Web site.

Perception Checking

2.3   *Write well-phrased perception checks for each of the following situations:*

Franco comes home from the doctor's office with a pale face and slumped shoulders. Glancing at you with a forlorn look, he shrugs his shoulders.

You say:

As you return the tennis racket you borrowed from Liam, you smile and say, "Here's your racket." Liam stiffens, grabs the racket, and starts to walk away.

You say:

Natalie dances into the room with a huge grin on her face.

You say:

In the past, your advisor has told you that almost any time would be all right for working out your next term's schedule. When you tell her you'll be in on Wednesday at 4 p.m., she pauses, frowns, sighs, says "Uh-huh," and nods.

You say:

Compare your written responses to the guidelines for effective perception checking discussed earlier. Edit your responses where necessary to improve them. Now say them aloud. Do they sound natural? If not, revise them until they do.

Inter-Act with Media

Television

American Idol

American Idol is a popular television competition that aims to discover the latest solo singing talent. Hosted by radio DJ Ryan Seacrest, the show seeks to discover the best singer in the country, where viewers telephone or text message their votes to determine the winner. Throughout the season, contestants appear before a panel of judges who critique their performances. The composition of the judging panel has changed over the years. Famous judges included singer and choreographer Paula Abdul and music executive Simon Cowell. The panel for the 2011 season included Randy Jackson, Jennifer Lopez, and Steven Tyler. In past seasons, Abdul was praised as a sympathetic and compassionate judge of the competitors and was perceived as quite kind when compared to Cowell, who often harshly criticized competitors when their performances were simply dreadful. Cowell gained notoriety for his direct and often controversial criticisms, insults, and jokes about contestants and their abilities. Contestants often cried, while others quickly returned the barbs. Aside from its value as musical entertainment, *American Idol* might be viewed as an ad hoc demonstration of many varied styles of interpersonal communication and the delivery of criticism, both effective and ineffective.

IPC Concepts: Self-concept, self-esteem.

To the Point:

How might critical feedback affect a person's self-concept and self-esteem?
How do you react to critical feedback from a teacher, parent, or friend?
How does a person's critical feedback influence your perceptions of him/her as a competent communicator?

Cinema

Legally Blonde (2001). Robert Luketic (director). Reese Witherspoon, Matthew Davis, Selma Blair.

Elle Woods (Witherspoon), an enthusiastic and cheerful sorority president and fashion merchandising major, is passionately in love with her boyfriend, Warner Huntington III (Davis). Warner hails from a prominent political family and plans to attend Harvard Law School to continue his family's storied political success. Elle expects Warner to propose marriage, but he breaks up with her instead and claims that he needs a more serious girlfriend to help his political career. In an effort to win Warner back, Elle applies and is admitted to Harvard. While her Harvard Law colleagues view her as unsuitable for law school, she learns that Warner is engaged to fellow law student Vivian Kensington (Blair). Elle talks with Warner and comes to the conclusion that he will never accept her as a girlfriend or respect her as a serious and potential lawyer. Elle is more determined than ever to succeed in law school. She studies hard and wins an internship at a professor's law firm. During her internship, she defends an innocent woman who is on trial for murder. At the end of the film, Elle graduates with high honors; her class elects her speaker at the commencement ceremony; and one of Boston's best law firms offers her a job.

IPC Concepts: Self-concept, self-esteem.

To the Point:

> How might you describe Elle's self-concept and self-esteem at the beginning of the movie compared to the end?
> Have you ever experienced similar criticism from a friend or romantic partner? How did you react?
> What effect did this criticism have on your relationship with the person?

What's on the Web

Find links and additional material, including self-quizzes, on the companion Web site at www.oup.com/us/verderber.

3

Intercultural Communication

"Hi, Terrell. What are you still doing on campus?" asked Professor Green as he climbed onto the treadmill next to where Terrell was running. "Most students have already left for the Thanksgiving holiday. You're going home, aren't you?"

"Um, maybe," Terrell mumbled in reply.

"Well, you better decide. I mean, you live on campus, right? And the dorms close at 5 P.M. today."

"Yeah, sure, I guess. Whatever," Terrell answered and then abruptly changed the subject. "So, Professor Green, do you think the football team's record is good enough to get a bowl bid?"

What's happening in this conversation between Professor Green, a middle-aged, middle-class, white man, and Terrell, a young adult, black student who grew up in the city, is a microcosm of what can occur when people from different cultural backgrounds communicate. Green, whose middle-class, white culture having taught him to value planning, intended to show his concern about Terrell's seeming lack of preparation for the holiday vacation. Meanwhile Terrell's answers, although noncommittal, were his attempt to behave in accord with his black cultural upbringing by showing respect for Professor Green's higher status. At the same time he parried what his inner-city-youth cultural lens saw to be inappropriately patronizing and intrusive questions. Both Professor Green and Terrell were behaving in accord with their respective cultural backgrounds, yet this conversation was probably not very satisfying to either because of these cultural differences.

People are so familiar with their own culture, its language, gestures, facial expressions, conversational customs, and norms, that they may experience anxiety when these familiar aspects of communication are disrupted. Yet this occurs frequently when we interact with people from different cultures. **Culture shock** is the psychological discomfort you experience when you must interact in a new culture (Klyukanov, 2005). Culture shock results when taken-for-granted meanings are not shared by others. You are likely to feel it most profoundly when you are thrust into another culture through international travel, business, or study. The 2006 movie *Outsourced,* for example, depicted cultural misunderstandings between an American manager and his Indian employees.

Culture shock can also occur when you come in contact with people from co-cultures within your home country. For example, Brittney, who is from a small town in Minnesota, may experience culture shock on her first visit to see her sister who has moved to Miami, Florida. She may be overwhelmed by the

Culture shock—the psychological discomfort you experience when you must interact in a new culture.

distinctly Hispanic flavor of the city, by hearing Spanish spoken among people on the street, by the prevalence of Latin beat music, by the prominence of billboards in Spanish, and by the way people look and dress. Brittney is likely to be disoriented not only because of the prominence of the Spanish language but also because the beliefs, values, and attitudes of the people she encounters might seem quite foreign to her. If Brittney is to overcome her culture shock and enjoy the scene on South Beach, she will need to become adept at talking with people from this different culture.

Intercultural communication refers to interactions that occur between people whose cultures are so different that the communication between them is altered (Samovar, Porter, & McDaniel, 2010, p. 12). In other words, when communicating with people whose beliefs, values, and attitudes are culturally different from our own, we are communicating across cultural boundaries, which can lead to misunderstandings that would not ordinarily occur between people who are culturally similar. It is important to recognize that not every interaction between persons of different cultures exemplifies intercultural communication. For example, when Brittney is on the beach in Miami and joins a group of Latinos in a friendly game of beach volleyball, their cultural differences are unlikely to affect their game-related exchanges. However, when Brittney joins her sister for a night of club-hopping on South Beach, she is likely to experience conversations in which cultural differences lead to difficulty in understanding or interpreting what is said. The first step toward becoming effective at intercultural communication is to understand what a culture is and be able to identify how cultures systematically differ from one another and how that affects interpersonal messages.

In this chapter, we examine how culture affects our communication behaviors and how it influences our perception of the communication we receive from others. We begin by explaining culture and several basic culture-related concepts. Then we describe six ways that cultures systematically differ in their values, attitudes, norms, and orientations. We end the chapter by describing how to develop intercultural communication competence.

> **Intercultural communication**—interactions that occur between people whose cultures are so different that the communication between them is altered.

Culture and Communication

Culture is the system of shared values, beliefs, attitudes, and orientations learned through communication that guide what is considered to be appropriate thought and behavior in a particular group of people. It is a way of life, the taken-for-granted rules of how and why you behave as you do. Your culture influences not only important behaviors and decisions, but also more trivial ones as well. For example, do you routinely address higher status people by a title like Ms., Reverend, Doctor, or Professor and feel uncomfortable when you don't? If so, you probably come from a culture where you learned to use titles to show respect.

At the heart of any culture are its values. **Values** are the commonly accepted preference for some states of affairs over others. They include agreed-on standards of what is considered right and wrong, good and evil, fair and unfair, just and

> **Culture**—the system of shared values, beliefs, attitudes, and orientations learned through communication that guides what is considered to be appropriate thought and behavior in a particular segment of the population.

> **Values**—the commonly accepted preference for some states of affairs over others.

unjust, etc. Although members of a culture may not be able to state these values, you can guess what they are by how people behave.

Cultures have both real and ideal values. Ideal values are those that members of a culture profess to hold, whereas the real values of the culture are those that can be seen guiding the actual behavior of members of that culture. For example, Iran is a Muslim state and Israel is a Jewish state both of whose constitution offers protections for members of religious minorities (ideal value). But both the legal system and the everyday treatment of religious minorities in each country belies this ideal. In both countries religious minorities are routinely subjected to legal hassles and mistreatment by their fellow citizens (real value in action).

Communication plays a central role in culture. First, as the definition of culture makes clear, communication is the way that culture is transmitted to members. If you address higher status people by their title, you probably remember a parent or teacher prompting you to do this. In Western cultures we eat using forks, knives, spoons, individual plates, and bowls that we learned to use in childhood. In China people eat with chopsticks, and in other cultures people use bread, or leaves, or eat with their fingers, and share a common bowl. All these dining rituals are culturally based and taught by one generation to the next through communication.

Not only is a culture transmitted through communication, but communication is also the mechanism through which a culture is modified. For example, several generations ago most American children were taught to show respect by addressing adult family friends with a title and the friend's last name (Mr. Jones, Miss Smith, etc). Today, it is commonplace for even young children to address family friends by their first name. How did this cultural custom change? In earlier generations, when a parent corrected a young child who had mimicked the parent's use of an adult friend's first name, the friend remained silent, reinforcing the correction. So the child learned to say "Mr.," "Mrs.," "Doctor," etc. But during the last half of the twentieth century, adults began to communicate their permission for children to use their first name, stopping parents in mid-correction or correcting children who addressed them using a title with their last names. Over time, the cultural norm changed, and today it is common for American children to address all adult family friends as well as others by their first name. Communication is both the means by which culture is transmitted and the way that a culture is changed.

Dominant and Co-Cultures

Although the United States is a diverse society, there are many attitudes, values, beliefs, and customs that the majority of people hold in common and that the minority feel they must follow. The **dominant culture** is the learned system of values, beliefs, attitudes, and orientations held by the people who are in power in a society. Generally these people historically and presently have controlled the major institutions of the society (Samovar, Porter, McDaniels, 2010, p. 12). The less diverse the population of a society, the stronger is its dominant culture. In the United States, the dominant culture has evolved over time. It once strictly reflected and privileged the values of white, Western European, English-speaking, Protestant, heterosexual men. Before the 1960s, people coming to the United States from other cultural backgrounds were expected to assimilate into this dominant cultural perspective and to sublimate or abandon their native culture. In many cases, immigrants arriving from other countries changed their names to sound more American. They were expected to learn English as quickly as possible and follow the norms of conversation of the dominant culture. But since the 1960s the United States has experienced a cultural revolution that has resulted in an adjustment of the dominant cultural perspective to be more reflective of the diverse cultures with which its citizens identify. We have come to understand and expect that different people may follow different communication patterns and that to be competent communicators we need to be able to adjust to diversity.

While there is a dominant culture, many Americans also identify with one or more **co-cultures** that exist side by side with the dominant culture and are comprised of smaller numbers of less powerful people who hold common values, attitudes, beliefs, and orientations that differ from those of the dominant culture. Co-cultural groups form around one or more shared demographic characteristics such as gender, race, ethnicity, sexual orientation/gender identity, religion, social class, and generation.

Gender

Most dominant cultures differentiate between the behavior valued in men and the behavior valued in women. They socialize children in ways that lead girls and boys to act in accord with the roles that the dominant culture

Dominant culture—the learned system of values, beliefs, attitudes, and orientations held by the majority of people in a society.

Co-cultures—cultures that exist side by side with the dominant culture and are comprised of smaller numbers of people who hold common values, attitudes, beliefs, and orientations that differ from those of the dominant culture.

OBSERVE AND ANALYZE

Communicating within Co-cultures

Attend an event of a co-cultural group on campus or in your community. Consider visiting an ethnic festival, an unfamiliar house of worship, or a senior center. Observe the behavior of others, and communicate with as many people as possible. Then write a paper describing the experience and discussing the concepts of intercultural communication, culture shock, ethnocentrism, and stereotyping. Provide specific examples of any of these concepts you experienced.

expects them to play. Because they belong to different co-cultures, women and men communicate differently. Research shows that women, for instance, are primarily concerned with personal relationships when they communicate. They talk more about relationships and feelings, tend to include others in conversations, and actively respond to others. Men more often focus on tasks or outcomes when they communicate. They talk more about content and problem solving, tend to emphasize control and status, and are less responsive to others (Wood, 2007).

Race

The term "race" was traditionally used to classify people based on widely evident—or visible—biological traits, such as skin and eye color, hair texture, and body shape (Kottak, 2012). However, recent genetic studies such as the Human Genome Project (2001) show that racial groups are not biologically distinct (Smedley and Smedley, 2005). Yet race as a social concept is very much a part of our lives. People have experienced the social effects of perceived race and have formed communities and cultures based on racial experiences. As a result, race is an important co-culture for many people.

Racial co-culture influences not only attitudes but also communication behavior. For example, Asian Americans, as well as other co-cultural group members, may **codeswitch**, altering their linguistic and nonverbal patterns to conform to the dominant culture or co-culture depending on the topics or co-participants in a conversation (Bonvillain, 2003). When Ling joins her family for dinner, she may speak Vietnamese and defer to her older relatives. At school, however, she may speak only English, and while hanging out at the local youth center with her friends from the neighborhood, she may speak a mixture of Vietnamese and English.

Codeswitch—to alter linguistic and nonverbal patterns to conform to the dominant or co-culture depending on the topics or co-participants in a conversation.

Ethnicity

Like race, ethnicity is an inexact distinction. **Ethnicity** is a classification of people based on shared national characteristics such as country of birth, geographic origin, language, religion, ancestral customs, and tradition. People vary greatly in terms of the importance they attach to their ethnic heritage and the degree to which it affects their attitudes, values, and behaviors. Generally, the further you are from your family's immigrant experience, the less you will be influenced by your ethnic co-culture. Language or mother tongue is an obvious influence of ethnicity on communication. Immigrants bring with them the language of their original country and may or may not speak English when they arrive. Even after they learn English, many immigrants choose to speak their mother language at home, live in proximity to other people from their home country, and interact with them in their native language. Although the United States is considered an English-speaking country, it now has the third-largest Spanish-speaking population of any country in the world, and 70 percent of Latinos in the United States mainly speak Spanish at home (Carlo-Casellas, 2002). To accommodate Spanish speakers, businesses and government agencies offer automated phone services with bilingual menus and employ bilingual customer-service professionals.

Ethnicity—a classification of people based on shared national characteristics such as country of birth, geographic origin, language, religion, ancestral customs, and tradition.

Spotlight on Scholars

Read about the inter-ethnic identification research of Michael L. Hecht at www.oup.com/us/verderber.

How were you encouraged to maintain your ethnic identity?

Sexual Orientation and Gender Identity

In the United States, as in most other countries, the dominant culture historically has valued and privileged heterosexuality and encouraged children to identify with their birth gender. People who deviated from the preferred pattern of behavior were severely mistreated. As a result, gay, lesbian, and transgender people formed underground communities that developed co-cultures where homosexual and transgender behaviors were valued and members received social support. Over the past 40 years, gay activism has modified the dominant culture so that homosexual and transgender people face less discrimination. Nevertheless, today there are still gay, lesbian, and transgender co-cultures that provide important social support to members.

Religion

A **religion** is a system of beliefs, rituals, and ethics based on a common perception of the sacred or holy. Although the ideal value of the dominant culture of the United States is religious freedom and diversity, historically its real values reflected monotheistic Judeo-Christian perspectives. All observant practitioners of a religion participate in a co-culture. Those who strongly identify with a religious group outside the Judeo-Christian tradition will have different orientations that shape relationships and their communication behaviors. For example, Buddhism advises individuals to embrace rather than resist personal conflict. Adversity, emotional upheaval, and conflict are seen as natural parts of life (Chuang, 2004). Accordingly, a Buddhist is apt to communicate openly and calmly during an interpersonal conflict and embrace the positive aspects of conflict in strengthening interpersonal ties.

Religion—a system of beliefs, rituals, and ethics based on a common perception of the sacred or holy.

Social Class

Social class is a level in the power hierarchy of a society whose membership is based on income, education, occupation, and social habits. Most Americans are uncomfortable talking about social class and identify with the middle class even though they may really be members of more elite or lower classes (Ellis, 1999). But social classes exist in the United States just as they exist in all societies. Your social class often determines where you live and with whom you come in contact. As a result, over time members of a social class develop and reinforce their co-cultures with distinct values, rituals, and communication practices. For example, social class may influence aspects of verbal communication including grammar, vocabulary, and slang.

Generation

The time period in which we are born and raised can have a strong formative influence on us. People of the same generation form a cultural cohort group whose personal values, beliefs, and communication behaviors have been influenced by the common life experiences and events they encountered as they aged. People who grew up influenced by the Great Depression tend to be frugal; those alive during World War II value sacrifice of self for cause and country. Baby Boomers, who include large numbers of people who came of age during the counterculture of the 1960s, are likely to judge, question, and compete. Those we call Generation X, who experienced latchkey childhoods and the consequences of widespread divorce, value self-sufficiency and are adaptable, creative, and comfortable with technology. Millennials (also called Generation "Y" or the Echo Boomers) never knew life without computers, were exposed to school and world violence at an early age, experienced corporate failures and globalization, and grew at the start of the trend for parents to place their children on pedestals. They are adept at using technology to multitask, have a high sense of morality, are cautious about issues of safety, and appreciate diversity. Finally, the latest generation, known as Digital Natives (or Generation "Z" or Generation "I"—for Internet), have never known a world without portable technology, Internet access, notebook PCs, iPods, DVDs, and, of course, social media sites like Facebook and MySpace. According to educational leader and learning software developer Marc Prensky, who coined the term

> *Digital Natives are used to receiving information really fast. They like to parallel process and multi-task. They prefer their graphics before their text rather than the opposite. They prefer random access (like hypertext). They function best when networked. They thrive on instant gratification and frequent rewards. They prefer games to "serious" work. (Prensky, 2001)*

While Generation Y members are group oriented, Digital Natives are highly individualistic.

Whether in family relationships or in the workplace, when people from different generations interact, their co-cultural orientations can create communication difficulties. For example, when members of different generations work together, miscommunication, misunderstandings, and conflict are likely to occur more than when people work with others of the same generation. Generally, people from earlier generations are less likely to question authority figures. They demonstrate their respect by using formal terms of address such as referring to people as Mr., Ms., Dr., Sir, and so forth. People who came of age in the 1960s or later, on the other hand, tend to be more skeptical of authority and less formal in dealing with authority figures. They are more likely to question their managers and to openly disagree with decisions that are made by those in authority (Zemke, Raines, & Filipczak, 2000). We speculate that the profound differences between Digital Natives and the earlier generations, who have been called "Digital Immigrants," will create new challenges for co-cultural relationships.

Cultural Identity

In addition to the dominant culture, most of us belong to one or more co-cultures. Your **cultural identity** is that part of your self-image that is based on the cultural group or groups with which you most closely associate and align yourself. It is determined by the importance that you assign to your membership in a cultural group (Ting-Toomey et. al., 2000). You may closely identify with one co-culture group into which you fit and not identify with another. You may choose to embrace a co-cultural identity at odds with the dominant culture, or you may work hard to distance yourself from a co-cultural group and adopt the values and mores of the dominant culture. You may be proud that you are a third-generation Polish American who embraces this heritage through your verbal and nonverbal mannerisms, your religion, your diet, and many other aspects of your identity. On the other hand, your roommate, also a third-generation Polish American, may be more assimilated to the dominant American culture, rarely thinking of or identifying herself as from a Polish background. She may not adhere to any of the cultural communication norms common to this ethnic background. When the dominant culture stigmatizes a co-culture, some members of the co-culture may downplay or obscure this part of their identity to fit into the dominant culture, or they may more closely identify with the co-culture and become activists or advocates for it.

Cultural identity—that part of your self-image that is based on the cultural group or groups with which you most closely associate and align yourself.

Many contemporary Muslim women honor their religious beliefs by wearing hijabs. Do you wear symbols of any religious affiliation?

How Cultures Differ

We may be able to figure out people's culture based on their language, dress, or personal artifacts, such as religious markers worn as jewelry or placed in the home. For example, when people meet Deen Singh, his turban tells them that he is a Sikh. But while these things may help you recognize that someone belongs to a specific culture, they do not help you understand the values or the communication practices you can expect from members of that culture. Appearance alone does not explain who people are inside, how they perceive the world, and how they interact with others. Beyond wearing a turban, what does it really mean to be a Sikh? How are Sikhs similar or different from other cultural groups?

The work of Geert Hofstede and the earlier work of Edward T. Hall give us a way to understand how cultures are similar to and different from one another and how cultural variation affects communication. As a manager in the personnel research department at IBM Europe, Hofstede (1980) conducted a large-scale research project that studied fifty countries and three regions. His work identified four ways in which cultures differ that are important for intercultural communication: (1) the extent to which the individual is valued versus the group or collective; (2) the extent to which predictability is valued versus tolerating uncertainty; (3) the extent to which the norms of the culture support equality or uneven distribution of power; and 4) the extent to which the culture is oriented to traditional masculine or feminine gendered behavior. Figure 3.1 shows where the United States falls on each of these dimensions. Edward T. Hall, an anthropologist who is considered the father of intercultural communication, identified two ways in which cultures differ that have important implications for intercultural interaction: (1) cultural norms about time and (2) the importance of context for understanding a message (Rogers, Hart, & Miike, 2002). Let's look at each of these six ways in which cultures may differ from one another.

The Value of the Individual vs. the Group

Individualistic culture—a culture that values personal rights and responsibilities, privacy, voicing one's opinion, freedom, innovation, and self-expression.

Hofstede found that cultures differed in the extent to which individualism or collectivism was valued (1997). An **individualistic culture** is a culture that values personal rights and responsibilities, privacy, voicing one's opinion, freedom, innovation, and self-expression (Andersen, Hecht, Hoobler, & Smallwood, 2003). People in individualistic cultures place primary value on the self and on personal achievement, which explains the emphasis on personal opinion, innovation, and self-expression. In individualistic cultures, people's connections to groups are loose. They consider the interests of others only in relationship to how those interests affect the interest of the self. If you come from an individualistic culture, you may consider your family and close friends when you act but only because your interests and theirs align. People in individualistic cultures also view competition as desirable and useful. Because of this, they value personal rights, freedom, and privacy that support fair competition. According to Hofstede, individualistic

Individualism	High uncertainty avoidance	High power distance	Masculinity
X (1st)			
			X (15th)
		X (38th)	
	X (43rd)		
Collectivism	Low uncertainty avoidance	Low power distance	Femininity

FIGURE 3.1 Dimensions of Culture—U.S. Ranking Among 53 Countries/Regions

How comfortable would you be in a collectivist culture like this? What if you didn't feel like exercising?

cultures include those in the United States, Australia, Great Britain, Canada, and northern and eastern European countries.

In contrast, a **collectivist culture** is a culture that values community, collaboration, shared interests, harmony, the public good, and avoiding embarrassment (Andersen et al., 2003). Early in life, people in collectivist cultures are integrated into strong, close-knit groups that will protect them in exchange for loyalty. Collectivist cultures place primary value on the interests of the group and group harmony. An individual's decisions are shaped by what is best for the group, regardless of whether they serve the individual's interests. Collectivist societies are highly integrated, and the maintenance of harmony and cooperation is valued over competitiveness and personal achievement. According to Hofstede, collectivist cultures are found in South and Central America, East and Southeast Asia, and Africa.

The values of individualism and collectivism influence many aspects of communication, including self-concept and self-esteem formation, approaches to conflict, and working in groups (Samovar et al., 2007).

First, individualism and collectivism affect self-concept and self-esteem. You'll recall from our discussion of self-perceptions in Chapter 2 that people in individualist cultures form independent self-concepts and base their self-esteem on individual accomplishments. People in collectivist cultures form interdependent self-concepts and base their self-esteem on how well they fit into a group. If, for example, Marie, who was raised in an individualistic culture, is the highest-scoring player on her basketball team, she will feel good about herself and identify herself as a "winner" even if her team has a losing season. But if Marie is from a collectivist culture, the fact that she is the highest-scoring player will have little effect on her self-esteem. Her team's losing season will likely cause her to feel lower personal self-esteem.

Collectivist culture—a culture that values community, collaboration, shared interests, harmony, the public good, and avoiding embarrassment.

Individualism and Collectivism

by Min Liu, Assistant Professor of Communication, Southern Illinois University at Edwardsville

I was born and raised in China, which is a collectivist country. I arrived in the United States for the first time in August of 2002 when I entered the Ph.D. program as a graduate student at North Dakota State University (NDSU) in Fargo, North Dakota. I chose NDSU for a number of reasons, but one that stands out in my mind as important is the fact that Fargo was listed as one of the safest cities in the USA at the time. You see, my family was concerned about sending their daughter to study in the USA, which is the most individualistic country in the world. They felt a bit more at ease knowing I would be studying in one of the safest cities in that country. Even my decision to come to NDSU was influenced by my family and our collectivist ideals. Little did I know, however, how much "culture shock" I would experience beginning with the first day I set foot on the NDSU campus.

I officially became an international student studying Communication at North Dakota State University in August of 2002. I felt prepared to study in the USA because I had learned English and was trained to become a college English instructor back in China. I had also aced the English proficiency test (TOEFL) required of international students. I remember feeling pretty confident about communicating with my American colleagues. As I walked across campus for my first day of orientation, I thought to myself, "Worst-case scenario I'll forget how to say something in English and that's what my digital Chinese-English dictionary is for."

I would soon learn, however, that the issue of translating vocabulary was not the worst-case scenario. For most of my communication struggles, I could not find an answer in the dictionary. For example, in one of the first graduate classes I took, the professor asked everyone to call her by her first name (Deanna). Without hesitation, all my American classmates began doing so. Calling a professor by her first name was unheard of for Chinese students like me!

As a sign of respect, we always call our teachers by their titles—Dr. Sellnow, Professor Sellnow, or Teacher Sellnow. Wherever you are on a college campus in China, it's clear who is the teacher and who are the students. I thought, "How I am to call a professor of mine by her first name?"

For a long time, I felt torn as to what to do—continuing to call her Dr. Sellnow may seem too distant and she might correct me. I want to honor her request out of respect for her authority. But, everything in my collectivist values suggested that calling her Deanna was simply too disrespectful. So, I simply avoided calling her anything. This solution worked fairly well in face-to-face communication situations—I would walk up to her, smile, and then start the conversation. This approach was working fairly well for me until the day came when I needed to email her. I remember sitting in front of my computer for almost an hour trying to fine-tune a one-paragraph email. Soon I realized the email message was fine. The reason I couldn't bring myself to press "SEND" was with the beginning of the email, which read, "Hello Deanna." I finally changed it to Dr. Sellnow, followed by an apologetic explanation asking her to understand my dilemma and why I addressed her in this way. To my surprise, she responded by saying there was nothing wrong in addressing her as "Dr. Sellnow" and that I should continue to do so if that is what feels most appropriate to me.

In another class, I studied intercultural communication concepts. What I learned there proved helpful to me in reconciling my collectivist-individualistic predicament and better understand the cultural shock I was experiencing. As a Chinese, I grew up in a high power distance culture. Professors and teachers are seen as having more power than students because, in my culture, people hold more or less power depending on where they are situated in certain formal, hierarchical positions. Students are to respect and honor their teachers by acknowledging their higher

Second, people from each of these cultural perspectives view conflict differently. The emphasis placed on the individual leads members of individualistic cultures to value and practice assertiveness and confrontational argument, whereas members of collectivist cultures value accord and harmony and thus practice collaboration or avoidance in arguments. In the United States, we teach

position of authority and status. The United States, however, is a low power distance culture. People demonstrate respect for one another by addressing each other more as equals regardless of the formal positions they may hold. So, as uncomfortable as I felt, I tried to call my professors by their first names when they suggested it was appropriate to do so. I reminded myself that, in the USA doing so was culturally appropriate and not a sign of disrespect.

Another culture shock experience I had to reconcile as a result of the differences between my collectivist values and the individualistic values of the USA had to do with disagreeing with my professor. In the USA, students learn to form opinions and defend their viewpoints and are rewarded for doing so in classroom presentations and debates. Professors perceive students who challenge their viewpoints with evidence and reasoning as intelligent and motivated. Students who do so are perceived very differently in the Chinese culture, where public disagreement with an authority figure is not only rare, but also inappropriate. Because of this value clash, I found it difficult to express and defend my opinions in class, especially if they differed from something the professor said. Doing so, it seemed to me, would be extremely disrespectful. Yet, I observed classmates doing so and being lauded for their comments. Many times, I chose not to say anything during a face-to-face meeting with a professor, but found the courage to write an email later. In the online environment, I found I could be honest and explain my disagreement with respect. Fortunately, many of my professors soon realized my cultural values dilemma and adapted their communication styles toward me. Still today, though, I prefer to present my viewpoints concerning controversial issues in a paper, a letter, an email message, or an online post, rather than in a meeting or other face-to-face discussion. I have found a way to honor my collectivist values in a way that also allows me to express myself in an individualistic cultural setting.

Finally, I recall struggling with how to behave in group settings as a result of the cultural differences along the individualism vs. collectivism continuum. When I first arrived in the USA, I was very conflict avoidant, probably because in collectivistic cultures maintaining the harmony of the collective is an important priority. The approaches I had learned to value and enact in small group settings were actually perceived negatively by my peers and professors in the USA. My conflict avoidant style—which I engaged in as a sign of respect—would actually frustrate some of my group members. They perceived it as a sign that I did not care about the group's success and was a "slacker." I felt frustrated, too, as I tried to help the group become more cohesive and successful by avoiding conflict! I eventually learned that, to be successful, we all had to begin by being upfront about where we come from and our values. Once we all understood the differences, we could create a workable plan for success.

I have been in the U.S. for seven years now, am married, and have a son. I have also earned my Ph.D. and am working as an Assistant Professor of Communication at the University of Southern Illinois at Edwardsville. Even now, I continue to learn new things about how to communicate best in this individualistic culture as compared to my collectivist home in China. Based on my experiences, I would have to say the most important thing for successful communication when interacting with people who come from a different place on the collectivism–individualism continuum is for all of us to always be mindful.

For Consideration:

1. In collectivist cultures respect is communicated by formalities like naming, unquestioning acceptance of the authority, and avoiding conflict. How is respect communicated in individualist cultures?

2. While the dominant culture in the USA seems to follow the patterns that Dr. Liu lays out in her essay, there are subcultures and family cultures that do not adhere to the patterns she describes. Were you raised to call your elders Mr., Mrs, Ms., Dr., etc? Are you still most comfortable doing so? How questioning of authority are you? Does this reflect a cultural or family norm? Finally, how likely are you to directly express your disagreements with others? Is this pattern one that is valued by your culture or family?

assertiveness and argumentation as useful skills and expect them to be used in interpersonal and work relationships, politics, consumerism, and other aspects of civic life. In contrast, the collectivist culture of Japan has developed business practices that maintain harmony and avoid interpersonal clashes. For example, in Japanese business, an elaborate process called *nemawashii* (a term that also means "binding the roots of a plant before pulling it out") has evolved. In Japan, any subject that might cause conflict at a meeting should be discussed in advance so that the interaction at the meeting will not seem rude or impolite (Samovar et al., 2010). In collectivist societies like Japan, a communication style that respects the relationship is preferred to one that expedites the exchange of information (Jandt, 2001). In collectivist societies, group harmony, sparing others embarrassment, and a modest presentation of self are important ways to show respect and avoid conflict. Direct speech that might hurt others in the group is discouraged.

Finally, individualism and collectivism influence how people work in groups. Because members of collectivist cultures consider group harmony and the welfare of the group to be of primary importance, they strive for consensus on group goals and may at times sacrifice optimal outcomes for the sake of group accord. In individualistic cultures, however, optimal outcomes are paramount, regardless of whether that results in group disharmony. Your cultural assumptions affect how you work to establish group goals, how you interact with other group members, and how willing you are to sacrifice for the sake of the group. Groups whose members come from both individualistic and collectivist cultures may experience difficulties because of their diverse cultural assumptions.

Attitudes toward Predictability and Uncertainty

Hofstede found that cultures differed in their attitudes toward **uncertainty avoidance**, the extent to which people in a culture look for ways to predict what is going to happen as a way of dealing with the anxiety caused by uncertain situations or relationships. A **low uncertainty-avoidance culture** (such as the United States, Sweden, and Denmark) is a culture that tolerates uncertainty and is less driven to control unpredictable people, relationships, or events. As you might expect, the more diverse the people in a society, the more likely the dominant culture will be low on uncertainty avoidance. People in low uncertainty-avoidance cultures tend to easily accept life's unpredictability and ambiguity, tolerate the unusual, prize initiative, take risks, and prefer as few rules as possible. People from these cultures are also more comfortable accepting multiple, diverse, and at times contradictory perspectives on "truth" rather than searching for one "Truth."

A **high uncertainty-avoidance culture** is a culture characterized by a low tolerance for and a high need to control unpredictable people, relationships, or events. Societies whose members are more homogeneous are likely to be high on uncertainty avoidance, as there are likely fewer co-cultural groups with which they must interact. These cultures create systems of formal rules and believe in absolute truth as ways to provide more security and reduce risk. They also tend to be less tolerant of people or groups with deviant ideas or behaviors. Because their culture emphasizes the importance of avoiding uncertainty, they often view life as hazardous, experiencing anxiety and stress when confronted with unpredictable people, relationships, or situations. Nations whose cultures are marked by high uncertainty avoidance include Germany, Portugal, Greece, Peru, and

Uncertainty avoidance—the extent to which the people in a culture look for ways to predict what is going to happen as a way of dealing with the anxiety caused by uncertain situations or relationships.

Low uncertainty-avoidance culture—a culture that tolerates uncertainty and is less driven to control unpredictable people, relationships, or events.

High uncertainty-avoidance culture—a culture characterized as having a low tolerance for and a high need to control unpredictable people, relationships, or events.

Belgium (Samovar et al., 2007). How our culture has taught us to view uncertainty affects our communication with others. It shapes how we use language and develop relationships.

First, uncertainty avoidance affects the use of language. People from high uncertainty-avoidance cultures use and value specific and precise language because they believe that through careful word choice we can be more certain of the meaning of a person's message. Imagine a teacher declaring to a class, "The paper must be well-researched, cite evidence, and be professional in format and appearance." Students from high uncertainty-avoidance cultures would find the teacher's remarks to be too general and vague. They would most likely experience anxiety and, to reduce their uncertainty, would probably ask a lot of questions about what kind of research is appropriate, how to cite evidence, how much evidence is needed, what writing style to use, and the desired length of the paper. These students would welcome a specific checklist or rubric that enumerated the exact criteria by which the paper would be graded. By contrast, students from a low uncertainty-avoidance cultural background would be annoyed by an overly specific list of rules and guidelines, viewing it as a barrier to creativity and initiative. As you can imagine, a teacher with students from both cultural backgrounds faces a difficult challenge when trying to explain an assignment.

Second, uncertainty avoidance influences how people approach new relationships and how they communicate in developing relationships. People from high uncertainty-avoidance cultures are wary of strangers and may not seek out new relationships or relationships with people they perceive as different from them, since these would be unpredictable. They generally prefer meeting people through friends and family, and they refrain from being alone with strangers. When developing relationships, people from high uncertainty-avoidance cultures tend to guard their privacy, to refrain from self-disclosure early in a relationship, and to proceed more slowly through relationship development. Members of low uncertainty-avoidance cultures, on the other hand, are likely to initiate new relationships with people who differ from them and enjoy the excitement of disclosing personal information in earlier stages of relationship development.

Attitudes about Social Power Distribution

How members of the culture view unequal distribution of power is a third way in which cultures differ that affects communication. **Power distance** is the extent to which members of a culture expect and accept that power will be unequally shared. A culture can be either a high power-distance culture or a low power-distance culture. A **high power-distance culture** is a culture in which both high- and low-power holders accept the unequal distribution of power. In these cultures the power imbalances are endorsed as much by less powerful members as they are by those with power. While no culture distributes power equally, in high power-distance cultures more inequality is seen and viewed by members as natural. High power-distance cultures include most Arab countries of the Middle East, Malaysia, Guatemala, Venezuela, and Singapore. The recent Arab Spring political movements in Middle Eastern countries suggest that the acceptance of

Power distance—the extent to which members of a culture expect and accept that power will be unequally shared.

High power-distance culture—a culture in which both high- and low-power holders accept the unequal distribution of power.

high power distance in a culture will only continue when less powerful people believe that the powerful are working in the collective best interest.

A **low power-distance culture** is a culture in which members prefer power to be more equally distributed. In cultures characterized as having low power-distance, inequalities in power, status, and rank are underplayed and muted. People know that some individuals have more clout, authority, and influence, but lower-ranking people are not awed by, more respectful toward, or fearful of people in higher positions of power. Even though power differences exist, these cultures value democracy and egalitarian behavior. Austria, Finland, Denmark, Norway, the United States, New Zealand, and Israel are examples of countries whose dominant cultures are characterized by low power-distance.

Our cultural beliefs about power distance naturally affect how we interact with others in authority positions. If you were a student, an unskilled worker, or an average citizen in a high power-distance culture, you would not argue a person in authority. You would expect the more powerful person to control any interaction; you would listen with attention to what that person said to you; and you would do what was ordered without question. Proper and polite forms of language, and nonverbal signals of your status differences would be evident in the exchange. In contrast, if you come from a low power-distance culture, because differences in status are muted, you are more comfortable arguing with those in authority. When interacting with a higher-power person, you feel comfortable directing the course of the conversation, and you question or confront power-brokers if needed. You do not feel compelled to use formal titles when addressing more powerful people.

Masculine vs. Feminine Orientation

A fourth way in which cultural differences affect communication is the extent to which traditionally masculine or feminine orientations are valued in a culture. Cultures differ in how strongly they value traditional sex-role distinctions. According to Hofstede, a **masculine culture** is a culture in which men are expected to adhere to traditional sex roles. Hofstede called these cultures masculine because, for the most part, groups that maintain distinct sex-based roles also value masculine roles more highly than feminine ones. If you come from a masculine culture like those dominant in Mexico, Italy, and Japan, you are likely to expect men to act assertively and dominantly and expect women to be nurturing, caring, and service oriented. Encounters with people who don't meet these expectations may make you uncomfortable. If you come from a masculine culture, your culture has likely taught you that masculine behaviors are more worthwhile, regardless of your own sex. Accordingly, you will probably value the traditionally masculine characteristics of performance, ambition, assertiveness, competitiveness, and material success more than you value traditionally feminine traits and behaviors that are relationship oriented such as nurturing and helping (Hofstede, 2000).

A **feminine culture** is a culture in which people regardless of sex can assume a variety of roles depending on the circumstances and their own choices. Men

Low power-distance culture—a culture in which members prefer power to be more equally distributed.

Masculine culture—a culture in which men are expected to adhere to traditional sex roles.

Feminine culture—a culture in which people regardless of sex can assume a variety of roles depending on the circumstances and their own choices.

In feminine cultures like Denmark, people, regardless of sex, assume a variety of roles. Did your family tend to have a masculine or a feminine culture?

as well as women in feminine cultures are accustomed to being nurturing, caring, and service oriented. If you are from a feminine culture, like Sweden, Norway, or Denmark you will also value those traits that have traditionally been associated with feminine roles (Hofstede, 1998).

Whether you come from a masculine or a feminine culture has a significant effect on how much behavioral flexibility you demonstrate in communicating with others. People from masculine cultures have strict definitions of what behavior is appropriate for people of a particular sex. As a result, they learn and are rewarded only for those behaviors seen as appropriate for their sex. Men in these cultures may be unprepared to engage in nurturing and caring behaviors, such as empathizing and comforting, and women are unprepared to be assertive or argue persuasively. Both men and women in feminine cultures learn and are rewarded for demonstrating both traditionally masculine and feminine behaviors. Consequently, people from feminine cultures are more flexible in how they communicate. Both men and women learn to nurture, empathize, assert, and argue, although any single individual may still lack skill in one or more of these behaviors.

Time Orientation

Edward T. Hall pioneered the field of **chronemics**, the study of how perception of time differs between individuals and cultures (Hall, 1976). Some people and cultures are **monochronic**, perceiving time as being small, even units that occur sequentially. Monochronic people adhere to schedule and do things one at a time. Monochronic cultures value punctuality, uninterrupted task completion, meeting deadlines, and following plans. For instance, when Margarite, who perceives time in a monochronic way, is interrupted by her sister,

Various cultures treat time differently. Social media have changed how members of the American culture view time. Think for a moment about how quickly you respond to a friend's text message. Why might you feel a burning desire to respond so quickly? Does the same hold true for messages you receive through other forms of social media such as e-mail or Facebook? As you learn about culture in this chapter, think about how social media might influence how members of other cultures treat time. Is the burning desire to respond quickly to text messages unique to the American culture? Why or why not?

Chronemics—the study of how perception of time differs between individuals and cultures.

Monochronic—a time orientation that views time as being small, even units that occur sequentially.

who is excited to share some good news, Margarite may snap, "Get out of here right now. You know it's my study time!" The dominant culture of the United States is monochronic.

Other people and cultures are **polychronic**, seeing time as a continuous flow. Polychronic people understand that appointment times and schedules are approximate and fluid. Rather than doing one thing at a time, they are comfortable doing several things at once, having flexible schedules or none at all, and disregarding deadlines and appointment times to satisfy task or relationship needs (Chen & Starosta, 1998). People who take a polychronic approach to time do not perceive interruptions as annoying departures from plans but as natural occurrences. Latin American, Arab, and southern European cultures are polychronic.

Differences in time orientation can make intercultural communication challenging. For example, Dante, who perceives time in a polychronic way, may show up for a noon lunch with Stephen at 12:47 and not think of that as a problem, since his co-worker stopped him to ask for help with a project. Stephen was annoyed and impatient, however, when Dante arrived a half an hour late to their planned lunch and then proceeded to ignore his attempts to quickly move the discussion to the business they needed to complete. Meanwhile, Dante found Stephen's attitude confusing and off-putting. Stephen's abrupt transition to business seemed rude to Dante. In polychronic cultures engaging in conversation to enhance the relationship is seen as much more important than quickly concluding business. Differences in time orientation make the lunch and conversation uncomfortable for both men. Like other cultural differences, monochronic and polychronic perceptions of time are only general tendencies of certain cultures and individuals, and one orientation is not better than the other.

The Importance of Context for Sharing Meaning

The difference between cultures perhaps most related to intercultural communication is the extent to which members rely on contextual cues to convey the actual meaning of a message. According to Edward T. Hall (1976), cultures differ not only in the languages spoken but also in the degree to which people rely on factors other than words to convey their meaning. In some cultures, the speaker's words convey most of the meaning. In other cultures, much of the speaker's message is understood from the context. Thus, cultures may be either high or low context.

A **low-context culture** is a culture in which message meanings are usually encoded in the verbal part of the message. The words spoken are more important in understanding the message than contextual cues like nonverbal behaviors, previous interactions, or cultural cues. Verbal messages are direct, specific, and detailed. Speakers are expected to say exactly what they mean and get to the point. In low-context cultures people use forceful verbal messages

Polychronic—a time orientation that views time as a continuous flow.

OBSERVE AND ANALYZE

Observing Dimensions of Culture

Interview someone who was born and raised in a country other than yours. During the discussion, explain the cultural dimensions of (a) individualism–collectivism; (b) uncertainty avoidance; (c) power distance; (d) masculinity/femininity; (e) monochronism/polychronism; and (f) high-context/low-context cultures. Solicit an example from this person of each of these four dimensions to determine where his or her culture falls on each one of the dimensions. Then analyze what you have learned about these four cultural dimensions as a result of this activity.

Low-context culture—a culture in which message meanings are usually encoded in the verbal part of the message.

in persuading others. The United States, Germany, and Scandinavia are low-context cultures.

A **high-context culture**, on the other hand, is a culture in which much of the real meaning of a message is indirect and can only be accurately decoded by referring to unwritten cultural rules and subtle nonverbal behavior. In a high-context culture verbal messages are general and ambiguous, with the real meaning implied and understood by "reading between the lines." In high-context cultures speakers are cautious and tentative in their use of language. Most Native American, Latin American, and Asian countries are high-context cultures (Chen & Starosta, 1998).

Effective communication between members of high- and low-context cultures is very difficult. Consider the following conversation between Isaac, a member of a low-context culture, and Zhao, a member of a high-context culture, who are trying to conduct business together.

High-context culture—a culture in which much of the real meaning of a message is indirect and can only be accurately decoded by referring to unwritten cultural rules and subtle nonverbal behavior.

> **Isaac:** *Let's get right down to business here. We're hoping that you can provide 100,000 parts per month according to our six manufacturing specifications spelled out in the engineering contract I sent you. If quality control finds more than a 2 percent margin of error, we'll have to terminate the contract. Can you agree to these terms?*
>
> **Zhao:** *We are very pleased to be doing business with you. We produce the highest quality products and will be honored to meet your needs.*
>
> **Isaac:** *But can you supply that exact quantity? Will you commit to meeting all of our engineering specifications? Will you consistently have a less than 2 percent margin of error?*
>
> **Zhao:** *We are an excellent, trustworthy company that will send you the highest quality parts.*

Isaac was probably frustrated with what he perceived as general, evasive language on Zhao's part. Zhao was probably offended by the direct questions and specific language, which he perceived as threatening and embarrassing.

Both Isaac and Zhao could have been more effective in this exchange if each had been mindful of how messages are formed and understood in the other's culture. When low-context communicators like Isaac interact with high-context communicators like Zhao, they should be aware that building a good relationship is important for long-term effectiveness. Therefore, polite social conversation should precede business; nonverbal messages and gestures will be as important as what is said; status and identity are communicated nonverbally and need to be acknowledged; face-saving and tact are important and can often supersede being frank; and indirect expressions must be interpreted within the context and rules of the speaker's culture. When high-context communicators like Zhao interact with low-context communicators like Isaac, they should recognize that what is said should be taken at face value rather than examined for underlying meaning. They need to be mindful that direct questions, assertions, and observations are not meant to be offensive. Finally, they need to recognize that low-context people usually do not interpret or understand indirect contextual cues.

Developing Intercultural Communication Competence

As you have read this chapter, you have probably begun to realize how difficult it is to effectively communicate with someone from a different culture. Yet you know that immigration, the Internet, and increasing globalization of business require effective intercultural communication. Developing your intercultural competence means overcoming several barriers. Let's quickly look at several of the most common barriers to effective intercultural communication and then turn our attention to a model that describes how you can develop intercultural competence.

Barriers to Effective Intercultural Communication

The most common barriers to effective communication between members of different cultures include anxiety, assuming similarity or difference, ethnocentrism, stereotyping, incompatible communication codes, and incompatible norms and values.

Anxiety

It is normal to feel some level of discomfort or apprehension when we recognize that we are different from most everyone else or when entering a cultural milieu whose customs are unfamiliar. Most people experience fear, dislike, and distrust when first interacting with someone from a different culture (Luckmann, 1999). If you have ever traveled to a foreign country or been the only member of your cultural group in some setting, you probably experienced anxiety.

When you found yourself in the midst of others from a different culture, what was your initial feeling?

Assumed Similarity or Difference

When people enter an unfamiliar cultural environment, they often assume that the familiar norms that have always applied will apply in a new situation. When traveling internationally from the United States, for example, many people expect to eat their usual hamburgers and fries provided with rapid and efficient service. They may be annoyed with shops and restaurants closing during midday in countries that observe the custom of siesta. It can be just as great a mistake to assume that everything about an unfamiliar culture will be different. For example, Marissa, a Mexican American student from California who is studying at a small private college in Vermont may feel that no one understands her and her experiences. As she makes friends, however, she may learn that while Rachel, who is Jewish, didn't have a quinceañera, she did have a bat mitzvah, and Kate, who is Irish Catholic, had a big confirmation party. While these occasions are different, each rite celebrates coming of age in their respective cultures. As Marissa makes these and other connections, she will be able to accurately notice similarities and then key in on real rather than apparent differences.

Ethnocentrism

Ethnocentrism is the belief that one's own culture is superior to that of others. The stereotype of the immigrant in the host country, loudly complaining about how much better everything was back home, is the classic example of ethnocentrism. In varying degrees, ethnocentrism is found in every culture (Haviland, 1993) and can occur in co-cultures as well. An ethnocentric view of the world leads to attitudes of superiority and messages that are directly and subtly condescending in content and tone. As you would expect, these messages are offensive to receivers from other cultures or co-cultures and get in the way of intercultural communication.

Ethnocentrism—the belief that one's own culture is superior to that of others.

Stereotyping

As you will recall from Chapter 2, stereotyping is a perceptual shortcut in which we assume that everyone in a cultural group is the same. For example, thinking that a Chinese international student in your class will get the best grade in the course because all Asian students excel intellectually; assuming that Jean Marc, who is Haitian, is working in the United States as an undocumented worker; or anticipating that all European Americans are out to take advantage of people of color are all examples of stereotyping. When we interact based on stereotypes, we risk creating inaccurate messages that damage our relationships. When we listen with our stereotypes and prejudices in mind, we may misperceive the intent of the person with whom we are talking.

Incompatible Communication Codes

When others speak a different language, it is easy to see that we have incompatible communication codes. But even among people who speak the same language, there will be cultural variations that result from the co-cultures to which they belong. For example, people from Great Britain take a "lift" to reach a higher floor and eat "chips" with their fish, while Americans ride an "elevator" and eat "french fries" with their burgers. Within the United States, Midwesterners drink "pop," while New Yorkers drink "soda." Co-cultural groups will often purpose-fully develop "in-group" codes that are easily understood by co-culture members but unintelligible to outsiders. Just try to have a conversation about your com-puter problem with your friend Sam, who is a "techno-geek." As an insider, Sam is likely to talk in a vocabulary as foreign to you as Icelandic. "BTW," "OMG," and other initialisms once confined to text messages are now sprinkled in the verbal messages of teens and other heavy IMers. To get past incompatible com-munication codes, we may use nonverbal signing in an effort to overcome the language barrier. However, significant differences in the use and meaning of nonverbal behaviors may also render those codes incompatible.

Incompatible Norms and Values

What is normal or of high value in one culture may be offensive in another. The Vietnamese, for example, consider dog a delicacy. Most Americans find this practice disgusting, yet think nothing of eating beef. Hindus, on the other hand,

---

LEARN ABOUT YOURSELF ● Ethnocentrism

Take this short survey to learn something about yourself. Answer the questions honestly based on your initial response. There are no right or wrong answers. For each statement, record the number to the left of the response that best describes your beliefs.

1 = Strongly agree
2 = Agree somewhat
3 = Neutral
4 = Disagree somewhat
5 = Strongly disagree

_____ 1. My country should be the role model for the world.
_____ 2. Most other countries are backward in comparison to my country.
_____ 3. People in my culture have just about the best lifestyle of anywhere.
_____ 4. People in other cultures could learn a lot from people in my culture.
_____ 5. Other cultures should try to be more like my culture.
_____ 6. I respect the customs and values of other cultures.
_____ 7. I am interested in the customs and values of other cultures.
_____ 8. Each culture should preserve its uniqueness.
_____ 9. People from my culture behave oddly when they interact with other cultures.
_____ 10. Although different, most countries have value systems as valid as ours.

Scoring the survey: To find your scores, add up your responses for items 1, 2, 3, 4, and 5. Then add up separately your responses for items 6, 7, 8, 9, and 10. Each score can range from 5 to 25. Each score measures ethnocentrism. On the first score, the lower the number, the higher your ethnocentrism. On the second score, the higher the number, the higher your ethnocentrism.

Adapted from Neuliep, J. W., & McCroskey, J. C. (1997). The development of a U.S. and generalized ethnocentrism scale. *Communication Research Reports, 14*, 385–398.

consider beef eating abominable, as the cow is sacred to their religion. Cultural incompatibilities can cause serious problems in personal relationships and even war on a societal level.

The Pyramid Mode of Intercultural Competence

Intercultural scholars define **intercultural competence** as "the effective and appropriate behavior and communication in intercultural situations" (Deardorff, 2006). The Pyramid Model of Intercultural Competence (Deardorff, 2006) in Figure 3.2 depicts how the lifelong process of acquiring intercultural competence occurs. This tiered model suggests that competence begins with attitudes that support intercultural exchanges. Then you can use learning skills to develop knowledge and understanding of your own and other cultures. This knowledge will equip you with a cultural frame of reference that can guide you to communicate effectively and appropriately with people from another culture. Let's take a closer look at how this model works.

Requisite Attitudes

According to the Pyramid Model, intercultural competence begins by having the right attitudes toward learning about another culture. These attitudes are respect, openness, and curiosity or discovery. When we respect another culture,

Intercultural competence—the effective and appropriate behavior and communication in intercultural situations.

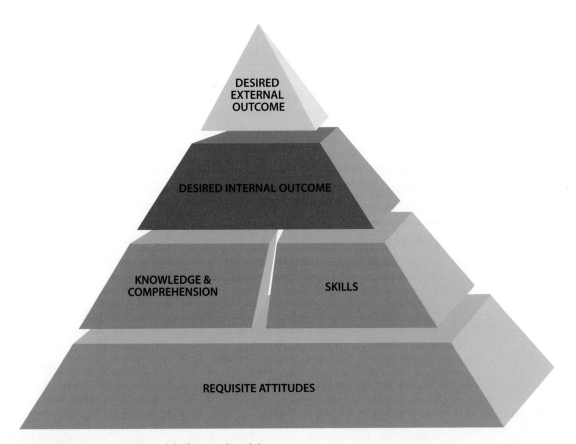

FIGURE 3.2 The Pyramid Model of Intercultural Competence

we appreciate and try to see the value of the ways in which another culture differs from our own. This respect guides our desire to learn how to behave in interculturally appropriate ways. For example, when Clarise, a store manager, wanted to reward her team with lunch, she chose a vegan restaurant because she respects the cultures of two members of her team, a conservative Jew and a Muslim who don't eat pork and are not allowed to eat meat unless it has been killed according to the dietary laws of each religion.

If you are to become effective in intercultural interactions, you must also be open to new ideas and to meeting people from other cultures. This requires that we withhold our judgments about their values, norms, attitudes, and orientations. One of the most difficult things for many of us is being open to eating new things. When in Taiwan, my colleague was honored at a banquet where the hosts served an expensive Taiwanese delicacy—a whole newt submerged in a delicate broth served in a soup bowl. My colleague watched as those around her, using their chopsticks to pick up the amphibian, began to eat. To save face for her host, my colleague bravely took her chopsticks and dug in.

Finally, if we are to become effective, we must let our curiosity overcome our anxiety and fear of the unknown. We must work hard to tolerate the uncertainty and ambiguity that accompanies interacting with someone who is very different and in perhaps a foreign environment. My colleague reported that despite its not unpleasant flavor, being open to the idea of dining on what looked to her like "The GEICO Gecko®" was very difficult. My colleague demonstrated an attitude of curiosity when she bit into that newt. And much to her relief, it tasted OK.

Developing Culture-Specific Knowledge and Understanding

To become competent in intercultural interactions, we need to develop a deep understanding of the culture, the cultural history, the extent to which the people with whom we are interacting identify with their culture, and the likely worldview of someone from this culture. We will also need to learn specific information such as the social customs expected on specific occasions. We may need to develop specific language skills to understand how the other's culture has influenced the way that our common language is used. The more we know about other cultures, the more likely we are to be competent intercultural communicators (Neuliep, 2006). There are various ways to learn about other cultures. These include observation, language study, formal cultural study, and cultural immersion.

1. **Observation.** You can simply watch members of another culture interact with each other. As you observe, you will notice how the values, rituals, and communication styles of that culture are similar to and different from your own and from other cultures with which you are familiar. Passive observers who study the communication behaviors used by members of a particular culture become better intercultural communicators as a result.

2. **Language study.** Because communication is culture and culture is communication, it is difficult to understand a culture without understanding its

language. The United States lags behind most other developed countries in being multilingual. According to a 2001 Gallup poll, only 25 percent of Americans can hold a conversation in a language other than English and for 55 percent of them that language is Spanish (McComb, 2001). In a similar report, the European Union found that 47 percent of EU citizens could converse in a second language and 27 percent of them were fluent in a third language (European Commission, 2001). Regardless of statistics, if you really want to be effective at intercultural communication, language study is critical.

3. Formal cultural study. You can learn more about another culture by reading accounts written by members of that culture; looking at ethnographic research studies; taking courses; or interviewing a member of the culture about his or her values, rituals, and so on. Formal study and observation can go hand-in-hand, working together to help you achieve greater intercultural understanding.

4. Cultural immersion. Active participation is the best way to learn about another culture. When you live or work with people whose cultural assumptions are different from yours, you not only acquire obvious cultural information but also learn the nuances that escape passive observers and are generally not accessible through formal study. Study abroad programs often include homestays to provide students the opportunity to be surrounded by the culture of the host country. We hope that you will consider participating in a study abroad experience. The international or global studies office at your college or university can point you to a variety of study abroad opportunities and may even guide you to scholarships or grants to help pay your expenses.

Skills for Acquiring Cultural Knowledge

Several skills can help you learn another culture. The first of these is the communication skill of listening. As you will see when you study Chapter 7, listening is not a passive activity. It includes active behaviors for paying attention, carefully observing, and aiding understanding by asking questions and probing for additional information. It requires that you analyze, evaluate, and interpret what you have observed. Finally, you must be able to relate what you have learned to other things you know about your own and the new culture. When Ian found out that in two months he was going to be transferred to Milan, Italy for three years to work on a joint venture between an Italian company and his company, he knew that the success of the project depended on how well and how quickly he could understand Italian culture. Before he left he read everything he could about Italian culture and history, used a Rosetta Stone® program to begin learning the language, and spent time with a co-worker's family who was from Italy.

But when he arrived in Milan, he still felt like a fish out of water. As he interacted with his Italian neighbors and co-workers, he observed things about the culture that were foreign to him. For instance, he noticed that people adjourned for coffee or espresso at about 10 A.M. While he was used to the concept of a coffee break, he was surprised that instead of a ten-minute run to the company cafeteria, this was often an hour break taken at a local café. Moreover, it wasn't unusual for his co-workers to have a little grappa (a grape brandy) either alongside as a chaser or added to the espresso and called *caffè corretto* (corrected coffee). As an American, Ian was initially appalled until he noticed that his Italian co-workers extended or contracted their workday depending on how much time they had spent on breaks so that they always put in the expected eight hours of work. As for the *caffè corretto,* further observation showed that the typical barista added only a teaspoon of the liqueur to the espresso, not enough to give anyone a buzz. After being in the country for six months, Ian's Italian had really improved as had his understanding of northern Italian culture. When sent on a short business trip to Sicily, however, he once again experienced culture shock and had to refocus on using his skills to learn the subtle differences in Sicilian culture.

Internal and External Outcomes

Developing intercultural knowledge will enable you to make several changes in your mental library or map. Your revised mental map will include canned plans that allow you to adapt and adjust to the new cultural environment using a different style and communication behaviors. These new canned plans will help

---

A QUESTION OF ETHICS ● What Would You Do?

Tyler, Jeannie, Margeaux, and Madhukar are sitting around Margeaux's dining room table and working on a group marketing project. It was 2:00 A.M. They had been at it since 6:00 P.M. and still had several hours of work remaining.

"Oh, the agony," groans Tyler, pretending to slit his throat with an Exacto knife. "If I never see another photo of a veggie burger, it will be too soon. Why didn't we choose a more appetizing product to base our project on?"

"I think it had something to do with *someone* wanting to promote a healthy alternative to greasy hamburgers," Jeannie replies sarcastically.

"Right," Tyler answers. "I don't know what I could have been thinking. Speaking of greasy hamburgers, is anyone else starving? Anyone up for ordering a pizza or something?"

"Sorry, but no one will deliver up here so late," Margeaux apologizes. "But I have a quiche that I could heat up."

"Oh, oui, oui," Tyler quips.

"You wish," Margeaux says. "It came out of a box."

"Sure, it sounds great. Thanks," Jeannie says. "I'm hungry too."

"It doesn't have any meat in it, does it?" asks Madhukar. "I don't eat meat."

"Nope, it's a cheese and spinach quiche," Margeaux answers.

Tyler and Margeaux go off to the kitchen to prepare the food. Tyler takes the quiche, which is still in its box, from the refrigerator. "Uh-oh," he says. "My roommate is a vegetarian, and he won't buy this brand because it has lard in the crust. Better warn Madhukar. He's a Hindu, so I imagine it's pretty important to him."

"Shhh!" responds Margeaux. "I don't have anything else to offer him, and he'll never know the difference anyway. Just pretend you didn't notice that."

For Consideration:

1. What ethical principles are involved in this case?
2. What exactly are Margeaux's ethical obligations to Madhukar in this situation?
3. What should Tyler do now?

you overcome your ethnocentrism and provide you instead with an ethnorelative way of viewing things. **Ethnorelativism** is a point of view that allows you to see the value in other cultural perspectives. Because your new canned plans will also include scripts, you will gain behavioral flexibility, which means that when you interact with someone from another culture you will be able to choose scripts appropriate to that cultural setting.

The external result or outcomes of becoming culturally competent is the ability to behave and communicate effectively and appropriately in the new culture. After being in Italy for a year and a half, Ian was still working on developing intercultural competence. One day after work he stopped at his neighborhood bar for a drink. On his initial visit to the café, he had chosen to sit at a table (*al tavolo)* only to discover that his drink cost more than had he chosen to stand at the bar. So this time, he sidled up to the bar to enjoy his drink and to talk with a couple of his neighbors. As with most people who are learning another language, Ian was still translating from English into Italian when he spoke and doing the reverse when he was listening. But this evening, as he was talking, Ian was amazed to realize that he had made a breakthrough. He was no longer translating; rather, he was thinking in Italian, the ultimate experience for someone learning a foreign language. But it came about because he had started with attitudes that supported his learning about Italian culture and trying to learn the language. He had not only read about Italy but had immersed himself in Italian life, even choosing to live outside the normal districts frequented by Americans in favor of a "real" Italian neighborhood. Still, it took over a year and a half before Ian was able to be completely absorbed in the culture and think as an Italian. You may never have the opportunity to become so thoroughly immersed in another culture that you develop this level of cultural competence. But you can use the pyramid model of intercultural competence to identify ways to improve your intercultural communication. Ian is not entirely fluent in Italian culture, and having recently learned of his upcoming transfer to New Zealand to begin another project, he will continue his intercultural competence quest elsewhere.

Ethnorelativism—the point of view allows you to see the value in other cultural perspectives.

Summary

Contact among people of diverse cultures is increasing. Culture is the system of shared values, beliefs, attitudes, and orientations learned through communication that guide what is considered to be appropriate thought and behavior in a particular segment of the population. Culture shock refers to the psychological discomfort people have when they attempt to adjust to a new cultural situation. Intercultural communication involves interactions that occur between people whose cultures are so different that the communication between them is altered. Within a society there are both dominant and co-cultures. A shared system of meaning exists within the dominant culture, but meanings can vary within co-cultures based on gender, race, ethnicity, sexual orientation and gender identity, religion, social class, and generation.

Cultures vary according to how they value individualism versus collectivism, predictability versus tolerating uncertainty, equality versus an unequal distribution of power, and masculine versus feminine ways of behaving; whether they are monochronic or polychronic; and how important context is for understanding the meaning of verbal messages. Intercultural competence enables us to overcome common barriers to intercultural communication including anxiety, assumptions about differences and similarities, ethnocentrism, stereotyping, incompatible communication codes, and incompatible norms and values.

The Pyramid Model of Intercultural Competence depicts how you can develop intercultural competence. It begins with developing the requisite attitudes that support using learning skills to acquire cultural knowledge that increases your mental libraries and maps and provides you with new scripts to form effective messages.

Chapter Resources

What You Should Be Able *to Explain:*

- What defines a culture
- The role of communication in defining, transmitting, and changing culture
- The relationships between dominant and co-cultures
- How cultural identity affects communication
- Six systematic ways in which cultures differ and how that affects intercultural communication
- The barriers we face when communicating with others from different cultures
- How to develop intercultural communication competence

What You Should Be Able *to Do:*

- Develop a plan for acquiring intercultural competence

Self-test questions based on these concepts are available on the companion Web site (www.oup.com/us/verderber) as part of Chapter 3 resources.

Key Words

Flashcards for all of these key terms are available on the *Inter-Act* Web site.

Apply Your Knowledge

The following questions challenge you to demonstrate your mastery of the concepts, theories, and frameworks in this chapter by using them to explain what is happening in a specific situation.

3.1 *Name the co-cultural group with which you most identify. It might be your religious group, your sorority or fraternity, your ethnic group, etc.*

   a. Describe this culture. Who belongs? How do you become a member? What are its top three ideal values? What are two of its real values? Cite at least one attitude widely shared by co-culture members. Describe two important rites or rituals in which members participate. What is the purpose of these?

   b. Locate this culture on each of the six dimensions that differentiate cultural groups. Explain your reasoning.

   c. On which of these dimensions is your co-culture most different from the dominant culture? How do you deal with these differences?

3.2 Recall a conversation you have had with someone whose culture or co-culture was very different from your own. Describe the difficulties you had in communicating with this person. Which of the barriers to intercultural communication seemed to be in play? How would better intercultural competence have helped you in this situation?

Skill Practice

Skill Practice activities give you the chance to rehearse a new skill by responding to hypothetical or real situations. Additional skill practice activities are available at the companion Web site.

Intercultural Communication

3.3 Identify a country where people speak a language you don't know and that you know very little about. Pretend that you have agreed to take part in a sister cities cultural exchange program in that country six months from now. You will be there for one month and will be staying in a home with citizens of that country. Use the pyramid model to help you develop a plan for acquiring as much cultural knowledge about this country as you can before you leave. Your plan should include a timetable.

Communication Improvement Plan: Intercultural Communication

How would you like to improve your ability to communicate across cultures, as discussed in this chapter?

- Develop requisite attitudes
- Gain culture-specific knowledge and understanding
- Improve cultural learning skills

3.4   Pick the area in which you would like to improve and write a communication improvement plan. You can find a communication improvement plan worksheet on our Web site at www.oup.com/us/verderber.

Inter-Act with Media

Television

Family Guy, episode: "From Method to Madness" (2002).

As they arrive for dinner at a friend's home, Peter and Lois shockingly discover that Mark, his wife, Dottie, and children are nudists. They freely walk around the house naked and are comfortable doing so. Jeff, the teenage son of Mark and Dottie, becomes quite interested in Meg, a daughter of Peter and Lois. They discourage Meg from dating Jeff because he is a nudist. A few days later, Jeff visits Meg's home for dinner and Peter and Lois take off their clothes in an effort to make Jeff feel welcome. This confuses and shocks Meg. When he leaves, Jeff says that he appreciates Meg's parents' decision to pretend to be nudists to make him feel at home.

IPC Concepts: Culture shock, co-culture, cultural identity.

To the Point:

> When did you last experience culture shock?
> How did this feeling influence your effectiveness as a communicator in the particular situation?
> How did the experience contribute to your thoughts about your own cultural identity?

Cinema

Lost in Translation (2003). Sofia Coppola (director). Bill Murray, Scarlett Johansson.

American actor Bob Harris (Murray) arrives in Tokyo to film a commercial that showcases a popular whiskey. Because he is far away from his wife and in a very unfamiliar culture, he feels lonely and easily becomes frustrated because he can only understand a fraction of what members of the Japanese culture are saying. After experiencing many sleepless nights, Bob meets a young (about half his age) American woman, Charlotte (Johnasson). She too feels lonely because her husband is quite busy and suggests that he is more interested in his photography work than in her. Like Bob, she has been wandering the streets of Tokyo to better wrap her head around this very unfamiliar culture. Bob and Charlotte become close friends and maintain a relationship that is built on respect and trust. Viewers are left wondering whether their relationship will become romantic in nature or if they will just remain friends.

IPC Concepts: Intercultural communication, culture shock, stereotyping.

To the Point:

When did you last share the experience of culture shock with another person?
How did this experience influence your relationship with the person?
What did you learn about yourself as a communicator?

What's on the Web

Find links and additional material, including self-quizzes, on the companion Web site at www.oup.com/us/verderber.

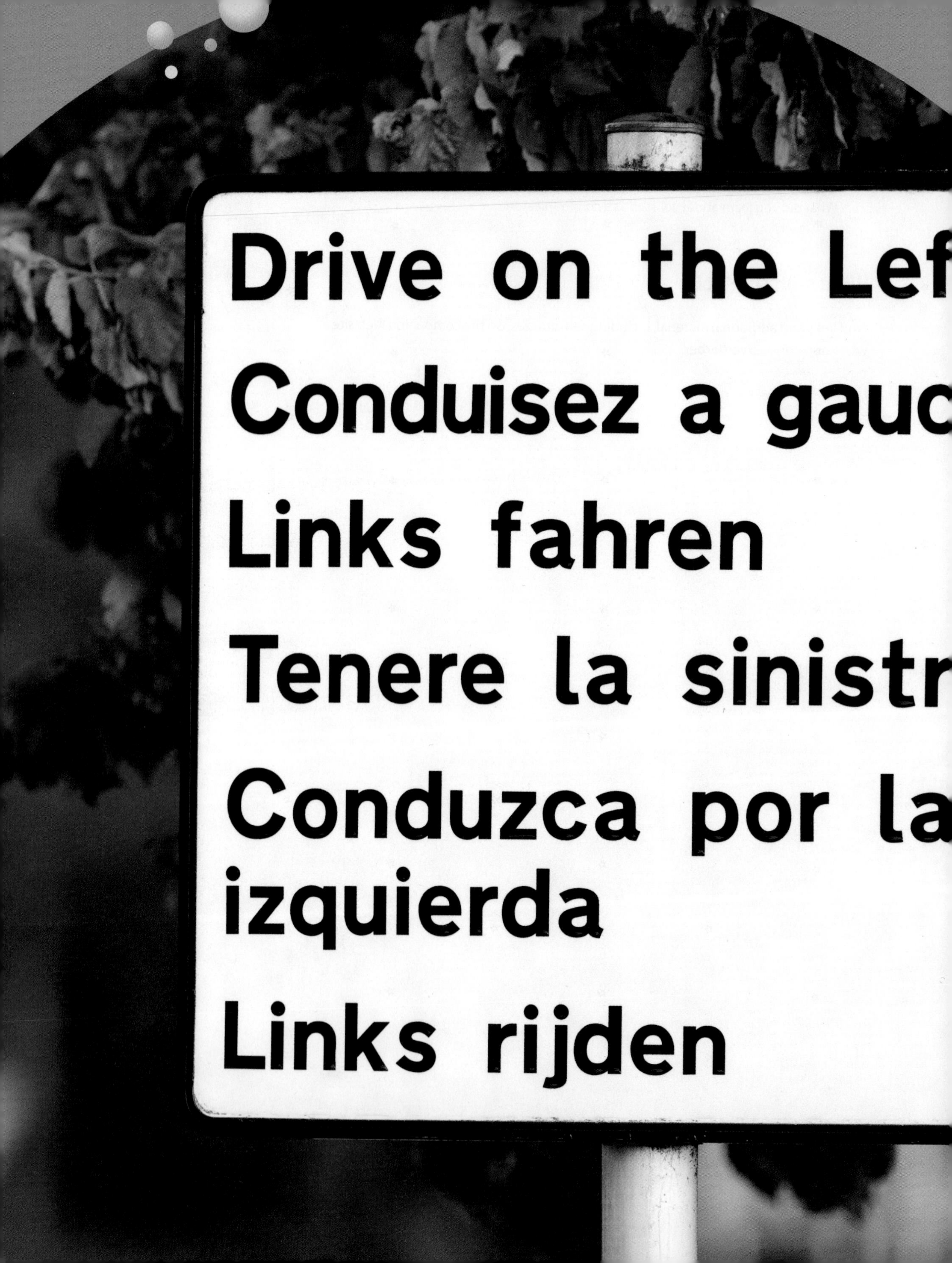

Drive on the Lef

Conduisez a gauc

Links fahren

Tenere la sinistr

Conduzca por la izquierda

Links rijden

Verbal Messages

The study group meeting had begun and everyone was there
except Maria, who had been late to every meeting. Ten minutes into the discussion, Maria rushed into the room.

"The sitter, she didn't show up," said Maria in heavily accented English
as she pulled up a chair to join the group.

"Oh, so that's why you're late, again. You should just fire her," Louisa
replied.

"Well, that's what I thought too. When she didn't show up, though, I just
called her house, and her husband told me that she was sick, but her
sister was on the way over, and she got there just as I was hanging up.
Actually, I'm glad her sister came. She straightens up the house while
she's there and makes the kids put away their toys when they are
done playing."

"I'm so happy to hear all that," Kai piped in. "You're childcare situation
is of grave concern to all of us here, and we can't think of anything
we'd rather do than discuss it."

"So I give. Why were you late, again?" Louisa asked.

"Well, on my way up the stairs I ran into Professor Green so I stopped to talk with him a bit. I was thinking that well, if I spend a little time with him, I might be able to get a little inside information that would help us study for the test," Maria replied.

"Yeah, right. You flash him a toothy smile, and he just hands you an advance copy of the test," Terrell mumbled.

"Oh, Terrell, that's so silly. But while we were talking, he did mention that there would be two essays, and he gave me a little hint about what one of them would be. So if all of you will stop making fun of me, I might even tell you what I learned."

What you should be able *to explain* after you have studied this chapter:

- How interpersonal communication meaning is conveyed through verbal and nonverbal parts of messages
- What a language is
- What a dialect is
- What an idiolect is
- How language and dialects are related
- How the meaning of a verbal message depends on the language itself
- How a verbal message's meaning depends on the conversational context
- How a verbal message's meaning depends on the social or cultural context

What you should be able *to do* after you have studied this chapter:

- Form clear and precise messages.
- Create messages that are appropriate and effective within a conversational context.
- Tailor messages to the social and cultural context.

What's your impression of this conversation? Why did Maria bother to tell the group that the sitter was late? Did Louisa think Maria's statement was providing an excuse or apologizing? Was Kai really happy to hear about Maria's childcare situation? Did Terrell really think that Professor Green had given Maria a copy of the test? What did Maria do when she answered Terrell? Why did she do this? After studying this chapter, you should be able to answer all of these questions.

In this chapter we're going to look at the verbal parts of messages to help you understand how language is used to share meaning and how you can increase your ability to form and to interpret the verbal parts of messages. We begin by explaining several fundamental concepts regarding verbal messages. The bulk of this chapter is devoted to describing each of the levels of meaning in verbal messages as well as how you can improve your ability at each level.

Verbal Message Fundamentals

An **utterance** is a complete unit of talk that is bounded by the speaker's silence (Arnoff & Rees-Miller, 2001). By definition, then, utterances are spoken to someone else. In a conversation an utterance is the same thing as a "turn." When you talk with someone, your utterance includes both verbal and nonverbal parts. **Verbal messages** are the parts of an utterance that use language to convey meaning. Let's begin our study of verbal messages by defining and describing several related concepts: language, language community, dialect, speech community, and idiolect.

Utterance—a complete unit of talk that is bounded by the speaker's silence.

Verbal messages—the parts of an utterance that use language to convey meaning.

What Is a Language?

Language is a symbolic system used by people to communicate verbal or written messages. Each language includes a **lexicon**, the collection of words and expressions, a **phonology**, the sounds used to pronounce words, and a **syntax and grammar**, the rules for combining words to form sentences and into larger units of expression. A **language community** includes all people who can speak or understand a particular language. For example, the English language community includes Australians, Scots, Irish, Canadians, Indians, and Americans as well as others who speak English. The five largest language communities, in order, are Chinese, Spanish, English, Arabic, and Hindi (Lewis, 2009). A quick look at the definition of a language makes it all seem so simple. But it is not. This definition implies that everyone in a particular language community knows all the words, pronounces them the same, and uses the same rules of grammar and syntax. But you know from experience that this is not the case. For example, you know that the English spoken in England is not the same as the English spoken in the United States. And the English spoken in Boston, Massachusetts differs from that spoken in Biloxi, Mississippi, and in Fargo, North Dakota.

Language—a symbolic system used by people to communicate verbal or written messages.

Lexicon—the collection of words and expressions in a language.

Phonology—the sounds used to pronounce words.

Syntax and grammar—the rules for combining words to form sentences and into larger units of expression.

Language community—all people who can speak or understand a particular language.

Languages are really collections of dialects. A **dialect** is a form of a more general language spoken by a specific culture or co-culture that, while differing from the general language, shares enough commonality that most people who belong to a particular language community can understand it (O'Grady et. al., 2001). A **speech community** is comprised of members of a larger language community who speak a common dialect with a particular style and observe common linguistic norms or scripts. Dialects of a language fall on a continuum, being situated closer to dialects with more commonalities and farther from those with fewer. If you have you ever had a conversation with someone from Scotland, you probably had trouble understanding this person. Even though you were both speaking English, the way that Scots pronounce most words is very different from the way that Americans do. On the other hand, while Canadians pronounce a few words differently than Americans and use some different words, most Americans can easily understand English-speaking Canadians and vice versa. On a dialect continuum, American and Canadian dialects are close, whereas Scottish dialects would be more distant.

Dialect—a form of a more general language spoken by a specific culture or co-culture that, while differing from the general language, shares enough commonality that most people who belong to a particular language community can understand it.

Speech community—the members of a larger language community who speak a common dialect with a particular style and observe common linguistic norms or scripts.

There are several popular misconceptions about dialects, including the belief that they are substandard, incorrect, or slang. From a linguistic perspective, one dialect is not better or worse than another. They just have differences in lexicon, phonology, and grammar and syntax. Nevertheless, certain dialects are more privileged and perceived to be "better" than others because the power elite of a language group speaks them. Speaking a privileged dialect marks someone as part of the powerful "in-group" of the society or country. Those who speak other dialects, particularly if they are distant from the ones associated with the powerful people are marked as the "out-group," whose speakers are less likely to achieve positions of influence in the society or country. People may, therefore, learn and use the in-group dialect to improve their opportunities or learn and use the out-group dialect to show solidarity with out-group co-cultures. As you will recall, from Chapter 3, this is called codeswitching.

As the in-group solidifies its position, its dialect is idealized and seen as the "proper" or real form of a language, a power disparity captured by the old linguistic saying that "a language is a dialect with an army and a navy" (Fasold, 1984).

What is called a language and what is called a dialect is usually a matter more political than linguistic, as the recent cases of the former Yugoslavia and China demonstrate. Serbo-Croatian, the official language of the former country of Yugoslavia, was comprised of a variety of very similar dialects. But since the collapse of Yugoslavia in the mid- to late 1990s, each of the former regions became a separate nation claiming their own unique language. Serbian is spoken in Serbia, Croatian in Croatia, Bosnian in Bosnia, and Montenegrin in Montenegro. Nevertheless, people from all these countries can still easily understand one another. So from a linguistic perspective, they all speak dialects of the same language (Cvetkovic, 2009).

In contrast, the official language of China is, for political purposes, called Chinese. All literate people in China use the same written symbol system developed in ancient times. In general, people from one part of the country can easily read writing from another part of the country, but the written symbols do not have a commonly shared pronunciation. Although the government of China considers the regional tongues of Mandarin, Wu, Cantonese, and Min to be dialects of Chinese, speakers of one dialect can't understand someone speaking another (Wright, 2010). In the "Diverse Voices" article, "Mommy, Why Does Raj Talk Funny?," we read about how Indian English differs from the English spoken in America.

This linguistic situation is even more complex, however, for no one really speaks a dialect. Rather, each of us has our own personal symbolic system called an **idiolect** that includes our active vocabularies, our pronunciation of words, and our grammar and syntax when talking or writing (Higginbotham, 2006). We may have words in our lexicon that are understood by very few people as well as words whose meaning is shared by many. We may pronounce words in an idiosyncratic way or use a creative grammar and syntax. Those who know us well and talk with us frequently understand our idiolect best. That's why parents

Idiolect—our personal symbolic system that includes our active vocabularies, our pronunciation of words, and our grammar and syntax when talking or writing.

can understand the utterances of toddlers whose speech is unintelligible to others. Those who speak a common dialect, those who speak similar dialects, and finally those who share a common language can also understand much of what we say.

With these background concepts in mind, let's consider some of the general characteristics of language that will help us understand why sharing meaning is so tricky.

Characteristics of Language

All languages, dialects, and idiolects share seven characteristics. They are arbitrary, ambiguous, abstract, self-reflexive, changeable, revealing, and hierarchical.

1. Language is arbitrary. The words used to represent things in all languages are arbitrary symbols. There is no physical connection between a word and its referent. The words used to represent objects, ideas, or feelings are arbitrary, yet for a word to have any meaning, it must be recognized by members of the language or speech community as standing for a particular object, idea, or feeling. Different language communities use different word symbols for the same phenomenon. Speech communities within a language community may also have words that differ from other speech communities within the language group. As long as members of the speech and/or language community accept the use of a particular word, it carries meaning. For example, the storage compartment of a car is called a "trunk" in America and a "boot" in England.

OBSERVE AND ANALYZE

Language and Dialects

Identify someone who comes from your language community but who belongs to a speech community that speaks a dialect different than yours. Arrange to interview this person about their dialect and idiolect. When did this person first notice that her or his dialect differs from that of others who speak the common language? What are some of the key differences between this person's dialect and the common language? Does he or she codeswitch, speaking the dialect when interacting with others in the speech community but speaking differently when interacting with others outside this group? If so, why does codeswitching occur, and how was it learned? Based on your interview, write a short paper describing what you have learned about how someone experiences language and dialect.

"Mommy, Why Does Raj Talk Funny?"

by Raj Gaur, ABD, University of Kentucky

I grew up in India. In my home we spoke Hindi, but from the time I began school at five years old, I was also taught English. By the time I was fourteen years old I was fluent in English—at least what I thought of at the time as English. Ten years ago, I came to the United States and have since learned that the English I speak is somewhat different from the English that is spoken here in the United States. These differences sometimes make it difficult for me to be understood by some Americans. You see, the English I learned as a child is a *nativization* of English that might more accurately be called "Indian English." What is nativization?

Nativization is the unconscious process of adapting a foreign language so it conforms to the linguistic style and rhetorical patterns of the native language spoken in a particular culture. You are familiar with the ways American English differs between regions and among groups within the United States, as well as differences between British English and American English. If there are differences among native English speakers, imagine what happens when a cultural group like Indians whose native language is Hindi adopts English as a second language! As you would probably expect, they adapt English by using some of the grammar, syntax, and pronunciation rules that characterize their first language, as well as by adopting some of the rhetorical and idiomatic expressions that they use in their mother tongue. It's not that Indians consciously decide to make these changes. Rather, the changes simply occur as the new language, in this case English, is used in everyday conversations with other Indians.

Prior to coming to the United States, most of the people I knew spoke English just like I did, and I had no problem understanding them or being understood by them. So imagine my consternation when after arriving in the United States some of my American colleagues, professors, and students had trouble understanding me when I spoke. What made this particularly interesting was that I didn't seem to have as much trouble understanding others or being understood when I wrote in English. Rather, it was when I spoke that I got quizzical looks and repeated requests to repeat myself.

What I now understand is that there are major differences between the way certain words are pronounced by those speaking American English and those speaking Indian English. Some of these differences are due to the rules each type of English uses for accenting the syllables within a word. In American English, as a general rule, words with more than one syllable alternate between accented and unaccented syllables. So if the first syllable is accented the second is not and vice versa. But in Hindi, whether a particular syllable is accented or not depends on the sounds in the word. Some sounds always receive an accent and

2. Language is ambiguous. No matter how specific you try to be with your verbal messages, there can always be multiple interpretations. This is because the real meaning being captured by the words in any utterance is not found in a dictionary, a written lexicon for the language community. Rather, the real meaning is conveyed by the person using the word as part of the lexicon, grammar, and syntax in her or his personal idiolect. Those same words, grammar, and syntax may have a different meaning for you, and you will interpret what is said using your idiolect.

3. Language is abstract. The word is not the thing that it represents. The words, "I am so sad," represent your internal emotional state, but they are not your feelings. Another way to say this is that "the map is not the territory." Words vary in how abstract we perceive them to be. If Rema refers to her "pet," a fairly

others do not, regardless of their position in a word. So in Indian English, "pho" is pronounced the same whether the speaker is using the word "photo" or "photography." If you speak American English, you are used to hearing "pho·TOG·gra·phy," but when I pronounce it in Indian English, I say "PHO·to·GRAPH·y." If you're an American English speaker and you hear me say this, you may not understand me or may think, "Oh he just mispronounced that word." But to me, your pronunciation sounds just as strange because in India, that is how we pronounce the word.

There are also syntactic differences between Indian and American English. You will recall that syntax is the rules of a particular language for how words are supposed to be put together to form complete ideas. The syntactic issue that I have struggled most with is the use of articles (*a, an, the,* etc.). In Hindi, we may or may not use articles, and this practice also guides our Indian English. So an Indian English student may say, "I go to university in city of Mumbai," rather than "I go to *the* university in *the* city of Mumbai. Another syntactic difference that is common to speakers of Indian English is to form questions without using an auxiliary verb (*do, should, can, must,* etc.). In Hindi, auxiliary verbs are not required when forming an interrogatory sentence. So in Indian English I may ask "I know you?" rather than "*Do* I know you?" or "I finish it?" rather than "*Should* or *can* or *must* I finish it?"

Nativization of English can also be perceived at the idiomatic level when I attempt to express Indian sensibilities and Indian realities to my American friends. To clarify, as a speaker of Indian English, I sometimes exploit the syntactic structures of the language by directly translating Hindi idioms to English. For example, I might say "wheatish complexion" in Indian English to mean "not dark skinned, tending toward light." Or I might use the phrase "out of station" to mean "out of town," which has its origins to denote army officers posted to far-off places during the British rule. Indians also commonly substitute "hotel" for "restaurant," "this side" and "that side" for "here" and "there," "cent per cent" for "100 percent," and "reduce weight" for "lose weight."

Any one of these English adaptations might not pose problems, but taken together they make the brand of English that I speak very different from that of my American friends. Indian English has evolved over a long period of time, and English is now integrated into much of Indian culture. English is taught in schools, business is conducted in English, and English is used in government dealings. Nonetheless, the English of Delhi is not the English of London, or Berlin, or New York, or Lexington, Kentucky. And I find it ironic that after living in the United States for nearly ten years now and struggling to be understood by Americans, my friends in India now complain about my English too. They say it's too American!

For Consideration:

1. How does this article help you to understand the variety within a "language?" How do the concepts of language communities aid this understanding?
2. Based on what you have learned in this article, is Black English (Ebonics) a nativization of American or British English? Argue your conclusion based on the characteristics identified in the article.

concrete word, her co-worker Margi may think of a dog, cat, snake, bird, or hamster. Even if Rema specifically mentions her dog, Margi still has many possibilities for interpretation, including dogs of various breeds, sizes, colors, and temperaments. If words that refer to tangible entities like cars and pets vary in abstraction, imagine all the possibilities of meaning for intangible concepts such as honesty, love, patriotism, or justice.

4. Language is self-reflexive. Not only does language refer to other things, but it can also refer back to itself. In other words, it is self-reflexive. We can use language to talk about language itself and about its possible uses. As a result of the reflexivity of language, humans are able to explore concepts that animals cannot. For instance, people have the capacity to think and talk about themselves, to speak hypothetically, to talk about past and future events, and to communicate about people and things that are not present. Language enables us to learn from others' experiences, to share a common heritage, and to develop a shared vision for the future. In addition, language, coupled with the ability to reflect on ourselves, allows for higher-order communication, or communication about communication. Think of the possibility for improving interpersonal communication when people can comment on the very process of communicating.

5. Language changes. Language changes over time in a number of ways. First, new words are constantly being invented. Younger generations and other subcultures invent new words or assign different meanings to the words they learn, use different grammars, and alter word pronunciation. New inventions produce new words. Think of the technology-related words that have entered our common vocabulary: "texting," "googling," "e-books" "cyberbullying," and "podcasting," among others. Language used by previous generations, such as "cassette tape," may fade from use over time and may even be removed from dictionaries. Members of a co-culture may redefine common words whose new meanings will initially be understood only by other speech community members. Finally, members of an ethnic subculture who also speak a heritage language may introduce parts of the heritage language into the common language. For example, you "take a *siesta*," or "live on a *cul-de-sac*," or "go to *kindergarten*."

6. Language reveals. Most us do not realize the extent to which our word choice reveals our attitudes, judgments, or feelings. Imagine, for instance, that Shana routinely saves 60 percent of the money she earns. She lives in a very modest apartment, drives an old car, makes her own clothes, and rarely buys material possessions. What word comes to your mind to describe Shana's approach to money? Do you call her "thrifty," "budget-conscious," or "frugal"? Or do you select words such as "tightwad," "penny-pincher, "or "stingy"? Notice how the first set of words tends to leave a positive impression, whereas the second set seems negative. From the words you choose, a listener may infer your attitudes toward saving and spending.

7. Language is hierarchical. Kenneth Burke tells us that language allows us to compare and judge, which results in social orderings (1968). Once we are able to compare, then notions of better and worse inevitably follow. When people compare anything with anything else and notice difference, seldom is that difference seen as merely a difference. Instead, humans tend naturally to judge or evaluate difference in some way. This tendency to judge difference creates hierarchy, with some things (and people) seen as better or worse than others. So when Callie points to one of the three guys walking by and says, "Wow, look at the guy in the middle. He's really hot," she is not only commenting on him but also implying that he is better looking than his companions.

As you can see from these characteristics, language is by nature an imprecise vehicle for transferring meaning from one person to another. The meaning of any verbal message is conveyed and understood through the following factors: (1) the meaning of the language itself; (2) the meaning of the language in the verbal message within the context of the conversation; and (3) the meaning of the language in the verbal message within the social and cultural background of the interaction. In the next sections we explain each of these and provide guidelines to help you form and correctly interpret the meaning of verbal messages.

Meaning in the Language Itself

The **semantic meaning** of an utterance is the meaning derived from the language itself. At the semantic level, we are interested in the truth of the words.

Semantic meaning—meaning of a verbal message derived from the language itself.

Understanding Semantics

At this level we understand a verbal message through its words and how the grammar and syntax of the language are used to combine them into sentences that comprise the utterance.

Words are the arbitrarily chosen symbols used by a language or speech community to name or signify things. Words allow us to identify parts of the world and to make statements about it (Saeed, 2003). Each of us has a lexicon of words for each of the languages that we speak. Although we learn new words, the size and accuracy of our vocabulary limit our ability to express what we are thinking and feeling, as well as our ability to understand the verbal messages we receive on a day-to-day basis. The extent to which you are able to share semantic meaning with someone depends on how much your personal lexicons overlap. As previously discussed, identifying word meaning is tricky. This is because words have two types of meanings.

Words—the arbitrarily chosen symbols used by a language or speech community to name or signify things.

Denotation is the direct, explicit meaning of a word found in a written dictionary of the language community. Denotative meanings, however, diverge from dictionary to dictionary, change over time, and can vary by dialect. In addition, dictionaries use words to define other words that also depend on words for their meaning. Not only that, the lexicon of our idiolect rarely corresponds to the definitions of the same words found in formal dictionary definitions. Thus, your definition of a word may be different from mine. Suppose the president of our club says, "Please go upstairs and get a few more chairs for the meeting." When you hear the word "chair," you might picture a straight-backed, wooden object, whereas I picture a metal folding chair. Our own idiosyncratic definitions, while similar, may or may not refer to the same real-world referent.

Denotation—the direct, explicit meaning of a word found in a written dictionary of the language community.

Connotation is the feelings or evaluations we personally associate with a word. For example, think of the different meanings that people bring to the word "family" based on their positive or negative experiences growing up in their unique family situation. To you, a family may be a safe place where you are unconditionally loved, accepted, and cared for. To someone else with a different upbringing, family may be a dangerous brutal place where everyone fends for himself or herself. There may be even greater variation of connotative meaning with more strictly emotion-based words such as love, freedom, harmony, hate,

Connotation—the feelings or evaluations we personally associate with a word.

OBSERVE AND ANALYZE

Language and Meaning

Answer the questions for each word or phrase that follows. Then ask someone who is at least one generation older than you to do the same without seeing your answers.

Expensive car: How much does it cost?

Staying up late on a weeknight: What time did you go to sleep?

Spending a lot of time writing a report: How much time did you prepare?

He's rich: How much money does he have?

She's liberal: What are her views on immigration, abortion, capital punishment, global trade, gay marriage?

He's got one of those hybrid cars: What make and model is the car?

They're tree-huggers: What environmental practices do they follow?

Compare the similarities and differences in the interpretation of these phrases between the two of you. Based on the meaning that you and your partner gave to these words, what can you conclude about idiolects and language denotation and connotation?

oppression, and so on. So when we choose words or when we interpret the words of others, there is no guarantee that the physical representation intended by the person speaking the word will match that of the person who hears the word.

The meaning of the sentences in a verbal message is based not only on the words but also on how those words are related to one another. You'll recall that grammar and syntax are the rules for combining words into meaningful phrases, sentences, and larger units of expression. Your vocabulary is somewhat set, but your ability to use the rules of grammar and syntax to create unique sentences is unlimited. For example, you might communicate the same meaning by saying:

"When he went to the pound, he adopted a 3-pound puppy."
"He went to the pound and adopted a 3-pound puppy."
"Upon arriving at the pound, he adopted a 3-pound puppy."
"The 3-pound puppy he adopted came from the pound."

These four sentences use different syntax and grammar and slightly different vocabulary but convey the same semantic meaning or "truth": Someone who was male procured a young canine weighing 3 pounds from a place where animals without an owner or whose owner is unknown are kept. But notice how we alter the meaning of these words by changing the grammar and syntax and deleting one word:

"He, the 3-pound adopted puppy, went to the pound."

Now the truth in the semantics of the sentence is that an adopted three-pound immature canine went to the place where animals who are not owned or whose owner is unknown are kept. In addition, the meaning of a word may vary depending on its position in a sentence and the surrounding words. In the example above, the word "pound" is used twice in each sentence, but its meaning or sense changes. In one instance, it signifies a unit of weight, and in the other, it signifies a place. But you knew which meaning to apply by the syntactical context. With this in mind, what can we do to make it more likely that others will understand our semantic meaning? Let's look at several guidelines for forming verbal messages with clearer semantic meaning.

Guidelines for Improving Message Semantics

1. Use specific, concrete, and precise language to improve message clarity.
As we try to express our thoughts, we tend to use the first word that comes to mind, often a very generalized term that creates an ambiguous message. We can get a message across better if we use **specific language.** Specific language is language in an utterance that uses concrete and precise words as well as details and examples, combining them in accord with the rules of grammar and syntax for that language. Compare the speaker's use of language in the following two descriptions of a near miss in a car:

Specific language—language in an utterance that uses concrete and precise words, as well as details and examples, combining them in accord with the rules of grammar and syntax for that language.

"Some nut almost got me a while ago."

"An hour ago, an older man in a banged-up Honda Civic ran the red light at Calhoun and Clifton and almost hit me broadside while I was in the intersection waiting to turn left."

In the second description, the semantic meaning of the language is much clearer. Consequently, the listener is likely to have a more accurate or "truer" understanding of exactly what happened. Let's look more closely at what we mean by concrete words, precise words, details, and examples.

Concrete language is words that describe something that can be sensed: seen, heard, felt, tasted, or smelled. For example, instead of saying that Jill "speaks in a weird way," it is clearer to say, "Jill mumbles, (or whispers, or blusters, or drones)." Each of these alternative words provides a specific description of the sound of Jill's voice.

Precise words are words that identify a smaller grouping within a larger category. For instance, notice the difference between

"Ruben is a blue-collar worker."
"Ruben is a construction worker."
"Ruben is a bulldozer operator."

Choosing concrete and precise words enables us to improve clarity, but there are times when a word may not have a more specific or concrete synonym, in which case a detail or an example may clarify or increase specificity. Suppose Lala says, "Rashad is very *loyal.*" Since the meaning of loyal (faithful to an idea, person, company, etc.) is abstract, Lala might add, "I mean he never criticizes a friend behind her back." By following her use of the abstract concept of loyalty with an example, Lala makes it easier for her listeners to ground their idea of this personal quality and see more accurately how it applies to Rashad. Figure 4.1 provides additional examples of how concrete and precise words and details or examples add semantic clarity to messages.

Concrete language—words that describe something that can be sensed.

Precise words—words that identify a smaller grouping within a larger category.

Message	Improved Message
The senator brought *several things* to the meeting.	The senator brought *recent letters from her constituency* to the meeting.
He lives in a *really big house.*	He lives in a *fourteen-room Tudor mansion.*
The backyard has *several different kinds of trees.*	The backyard has *two large maples, an oak, and four small evergreens.*
Morgan is a *fair grader.*	Morgan *uses the same standards for grading all students.*
Many students *aren't honest* in class.	Many students *cheat on tests* in class.
Judy *hits* the podium when she wants to emphasize her point.	Judy *pounds on* the podium when she wants to emphasize her point.

FIGURE 4.1 Improving Message Semantics through Clear and Specific Language

2. Date information to specify when an utterance was true.

Dating information—the communication skill that improves the semantic accuracy of verbal messages by pointing out when the information in a message was true.

Dating information is the communication skill that improves the semantic accuracy of verbal messages by pointing out when the information in a message was true. A common source of semantic misunderstanding is leaving the impression that information in an utterance is currently true when you don't know that it is. For instance, Parker says, "I'm going to be transferred to Henderson City. Do you know anything about the city?" Laura replies, "Yes I do. Let me just say that they've had some real trouble with their schools." On the basis of Laura's statement, Parker may worry about the effect the move will have on his children. What he doesn't know is that Laura's information about this problem in Henderson City is fifteen years old! Henderson City may still have problems, but then again, it may not. Had Laura dated the truth claim of her message and replied, "I know that fifteen years ago they had some real trouble with their schools. I'm not sure what the situation is now, but you may want to check," Parker would have received more accurate information.

The skill of dating our messages requires that we consider and determine when the information was true and verbally acknowledge this time frame. This seems like a simple skill to put into practice—and it is. We have no power to prevent change. But we can increase the semantic accuracy of our messages if we verbally recognize the reality of change by dating the statements we make. Figure 4.2 provides several examples of the skill of dating messages.

3. Index to qualify generalizations.

Indexing generalizations—the communication skill that improves the semantic meaning of a verbal message by acknowledging that individual instances may differ from the truth statement of our message.

Indexing generalizations is the communication skill that improves the semantic meaning of a verbal message by acknowledging that individual instances may differ from the truth of our message. For instance, Jerome's statement, "With a degree in computer science you never have to worry about getting a job," is a generalization to which there may be many exceptions.

Message	Dated Message
Cancún is really popular with the college crowd.	When we were in Cancún *two years ago*, it was really popular with the college crowd.
Professor Powell brings great enthusiasm to her teaching.	Professor Powell brings great enthusiasm to her teaching—at least she did *last quarter* in communication theory.
You think Mary's depressed? I'm surprised. She seemed her regular high-spirited self when I talked to her.	You think Mary's depressed? I'm surprised. She seemed her regular high-spirited self when I talked with her *last month.*
The Apple iPhone is the most expensive PDA on the market.	The Apple iPhone was the most expensive PDA on the market when I brought my Droid last summer.

FIGURE 4.2 Improving Semantic Accuracy by Dating Messages

SKILL BUILDERS ● Dating Information

SKILL	USE	PROCEDURE	EXAMPLE
Including a specific time referent to clarify a message	To avoid the pitfalls of language that allow you to speak of a dynamic world in static terms	1. Before you make a statement, consider or find out when the information was true. 2. If not based on present information, verbally acknowledge when the statement was true.	When Jake says, "How good a hitter is Steve?," Mark replies by dating his evaluation: "When I worked with him two years ago, he couldn't hit the curve ball."

He can improve the semantic truth meaning of this statement by indexing or qualifying it, by saying something like this: "With a degree in computer science you never have to worry about getting a job. At least eleven of my friends who majored in computer science had no problem." All people generalize at one time or another, but by indexing, we can avoid the semantic problems of generalized statements. To index your verbal messages, first consider whether your statement is about a specific object, person, or place or whether it is a generalization about a class to which the object, person, or place belongs. If what you want to say is based on a generalization, qualify your statement appropriately so that your assertion does not exceed the evidence that supports it. Figure 4.3 provides several examples of generalized statements and indexed statements.

Message	Indexed Message
Men are stronger than women.	*Most* men are stronger than most women.
State U must have a good economics department; the university is ranked in the top twenty in the U.S.	Because State U is among the top twenty schools in the nation, the economics program should be a good one, *although it may be an exception.*
Jack is sure to be outgoing; Don is, and they're brothers	Jack is likely to be outgoing because his brother Don is, *but Jack could be different.*
Your Sonic should go fifty thousand miles before you need a brake job; Jerry's did.	Your Sonic may well go fifty thousand miles before you need a brake job; Jerry's did, *but, of course, all Chevys aren't the same.*
Don't play the lottery; you won't win.	Don't play the lottery; *it's highly unlikely that you will win.*

FIGURE 4.3 Improving Semantic Accuracy by Indexing Messages

SKILL BUILDERS ● Indexing Generalizations

SKILL	USE	PROCEDURE	EXAMPLE
Mentally or verbally accounting for individual differences when generalizing	To avoid "allness" in speaking	1. Before you make a statement, consider whether it pertains to a specific object, person, or place. 2. If you use a generalization, inform the listener that it does not necessarily apply in the situation being discussed.	"He's a politician and I don't trust him, although he may be different from most politicians I know."

IT'S THE LAW

IF YOU HAVE A MEDICAL EMERGENCY OR ARE IN LABOR YOU HAVE THE RIGHT TO RECEIVE, within the capabilities of this hospital's staff and facilities:
- An appropriate medical SCREENING EXAMINATION
- Necessary STABILIZING TREATMENT (including treatment for an unborn child)...and if necessary
- An appropriate TRANSFER to another facility...even if YOU CANNOT PAY OR DO NOT HAVE MEDICAL INSURANCE...or YOU ARE NOT ENTITLED TO MEDICARE OR MEDICAID
This hospital does participate in the Medicaid program.

How does jargon improve or hinder communication?

Jargon—technical terminology whose meaning is understood by only a select group of people in a specialized speech community based on shared activities or interests.

Slang—the informal vocabulary developed and used by particular co-cultural groups in a society.

4. Adapt your language to your listeners.

Because we want to be understood, we need to choose our words carefully by using vocabulary our listener understands, using jargon sparingly, and using slang only when we are certain that the person with whom we are communicating not only understands the slang but will not be offended by our word choice.

People vary in the extent to which they know and use a large variety of words. The larger your vocabulary, the more choices you have for the language of your message. Having a larger vocabulary, however, can present challenges when you are communicating with people whose vocabulary is more limited. One strategy for assessing another's vocabulary level is to listen to the types and complexity of words the other person uses—that is, take your signal from your communication partner. If you determine that your vocabulary is larger than your partner's, you can choose simpler synonyms for your words or use word phrases composed of more familiar terms. Adjusting your vocabulary to others does not mean talking down to them, however. It is merely polite behavior and effective communication to select words that others understand.

A second way to adapt to your listeners is to use jargon sparingly. **Jargon** refers to technical terminology whose meaning is understood by only a select group of people in a specialized speech community based on shared activities or interests. The key to effective use of specialized terms is to employ them only with people who speak the same jargon. Among people who understand the same jargon, its use facilitates communication. If you must use jargon with people outside that specialized speech community, remember to explain the terms you are using. Without this explanation for outsiders, jargon becomes a type of foreign language.

A third way to adapt your language to your listeners is to use slang appropriately. **Slang** is the informal vocabulary developed and used by particular co-cultural groups in a society. Slang bonds those who use the same words by emphasizing a shared experience while simultaneously excluding others who don't share the terminology. Some slang words, which may be inoffensive when used by an in-group with other in-group members, become highly offensive when used by non-members or when used outside the in-group speech community. The "n" word and many swear words would exemplify this. Unless you want to risk offending your listener, use slang only with people who understand and appreciate it. If your communication goal is to be realized, your partner needs to understand you.

5. Demonstrate linguistic sensitivity.

Linguistic sensitivity is using language that respects others while avoiding language that offends. Some of our mistakes result from using expressions perceived by others as sexist, racist, or otherwise biased. Any language that is perceived as belittling any person or group of people can become the real meaning of our message, undermining our intended meaning.

Use inclusive language when you are referring to a wide swath of people. According to traditional rules of English usage, male references were employed as though they included both men and women. Masculine pronouns were used when referring to both men and women, as in the sentence, "When a person shops, *he* should have a clear idea of what *he* wants to buy." In modern English grammar, we are aware that this sentence is sexist because it encourages us to visualize a male person. Linguistic sensitivity means avoiding sexist language by using plurals or using both male and female pronouns. Stewart, Cooper, Stewart, and Friedley (2003) cite research to show that using *he or she* and to a lesser extent *they* alerts listeners to the importance of gender balance in both language and life.

In addition, English is rife with words that have single-sex markers for concepts that are really generic; for example, using "man" as a prefix or suffix (mankind, policeman, fireman, etc.). When some of these words were coined, a single-sex marker was appropriate since women or men were barred or discouraged from participating in those occupations or groups. Today, however, it is insensitive, for instance, to refer to a "flight attendant" as a "stewardess," and we recognize that it is more accurate to say "all people" rather than "mankind."

Verbal Meaning Within the Conversational Context

The **pragmatic meaning** of the language in a verbal message is the meaning that arises from understanding the practical consequences of an utterance. At the semantic level, we are interested in what the words mean (Korta & Perry, 2008). At the pragmatic level, we are interested in what people mean; more specifically, we are interested in what a specific speaker talking to a specific other in a conversation means at a certain point in time. So, while the semantic meaning of a message remains the same across speakers and conversations, its pragmatic meaning changes.

A **speech act** is the action the speaker takes by uttering a verbal message that implies how the listener should respond. At the pragmatic level, when we speak, we do. At times, our speech acts are explicit, but in many instances

Linguistic sensitivity—using language that respects others while avoiding language that offends.

Pragmatic meaning—meaning of a verbal message that arises from understanding the practical consequences of an utterance.

Speech act—the action that the speaker takes by uttering a verbal message that implies how the listener should respond.

what we are doing is implicit. As we search for the pragmatic meaning of the message, we ask ourselves, "What is the speaker doing by saying these words to me right now?" Similarly, when forming our message, we choose language intended to create a certain response in our listener. For example, suppose I say, "Karen, pass me the bowl of potatoes." This imperative statement directly orders Karen to pick up the bowl of potatoes and hand them to me. Instead, suppose I ask, "Karen, do you mind passing me the potatoes?" At the semantic level, this question appears to give Karen a choice, yet at the pragmatic level, what I am trying to do is the same: direct Karen to pass me the bowl of potatoes. We can accomplish the same pragmatic goal with either a direct/explicit or indirect/implicit speech act.

The meaning of a speech act depends on the context. We can use a verbal message whose semantic meaning is exactly the same to perform very different speech acts whose pragmatic meanings are quite different. Let's look at a simple example. One morning after his car failed to start, Harry made three phone calls:

> Phone Call 1:
> *Harry:* The car won't start.
> *Katie:* Sorry about that. I'll just take the bus.
> Phone Call 2:
> *Harry:* The car won't start.
> *AAA Customer Service Representative:* Where is the car, sir? I'll send a tow truck right away.
> Phone Call 3:
> *Harry:* The car won't start.
> *Previous owner who recently sold the car to Harry:* Wow, that never happened to me. But I told you I was selling the car "as is."

In all three cases, the verbal utterance and the semantic meaning of Harry's message is the same, but from a pragmatic standpoint, Harry performed three different speech acts. What he was doing when he talking to Katie was different from what he was doing when he was talking with the customer service representative at AAA and different still from what he was doing when he made the statement to the person who sold him the car. With Katie, he was expressing his feelings, apologizing and/or explaining. By this speech act, he implies that Katie should understand, comfort, and release him from his obligation to take her to school. With the AAA rep, Harry was directing him to act, calling in a promise of service that comes with his AAA membership. This speech act was a demand for assistance. When Harry called the previous owner of the car, he was complaining and implying that the previous owner of the car should accept responsibility. In all cases, same words, same syntax, but three different speech acts.

Each of the people he talked to understood the pragmatic meaning of his speech act and how Harry expected them to behave. Katie "read" what he said as frustration and that she needed to find her own way to school. So she offered a "sorry" and relieved him of the responsibility for getting her to class. The customer service rep at AAA expected that the person on the line would be calling to report car trouble and request a tow truck be dispatched, so his response to

Harry's speech act was to find out where the car was located. The previous car owner correctly understood Harry's speech act, but his response refused ownership of the problem. While the semantic level of Harry's three messages was identical, he performed at least three different speech acts.

As you can see, accurately conveying and interpreting the pragmatic meaning of messages can be challenging. The next section explains why we are able to understand what someone is doing or implying when speaking. Based on this, we'll present several guidelines for improving how well others are able to understand the pragmatic meaning of your verbal messages and how you can improve your understanding of what others are doing or implying with their verbal messages.

Guidelines for Improving Pragmatic Understanding

Paul Grice, a noted linguist, provides important insights into the assumptions that we make during conversation that allow us to make sense of speakers' verbal messages. His general premise, the **cooperative principle**, states that conversational partners are able to understand what others mean to do with their verbal messages because they assume that their partners are collaborating. They are sharing verbal messages in line with the shared purpose of the conversation (Grice, 1975). By assuming cooperation, we can go beyond the semantic level of meaning and understand the speaker's purpose for uttering a verbal message. Grice identified four **conversational maxims**, specific rules that cooperating partners count on others to follow. You can use these to help develop pragmatic competence.

1. Tell the truth, the whole truth, and only the truth. This is called the "quality maxim." This guideline directs us to say things we believe to be true and we have enough evidence to support. We also comply with this guideline when we fully disclose all that we know about something. Finally, we follow this guideline by not saying things we know or suspect to be false. Obviously, lying, distorting, or misrepresenting what we know to be true violates this guideline and results in our misleading others. When we do this intentionally, we are also acting unethically.

Often, however, we tell partial truths that we rationalize with the claim that we are "protecting" our conversational partners or ourselves. For example, when your friend asks you what you think of her new boyfriend, you may offer a non-committal response that masks your immediate dislike for the guy: "Well, he certainly appears to like you." Your friend may interpret your remark about her new boyfriend as your approval rather than your attempt to parry the question and spare her feelings. As you can see, providing ambiguous responses makes it more difficult for people to correctly understand what we truly believe, or they may misinterpret what we are doing. In this case, you disapproved of your friend's new love interest, but your disapproval may go undetected. Suppose a classmate known for freeloading on group projects asks if you have a partner for the upcoming lab, and you don't. If, out of self-interest and to spare this person's feelings, you reply, "I think that I may have," you have violated the quality maximum by

OBSERVE AND ANALYZE

Semantic Meaning vs. Pragmatic Understanding

An interesting place to observe the divergence between semantic meaning and pragmatic understanding is in the dialogs of situation comedies. Select an episode of *The Big Bang Theory* to analyze. Watch the show. Find three instances when a character correctly interprets the semantic meaning of the message while misinterpreting the pragmatic level of the message. Record what was said, what was meant, and what alternative pragmatic meaning was interpreted. For each case, explain why the misunderstanding occurred.

Cooperative principle—the pragmatic principle that states that conversational partners are able to understand what the other means to do with their verbal messages because they assume that their partners are collaborating by sharing verbal messages in line with the shared purpose of the conversation.

Conversational maxims—specific rules that cooperating partners count on others to follow.

allowing him to assume that you discussed partnering with someone else rather than learn that there was no way you were going to work with him. In some cultures, speech acts that violate the quality maxim will be properly understood, but in other cultures, they will mislead.

2. Provide the "right" amount of information. What you may informally think of as the "Goldilocks" maxim (not too much, not too little, but just right) is formally known as the "quantity maxim." This guideline directs us to cooperate with our partner by giving the right amount of information. We violate this by providing either too much or too little information. For instance, when Sam, who is getting ready to leave for work, asks Randy where he parked Sam's car, Randy's answer "a couple of streets over" is uncooperatively brief. Sam needs to know the car's exact location. At the other extreme, should Randy begin, "You just wouldn't believe the trouble I had . . ." as he launches into a five-minute monologue on his difficulties finding a parking space in the neighborhood after midnight, his excessively detailed narrative would also violate the quantity guideline.

3. Relate what you say to the topic being discussed. The "relevancy maxim" is the guideline that directs us to link our messages to the purpose or topic of the conversation and to interpret others' messages as though they are relevant to the conversation at hand. Much of how we interpret what others mean is based on our assumption that their verbal messages are relevant. For example, Barry asks, "Who's going to pick up Mom from work today?," and his brother answers, "I've got a big test tomorrow." Barry, assuming that his brother's remark is relevant, interprets it as, "I can't; I have to study" rather than as just some random unrelated remark. Barry was able to correctly understand the pragmatic meaning of his brother's answer because he assumed it was relevant to figuring out how to get their mother home.

Comments that are only tangential to the subject or that seek an abrupt subject change when other conversational partners are still actively engaged with the original topic are uncooperative. You can improve the likelihood of your pragmatic meaning being understood if you cooperate with your partner and avoid making random unrelated comments or abruptly shifting topics.

4. Be orderly in what you say. The "manner maxim" is the guideline that directs us to cooperate with our conversational partners by choosing specific language and organizing our words in a manner that allows our partners to easily understand our implicit meaning. For example, when D'wan, a new MacBookPro®4GS owner, asks Raphael how to compose a song using Garage Band®, Raphael will help D'wan grasp the process if he describes it one step at a time, using language that D'wan, a novice, can understand.

In practice, we frequently violate the first four guidelines yet are still understood because we adhere to one of these last two:

5. Acknowledge when you are violating a maxim. By signaling that we are violating one of the maxims, we will help our partner understand how to interpret what we are saying. For example, "I don't know if this is true, but my sister said . . ." acknowledges violating the quality maxim. "If I told you, I'd have to kill you . . ." acknowledges violating the quantity maxim. "This may be beside the point, but . . ." acknowledges violating the relevancy maxim. And, "This is just off the top of my head . . ." acknowledges violating the manner maxim. So when you recognize that your verbal message violates a maxim of the cooperative principle, you can still help your partner understand your intention if you acknowledge your violation. Similarly, pay attention when your partner acknowledges a violation so that you don't overinterpret or misinterpret what is being said.

6. Rely on the cooperative principle when interpreting violations of the maxims. There are times when we intentionally violate a maxim to imply something with our statement. In this case, we don't signal our violations but we trust that our partner, who expects us to be cooperating, will understand our intended meaning. For example, when Jeremy asks his roommate, "What's for dinner?," and his roommate replies, "Ramen or filet mignon," his roommate violates the quantity maxim by not giving Jeremy the exact information. But Jeremy, assuming that his roommate is cooperating in the conversation, will probably correctly interpret the comment as sarcasm meaning his roommate has no idea what they will eat. Similarly, when Kent tells his mom that he's going to go to Mexico with some friends on spring break and she replies, "Oh sure, like that's going to happen," she violates the quality maxim, but Kent still understands that she is not on board with his plans. When encountering violations of conversational maxims, we should rely on the cooperative principle to help us identify what the speaker means when uttering the verbal message.

Meaning within the Social and Cultural Context

In the last chapter we discussed how cultures vary and how this variation generally affects communication. The **sociolinguistic meaning** of a message is the meaning of a verbal message that varies according to the language norms and

Sociolinguistic meaning—the meaning of a verbal message that varies according to the language norms and expectations of a particular cultural or co-cultural group.

How might culture affect the conversation between the children in this picture?

expectations of a particular cultural or co-cultural group. Since we learn to speak within the context of our culture and co-cultural groups, our canned plans and scripts come from modeling the verbal messages of others in our group. Socio-linguistic misunderstandings occur when we interact with someone from a different culture or co-cultural background. Cultures develop different norms and expectations about the way words are combined, about how to say what to whom and when, and about speech style.

LEARN ABOUT YOURSELF ● Verbal Style

Take this short survey to learn about your preferred verbal style. There are no right or wrong answers. Just be honest in reporting how you act in most situations. For each item, select the number to the left that best reflects how you talk.

1 = Rarely
2 = Occasionally
3 = Frequently
4 = Most of the time

_____ 1. I tell the truth regardless of the consequences.

_____ 2. When I want something, I drop a hint and expect the other person to figure out what I need.

_____ 3. If a conversation becomes heated I join in, or tell them to cool it.

_____ 4. If a conversation becomes heated, I change the subject.

_____ 5. I like to hear a clear "no" if someone disagrees with me.

_____ 6. When people dispute what I have said I acknowledge the point they have made but do not directly disagree with them.

_____ 7. I enjoy a good verbal argument.

_____ 8. If I don't want to do something, I say "maybe" rather than hurt someone with my refusal.

_____ 9. If I see people make a mistake, I immediately tell them what they did and how to correct it.

_____ 10. If I see people make a mistake, I take them aside and ask them what they were trying to do.

_____ 11. If someone compliments me, I acknowledge it by saying, "Thank you."

_____ 12. If someone compliments me, I point out how what I did was not exceptional.

Scoring this survey: Add up your scores on the odd-numbered items for your direct verbal style score. Then add up your scores on the even-numbered items to get your indirect verbal style score.

Direct Verbal Score: _____   Indirect Verbal Score: _____

Both scores can range from 6 to 24. The more divergent your scores, the more you rely on either a direct or indirect verbal style; the more similar your scores, the more flexible your style. Take a moment to think about how your style affects the people with whom you interact. Do most of your family and friends have similar styles? Can your style create problems for a relationship?

First, cultures have norms that assign meaning to specific combinations of words that differ from the semantic meaning of those word combinations. For example, in English we associate the word "pretty" with women and "handsome" with men, even though both refer to physical beauty. So choosing to say "She is a pretty woman" sends a different message than "She is a handsome woman" (Chaika, 2007). In addition, all cultures develop **idioms**, expressions used by members of a language or speech community whose meaning differs from the usual meanings associated with that combination of words. Imagine how confusing it is to someone who is just learning the language to hear, "That test was *a piece of cake*," which literally means the test was a slice of baked goods. The French, for example, would say, "Il s'est jeté *à corps perdu* dans son nouveau projet." This literally means "He threw himself *with body lost* into his new project." Both the French and the English use the idiom "to throw oneself into something," but the French use the expression *à corps perdu* to signify what in English would be idiomatically expressed as "body and soul," "wholeheartedly," or "headlong." It is necessary to understand French cultural idioms to correctly translate and interpret this statement as "He threw himself wholeheartedly into his new project."

Second, cultures develop different norms about what language should be used to convey certain meanings, what it means when a particular person uses a specific verbal message, and what it means when a specific language is used in addressing a particular person. For example, complimenting others and accepting compliments are common to all language communities, but the sincerity of the compliment can depend on the language employed. In American culture, our compliment messages often use hyperbole or exaggerations. For instance, you might compliment your new Japanese friend by saying, "Miki, this is the *best* Miso soup I have ever tasted." To Miki, a new Japanese exchange student, your compliment sounds insincere because in Japanese culture the language of compliments is less effusive. To mitigate your error, she may reply, "Oh, it's nice of you to say that, but I am sure that you have had better Miso soup at sushi restaurants in the city." Similarly, in the American Midwest, we often smile and say "Hi" to strangers on the street as a way of being friendly. In China, acknowledging a stranger in this way assumes a familiarity that is unwarranted and even rude.

Third, different cultures also prefer different verbal styles. These may vary in a number of ways, but the degree to which the style is direct or indirect has the greatest effect on sociolinguistic meaning (Ting-Toomey & Chung, 2005). A **direct verbal style** is characterized by message language that openly states the speaker's intention and by message content that is straightforward and unambiguous. An **indirect verbal style** is characterized by message language that masks the speaker's true intentions and by roundabout, vague message content whose real meaning is embedded in the social or cultural context. As you have probably inferred, low-context cultures value direct verbal styles, while high-context cultures value indirect styles. Let's look at an example of how these diverse styles can create difficulty in interpreting the language that people use to express their meaning.

Idioms—expressions used by members of a language or speech community whose meaning differs from the usual meanings associated with that combination of words.

Direct verbal style—message language that openly states the speaker's intention and message content that is straightforward and unambiguous.

Indirect verbal style—message language that masks the speaker's true intentions and roundabout, vague message content whose real meaning is embedded in the social or cultural context.

College roommates Jorge and Kevin are from the same hometown as Sam, who lives across the hall and has a car. Thanksgiving is fast approaching, and both men need to find a ride home. One night while watching a football game in Sam's room, the following conversation occurs:

Jorge says to Sam: "Are you driving home for Thanksgiving?" [Maybe he'll give me a ride.]

Sam: "Yep." [If he wanted a ride, he'd ask.]

Kevin: "Well, I'd like a ride home."

Sam: "Sure, no problem."

Jorge: "Are you taking anyone else?" [I wonder if he still has room for me.]

Sam: "Nope. I'm leaving early, after my last class on Tuesday and not coming back until late Sunday evening." [I guess Jorge already has a ride home.]

Jorge: "Well, enjoy Thanksgiving." [If he wanted to give me a ride, I gave him several opportunities to offer. I guess I'll take the bus.]

In this conversation Jorge, the son of Nicaraguan immigrants, uses the indirect style he learned as a child growing up in the Latin American neighborhood of the city they all come from. His questions were meant to prompt Sam to offer him a ride. But Sam, whose parents grew up in New York, where being direct is the preferred style, completely misses what Jorge meant. Consequently, Jorge will ride the bus, even though Sam would have driven him home had he just asked in a way that Sam understood.

Evidence supports differences in the verbal styles of ethnic, national, cultural, and co-cultural groups; however, current scholarship has debunked the earlier research findings of distinct masculine and feminine verbal styles. Still, the popular and online media continue to erroneously report widespread differences. Today linguistic scholars acknowledge that language use is so particular to the conversational context that no reliable differences appear to exist between men and women in the same cultural or co-cultural group. Rather, the differences that are sometimes observed may be due to unequal power, conversational topic, individual identity, and same-sex or mixed-sex groups (Freed, 2003).

Guidelines for Improving Sociolinguistic Understanding

1. Develop intercultural competence. In the last chapter we described how to develop intercultural competence. The more you learn about other cultures, the better you will be able to form messages whose sociolinguistics align with your intended meaning and the better you will be able to understand the sociolinguistic meaning of others' messages.

Mindfulness—the process of drawing novel distinctions.

2. Practice mindfulness. Mindfulness is the process of drawing novel distinctions (Langer & Moldoveanu, 2000). If we are mindful when interacting with others, we are focused on the present moment and noticing how we are similar to and different from our conversational partners. How do our partners differ in this moment from how they were in the last moment? How does what is happening now differ from what has happened or from what we expected to have happen? How are our partners' verbal messages distinct from other things they have said or from what we would have said? In other words, when we practice mindfulness, we pay close attention to what is happening in the conversation at that moment and work hard to understand both our partners and ourselves.

3. Recognize, respect, and adapt to the sociolinguistic practices of others. As the old saying goes, "When in Rome, do as the Romans do." If, for example, you travel to Jakarta or are invited to your Indonesian American friend's home for the weekend, you should adapt your verbal style to that of your hosts. Or if you are from a low-context culture and are talking with someone who you think is from a high-context culture, be sensitive to the indirect meaning of verbal messages. Fluency in more than one language or in more than one dialect of a language allows you to codeswitch and use the dialect of your conversational partner.

A QUESTION OF ETHICS ● What Would You Do?

Abbie, who was from San Antonio, Texas, was adding sweetener to her iced latte in the coffee bar when she spied Ethan and Nate, two friends she knew from the gym. She flounced over to their table in the corner, dropped into the empty seat, and greeted them cheerily: "Hi, guys. How y'all doin'?"

"Not bad. Ethan and I were just chillin' between classes. What about you?"

"Well, I'm really annoyed," Abbie replied. "It took that guy behind the counter three times to get ma order. I mean, if you cain't understand English, I don't thank you should be workin' in a customer service position. And after he finally understood what I was sayin', he started to rattle off somefen in what I guess he thought was English. But damned if I could understand a word he said. You'da thank with all the people out of work that they could find someun who spoke good English."

"Who are you talking about, Abbie?" asked Ethan.

"That guy over yonder with the green shirt and the little bitty mustache at the second cash register."

"Abbie, that's Jean-Paul. He's French Canadian, and he speaks excellent English. Yes, he has an accent, but so do you," Ethan pointed out.

"Ah don't have an accent!" Abbie drawled. "I talk just fine. Both'a y'all have accents, but I understand you just fine. It's just those quote unquote immigrants who come over here and expect us all to put up with 'Press one for Spanish, two for English.' I mean come on, if ya cain't speak the language, don't 'spect us to cater to ya. I'm just sick of all of it. And . . ."

"Well," Nate interrupted. "You're right. I do have an accent—a Boston accent—and I'm proud of it. It lets people know where I'm from. And I have no problem understanding Jean-Paul, but I sure don't understand you sometimes."

For Consideration:
1. What ethical principle is at issue in this case?
2. What do you think about the issues that Abbie raises?
3. Based on what you have learned about language in this chapter, what could you tell Abbie that might help her become more tolerant of others?

Summary

Utterances, complete units of talk bounded by silences, have verbal and non-verbal parts. Verbal messages are those parts that use language to convey meaning. Language is the symbolic system that includes a lexicon, phonology, and syntax and grammar. A language community includes all the people who can speak or understand a particular language. Languages are really collections of dialects, and a speech community is comprised of the members of a language community who speak a common dialect. None of us speaks a language or a dialect; rather, we have our own personal idiolect. All languages, dialects, and idiolects share seven common characteristics. They are arbitrary, ambiguous, abstract, self-reflexive, changing, revealing, and hierarchical. To understand the full meaning of a verbal message, you need to interpret its semantics, pragmatics, and sociolinguistics. The semantic meaning of a message is contained in the language itself. You can improve a message's semantic level of verbal meaning by using specific language, dating information, indexing generalizations, adapting your language to your listener, and demonstrating linguistic sensitivity. The pragmatic meaning of a verbal message is the practical meaning of the language within the context of the conversation. You can improve a message's pragmatic level of verbal meaning by telling the truth, providing the right amount of information, relating what you say to the topic of discussion, and acknowledging when you are violating one of these guidelines. The sociolinguistic meaning of a verbal message varies from culture to culture depending on its norms and expectations about verbal message forms. You can improve a message's sociolinguistic level of verbal meaning by developing intercultural competence, practicing mindfulness, and recognizing, respecting, and adapting to the sociolinguistic practices of others.

Chapter Resources

What You Should Be Able *to Explain:*

- How interpersonal communication meaning is conveyed through verbal and nonverbal parts of messages
- What language, dialect, and idiolect are
- How language and dialects are related
- How the meaning of a verbal message depends on the language itself
- How a verbal message's meaning depends on the social or cultural context

What You Should Be Able *to Do:*

- Form clear and precise messages
- Create messages that are appropriate and effective within a conversational context
- Tailor messages to the social and cultural context.

Self-test questions based on these concepts are available on the companion Web site (www.oup.com/us/verderber) as part of Chapter 4 resources.

Key Words

Flashcards for all of these key terms are available on the *Inter-Act* Web site.

Concrete language, p. 111
Connotation, p. 109
Conversational maxims, p. 117
Cooperative principle, p. 117
Dating information, p. 112
Denotation, p. 109
Dialect, p. 103
Direct verbal style, p. 121
Idiolect, p. 104
Idioms, p. 121
Indexing generalizations, p. 112

Indirect verbal style, p. 121
Jargon, p. 114
Language, p. 103
Language community, p. 103
Lexicon, p. 103
Linguistic sensitivity, p. 115
Mindfulness, p. 122
Phonology, p. 103
Pragmatic meaning, p. 115
Precise words, p. 111
Semantic meaning, p. 109

Slang, p. 114
Sociolinguistic meaning, p. 119
Specific language, p. 110
Speech act, p. 115
Speech community, p. 103
Syntax and grammar, p. 103
Utterance, p. 103
Verbal message, p. 103
Words, p. 109

Apply Your Knowledge

The following questions challenge you to demonstrate your mastery of the concepts, theories, and frameworks in this chapter by using them to explain what is happening in a specific situation.

4.1 Reread the study-group scene at the beginning of this chapter. Then statement by statement, compare what is said at the linguistic level to what is meant at the pragmatic level and explain how sociolinguistics plays a role in the meaning of the verbal messages.

4.2 Write a short dialogue that demonstrates the unique ways in which semantics, pragmatics, and sociolinguistics each contributes to the meaning of verbal messages. Annotate your dialogue to explain what is happening at each level with each utterance.

Skill Practice

Skill Practice activities give you the chance to rehearse a new skill by responding to hypothetical or real situations. Additional skill practice activities are available at the companion Web site.

4.3 Reword the following messages to make the language more specific with concrete and precise words:

a. "You know that I really love baseball. Well, I'm practicing a lot because I'm hoping to get a tryout with the pros."

b. "I'm really bummed out. Everything with Corey is going down the tubes. We just don't connect anymore."

c. "She's just a pain. Ya know, always doing stuff to tick me off. And then just acting like, ya know."

4.4   Improve each of the statements below using the skills of indexing and dating:

    a. "The Mortensons always drive a new car."

    b. "Grady is always on Facebook. He has more "friends" than anyone I know."

    c. "The Scoop has the best ice cream in Southwest Florida."

    d. "Just watch, when Cameron walks in he'll look like he just walked off the set of a *GQ* shoot."

    e. "He'll be on time. He was in the military."

    f. "*Law and Order: Los Angeles* is going to be a hit. It's a Dick Wolf show."

Communication Improvement Plan: Verbal Communication

4.5   How can you improve your ability to use language in producing or interpreting the meaning of verbal messages? Identify a problem you have forming or understanding verbal messages. Review the guidelines for improving the semantic, pragmatic, and sociolinguistic meanings of verbal messages. Select at least one of these as a goal. Then using the interpersonal communication skills you have studied in the course, write a communication improvement plan. You can find a communication improvement plan worksheet on our Web site at www.oup.com/us/verderber

Inter-Act with Media

Television

Miss Teen USA, Ms. South Carolina (2007)

In 2007, Miss South Carolina Teen USA placed fourth in the 2007 *Miss Teen USA* pageant. She gained international notoriety for her convoluted and nonsensical response to a question posed to her during the national pageant: *"Recent polls have shown a fifth of Americans can't locate the U.S. on a world map. Why do you think this is?"* Upton responded:

"I personally believe that U.S. Americans are unable to do so because, uh, some . . . people out there in our nation don't have maps and, uh, I believe that our, uh, education like such as in South Africa and, uh, the Iraq, everywhere like such as, and, I believe that they should, our education over HERE in the U.S. should help the U.S., uh, or, uh, should help South Africa and should help the Iraq and the Asian countries, so we will be able to build up our future, for our children."

YouTube video clips of her answer had over 46.5 million views.

IPC Concepts: Verbal messages, words, denotation, connotation, specific language, improving message semantics.

To the Point:

> How would you characterize Miss South Carolina's communication competence?
> What recommendations would you offer Miss South Carolina for improving her message semantics?
> Try your hand at crafting a more effective response that illustrates your knowledge of the content from this chapter.

Cinema

Mickey Blue Eyes (1999). Kelly Makin (director). Hugh Grant, Jeanne Tripplehorn, James Caan.

British auctioneer Michael Felgate (Grant) is shocked when his girlfriend, Gina Vitale, (Tripplehorn) rejects his marriage proposal. A crying Gina explains that her father, Frank (Caan), and many of her family members are entrenched in a Mafia crime family. Gina fears that Michael may also become part of the Mafia game and begin to lead a very dangerous life. Shortly after Michael says that he will never let this occur, Michael becomes involved in a money laundering scheme. First, he does a few "favors" for Gina's relatives, but soon he is helping to bury dead bodies. Gina's father coaches Michael to change his *t*'s to *d*'s and drop his *r*'s, hoping he'll be able to say *fuhgeddaboudit* like a true mobster. Although his first attempts at using the Mafia "language" are laughable, he still manages to deceive a few people.

IPC Concepts: Verbal messages, speech community, dialect, codeswitching.

To the Point:

> How might you describe the speech communities present in this film?
> What challenges often accompany dialect differences that we experience in our interactions with others?
> When did you last engage in codeswitching?
> How did others react to your codeswitching ability?

What's on the Web

Find links and additional material, including self-quizzes, on the companion Web site at www.oup.com/us/verderber.

5

Nonverbal Messages

TAKE I

Amber enters the suite.

Amber: "I'm home. Are we going to dinner soon?"

Louisa: "Uh huh."

Amber: "Good, because I'm starving. I worked so long in chem lab that I completely missed lunch and had to do with a power bar that was at the bottom of my backpack. And it was stale, so I barely ate two bites."

Louisa: "Uh huh."

Amber: "Hey, I've been thinking about spring break. What would you think about doing an alternative spring break? Student government is sponsoring three different trips, and one is to Haiti. I thought we could do some good and get some sun. What do you think?"

Louisa: "Whatever."

Amber: "Crap. What did I do wrong this time? Sometimes I just don't understand her."

What just happened? From the verbal transcript of this scene, it's hard to tell because it only records the verbal message part of each of these utterances. Let's look at a different account of the conversation:

TAKE II:

As Amber enters the suite, Louisa is sitting cross-legged on the bed typing furiously on her laptop.

"I'm home. Are we going to dinner soon?" Amber asks, smiling brightly as she drops her backpack on the floor and flops down on the red futon across the room.

"Uh huh," mumbles Louisa as she furrows her brow, continuing to type and stare intently at the screen.

"Good, because I'm starving. I worked so long in chem lab that I completely missed lunch and had to do with a power bar that was at the bottom of my backpack. And it was stale, so I barely ate two bites," Amber continues brightly, wrinkling her nose.

"Uh huh," Louisa mutters, exhaling loudly as she turns her back to Amber and remains wholly focused on her typing.

"Hey, I've been thinking about spring break. What would you think about doing an alternative spring break? Student government is sponsoring three different trips, and one is to Haiti. I thought we could do some good and get some sun. What do you think?" Amber asks eagerly as she gets up from the futon and plops down on the bed in front of Louisa, sending books and papers flying.

"Whatever," Louisa shouts as she bangs her laptop closed, gathers her papers, and storms out of the room.

"Crap," Amber thinks as she stares wide-eyed at the door that was rebounding from the force with which Louisa had slammed it. "What'd I do wrong this time? Sometimes I just don't understand her."

What you should be able *to* explain after you have studied this chapter:

- The characteristics of nonverbal messages
- The functions of nonverbal messages
- The types and meanings of body motions in messages
- The types and meanings of paralanguage in messages
- The types and meanings of physical space in messages
- The types and meanings of self-presentation
- Cultural and gender differences in nonverbal behavior
- How to improve the nonverbal messages you send and interpret the nonverbal messages you receive

What you should be able *to* do after you have studied this chapter:

- Improve the content of your nonverbal communication
- Apply the skill of perception checking

So now can you help Amber out? Can you tell her what she was failing to notice and why Louisa left? After reading the second description, you probably recognized that Amber had completely ignored the nonverbal messages that Louisa was sending by her eye contact, her tone of voice, and her body language. In the last chapter you learned about how language creates meaning in the verbal message part of an utterance. In this chapter you will learn about **nonverbal communication**, the term commonly used to describe all human communication events that transcend spoken or written words (Knapp & Hall, 2009). More specifically, it describes how actions and vocal tone, among other things, create meanings that stand alone or that support, modify, or contradict the meaning of a verbal message.

Nonverbal messages are so important to our communication. In fact researchers have estimated as much as 65 percent of the social meaning we convey in face-to-face interactions is a result of nonverbal behavior (Burgoon and Bacue, 2003). In other words, the meaning we assign to any utterance is based on both the content of the verbal message and our interpretation of the nonverbal message, the behavior that accompanies and surrounds the verbal message. As we can see from Take I and Take II of the conversation between Amber and Louisa, noticing and correctly interpreting these nonverbal actions are critical to understanding what our partner is "saying." In this chapter we provide a framework for understanding and improving nonverbal communication message behaviors. We begin this chapter by describing the characteristics and functions of nonverbal messages. Next, we identify the types of behaviors used in nonverbal messages, including body motions (kinesics), nonverbal sounds (paralanguage), spatial cues (proxemics), and self-presentation cues. Then, we discuss how these types of nonverbal messages vary with culture and gender. Finally, we offer suggestions for improving the ways you send and interpret nonverbal communication.

Nonverbal communication—all human communication events that transcend spoken or written words.

Characteristics and Functions of Nonverbal Messages

Regardless of the type of nonverbal behavior, all nonverbal messages share common characteristics and functions. Understanding these commonalities provides a foundation for our study of nonverbal messages.

THUMPA
THUMPA
THUMPA

In negotiations, he appeared to have ice in his veins, but his tail betrayed him.

Characteristics of Nonverbal Communication

Nonverbal communication has five distinct characteristics: It is intentional or unintentional, primary, ambiguous, continuous, and multichanneled. Let's look at these characteristics more closely.

1. Nonverbal communication can be *intentional* or *unintentional*. Sometimes we are aware of the nonverbal messages we are sending, but most often we are not consciously aware of them. For example, Zach smirks when he is nervous, taps his foot when impatient, speaks forcefully when angry, and stands tall when confident. Although he consistently uses these behaviors, he may be unaware of them, but people close to him "read" his emotional state by noticing these mannerisms. Because we are generally unaware of our emotional signals, many of us react to seeing video of ourselves, saying things like, "I didn't know that I sounded like that, frowned so much, walked like that, gestured like that, or stood that close to people." While we may be acting naturally and without any conscious intent to send nonverbal messages, the people we talk with interpret nonverbal cues as intentional (Burgoon, 1994).

2. Nonverbal messages are *primary*. We interpret how speakers feel about what they are saying based on the nonverbal messages in the utterance. In other words, nonverbal communication is primary, taking precedence over verbal communication. For instance, when Janelle frowns, clenches her fists, and forcefully says, "I am *not* angry!" her sister Renée ignores the verbal message in favor of the contradicting nonverbal behaviors, which indicate that Janelle is, indeed, very angry. In a classic study of nonverbal communication and emotion, psychologist Albert Mehrabian (1972) found that about 93 percent of the emotional meaning of utterances is conveyed nonverbally. Think about it, 93 percent! In addition, the nonverbal message is perceived to be more believable than the verbal. It is easy to deceive others with our scripted words. Nonverbal behavior, however, is harder to fake because it is more spontaneous. Was your gut-level response to someone you encountered ever discomfort or distrust? The other person's verbal messages may have seemed friendly or kind, but your reaction was based on nonverbal cues. Though you may not have been conscious of or able to pinpoint the person's nonverbal behaviors that bothered you, you were reacting more strongly to these subtle signals than to the content of the verbal message.

3. Nonverbal behavior is frequently *ambiguous*. Most nonverbal behaviors are not codified; that is, there is no agreed on lexicon of definitions for what it means to behave a certain way. For example, the word "smile" means a pleasant facial expression in which the corners of the lips turn up and the outside of the eyes crinkles. When we say, "She was smiling," we are describing her facial expression. But the nonverbal meaning of that same smile is ambiguous. It can depend on the smiler's personality, culture, the conversational context, and the relationship of the nonverbal behaviors to the verbal message. The nonverbal act of smiling may convey nervousness, happiness, or excitement. A smile can also be used to mask anger, hatred, boredom, or embarrassment. You may display your anger by frowning or by being poker-faced. You may speak loudly or softly, quickly or slowly. You may glare at someone or avoid eye contact altogether. You may cry. In short, it is difficult to interpret nonverbal behaviors accurately, especially when you do not know someone well. When we are in a relationship with someone, however, we learn to read and more accurately decode our partner's nonverbal behaviors.

4. **Nonverbal communication is** *continuous.* Although your verbal message is bounded by silence, as long as you are in the presence of another person, your behavior may be noticed and interpreted as a message. You never stop communicating nonverbally. For instance, when Austin yawns and nods off during a meeting at work, his co-workers will notice this behavior and make assumptions about him. Some may think he is rude; others, bored. Paul, however, may correctly recognize that his friend Austin is exhausted from studying for exams. Meanwhile, Austin snoozes unaware of the various meanings he is sending with his nonverbal "message."

5. **Nonverbal messages are** *multichanneled.* When interpreting someone's nonverbal behavior, we use a variety of cues or channels to make sense of what is happening. These cues include the vocal tone, body position, gestures, facial expressions, and general appearance of the other person. For example, when Alisha first meets her new neighbor, Mimi, she will notice many things at once, including Mimi's smile, twinkling eyes, fast rate of speech, erect posture, designer suit, perfume, and apartment décor. Alisha will consider these as she interprets Mimi's comments about the way other neighbors violate the rules. We not only notice a variety of nonverbal behaviors to interpret someone's meaning but also typically perceive these behaviors together rather than in isolation. We interpret all these behaviors jointly with any verbal messages that accompany them to determine the real meaning the speaker intended.

Functions of Nonverbal Messages

In addition to having the specific characteristics we just discussed, nonverbal messages serve five primary functions: They provide information; regulate interaction; express or hide emotion and affect; present an image; and express status, power, and control. In this section we will describe each function separately, yet it is important to recognize that in conversations, these functions overlap, and nonverbal messages can fulfill more than one of these functions at the same time.

1. **Nonverbal behavior** *provides information.* Our nonverbal behaviors provide information by repeating, substituting for, emphasizing, or contradicting our verbal messages. First, we may use nonverbal cues to *repeat* what we have said verbally. For instance, if you say "no" and shake your head at the same time, your

---

INTER-ACT WITH SOCIAL MEDIA

You might use social media to remain connected with your romantic partner throughout the course of a day. Since we likely experience a stronger emotional connection with romantic partners than we do with our friends, we often want to convey that emotion through social media—perhaps through a text message or Facebook message. How do you communicate emotion in the messages that you send through social media? What are some of the challenges associated with using certain forms of social media— such as texting, Facebook, and video conferencing services (e.g., Skype)— to fully express how you are feeling?

nonverbal message repeats what you have said verbally. Second, some nonverbal behaviors *substitute* for words. A wave, for example, has the symbolic meaning of "hello" or "good-bye." In some cultures, curling your index finger and motioning toward yourself substitutes for the verbal message "come here," but in other cultures, the same gesture carries the nonverbal message meaning "go away" or "good-bye." Third, nonverbal behaviors can *emphasize* a verbal message by accenting, complementing, or adding information to the words. For instance, a teacher may smile, clap, or pat a student on the back when saying, "Good job on the test." In this case, facial expression, body motions, and voice volume emphasize the verbal praise message. Finally, nonverbal behaviors may send messages that *contradict* the verbal message. This can confuse the listener. For example, when Sadie says in a quiet, monotone voice, "I am really interested in your project," while avoiding eye contact and moving away, her nonverbal message has contradicted her verbal message. People who receive mixed messages use the nonverbal message to interpret the pragmatic meaning of the verbal message.

2. Nonverbal messages *regulate interaction*. We manage a conversation through subtle and sometimes obvious nonverbal cues. We use shifts in eye contact, slight head movements, posture changes, raised eyebrows, and nodding to tell another person when to continue, to repeat, to elaborate, to hurry up, or to finish what he or she is saying. Think of the times you have used nonverbal cues in an attempt to end a conversation. You may have decreased the amount of eye contact you gave the other person, given abrupt or abbreviated responses, shown less animated facial expression, or turned away from the other person. Students in a classroom regularly signal to the instructor that class time is nearly over by packing away their laptops, putting on their coats, fidgeting in their seats, or mumbling to each other. Effective communicators learn to adjust what they are saying and how they are saying it on the basis of the nonverbal cues of others.

3. Nonverbal behaviors *express or hide emotions and affect*. While we can easily hide from others the things we are thinking, we can't hide the things we are feeling. As we experience them, our emotions are instantaneously conveyed by our nonverbal behavior. People will use these signals to interpret our verbal messages (Ekman, 2003). So, if you knit your brows together, tighten your jaw, and scream at your mother, "I'm not angry," your emotional nonverbal language drowns out your verbal message. The TV show *Lie to Me,* a detective who-done-it, was premised on the ability of the lead character to solve the case by reading the micro-expressions of suspects that expose whether they are lying or telling the truth. The show was based on the work of Paul Ekman, a well-respected social scientist who serves as a scientific consultant to the show. Among other things, Ekman's research has identified universal facial expressions that convey the emotions of sadness, anger, surprise, fear, disgust, contempt, and happiness. His work also suggests that although training may enable us to moderate our nonverbal reactions, it is unlikely that we will be able to eliminate them (Ekman, 2003).

INTER-ACT WITH SOCIAL MEDIA

When we have a face-to-face conversation with another person, we are expected to make eye contact to indicate that we are attentive and fully engaged in the conversation. In a face-to-face conversation with one person, however, we can simultaneously use social media (such as texting and Facebook) to communicate with another. How often do you find yourself in this situation, either as the person communicating with two people at once or as the person conversing with someone who is using social media at the same time? How does your use of social media affect the quality of the face-to-face conversations that you have with others?

4. Nonverbal communication *presents an image.* Much of our efforts to manage the impression that others form about us are done with nonverbal cues and messages. People may carefully develop an image through the clothing, grooming, jewelry, and personal possessions they display. For example, when you see a man dressed in an expensive suit briskly walking down the street sending a text message on his iPhone while wearing a Bluetooth headset, what do you think? How people handle, use, accessorize, and wear their cell phones communicates something about them and their lifestyles (Kleinman, 2007). Not only do people use nonverbal communication to communicate a personal image, but they may also use nonverbal cues to signal their relationship status. So when you see two people of similar ages with identical tee-shirts walking together holding hands, their dress and hand holding signals that they are a couple. Likewise, if you notice that the woman who sits next to you in class no longer is wearing her wedding ring, you may infer that she is getting divorced. Sometimes the image presented is not accurate, however. For example, couples in a distressed marriage may publicly project a positive image by holding hands or being attentive to each other through facial expressions (Patterson, 1994).

5. Nonverbal communication *expresses status, power, and control.* Many nonverbal behaviors are signs of dominance, regardless of whether the person displaying them intends to convey power and control. Consider how a high-level manager conveys status and how subordinate employees acknowledge that status through nonverbal behavior. The manager may dress more formally, have a larger and more expensively furnished office, and walk and speak authoritatively. Subordinates may show respect to the manager by using eye contact and listening attentively when the manager speaks, by not interrupting, and by seeking permission (appointments) to enter the manager's office. As another example, imagine a parent who says to a child, "Look at me when I'm speaking to you." The parent expects that the child will nonverbally accept parental dominance by directing steady eye contact at the parent as a sign of respect.

Types of Nonverbal Communication

Nonverbal behaviors used in messages can be classified into four general categories or types. These categories are body language (body motions used in communication, such as eye contact, facial expressions, gestures, posture, and touch), paralanguage (nonverbal sounds such as pitch, volume, rate, quality, and intonation that accompany words), spatial usage (the use of acoustic space, territory, and artifacts during communication), and self-presentation cues (use of physical appearance cues, time cues, and smell cues).

Body Language

Of all the categories of nonverbal behavior, you are probably most familiar with **body language**, the intentional or unintentional movement of various body parts that sends nonverbal messages. **Kinesics** is the study of body language.

OBSERVE AND ANALYZE

Truth or Lie?

Locate and watch an episode from the third season of the canceled show, *Lie to Me.* Pause every time the Lightman character is about to "read" someone. Predict whether the person is lying or telling the truth, Then view Dr. Lightman's read and compare it to yours. After watching the show, go to Paul Ekman's website and read his blog on the show you watched. Write a short paper about what you learned from this. How well do you read people?

Body language—the intentional or unintentional movement of various body parts that sends nonverbal messages.

Kinesics—the study of body language.

Body motions serve five functions. First, body motions may be used to take the place of a word or phrase. For instance, a head nod means "yes," and pointing a thumb toward the ceiling while curling the other fingers literally means "thumbs up," a symbol for "everything is OK." Second, body motions that accompany a verbal message may complement it by emphasizing what has been said, demonstrating what is being said, or indicating the physical placement of something. Third, body motions convey emotional states. Fourth, body motions can control or regulate the flow of conversation. By vigorously nodding your head, you can let a speaker know that you need no further explanation, or by holding your hand in front of you with your palm perpendicular, you can signal that someone should stop talking. Finally, body motions may help us relieve our internal tensions. Body language includes eye contact, facial expression, gesture, posture, and touch. Let's take a closer look at each of these.

1. Eye contact. Eye contact (or gaze) is using eye focus to signal attention, respect, emotional reactions, or dominance.

Eye-contact messages convey many meanings that vary with person, situation, and culture. Your eye contact can signal that you are paying attention or that you respect the person with whom you are speaking. It can convey a range of emotions. When your professor, looking out over the class, sees that most of the students are not looking back, she knows that they are not paying attention to her lecture. Or if you inappropriately mention at dinner with his parents that your friend is contemplating dropping history this semester, he may glare at you to signal your transgression. Intense eye contact may also be an attempt to dominate (Pearson, West, & Turner, 1995). Accordingly, we speak of "looks that could kill" or "staring another person down." The use of eye contact can signal aggression or status.

Eye contact—using eye focus to signal attention, respect, emotional reactions, or dominance.

In many Eastern cultures (and some American subcultures), a person will avoid direct eye contact when talking to someone of higher status to show respect. Violating this cultural expectation is seen as rude or aggressive. In Western cultures, holding someone's gaze for too long or staring tends to be interpreted as a sign of dominance or aggression. Indeed, in some segments of society, a prolonged stare may be an invitation to a physical fight. Yet, ironically, not making any eye contact at all can also be seen as a sign of dominance. The dominant person in an exchange, such as a boss, an interviewer, a teacher, or a police officer, has the freedom to maintain eye contact or look away at will, but the subordinate person in the situation is expected to maintain steady and respectful eye contact.

2. Facial expression. **Facial expression** is arranging facial muscles to communicate emotion or provide feedback. Three groups of muscles are manipulated to form facial expressions: those in the brow and forehead; those surrounding the eyes, eyelids, and root of the nose; and those in the remainder of the nose, the cheeks, mouth, and chin. As we discussed earlier, facial expressions are especially important in conveying the six basic emotions of happiness, sadness, surprise, fear, anger, and disgust. In fact, facial expressions are so central to shared meaning that when we use digital media we employ **emoticons**, typed or graphic symbols that convey facial expressions in online messages (Walther & Parks, 2002). Facial expressions also provide nonverbal feedback to speakers. For instance, people knit their brows and squint their eyes into a quizzical look when they don't understand what someone is saying, or they purse their lips and raise one eyebrow to convey skepticism.

> **Facial expression**—arranging facial muscles to communicate emotion or provide feedback.

> **Emoticons**—typed or graphic symbols that convey facial expressions in online messages.

3. Gesture. **Gesture** is using hand, arm, and finger movement to replace, complement, and augment a verbal message. Just as we learn what words mean, we also learn what certain gestures mean. **Emblems** are gestures that substitute completely for words. A hitchhiker's upward-pointing thumb, for example, is an emblem, a gesture that needs no words to accompany it. Likewise, a finger placed vertically across the lips means "Be quiet." Emblems have symbolic meanings in a particular culture, but the same gesture can mean different things in other cultures, or an emblem in one culture may have no symbolic meaning in another. Gestures can also complement a verbal message. For example, when a person says "about this high" or "nearly this round," we need to see a gesture accompanying the verbal description to understand the height or size of the object. Gestures can also augment or add to a verbal message by conveying emotional information. When the verbal message, "I told you not to do that," is accompanied by the speaker repeatedly slamming the fist of one hand into an open palm of the other, the extreme frustration of the speaker becomes evident.

> **Gesture**—using hand, arm, and finger movement to replace, complement, and augment a verbal message.

> **Emblems**—gestures that substitute completely for words.

4. Posture and body orientation. **Posture** is the position and movement of the whole body. Your posture is erect when you straighten your spine, open your chest, and settle your shoulders down and apart, with your head and neck aligned with your spine. Your posture is slouched when your spine curves in, your chest

> **Posture**—the position and movement of the whole body.

Body orientation—your position in relation to another person.

and shoulders roll forward, and your head and neck are forward of your spine. **Body orientation** refers to your position in relation to another person. Like eye contact, it can be described as direct or indirect. Facing another person squarely is called direct body orientation. When two people's postures are at angles to each other, this is called indirect body orientation. The combination of posture and body orientation can convey information about attentiveness, respect, and power. Consider, for example, how you would sit in a job interview. You are likely to sit up straight and face the interviewer directly because you want to communicate your interest, respect, and confidence, while the interviewer may also sit up straight, face you directly, and possibly lean forward to signal dominance. Interviewers tend to interpret a slouched posture and indirect body orientation as disinterest, disrespect, and lack of confidence, while interviewees may interpret a slouched, indirectly oriented, and back-leaning interviewer as not only uninterested and disrespectful but also a pushover. In other situations, such as talking with friends, a slouched posture and indirect body orientation may be appropriate and may not carry any messages about attention, respect, or power. This difference in meaning based on various situations demonstrates the ambiguous nature of nonverbal communication. Rarely does any one posture or body orientation absolutely mean any one thing.

Touch—putting part of the body in contact with something or someone.

5. Touch. Also known as haptics, **touch** is putting part of the body in contact with someone or something.

We use our hands, our arms, and other body parts to pat, hug, slap, kiss, pinch, stroke, hold, embrace, and tickle, communicating a variety of emotions and messages. Our touching can be gentle or firm, perfunctory or passionate, brief or lingering. Like many of the other types of body motion, touch can convey messages about power. Usually, the higher-status person in a situation is the one to initiate touch. Managers are more likely to touch their employees than vice versa, and faculty members are more likely to touch their students than vice versa.

There are three types of touch: spontaneous, ritualized, and task-related. *Spontaneous touch* is touch that is automatic and subconscious. Patting someone on the back when you hear that he or she has won an award, for example, is spontaneous touch. In addition, there are many forms of *ritualized touch*, touch that is scripted rather than spontaneous. Handshakes or high-five slaps of the hands, for example, are forms of ritualized touch that have rather definite meanings as greeting rituals and are expected in certain situations. *Task-related touch* is touch used to perform a certain unemotional function. For instance, a doctor may touch a patient during a physical examination, or a personal trainer may touch a client during a workout at the gym. We do not attach the same meanings to task-related touch as we do to

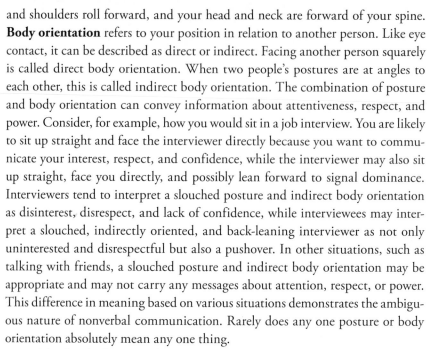

spontaneous or ritualized touch. We see task-related touch as part of the professional service we are receiving. There is also a type of touch that combines spontaneity and task-related touch to convey messages of closeness. In public, when someone adjusts your coat collar or removes some lint from your clothing, the person is not only doing a task-related favor for you but is also signaling, perhaps inadvertently, a degree of closeness between the two of you that they would not signal to a complete stranger or a casual acquaintance.

People differ in their touching behavior and in their reactions to unsolicited touch from others. Some people like to touch and be touched; other people do not. Although American culture is relatively non-contact-oriented, the kinds and amounts of touching behavior within our society vary widely. Touching behavior that seems innocuous to one person may be perceived as overly intimate or threatening to another. Moreover, the perceived appropriateness of touch differs with the context. Touch that is considered appropriate in private may embarrass a person in public or with a large group of people.

Paralanguage

The second category of nonverbal communication is paralanguage. **Paralanguage** (also known as vocalics) is using the voice to convey meaning. There are five vocal characteristics that comprise paralanguage: pitch, volume, rate, quality, and intonation. By controlling these, we can complement, supplement, or contradict the meaning conveyed by the language of our message.

Paralanguage—using the voice to convey meaning.

1. Pitch. Pitch is the rate of vibration of your vocal cords. The faster your vocal cords vibrate, the higher the pitch of your voice; the slower they vibrate, the lower the pitch of your voice. We raise and lower our vocal pitch to emphasize ideas, indicate questions, or show nervousness. Our pitch may rise when we are nervous and drop when we want to be forceful.

Pitch—the rate of vibration of your vocal cords.

2. Volume. Volume is the loudness of a person's voice. Whereas some people have naturally loud voices that carry long distances, others are normally soft-spoken. Regardless of our normal volume level, most of us vary vocal volume depending on the situation or topic of discussion. For example, people may talk loudly when they wish to be heard in noisy settings, raise their volume when angry, or speak more softly when being romantic or loving.

Volume—the loudness of a person's vocal tone.

3. Rate. Rate is the speed at which a person speaks. While some people's normal rate is faster than that of others, people tend to talk more rapidly when they are happy, frightened, nervous, or excited, and they tend to talk more slowly when they are problem solving out loud or trying to emphasize a point.

Rate—the speed at which a person speaks.

4. Quality. Quality is the sound of a person's voice. Each human voice has a distinct tone. Some voices are raspy, some smoky, some have bell-like qualities, and others are throaty. But regardless of voice quality, each of us uses a slightly different quality of voice to communicate a particular state of mind. We may convey a complaint with a whiny, nasal vocal quality; a seductive invitation with a soft, breathy quality; and anger with a strident, harsh quality.

Quality—the sound of a person's voice.

Intonation—the variety, melody, or inflection of a person's voice.

5. Intonation. Intonation is the variety, melody, or inflection of a person's voice. Some voices have little intonation and sound monotonous. Other voices are very melodious and may have even a childlike singsong quality. People prefer to listen to voices with a moderate amount of intonation.

Vocal interferences—extraneous sounds or words that interrupt fluent speech.

Pitch, volume, rate, quality, and intonation add nonverbal shades of meaning to words. **Vocal interferences**, however, are extraneous sounds or words that interrupt fluent speech. These vocalized sounds add little or no meaning to the verbal message and may even interfere with understanding. They are sometimes used as "place markers" designed to fill in momentary gaps in a verbal message while we search for the right word or idea. These place markers indicate that we are not done speaking and that it is still our "turn." The use of an excessive number of fillers can lead to the impression that you are unsure of yourself or confused about what you are attempting to say. The most common interferences that creep into our speech include "uh," "er," "well," and "OK," as well as the extraneous use of "you know" and "like."

Spatial Usage

The way we use the space that surrounds us during an interaction sends nonverbal messages to our partners. We send nonverbal messages by the way we use our personal space, the acoustic space of the setting, the space we claim as our territory, and the objects or artifacts we use to adorn our space.

Personal space—the area that surrounds a person, moves with that person, and changes with the situation as well as moment to moment.

Proxemics—the study of personal space.

1. Personal space. Personal space is the area that surrounds a person, moves with that person, and changes with the situation as well as moment to moment. **Proxemics** is the study of personal space. Have you ever been speaking with someone and become aware that you were uncomfortable because the other person was standing too close to you? Or maybe you've found yourself starting a conversation and then moving closer to someone as you begin to share an embarrassing story. If you have experienced either of these situations, you are already aware of the way that the space between conversational partners influences their interaction. We adjust our personal space depending on the conversation. Research suggests that most Americans comfortably converse at one of four distance ranges determined by the nature of our relationship with our partner and the topic of conversation (Hall, 1969):

- *Intimate distance,* up to 18 inches, is comfortable spacing for private conversations among intimates.
- *Personal distance,* from 18 inches to 4 feet, is comfortable spacing for casual conversations with a normal amount of background noise.
- *Social distance,* from 4 to 12 feet, is comfortable spacing for impersonal or professional interactions such as a job interview or team meeting.
- *Public distance,* anything more than 12 feet, is comfortable spacing for people in a public forum where interaction and conversation is not desired.

Of greatest concern to most people is the intimate distance—the distance we regard as the appropriate distance between people when we have a very personal conversation with close friends, parents, and younger children. People usually become uncomfortable when "outsiders" violate this intimate distance. For instance, in a movie theater that is less than one-quarter full, people will tend to leave one or more seats empty between themselves and people they do not know. If in such a setting a stranger sits right next to you, you are likely to feel uncomfortable or threatened, and you may even move away. Intrusions into our intimate space are acceptable only in certain settings and then only when all involved follow the unwritten rules. For instance, people will tolerate being packed into a crowded elevator or subway car, making physical contact with people they do not know, provided those involved follow the "rules." The rules may include standing rigidly, looking at the floor, and not making eye contact with others. In essence, we cope with this space violation by turning other people into objects. Only occasionally will people who are forced to invade each other's intimate space acknowledge the other as a person. Then they are likely to exchange sheepish smiles or otherwise acknowledge the mutual invasion of intimate distance.

2. **Acoustic space. Acoustic space** is the area over which your voice or other sounds can be comfortably heard. Competent communicators adjust the volume of their voices so that their conversations can be easily heard by their partners but not be overheard by others who are not part of the conversation. Speaking too loudly or too softly can annoy both your conversational partner and those around you. Mobile phone conversations and excessively loud car or headphone music can be seen as an acoustic invasion of space. This is why some communities

OBSERVE AND ANALYZE

Intruding on Personal Space

Find a crowded elevator. Get on it, and face the back. Make direct eye contact with the person you are standing in front of. Note their reaction. On the return trip, introduce yourself to the person who is standing next to you and begin an animated conversation. Note the reaction of others around you. Get on an empty elevator and stand in the exact center. Do not move when others board. Note their reactions. Be prepared to share what you have observed with your classmates.

Acoustic space—the area over which your voice or other sounds can be comfortably heard.

have ordinances prohibiting loud music from cars and restaurants, hospitals and theaters have rules against cell phone use, and public transportation passengers are increasingly bold about asking other passengers to turn down their music and keep their cell phone conversations to themselves.

Territory—the space over which we claim ownership.

3. Territory. Territory is the space over which we claim ownership. We expect others to respect this territory, and we may feel annoyed or even violated when they do not. Sometimes we are unaware of our territorial behavior, and other times we consciously mark or defend it. For example, when Rheanne decides to eat lunch at the company cafeteria, the space at the table she occupies unconsciously becomes her territory. If during lunch Rheanne leaves her territory to get butter for her roll, she is likely to leave her coat on her chair and her tray of food on the table, indicating that the chair and the space around her tray are "hers." If, when she returns, Rheanne finds that someone at the table has moved a glass or a dish into the area that she regards as her territory, she is likely to feel resentful.

In other instances, we purposefully and directly mark and defend our territory to others using visible signals. People use locks, signs, and fences to communicate ownership of their territory. For instance, Graham may have "his chair" in the family room because he has always used this chair and has positioned it in a certain way (he may even have verbally announced that it is his chair). As a result, other members of the family will avoid using it. Likewise, Regan may assert the kitchen as her territory by creating an organizational scheme for where various types of food, utensils, plates, and so on should go, and she will expect her roommates to know that she is the one who has decided where objects are placed. She is likely to be upset if anyone rearranges the kitchen layout.

Territoriality can also have a power dimension to it. For instance, higher-status people generally claim larger, more prestigious, and more protected territory (Henley, 1977). A top-level executive may have a large, expensively decorated, top-floor office with a breathtaking view, as well as one or more people to protect the space from intruders. An entry-level employee in the same organization may have a small cubicle that is neither private nor protected. Think of all the messages that we get from the amount and type of territory that someone claims. For instance, in a family, who shares bedrooms and who gets the largest one? Who sits where when the family members are watching TV? Who generally sits at the "head" of the dinner table? Not only do territoriality concerns permeate family, work, and friendship groups, but the power dimension is also played out in political and social areas. For example, consider where subsidized housing or environmentally harmful facilities are located in your community—usually in areas that are economically poor.

Artifacts—the objects we use to adorn our territory.

4. Artifacts. Artifacts are the objects we use to adorn our territory. We own and display things in our rooms, offices, and homes, not just for their function but also for their qualities we find pleasing. As a result, other people looking at these artifacts come to understand something about us. Think of all the types of cars and the images these cars project about their owners. Someone driving an SUV is likely to convey a different image than someone driving a brand new Chevy Volt®. People who walk down a street talking on a Droid® or listening to an iPod also send messages about themselves and their image.

Think what your home, apartment, or room says about you. You probably accumulated the objects in that space over a period of time, but taken together, they provide information to others about who you are and what you think is important, beautiful, and so on. We select and place furnishings and decorations to achieve certain effects. The chairs and couch in your living room may approximate a circle that invites people to sit down and talk. Or the seating in a room may be theater style and face the television, thereby discouraging conversation. A manager's office with a chair facing the manager across the desk encourages formal conversation. It says, "Let's talk business—I'm the boss and you're the employee." A manager's office with a chair at the side of the desk (absence of a physical barrier) encourages more informal conversation. It says, "Don't be nervous—let's just chat."

The colors we use in our territory can also be subtle nonverbal signals that encourage certain moods. Color stimulates both emotional and physical reactions. For instance, red excites and stimulates, blue comforts and soothes, and yellow cheers and elevates moods. Knowing this, professional interior designers may choose blues when trying to create a peaceful, serene atmosphere for a living room but reds and yellows when decorating a playroom.

Self-Presentation Cues

The third type of nonverbal behavior that sends messages is how we represent ourselves to others. This includes your physical appearance, your approach to time, and your use of smells and scents. Let's have a look at each of these.

1. Physical appearance. First, we learn a great deal about others and make judgments about others based on their physical appearance. Your physical appearance is how you look to others including your race, gender, body type, facial features, clothing, personal grooming, and body art. You control some parts of your physical appearance, while other parts you inherit from your family. In our sex- and race-conscious society, others use your gender, race, and ethnicity to form impressions of you. Although someone may claim to be "color blind," the first thing people notice about others is their race (DiTomaso, Parks-Yancy, & Post, 2003). The size and shape of your body are taken into consideration when people are trying to figure out who you really are, with some body types held in higher regard than others. American society places so much emphasis on physical appearance that entire industries are devoted to changing one's physical appearance through cosmetic surgery, weight loss, and grooming products. In addition, many people go to great lengths to select clothing to manage the impressions they portray. Brands and styles of clothing convey certain images. How you wear your hair and whether and how you use makeup and body art also convey something about you to others, though

"The boss finally noticed me today. He said I should wear deodorant."

the exact "message" will depend on another person's frame of reference. Magenta tinted and spiked hair coupled with large tattoos and ear lobe gauging may be read by one person as "He's really slammin'" and by another as "He's sure a loser." Since choice of clothing and personal grooming will communicate messages about us, most of us modify our dress and grooming to the situation. For example, at work Tiffany dresses conservatively, carefully covers her tattoo by wearing sleeved tops, and pulls her hair up into a neat ponytail or back in a barrette. But on the weekends when she goes out, she chooses short, tight skirts, 4-inch heels with crisscross straps and buckles, and halter tops that show off her tat, and she wears her hair long and loose. The image she projects at work sends the message, "I am a serious intelligent professional whom you can trust to perform," whereas the image she projects at the clubs sends the message, "I am confident, sexy, and ready to have a good time."

2. Use of time. In Chapter 3 we discussed how cultures differ in their approach to time. Just as cultures are monochronic or polychronic, so too are individuals. If your approach to time matches that of the people with whom you interact, they probably won't notice it or will view you as being appropriate. On the other hand, if your approach to time is different, your behavior will be

---

LEARN ABOUT YOURSELF ● Orientation to Time

Take this short survey to learn something about your perception of time. Answer the questions honestly based on your initial response. There are no right or wrong answers. For each question, select one of the numbers to the left that best describes your behavior.

1 = Always False

2 = Usually False

3 = Sometimes True, Sometimes False

4 = Usually True

5 = Always True

_____ 1. I do many things at the same time.

_____ 2. I stick to my daily schedule as much as possible.

_____ 3. I prefer to finish one activity before starting another one.

_____ 4. I feel like I waste time.

_____ 5. I would take time out of a meeting to take a social phone call.

_____ 6. I separate work time and social time.

_____ 7. I break appointments with others.

_____ 8. I prefer that events in my life occur in an orderly fashion.

_____ 9. I do more than one activity at a time.

_____ 10. Being on time for appointments is important to me.

Scoring the survey: To find your score, first reverse the responses for the odd-numbered items (if you wrote a 1, make it a 5; 2 = 4; leave 3 as is; 4 = 2; and 5 = 1). Next add the numbers for each item. Scores can range from 10 to 50. The higher your score, the more monochronic you are. The lower your score, the more polychronic you are.

Adapted from Gudykunst, W. B., Ting-Toomey, S., Sudweeks, S., & Stewart, L. P. (1995). *Building Bridges: Interpersonal Skills for a Changing World.* Boston: Houghton Mifflin.

viewed as inappropriate and will strain your relationship. For example, Carlos, a Brazilian national who is polychronic, often arrives late to meetings with his North American project team. His teammates resent his tardiness and see him as arrogant and self-important.

3. Use of smells and scents. Your intentional or unintentional odor and intentional use of scents either on your body or in your territory also send messages to others. **Olfactory cues** are messages sent through smells and scents. If you do not think that smells and scents have the power to communicate, think of the beauty care industry in the United States designed to manufacture and market scent-related products for both women and men. We buy not only perfumes and colognes but also scented soaps, shampoos, air fresheners, candles, cleaning products, and pet products, to name a few. Often we go to great lengths to influence the odors associated with our bodies, our cars, and our homes. Aromatherapy is used to relieve stress and alter mood (Furlow, 1996). Homeowners sometimes bake cookies or bread before holding an open house so that prospective buyers will perceive the house to be "homey." The meanings attached to certain odors and scents as well as other nonverbal behaviors are firmly based in culture, as we will see in the next section.

Olfactory cues—messages sent through smells and scents.

Spotlight on Scholars

Read about the nonverbal expectancy research of Judee K. Burgoon at www. oup.com/us/verderber.

Cultural and Gender Variations in Nonverbal Communication

Throughout this chapter we have pointed out that the meanings conveyed by nonverbal behaviors vary with culture and with gender. Let's now look at some of the specific differences, following the four categories of nonverbal communication outlined in the preceding sections.

Variations in Body Language

The use of body motions, as well as the meanings they convey, differs among cultures and by gender. Several cultural differences in body motions are well documented.

First, eye contact is a major variant. Cultures vary widely in what eye contact behavior is appropriate and what different uses of eye contact mean. Studies show that in Western cultures, talkers hold eye contact about 40 percent of the time and listeners nearly 70 percent of the time (Knapp & Hall, 2006). In Western cultures people also generally maintain better eye contact when discussing topics with which they are comfortable, when genuinely interested in another person's comments or reactions, or when trying to influence the other person. Conversely, they tend to avoid eye contact when they are discussing topics that make them uncomfortable; when uninterested in the topic or the person talking; or when embarrassed, ashamed, or trying to hide something.

The majority of people in the United States and other Western cultures expect those with whom they are communicating to "look them in the eye." Samovar, Porter, and McDaniel (2010), however, conclude that direct eye contact is

OBSERVE AND ANALYZE

Cultural Differences in Nonverbal Behavior

Interview or converse with two international students from different countries. Try to select students whose cultures differ from each other and from the culture with which you are most familiar. Develop a list of questions related to the material discussed in this chapter. Try to understand how people in the international students' countries differ from you in their use of body language, paralanguage, space, and self-presentation cues. Write a short paper explaining what you have learned.

not universally considered appropriate. For instance, in Japan people direct their gaze to a position around the Adam's apple and avoid direct eye contact. Chinese people, Indonesians, and rural Mexicans lower their eyes as a sign of deference—to them, too much direct eye contact is a sign of bad manners. Middle Easterners, in contrast, look intently into the eyes of the person with whom they are talking for longer periods—to them, direct eye contact demonstrates keen interest.

There are differences in the use of eye contact among co-cultures and by gender within the United States. For instance, African Americans tend to use more continuous eye contact than European Americans when they are speaking but less when they are listening (Samovar et al., 2010). A study of black kinesics (Johnson, 2004) reports that some African Americans may be reluctant to look authority figures in the eye because to do so would be a sign of disrespect carried over from the days of slavery and Jim Crow, when looking directly at whites signaled an inappropriate assumption of equality. Women tend to use more frequent eye contact during conversations than men (Miller, 2011). Moreover, women tend to hold eye contact longer than men regardless of the sex of the person with whom they are interacting (Wood, 2007). It is important to note that these differences, while often described as biological differences, are also related to societal status. For example, historically, women in the United States have had lower status than men, which may partially explain the differences between men and women in the eye contact that we observe today. People, whether male or female, will use more eye contact when displaying behaviors considered feminine than when displaying behaviors considered masculine.

Second, the use of facial expressions varies across cultures and by gender. But studies also reveal many similarities in nonverbal communication across cultures, especially in facial expressions. Several appear to be universal, including a slight raising of the eyebrow to communicate recognition and wriggling one's nose with a look of disgust to indicate social repulsion (Martin & Nakayama, 2006). In fact, at least six facial expressions (happiness, sadness, fear, anger, disgust, and surprise) carry the same basic meaning throughout the world (Samovar et al., 2010). However, the choice of whether to display emotions through facial expressions varies across cultural and gender lines. For instance, in some Eastern cultures, people have been socialized to downplay emotional behavior cues like frowning and smiling, whereas members of other cultures have been socialized to amplify their displays of emotion through facial expressions. In addition, research has shown that gender plays a role in the choice of displaying emotion through facial expressions. Women and men tend to smile more frequently when communicating in ways socially perceived as feminine and smile less frequently when communicating in so-called masculine ways, for instance, when being authoritative.

Third, the use of gesture varies across cultures and by gender. Men, for instance, are more likely to use large gestures than are women (Woods, 2011). The meanings of gestures also differ considerably across cultures. For example, making a circle with the thumb and forefinger signifies "OK" in the United States, zero or worthless in France, money in Japan, and something vulgar in Germany and Brazil (Axtell, 1998). When communicating with people from cultures other than your own, be especially careful about the gestures you use, as they are by no means universal.

Finally, cultures have different rules about touch. Latin America and Mediterranean countries are high-contact cultures. Northern European cultures are medium to low in contact. And Asian cultures are for the most part low-contact cultures. The United States, a country of immigrants, is generally perceived to be in the medium-contact category, though there are wide differences among individual Americans because of variations in family heritage (Ting-Toomey & Chung, 2011). In terms of gender, women tend to touch others less than men because they generally value touching more than men. Women view touch as an expressive behavior that demonstrates warmth and affiliation, whereas men view touch as instrumental behavior; for instance, touching females is considered as leading to sexual activity (Pearson et al., 1995).

Variations in Paralanguage

There are a few cultural and gender variations in use of paralanguage as well. In the Middle East, speaking loudly signifies being strong and sincere. People from Hong Kong use high-pitched, expressive voices. What we call vocal interferences in the United States are not considered interferences in China, where using fillers signals wisdom and attractiveness (Chen & Starosta, 1998). In the United States, stereotypes exist about masculine and feminine vocalics. We expect male voices to be lower pitched and loud, with moderate to low intonation, and we expect female voices to be higher pitched, softer in volume, and more expressive. Both sexes have the option to portray a range of vocalics, yet most people conform to the expectations for their sex. One voice feature, pitch, is a direct result of physical differences between men and women. On average, men have larger and thicker vocal cords than women, which accounts for their lower pitch. Despite this physical reason for differing voice pitches, societal expectations about masculinity and femininity still play a part. Before puberty, the vocal cords of males and females do not differ. Yet, even before a physical reason develops for sex differences in pitch, little boys frequently speak in a lower pitch than little girls (Wood, 2007).

Variations in Spatial Usage

Problems in our relationships occur when our use of space violates the expectations of our partner or when our partner's use of space violates our expectations. Violations may be caused by cultural and gender differences in how space is used. As you would expect, the spatial environments in which people feel comfortable depend on cultural background. In the United States, where many people live in single-family homes or in large apartments, we expect to have greater personal space. In other countries, where population densities in inhabited regions are high, people live in closer quarters and can feel "lonely" or isolated in larger spaces. In Japan and Europe, most people live in spaces that by American standards would be called cramped. Similarly, people from different cultures have different ideas about what constitutes appropriate distances for various interactions. Recall that in the dominant culture of the United States, the closest

Latin American and Anglo American Use of Personal Space in Public Places

by Elizabeth Lozano

How we use space and how we expect others to treat the space around us are determined by our culture. In this excerpt the author focuses our attention on the ways in which the body is understood and treated by Latin Americans and Anglo Americans and the cultural differences that become apparent when these two cultural groups find themselves sharing common space.

It is 6:00 P.M. The Bayfront, a shopping mall near a Miami marina, reverberates with the noise and movement of people, coming and going, contemplating the lights of the bay, sampling exotic juice blends, savoring the not-so-exotic foods from Cuba, Nicaragua, or Mexico, and listening to the bands. The Bayfront provides an environment for the exercise of two different rituals: the Anglo American visit to the mall and the Latin American paseo, the visit to the outdoor spaces of the city.

Some of the people sitting in the plaza look insistently at me, making comments, laughing, and whispering. Instead of feeling uneasy or surprised, I find myself looking back at them, entering this inquisitive game and asking myself some of the same questions they might be asking. Who are they, where are they from, what are they up to? I follow their gaze and I see it extend to other groups. The gaze is returned by some in the crowd, so that a play of silent dialogue seems to grow amidst the anonymity of the crowd. The crowd that participates in this complicity of wandering looks is not Anglo American. The play of looks described above has a different "accent," a Hispanic accent, which reveals a different understanding of the plaza and public space.

The Anglo American passers-by understand their vital space, their relationship with strangers, and their public interactions in a different manner. If I address them in the street, I better assume that I am confronting them in an alley. But when I am walking by myself along the halls of a Hispanic mall, I am not alone. I do not expect, therefore, to be treated by others as if they were suddenly confronting me in a dark alley. I am in a crowd, with the crowd, and anyone there has access to my attention.

Anglo Americans are alone (even in the middle of the crowd) if they choose to be, for they have a guaranteed cultural right to be "left alone" on their way to and from anywhere. To approach or touch someone without that person's consent is a violation of a fundamental right within Anglo-Saxon, Protestant cultural tradition. This is the right to one's own body as private property. Within this tradition, touching is understood as an excursion into someone else's territory. With this in mind then, it is understandable that Anglo Americans excuse themselves when they accidentally touch someone or come close to doing so. To accidentally penetrate someone else's boundary (especially if that person is a stranger) demands an apology, and a willingness to repair the damage by stepping back from the violated territory.

One can see how rude a Latin American might appear to an Anglo American when the former distractingly touches another person without apologizing or showing

boundary of personal space is about 18 inches, although men are usually more comfortable being further apart. In Middle Eastern cultures, however, men move much closer to other men when they are talking (Samovar et al., 2010). Thus, when an Egyptian man talks with an American man, one of the two is likely to be uncomfortable. Either the American will feel uncomfortable and encroached upon, or the Egyptian will feel isolated and too distant for serious conversation. But we don't have to leave the North American continent to see variations in the way uses of space may differ. In the "Diverse Voices" box in this chapter, notice how Latin American and Anglo American spatial usage differs.

concern. But within Latino and Mediterranean traditions, the body is not understood as property. That is, the body is not understood as belonging to its owner. It does not belong to me or to anyone else; it is, in principle, public. It is an expressive and sensual region open to the scrutiny, discipline, and sanction of the community. It is, therefore, quite impossible to be "left alone" on the Latin American street. For Latin Americans, the access to others in a public space is not restricted by the "privacy" of their bodies. Thus, the Latin American does not find casual contact a form of property trespassing or a violation of rights. Walking the street in the Anglo United States is very much an anonymous activity to be performed in a field of unobstructive and invisible bodies. Since one is essentially carrying one's own space into the public sphere, no one is actually ever in public. Given that the public is private, no intimacy is granted in the public space. Thus while the Latin American public look or gaze is round, inquisitive, and wandering, the Anglo American is straight, nonobstructive, and neutral.

Civility requires the Anglo American to restrict looks, delimit gestures, and orient movement. Civility requires the Latin American to acknowledge looks, gestures, and movement and actively engage with them. For the Latin American, the unavoidable nature of shared space is always a demand for attention and a request to participate. An Anglo American considers "mind your own business" to be fair and civil. A Latin American might find this an unreasonable restriction. What takes place in public is everybody's business by the very fact that it is taking place in public.

One can understand the possible cultural misunderstandings between Anglo Americans and Latin Americans. If Anglo Americans protest the "impertinence" of Latin Americans as nosy and curious, Latin Americans would protest the indifference and lack of concern of Anglo Americans. The scene in the Miami mall could happen just as easily in Los Angeles, Chicago, Philadelphia, or New York, cities in which Latin Americans comprise an important segment of the population. The influence of this cultural heritage is going to have growing influence in the next few decades on the Anglo American scene, as Hispanics become the largest ethnic and linguistic minority in the United States. The more knowledge we can gain from what makes us culturally diverse, the more we will be able to appreciate what unifies us through the mixing and mutual exchanges of our cultures.

Excerpted from Lozano, E. (2007). The cultural experience of space and body: A reading of Latin American and Anglo American comportment in public. In A. Gonzalez, M. Houston, & V. Chen (Eds.), *Our Voices: Essays in Culture, Ethnicity, and Communication: An Intercultural Anthology* (4th ed., pp. 274–280). New York: Oxford University Press.

For Consideration:

1. How comfortable would you be on South Street in Miami? Would you be more or less comfortable having read this article?
2. What do you think about the author's following statement?

   But within Latino and Mediterranean traditions, the body is not understood as property. That is, the body is not understood as belonging to its owner. It does not belong to me or to anyone else; it is, in principle, public. It is an expressive and sensual region open to the scrutiny, discipline, and sanction of the community.

   How well does that reaction map onto the author's dichotomy that contrasts Anglo American concepts of space with Latin American ones?

Unfortunately, there are times when one person intentionally violates the space expectations of another, usually in the context of gender variations regarding personal space. When the violation is between members of the opposite sex, it may be considered sexual harassment. For instance, Glen may, through violations of informal space, "come on" to Donnice. If Donnice does not welcome the attention, she may feel threatened. In this case, Glen's nonverbal behavior may be construed as sexual harassment. To avoid perceptions of harassment, people need to be especially sensitive to others' definitions of intimate space.

The objects and artifacts that people treasure and display in their territories differ by culture. What constitutes art is a function of culture, as are certain decorating aesthetics. Chinese and Japanese approaches to interior design follow feng shui, the ancient Chinese approach of arranging objects to achieve harmony in one's environment. Rooms arranged according to these principles communicate messages that are different from rooms arranged according to other design principles. Even the meanings that we assign to colors vary among cultures, mostly because of religious beliefs. In India, white, not black, is the color of mourning, and Hindu brides wear red. In Latin America, purple signifies death, and in Japan, green denotes youth and energy.

Variations in Self-Presentation Cues

The self-presentation cues of physical appearance, time perception and orientation, and olfactory communication also vary widely by culture and across gender lines.

First, standards of physical appearance and beauty vary widely by culture and gender. For example, in India and Pakistan, both females and males who are more heavy-set in appearance are considered more attractive than is socially acceptable in the United States, where being thin and/or physically fit is considered the standard of physical attractiveness. Conversely, in Japan, even more emphasis is placed on being thin than in the United States, which has resulted in a severe occurrence of anorexia and bulimia among teenage girls, rivaling an already serious problem in America. In terms of body decoration, cultures vary greatly as to how much or how little decoration is considered appropriate. In the United States, women's clothing and accessories are more decorative, while men's clothing and accessories are more functional. Think of the variety of clothing and accessories aimed at women: shoes and purses in every color and style; jewelry for ears, neck, wrists, ankles, toes, and clothing; hair decorations; decorative belts and scarves; patterned hose and colorful socks; not to mention the enormous variety of clothing itself. While the accessory options for men are increasing, the emphasis on decorative accessories for men remains minimal. Religious customs also influence how people, especially adult women, present themselves. Many Muslim women follow the traditions of Islam by wearing modest clothing and covering their hair when in public. It is also customary for orthodox Jewish women to cover their hair with either a scarf or wig when in public. In India, most married Hindi women wear the bindi, a customary red dot between the eyes, as a sign of fidelity in marriage. Sikh men do not cut their hair and wear a dastar (turban) as a sign of Sikh identity.

Second, not only can cultures can be monochronic or polychronic with respect to time, but they also differ in their orientations to time. Some cultures are past oriented, some present, and some future. For example, China is oriented toward the past and so adherence to tradition, respect for elders, and ancestor worship are widely regarded as appropriate. The United States is considered to be oriented toward the present and near future so businesses emphasize short-term profits. People "live in the moment" and are always on the lookout for the "next big thing."

Finally, while cultural and gender variations are not great with regard to the olfactory aspect of nonverbal communication, there are some points worth noting. The fact that certain scents are marketed differently to men and women in colognes and perfumes does show different expectations or stereotypes about male and female preferences. In some cultures, artificial scents from colognes and perfumes are considered annoying, while in other cultures, such as the dominant United States culture, natural body odors are offensive.

Guidelines for Improving Nonverbal Messages

Sending Nonverbal Messages

1. Be mindful of the nonverbal behavior you are displaying. Remember that you are always communicating nonverbally. Some nonverbal cues will always be subconscious, but you should work to bring more of your nonverbal behaviors into your conscious awareness. Paying attention to what you are doing with your eyes, face, posture, gestures, voice, use of space, and appearance, as well as your handling of time and scents, allows you to adjust your nonverbal behavior so that it is appropriate. To help you develop mindfulness, you might ask a friend to give you feedback about how well your nonverbal behaviors compliment your verbal messages.

2. Adapt your nonverbal behaviors to your purpose. Choose to display nonverbal behavior appropriate to your interaction goals. For instance, if you want to persuade your partner to your way of thinking, you should adopt nonverbal cues that demonstrate confidence and credibility. These may include direct eye contact, a serious facial expression, a relaxed posture, a loud and low-pitched voice with no vocal interferences, and professional clothing and grooming. If you want to communicate empathy and support, you would use different nonverbal behaviors, including a moderate gaze, caring facial expressions, posture in which you lean toward the other, a soft voice, and touch.

3. Adapt your nonverbal behavior to the situation. Situations vary in their formality, familiarity, and purpose. Just as you would select different language for different situations, you should adapt your nonverbal messages to the situation. Assess what the situation calls for in terms of body motions, paralanguage, spatial usage, artifacts, physical appearance, and use of time and scents. Of course, you already do some situational adapting with nonverbal communication. You wouldn't dress the same way for a wedding as you would to walk the dog. You would not treat your brother's territory the same way you would treat your doctor's territory. But the more you can consciously adapt your nonverbal behaviors to what seems appropriate to the situation, the more effective you will be as a communicator.

4. Align your nonverbal cues with your verbal communication. When we presented the functions of nonverbal communication earlier in this chapter, we explained how nonverbal communication may contradict verbal communication, creating a mixed message. Effective interpersonal communicators try to avoid mixed messages. It is important to make your verbal and nonverbal messages match, yet it is also important that the various types of nonverbal cues should complement each other. If you are telling your friend that you feel sad, a soft and less expressive voice will complement your words. Similarly, your friend will expect your facial expression to convey sadness and will be confused if you smile brightly, using the facial signals for happiness. People get confused and frustrated when they have to interpret inconsistent verbal and nonverbal messages.

5. Eliminate nonverbal behaviors that distract from your verbal message. Fidgeting, tapping fingers or feet, pacing, mumbling, head nodding, and vocal interferences (e.g., ums, ers, you knows, etc.) send messages that influence the way your partner interprets your message. While controlling the nonverbal cues that telegraph nervousness, impatience, and disapproval can be difficult, it is important to try so that our partners are not distracted from our meaning.

A QUESTION OF ETHICS ● What Would You Do?

After the intramural mixed-doubles matches on Tuesday evening, most of the players adjourned to the campus grill to have a drink and chat. Although the group was highly competitive on the courts, they enjoyed socializing and talking about the matches for a while before they went home. Marquez and Lisa, who had been paired together at the start of the season, sat down with another couple, Barry and Elana, who had been going out together for several weeks. Marquez and Lisa had played a particularly grueling match that night against Barry and Elana, a match that they lost largely because of Elana's improved play.

"Elana, your serve today was the best I've seen it this year," Marquez said.

"Yeah, I was really impressed. And as you saw, I had trouble handling it," Lisa added.

"And you're getting to the net a lot better too," Marquez added.

"Thanks, guys," Elana said with gratitude. "I've really been working on it."

"Well, aren't we getting the compliments today," sneered Barry in a sarcastic tone. Then after a pause, he said, "Oh, Elana, would you get my sweater? I left it on that chair by the other table."

"Come on, Barry. You're closer than I am," Elana replied.

Barry got a cold look on his face, moved slightly closer to Elana, and said emphatically, "Get my sweater for me, Elana—now."

Elana quickly backed away from Barry as she said, "OK, Barry—it's cool." Then she quickly got the sweater for him.

"Gee, isn't she sweet?" Barry said to Marquez and Lisa as he grabbed the sweater from Elana.

Lisa and Marquez both looked down at the floor. Then Lisa glanced at Marquez and said, "Well, I'm out of here—I've got a lot to do this evening."

"Let me walk you to your car," Marquez said as he stood up.

"See you next week," they said in unison as they hurried out the door, leaving Barry and Elana alone at the table.

For Consideration:

1. What ethical principles are violated in this case?
2. Analyze Barry's nonverbal behavior. What was he attempting to achieve?
3. How do you interpret Lisa's and Marquez's nonverbal reactions to Barry?
4. Was Barry's behavior ethically acceptable? Explain.

Interpreting Nonverbal Messages

1. Be mindful that most nonverbal cues are not emblems. Most gestures have no set meanings. They vary from person to person and culture to culture. Just because you fidget when you are lying, doesn't mean that others do. What is a loud, angry tone for one person may be a normal paralanguage level for another person. The more you interact with someone, the more you will learn how to read the nonverbal cues sent. Even then, quick interpretations and rapid conclusions about the meaning of another's nonverbal cues can lead to misunderstandings.

2. Recognize culture, gender, and other speech community diversity when interpreting nonverbal cues. As you gain intercultural competence, you will become more accurate in interpreting others' nonverbal cues.

3. Attend to all of the nonverbal cues and their relationship to the verbal message. Do not take nonverbal cues out of context. In any one interaction, you are likely to get simultaneous messages from a person's eyes, face, gestures, posture, voice, spatial usage, and touch. Most nonverbal cues occur in conjunction with verbal messages. By taking into consideration all the channels of communication, you will more effectively interpret the messages of others.

4. Use the skill of perception checking. The skill of perception checking, introduced in Chapter 2, lets you see if your interpretation of another person's message is accurate or not. It is especially useful for testing your interpretation of nonverbal messages. By describing the nonverbal behavior you have noticed and tentatively sharing your interpretation of it, you can receive confirmation or correction of your interpretation. For instance, suppose a person smiles and nods her head when you tell her about a mistake she has made. Before you conclude that the person agrees with your observation and accepts your criticism, you might say, "From the smile on your face and your nodding, I get the impression that you had already recognized a problem here, or am I off base?" Perception checking should also be used when you are not sure of the cultural or gender norms surrounding specific nonverbal cues. Perception checking is critical when the person's verbal message and nonverbal cues contradict each other.

Summary

Nonverbal communication is the term commonly used to describe all human communication events that transcend spoken or written words. It includes how actions, vocal tone, and other things create meanings that stand alone, support, modify, or contradict the meaning of a verbal message. The characteristics of nonverbal communication are that it varies in intentionality, and it is ambiguous, primary, continuous, and multichanneled. The functions of nonverbal communication are that it provides information, regulates interactions, expresses or hides emotions, presents an image, and conveys power.

There are different types of nonverbal communication. Perhaps the most familiar type of nonverbal communication is body language, how a person communicates using eye contact, facial expression, gesture, posture, and touch. A second type of nonverbal communication is paralanguage, which includes our use of pitch, volume, rate, quality, and intonation to give special meaning to the words we use. These vocal characteristics help us interpret the meaning of a verbal message, whereas vocal interferences ("ah," "um," "you know," and "like") often impede a listener's ability to understand. A third type of nonverbal communication is spatial usage. People communicate through the use of physical space, acoustic space, posture and body orientation, and territory. We also communicate through artifacts, such as personal possessions and the ways we arrange and decorate our space. The final type of nonverbal communication is self-presentation cues, including personal appearance, use of time, and choice of scents and smells.

The many types of nonverbal communication may vary depending on the individual's culture and gender. As a result, our body language, paralanguage, spatial usage, and self-presentation cues may differ considerably. You can improve the nonverbal messages that you send by being mindful of the nonverbal behavior you are displaying, adapting your nonverbal behaviors to your purpose, adapting your nonverbal behavior to the situation, aligning your nonverbal cues with your verbal message, and eliminating nonverbal behaviors that distract from your verbal message. You can improve the accuracy of your interpretations of others' nonverbal communication by being mindful that most nonverbal cues are not emblems; by recognizing culture, gender, and other speech community diversity in the use of nonverbal cues; attending to all the nonverbal cues and their relationship to the verbal message; and by using the skill of perception checking.

Chapter Resources

What You Should Be Able *to Explain:*

- The characteristics of nonverbal messages
- The functions of nonverbal messages
- The types and meanings of body motions in messages
- The types and meanings of paralanguage in messages
- The types and meanings of physical space in messages
- The types and meanings of self-presentation
- Cultural and gender differences in nonverbal behavior
- How to improve the nonverbal messages you send and interpret the nonverbal messages you receive

What You Should Be Able *to Do:*

- Follow the guidelines for sending and interpreting nonverbal messages
- Use the skill of perception checking to verify the meaning of nonverbal messages

Self-test questions based on these concepts are available on the companion Web site (www.oup.com/us/verderber) as part of Chapter 5 resources.

Key Words

Flashcards for all of these key terms are available on the *Inter-Act* Web site.

Acoustic space, p. 141
Artifacts, p. 142
Body language, p. 135
Body orientation, p. 138
Emblems, p. 137
Emoticons, p. 137
Eye contact, p. 136
Facial expression, p. 137

Gesture, p. 137
Intonation, p. 140
Kinesics, p. 135
Nonverbal communication, p. 131
Olfactory cues, p. 145
Paralanguage, p. 139
Personal space, p. 140
Pitch, p. 139

Posture, p. 137
Proxemics, p. 140
Quality, p. 139
Rate, p. 139
Territory, p. 142
Touch, p. 138
Vocal interferences, p. 140
Volume, p. 139

Apply Your Knowledge

The following questions challenge you to demonstrate your mastery of the concepts, theories, and frameworks in this chapter by using them to explain what is happening in a specific situation.

> *Jesa and Madison were lounging on a blanket in the quad one spring afternoon, enjoying the sun as they reviewed for the upcoming test in their art history course, when Jesa jerked her head around, bolted upright, quickly gathered her things, and quietly said, "See you back upstairs." With that, she took off toward their building at a fast clip.*
>
> *Madison quickly glanced in the direction that Jesa had been looking just before she bolted and shouted, "Wait a sec. I'm coming too."*
>
> *Once they were back in their apartment, Madison sighed and said, "Okay, Jesa, what's really going on with you? Who was that guy? And why are you acting so scared?"*
>
> *"What guy? I don't know what you're talking about," mumbled Jesa looking down at her feet. "And I'm not scared," she added as she turned to the window, pulled back the corner of the curtain, and peeked down into the quad.*

5.1 How is each of the characteristics of nonverbal behavior exemplified in this scene?

5.2 Do you think that Jesa was telling the truth? How does her nonverbal behavior support your conclusion?

Skill Practice

Skill practice activities give you the chance to rehearse a new skill by responding to hypothetical or real situations. Additional skill practice activities are available at the companion Web site.

Perception Check

Recall the three steps of perception checking before beginning this activity:
(1) watch the behavior of another; (2) ask yourself what the behavior means to you; and

(3) describe the behavior and interpret the nonverbal elements in words. Provide a perception check for each of the following situations.

5.3   Perception check:

   a. *Larry walks into the cubicle, throws his report across the desk, smiles, and loudly proclaims, "Well, that's that!"*

5.4   Perception check:

   b. *Christie, dressed in her team uniform, with her hair flying every which way, charges into the room, and announces in a loud voice, "I'm here, and I'm ready."*

5.5   Perception check:

   c. *It was dinner time, and Anthony was due home from work at any minute. Suddenly the door flies open, banging against its hinges, and Anthony stomps in. Crossing the room in three long strides, he plops onto the sofa, folds his arms, and with a sour expression stares straight ahead.*

Communication Improvement Plan: Nonverbal Communication

5.6   How can you improve your nonverbal behavior? Identify a problem you have with nonverbal message cues. Review the guidelines for improving nonverbal messages. Select at least one of these as a goal. Then using the interpersonal communication skills you have studied in the course, write a communication improvement plan. You can find a communication improvement plan worksheet on our Web site at www.oup.com/us/verderber.

Inter-Act with Media

Television

Hell's Kitchen (2010)

Featured on FOX and hosted by celebrity chef Gordon Ramsay, *Hell's Kitchen* is a reality-television cooking competition. The program format features two teams of chefs that compete in various cooking challenges. When a small number of chefs remain after others are eliminated, the two teams combine to become a single team whose members also compete individually. Throughout a series of food service challenges including a full restaurant dinner service, the teams must prepare food to Chef Ramsay's demanding expectations. The teams must do this all within a very limited amount of time. Ramsay supervises the chefs and sends only the most perfect preparations to the dining room. He regularly throws away an entire plate of food due to one minor issue (e.g., too much salt or ugly garnish) and requires the team to re-prepare the dish. During dinner service, the underperforming chef or team must endure Ramsay's storm of verbal insults and obscenities. He often screams in the faces of poorly performing chefs, chucks items in the kitchen, and at times throws chefs out of the kitchen.

IPC Concepts: Nonverbal communication, body language, paralanguage, artifacts, personal space, acoustic space.

To the Point:

> What specific recommendations would you give to Chef Ramsay to improve his communication with others?
>
> When are we more likely to violate the personal space of others?
>
> What nonverbal communication behaviors best reinforce the emotions that we attempt to verbally communicate?

Cinema

21 (2008). Robert Luketic (director). Jim Sturgess, Kate Bosworth, Laurence Fishburne, Kevin Spacey.

MIT student Ben Campbell (Sturgess) needs to earn additional tuition money and signs on as a member of an undercover student card-counting team in Vegas. He quickly learns the lingo of counting and memorizes many of the nonverbal gestures that are necessary for effective communication among team members. Folded arms refer to a table as hot; a touch to the eye means, "We need to talk"; and when a hand is placed on the forehead, the deck is cooling off. The most serious gesture—fingers through the hair—means, "Get out now." Cole Williams (Fishburne), chief of security, catches Ben who, unknown to Ben, has an old feud with Rosa. Ben and his team must change any and all outward signals. Throughout the movie, nonverbal signals such as glances and gestures play a meaningful part of the action of both communication and deception necessary to win at this level of competition.

IPC Concepts: Functions of nonverbal communication, gesture, eye contact, touch, physical appearance.

To the Point:

> How might a person's gestures and eye contact suggest that he or she is attempting to engage in deception?
>
> In your opinion, which nonverbal communication cues can transmit the most information to a receiver?

What's on the Web

Find links and additional material, including self-quizzes, on the companion Web site at www.oup.com/us/verderber.

Communication in the Life Cycle of Relationships

"Kai, wasn't that Brian I saw you with again? I thought you've been dating Ben."

"Yeah, I was hanging out with Brian, but we're just friends."

"Just friends! Come on, girl, I see you with him a lot. Are you sure he doesn't think it's serious between the two of you?"

"Terrell, I see him a lot because I am really able to talk with him. We're just comfortable with each other. But before you get too worried about his feelings, he and Amber are getting pretty close."

"And she doesn't mind you spending time with him? Are you sure you're not just kidding yourself?"

"Hey, I don't know if she minds, but Brian and I just aren't together—there's no chemistry. Actually, he's more like a brother to me. I tell him my problems as well as what's going right with me. He's been a lot of help. And he talks with me about his problems, too. It's great to have a close guy friend to confide in. If something happened between us, I'd really miss him."

What you should be able *to* explain after you have studied this chapter:

- The functions communication plays in relationships
- How relationships change
- Types of relationships

- Dimensions of relationships
- How self-disclosure and feedback work in relationships
- How relationships begin
- How relationships develop
- How relationships are sustained

- The dialectical tensions in relationships and how to manage them
- Turning points in relationships
- How relationships deteriorate and end

Relationship—a set of expectations two people have for each other based on their pattern of interaction.

Good relationship—a relationship in which the interactions are satisfying and healthy for those involved.

Abusive relationship—a relationship in which the interactions are physically, mentally, or emotionally harmful to one or both partners.

Kai is lucky because she has someone she can really talk with—she has a healthy relationship. A **relationship** is a set of expectations two people have for each other based on their pattern of interaction (Littlejohn & Foss, 2011). Some relationships are good, while others are abusive. A **good relationship** is a relationship in which the interactions are satisfying and healthy for those involved. An **abusive relationship** is a relationship in which the interactions are physically, mentally, or emotionally harmful to one or both partners. Abusive relationships take many forms, but all are characterized by unhealthy patterns of communication. The interpersonal skills you will learn in this course can help you start, build, and sustain healthy relationships with others and they can help you gracefully end relationships when necessary. However, while improving the communication skills of partners can help to improve abusive relationships, in general, most abusive relationships also require intense professional intervention including individual and couple counseling.

Most of us intuitively understand that relationships require work. Good relationships do not just happen, nor do they grow and sustain themselves automatically. Partners must invest time and effort in sustaining their relationships or they will deteriorate (Canary & Dainton, 2002). In this chapter you will see that without communication we couldn't have relationships. Specifically you will study the ways that communication functions in relationships. Then you will learn about the various ways that relationships differ and can be categorized. Next, you'll come to understand how relationships change during their life cycles.

Finally, you will study each stage in the life cycle of a relationship, examining the issues that require effective communication if the relationship is to be satisfying and healthy for you and your partner.

The Functions of Communication in a Relationship

Communication has three main functions or purposes in a relationship. First, communication forms or constitutes our relationships—it is how we "do" our relationships. Second, communication is instrumental: We use communication to get things done with our relationship partner. Third, communication provides an index or measure of our relationship. It signals the state of our relationship. Let's take a closer look at each of these functions.

The Constitutive Function

How do you do or perform your relationships? At first glance, this may seem like a strange question. When we say that communication serves a **constitutive function**, we mean that the communication messages that are exchanged in a relationship form it. Put another way, a relationship consists of the sum of all of the messages partners have exchanged. Whenever you talk with a relationship partner, the meanings you share become part of your relationship. If we use a piece of cloth as a metaphor for a relationship, then the relationship has been woven from the messages that have been exchanged. Each time you send or receive a message, you add a thread to the fabric of your relationship. Just as each thread adds color and texture and affects the strength of the fabric, so too our messages interweave to create the type and quality of the relationship we have with someone. Think about the two people whom you consider closest to you. Would you say that you have the same exact relationship with each of these people? Probably not. Why? Because each relationship is unique. It is the sum and substance of what you have shared with each other and that differs from person to person, from relationship to relationship, and within one relationship from one time to another. Some of our relationships are created with rich, confirming interactions that are healthy for both partners. Other relationships are fraught with tense interactions and unresolved arguments that create friction between partners. So, the relationships that you have with others come about through your interactions.

> **Constitutive function**—the communication messages exchanged in a relationship form the relationship.

The Instrumental Function

How do you get your relationship partner to do something? When we say that communication serves an **instrumental function** in a relationship we mean that the communication messages exchanged in a relationship are the means through which we accomplish our personal and our relationship goals. Communicating is how we get things done. We send messages hoping that our relationship partners will help us accomplish our goals. Our personal goals may vary from simple to difficult: conveying information, planning activities, negotiating expectations and responsibilities, managing conflict, and conveying

> **Instrumental function**—the communication messages exchanged in a relationship are the means through which we accomplish our personal and our relationship goals.

support when our partners face difficulties. If a metaphor for the constitutive function of communication is weaving cloth, then the metaphor that would describe the instrumental function is a toolbox with different tools that we pull out at the appropriate time to accomplish our purposes. Learning communication skills and developing behavioral flexibility increase our competence by giving us tools that we can use when we need them. The greater our skill with a particular tool, the better we are able to fully craft our messages and the more likely it is that we will accomplish our goals. For example, Zack needs to go home because his dad is having surgery next week. But he can't take his dog because his younger sister is allergic to dogs. He would like to leave his dog with Maggie, his girlfriend. How does he accomplish this? He can promise, bargain, appeal to her emotions, or use some other message strategy to convince her to keep the dog. But to accomplish his purpose, he will have to effectively communicate his need. How competently he communicates his desire will not only determine whether his girlfriend agrees to keep his dog, but it may also affect the relationship itself.

At times we also use communication as the instrument to change our relationships. For example, if you are sexually attracted to a friend, you might initiate a "relationship talk" with the hope of changing it from a platonic friendship into a romantic relationship. When you no longer want to be in the romantic relationship, you will have to break up with that person and again you will communicate to accomplish this relationship goal. We also mend our relationships when we talk through problems and transgressions that have damaged them.

The Indexical Function

How do you measure the health or status of your relationship? When we say that communication serves an **indexical function** in relationships, we mean that embedded in exchanged messages are measures of who is in control, how much partners trust each other, and the level of intimacy in the relationship (Millar & Rogers, 1976). One level of a message transmits the content of what is said. For example, Trey, talking with his high school son, demands, "I need to see your homework." The content of the message is that this father wants his son to show him the homework that he was supposed to have completed. But on another level, the father is asserting control over his son. Notice, he doesn't ask to see the homework, he makes a demand. If the son responds, "O.K., here it is," then the form of this exchange demonstrates that the son accepts his father's control of the relationship. If, however, the son replies, "I don't need you looking over my work. I'm almost 18," then the son has rejected his father's control move and is signaling his own desire to control the relationship. This level of message not only indexes who is dominant or whether there is a power struggle in the relationship, it also indicates how much faith or confidence partners place in each other and how close and warm their relationship is. By demanding to see his son's homework, the father in our example signals that he doesn't trust the son to truthfully respond to a simple query, "Have you finished your homework?"

Indexical function—embedded in the communication messages that are exchanged in a relationship are measures of who is in control, how much partners trust each other, and the level of intimacy in the relationship.

or to have completed his assignments without the father checking up on him. A metaphor for the indexical function of communication would be a thermometer that measures the temperature of the relationship. It may change slowly or abruptly. It may vary only slightly, or it might have wide swings. But in all cases, the communication between partners provides a measure of the control, trust, and intimacy in the relationship.

Describing Relationships

At the most basic level all relationships are either impersonal or personal, either voluntary or involuntary, and either platonic or romantic.

First, relationships vary in their intensity from impersonal to personal (La-Follette, 1996). An **impersonal relationship** is a relationship in which you relate to another person merely because the other fills a role that satisfies an immediate need. For instance, at a restaurant Emma may prefer a particular server, but she will be satisfied if whoever waits on her does it competently. By contrast, a **personal relationship** is one in which people care about each other, share at least some personal information, and meet at least some of each other's interpersonal needs. So if Carlos and Derek are teammates who enjoy talking about *World of Warcraft* as they work out together, they have a personal relationship.

Second, while some of our relationships are **voluntary relationships**—we freely choose the people with whom we interact—others are **involuntary relationships**—we have no choice about the other people with whom we interact. For example, you choose your friends, but not your family, co-workers, managers, or customers. Carla may not like her sister-in-law, but because she loves her brother, she has a relationship with his wife.

Third, some relationships are **platonic relationships** in which partners are not sexually attracted to each other or choose not to act on their sexual attraction. Others are **romantic relationships** in which partners act on their mutual sexual attraction. Although what you will learn in this course will be useful for all relationships, in this book we will focus our discussion on personal relationships—voluntary and involuntary, platonic and romantic.

Types of Relationships

We also describe our relationships by our familiarity with or closeness to our partners. We differentiate among our relationships with others, thinking of them as acquaintances, friends, or close friends/intimates.

Acquaintances

Acquaintances are people we know by name and talk to when the opportunity arises but with whom our interactions are limited. Many of your acquaintance relationships grow out of a particular context. You become acquainted with those who live in your apartment building, dorm, or the house next door, who sit next to you in class, who go to your place of worship, or who belong to the same club. For example, Melinda and Paige are acquaintances. They met in biology class

Impersonal relationship—a relationship in which one person relates to another merely because the other fills a role that satisfies an immediate need.

Personal relationship—a relationship in which people care about each other, share at least some personal information with each other, and meet at least some of each other's interpersonal needs.

Voluntary relationship—a relationship in which we freely choose the people with whom we interact.

Involuntary relationship—a relationship in which we have no choice about the other people with whom we interact.

Platonic relationship—a relationship in which partners are not sexually attracted to each other or choose not to act on their sexual attraction.

Romantic relationship—relationships in which partners act on their mutual sexual attraction to each other.

INTER-ACT WITH SOCIAL MEDIA

Log on to your Facebook account and scan your list of friends. Think about the type of relationship that you have with each individual. Can you place individuals in categories that reflect the nature of your relationship? Do you have more acquaintances, friend or close friends/intimates?

Acquaintances—people we know by name and talk to when the opportunity arises but with whom our interactions are limited.

and talk regularly with each other about class-related topics, but they haven't shared any personal information or ideas, and they haven't made plans to meet outside of class.

Friends

Friends—people with whom we have voluntary personal relationships characterized by equality, mutual involvement, reciprocal liking, self-disclosure, and reciprocal social support.

Some acquaintances become our friends. **Friends** are people with whom we have voluntary personal relationships characterized by equality, mutual involvement, reciprocal liking, self-disclosure, and reciprocal social support (Fehr, 1996). As your friendships develop, you spend less time on small talk or task-related information sharing, and more of your interactions center on personal topics. For example, as the semester progresses, Melinda and Paige continued to sit next to each other in biology class. They began to talk about non-class-related topics and found that each of them enjoys Pilates, so they began going to a campus Pilates class together. As they continued to discover other things they had in common and found that they enjoyed each other's company, they slowly became friends who looked forward to the time they spent together.

Some of our friendships are context bound. For example, you may have soccer friends, work friends, or college friends. Because these context friendships exist within a limited situation, your work friends may never meet your college friends—and these friendships may fade when the context changes. For instance, close high school friends may lose touch if they go to different colleges, choose different careers, or if one friend leaves the area.

Intimates or Close Friends

Intimates or close friends—those few people with whom we share a high degree of interdependence, commitment, disclosure, affection, understanding, and trust.

Public opinion polls consistently show that the number one thing that gives meaning to people's lives is their close personal relationships (Moore, 2003). **Intimates** or **close friends** are those few people with whom we share a high degree of interdependence, commitment, disclosure, affection, understanding, and trust. Research suggests that although people may have up to 150 relationships, they have 10 to 20 close friends and intimates (Gladwell, 2000; Parks, 2007). In very intimate relationships, there is a fusion of self and other to the point where each person's self-concept tends to become closely related to the other person. In other words, you define who you are in part through your most intimate relationships (Aron, Aron, Tudor, & Nelson, 2004). This is why it is so painful when intimate relationships end.

Research shows that women and men tend to differ regarding the factors that lead to close friendships. This may be because society teaches women and men to behave differently to follow norms of femininity and masculinity. Women tend to develop close relationships with others through talking, disclosing personal history, and sharing personal feelings. Women seem to develop their sense of "we-ness" by gaining this knowledge of the innermost being of their partner. Men tend to develop close friendships through joint activities, doing favors for each other, and successive tests of how dependable their friend is. When asked to define a close friend, men are less likely than women to mention someone with whom they can share feelings. For men, close friends are the people they can depend on to help them out of a jam and the people with whom they regularly choose to pursue enjoyable activities (Wood & Inman, 1993). It is important to note that these differences are more pronounced in same-sex friendships. When men and women develop close friendships or intimate relationships with each other, these distinctions usually disappear.

In Chapter 13 you will learn more about communicating in intimate relationships, including those with friends, spouses, and families.

Dimensions of Relationships

Personal relationships are complex. Therefore, we need to understand their basic dimensions or aspects and how these vary from the beginning to the end of the relationship. In general, relationships develop as these dimensions increase and deteriorate as they decrease. Relationships vary on interdependence, breadth, depth, commitment, predictability, communication code change and shared social networks (Parks, 2007), and trust. Let's take a look at each dimension:

   1. Interdependence. Relationships vary in **interdependence**—the extent to which partners rely on each other to meet their needs. The more interdependent the partners, the more each partner's behavior will affect the other. When you first meet someone, you are independent. Neither of you expects the other to go out of his or her way to help. Likewise, as you are just getting to know people, you are less likely to be swayed by their opinion, adapt your behavior to please them, or depend on them to meet your needs. But when you are intimate with someone, you are both more likely to consider each other's preferences, make joint decisions, and mutually rely on the other.

   2. Breadth. Relationships vary in their **breadth**, the variety of conversational topics and activities that are shared by partners, as well as the number of contexts in which they interact. If you meet someone on a blind date where you go to a movie and then for a drink, you may find your conversation centering on your opinions of that movie and others you've seen. But as your relationship develops, you may share your political and moral viewpoints and talk about your families, personal histories, and previous relationships. You may begin to study together, hang out on weekends, or even do wash together. The increased time you spend together will lead you to discuss other topics and to see your partner in other contexts.

   3. Depth. Relationships vary in **depth**, which is how intimate the partners have become through disclosing personal and private information. Generally, as your relationship with someone develops, you and your partner are more willing to disclose private information, mutual disclosure that helps deepen your relationship as you come to know each other better. While this is the normal course of relationship development, some of us have had the unfortunate experience of sitting next to a stranger on a bus, train, or airplane who was emotionally distraught and used us to talk through a painful situation.

   4. Commitment. Relationships vary in terms of how dedicated or loyal partners are to each other. **Commitment** is how obligated partners feel to continue the relationship. Committed partners feel obliged to continue the relationship.

Interdependence—a dimension of relationships that gauges the extent to which partners rely on each other to meet their needs.

Breadth—a dimension of relationships that gauges the variety of conversational topics and activities that partners share, as well as the number of contexts in which they interact.

Depth—a dimension of relationships that gauges how intimate the partners have become through disclosing personal and private information.

Commitment—a dimension of relationships that gauges how dedicated or loyal partners are to each other.

In a relationship, you may feel committed to your partner because you enjoy being with him or her; therefore you have a personal desire to continue the relationship. In addition, you may feel a moral commitment to the relationship and feel guilty if you think about ending it. For example, if you have had a friend since grade school, you may feel compelled to continue your relationship. Sometimes there may be external forces or structural reasons to be committed to the relationship. For instance, a legally binding relationship such as a marriage or a shared apartment lease may increase your sense of commitment. If you have a child with someone, even if your romantic relationship ends, for the sake of your child, you may feel obligated to maintain some type of functional relationship with the other parent.

Understanding and predictability—a dimension of relationships that gauges how well partners understand and can predict each other's behaviors.

5. **Understanding and predictability.** Relationships vary in the extent to which there is **understanding and predictability**, how well partners understand and can predict each other's behaviors. The closer you become to your partners, the better you know them, knowledge that reduces uncertainty and enables you to predict how your partners will feel and act in a particular situation. Over time, you become experts about each other's feelings and behaviors. This is why couples who have been married for years are able to anticipate each other's needs and finish the other's sentences.

Communication code change—a dimension of relationships that gauges how much partners developed scripts that are exclusive to their relationship.

6. **Communication code change.** Relationships vary on **communication code change**, how much partners have developed scripts that are exclusive to their relationship. As a relationship develops, the partners develop unique lexicons, idioms, and personal references. For example, in our family, if a conversation is becoming embarrassingly heated or uncomfortable, one person may interrupt saying, "How about that chandelier?," which all family members understand as a request to change to a less stressful topic. We all understand this because we shared an experience where Kathie's father interrupted what was becoming a parent and adult child argument by commenting on the dining room chandelier. Some code changes like this one come about because of shared experiences, and others simply develop over time. Code changes include pet names and inside jokes. It can also include relationship symbols like "our" song, our movie, or other personalized references. Because of shared scripts, partners may begin to finish each other's sentences, learn to read each other's nonverbal messages, and in other ways shortcut the need for verbal conversation.

Shared social networks—a dimension of relationships that gauges how much the partners' interactions and relationships with other people overlap.

Social network—the structure of your relationships.

7. **Shared social networks.** Relationships vary in **shared social networks**, how much the partners' interactions and relationships with other people overlap. Your **social network** is the structure of your relationships. For example, Kareem's social network consists of a group of friends from high school with whom he keeps in contact; a group of college friends, one of whom went to high school with him but was not part of his high school friendship group; the members of his co-ed volleyball team, two of whom are also college friends; a group of co-workers; a romantic relationship with one of his co-worker's sisters; and his blended family consisting of one sister, two half-brothers, three step-siblings, a mother, stepmother, and father. When you first meet someone, you may not have any friends, co-workers, and so on in common. As relationships

develop, not only do partners become better acquainted with each other, but they also begin to meet and interact with each other's friends, co-workers, and family. So they blend their networks resulting in mutual friends and shared family.

8. Interpersonal trust. Relationships vary in the level at which partners trust each other. **Interpersonal trust** is the extent to which partners believe that they know what to expect from the relationship partner, know how they are supposed to act, and know that they want to act according to expectations (Pearce, 1974). Trust is lowest with strangers but can increase if our partners

Interpersonal trust—a dimension of relationships that gauges the extent to which partners believe that they know what to expect from the relationship, know how they are supposed to act, and know that they want to act according to expectations.

LEARN ABOUT YOURSELF ●

Take this short survey to learn something about one of your close relationships. Answer the questions based on your first response. There are no right or wrong answers. Just be honest in reporting your beliefs. Respond to these items with one relationship in mind. Choose someone you are close to, such as a romantic partner. For each question, select one of the numbers to the right that best describes your assessment:

_____ 1. My partner is primarily interested in his (her) own welfare.
_____ 2. There are times when my partner cannot be trusted.
_____ 3. My partner is perfectly honest and truthful with me.
_____ 4. I feel that I can trust my partner completely.
_____ 5. My partner is truly sincere in his (her) promises.
_____ 6. I feel that my partner does not show me enough consideration.
_____ 7. My partner treats me fairly and justly.
_____ 8. I feel that my partner can be counted on to help me.

7 = Very Strongly Agree
6 = Strongly Agree
5 = Mildly Agree
4 = Neutral
3 = Mildly Disagree
2 = Strongly Disagree
1 = Very Strongly Disagree

Scoring the Survey: This survey measures the trust you have in your partner. To find your score first reverse the response scores for Items 1, 2, and 6 (if you wrote 7 make it a 1, 6 = 2, 5 = 3, 4=4, 3=5, 2=6,1=7). Now add up your numbers for all eight items on the survey. Total scores can range from 8 to 56. The higher your score, the more you trust your partner; the lower your score, the less you trust your partner. You can compare your score to those of people who took this survey when it was developed.

Score	Percentile
< 40	Bottom 25%
40–47	26%–50%
48–52	51%–75%
53–56	76%–99+%

Based on Larzelere, R. E., & Huston, T. (1980). The dyadic trust scale: Toward understanding interpersonal trust in close relationships. *Journal of Marriage and Family, 42,* 595–604.

The Dyadic Trust Scale is copyrighted by R.E. Larzelere and used with permission.

meet our relationship needs, choosing to act in ways that enhance the relationship. Trust almost always involves some level of risk. There is a chance that your partner will disappoint you. Research suggests that four factors lead to trust (Boon, 1994): dependability, responsiveness, collaboration, and faithfulness. Dependable partners can be relied on to behave in consistent and expected ways. Responsive partners act to meet each others' needs. Collaborative partners resolve conflicts using problem-solving approaches that result in win-win situations. Faithful partners are loyal to the relationship by honoring each other's privacy wishes; by defending each other's reputation even when it is personally inconvenient; and in romantic relationships, by refraining from sexual behavior with others.

Self-Disclosure and Feedback in Relationships

As you interact in a relationship, you will begin to tell the other person things about yourself and share what you observe about your partner. Likewise, your partner will disclose things and will share observations about you. The mark of a healthy relationship is an appropriate balance of **self-disclosure**, verbally sharing personal, private information and feelings, and **feedback**, providing verbal and physical responses to relationship partners and/or their messages.

Understanding Self-Disclosure and Feedback: The Johari Window

Self-disclosure—verbally sharing personal, private information, and feelings.

Feedback—providing verbal and physical responses to relationship partners and/or their messages.

Johari window—a visual framework for understanding how self-disclosure and feedback work together in a relationship.

The **Johari window** (named after its two originators, Jo Luft and Harry Ingham) is a visual framework for understanding how self-disclosure and feedback work together in a relationship (Luft, 1970). The window represents all of the information about you that there is. You and your partner each know some (but not all) of this information. The window has four "panes," or quadrants, as shown in Figure 6.1: the open pane, the secret pane, the blind pane, and the unknown pane.

The first quadrant, the open pane of the window, represents the information about you that both you and your partner know. It includes information that you have self-disclosed and the observations about you that your partner has shared with you through feedback. It might include basic information that you share with most people, such as your college major, but it also may include information that you disclose to relatively few people. Similarly, it can include simple observations that your partner has made, such as how cute you look when you wrinkle your nose, or more serious feedback from your partner about your interpersonal style.

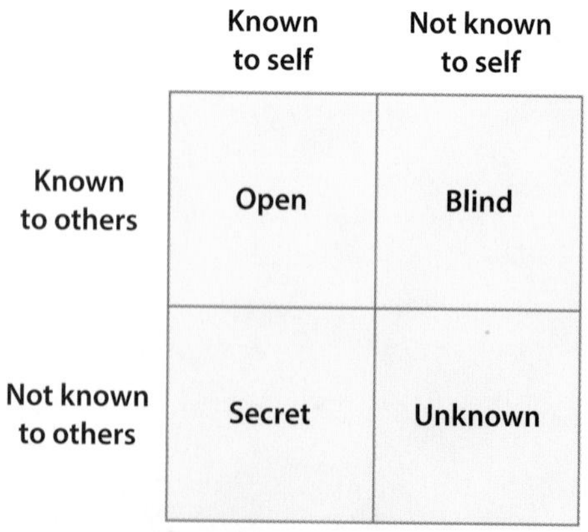

The second quadrant, the secret pane, represents all those things that you know about yourself but have chosen to maintain as private. So your partner does not know these things about you. When you self-disclose secret information to your partner, the information moves into the open pane of the window. For example, suppose that you had been engaged once, but on the day of the wedding, your fiancé

FIGURE 6.1 The Johari Window

backed out. You may keep this embarrassing and painful part of your history private and in the secret pane of your window in many of your relationships. But when you disclose this fact to someone, it moves into the open part of your Johari window with this person. As you disclose more information, the secret pane of the window becomes smaller, and the open pane is enlarged.

The third quadrant, the blind pane, represents the information that the other person knows about you but of which you are unaware. Most people have blind spots—parts or effects of their behavior about which they are unaware. Information moves from the blind area of the window to the open area through feedback from others. When someone provides an insight about yourself and you accept the feedback, then the information will move into the open pane of the Johari window you have with this person. Feedback also enlarges the open pane of the Johari window, and in this case, the blind pane becomes smaller.

The fourth and final quadrant, the unknown pane, represents information about you of which neither you nor your partner is aware. This is the information that we periodically "discover." If, for instance, you have never tried hang gliding, then neither you nor anyone else can really know how you will react at the point of takeoff. You might chicken out or follow through, do well or crash, love every minute of it or be paralyzed with fear. But until you try it, all this information is unknown. Once you try it, you gain information about yourself that becomes part of the secret pane, which you can move to the open pane through disclosure. Also once you have tried it, others who observe your flight will have information about your performance that you may not know unless they give you feedback.

As you disclose and receive feedback, the sizes of the various windowpanes change. These changes taken together reflect the closeness of the relationship. The panes of the Johari window you have with different people will vary in size. Figure 6.2 shows four Johari windows, with a different level of self-disclosure and feedback represented. Figure 6.2A depicts the pattern we would expect in a new relationship or one between casual acquaintances. There is little self-disclosure or feedback occurring. Figure 6.2B shows a relationship in which a person is disclosing to a partner, but the partner

A 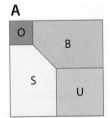 **B** 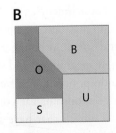 **C** 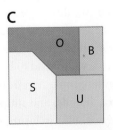 **D**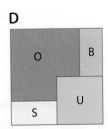

FIGURE 6.2 Sample Johari windows: (A) low disclosure, low feedback; (B) high disclosure, low feedback; (C) low disclosure, high feedback; (D) high disclosure, high feedback

is providing little feedback. Since part of the way that we learn about who we are comes from the feedback we receive from others, relationships in which one partner does not provide feedback can become very unsatisfying to the other individual. Figure 6.2C shows a relationship where a partner is good at providing feedback, but the other individual is not self-disclosing. Since most of us disclose only when we trust our partners, this pattern may be an indication that the nondisclosing individual does not have confidence in the relational partner. Finally, Figure 6.2D shows a relationship in which the individual has self-disclosed a good deal of information and received generous feedback. Windows that look like this indicate that close relationships have developed. Obviously, to get a complete picture of a relationship, each partner's Johari window would need to be examined. A balance of self-disclosure and feedback mark a healthy interpersonal relationship.

The Role of Self-Disclosure in Relationships

Social penetration theory—the premise that self-disclosure is integral to all stages of relationships, but the nature and type of self-disclosure change over time as people move from being strangers to being intimates.

According to **social penetration theory**, self-disclosure is integral to all stages of relationships, but the nature and type of self-disclosure change over time as people move from being strangers to being intimates (Altman & Taylor, 1973). According to this theory, we can think of our personality as an onion. On the outside are the public layers that contain factual information like your major, where you grew up, how you like your steak cooked, etc. Deeper in the onion of your personality are the layers of your inner self that house your attitudes, beliefs, and feelings. Just as in an onion, these layers are thicker. They take longer to share. Finally, we all have an inner core that consists of our values, deep emotions, and self-concept. When we meet someone, our initial conversations expose the public layers of our personality. We disclose a lot of this information. If our disclosures are reciprocated, we quickly disclose this outer layer. People who know us at this level are our long-term acquaintances. Most of our relationships remain at this level. As we begin to trust our partners, we will allow them to penetrate our outer layers and begin to share our inner self. During this time, our disclosures become somewhat deeper and more risky, and we make them less frequently as we gauge the trustworthiness of our partners. People with whom we share this type of information become our casual friends. Few relationships ever go past this point. But if we trust our partner and choose to disclose private and very personal things, we vastly increase the depth of our disclosures and share our inner core. When these types of disclosure are reciprocated, the relationship becomes intimate. We develop emotional attachments, and if partners are sexually attracted to one another, the relationship may become physically intimate. True intimate relationships are both deep and broad. Although truly intimate relationships are rare, they also tend to be deeply meaningful and stable. When relationships deteriorate, people refrain from deep, broad, and frequent self-disclosure. Acquaintances, friends, and intimate relationships vary on the depth, breadth, and frequency of self-disclosure and feedback that have been exchanged, and this type of communication plays a critical role in moving relationships from one stage of their life cycle to another.

Guidelines for Self-Disclosure

While self-disclosure helps us develop our relationships, indiscriminate self-disclosure can be damaging to people and relationships. So it's important to make appropriate disclosures. The following guidelines can help you decide when and what to disclose.

1. Self-disclose the kind of information that you want others to disclose to you. Since we expect self-disclosures to be reciprocated, you should only share the type of information that you would like others to share with you. For example, if you want to know about your partner's previous romantic partners, you should be willing to talk about yours.

2. Self-disclose information appropriate for the type of relationship you have. Disclosures about fears, loves, and other deep or intimate matters are most appropriate in close, well-established relationships. When people disclose deep secrets to acquaintances, they are engaging in potentially threatening behavior. Making such disclosures before a bond of trust is established risks alienating the other person. Moreover, people are often embarrassed by and hostile toward others who saddle them with personal information in an effort to establish a relationship where none exists.

3. Self-disclose more intimate information only when you believe the disclosure represents an acceptable risk. There is always some risk involved in disclosing, but as you gain trust in another person, you perceive that the disclosure of more revealing information is less likely to have negative consequences. We might expect this to occur in the context of an ongoing relationship, yet people sometimes inappropriately disclose very personal information to strangers because they perceive the disclosure to be safe since they will never see the person again.

4. Be sensitive to your partner's ability to absorb your disclosure. Because receiving self-disclosure from a partner can be as threatening as making the disclosure, be sensitive to your partner's capacity to handle what you might disclose. This means that you should avoid dumping deep and potentially disturbing disclosures without first considering your partner and even asking if your partner is willing to hear what you want to reveal. For example, B.J., who had fathered a child when he was in high school, had been seeing Julia for a while and wanted to tell her about his son. But he didn't know if Julia could accept knowing this about him and how that would affect their promising relationship. So one evening after dinner, he said, "Julie, there is something that happened when I was in high school that is important to me, but that you may not like. I'd like to share it with you. Are you willing to hear it?"

5. Reserve intimate or very personal self-disclosures for ongoing relationships. Disclosures about fears, loves, and other deep and intimate matters are most appropriate for close, well-established relationships.

6. Continue intimate self-disclosure only when it is reciprocated. We expect a kind of equity in self-disclosure. When it is apparent that

INTER-ACT WITH SOCIAL MEDIA

Scan your Facebook newsfeed or Twitter feed throughout the course of your day. Look at the information that your friends and followers are sharing with others. Do they appear to be following the "Guidelines for Self-Disclosure" explained in this chapter? As you reflect on your use of social media, have you been following these guidelines?

self-disclosure is not being returned, you should not continue to self-disclose. Lack of reciprocation generally suggests that your partner does not feel that the relationship is intimate enough for the type of disclosures you are making.

Relationship Life Cycles: How Relationships Change

Even though no two relationships develop in exactly the same manner, all relationships tend to move through identifiable stages of coming together, maintaining, and coming apart. (Baxter, 1982; Duck, 1987; Knapp & Vangelisti, 2005; Taylor & Altman, 1987). Your relationships can move through this life cycle in a linear fashion, but they will more likely cycle back and forth through the stages over time. A relationship's movement through these stages and its life cycle depend on the interpersonal communication that occurs between relationship partners. In this section we begin by describing how relationships are changed. Then we will take a closer look at each stage of a relationship, focusing on how interpersonal communication functions.

Turning point—any event or occurrence that marks a relationship's transition from one stage to another.

Turning Points

The movement from one stage of a relationship to another is usually associated with a **turning point** event, any event or occurrence that marks a relationship's transition from one stage to another. Turning points are crucial junctures that affect the nature of the relationship and its future. Relationships can change abruptly with a dramatic turning point, or they may change so gradually that only when partners reflect back are they able to identify the turning point.

The changes created by turning points can move a relationship to greater intimacy. For example, Caitlyn ran into an acquaintance on the day that her best friend died in a car accident. Her acquaintance spent several hours comforting Caitlyn. From this simple act of kindness, they both recognized that this was a relationship worth developing. They began to do things together, enjoyed long, deep conversations, and over time became good friends. Their chance meeting the day that Caitlyn's best friend died was the turning point in their relationship.

Not all turning points result in a closer relationship. In fact, some of these events like those that highlight differences in values and morals, gross violations of trust, infidelity, and other ethical violations, can end a relationship. For example, Will and Mikela, who have been dating for three months, seem to be heading toward a committed relationship—until a dinner with Will's parents at which Mikela witnessed how both Will and his father demean Will's mother. Because of this encounter, Mikela began to notice that Will had little regard for the opinions of women. She subsequently decided that while Will is attractive, smart, and generally easy to be with, she doesn't want to be in a long-term relationship with someone who doesn't respect women.

Turning points occur at all stages in a relationship and vary from relationship to relationship. In parent-child relationships, turning points often signal a change in the level of the child's dependence. A child's first day of school, a religious coming-of-age ceremony, earning a driver's license, graduating from high school, beginning or graduating from college, permanently moving out of the family home, and marriage are common turning points that mark a significant change in this type of relationship. Studies of romantic relationships (Baxter & Bullis, 1993; Baxter & Erbert, 1999) have identified going on a first date, experiencing a first kiss, meeting the family, dealing with an old or new rival, engaging in sexual activity, going on vacation together, deciding to date exclusively, having a big fight, making up, separating, living together, or getting engaged as important turning points. A study of romantic relationships that began online identified the first phone call and first face-to-face meeting as important turning points unique to developing relationships in cyberspace (McDowell, 2001). In this chapter's "Diverse Voices" selection, Saba Ali explains how simply holding hands ended a promising romantic relationship.

Discussing turning points with your partner before and after they occur can help you both understand what these events mean and how they may affect your relationship. Now that you understand turning points, let's take a closer look at each of the stages of a relationship.

Stage One: Beginning Relationships

For most of us, starting a new relationship is scary because we are uncertain about how we should act, how our partner will act, and how the relationship will develop (Knobloch & Miller, 2008). In most cases our first few conversations involve finding out more about our partner to reduce some of our uncertainty. According to **predicted outcome value theory**, in our early conversations with potential relationship partners, we gather information to predict whether the benefits of future interactions will outweigh the costs (Sunnafrank, 1990). The conversations that occur at the beginning of relationships actually progress through three identifiable phases (Berger & Calabreeze, 1975).

During the first or entry phase, we follow the norms of our culture, sharing appropriate basic demographic and interest information ("Where are you from?" "Do you have any brothers or sisters?"; "What is your major?"; "Do you follow sports?," etc.). After initial conversations, we decide whether or not spending additional time with someone will be worth it. We start by excluding people we dislike or don't think are appropriate partners (Fehr, 2008; Rodin, 1982). For example, when Kelly joined the marching band at college she didn't know anyone, so she was interested in finding others who might become friends. At the first practice, after talking with six of the band members, Kelly decided to avoid two of the guys because they were loud and obnoxious. She also ruled out one girl

OBSERVE AND ANALYZE

Turning Points in Relationships

Select one long-term relationship in which you have been or are currently involved. Identify what you consider to be the turning points in that relationship. For each turning point, indicate whether in your opinion this was a positive event that strengthened the relationship or a negative event that weakened relationship intimacy. Indicate whether you discussed these turning points with the other person.

Predicted outcome value theory—the premise that in our early conversations with potential relationship partners, we gather information to predict whether the benefits of future interactions will outweigh the costs.

Modern Love: Close Enough to Touch Was Too Far Apart

By Saba Ali, New York Times News Service

Excerpted from Naples Daily News—Friday, October 12, 2007

Who knew that holding hands, the very act that signals the start of so many relationships, would be the end of mine? It seems the mullahs were onto something when they wagged their fingers against premarital relations, of any kind.

Born in Kenya, I came to the United States at age 6, settling with my family in upstate New York. Growing up Muslim, I missed out on the "Dawson's Creek" method of courtship.

For scarf-wearing Muslims like me, premarital interaction between the sexes is strictly controlled. Men and women pray, eat and congregate separately. At private dinner parties, women exit the dining room so the men can serve themselves. Boys sit on one side of the hall, girls on the other, and married couples in the middle.

When out in public interactions with non-Muslim boys, we tend to be less constrained but still formal. A playful push from a boy would bring an awkward explanation of how touching is against my religion.

So my friends and I had high expectations for marriage which was supposed to quickly follow graduation from college. That's when our parents told us it was time to find the one man we would be waking up with for the rest of our lives, God willing. They just didn't tell us how.

There were no tips from our mothers or anyone else on how to meet the right man or to talk to him. It's simply expected that our lives will consist of two phases: unmarried and in the company of women, and then married and in the company of a man.

It's all supposed to start with a conversation, but not a private one. My friends and I call them "meetings." The woman comes with her chaperone, a family member, and the man comes with his. Talking points include such questions as "What do you expect from your husband?" and

"Would you mind if my parents were to move in with us after the reception?"

Yet now, at 29, despite all of my "meetings," I remain unmarried. And in the last five years I've exhausted the patience of my matchmaking aunties and friends who have offered up their husbands' childhood playmates.

All I wanted was to feel secure, to look forward to spending my days and nights with my match. Which is why my interest was piqued last year when a friend from college told me about a radiologist in his early 30s who was also frustrated by the challenges of the contemporary Muslim hookup. We lived hours from each other, but I agreed to do the traveling for our first get together, which we decided would be for brunch at a little French café near Central Park. I listened as he talked about his past relationships. Not the most appropriate topic for a first date, perhaps, but more comfortable for me than some typical pressurized questions: "Do you cook?" and "How many children do you want?"

After brunch, we walked through the park. I spoke with ease about my own confusions, ambitions, faith and fear of making the wrong decision about marriage. I told him I wanted someone who liked eating out. He said he wanted a wife who wasn't conservative and could fit in with his non-Muslim friends.

After meeting him, we kept getting to know each other by phone, often talking for hours at a time. If I was driving when he called, I would roam around aimlessly just so our exchange wouldn't end when I reached my destination. I hadn't yet told my parents about him, not wanting to get my mother's hopes up.

Our lingering problem, however, was the difference in how religious we each were; he hadn't planned on marrying someone who wore the traditional head scarf. His ideal woman was less strict, more secular. But I reveled in the recognition. Covering was a choice I had made in high

who openly bragged to anyone who would listen that she could "hook them up with a supplier." That left three possibilities for developing relationships.

After we have excluded people we don't like or don't think appropriate, we continue to evaluate the people we have talked with based on their physical attractiveness, social skills, and responsiveness to our overtures (Fehr, 2008). Kelly

school, partly out of a need for identity, and partly out of fear. The fear came from what I had heard at Muslim summer camp, which scared me enough to start covering and praying.

In the years since, that fear has evolved into understanding. Most girls will say the scarf is for modesty. I see it as a protection. It keeps me from making stupid decisions.

In order to get him over his hesitation, I planned our dates to take place in very public places. We played miniature golf, ate out at restaurants and went blueberry picking. I had my own doubts, although I was afraid to admit them: Namely, why should I push forward with this when we weren't aligned in terms of our faith? How could we be a good match if he didn't approve of my hijab? Would I have to change? Should I?

One evening he called to tell me he had gone to a lounge with a few of his buddies. "I visualized what it would feel like to have you sitting next to me," he told me.

"And how did I feel?" I asked.

"Pretty good," he said. "Manageable."

After, I finally called my mother and told her about him.

Before him, I had never gone past the second date. But by now he and I were approaching our fourth date—plenty of time, in my mind, to decide whether a man is right for you.

And then came the night of the movie, his idea. I'm a movie fanatic and remember the details of almost every movie I've ever seen. I can't remember the title of the one we saw that night. I looked over at him and smiled, convincing myself that the weightiness I felt was because I was in uncharted territory. We were moving forward, talking about meeting each other's families. So when he leaned over and asked, "Can I hold your hand?" I didn't feel I could say no. I liked him for taking the risk.

Nearly 30 years old, I had thought about holding hands with a boy since I was a teenager. But it was always in the context of my wedding day. Walking into our reception as husband and wife, holding hands, basking in that moment of knowing this was forever.

Non-Muslim girls may wonder about their first kiss or, later, about losing their virginity. I thought I was running the same risk, though for me it would be the first time actually touching the hand of a potential husband. How would it feel? Would it convince me that he was the one?

A lifetime's worth of expectations culminated in this single gesture in a dark theater over a sticky armrest. I'm not sure it's possible to hold hands wrong, but we were not doing it right. It felt awkward with my hand under his, so we changed positions: my arm on top, his hand cradling mine. It was still uncomfortable, and soon my hand fell asleep, which was not the tingling sensation I was hoping for. Finally, I took it away.

But the damage had been done. We had broken the no-contact rule, and in doing so, I realized I wasn't willing to be the kind of girl he wanted. I believe in my religion, the rules, the reasons and even the restrictions. At the same time, I've always wanted to be married, and the thought of never knowing that side of myself, as a wife and a mother, scares me. Being with him made me compromise my faith, and my fear of being alone pushed me to ignore my doubts about the relationship.

When we took it too far, I shut down. It wasn't supposed to happen that way. So after the date, I split us up. And I never saw him again.

For Consideration:

1. There are a variety of opportunities for turning points in a relationship. On their first date the doctor told Saba that he was interested in finding someone "who wasn't very conservative." How could Saba have used this comment as a turning point that perhaps would have led to a different outcome later?

2. Have you ever faced a relationship turning point where continuing the relationship meant that you would have compromised your values or beliefs? If you have, did you choose to compromise? What impact did your decision have on the relationship long term? Do you regret your choice?

found that while all of the remaining three people she had met were good looking, one of the women was really shy and difficult to talk with. Another guy seemed interesting, but when she tried to continue talking with him he seemed distracted and aloof. That left her with one woman who was easy to talk with and seemed to enjoy Kelly's company. So Kelly asked her if she wanted to get a bite to eat.

When you meet someone new, how do you decide if you like the person enough to spend more time with him or her?

After one or more entry stage conversations, we move to the second or personal phase of beginning the relationship. Conversations in this phase move beyond basic demographic information exchange as we begin to disclose somewhat more personal stories and relate critical incidents in our lives. From these more personal disclosures, we can learn about the attitudes, beliefs, and values of our partner and judge whether they are compatible with our own. During dinner at the Union Café, Kelly learned that both she and the other woman held similar political views, were close to their families, were majoring in public relations, and were avid environmentalists. It appeared that they shared a lot in common and even had a similar sense of humor. So at the end of the meal, they made plans to meet again for coffee before the next band practice.

At some point, partners will transition into the third or exit phase of the beginning relationship stage. If the former strangers decide that they like each other, that they have enough in common, and that the advantages of pursuing the relationship outweigh the disadvantages, they will continue to meet and invest in the relationship with self-disclosures. Or one or both of them may choose not to pursue a deeper relationship. After meeting and talking together several more times, Kelly recognized that although she had initially enjoyed the other woman's company, the more she got to know her the more boring she found her. Consequently, Kelly continued to talk with her bandmate at rehearsals and games, but she made excuses to avoid her outside of this context, and the women remained simply acquaintances.

Stage Two: Developing Relationships

We develop our relationships by choosing to continue investing our time in pursuing conversation, sharing joint activities, and engaging in deeper, reciprocated self-disclosure with our partner. Why do we continue to invest in and develop some relationships yet not others?

Choosing Which Relationships to Develop

Interpersonal needs theory—the premise that all of us have inclusion, affection, and control needs that we try to meet through our relationships, although our need for each of these varies in degree from person to person.

Inclusion need—our desire to be in the company of other people.

Two theories can help us understand our choice to develop a specific relationship. According to **interpersonal needs theory**, all of us have inclusion, affection, and control needs that we try to meet through our relationships, although our need for each of these varies in degree from person to person and over time (Schutz, 1966). **Inclusion need** is our desire to be in the company of other people, which stems from our nature as social animals. But people differ in how much interaction they need and how many people they need to have social relationships. Some people are happy spending time with one or two others and enjoy spending many hours alone. Other people enjoy having many relationships of varying intensities and find they are happiest if they spend most of their time with others. Most of us find ourselves somewhere between these two extremes. **Affection need** is our desire to love and be loved. The people you know probably run the gamut. Some people tend to avoid close ties, seldom show their loving feelings, and shy away from people who try to show them affection. Other people thrive on developing close and loving relationships with many others. They enjoy developing deep friendships, both verbally and nonverbally display their loving feelings, and thrive on the affection others show them. Again, you may find yourself somewhere between these two extremes. Finally, **control need** is our desire to influence the events and people around us and to be influenced by others. Like the other two needs, people also vary in their need for control. Some people feel a strong need to be in control, calling the shots, organizing their own lives and the lives of those around them, whereas other people seem happiest when someone else is making the decisions, taking charge, and being responsible. Most of us need to be in control some of the time when the outcome of events is important to us, but we also need to have our relationship partners "step up" and take control of other situations, decisions, and so forth.

According to **social exchange theory**, we continue to develop a relationship as long as we feel that its rewards outweigh its costs and we perceive that what we get from a particular relationship is more than we would be able to get if we invested elsewhere (Thibaut & Kelley, 1986). **Relationship costs** include the time and energy we spend developing a relationship and the negative experiences that may arise like hurt feelings, conflict episodes, jealousy, and so forth. **Relationship rewards** include having basic relationship needs for affection, control, and inclusion met. As long as we perceive a relationship's benefits are worth its costs, we will continue to develop it.

Let's look at an extended example of how interpersonal needs and social exchanges affect our decision to develop relationships. Zeke met Madison and Halley during freshman orientation week. Since then he had texted with Madison several times and spent one evening hanging out with her at the dorm where they talked all night. He found that Madison was easy to talk with, enjoyed several of his favorite bands, and laughed at his jokes. He really enjoyed spending time with her, and she seemed to be fine when they didn't talk for a couple of days. He also had several long phone conversations with Halley, and they had actually had a date that she initiated. While the date was OK, Halley had annoyed him by calling several times a day including very late every night and texting him almost every hour. A couple of times she woke him up, and at other times she interrupted his study time. He concluded that Halley was too needy and very high maintenance. Madison, on the other hand, seemed to be a good fit and he found that he looked forward to seeing her. As the semester progressed, Zeke spent more time getting close to Madison, and although he continued to be pleasant when he saw Halley, he used caller ID to avoid answering her calls, didn't respond to her text messages, and turned down her requests for another date. When his roommate asked him why he was pursuing Madison and keeping Halley at arm's length, he explained: "Madison gets me. She understands that

Affection need—our desire to love and be loved.

Control need—our desire to influence the events and people around us and to be influenced by others.

Social exchange theory—the premise that we continue to develop a relationship as long as we feel that its rewards outweigh its costs and we perceive that what we get from a particular relationship is more than we would be able to get if we invested elsewhere.

Relationship costs—negative outcomes to a relationship, including the time and energy we spend developing a relationship and the negative experiences that may arise like hurt feelings, conflict episodes, jealousy, etc.

Relationship rewards—positive outcomes to a relationship, including having basic relationship needs for affection, control, and inclusion met.

my classes and labs take a lot of time, and I need my space (meets my inclusion need/reward). Because we share so many common interests, she's always willing to do what I want to do (meets my control need/reward). And I can tell that she likes me, yet she's not overly expressive or possessive and recognizes that I'm not yet ready to declare my undying love (meets my affection need/reward). Halley just didn't get me. She needed much more attention than I have time to devote to anyone (too inclusive/cost) and wanted to take over my life (too controlling/cost). She had already told me how much she liked me and expected me to reciprocate, but I just didn't have those kinds of feelings for her (too affectionate/cost). So compared to Halley, Madison and I are just more compatible (weighing the alternatives and choosing the most rewarding)."

Throughout our relationships we continue to compare our costs to the rewards that we receive. As long as we feel that what we are getting from the relationship is worth what we are giving, and we don't see another relationship where our outcomes would be better, we continue developing or sustaining the relationship that we are in.

Activities in Developing Relationships

The developing stage of the relationship life cycle is a very intense period that results in our feeling closer and more committed to our partner. During this phase we increase the time we spend together by interweaving some of our daily activities, share more intimate disclosures, and test the relationship. For example, Zeke and Madison began to study together in the late afternoon, followed by dinner in the cafeteria. During dinner one Friday, Madison mentioned that she was going to do wash Saturday morning, and Zeke, who hadn't done laundry in two weeks, joined her. This became a Saturday morning "date," which they laughed about but continued to observe. As they spent more time together, each learned a great deal about the other. Among other "secrets," Zeke shared the painful breakup he had with his longtime girlfriend who dumped him two days before their senior prom. Madison confided that she worried about her father who drank too much and had lost his driver's license but continued to drive. Over the next three months, both Zeke and Madison tested the relationship. Madison, who had trouble trusting others, was pleased when Zeke kept what she had told him about her dad to himself. Several times Zeke purposely didn't follow his tradition of calling Madison to say goodnight to see how she would react. They also tested their chemistry and quickly agreed that although they really cared about each other, neither was physically attracted to the other. Consequently, they became really close friends in a platonic rather than romantic relationship. Rather than calling Zeke her "boyfriend," Madison referred to him as her "friend guy." When she marries she wants Zeke to be her "man of honor" and when he marries, Zeke wants Madison to be his "best woman."

Like Zeke and Madison's experience, developing any relationship occurs over time and through the self-disclosure process. As we disclose more and learn that our partner is trustworthy, we deepen our relationship. As long as we perceive that on balance the relationships rewards outweigh its costs, we will continue to invest in it. The more we have invested, the more we become committed to our partner. Over time, many relationships we develop become social friendships, some become close friendships, and a few become platonic or romantic intimate relationships.

Stage Three: Sustaining Relationships

The periods during which we are developing a close relationship can be very exciting. Getting to know someone, learning to trust him or her, and sharing activities are heady stuff. But once the relationship has stabilized, it cannot be taken for granted. Relationships that last are those in which the partners continue to emotionally invest in the relationship and maintain their commitment to their partner while managing the tensions inherent in any relationship. Let's look at the behaviors that characterize healthy ongoing relationships and then discuss the tensions that arise in all relationships and how you can effectively handle these.

Behaviors That Sustain Relationships

People use various types of behaviors to maintain healthy relationships (Canary, Stafford, & Semic, 2002; Dindia & Baxter, 1987). First, people continue to use prosocial behaviors. They are friendly and polite to one another, and they avoid becoming overcritical of their partner. Unfortunately, it's very easy to begin to take a partner for granted. For example, instead of politely asking our roommate to pick up a needed item, we may phrase this request as an order: "Stop by Kroger on your way home and pick up a loaf of bread."

Second, people who sustain a relationship continue to observe ceremonial occasions like birthdays and anniversaries. They share vacations and spend time together recounting pleasant, memorable events from their common past. Fifteen years ago, when our daughter was in college, she developed a very close group of friends. They are now spread out across the country, yet they continue to exchange e-mails, send birthday cards, and get together either at a college reunion or for group vacations with spouses, significant others, and kids. During these times they relive their favorite memories from college as well as make new memories.

Third, partners who sustain relationships make it a habit to spend time together as a couple and with mutual friends. Many happily married couples have a weekly "date" night when they go out to have fun, seeing a movie, sharing a quiet dinner, or just taking a long walk. These planned times allow them to withdraw from the busyness of day-to-day living and to focus on each other. Doing things together with mutual friends can help sustain a relationship since it provides an opportunity for partners to observe each other in a social setting and to privately discuss what happened at the gathering. Fourth, partners who sustain relationships communicate frequently and talk about deep and everyday topics. Their communication is characterized by honesty and openness. Fifth, those who sustain relationships use words and actions to reassure their partners of their continuing affection, discretion, and trustworthiness. "You're my best friend," "I really can't imagine not having you to talk with," and "I love you" exemplify statements that reassure a partner of the relationship's status.

Finally, relationships are sustained when partners share the tasks that must be done. For example, Chas and Raj share an off-campus apartment, and both men do household chores and contribute to a household fund from which they pay joint expenses. All these behaviors are investments in the other person and the relationship. Just like a checking account, when the relationship account is flush, the relationship is healthy, but when one or both members continually make relationship withdrawals that exceed relationship deposits, the reward/cost ratio tilts, and the partners may look for alternative relationships in which to invest. The deposits that we make in our relationship are what keep it from stagnating or deteriorating. Not only will you need to be proactive in your relationships, but you will need to be able to manage the relationship tensions that inevitably arise.

Understanding and Managing Dialectical Tensions in Relationships

We enjoy getting to know all about a new relationship partner and sharing large parts of ourselves with our partner, but at some point we will feel that we need to step back and keep some of our secrets private. While the relationship was developing, we may have been enjoying feeling connected to our partner. But at some point, we realize that it would be nice to be independent. When getting to know our partners, we did a lot of new things that were exciting because they were not part of our normal routine, but we may begin to long for the old days when our lives were more predictable. The competing feelings you experience are called relational dialectics (the word "dialectic" means a tension between conflicting forces). **Relational dialectics** are the conflicting pulls that exist in relationships as well as within each individual in a relationship. At any one time, one or both people in a relationship may be aware of these tensions. The secret to sustaining healthy relationships is effectively balancing these tensions.

Relational dialectics—the conflicting pulls that exist in relationships as well as within each individual in a relationship.

How does this image demonstrate the tension between connection and autonomy?

Three dialectics common to most relationships are the tugs between openness and closedness, autonomy and connection, and novelty and predictability (Baxter & Montgomery, 1996; Baxter & West, 2003). **Openness** is the desire to share intimate ideas and feelings with your relationship partner. **Closedness** is the desire to maintain privacy. This openness-closedness dialectic is also referred to as the disclosure-privacy dialectic. When getting to know one another, both Zeke and Madison disclosed quite a bit to each other. But Zeke always told Madison more than she told him. In other words, the open quadrant of Zeke's Johari window in their relationship is quite large. Because Madison comes from an alcoholic family, she has learned to keep secrets, making disclosure harder for her. As their relationship stabilized, Zeke continued to disclose but noticed that Madison seemed to be withdrawing and not sharing as much as he was. The fact that Zeke and Madison differ in their preferred levels of self-disclosure is one source of tension they needed to manage to sustain the relationship. Zeke does not always want complete openness, feeling that at times it is appropriate to be closed or to refrain from self-disclosure with Madison. He seeks both openness and closedness in this relationship. Madison, while wanting more closedness than Zeke, still wants some openness. So, like Zeke, she experiences opposite forces occurring simultaneously in their relationship. In Chapter 10 we will discuss the theory of privacy management and identify specific skills and strategies for handling this important relational dialectic.

Autonomy is the desire to act and make decisions independent of your relationship partner. **Connection** is the desire to link your actions and decisions with those of your relationship partner. Imagine that Madison and Zeke have been best friends for about a year. At this point in their relationship, Zeke wants to spend most of his free time with Madison and enjoys talking with her before acting or making decisions, but Madison has begun to feel hemmed in. For example, she wants to spend some time hanging out with her roommates, her new boyfriend, or studying alone. At the same time, however, she doesn't want to hurt Zeke's feelings or ruin the closeness in their relationship. Although Zeke is at peace and may not recognize any tension between autonomy and connection in the relationship, Madison is feeling the conflict of wanting to be more autonomous but without jeopardizing her connection to Zeke. If Madison begins to act autonomously, she may relieve her own tension, yet she may create tension in the relationship.

Novelty is the desire for originality, freshness, and uniqueness in your partner's behavior or in your relationship. **Predictability** is the desire for consistency, reliability, and dependability. People in relationships frequently experience tension between their desires for novelty and predictability. While Madison and Zeke know each other well, can predict much about each other, and have several routines in their relationship, they also want to be surprised and have new experiences with each other. Madison and Zeke may differ in their needs for novelty and predictability. Zeke may wish that Madison would surprise him by proposing that they try something different ("Let's go parasailing!"), or he may shock Madison by spontaneously breaking into her favorite song in the

Openness—the desire to share intimate ideas and feelings with your relationship partner.

Closedness—the desire to maintain privacy.

Autonomy—the desire to act and make decisions independent of your relationship partner.

Connection—the desire to link your actions and decisions with those of your relationship partner.

Novelty—the desire for originality, freshness, and uniqueness in your partner's behavior or in your relationship.

Predictability—the desire for consistency, reliability, and dependability in your partner's behavior or in your relationship.

middle of campus. At this point in their relationship, Madison may be comfortable operating by the routines they have established, and given her father's erratic behavior, she may appreciate that she can count on Zeke to behave in predictable ways. As a result, his spontaneous song may shock and embarrass her. Zeke may need more novelty at this moment, and eventually Madison may experience this as well. But to effectively sustain their relationship, they will need to adjust their behavior to relieve the tensions that arise between their needs for novelty and predictability in the relationship.

It is important to remember that dialectical tensions exist in all relationships and they are ongoing and changing. In other words, relationship dynamics are always in flux. Sometimes these dialectical tensions are active and in the foreground; at other times, they are not prominent and are in the background. Nevertheless, when these tensions are experienced, they change what is happening in the relationship (Wood, 2000).

After reading about dialectical tensions, you are probably asking yourself, "How can I cope with dialectical tensions in my relationships?" How do people satisfy opposite needs at the same time in relationships? Several scholars (Baxter & Montgomery, 1996; Wood, 2000) have studied how people actually manage the dialectical tensions in their relationships. People report using four strategies to manage these dialectics: temporal selection, topical segmentation, neutralization, and reframing.

Temporal selection—the strategy of dealing with dialectical tensions by choosing one side of a dialectical opposition while ignoring the other for a period of time.

1. Temporal selection is the strategy of dealing with dialectical tensions by choosing one side of a dialectical opposition while ignoring the other for a period of time. For example, perhaps you and a friend realize that you have spent too much time apart lately (autonomy), so you make a conscious decision to pursue connection. That is, you agree that over the next few months, you will make a point of spending more time together. You schedule many activities together to be more connected. Over time, however, if you feel that you are spending too much time together, you may find yourself canceling dates. Seesawing back and forth like this is one way to manage a relational dialectic.

Topical segmentation—the strategy of dealing with dialectical tensions by choosing certain areas in which to satisfy one side of a dialectical tension while choosing other areas to satisfy the opposite side.

2. Topical segmentation is the strategy of dealing with dialectical tensions by choosing certain areas in which to satisfy one side of a dialectical tension while choosing other areas to satisfy the opposite side. For instance, if you and your mother want more openness in your relationship, you may choose to be open about certain topics or aspects of life, such as feelings about school, work, or politics, but remain closed about your sex lives. This segmentation can satisfy both parties' needs for balance in the openness-closedness dialectic.

Neutralization—the strategy of dealing with dialectical tensions by compromising between the desires of those in the relationship.

3. Neutralization is the strategy of dealing with dialectical tensions by compromising between the desires of those in a relationship. This strategy partially meets the needs of both people in the relationship but does not fully meet the needs of either. For example, a couple might pursue a moderate level of novelty and spontaneity in their lives, which satisfies them both. The degree of novelty in the relationship may be less than what one person would ideally want and more than what the other would normally desire, but they have reached a middle point comfortable to both.

4. Reframing is the strategy of dealing with dialectical tensions by changing perceptions about the level of tension. Reframing involves putting less emphasis on the dialectical contradiction, looking at your desires differently so that they no longer seem quite so contradictory. For instance, maybe you are uncomfortable because you perceive that you are more open and your partner is more closed. As a result, you think about how much you disclose to him and how little he discloses to you. You might even discuss this issue with your partner and begin to realize the times that you have held back (closedness) as well as the instances where he was open. After the conversation, you no longer see such a strong contradiction. You see yourselves as more similar than different on this dialectic. You have reframed your perception of the tension.

In most cases, when you are trying to sustain a relationship by managing dialectical tensions, it helps if you and your partner talk about the tensions that you are feeling and come to an agreement about how you will manage the dialectic going forward. By disclosing your anxiety and receiving your partner's feedback, you and your partner may be able to negotiate a new balance satisfying to you both. When tensions cannot be managed and/or when partners quit investing in the relationship, it will begin to decline and may eventually end.

Stage Four: Relationship Decline

Less well-developed relationships like those with acquaintances, casual friends, co-workers, and neighbors are more likely to end than are highly developed relationships (Parks, 2007). Yet any relationship can decline. As a relationship declines, interdependence, depth, breadth, commitment, frequency of communication, and trust decrease. Several scholars have offered descriptive-stage models of how relationships decline and end (Duck, 1982; Knapp & Vangelisti, 2011), but there is little research to support any one model. Nevertheless, relationship decline is obviously a process that at its most basic level involves the following: one or both partners recognizing that the relationship is somehow less satisfying than in the past, a successful attempt to repair the relationship, and/or a series of steps to disengage from the relationship that results in either a less intimate relationship or a complete break in or end to the relationship. Let's look at these processes.

Your relationships are like living things that need to be continually fed if they are to flourish. When they are neglected or conflict laden, you or your partner eventually notice that the relationship has become dissatisfying—that the rewards you are receiving from the relationship are not worth the costs you're paying. This may be caused by unmet interpersonal needs, unresolved dialectical tensions, benign neglect, or by continual unresolved conflict (including nagging and fighting). At this point, there are three choices. First, you can ignore what you are feeling and hope that the relationship spontaneously improves. Perhaps it will, but more likely, it will not since your partner will remain unaware of your

Reframing—the strategy of dealing with dialectical tensions by changing perceptions about the level of tension.

Spotlight on Scholars

Read about the relationship theory research of Steven Duck at www.oup. com/us/verderber.

dissatisfaction or your partner will sense it but not really understand what is happening. Ignoring your dissatisfaction may be a temporary strategy, yet in the long run you will end up doing something else.

Second, you can decide to talk with your partner about your dissatisfaction. People tend to take this route when they have heavily invested in the relationship and don't have readily available alternative relationships that are promising. When someone who has been married for a long time and has small children feels dissatisfied with the marriage but doesn't have immediate romantic options, he or she will probably opt for talking with his or her spouse. Choosing this option means that you honestly disclose what you think is causing your dissatisfaction. If your partner is receptive to your message, then the two of you may decide to work on your relationship and try to reestablish the level of intimacy, trust, and closeness that you previously felt. Your conversations about your relationship may include discussions of how to better meet each other's interpersonal needs and resolve the dialectical tensions you are experiencing, as well as acknowledging and apologizing for trust violations and attempting to resolve other issues in the relationship.

For example, Danita and Faith had been best friends since childhood, sharing everything with each other and spending most Saturdays shopping and taking in a movie, that is, until Faith started going out with Troy. Then it seemed to Danita that Faith didn't need or have time for her. Over the last two months, Faith had cancelled their Saturday plans five times. But Danita, who didn't have many friends, wasn't willing to let her relationship with Faith deteriorate, so she sent Faith an e-mail asking to see her to talk about their relationship. When they met, Danita was careful to just describe what she perceived to be happening, indicating that although she was happy that Faith was with Troy, Danita missed their talks and time together. Faith acknowledged that she had been taking Danita for granted. She explained that Saturdays were the only day Troy had off work and that she wanted to spend time with him but didn't want to lose her great relationship with Danita, and she certainly didn't want to have to choose between them. After a lengthy conversation, they agreed to move their shopping day to Sunday afternoon, and Faith also suggested that Danita join Troy and her for coffee tomorrow. At times a moderator for these conversations can be useful. Impartial outsiders and professional counselors can offer a different perspective, helping partners listen and respond to what is being said. Many relationships can be repaired when both partners decide to reinvest in them.

Third, one or both partners may begin consciously disengaging from the relationship. Disengaging partners may feel less connected to the other, share fewer activities, and communicate less frequently. They may begin to emphasize the other's faults and downplay virtues. Subjects (that once inspired deep, private, and frequent communication) may become off-limits or sources of conflict. As the relationship begins to be characterized by more touchy subjects and more unresolved conflicts, partners become increasingly defensive and less able to foster a positive communication climate. Statements, such as "I don't want to talk about it anymore (or right now)" or "Stop bugging me," become more frequent. For example, if roommates Walt and Mark have been arguing about the cleanliness of their room, frequency of visitors, and unpaid personal loans, they may begin to avoid any discussion of these subjects.

As the relationship continues to deteriorate, people disengage from each other or drift apart. They become less willing to sacrifice for or forgive each other. Their communication patterns change from a pattern of sharing ideas and feelings to a pattern of mostly small talk and other "safe" communication and finally to a pattern of no significant interaction at all. It may seem strange that people who once had so much to share find themselves with nothing to talk about. They may begin to avoid each other altogether and seek out other people with whom to share interests and activities. They may depend less on each other and more on other people for favors and support. Hostility need not be present; rather, the overriding emotional tone is usually indifference.

When a relationship can't be maintained at a less developed level, it ends. A relationship has ended when the people no longer interact with each other at all. People give many reasons for terminating relationships, including poor communication, lack of fulfillment, differing lifestyles and interests, rejection, outside interference, absence of rewards, and boredom (Cupach & Metts, 1986). Unfortunately, many people who want a relationship to end don't want to be seen as the person who makes the first move. These people are likely to use strategies of manipulation, withdrawal, and avoidance (Baxter, 1982). Misguided and inappropriate, manipulation involves being indirect and failing to take any responsibility for ending the relationship. Manipulators may purposely sabotage the relationship in the hope that the other person will break it off. Withdrawal and avoidance, also less than competent ways of ending relationships, involve taking a passive approach, which leads to a slow and often painful death of a relationship.

The most competent way to end a relationship is to be direct, open, and honest. It is important to clearly state your wish to end the relationship while being respectful and sensitive to the resulting emotions. If two people have had a satisfying and close relationship, they behave ethically by being forthright and fair about communicating during its final stage. Whitney and Madeleine may decide separately that their friendship has reached an end and that they both want to room with different people next year. As effective communicators, they should discuss this sensitive topic with each other without blame or manipulation, acknowledge that their relationship is less close than it once was, and agree perhaps to move in with new roommates the following year.

Even when the participants agree that their relationship is over, they may choose a **relationship transformation**, continuing to interact and influence a partner through a different type of relationship after one type has ended. Romantic relationships may transform into friendships; best friends may become casual friends. Even people who end their marriage through divorce may continue on friendly terms or develop a type of "business" relationship that coordinates child-rearing practices and expenses (Parks, 2007). For example, although

Relationship transformation— continuing to interact and influence a partner through a different type of relationship after one type of relationship has ended.

arguing and mistrust damaged the intimate relationship of Whitney and Madeleine, who decided to no longer share a room, they may continue to talk when they run into each other on campus. Or R. J. and Liz divorce but work with a counselor to develop a functional joint-custody parenting relationship, which allows them to be cordial, make joint decisions about the children, and even share important events with them.

Although we have discussed these stages in a sequential order, it is important to remember that over their life many relationships cycle back and forth between stages, transforming themselves through the messages that partners exchange. Your cognitive maps, interaction scripts, and communication skills equip you to form and develop your relationships.

THE SOCIAL MEDIA FACTOR

Social Media and Relationship Closeness

One of the hallmarks of social media is that they not only approach the feeling of face-to-face interactions by facilitating the rapid exchange of messages but they also create and sustain relationships. For example, if you have left home to go to college in another city or state, you may have left your boyfriend, girlfriend, or best friend behind. In these long-distance relationships, you no longer have daily face-to-face contact, but social media can help you maintain an interpersonal dialog (O'Sullivan, Hunt, & Lippert, 2004).

Interestingly, some studies have shown that social media dialogs may help you feel even closer than before (Baron, 1998; Carnevale & Probst, 1997; McKenna & Bargh, 1998). Social media can also allow you to maintain relationships when your schedules don't permit synchronous interactions. This is where e-mail often comes in. In addition, carefully composing an e-mail also enables a more strategic presentation of you to others. Asynchronous communication lets you spend as much time as you need crafting a carefully worded message, whether to coax a deadline extension from your professor or to resolve a heated argument with a romantic partner. In addition, asynchronous social media are less demanding since our partners can reply to us when it is convenient for them.

Media Richness and Social Cues

When you call someone there are audible cues in the form of background noise and the tone of voice of your partner that help you understand what is going on around them. In social media where these cues are absent, it is difficult to ascertain the mood or reaction of your partner. Are they annoyed or happy to be distracted by your message? The richer the media, the more context cues available to fully understand the message. When we use lean media we may use questions to solicit context information to clarify communication.

When was the last time you accidently misinterpreted the meaning of a text message because of a typo or the lack of a smiley face? Face-to-face conversations allow us to take advantage of available social cues and simultaneously send and receive messages that communicate our intended meaning.

The ability to identify the other party is also affected by the relative richness of the social media tool. Social media also vary in the extent to which they enable us to verify the person with whom we are communicating. Leaner forms of social media convey very little information about the identity of the sender. Lean media—such as those on the left side of the continuum—have a dark side. People may remain anonymous, inaccurately portray themselves, or even assume a bogus identity. Lean media may make senders feel safer and give them permission to write a nasty anonymous letter to the editor of a newspaper, post a frank comment on someone's online blog, or send a vicious text message to a boyfriend's ex-girlfriend, assuming the number would not be stored in the receiver's cell phone. Anonymity can have some advantages as well. If you are a new employee in an organization, you may hesitate to voice your concerns over recent budget cuts. You may not want your colleagues to negatively perceive your desire to share your strong opinions. Writing an anonymous letter and dropping it in your supervisor's mailbox can allow you to express yourself but also protect your identity as you become more experienced at the specific job.

As you think about the most effective way to get your point across, consider the influence of media richness. Face-to-face conversations are one of the best ways to communicate that we care deeply for another person. If a good friend's grandmother passes away, it would be difficult to truly communicate your sympathies in a text message. A formal greeting card would be nice, but actually talking with your friend on the phone or sharing your condolences with them in person would better communicate your feelings and confirm your interpersonal relationship. While we might enjoy sharing good news face-to-face so others can share in our joy, we often rely on leaner social media to send that news to many people. If you just got engaged, it would be difficult to meet with each and every

---

A QUESTION OF ETHICS ● What Would You Do?

Grant and Amy have been in a committed relationship for two years. They maintain their relationship by spending almost all their free time together and having a common circle of friends. They are each other's best friends, share many hobbies and interests, and confide in each other on virtually all topics. A few months ago, Grant met Devon online through Facebook because of a common childhood friend. They began to exchange messages on Facebook and text each other on a daily basis. Occasionally, they would Skype or talk on the phone. Recently, when Devon was in town, they met at Starbucks for coffee and ended up spending the day together. Their relationship seems to be developing such that they share personal information, connect with each other easily, interact frequently, and expect the relationship to continue. Amy and Devon do not know about each other.

For Consideration:
1. What if any ethical principles is Grant violating?
2. What is likely to happen if Amy and Devon find out about each other?
3. What should Grant do?

one of your friends to tell him or her good news. Instead, you can tweet about your joy on Facebook and Twitter and easily reach hundreds, if not thousands, of people.

Summary

A relationship is a set of expectations that two people have for each other based on their pattern of interaction. There are good relationships, but there are also abusive relationships. Serving constitutive, instrumental, and indexical functions, communication is integral to relationships. We can describe relationships in several ways: personal or impersonal, voluntary or involuntary, platonic or romantic. We distinguish among our relationships, considering others as acquaintances, friends, and close friends or intimates. Relationships vary on eight dimensions: interdependence, breadth, depth, commitment, predictability, communication code change and shared social networks, and trust. At the heart of our relationships are two interpersonal communication behaviors: self-disclosure and feedback. The Johari window is a visual framework for understanding how self-disclosure and feedback work together in a relationship. Social penetration theory holds that self-disclosure and feedback are integral to all stages of relationships but that the nature and type of self-disclosure change over time. Relationship life cycles include beginning, developing, sustaining, and perhaps deteriorating and ending stages. Relationship stage changes are marked by turning points. At the beginning stage of a relationship, we use early conversations to predict whether the benefits of future interactions will outweigh the costs. Beginning relationships pass through three phases: an entry phase when we exclude people we don't like, a personal phase when we use mid-level disclosures to probe and assess our compatibility, and an exit phase when partners determine whether to invest in developing the relationship. We choose to develop relationships with people who can meet our interpersonal needs for inclusion, affection, and control and with whom social exchanges are more beneficial than costly and better than our other options. We sustain relationships by continuing to invest in them through prosocial behavior; by observing ceremonial occasions; by spending time together; by conversing frequently about day-to-day and intimate topics; by verbally and nonverbally reassuring our partners of our continuing affection, discretion, and trustworthiness; and by successfully managing relationship dialectics. Relational dialectics are the conflicting pulls that exist in a relationship, for example, the tugs between openness and closedness, autonomy and connection, and novelty and predictability. We can manage these tensions through temporal selection, topical segmentation, neutralization, and reframing. Relationships decline and perhaps end when one or both partners, recognizing that the relationship is less satisfying, unsuccessfully attempt to repair the relationship or begin to disengage from the relationship, which results in either its transformation or its termination. At all times, communication skills or lack of communication skills affects how relationships move through their life cycle.

As you think about how to most effectively get your point across, consider the influence of media richness on interpersonal communication. When you call someone, the background noise that you hear and the other party's tone of voice provide cues that help you understand what is going on around your partner and how they are feeling. In social media where these cues are absent, it is difficult to ascertain the mood or reaction of your partner. The richer the media, the more context cues are available to fully understand the message.

Chapter Resources

What You Should Be Able *to Explain:*

- The functions communication plays in relationships
- How relationships change
- Types of relationships
- Dimensions of relationships
- How self-disclosure and feedback work in relationships
- How relationships begin
- How relationships develop
- How relationships are sustained
- The dialectical tensions in relationships and how to manage them
- Turning points in relationships
- How relationships deteriorate and end

Self-test questions based on these concepts are available on the companion Web site (www.oup.com/us/verderber) as part of Chapter 6 resources.

Key Words

Flashcards for all of these key terms are available on the *Inter-Act* Web site.

Apply Your Knowledge

The following questions challenge you to demonstrate your mastery of the concepts, theories, and frameworks in this chapter by using them to explain what is happening in a specific situation.

6.1   *On the first day of his internship with a local TV station, Chase met Mia, a new sales assistant, when both were waiting for an orientation session with the human resources manager. Since they finished the session at lunchtime, Mia suggested that they grab a bite to eat at the diner next to the station. Over burgers and fries, they rehashed what they had learned from the H.R. manager and then moved on to exchanging basic information about their school backgrounds, career ambitions, and first impressions of the TV station. Over the next few weeks, they'd run into each other at the station but really didn't have much of a chance to talk: Chase was interning in production and worked the late shift on the 11:00 news show, while Mia worked 9 to 5 and spent most of her time out of the station calling on clients. One afternoon as Chase was arriving at the station, he ran into Mia as she was returning from a call. On a whim, Chase stopped her and asked her out. He was excited when she accepted, and they quickly agreed on a time, exchanging phone and e-mail information. The date went well, and Chase and Mia began to text each other during the day and spend much of the weekend hanging out and talking. The more time they spent together, the more they seemed to be attracted to each other. It was clear to Chase that both of them were falling in love. Over the next few months, they continued to see each other and shared deep conversations with revealing disclosures. As their relationship increased in its intimacy, Mia sidestepped Chase's sexual advances, which Chase attributed to her religious upbringing. Six months later Chase proposed, expecting Mia to be thrilled. Instead, she turned him down, leaving him hurt and confused. Sobbing, Mia explained, "I'm so sorry. I'm so sorry. This isn't about you. You're the best friend I've ever had! I just can't marry you! Oh, I'm so sorry. I never meant to mislead you. I just didn't want to lose you. Don't hate me. I'm so sorry, Chase. I'm bisexual."*

    a. How would you describe this relationship from each person's perspective?

    b. It seems like Mia was reluctant to come out to Chase. Was there anything that Chase could have done to uncover this secret?

    c. Write a script for a conversation that Chase and Mia should have next.

Identifying Personal Self-Disclosure Guidelines

6.2   The following exercise will help you recognize the types of self-disclosures you consider risky. Label each of the following information as L (low risk), meaning you believe that it is appropriate to disclose this information to almost any person; M (moderate risk), meaning that you believe this information is appropriate to disclose to people you know fairly well and consider friends; or H (high risk), meaning that you would disclose such information only to the few friends you trust deeply and to your most intimate friends; or X (unacceptable risk), meaning that you would not disclose this information to anyone.

_____ a. Your hobbies or how you like to spend your free time.

_____ b. Your music likes and dislikes.

_____ c. Your educational background and your feelings about it.

_____ d. Your views on current political issues including your opinion on the President.

_____ e. Your personal religious beliefs and the nature of your religious participation.

_____ f. Your habits and reactions that bother you.

_____ g. Your accomplishments and personal characteristics in which you take pride.

_____ h. Your most embarrassing moment recounted in detail.

_____ i. Your life's unhappiest moment.

_____ j. Your life's happiest day.

_____ k. Your deepest regret.

_____ l. Your fondest wish and biggest dream.

_____ m. Your views on an ideal marriage.

_____ n. Your physical fitness routine.

_____ o. Your physical features that make you most proud.

_____ p. Your physical features that most displease you.

_____ q. Your most resented person and why you feel as you do.

_____ r. Your use/abuse of alcohol, drugs, gambling, or sex.

_____ s. Your opinions on hooking up and friends-with-benefits relationships.

_____ t. Your personal hook-up and friend-with-benefits experiences.

Review your responses. What do you conclude about your willingness to disclose? Write a set of personal self-disclosure guidelines based on what you have learned about yourself.

6.3 Think about one of your relationships that ended badly. Considering what you have learned about relationship endings, how would you change the way that relationship ended if you could end it again? Write a script of the key parts of the final conversation you would like to have had.

6.4 Describe one of your relationships that has not progressed beyond an acquaintanceship even though you have known the person for a long time. Use the concepts in this chapter to explain why this relationship has not developed.

Communication Improvement Plan: Relationships

6.5 Relationships are developed through self-disclosure and feedback. Do you have problems either disclosing personal information or providing your relationship partner with feedback? Using the interpersonal communication skills you have studied in the course, write a communication improvement plan. You can find a communication improvement plan worksheet on our Web site at www.oup.com/us/verderber.

Inter-Act with Media

Television

Sex and the City (2004).

Viewers tune in to the syndicated show *Sex and the City* to watch Carrie Bradshaw (played by Sarah Jessica Parker) and her friends stumble through romances with a multitude of men. Throughout these experiences, the relationships among the friends grow and adapt to changing life circumstances. During the series, Carrie offers interesting insights on the nature of relationships. At one point, Carrie, a habitual smoker, becomes very interested in a man named Aidan. She quickly learns that Aidan cannot date a woman who smokes. Carrie begins to weigh her feelings for him against her addiction to cigarettes. For any smoker, quitting the habit is difficult to even consider. Carrie, however, recognizes the potential for a worthwhile relationship with a man who is handsome, charming, and kind. Consequently, she stops smoking with the aid of a nicotine patch.

IPC Concepts: Social exchange theory, relationship costs, relationship rewards.

To the Point:

How might social exchange theory explain this situation?
How might you describe the relationship costs and relationship rewards in Carrie and Aidan's potential relationship?

Cinema

Knocked Up (2007). Judd Apatow (director). Leslie Mann, Paul Rudd.

Debbie (Mann) and Pete (Rudd) reach a turbulent time in their marriage. Debbie's communication style is rather controlling, and she constantly nags Pete to settle down and spend more time at home with her and their children. Pete is employed as a talent scout for various bands. He leaves the home at odd hours in the middle of the night. This naturally makes her suspect that he is engaging in an extramarital affair. When she investigates the situation, she quickly learns that Pete is actually playing in a fantasy baseball draft with a few of his close friends. Pete explains to her he is part of the draft so he can have some time away from Debbie's controlling behavior. Pete's lying is the final straw for their relationship, and they agree to spend some time apart. They eventually get back together, though, recognizing the importance of their relationship while realizing the importance of time away from each other.

IPC Concepts: Relational dialectics, novelty, predictability, autonomy, connection.

To the Point:

How might relational dialectics explain the obstacles Debbie and Pete are experiencing in their marriage?
How might a person's time away from his/her partner lead to a greater appreciation for their interpersonal relationship?

What's on the Web

Find links and additional material, including self-quizzes, on the companion Web site at www.oup.com/us/verderber.

7

Listening
Effectively

As Terrell, Maria, Kai, and Ben walked toward the Union after Professor Green's class, Terrell commented:

"Professor Green drives me crazy. Why doesn't he just tell us what the bottom line is. I mean, every lecture he spends most of the time telling us about all the previous theories that research has found to be bogus. Who cares about that stuff? All we really need to know is what the current thinking is. I mean, that's what really matters."

"Well," responded Kai, "I disagree. This is my major, and besides, I really enjoy hearing all the background stuff. It's interesting, and I like hearing the details. It's like we're learning about how someone solved a mystery. Kind of like CSI on TV. And I really . . ."

"I'm with Terrell," Ben interrupted, "I mean, he needs to get to the point quicker. All that background is just wasting my time, and I get really annoyed when he starts with the stories. I mean, what do I care about how some scholar got started in researching a topic? I'm busy and could use the time he wastes with stories studying for my other classes."

"I totally disagree with you about the stories," Maria snapped. "The stories are the best part. They let you feel like you know the researchers and it's important to understand what makes people do what they do. How can you really appreciate their theories if you don't know anything about them? It easier to listen when you understand why someone was thinking the way they were."

What you should be able *to explain* after you have studied this chapter:

- The definition of listening
- The challenges to effective listening
- The personal and cultural styles of listening
- Listening apprehension
- The dual approaches we use when we listen
- The processes we use when we actively listen

- Guidelines to improve your attention to messages you receive
- Guidelines to understand messages more accurately
- Techniques to remember and retain information more accurately
- Guidelines to critically evaluate information
- Guidelines to provide feedback to a message
- Principles guiding effective digital listening

What you should be able *to do* after you have studied this chapter:

- Apply techniques to improve active listening skills
- Use listening techniques for clarifying and understanding messages
- Ask clarifying and probing questions
- Paraphrase a message to demonstrate what you have understood

---

All four classmates heard the same lecture, yet each adopted a different perspective on what was heard. Listening is a fundamental communication activity. How well we listen affects the quality of our conversations and shapes the course of our relationships (Halone & Pecchioni, 2001). In fact, listening creates reality. We listen and create reality based on what we hear in each moment (Ellinor & Gerard, 1998). If we are poor listeners, the personal reality we create may be very different from the one that others are trying to help us understand.

Of the basic communication skills (reading, writing, speaking, and listening), we use listening the most. What is listening? According to the International Listening Association, **listening** is the process of receiving, constructing meaning from, and responding to spoken and/or nonverbal messages.

According to one study, from 42 to 60 percent (or more) of communication time is spent listening. This percentage varied with the occupation of the listener, whether they were students, managerial trainees, doctors, counselors, lawyers, or nurses (Purdy, 1996). After 48 hours, however, many listeners can remember only about 25 percent of what they heard (Steil, Barker, & Watson, 1983). And

Listening—the process of receiving, constructing meaning from, and responding to spoken and/or nonverbal messages.

listeners who heard the same message may remember different things. Considering the importance of listening, it is unfortunate that we don't spend more time trying to understand and improve this important skill. To that end, this chapter is devoted to listening. We begin our study by looking at three challenges that make it difficult for us to effectively listen. Then we describe each of the steps in the active listening process (attending, understanding, remembering, critically evaluating, and responding) and present guidelines and skills that can help you improve your ability to listen at each.

Challenges to Effective Listening

Even before we hear a message, three things can affect how we listen to it: our personal and cultural styles of listening, our level of listening apprehension, and which of the dual processes of listening we adopt in a specific situation.

Personal and Cultural Styles of Listening

Most often when we listen, we do so based on our personal habits or style. Your **listening style** is your favored but usually unconscious approach to attending to your partner's messages (Watson, Barker, & Weaver, 1995). It reflects your preferences, attitudes, and predispositions about the how, where, when, who, and what of receiving messages (Sargent & Weaver, 2007). Research suggests that there are four styles of listening and that most of us favor one, though some people have two and a few can switch between all four (Weaver & Kirtley, 1995). We also know that adapting your listening style, even if another would be more effective, is difficult (Wolvin & Coakly, 1992).

Listening style—your favored but usually unconscious approach to attending to your partner's messages.

LEARN ABOUT YOURSELF ● Personal Listening Style Profile

Use the scale below to indicate the extent to which each of these statements captures how you listen. Always (4), Frequently (3), Sometimes (2), Infrequently (1), Never (0):

_____ 1. I focus my attention on the other person's feelings when listening to them.

_____ 2. I am frustrated when others don't present their ideas in an orderly, efficient way.

_____ 3. I prefer to listen to technical information.

_____ 4. When hurried, I let the other person(s) know that I have a limited amount of time to listen.

_____ 5. When listening to others, I quickly notice if they are displeased or disappointed.

_____ 6. When listening to others, I focus on any inconsistencies and/or errors in what's being said.

_____ 7. I prefer to hear facts and evidence so I can personally evaluate them.

_____ 8. I begin discussions by telling others how long I have to meet.

_____ 9. I become involved when listening to the problems of others.

_____ 10. I jump ahead and/or finish thoughts of speakers.

_____ 11. I like the challenge of listening to complex information.

_____ 12. I interrupt others when I feel time pressure.

_____ 13. I nod my head and or use eye contact to show an interest in what others are saying.

_____ 14. I am impatient with people who ramble on during a conversation.

_____ 15. I ask questions to probe for additional information.

_____ 16. I look at my watch or clocks in the room when I have limited time to listen to others.

Scoring the survey: This survey identifies your personal listening style. Sum your responses to Items 1, 5, 9, and 13. This is your people-oriented listening style score. Sum your responses to Items 2, 6, 10, and 14. This is your action-oriented listening style score. Sum your responses to Items 3, 7, 11, and 15. This is your content-oriented listening style score. Sum your answers to Items 4, 8, 12, and 16. This is your time-oriented listening style score. The style for which you have the highest sum is your preferred personal listening style. Some people have one dominant style, while others will have two with close scores. A few people do not have a dominant style and can switch listening modes as needed.

Based on: Watson, K. W., Barker, L. L., & Weaver, J. B., III. (1995). The listening styles profile (LSP-16): Development and validation of an instrument to assess four listening styles. *International Journal of Listening, 9,* 1–13.

Used with permission.

Some of us have a **content-oriented listening style**, which means that we prefer to focus on the facts and evidence in a message. We appreciate detail and enjoy the challenge of listening to complex messages. We prefer to pay attention to facts and evidence in messages so that we can evaluate them. We like messages that provide technical information, and we ask questions to get even more information that we can think about.

Others have a **people-oriented listening style**, which means that when we listen to a message we prefer to focus on what it tells us about our conversational partners and their feelings. For example, we notice whether our partners are pleased or upset about the message that they are sending. When speakers tell people-oriented listeners about their problems, these listeners become personally involved. People-oriented listeners also provide nonverbal cues like head nods that encourage their partners and indicate their interest in what is being said.

Those who have an **action-oriented listening style** prefer to focus on the point that the speaker is trying to make with a message. These listeners are task oriented and get frustrated when ideas are disorganized or when people ramble on during a conversation. They anticipate what the speaker is going to say and may even finish the speaker's sentence. Because we focus on the point of a message, we notice inconsistencies or errors in the details of what is being said.

Finally, some of us have a **time-oriented listening style**, which means that when we listen, we prefer brief and swift conversations. We use nonverbal and verbal cues to signal to our partners that they need to be more concise. We may tell our partners exactly how much time we have to listen, interrupt our partner when we feel time pressures, look at our watches or clocks, or rapidly nod our heads to nonverbally encourage our partners to pick up their pace.

As you can imagine, each of these styles has advantages and disadvantages. Those of us who are content oriented in our style of listening are more likely to correctly understand and remember the details of what has been said but may miss the overall point of the message and be unaware of how the speaker feels about the message. Our preference for details also means that we are insensitive to how much time may pass while we are listening.

Because those of us who are people oriented pay close attention to the emotional tone of a message, we are better able to understand what the message means to the speaker, which allows us to empathize and offer appropriate comfort and support. But as people-oriented listeners, we can become too involved with the speaker's feelings and may miss inconsistencies in what has been said or fail to personally evaluate what the speaker has said. Our focus on our partner and our involvement with our partner's problems result in the tendency to devote too much time to listening to others when we may have more important things to do.

Content-oriented listening style—the personal listening style that prefers to focus on the facts and evidence in a message.

People-oriented listening style—the personal listening style that prefers to focus on what a message tells us about our conversational partners and their feelings.

Action-oriented listening style—the personal listening style that prefers to focus on the point that the speaker is trying to make with a message.

Time-oriented listening style—the personal listening style that prefers brief and swift conversations.

OBSERVE AND ANALYZE

Listening Styles

Identify six people you talk with daily. What personal listening style do you think each uses most often? During the next few days, note whether each of their listening behaviors corresponds to your original perception. Then have a short conversation with each person. Begin by quickly explaining the four personal listening styles and ask them to identify the one they believe they use most frequently. Write a paragraph explaining what you have learned.

Those of us who are action-oriented listeners focus on understanding the point of a message and how the message is organized. We are, therefore, able to notice inconsistencies in what we have heard. But because we focus on the point of the message, we can be insensitive to the speaker and the speaker's feelings, and our nonverbal feedback may communicate our preference for organized and succinct messages. In our rush to understand the point of a message, we anticipate what the speaker is going to say and may consequently miss what the speaker actually says.

Finally, those of us who are time-oriented listeners have limited time to attend to a message and make that clear to conversational partners. Through both verbal and nonverbal messages, we encourage our partners to form succinct messages that we can quickly understand and respond to. As a result, we may not hear and properly evaluate detailed messages. And we may miss how the speaker feels about the message. Time-oriented listeners tend to half-listen to the message, stress about their time constraints, and respond insensitively to the needs of their partners.

While preferred listening styles are personal, they are also influenced by gender and culture. Research has shown that women are more likely to describe themselves as person oriented in their listening style than men. Men, on the other hand, are more likely to be time oriented in their preferred listening style (Salisbury & Chen, 2007). Our culture also influences our preferred listening style. As you would expect, research has found differences between the listening styles of people from collectivist cultures and those of people from individualistic cultures. People in collectivist cultures like Israel, where maintaining group harmony is highly valued, are more likely to have people-oriented listening styles. People from individualistic cultures like the United States are more likely to have action-oriented listening styles (Kiewitz et al., 1997). Other research has found that people from high-context cultures like France, Japan, and Vietnam favor people-oriented listening styles, whereas people from low-context cultures like the United States, Germany, Switzerland, and Scandinavian countries favor action-oriented styles (Harris, 2003). Although our personal preferred style may differ from the style preferred by our gender or culture, most of us adopt a listening style seen as appropriate for our gender and culture.

Listening Apprehension

Listening apprehension—the anxiety we feel about listening that interferes with our ability to be effective listeners.

Listening apprehension, the second challenge to effective listening, is the anxiety we feel about listening that interferes with our ability to be effective listeners. Listening anxiety may be due to our fear of misinterpreting the message, our fear of not being able to understand the message, or our fear of how the message may psychologically affect us (Brownell, 2006; Wheeless, 1975). For example, if you are in an important meeting or job training, you may feel undue stress about having to absorb all the important technical information that you know you need to remember to do your job well. Or your anxiety may escalate if you find yourself in a situation where the material you need to absorb is difficult or confusing. Likewise, your anxiety may increase when you have to listen closely to a message but are feeling ill, tired, or stressed. Or suppose that your spouse confronts you with a lie that you told. You may experience listening apprehension that stems from the emotionally charged atmosphere, from the psychological turmoil caused by being confronted with your own ethical lapse, or from your concern about how what you are hearing will affect your relationship. Whatever the reasons for listening apprehension, anxiety makes it more difficult for us to focus on what we are hearing. In the Diverse Voices selection, "How I Learned to Shut Up and Listen," blogger Eileen Smith describes how her listening apprehension taught her the value of listening.

Dual Processes in Listening

You may recall from Chapter 2 that we use one of two approaches to process the information that we receive—automatic or conscious. **Passive listening** is the effortless, thoughtless, and habitual process of receiving the messages we hear. When we listen this way, we are on automatic pilot. We may attend to only parts of the message and then assume that what our conversational partner is saying is predictable from one of our scripts. Passive listening is the default setting of our listening behavior. Sometimes we passively listen because we aren't really interested in the subject. At other times we passively listen because we are multitasking—trying to do several things at once. Think of how you normally listen to music or watch TV. Most of us are passive listeners to these media. Some of us have either music or TV on when we are doing other activities. Some of us will continue to "listen" to our M3P or iPods even when talking with others. If asked about what we are hearing on this background media, we may be able to give the title of the song playing, but unless we know the song, we usually will be unable to accurately report its lyrics.

By contrast, **active listening** is the skillful, intentional, deliberate, conscious process of attending to, understanding, remembering, critically evaluating, and responding to messages that we hear. Active listening is a fundamental communication skill that requires mindfulness and practice. Although we usually passively listen to music, you have probably actively listened to a song so you could learn its lyrics. When you did this, you listened differently than you normally do. The process you used was intentional and aimed at attending to, understanding, and remembering the words, phrasing, and tone of the lyrics. If you succeeded in learning the words, you understand how much work is involved in active listening.

As you have seen, our ability to be effective listeners is challenged by our listening style, our level of listening anxiety, and our tendency use a passive listening approach. If we are to improve our listening effectiveness, we must understand the active listening process and master and use listening skills. In the rest of this chapter, we will look at each step in the active listening process and suggest guidelines and listening skills that will help you overcome listening challenges.

Passive listening—the effortless, thoughtless, and habitual process of receiving the messages we hear.

Active listening—the skillful, intentional, deliberate, conscious process of attending to, understanding, remembering, critically evaluating, and responding to messages that we hear.

How I Learned to Shut Up and Listen

by Eileen Smith, Bearshapedsphere.com

Living in the "wrong" country for nearly seven years now, Elieen bikes, photographs, writes, eats and talks about language, but not in that order. Chile is home now, and probably will be for a while. She was raised in Brooklyn, New York.

I sat at a table of no fewer than fifteen people on the street Pio Nono, entry to Bellavista, the down-home party section of Santiago, Chile. I'd been invited to go out for a beer after the monthly critical mass bike ride. We sat at a long series of card tables extending down the street, serving ourselves beer from the liter bottles of Escudo on the center of the tables. Some, drinkers of fan-schop (a Chilean specialty), mixed theirs with Fanta. I drank mine plain, and listened.

I arrived to Chile in 2004, with way more than a passing knowledge of Spanish. Between high school and a couple of travel and study stints in the *mundo hispanohablante* (Spanish-speaking world), I could express myself fairly well, if not cleverly. Hadn't I explained the electoral college to a group of teachers in Antigua, Guatemala in the 90s? Wasn't it me who grabbed other travelers by the hand to take them to the post office, the bus station, to get their hair cut? I enjoyed helping, expressing, being in charge. I could get you a seat on the bus, a doorstop, tape to fix a book—you name it. I could ask for it directly or circumlocute it. I spoke, and people understood. At the time, I felt that this was the only necessary linguistic accomplishment. You listen to me. And then it was over.

While output was the feather in my linguistic cap, my listening wouldn't have won any awards. Still, I was skilled enough (or so I thought). Ask a predictable question while travelling, and get a predictable answer. "Where" questions should lead to a location. "When" questions should yield a time, or a day. "I don't know" might come up at any time, so be prepared. Other times you might get a "probably," or "No, we're out of that (on the menu), what about this?" These little sayings are repetitive, predictable, often accompanied by hand and head motions, and occasional pointing. Understandable.

But what happens when you get out of the predictable, and put fifteen of your new closest friends on a loud sidewalk, add an unfamiliar accent, country-specific slang and not just a touch of cheap beer? As an ESL teacher I'd seen students reduced to frustration, to squinching their eyes shut against visual input while they leaned their heads closer to the audio, hoping that the problem wasn't their ear for English, but their hearing. Try as I might there on the sidewalk, no matter of eye squinching or head leaning was going to fix the fact that I was simply not up to the task. My Chilean friends could understand me, but of the reading/writing/listening/speaking quadrifecta that make up second-language learning, clearly my listening was the weakest. I'm loquacious at the best of times, grate-on-your-nerves chatty when it's worse. But here, on the street in Santiago, 5,000 miles from a place where

Spotlight on Scholars

Read more about the active-listening process and the research of Judi Brownell at www.oup.com/us/verderber.

Attending—the process of willfully striving to perceive selected sounds that are being heard.

The Active Listening Process

The active listening process includes five steps: attending, understanding, remembering, critically evaluating, and responding to the messages we receive.

Attending

Active listening begins with **attending**, the process of willfully striving to perceive selected sounds that are being heard (O'Shaughnessey, 2003). To get a clearer idea of what attending is, stop reading for a minute, and try to become

I could understand easily (and foolishly had taken this for granted), I was relegated to good listener status. It wasn't that I couldn't exactly understand what anyone was saying. I could understand enough to follow, kind of, but not fast enough to say anything relevant to the conversation while the topic was still hot.

I was also in Chile, which, with the exception of not letting people off the metro before getting on, is one of the most polite places I'd ever been. What this means is that any time I so much as appeared to want to say anything, a hush would fall over the string of tables. People knew they might not understand me easily, so they wanted to give me their complete attention.

Between the hot topic issue and the *plancha* (embarrassment) I felt at having all eyes on me, the venerable communicator, I simply had to take a different tack. No longer was I Eileen, wordsmith extraordinaire. I was Aylín, the good listener. I was polite. It was cute. People described me as quiet. Not being able to participate in a conversation is like being in disguise. I would sit there in my shy suit and let the words whirl around me, swirl past me. For the first time in my life I was getting to know the patient people, the ones that reach out to quiet ones. I'd never met them before because I was so busy with my soundtrack. It made people want to take me into their confidence, their inner circle. I was not a person who repeated private information. As far as they could tell, I didn't even speak.

After several months of more listening than speaking, I took it up as a new challenge: To follow every conversation with surgical precision, and say nothing, or nearly nothing. I could feel the cloud of wonder and panic lifting, and still I chose to stay quiet. I learned about body language and turn-taking, Chilean social niceties, and watched the other quiet people to see what they were doing. Following along as well, in most cases. They weren't bland, just quiet. It was a revelation.

Nearly five years later, I don't have to just listen any more. I can exchange jokes and fling around slang with abandon. But what I've found is that I often don't want to. I'm often happy to let events take place without interrupting them, just listening to people say what they have to, what they want to. I don't interrupt as much and I've discovered this whole new world, even among my very own family, the self-professed masters of interrupting and simultaneous yammering (I blame Brooklyn). Sometimes I just try to let them talk themselves out before chiming in. Because when people are talking, they tend not be great listeners. I'd rather have their attention before saying something.

I'm often told I've changed quite a bit since being in Chile. Years have passed, and in that time we've all changed. But what I learned here is that you don't have to be on your game at every possible second. You can watch from the sidelines and participate at the same time. Sometimes the story we tell when we're not saying a word is the most important story of all.

For Consideration:

1. Have you ever been in a similar situation where you couldn't really follow a conversation because it was in a different language or dialect? Did you respond as this author did?
2. The author describes how not being able to be verbally active in conversations taught her to enjoy a whole different part of interaction. Can you list the benefits she described? Which of these benefits would enrich you the most?

Originally posted April 2, 2009, at Travelblogs.com. Used with permission of the author.

conscious of all of the sounds you hear around you. Perhaps you notice the humming of an electrical appliance, the rhythm of street traffic, the singing of birds, footsteps in the hall, a cough from an adjoining room. Yet while you were reading, you were probably unaware of most of these sounds. Although we physically register any sounds emitted within our hearing range, we exercise psychological control over the sounds to which we attend. Improving your listening, then, begins with attending—learning to keep your mind on or pay attention to what you hear in a more focused manner. The following guidelines can help you better attend to what you hear.

Guidelines to Improve Attending

1. Get physically and mentally ready to attend. To get ready to attend, good listeners prepare physically and mentally. Physically, good listeners create an environment conducive to listening, and they adopt a listening posture. It is easier to pay attention to what someone is saying when you have eliminated possible sources of distraction. For example, turning off your iPod before you answer the phone creates a better environment for you to focus on the caller's message. You can also improve your attention if you align your body so your senses are primed to receive messages. Moving toward the speaker, adopting a more upright stance, and making direct eye contact with the speaker are all physical actions that stimulate your senses and prepare you to perceive. You've probably noticed that when the professor tells the class that the next item of information will be on the test, students adjust their posture, sitting upright in their chairs and leaning slightly forward. They stop any extraneous physical movement and look directly at the professor. Their bodies are poised to attend to what will be said.

Attending to unrelated and competing thoughts and feelings rather than your partner's message is one of the leading causes of poor listening. Accordingly, active listeners also mentally prepare to attend. Active listeners make a conscious decision to ignore competing stimuli and focus on what the speaker is saying. If their minds wander, they quickly refocus on their partner's message. They deliberately block out miscellaneous thoughts that compete for their attention and put aside emotional distractions.

2. Make the shift from speaker to listener a complete one. In conversation, you are called on to quickly switch back and forth from being a speaker to being a listener. As a result, at times you may find it difficult to completely shift roles. We passively listen when we rehearse what we're

going to say as soon as we have a chance rather than focus on what our partner is saying. We actively attend when we discipline our thoughts so that we pay attention to what our partner is saying. Especially when engaged in a heated conversation, take a second to check yourself: Are you preparing your next remark instead of listening? Shifting completely from the role of speaker to listener requires constant and continuous effort.

3. Stay tuned in. Far too often, we stop attending before our partner has finished speaking because based on our scripts library, we "know what they are going to say." "Knowing" what a person is going to say is really only a guess. So active listeners cultivate the habit of waiting for the speaker to finish before searching their mental script library.

Understanding

The second part of the active listening process is understanding what is being said. **Understanding** is accurately decoding a message so you comprehend the semantic, pragmatic, and sociolinguistic meaning of a message. Having attended to and perceived the message being sent, you are now ready to understand, or "make sense" of it. To improve your understanding skills use the following guidelines and skills.

Guidelines and Skills for Improving Understanding

1. Identify the speaker's purpose and key points. Even in casual social conversations, speakers have some purpose or point they are trying to make. Sometimes people's thoughts are spoken in well-organized messages whose purposes and key ideas are easy to follow and identify. Other times, however, we must work harder to grasp the essence of what the speaker is trying to get across. If you can't figure out the speaker's purpose or key ideas, you will have trouble understanding the message. As you listen, ask yourself, "What does the speaker want me to understand?" and "What is the point being made?" For example, if Manuel spends two minutes talking about how much he likes the Cubs and asks Corella about her interest in baseball, casually mentioning that he has tickets for the game this weekend, Corella may recognize that he would like her to go with him.

Because speakers use messages to do things, you need to understand the pragmatic meaning of a message. When the speaker's purpose is to persuade you to think or do something, you will also want to identify what specific arguments the speaker is making. For instance, when Marlee, who is running for city council, asks Joanna what she thinks about the plan for the new arts center and begins to talk about some of its pros and cons, Joanna understands that Marlee is not making idle conversation. Beneath the surface of what Marlee is saying, she is attempting to persuade Joanna to vote for her.

2. Interpret nonverbal cues. In Chapter 5 we noted that up to 65 percent of the meaning of a message is transmitted nonverbally. Therefore, to understand

Understanding—accurately decoding a message so you comprehend the semantic, pragmatic, and sociolinguistic meaning of a message.

Listening means paying attention to nonverbal as well as verbal cues. What message is the speaker conveying through nonverbal cues?

what a speaker means, you need to understand not only what is said verbally but also the nonverbal behaviors that accompany what is said. For instance, if Deborah says to Gita, "Go on. I can walk home from here," what do these words mean? Without understanding the message cues transmitted through her tone of voice, body language, and facial expression, Gita can't really tell if Deborah truly prefers to walk or if she's just being polite but would really like a ride. Whether you are listening to a coworker describing her stance on an issue, a friend explaining the process for hanging wallpaper, or a loved one expressing why he or she is upset with you, you must look to how something is said as well as to what is said if you want to understand the real message.

Sometimes there is a message in silence, which can be the subtlest form of nonverbal communication that needs to be understood.

Clarifying question—a response designed to get further information or to remove uncertainty from information already received.

3. Ask clarifying questions. The skill of asking a clarifying question provides an easy way to better understand what a speaker is saying to you. A **clarifying question** is a response designed to get further information or to remove uncertainty from information already received. It also encourages the speaker to continue speaking. In addition to helping the listener, good clarifying questions help speakers sharpen their thinking about the points they make. Although you may have asked clarifying questions for as long as you can remember, you may notice that at times your questions either fail to yield the information you wanted or, worse, provoke an unwanted response—perhaps the other person becomes irritated, flustered, or defensive. To become skilled at questioning, you should follow these procedures:

- *Be specific about the kind of information you need to increase your understanding.* Suppose Maria calls you and says, "I am totally frustrated. Would you stop at the store on the way home and buy me some more paper?" At this point, you may be somewhat confused and need more information to understand what Maria is telling you. Yet if you respond by simply saying, "What do you mean?," you are likely to add to the confusion because Maria, who is already uptight, won't know precisely what it is you don't understand. So be more specific by asking for details, definitions, and causes. You might ask:

  "What kind of paper would you like me to get, and how much will you need?" (*clarify the important details*).
  "What do you mean by 'frustrated?'" (*clarify the definition*).
  "What is it that's frustrating you?" (*clarify the cause of the feelings the person is expressing*).

- *Deliver questions in a sincere tone of voice.* Ask questions with a tone of voice that is sincere—not a tone that could be interpreted as accusing, affected, sarcastic, cutting, superior, or judgmental. We need to remind ourselves that how we ask a question may be more important to getting a useful answer than the way we phrase the question.
- *Limit questions or explain that you need to ask multiple questions.* Sometimes asking several clarifying questions in a row can seem like an interrogation. If you can, limit your number of clarifying questions to the most appropriate ones. But if you need to ask several, you might explain why you are asking them. For instance, Vanessa could say to her dad, "I really want to understand why you won't pay my tuition this year, so I need to ask a few questions to get more information. Is that OK?"
- *Put the "burden of ignorance" on your own shoulders.* To minimize unplanned or unwanted reactions, phrase your clarifying questions in a way that puts the burden of ignorance on your own shoulders. Preface your questions with a short statement that suggests that any problem of misunderstanding may be the result of *your* listening skills. For instance, when Drew says, "I've really had it with Malone screwing up all the time," you might say, "Drew, I'm sorry. I'm missing some details that would help me understand your feelings better. What kinds of things has Malone been doing?"

Let's look at two examples that contrast inappropriate with more appropriate questioning responses.

> **I. Tamara:** They turned down my proposal again!
> **Art:** Well, did you explain it in the way you should have?
> *(Inappropriate: This question is a veiled attack on Tamara in question form.)*
> ***Art:*** Did they tell you why?
> *(Appropriate: This question is a sincere request for additional information.)*

> **II. Renée:** With all those executives at the party last night, I really felt weird.
> **Javier:** Why?
> *(Inappropriate: With this abrupt question, Javier is making no effort to be sensitive to Renée's feelings or to understand them.)*
> ***Javier:*** What is it about your bosses being there that made you feel weird?
> *(Appropriate: Here the question is phrased to elicit information that will help Javier understand and may help Renée understand as well.)*

Note how the appropriate, clarifying questions are likely to get the necessary information while minimizing the probability of an unplanned or unwanted reply. The inappropriate questions, on the other hand, may be perceived as an attack. To become skillful at questioning, follow the procedure in the Skill Builder on Questioning.

4. Paraphrase what you hear. Another way to affirm your understanding of what others say is to paraphrase what you hear. A **paraphrase** is an attempt to verify your understanding of a message by putting it into your own words and

Paraphrase—an attempt to verify your understanding of a message by putting it into your own words and sharing it with the speaker.\

sharing it with the speaker. When you paraphrase you don't just repeat what the speaker has said. Rather, you convey and try to verify the ideas and emotions you have perceived from the speaker's message. For example, during an argument with your sister, you might paraphrase what she said as follows: "So you are saying that you think I try to act superior to you when I talk about my successes at work?" Your sister can respond by saying, "Yes, exactly! It feels like you are trying to put me down when you do that." Or she may correct your paraphrase by saying, "Well, actually, I'm not feeling that you are trying to act like a big shot. It just makes me feel bad about the fact that I got laid off."

There are two types of paraphrases: a **content paraphrase** conveys your understanding of the denotative meaning of a verbal message; a **feelings paraphrase** conveys one's understanding of the emotional meaning behind a speaker's verbal message. You can also combine these into a paraphrase that conveys one's understanding of both the denotative and emotional meaning of your partner's verbal message. Whether a content or feelings paraphrase is most useful for a particular situation depends on what you perceive as the pragmatic meaning of the message. Let's look at an example.

> *Statement:* "Five weeks ago, I gave the revised paper for my independent study to my project advisor. I felt really good about it because I thought the changes I had made really improved my explanations. Well, yesterday I stopped by and got the paper back, and my advisor said he couldn't really see that this draft was much different from the first."
>
> *Content paraphrase:* "So you really thought that you had provided more depth and detail to your explanations, but Professor Delgato didn't notice."
>
> *Feelings paraphrase:* "You seem really frustrated that Professor Delgato didn't notice the changes you'd made."

Content paraphrase—a feedback message that conveys your understanding of the denotative meaning of a verbal message.

Feelings paraphrase—a feedback message that conveys one's understanding of the emotional meaning behind a speaker's verbal message.

SKILL BUILDERS ● Questioning

SKILL	USE	PROCEDURE	EXAMPLE
Phrasing a response designed to get further information or to remove uncertainty from information already received	To help get a more complete picture before making other comments; to help a shy person open up; to clarify meaning	1. Be specific about the kind of information you need to increase your understanding of the message. 2. Deliver questions in a sincere tone of voice. 3. Limit questions or explain that you need to ask multiple questions. 4. Put the burden of ignorance on your own shoulders.	When Connie says, "Well, it would be better if she weren't so sedentary," Jeff replies, "I'm not sure I understand what you mean by 'sedentary'—would you explain?"

Combination: "So Professor Delgato told you that he didn't notice the work you had done. What a bummer. No wonder you sound so disgusted."

Common sense suggests that we need not paraphrase every message we receive, nor would we paraphrase after every few sentences. So when should you use the skill of paraphrasing to better understand what you hear? We suggest that you paraphrase when you need a better understanding of a message's content, feelings, or both; when misunderstanding the message will have serious consequences; when the message is long and contains several complex ideas; when the message seems to reflect emotional strain; and when you are talking with people whose native language is not English.

To become skillful at paraphrasing follow the procedure in the Skill Builder on paraphrasing.

Remembering

The third step of the active listening process is **remembering**, the process of moving information from short-term memory to long-term memory. Too often people forget almost immediately what they have heard. Several things make remembering difficult. First, we often filter out the parts of the message that don't fit our personal listening style. As a result, this information, which is not stored in short-term memory, cannot be transferred to our long-term memory. For example, a people-oriented listener may be able to recall how someone felt about what she or he said but be unable to recall the details of the message. Second, when we are listening anxiously, we may be so stressed that we might not be able to recall anything we have heard. Some of us who become anxious when introduced to a large number of people at one time may be unable to remember any of the names five minutes later. Third, when we passively listen

Remembering—the process of moving information from short-term memory to long-term memory.

SKILL BUILDERS ● Paraphrasing

SKILL	USE	PROCEDURE	EXAMPLE
Verifying one's understanding of a message by putting it in one's own words and sharing it with the speaker	To increase listening efficiency; to avoid message confusion; to discover the speaker's motivation	1. Listen carefully to the message. 2. Notice what ideas and feelings seem to be contained in the message. 3. Determine what the message means to you. 4. Create a message in your own words that conveys these ideas and/or feelings.	Grace says, "At two minutes to five, the boss gave me three letters that had to be in the mail that evening!" Bonita replies, "I understand; you were really resentful that your boss dumped important work on you right before quitting time, when she knows that you have to pick up the baby at daycare."

to a message, we don't really pay attention to what is being said, so we don't remember it. Fourth, we are also selective in what we remember, finding it easier to recall messages that support our position and to forget information that contradicts our beliefs. For instance, if we watch a debate on television, we tend to recall the arguments for our point of view but forget some equally valid opposing arguments. Fifth, we are more likely to remember information at the beginning or end of a message and forget what comes in between. The **primacy effect** is the tendency to remember information that we heard first over what we heard in the middle, and the **recency effect** is the tendency to remember information that we heard last over what we heard in the middle. This explains why we are likely when given directions to remember the first few street names and turns as well as the last few but fail to recall the street names or turns in the middle of the route.

Let's look at several guidelines that can help you remember what has been said:

Guidelines for Improving Remembering

1. Repeat what was said. Repetition, saying something two, three, or even four times helps you store information in long-term memory (Estes, 1989). If information is not reinforced, it will be held in short-term memory for as little time as twenty seconds and then forgotten. The key to repetition is silently or vocally repeating something multiple times to aid the remembering process. When you are introduced to a stranger named Jon McNeil, if you mentally repeat, "Jon McNeil, Jon McNeil, Jon McNeil, Jon McNeil," you increase the chances that you will remember his name. Similarly, when a person gives you the directions, "Go two blocks east, turn left, turn right at the next light, and it's in the next block," you should immediately repeat to yourself, "Two blocks east, turn left, turn right at light, next block—that's two blocks east, turn left, turn right at light, next block."

2. Create mnemonics. A **mnemonic device** is a learning technique that associates a special word or short statement with new and longer information. One of the most common ways of forming a mnemonic is to take the first letter of each of the items you are trying to remember and form a word. For example, an easy mnemonic for remembering the five Great Lakes is HOMES (Huron, Ontario, Michigan, Erie, Superior). When you want to remember items in a sequence, try to form a sentence with the words themselves or assign words using the first letters of the words in sequence and form an easy-to-remember statement. For example, when you studied music the first time, you may have learned the notes on the lines of the treble clef (EGBDF) with the saying, "Every good boy does fine." Or to help students remember the colors of the spectrum in sequence, science teachers often ask them to remember the name "Roy G. Biv," standing for red, orange, yellow, green, blue, indigo, violet.

3. Take notes. Although note-taking may not be an appropriate way to remember information when you are engaged in casual interpersonal encounters, it

Primacy effect—the tendency to remember information that we heard first over what we heard in the middle.

Recency effect—the tendency to remember information that we heard last over what we heard in the middle.

Mnemonic device—a learning technique that associates a special word or short statement with new and longer information.

What are the advantages and disadvantages of taking notes during a meeting?

is a powerful tool for increasing your recall of information in telephone conversations, briefing sessions, interviews, and business meetings. Note taking provides a written record that you can revisit while promoting a more active role in the listening process (Wolvin & Coakley, 1992). In short, when you are listening to complex information, take notes.

What constitutes good notes will vary with the situation. Useful notes may consist of a brief list of main points or key ideas plus a few of the most significant details. Or the notes may take the form of a short summary of the entire concept; a type of paraphrase written after the message has been delivered. For lengthy and rather detailed information, however, good notes are best written in outline form, including the overall idea, the main points of the message, and key developmental material organized by category and subcategory. Good outlines are not necessarily long. In fact, many classroom lectures can be reduced to an outline of one page or less.

Critically Evaluating

The fourth step of the active listening process is critically evaluating. **Critically evaluating** is the process of determining how truthful, authentic, or believable you judge the message and the speaker to be. This may involve ascertaining the accuracy of facts, the amount and type of evidence supporting a position, and the relation of a position to your own values. For instance, when you get a tweet directing you to vote for a particular candidate for office or to sign a petition to add a skateboard park to the neighborhood, you will want to critically evaluate the message. Have supporting facts been presented for what you are being asked to do, and are they true? Have you been provided with the supporting information you need to make a judgment? Do you fundamentally agree with the basic

Critically evaluating—the process of determining how truthful, authentic, or believable you judge the message and the speaker to be.

idea? Critically evaluating also means assessing the speaker's credibility, including his or her expertise and character. You can improve your ability to critically evaluate the messages you receive if you follow the following guidelines and use these skills.

Guidelines for Improving Critical Evaluation

Facts—statements whose accuracy can be verified or proven.

Inferences—claims or assertions based on the facts presented.

1. Separate facts from inferences. Facts are statements whose accuracy can be verified or proven; **inferences** are claims or assertions based on the facts presented. Separating facts from inferences requires us to distinguish between a verifiable observation and an opinion related to that observation. Too often people treat inferences as factual. Let's clarify this distinction with an example. If we can document that Cesar received an A in geology, then saying that Cesar received an A in geology is a fact. If we go on to say that Cesar studied very hard, without knowing that this was the case, our statement is an inference. Cesar may have studied hard to receive his grade, but it is also possible that geology comes easily to him or that he had already learned much of the material in his high school physical science course.

Separating facts from inferences is important because inferences may be false, even if based on verifiable facts. Making sound judgments entails basing our inferences on facts whose correctness we have evaluated. Consider the following statements: "Better watch it. Carl is really in a bad mood today. Did you see the way he was scowling?"; or "I know you're hiding something from me. I can hear it in your voice"; or "Olga and Kurt are having an affair—I've seen them leave the office together nearly every night." Each of these conveys an inference, which may be—but is not necessarily—true.

Probing questions—questions that search for more information or try to resolve perceived inconsistencies in a message.

2. Probe for information. Sometimes to critically evaluate a message, we need to encourage the speaker to delve deeper into the topic. Or we may need to challenge the information to see if it holds up under scrutiny. To do this, we can ask **probing questions**, questions that search for more information or try to resolve perceived inconsistencies in a message. For example, suppose that Jerrod's landlord was talking with him about the need to sign a lease. Before signing this legally binding document, Jerrod should ask the prospective landlord probing questions such as the following:

> "You said that I would need to sign a lease, but you did not state the term of the lease. What's the shortest lease I could get?"
> "Your ad in the paper said that utilities would be paid by the landlord, but just now you said that the tenant pays the utility bill. Which way will it work with this apartment?"
> "Is there a deposit, and if so, what must I do to get my deposit back when the lease is up?"

With questions like these, Jerrod is testing what the landlord has said and trying to resolve inconsistencies.

When we ask probing questions, our nonverbal communication is especially important. We must pay attention to our tone of voice and body language so we do not appear arrogant or intimidating. Too many probing questions accompanied by inappropriate nonverbal cues can cause the other person to become defensive.

Responding

The final step of the active listening process is **responding**, the process of providing feedback to your partner's message. You can listen without providing any external cues that would indicate to others that you are listening (Bostrom, 2006). If you have ever talked with someone who appeared totally unresponsive to what you were saying, you can appreciate the importance of responding to messages you hear. The active listening process is not complete without responses on the part of the listener to indicate that he or she hears the speaker, understands the message, and is willing to comment on what has been understood. Although responding means that you are sending a message, it remains the critical final step of active listening. You can more effectively respond if you adopt the following guidelines.

Responding—the process of providing feedback to your partner's message.

Guidelines to Improve Responding

1. Provide back-channel cues. One way to indicate that you are listening to the message is to provide **back-channel cues**, verbal and nonverbal signals that indicate you are listening and attempting to understand the message. These cues include nodding, head shaking, smiling, laughing, head cocking, frowning, eyebrow knitting, or saying "huh?" "uh huh," "yeah," or other short vocalized utterances. Back-channel cues are useful and appropriate when they provide feedback to the speaker without becoming distractions.

Back-channel cues—verbal and nonverbal signals that indicate you are listening and attempting to understand the message.

2. Reply only when the message is complete. Except for back-channel cues, listeners should respond to a message only when the speaker has finished talking. One of the most common signs of poor listening is interrupting. A study of college students cited interrupting as the behavior that most interferes with really listening to what another person is saying (Halone & Pecchioni, 2001). Learning to wait can be especially challenging for those with a time-oriented listening style, when a group of people is talking, when you are in a heated conversation, or when you are excited and enthusiastic about what you have just heard. With concentration and practice, however, you can become better at waiting until a speaker is finished talking and you have had a chance to understand, remember, and critically evaluate what he or she is saying before you respond.

3. Respond to the previous message before changing the subject. Abrupt topic changes are inappropriate because they don't acknowledge what your partner has said. It is important to acknowledge your partner's message before changing the subject. Besides asking questions or paraphrasing what was said, you might respond to a message by agreeing or disagreeing with what was said, expanding on the ideas, challenging some of the message, indicating empathy or support, and offering advice. Let's look at an example that demonstrates different ways to respond to the same message from a friend:

> **Message:** "I need to look for a better job, and I'm probably going to quit school. I'm in a major financial mess with credit card debt, monthly living expenses of $1200, and late child support payments. And on top of all of this, my hours at work are being cut back. I'm in deep trouble here and pretty stressed out. I don't know what to do. Got any ideas?"
>
> **Paraphrase:** "So you're having trouble paying your bills at the same time that your paycheck is being reduced."
>
> **Question:** "What's the difference between your bills and your take-home pay each month?"
>
> **Agreement:** "Yeah, it makes sense to look for a higher-paying job."
>
> **Challenge:** "Is there a way that you can continue to make progress toward your degree even though you have to work more?"
>
> **Advice:** "You may want to meet with a debt consolidator who could help you work on a long-term plan for getting back into good financial shape."
>
> **Support:** "Wow, off the top of my head I can't really think of any, but I'm willing to talk with you about things, and maybe together we can figure this out."

As you can see, some responses are aimed at developing a clearer understanding of the original message, whereas others focus on helping the speaker. As we discussed in Chapter 1, it is important for you to develop behavioral flexibility so that you are skilled at responding in a variety of ways.

THE SOCIAL MEDIA FACTOR

Digital Listening Skills

Sending messages has never been easier, but effectively receiving the proliferation of messages that social media enable presents many challenges. How many digital messages do you send in one day? In 24 hours, you probably respond to many texts, answer several e-mails, listen to voicemails, and reply to Facebook posts and instant messages. You must attend to these messages, make sense of them, respond appropriately, and in some cases, remember them. In fact, research suggests that many teenagers send at least 50 text messages a day, while others send over 100 texts per day (Pew Internet and American Life Project, 2010). Being an effective digital listener requires **digital communication literacy**—the ability to critically attend to, analyze, evaluate, and express digital messages. This includes understanding how digital messages are created; recognizing a sender's underlying motives, values, or ideologies; and avoiding overdependence on social media. Let's briefly look at some of the problems and the solutions to the unique challenges we face in digital listening.

Digital communication literacy— the ability to critically attend to, analyze, evaluate, and express digital messages.

Attending and Understanding Digital Messages

Because social media permit the convenient and rapid exchange of short messages lacking in nonverbal cues, it is easy to make mistakes when interpreting digital messages. When your girlfriend sends a terse text message, do you automatically think she is mad at you? It is important to focus carefully on the message, ask questions, and consider the possibility of multiple, alternative meanings. Do not jump to a conclusion because of an omitted smiley face or because a partner's reply may be very brief. You can run the risk of misunderstandings, bad feelings, and unnecessary frustrations.

One of the biggest problems we face when attending to a digital message is the issue of multitasking. How many times have you texted a friend while talking to another friend face-to-face? Not only are nonverbal cues absent from the text message, but also you may only be paying "half attention" to the text or your friend. So anticipate that the people who get your messages will also be distracted. When you send a message, strive for clarity. One simple typographical error can communicate a completely different message. When you type a text message, many smartphones will automatically "correct" an unfamiliar word to something very different. As it turns out, our smartphones are not as "smart" as we think. In addition, if you are multi-tasking and a message you receive seems "off," don't respond until you can focus on the message. Then, if you are still concerned about what your partner said, help your partner to clarify the message with a question or paraphrase.

Social media are undoubtedly convenient. In fact, some people become so immersed in digital interactions that they sacrifice the richness available in face-to-face interactions. Remember that digital media aren't as rich as face-to-face interaction. As a result, even when we try to be skillful at digital listening, much of the sender's message meaning can be lost. So don't allow the keyboards of your smartphone to lull you into forgoing face-to-face interactions—even if you are a shy person. Although research suggests that people who heavily use social media to maintain relationships tend to be shyer than those who do not, online and face-to-face interactions have their place (Ward & Tracey, 2004). Digitally literate users of social media recognize that digital communication should not completely replace the face-to-face conversations that they can experience on a daily basis. If you are angry with your significant other, do not try to resolve the conflict via text messaging. Emotionally laden texts do no good and can be grossly misinterpreted. Instead of attempting to resolve a conflict by texting back and forth with your partner, send a quick text that asks if he is willing to meet in person. No need to hide behind a cell phone. Resolving the conflict in person will strengthen your relationship and cause it to grow and develop.

Critically Evaluating Digital Messages

Research indicates that we identify with others more quickly online than in face-to-face conversations (Pew Internet and American Life Project, 2001). Yet it is easy to intentionally or unintentionally post inaccurate and misleading information online, so it is important to critically evaluate the digital messages that you "listen" to. If a new friend's Facebook profile contains unfamiliar information that piques your curiosity, ask the person questions, as long as you are comfortable discussing the topic. Then you will be better able to separate facts from inferences you may make about your new friend. Similarly, computer hackers often spread viruses through social media. If it appears that a Facebook friend has posted an odd item on his page, or uploaded bizarre photos that are uncharacteristic of his personality, those strange postings may be a computer virus in disguise. Recently, a news story began appearing throughout Facebook. The article reported that actor Charlie Sheen had died. This false news story was a virus that was transmitted through social media (Kanalley, 2011). The information that circulates on the web as "facts" are often urban legends. So before you act on or pass along inaccurate information check it out. A useful place to check out the accuracy of information is at Snopes.com, an award-winning Web site dedicated to ferreting out the truth of urban legends.

Recognizing Underlying Motives, Values, and Ideologies

We can select what we pay attention to and what we ignore. In the days before Internet pop-up blockers, when you opened a Web site, you were often bombarded with multiple pop-up windows that each advertised a different product or service. You probably closed these windows quite quickly. In other words, you chose to ignore these digital messages. Digitally literate consumers of social media also consider how ideology may motivate senders, and they understand that their messages can have significant effects on receivers. In the recent presidential campaign, many candidates took advantage of the tremendous reach provided by social networking Web sites to convey their values and positions on controversial political issues. Savvy listeners, however, critically evaluate these messages to discern facts from political propaganda.

Avoiding Overdependence

Even skillful digital listeners may not interpret all of a message's meaning correctly. Despite its potential hazards, digital communication is tremendously convenient, and some people become so immersed in these interactions that they sacrifice richer forms of interaction, allowing their smartphone to replace face-to-face conversations. Digitally literate users of social media recognize that digital communication should not completely replace the face-to-face conversations that they can experience on a daily basis.

Summary

Listening is the process of receiving, constructing meaning from, and responding to spoken and/or nonverbal messages. There are three primary challenges to our listening effectiveness: our personal listening style, our listening apprehension, and the dual approach we can take to listening. Our personal listening style, which is influenced by our culture, may be people oriented, content oriented, action oriented, or time oriented. Each style has advantages and disadvantages.

Listening apprehension is the anxiety we feel about listening that interferes with our ability to be effective listeners. We use a dual-process approach to listening. Most of the time we are passive listeners, automatically processing what we hear with little effort made to focus on the message. Alternatively, we use the active-listening process of attending, understanding, remembering, critically evaluating, and responding to the message we heard. Attending is the process of willfully striving to perceive selected sounds that are being heard. To improve your attending skills, get physically and mentally ready to attend, make the shift from speaker to listener a complete one, resist tuning out, and avoid interrupting. Understanding is the process of accurately decoding a message so that you share its meaning with the speaker. To increase your understanding skills, identify the speaker's purpose and key points, interpret nonverbal cues, ask clarifying questions, and paraphrase what you hear. Remembering is the process of moving information from short-term memory to long-term memory. To be more skilled at remembering, repeat what was said, use mnemonic devices, and take notes. Critically evaluating is the process of interpreting what you have understood to determine how truthful, authentic, or believable you judge the meaning to be. To

A QUESTION OF ETHICS ● What Would You Do?

Janeen always disliked talking on the telephone—she thought that it was an impersonal form of communication. Thus, college was a wonderful respite because when her friends would call her, instead of staying on the phone, she could quickly run over to their dorm or meet them at the campus coffeehouse.

One day, during reading period before exams, Janeen received a phone call from Barbara, a childhood friend. Before she was able to dismiss Barbara with her stock excuses, Janeen found herself bombarded with information about old high school friends and their whereabouts. Not wanting to disappoint Barbara, who seemed eager to talk, Janeen tucked her phone under her chin and began to check her e-mail, answering Barbara with the occasional "uh huh," "hmm," or "Wow, that's cool!" As the "conversation" progressed, Janeen signed on to her Facebook account and was reading posts. After a few minutes she realized there was silence on the other end of the line. Suddenly very ashamed, she said, "I'm sorry, what did you say? The phone . . . uh, there was just a lot of static."

Barbara replied with obvious hurt in her voice, "I'm sorry I bothered you; you must be terribly busy."

Embarrassed, Janeen muttered, "I'm just really stressed, you know, with exams coming up and everything. I guess I wasn't listening very well. You didn't seem to be saying anything really important. What were you saying?"

"Nothing 'important,'" Barbara answered. "I was just trying to figure out a way to tell you. I know that you were friends with my brother Billy, and you see, we just found out yesterday that he's terminal with a rare form of leukemia. But you're right. It obviously isn't really important." With that, she hung up.

For Consideration:
1. Which of the ethical principles did Janeen violate by how she listened to Barbara? Explain how each of these principles applies to listening.
2. Although Barbara was the one hurt by Janeen's comment about the importance of the call, did she violate any ethical principles by how she ended the call?
3. Has this case changed the way you view ethical listening? If so, how? If not, why not?

improve your critical evaluation skills, separate facts from inferences and probe for information. Responding is the process of reacting to what has been heard while listening and after listening. To improve your responding skills, provide back-channel cues and reply when the message is complete.

Chapter Resources

What You Should Be Able *to Explain:*

- The definition of listening
- The challenges to effective listening
- The personal and cultural styles of listening
- Listening anxiety
- The dual processes we use when we listen
- The processes that we use when we actively listen
- Guidelines to improve your attention to the messages you receive
- Guidelines to understand messages more accurately
- Skills to remember and retain information more accurately
- Guidelines to critically evaluate information
- Guidelines to provide feedback about a message you have heard

What You Should Be Able *to Do:*

- Engage in active listening
- Ask clarifying and probing questions
- Paraphrase a message to demonstrate what you have understood

Self-test questions based on these concepts are available on the companion Web site (www.oup.com/us/verderber) as part of Chapter 7 resources.

Key Words

Flashcards for all of these key terms are available on the *Inter-Act* Web site.

Apply Your Knowledge

The following activities challenge you to demonstrate your mastery of the concepts, theories, and frameworks in this chapter by using them to explain what is happening in a specific situation.

Inter-Action Dialogue: Listening Effectively

7.1 The following is a transcript of a conversation illustrating aspects and issues related to effective listening. Do a line-by-line analysis of this *Inter-Action Dialogue* and indicate where you see evidence of the participants using the active-listening process. Be sure to note which specific skills and guidelines each follows as well as noting any challenges or problems you see in their listening behavior. How is this conversation affected by the use of active listening? You can watch a video of this conversation on the *Inter-Act* Web site and follow a transcript of the dialogue, provided online, with analysis in the right-hand column.

DIALOGUE

Gloria and Jill meet for lunch on campus.

Gloria: I'm really hungry—I don't know whether I've been working out too hard or what.

Jill: I know. There are some days when I can't figure out what happened, but I just feel starved.

Gloria: Thanks for meeting me today. I know you're up to here in work, but . . .

Jill: No problem, Gloria. I feel bad that we haven't been getting together as much as we used to, so I've been really looking forward to seeing you.

Gloria: Well, I need to talk with you about something that's been really bothering me. (She notices that Jill is fumbling with something in her purse.) Jill—are you listening to me?

Jill: I'm sorry, Gloria. For a minute I couldn't find my cell phone. I wanted to turn it off while we talked, and then I worried that I might have dropped it. But everything's OK. I apologize—that was rude of me. (She then sits up straight and looks directly at Gloria.) I'm ready.

Gloria: Well, you know I'm working with Professor Bryant on an independent research project this term.

Jill: I recall you mentioning something about it, but remind me of the details.

Gloria: Last semester when I took her course on family communication I wrote a term paper on how shared dinnertime affected family communication. Well, she really liked it and asked me if I wanted to work with her on a study this term. She said I could get credit.

Jill: How?

Gloria: I had permission to sign up for four credit hours of independent study.

Jill: That sounds good—so what's the problem?

Gloria: Well, since she videotapes actual family discussions and then interviews family members, I thought I'd get to help with some of the interviews. But so far, all I've been assigned to do is transcribe the tapes and do some library research.

Jill: So you're disappointed because you're not being challenged?

Gloria: It's more than that. I thought Dr. Bryant would be a mentor and there'd be team meetings when we'd talk over ideas and stuff. But I don't really even get to see her. Her graduate assistant gives me my assignments, and he doesn't even stop to explain why I'm being asked to do stuff. I'm not really learning anything.

Jill: So, if I understand, it's not only the type of assignments you're getting, but it's also that instead of really being involved, you're being treated like a flunky.

Gloria: Exactly.

Jill: So when she asked you to work on her study, did she ever sit down and discuss exactly what the independent study would entail?

Gloria: Not really. I just signed up.

Jill: Well since the term began, have you had any contact with Dr. Bryant?

Gloria: No. Do you think I should make an appointment to see her?

Jill: I think so, but if you did, what would you say to her?

Gloria: Well, I'd just tell her how disappointed I am with how things are going. And I'd explain what I hoped to learn this term and ask if she could help me understand how the assignments I'd been given were going to help me learn about family communication research.

Jill: So the purpose of your meeting wouldn't be to get different assignments but to understand what you are supposed to be learning from the assignments you've done so far?

Gloria: Right. But I think I'd also like her to know that I really expected to have more contact with her.

Jill: Well, it sounds as if you're clear on what you'd like to ask her.

Gloria: Yes, but I don't want to get her angry with me. Four credit hours is a lot, and it's too late to drop the independent study.

Jill: So you're concerned that she would be offended and take it out on your grade.

Gloria: A little. But that's probably ridiculous. After all, she's a professional, and all the students I know who have gone to see her say that she's really understanding.

Jill: Well, then what do you want to do?

Gloria: Hmm. . . . I'm going to make an appointment to see her. In fact, I'll stop by her office on my way to my next class. Jill, thanks for listening. You've really helped me.

Skill Practice

Skill practice activities give you the chance to rehearse a new skill by responding to hypothetical or real situations. Additional skill practice activities are available at the companion Web site.

Writing Questions and Paraphrases

Provide an appropriate question and paraphrase for each of the following statements. To get you started, the first conversation has been completed for you.

7.2 **Luis:** It's Dionne's birthday, and I've planned a *big* evening. Sometimes, I think Dionne believes I take her for granted—well, I think after tonight she'll know I think she's someone special!

Question: What specific things do you have planned?
Content paraphrase: If I understand you, you're planning a night that's going to cost a lot more than what Dionne expects on her birthday.
Feelings paraphrase: From the way you're talking, I get the feeling you're really proud of yourself for making plans like these.

7.3 **Angie:** Brother! Another nothing class. I keep thinking one of these days he'll get excited about something. Professor Romero is a real bore!

Question:
Content paraphrase:
Feelings paraphrase:

7.4 **Jerry:** Everyone seems to be talking about that movie on Channel 5 last night, but I didn't see it. You know, I don't watch much that's on the idiot box.

Question:
Content paraphrase:
Feelings paraphrase:

7.5 **Kaelin:** I don't know if it's something to do with me or with Mom, but lately she and I just aren't getting along.

Question:
Content paraphrase:
Feelings paraphrase:

7.6 **Aileen:** I've got a report due at work and a paper due in management class. On top of that, it's my sister's birthday, and so far I haven't even had time to get her anything. Tomorrow's going to be a disaster.

Question:
Content paraphrase:
Feelings paraphrase:

Creating Mnemonics

7.7 Practice remembering the four personal listening styles and the steps in the active-listening process by creating a mnemonic for each. Record your mnemonics. Tomorrow morning while you are dressing, see whether you can recall the mnemonics you created. Then see how many of the personal listening styles and active-learning steps you can recall using the cues in your mnemonics.

Communication Improvement Plan: Listening

7.8 Would you like to improve the following skills discussed in this chapter?

- Questioning
- Paraphrasing

Pick a skill, and write a communication improvement plan. You can find a communication improvement plan worksheet on our Web site at www.oup.com/us/verderber.

Inter-Act with Media

Television

Hell's Kitchen, season 4 (2008). Gordon Ramsey.

World-renowned chef Gordon Ramsey heads a group of fifteen people who are vying for the executive chef position at one of Ramsey's famous restaurants. In this episode, finalists Christina and Petrozza compete against each other. Their voted-off competitors act as their sous-chefs for the last dinner service. To act as an effective work team and accurately fill orders for restaurant guests, all of the chefs must carefully listen to each other. This is quite the challenge in a fast-paced kitchen. For example, when cleaning the kitchen prior to service, Petrozza innocently asks Jen if she needs help. Jen sharply replies, "If I need help sweeping, I wouldn't trust me to work a line." Jen's interpretation of Petrozza's statement likely stems from her resentment that she's not a finalist on the reality show. Later, Petrozza tells Bobby that he needs an appetizer immediately. After Bobby plates a cold strudel, Petrozza asks him to please "touch everything before it comes to him." Bobby listens, acknowledges and apologizes for his mistake, and delivers another hot dish. Christina assigns Matt to help Lou Ross in the competing kitchen because he fell behind on salads. Matt immediately repeats and paraphrases each of Lou Ross's instructions on the salad. Lou Ross finds this behavior very annoying. Looking toward the camera, Christina sharply criticizes Matt and indicates that he should not need help making a dish as simple as a salad.

IPC Concepts: People-oriented listening style, action-oriented listening style, time-oriented listening style.

To the Point:

> How might you explain the influence of the chefs' diverse personalities on the listening process?
>
> How might you characterize the relationship between the chefs' cooking skill levels and his/her ability to listen to others during service?

Cinema

The Proposal (2009). Anne Fletcher (director). Sandra Bullock, Ryan Reynolds.

Margaret Tate (Bullock) is the editor-in-chief of a large New York publishing house. She is viewed as driven and demanding and is not well-liked by her staff. Struggling to advance his career in publishing, her assistant, Andrew Paxton (Reynolds), caters to her every need. He brings her coffee in the morning, takes her phone calls, and manages her mail, among other duties. Andrew ensures that her every demand is completed in a timely fashion. When Margaret, a Canadian citizen, learns that she is going to be deported because of her expired visa, she convinces Andrew to marry her to avert being deported. During a visit to the immigration office, the officer informs Margaret and Andrew that he suspects they are committing fraud. Facing significant legal issues, Andrew demands that Margaret appoint him as an editor following their marriage and guarantee the publication of his book. Margaret agrees.

During a trip to Alaska to meet Andrew's family, Margaret, noticing that nearly every shop in town carries the name Paxton, realizes that Andrew is an "Alaskan Kennedy." Andrew's family convinces them to get married while they are in Alaska. At the wedding ceremony, Margaret confesses the sham marriage to the entire assemblage, including the immigration officer in attendance, who informs her she has 24 hours to leave the country. Margaret returns to the Paxton home to pack her things. Andrew rushes to their room only to find she has already gone, having left his book manuscript with a kind note of praise and a promise to publish it. When Andrew gets back to New York, he loudly announces his love for Margaret so all members of the office staff can hear. Their engagement is on again, but this time for real.

IPC Concepts: People-oriented listening style, action-oriented listening style, time-oriented listening style, content-oriented listening style.

To the Point:

How might Margaret have learned more about the personal aspects of Andrew's life?
During the couple's interactions with the immigration officer, how might you
characterize the officer's ability to critically evaluate the information being
exchanged?

What's on the Web

Find links and additional material, including self-quizzes, on the companion Web site at
www.oup.com/us/verderber.

Holding Effective Conversations

On Tuesdays, Ben has a two-hour gap between classes around lunchtime. Today he decides to go to the campus food court to get a bag of chips and a soda to go with the sandwiches he brought from home. Standing at the cash register, he notices a very attractive girl sitting by herself at a nearby table, eating and looking around. Thinking of Professor Green's admonition, "Nothing ventured, nothing gained!" he approaches the table.

Ben says, "Hey, I see you have a crowd at this table."

The girl responds, "Huh? Oh, no. Just me."

Ben replies, "Mind if I sit here? I won't bite anything except sandwiches."

Laughing, the girl says, "I'll protect my sandwich, then. Sure, have a seat."

Ben sits down and arranges his food. After taking a bite and a swallow of soda, he notices the textbook open next to the girl's plate. "Is that Chemistry—or Biology?" he asks.

"Both: It's my BioChem class," the girl replies.

"Are you pre-Med, then?" Ben asks. "One of my friends is pre-Med, and he's taking BioChem this semester. His name is Evan—Evan Riehle."

The girl thinks about it for a second. "No," she says. "Sorry, I don't actually think I know Evan. But there are several sections of BioChem. And what about you? What's your major?"

"I'm in Construction Engineering. By the way, my name is Ben. What's yours?"

What you should be able *to explain* after you have studied this chapter:

- What defines a conversation
- The characteristics of conversation
- Six ways in which conversations vary
- Guidelines to be a more effective conversationalist

- Message strategies to initiate, sustain, and close conversations effectively
- Cultural variations in conversation
- Issues in mediated conversations
- Factors influencing your ability to engage in effective digital conversations

What you should be able *to do* after you have studied this chapter:

- Use effective turn-taking in a conversation
- Comfortably initiate a conversation with a stranger
- Skillfully sustain conversations
- Comfortably close conversations

Conversations are the stuff from which our relationships are made. All relationships are initiated, developed, sustained, and sometimes terminated through conversations that may be face-to-face or mediated. Conversing is one of the primary activities between friends and romantic partners (Duck, 2007). When our conversations go well, they are interesting, informative, stimulating, and just plain fun. Yet we experience some conversations as awkward and uncomfortable, even difficult. By examining how conversations work, we can see how much they depend on the collaborative effort of two (or more) participants. We can also learn to converse in ways that increase ease and enjoyment.

In this chapter, we explore conversation in detail. We begin by defining the word "conversation," using the definition to investigate the characteristics of conversation, and then we consider some important ways in which conversations vary: type, purpose, sequence, tone, participants, and setting. Next, we present general guidelines to help you become a more effective conversationalist and specific skills for improving first-time conversations with strangers, since this is a type of conversation that many people find challenging. Finally, we summarize how culture and technology affect conversation.

Conversation: Definition, Structure, and Variation

As a start, let's first define what a conversation is, explore some of its basic structure, and then consider how conversations vary. With this basic understanding, we can move on to focus on improving how we conduct conversations.

Characteristics of Conversation

A **conversation** is an interactive, extemporaneous, locally managed, and sequentially organized interchange of thoughts and feelings between two or more people. Why this complex definition? A number of adjectives are required because conversations differ from other forms of communication like speeches, interviews, group meetings, or debates in these particular ways.

1. Conversations are interactive. Conversations involve **turn-taking**, alternating between speaking and listening in an interaction. A turn can be as short as one word or as lengthy as a monologue. In ordinary conversation, people often overlap or speak "on top of" each other for brief segments. This can make it difficult to identify where one person's turn begins and another's ends. Nevertheless, the concept of a turn is significant for people conversing. For example, when you and your partner both try to take a turn speaking at the same time, various behaviors can occur that demonstrate that you both understand the importance of turn-taking. You may back down and let the other person speak. Or both of you may back down through a polite negotiation in which each says, "I'm sorry. You go ahead." Or both may continue trying to speak until the more persistent one "wins" a turn and the other gives way, though this can result in the "loser" feeling frustrated or annoyed by being interrupted.

2. Conversations are extemporaneous. Much more than presentations or interviews, for example, our social conversations are **extemporaneous**, with messages uttered in the spur of the moment without lengthy preplanning. For an ordinary or typical conversation, we do not script what we will say exactly at each turn. Instead, we reference our canned plans and scripts as the conversation unfolds and create messages based on them to pursue our goals. This makes conversation spontaneous and, in some ways, more creative than other forms of communication. The ability to move from one topic to another as the mood strikes is one of the characteristics that most of us find enjoyable about conversation. Still, you have undoubtedly also had conversations that were rather painful, a struggle to find things to talk about. Extemporaneous talk,

Conversation—an interactive, extemporaneous, locally managed, and sequentially organized interchange of thoughts and feelings between two or more people.

Turn-taking—alternating between speaking and listening in an interaction.

Extemporaneous—uttered in the spur of the moment without lengthy preplanning.

Local management—the way that conversational partners produce and monitor every aspect of the conversational give-and-take.

despite its apparent effortlessness, is actually a skillful form of communication to master.

3. Conversations are locally managed. Local management is the way that conversational partners produce and monitor every aspect of the conversational give-and-take, including not only turn-taking but also topic changes (Nofsinger, 1991). If Hector and Desirée are chatting casually before class, Desirée may introduce a topic based on their common ground, such as an upcoming exam in the class. They may briefly converse about that until subtle nonverbal cues signal that this topic is winding down. Each person's voice may become softer and less

LEARN ABOUT YOURSELF ● How Conversations Work

Take this short survey, which will help you get a better idea of how conversations work by exploring an actual conversation you have had. Pick a recent conversation (satisfactory or unsatisfactory) with a friend, colleague, family member, or anyone else, and then answer the following questions. There are no right or wrong answers, so answer the questions using your first instinct. For each question, select one of the numbers to the left that best describes your attitude toward the conversation you chose to explore.

1 = Strongly Agree

2 = Agree Somewhat

3 = Neutral

4 = Disagree Somewhat

5 = Strongly Disagree

_____ 1. I would like to have another conversation like this one.

_____ 2. I was very dissatisfied with this conversation.

_____ 3. During this conversation, I was able to present myself as I wanted the other person to view me.

_____ 4. The other person expressed great interest in what I had to say.

_____ 5. We talked about things I was not interested in.

_____ 6. I was annoyed by the other person's interruptions of me.

_____ 7. Turn-taking went smoothly in this conversation.

_____ 8. There were many uncomfortable moments during this conversation.

_____ 9. I did not get to say what I wanted in this conversation.

_____ 10. I was very satisfied with this conversation.

Scoring the survey: To find your score, first reverse the responses for the odd-numbered items (if you wrote a 1, make it a 5; 2 = 4; leave 3 as is; 4 = 2; and 5 = 1). Next add the numbers for each item. Scores can range from 10 to 50. The lower (closer to 10) your score, the more satisfied you were with the conversation. The higher (closer to 50) your score, the less satisfied you were with the conversation. Keep your score in mind as you work through this chapter and learn how to improve your conversational skills. If your conversation got a low satisfaction score, what could the participants have done to improve the conversation? If your conversation got a high satisfaction score, what did the participants do right?

Note: After an important conversation, it would be useful for both you and your partner to complete this survey separately, then compare and discuss your scores.

Adapted from Hecht, M. L. (1978). Measures of communication satisfaction. *Human Communication Research, 4*, 350–368.

animated, and there may be shorter remarks and more pauses between turns. Hector may notice this and make a conscious (or semiconscious) decision to introduce a new topic, such as the behavior of another student in the class. They may converse on that topic until nonverbal cues indicate the need for a further change. Or Desirée may abruptly change the topic while Hector is speaking by asking, "Have you had lunch yet?" Topic change can be gradual, following a natural progression from one topic to the next, or it can be abrupt and unpredictable, changing from one unrelated issue to the next. Regardless of how it is accomplished, topic change in conversation has to be locally managed by the interactants themselves. In contrast, topics and turns are often scripted beforehand at group presentations or meetings, for example, and participants follow a preplanned outline or agenda. In these settings, there may even be group sanctions for deviating from preset "rules."

4. Conversations are sequentially organized. Sequential organization means that conversations have identifiable beginnings (openings), middles (bodies), and ends (closings), similar to other forms of communication. Unlike communication in other settings, however, the sequential organization is not planned in advance but instead unfolds, turn by turn, through extemporaneous and locally managed talk.

> **Sequential organization**—the identifiable beginnings (openings), middles (bodies), and ends (closings) of conversations.

With these characteristics defined and explored, it becomes more evident that the most ordinary conversation is actually a complex form of communication. You can compare it to improvised music or dancing: conversational partners exchange the roles of leader and follower, make different moves, "dance" with quick or slow turns and topic changes, and so forth, all under their own direction. Most of us, much of the time, do a fairly good job of conversing. However, some conversational issues can be difficult to manage. Later in this chapter, we'll discuss some ways to improve your conversational dancing. But first, let's continue exploring conversation by looking at some of the ways that conversations vary.

Variation in Conversation

Conversations are like snowflakes—no two are exactly alike. We can appreciate the variation more fully if we look at conversational type, purpose, sequence, and tone, along with the influence of participants and setting on your conversational behavior.

Conversational Type

There are many different types of conversation. Some are common enough that we have shared names for them. **Small talk**, for example, is a type of conversation focused on inconsequential topics such as the weather, uncontroversial news topics, harmless facts, and predictions. We are familiar with small talk and use it to initiate conversations with strangers, break the ice with new acquaintances, or even begin conversations with intimates. For instance, Adrianna and Luis may engage in small talk as they wait for their bus, since Adrianna has introduced the weather as a topic. Or as they are waiting for a show to begin, Tom and Elena may chat about the upcoming playoff games, speculating on which teams will make the cut. **Gossip** is another easily recognized form of conversation, involving discussion of people who are not present for the conversation. Statements such as "Do you know

> **Small talk**—a type of conversation focused on inconsequential topics such as the weather, uncontroversial news topics, harmless facts, and predictions.

> **Gossip**—discussion of people who are not present for the conversation.

Conversational Profiling

Look at the list of conversation types in Figure 8.1 and think about the conversations you had yesterday. Which of the twenty-nine types did you participate in? Which did you have most frequently? Were there any types of conversation that don't fit in these categories? Now choose two different relationships in your life and go through the list, thinking about the conversations you've had with these two people over the past week. How does the "conversational profile" differ between the two relationships? In Chapter 6, you learned about the indexical function of communication in relationships. What do the two different conversational profiles tell you about control, trust, and intimacy in these two relationships?

Conversation purpose—what the conversation is intended to do.

Armando? I hear he has a really great job"; "Would you believe that Mary Simmons and Tom Johnson are going out? They never seemed to hit it off too well in the past"; and "My brother Omar is really working hard at losing weight. I saw him the other day, and all he talked about was his diet" are all examples of gossip.

One study identified twenty-nine distinct types of conversation common in friendships and romantic relationships (Goldsmith & Baxter, 2006). Along with small talk and gossip, the most-reported types were making plans, joking around, recapping the day's events (i.e., reviewing what happened to each person that day), and catching up (i.e., going over what has happened in each person's life since the last meeting). Other common types included complaining, talking about problems, decision making, conflict, making up, and relationship talk (Goldsmith & Baxter, 2006). Figure 8.1 presents a list of all twenty-nine types.

Purpose

Conversational types differ, in part, because they have distinct purposes. The **conversation purpose** is what the conversation is intended to do. Some conversations intend to entertain, but others might aim to persuade, inform, or comfort. Conversations can and do have multiple purposes, such as when we converse to pass time as well as to get acquainted with another person. The purpose of a conversation is typically linked to the goals of the individual participants. What each participant is trying to achieve during the conversation will obviously influence the direction of the conversation as a whole. Because conversation is interactive, however, the purpose of the conversation is not necessarily identical to either participant's goals. Instead, the purpose is "negotiated" by the participants as they interact. Usually, the negotiation isn't obvious because the participants' goals are compatible and result in a mutually agreeable purpose. The fact that we negotiate our goals to arrive at the purpose of the conversation becomes more evident when our goals are incompatible with our partner's goals. For example, if Adrianne meets Micah at a club and is physically attracted to him, she may have the goal of "hooking up," but the conversational purpose won't become a "pickup" if Micah isn't also interested in hooking up or isn't attracted to Adrianne.

The purpose of an interaction is usually evident in the type of messages exchanged and after the fact by what has happened as a result of the conversation. A conversation's purpose can be identified as "joking around" partly because of the teases and jibes that the participants exchange, but also because looking back later, they observe that nothing consequential occurred because of that conversation. Sometimes, the purpose of a conversation isn't evident until it's over and both participants can see what it has accomplished. This may be especially true when a conversation is a turning point in a relationship. Have you ever said, "That conversation was when we became friends"? or "I knew when we finished the conversation that the relationship was not going to last"? A particular outcome may help you realize that the conversation had a different purpose than you intended when you were engaged in it.

1. **Asking a favor:** talk with the specific purpose of getting someone to do something for you.

2. **Asking out:** the kind of talk one person uses when asking another out on a date.

3. **Bedtime talk:** the kind of routine talk you have right before you go to bed.

4. **Breaking bad news:** a conversation in which one person reveals bad news to another.

5. **Catching up:** the kind of conversation you have when you haven't talked with someone recently, and you talk about the events in your lives that have occurred since you last spoke.

6. **Class information talk:** informal conversations in which you find out about class assignments, exams, or course material.

7. **Complaining:** expressing frustrations, gripes, or complaints about some common experience, directing negative feelings toward the topic but not the other people in the conversation.

8. **Conflict:** conversations in which the two people disagree.

9. **Current events talk:** a conversation whose topic is limited to news and current events.

10. **Decision-making conversation:** a conversation whose goal is making a decision about some task.

11. **Getting to know someone:** the kind of small talk you have when you want to be friendly and get acquainted with someone.

12. **Giving and getting instructions:** a conversation in which one person gives another information or directions about how to do some task.

13. **Gossip:** exchanging opinions or information about someone else who isn't present.

14. **Group discussion:** group talk to exchange information, persuade other people, or make decisions.

15. **Interrogation:** a one-way kind of conversation in which one person grills another with questions.

16. **Joking around:** a playful kind of talk to have fun or release tension.

17. **Lecture:** a one-way kind of conversation in which one person tells another how to act or what to do.

18. **Love talk:** talk that has little content but gives attention and expresses love and affection.

19. **Making plans:** talk to arrange a meeting or an activity with someone.

20. **Making up:** a conversation in which one person or both apologize for violating expectations.

21. **Morning talk:** the kind of routine talk you have when you first wake up in the morning.

22. **Persuading conversation:** conversation in which one person aims to convince the other to do something.

23. **Recapping the day's events:** discussing what's up and what happened to each person during the day.

24. **Relationship talk:** talking about the nature and state of a relationship.

25. **Reminiscing:** talking with someone about shared events you experienced in the past.

26. **Serious conversation:** a two-way, in-depth discussion or exchange of feelings, opinions, or ideas about some personal and important topic.

27. **Small talk:** a kind of talk to pass time and avoid being rude.

28. **Sports talk:** the kind of talk that occurs while playing or watching a sporting event.

29. **Talking about problems:** a conversation in which one person talks about some problem he or she is having and the other person tries to help.

FIGURE 8.1 Twenty-nine Types of Conversations. Adapted from Goldsmith, D. J., & Baxter, L. A. (2006). Constituting relationships in talk: A taxonomy of speech events in social and personal relationships. *Human Communication Research, 23,* 87–114.

Sequence

While all conversations have openings, bodies, and conclusions, the turn-by-turn sequence of any conversation is unique. Much of the sequential variation is linked to the type and purpose of the conversation. Consider joking around and recapping the day's events, two types of conversation that occur frequently in the relationships of college students. The opening of a joking-around episode often involves some form of teasing, which will typically be returned in kind. Subsequent acts may include a combination of jokes, banter, humorous put-downs, amusing anecdotes, and so forth. A very different sequence is involved in "recapping the day's events," whose opening would be something like "So . . . how'd it go today?" The sequence for this episode involves each person talking about what happened, punctuated by questions and comments from the other party, and the ending might be a transition to another activity ("Let's get dinner started") or to another type of conversation such as planning ("What do you want to do tomorrow?").

In some types of conversation, the sequence becomes **scripted** or highly routinized. The canned plan is well learned and happens without any conscious thought or choice. For example, consider brief conversations whose only purpose is to greet and acknowledge someone you know. If Kimiko and Jesse have not seen each other for some time but bump into each other while jogging, the following conversation would follow a greeting script.

Jesse: *Hey, it's been a long time. How are you doing?*
Kimiko: *Yes, it's been forever since we've seen each other. I'm doing fine. How about you?*
Jesse: *I'm good. Can't complain. How is work going?*
Kimiko: *Work's keeping me busy. Are you still with KDC Software?*

Notice the reciprocal exchange of acknowledgements and inquiries in this conversation. Jesse greets Kimiko and asks a question; after acknowledging the greeting and answering the question, Kimiko asks the same question of Jesse. Certain topics are standard in a greeting script. We are likely to chat about health, work, school, and common friends rather than world politics, serious crises, or our financial status. Notice also how turns are very short. Greeting conversations have a quick give-and-take to them. Other scripted conversations might relate to giving and receiving compliments or the annual phone call to your great aunt to thank her for your birthday present.

A unique type of conversational scripting occurs between two individuals who have been interacting for a long time. **Co-narration** is a specific type of conversational sequencing in which people finish each other's sentences because they have intimate knowledge of the topic and each other's style (Sawyer, 2001). So they share a script. For example, if Dana

Scripted—Highly routinized.

Co-narration—Specific type of conversational sequencing in which people finish each other's sentences because they have intimate knowledge of the topic and each other's style.

Co-narration is expected of identical twins, but it is also experienced by others who are intimate. Do you know any couples that co-narrate?

and Armand have lived together for many years and Armand says, "In 1999, we went out West for a trip," Dana will say, "It was spring and we drove our RV." When Armand adds, "That RV always gave us trouble because . . ." Dana will finish, "the engine would overheat when you drove fast." Because this conversation is so routine and scripted, Armand and Dana may not perceive that they are interrupting each other. Instead, they are cooperating in narrating the story.

Tone

The **conversation tone** is its emotional and relational quality, or how it feels "inside" the interaction. Imagine you are at a social event and are forced into conversation with a former boyfriend or girlfriend who really hurt you by abruptly ending your relationship to be with someone else. Neither of you really wants to be interacting with the other, and your distaste for the situation (and for each other) will be indexed nonverbally through behaviors like limited eye contact and lack of facial expressiveness and verbally through very short and impersonal messages. These behaviors will create a conversational tone that is cold and "stiff." In contrast, a conversation with a friend you hadn't seen recently and were delighted to encounter would probably have a warm, easy tone.

One important dimension of tone is **formality**, the degree to which a conversation follows scripted norms, rules, and procedures. The formality of a conversation is strongly influenced by the participants' characteristics and their relationship to each other, especially their relative status and familiarity. Typically, when there is a recognized status difference between the participants, the tone of the conversation will be more formal. For example, if you were speaking to the president of your college or your company, the conversation tone would probably be formal. You might shake the president's hand rather than hug or slap hands. You would defer to the president and accept the president's topic choice. You would self-monitor so that you didn't interrupt the president and would self-censor to avoid using profanity. When participants are more familiar with each other, conversations are more informal. When you talk with a close friend, you stand or sit closer together. You both introduce topics. Interruptions are acceptable, and—depending on the sensitivity of the participants—profanity may be used and intimate topics discussed.

Participants

Obviously, conversations vary with the participants. This is because how conversational partners talk to each other is fundamentally influenced by their roles, their relationship to each other, and their individual characteristics and personality traits. Imagine an older married couple who have been regular customers at a small restaurant for several years. Because of their role as "regulars," they are likely to have conversations with the wait staff that are more extended and personal than the conversations that would occur with casual customers. For example, the regulars and the employees would likely have learned things about each other's families and pets, activities away from work, and some likes and dislikes, all of which would provide material for their conversations. If the couple had not come to the restaurant for a longer-than-usual period, the employees would almost certainly inquire about what they had been doing in their absence.

Conversation tone—emotional and relational quality, or how it feels "inside" the interaction.

Formality—degree to which a conversation follows scripted norms, rules, and procedures.

The audience for a conversation is not necessarily limited to the participants who speak. The couple who are regulars at the restaurant may be talking directly to one employee, but other customers and employees who are nearby are likely to overhear. These others might be "candidates" to participate actively in the conversation, depending on their interest and whether the current participants encourage them, by making eye contact and smiling in their direction rather than avoiding eye contact and leaning in toward each other to signal that others are not welcome to contribute.

Setting

How we experience any conversation is influenced by the setting or physical environment in which it occurs, and the setting often influences our perception of the kinds of conversation that are appropriate. Few people engage in casual joking around in a funeral parlor (though funeral home employees would certainly do it when clients were not around), nor would many people choose a crowded fast-food restaurant for a conversation that involved emotional reminiscing about someone who had died. Even when the physical setting remains the same, the "scene" within that setting can change, with consequences for the type of conversation that occurs. For example, the scene is different in an apartment when roommates are getting ready for work or school from when they are hosting a party. In the first scene, conversation will probably focus on mundane morning activities such as making breakfast, finding misplaced keys or phones, or planning for events that will take place later in the day. In the second scene, there will likely be a much wider range of topics, greater volume and more energetic expression, and the sense that the conversation is a key part of the fun rather than a way of getting things done.

Guidelines for Effective Conversationalists

Because conversations are highly varied, the kinds of skills necessary to be an effective conversationalist also vary according to type of conversation, setting, participants, and so forth. In the remainder of this chapter we will describe general guidelines you can use to become a better conversationalist. Then we will present specific skills that will help you when you converse with someone you don't really know.

General Conversation Guidelines

There are several general guidelines you can follow as you work to be a better conversational partner: develop an other-centered focus, engage in appropriate turn-taking, maintain conversational coherence, practice politeness, protect privacy, and engage in ethical dialog.

1. Develop an other-centered focus. To be other-centered in conversation means listening carefully, asking questions, and introducing topics that interest to your conversational partner. Being other-centered is also demonstrated by full involvement in the conversation. For example, looking at your partner rather than watching others who are entering or leaving the room, silencing cell phones and not responding to vibration, and not multitasking are all ways to be other-centered. Being other-centered does not mean leaving yourself out. If you are focused on others, you can still talk about yourself when the conversation naturally moves to your interests or when your conversational partner asks you for information.

2. Engage in appropriate turn-taking. Effective conversationalists show respect and consideration for others in the way they take turns. Two major elements of appropriate turn-taking are distributing the talk time evenly and avoiding interruption. **Talk time** is the share of time participants each have in a conversation. Generally, you should balance speaking and listening, and all participants should have roughly the same opportunity to talk. Certainly, it is acceptable to allocate more floor time to higher-status people and to accommodate those whose conversational style is more outgoing or reserved. However, people are likely to tune out or become annoyed at conversational partners who make speeches, filibuster, or perform monologues rather than engage in the ordinary give-and-take of conversation. Similarly, it is difficult to carry on a conversation with someone who provides one- or two-word replies to questions designed to elicit meaningful information. Turns do vary in length depending on what is being said, but if your statements average much longer or much shorter than your conversational partners, you probably need to adjust. If you discover that you are speaking more than your fair share, try to restrain yourself by mentally checking whether anyone else has had a chance to talk once you talk a second time. On the other hand, if you find yourself being inactive in a conversation, try to increase your level of participation. In group conversation, you can help others who are unable to get enough talk time by saying something like "Donna, I get the sense that you've been wanting to comment on this point," or "Tyler, what do you think?"

A second critical element of turn-taking is learning to wait for others to finish speaking. Some people are chronic interrupters and do not realize it. Pay

Talk time—the share of time participants each have in a conversation.

SKILL BUILDERS ● Turn-Taking

SKILL	USE	PROCEDURE	EXAMPLE
Engaging in appropriate turn-taking	Determining when a speaker is at a place where another person may talk if he or she wants	1. Take your share of turns. 2. Gear the length of turns to the behavior of partners. 3. Give and watch for turn-taking and turn-exchanging cues. Avoid giving inadvertent turn-taking cues. 4. Observe and use conversation-directing behavior. 5. Limit interruptions.	When John lowers his voice as he says, "I really thought they were going to go ahead during those last few seconds," Melissa, noticing that he appears to be finished, says, "I did, too. But did you notice…"

attention to your turn-taking behavior to make sure that you are not seizing the conversational floor from others. Interrupting for "agreement" (confirming) or clarification is generally considered to be interpersonally acceptable (Kennedy & Camden, 1983). For instance, if you say, "Good point, Max," or "Exactly!" most people won't object, even if you are talking right on top of them. Similarly, you can usually interrupt with questions or paraphrases to better understand what another person is saying without offending. For example, you could interrupt to ask, "What do you mean by you were 'on the struggle bus?'" or say "'On the struggle bus'—oh, you mean it was a tough day." If, however, your interruptions involve changing the subject, minimizing the contribution of the interrupted party, disagreeing, or attempting to turn conversational attention to yourself, they are likely to be viewed as disruptive and impolite.

3. **Maintain conversational coherence. Conversational coherence** is the extent to which the comments made by one person relate to those made previously by others in a conversation (McLaughlin, 1984, pp. 88–89). It is a way to create clear meaning in conversation (Littlejohn & Foss, 2005). The more directly messages relate to those that precede them, the more coherent or meaningful the conversation. If what you want to say is only tangentially related or unrelated to what was said before, then you should probably yield your turn to someone else who may have more relevant comments and wait for a lull in the conversation to introduce your new topic. If only two people are conversing, then the listener should at least respond to the speaker's message before introducing a change in topic. If at any point you must introduce a completely unrelated topic, it will appear somewhat more coherent if you acknowledge what you're doing, such as "Sorry to change the subject, but did you hear that . . .?"

4. **Practice politeness. Politeness** is relating to others in ways that meet their needs to be appreciated and respected. The effect of politeness is universal to all cultures and contributes greatly to effective conversation (Brown & Levinson, 1987). One way of showing politeness is to engage in **face-saving**, helping others to preserve their self-image or self-respect. Put another way, face-saving means helping another person to avoid embarrassment. There are many ways that we engage in face-saving during conversations. One way is to avoid potentially embarrassing topics. For example, if Chad knows that Charlie just lost his job, Chad is not likely to bring up that topic in a casual conversation among a group of friends at the coffee shop. To say, "Hey, Charlie, I hear you just got canned," would embarrass everyone. Another way to engage in face-saving is to choose our words carefully. For example, suppose your professor returns a set of papers and you believe the grade you received does not accurately reflect the quality of the paper. You could say, "You didn't grade my paper fairly. It deserves a much higher grade." Because saying this implies that the professor is wrong, however, it causes a loss of face and could lead to defensive behavior. You might, instead, say something diplomatic like, "Professor, I thought I did a better job than what the grade shows. I'm not sure why these sections were marked wrong. I've marked the places on the paper where my comments come from our textbook, and I've noted the textbook pages. I wonder if you would consider re-grading the paper or at least helping me understand the reasons for this grade."

Conversational coherence—the extent to which the comments made by one person relate to those made previously by others in a conversation.

Politeness—relating to others in ways that meet their needs to be appreciated and respected.

Face-saving—helping others to preserve their self-image or self-respect.

5. Protect Privacy. Being an effective conversationalist also includes protecting privacy. One aspect of protecting privacy is keeping confidences. If someone reveals private information in a conversation and asks you not to share this information with others, it is important to honor this request. Another aspect of protecting privacy is paying attention to any unintended audience to the conversation. To avoid revealing private things to strangers who don't need to know them and probably don't want to know them, you may need to move a conversation to a more secluded location, speak more softly, or have the conversation at another time.

6. Engage in ethical dialog. The final guideline followed by effective conversationalists is to engage in ethical dialog. **Ethical dialog** is conversation characterized by authenticity, empathy, confirmation, presentness, equality, and supportiveness (Johannesen, Valde, & Whedbee, 2008).

Authenticity is communicating information and feelings that are relevant and legitimate to the subject at hand directly, honestly, and straightforwardly. Completely disagreeing with what is being said but saying nothing in a discussion is inauthentic. Agreeing verbally with something that you really do not believe in is also inauthentic.

In the next chapter, we will discuss and formally define empathy. But in the meantime you can think of empathy as demonstrating an understanding of another person's point of view without giving up your own position or sense of self. So in an ethical dialog, comments such as "I see your point," or "I'm not sure I agree with you, but I'm beginning to understand why you feel that way" demonstrate empathy.

Confirmation is expressing a warm affirmation of others as unique persons without necessarily approving of their behaviors or views. Examples of confirmation might include, "Well, Keith, you certainly have an interesting way of looking at things, and I must say, you really make me think through my own views"; or "Well, I guess I'd still prefer that you didn't get a tattoo, but you really have thought this through."

Presentness is the willingness to become fully involved with another person by taking time, avoiding distractions, being responsive, and risking attachment. The most obvious way to exhibit presentness in a conversation is by listening actively. You can also demonstrate presentness during a conversation by asking questions that are directly related to what has been said.

Equality is treating conversational partners as peers, regardless of the status differences that separate them from other participants. To lord one's accomplishments, power, or social status over another during conversation is unethical.

Supportiveness, like empathy, will be covered extensively in the next chapter. In casual conversations, **supportiveness** encourages your partners to continue talking by acknowledging your appreciation of what they are saying.

When we engage in ethical dialog, we improve the odds that our conversations will meet our needs and the needs of those with whom we interact.

Ethical dialog—a conversation characterized by authenticity, empathy, confirmation, presentness, equality, and supportiveness.

Authenticity—communicating information and feelings that are relevant and legitimate to the subject at hand directly, honestly, and straightforwardly.

Confirmation—expressing a warm affirmation of others as unique persons without necessarily approving of their behaviors or views.

Presentness—the willingness to become fully involved with another person by taking time, avoiding distractions, being responsive, and risking attachment.

Equality—treating conversational partners as peers, regardless of the status differences that separate them from other participants.

Supportiveness—encouraging your partners to continue talking by acknowledging your appreciation of what they are saying.

OBSERVE AND ANALYZE

Analysis of a Media Conversation

Analyze a conversation between two people in a television show or movie. Evaluate the communicators according to the guidelines for effective conversationalists. To what extent do the people show an other-centered focus, take turns appropriately, maintain conversational coherence, practice politeness, protect privacy, and engage in ethical dialog? Provide examples of the characters following or violating these guidelines. If this is a comedy, how do violations add to the humor? If this is a drama, how do violations affect the emotional tone of the conversation?

Skills for Conversing with Strangers

Conversations often seem to have a life of their own, and when they're going well, they seem effortless. But as you have seen, creating a satisfying conversation is a complex and sometimes difficult activity. In particular, many of us find it challenging to talk to people we are meeting for the first time or don't know very well. You want to be able to converse successfully with strangers for many reasons. These include the need to network with others who might be good career contacts, to develop friendships in your new neighborhood, or to simply pass the time more pleasantly while waiting in the airport lounge for a delayed flight. To help you get the most from these conversations, this section focuses on developing skills for conversing with someone you do not know well or at all. The skills discussed will help you initiate, continue, and close conversations, leading to more enjoyable and effective interactions. Even if you typically like talking with unfamiliar people, you may find some suggestions that will make your first-time conversations flow more easily or that apply to other kinds of conversation.

Starting a Conversation

Are you comfortable initiating a conversation with a complete stranger? Many of us feel that just getting started is the most awkward part. Fortunately, four easy strategies can help break the conversational ice: make a comment, ask a question, introduce yourself, and pay attention to non-verbal cues.

1. Make a comment. One simple approach is to make a comment that invites the other person to respond. You might comment on your surroundings or situation, such as "Well, I guess the bus is running late this morning," or mention something you find interesting about the other person, such as "That's a unique book bag. I haven't seen one like that before." You could also comment on something you're thinking or feeling in the situation: "Another Monday . . . they always make me feel a little blah." Yet another possibility for opening conversation is to notice something you and the other person have in common—"Looks like we're both headed up to campus"—or possibly something that's different about you, particularly if the other person would find the comparison positive. For example, if it's raining and the other person has an umbrella and you don't, a conversation starter might be "You're a lot more organized than I am. I never remember to bring an umbrella!" A note of humor, especially at your own expense, can also help get things off to a good start. Researchers have found that a shared laugh can ease the initial awkwardness between strangers (Fraley & Aron, 2004). For example, if you got wet in the rain, you could say, "The drowned rat look is *always* in fashion!" or "I used to laugh when Grandma said I should take an umbrella. Guess who's laughing now?"

2. Ask a question. Another general strategy is to ask a question. Generally, this should be a **ritual question**, a question about the other person or the situation that is easy to answer and doesn't pry into personal matters (Gabor, 2001). For example, if you're in line at a smoothie shop, you might ask the person in front of you, "Do you recommend a particular flavor?" or if it's the first day of class and the professor hasn't arrived yet, you could ask, "Is this class for your major?" or

Ritual question—a question about the other person or the situation that is easy to answer and doesn't pry into personal matters.

"Do you know the instructor for this class?" It can be useful to pair comments and ritual questions, especially when the comment makes the question seem more natural or less intrusive. For example, just blurting out "What's your major?" to someone at a campus bus stop is rather awkward, but if you comment on something you see that gives a clue about the person's course of study ("Wow, that's a high-powered calculator. What's your major?" or "That's a really nice portfolio. Are you in Fine Arts?"), the observation creates a basis for asking the question.

3. Introduce yourself. Make a greeting, state your own name, and directly or indirectly ask for the other person's name. For example, "Hi. My name is Brianna. What's yours?" A variation on this approach is to add a simple disclosure that helps explain why you're introducing yourself: "Hello. My name's Evan. I just got added to this class. What's your name?" The introduction approach probably works best in situations where you expect to interact with the other person again (such as a classroom or work context), which makes an exchange of names highly appropriate. If you're talking to someone you probably won't see again (e.g., at the bus stop or smoothie shop), you could still use this strategy to open the conversation, but it could be seen as pushy because the other person will feel pressure to offer his or her name and may not want to do so. In such situations, you will probably get a more positive reaction if you start with a comment or ritual question and delay the introduction until some conversation has taken place. Once the conversational ball is rolling, there may not be an obvious time to introduce yourself, but you can always slide it in with a comment that indicates you know you're changing the topic: "Oh, by the way, I'm Brianna," or "I don't think I mentioned, but my name's Brianna." You may also find this opening helpful in situations where you know you have talked with people before, but can't remember their names. Saying something like, "It's good to see you again, my name is Brianna, and forgive me, but I can't recall your name," is a polite way to truthfully acknowledge the situation, and provide an opportunity for people to tell you their names.

4. Pay attention to nonverbal cues. Paying attention to nonverbal as well as verbal behavior will enhance your success at getting a conversation started.

SKILL BUILDERS ● Initiating Conversation

SKILL	USE	PROCEDURE	EXAMPLE
Initiating conversation with a stranger	To start an interaction with someone you don't know	Do one or more of the following: 1. Make a comment about the situation, the other person, or yourself. 2. Ask a ritual question. 3. Introduce yourself.	Jenna is waiting in line at the grocery store. The woman in front of her is looking at the candy bars. Jenna says "Don't those look good? I always seem to end up at the store when I'm hungry."

You are much more likely to have a positive interaction with someone who appears receptive to conversation. Clues that someone might be interested in talking with you include open arms, eye contact, and a smile. If someone does not look interested in conversation, this doesn't mean you can't or shouldn't try to talk to her or him, but it may take more skill and effort on your part, and you should be prepared for the other person to close the conversation quickly. Your own nonverbal behavior also matters. To show your interest in interaction, you can smile, keep your arms uncrossed and relaxed, approach to a distance that's appropriate for conversation (or, if seated, lean slightly forward toward the other person), and make eye contact.

Sustaining a Conversation

Once a conversation is underway, how do you keep it going? Several specific strategies facilitate conversation: using free information, asking questions, seeking topics of interest to the other person, providing self-disclosure, and listening.

Free information—information volunteered during conversation rather than specifically required or requested.

1. Use free information. One essential strategy for keeping a conversation going is making use of **free information**, information volunteered during conversation rather than specifically required or requested (Gabor, 2001). For example, if you asked, "Where are you headed after class today?" the person might respond, "Downtown. I have a job interview." The information about the interview is "free" because it isn't strictly necessary to answer your question. This information provides a natural basis for your next contribution to the conversation, enabling you to ask something like, "Oh, where are you interviewing?" or "I noticed you had a suit on. Interviewing makes me so nervous. How do you handle it?" Keep in mind that you need to provide free information for others to use, too. If you give only minimal responses to others' questions or comments, you are depriving them of material that will help them sustain the conversation with you.

Closed-ended questions—questions that can be answered with "yes," "no," or a few words.

Open-ended questions—questions that require answers with more elaboration and explanation.

2. Ask questions. Questions can open new topics of conversation, demonstrate interest in the other person, and ensure that all parties to the conversation get opportunities to speak. Skilled conversationalists use a mix of **closed-ended questions**, questions that can be answered with "yes," "no," or a few words, and **open-ended questions**, questions that require answers with more elaboration and explanation (Garner, 1997). Closed-ended questions are good for eliciting specific information ("Where are you headed?"), but if you use exclusively closed-ended questions, your conversation can end up feeling like an interrogation, especially if your conversational partner provides only the required information ("Where are you headed after class today?" "Downtown." "What takes you downtown?" "Shopping."). When you follow a closed-ended question with an open-ended question, you create a space for your conversational partner to expand. For example, "Hmm . . . why do you shop downtown rather than around here?" or "Where do you think are some of the better places to shop in town?" Notice how these open-ended questions would encourage disclosure of your conversational partner's thoughts and feelings.

3. Seek out topics of interest to the other person. Most people will jump at the chance to talk about things that they find personally interesting and important. If you can identify one of these topics and get the other person going, the conversation will practically run itself for a while. Often, what other people are wearing or items they are carrying will provide clues about where they devote their time, energy, and money, including their jobs, affiliations or associations, and hobbies or other activities. A brief comment such as "Looks like you're a Cubs fan!" or "I see the logo on your shirt. What do you do in that company?" can stimulate subsequent discussion. Free information also provides good clues about topics that others find interesting. For example, if you ask, "What neighborhood do you live in?" and the response is, "Well, because we have little kids . . .," or "You know, with our dogs, we decided we had to . . ." you can bet that it won't take much prompting to get that person talking about his or her kids or dogs. You can also use direct questions to elicit another person's high-interest topics, such as, "What do you do when you're not working?" As you seek out another person's high-interest topics, don't forget that your own interests can be part of the conversation, too. For example, if you've been talking with another person about his or her work, sharing something about your work or school can be a good way to continue the conversation. For example, "It sounds like you have a good time with your work. I like my job, too, especially interacting with the public. . . ." If you have indicated interest in things that matter to someone else, that person will likely show you the same respect. Even better, as each of you reveals some of what's interesting and important to you, you may have the joy of discovering that you have something in common.

    4. Self-disclose appropriately. Self-disclosure involves verbally sharing personal ideas and feelings with others. Although you don't want to disclose highly intimate or risky information to people you've just met, a willingness to share some of your personal experiences and perspective can result in more stimulating and meaningful conversation. So with new acquaintances, disclose factual information about yourself. For example, if you've been chatting with someone about the stores and restaurants in your neighborhood, you might disclose that you prefer to buy locally and support merchants who live near you rather than spending your money at national chains. This disclosure reveals something about your perspective and values, creating an opportunity for your conversational partner to know you a little better, reveal a shared—or different—point of view, or ask you questions about the practice of buying locally. At the same time, this disclosure would not be perceived as overly intimate, put your privacy at risk, or embarrass you. Overall, the best approach to self-disclosure in initial interactions is to disclose gradually, making sure that the thoughts and feelings you reveal are relevant to whatever topic is under discussion and appropriate to sharing with a stranger (or whatever relationship you may have with the other person). You should also observe whether your self-disclosure is reciprocated or matched by your conversational partner. If he or she doesn't reveal thoughts or feelings similar in quality and quantity, you may want to scale back on your disclosure so that both of you are comfortable.

    5. Actively listen. Use the listening skills you learned in Chapter 7. If you are prone to worrying about what you will say next, paying close attention to what the other person is saying will make coming up with a response less of a problem.

Self-disclosure—verbally sharing personal ideas and feelings with others.

Also, if your nonverbal behavior suggests that you're listening (eye contact, nodding, positive facial expression, etc.), you will likely encourage the other person to continue talking, making your side of the conversation that much easier.

Closing a Conversation

Knowing how to close a conversation smoothly is just as important as being able to get one started. A graceful exit leaves a good impression, which is valuable even if you don't expect to encounter the other person again. Also, on occasion you may be uncomfortable continuing to talk with someone, in which case knowing how to bring a conversation to a close quickly can be useful. Four strategies are useful for closing a conversation: notice and use nonverbal leave-taking cues, verbalize your desire to end the conversation, ask to see the other person again if appropriate, close with a brief stock message.

Leave-taking cues—nonverbal behaviors that indicate someone wants to end the conversation.

1. Notice and use leave-taking cues. Leave-taking cues are nonverbal behaviors that indicate someone wants to end the conversation. These include changes in eye contact and body position and movement. One nonverbal leave-taking cue is shifting eye contact from looking mostly at your conversational partner to scanning the scene around the two of you. Similarly, if someone you've been talking with rises, turns away, or begins rapidly nodding as you're talking, these are probably kinesic (bodily movement) cues of the desire to end the conversation. You can use these cues to signal your desire to end a conversation, and when you observe your partner using these cues, you should quickly finish talking and allow your partner to exit.

2. Verbalize your desire to end the conversation. You need to complement your use of nonverbal leave-taking cues with verbal indicators that the interaction

---

SKILL BUILDERS ● Sustaining Conversation

SKILL	USE	PROCEDURE	EXAMPLE
Sustaining conversation	To sustain a first-time conversation, pass time enjoyably, and get to know someone	Do the following throughout the conversation: 1. Use and provide free information. 2. Ask closed-ended and open-ended questions. 3. Seek high-interest topics. 4. Make appropriate self-disclosures. 5. Listen actively.	Roger and Eduardo are chatting while waiting for treadmills to become available at the gym. Roger says, "Man, I wish this place had more treadmills. I really need to step up my workouts." Eduardo replies, "Are you training for something in particular?" "Yes," says Roger. "I've signed up for a half-marathon in a couple of months." "Phew," Eduardo comments. "That's a lot of miles. What got you into running races?"

is nearing its end. You can do this indirectly by summarizing something interesting that has been talked about: "Alex, I'm glad I had the opportunity to learn about your work with the Literacy Center. You're making an important contribution to our community." You can thank or compliment the other person for the interaction: "I really enjoyed talking to you!" Or you can be more direct by stating your need to end the conversation: "I really need to get going." "Please excuse me, but I see someone I need to talk with."

3. Ask to see the person again if appropriate. If you are interested in seeing the other person again, this is the time to inquire about whether the other person is also interested, and if so, exchange phone numbers or e-mail addresses, or plan a specific date and time. For example, you might say, "Would you like to get together for coffee? I'm free during the week most afternoons after 3:00"; or "It was fun talking to you! I'm going to take my kids to the park Saturday morning. Would you and your kids like to join us?"

4. Close with a brief stock message. Just as there are ritualized ways to open a conversation, there are recognized messages to end a conversation. To politely close an interaction, say something like, "Take care," or "Have a great day, OK?"; or, if you've planned to meet again, "See you later," or "I'll see you in. . . ." If you have learned and remember the person's name, using it as you say goodbye adds a personal touch and shows respect: "Have a great afternoon, Marissa!"

SKILL BUILDERS ● Closing Conversation

SKILL	USE	PROCEDURE	EXAMPLE
Closing conversation	To end a conversation	Do one or more of the following: 1. Use and respond to others' nonverbal leave-taking cues. 2. Use verbal leave-taking cues such as summarizing something interesting in the conversation and thanking the other person for the opportunity to talk. If desired, make plans to talk again. 3. Use a brief closing statement. 4. Verbalize your desire to end the conversation.	Elena and Danh have been talking in the hallway of a campus building, but it's almost time for Danh to go to class. He picks up his backpack and says, "Hey, it's been fun talking. I have to go to class now, but you can look me up on Facebook. It's like "Dan," but with an 'h' on the end, and my last name is just Ng." Elena says, "Yeah, I'll do that. Bye now!" "Bye!"

Cultural Variation in Conversation

Throughout this chapter, we have assumed a Western cultural perspective on effective conversation, specifically, the perspective of low-context cultures. Verbal and nonverbal rules vary from low-context to high-context cultures, as do the guidelines for effective conversation. For example in the "Diverse Voices" article in this chapter, Nancy Masterson Sakamoto discusses how a conversation in Japan can be a very different experience than a conversation in the United States. Four differences in conversational patterns between people from low-context and high-context cultures have been observed (Gudykunst & Matsumoto, 1996).

First, conversations in low-context cultures (like the U.S.A.) are likely to include greater use of direct categorical words such as *"certainly," "absolutely,"* and *"positively,"* whereas in high-context cultures (like China), conversations rely on indirectness using verbal qualifiers such as *"maybe," "perhaps,"* and *"probably."*

Second, low-context cultures have a strong expectation that conversational contributions will be overtly relevant—clearly on topic with whatever has been talked about up to that point. In high-context cultures, however, individuals' responses are likely to be more indirect, ambiguous, and apparently less relevant because listeners rely more on nonverbal cues to help them understand a speaker's intentions and meaning.

Third, in low-context cultures, there is an expectation of verbal directness and honesty. People are expected to communicate their actual feelings verbally, regardless of how this affects others. Effective conversationalists in high-context cultures, however, put a high priority on maintaining harmony with others, and so conversationalists will sometimes send messages that mask their true feelings.

Fourth, in low-context cultures, periods of silence are perceived as uncomfortable because when no one is speaking, little information is being shared. In high-context cultures, silences in conversation are often meaningful. When three or four people sit together and no one talks, the silence may indicate agreement, disapproval, embarrassment, or disagreement, depending on the context.

In this chapter, you have learned a number of guidelines for conducting effective conversations. But because of these and other cultural variations, adhering too closely to particular guidelines may sometimes be ineffective. In other words, different cultures have different standards as to what constitutes an effective conversation. For example, people from other cultures observing a conversation between people from southern Europe or the Middle Easterners may misinterpret an interaction to be an argument because in these cultures conversational style is animated. People converse by talking loudly, yelling, confronting, interrupting, abruptly changing topics, and being passionately involved (Sawyer, 2001). Members of these cultures view this as part of a lively, engaging conversation and would see rules of politeness, turn-taking, topic changing, and conversational coherence as uninvolving and ineffective. Instead, a good conversationalist would be expected to discuss multiple topics at once, jump into the conversation without waiting for a turn, speak in a loud and emotional tone, and disagree strongly with others. So be aware that there are cultural norms but no absolute rules regarding conversation. By understanding and appreciating cultural variation in conversations, we can avoid judging others' conversational styles when they do not conform to our own rules. There are many ways to have a conversation.

THE SOCIAL MEDIA FACTOR

Digital Conversation Skills

Daily conversations, traditionally viewed as interactions that took place face-to-face or over the telephone, are now frequently conducted through social media. In today's digitally connected world, guidelines for conducting effective digital conversations have become as important as rules governing face-to-face inter-actions. The effectiveness of digital conversation largely depends on the level of engagement or attention given to such interactions (Shedletsky & Aitken, 2004). In Part 1, we learned that media richness theory focused directly on the social media device and its suitability for delivering certain kinds of messages. There is a human side to this as well. As we work to effectively use our digital conversation skills, we attempt to perceive our conversational partner as real and fully present in the interaction. **Social presence** is your personal sense that in a particular moment your conversational partners are immediately available to you—even if they aren't (Biocca & Harms, 2001). While social presence is a perception, media vary in their ability to help us sense that our partners are close by in time and space. For instance, we can more fully perceive our partner as present in a conversation through Skype than through a series of static text mes-sages. We should consider how important the feeling of social presence is when we choose to use mediated communication channels for conversations. Specifi-cally we need to consider how well the channel we choose affects our ability to be aware of our audience, appear to have conversational spontaneity, manage abrupt conversational disengagements, coordinate multiple conversations, and protect our privacy (Short et al., 1976).

Social presence—your personal sense that in a particular moment your conversational partners are immediately available to you—even if they aren't

Awareness of Audience

When you practice face-to-face communication, you know exactly who your conversational partner is when you begin the interaction. But, when you send a tweet, post to a blog or your Facebook page, you can't always be sure who your conversational partner will be. For example, you may text your boyfriend about your upcoming date, but what if your boyfriend's roommate picked up your boy-friend's cell phone and jokingly responded to your message? If you are upset over a co-worker's attitude, you may send to your close friend a private e-mail that ex-plains your frustration in detail, only to find out that your friend forwarded your e-mail to many other people. As you interact with others through social media, always remember that your message can make its way into the hands of an unin-tended recipient. Even though you expect certain people to visit your Facebook page, it is also open for the world to examine. Facebook can become a platform

Conversational Ballgames

by Nancy Masterson Sakamoto

Nancy Masterson Sakamoto is professor of American studies at Shitennoji Gakuen University, Hawaii Institute, and coauthor of *Mutual Understanding of Different Cultures* (1981). A former English teacher and teacher trainer in Japan, she co-wrote (with Reiko Naotsuka) a bilingual textbook for Japanese students called *Polite Fictions: Why Japanese and Americans Seem Rude to Each Other* (1982). "Conversational Ballgames" is excerpted from this book.

After I was married and had lived in Japan for a while, my Japanese gradually improved to the point where I could take part in simple conversations with my husband and his friends and family. And I began to notice that often, when I joined in, the others would look startled, and the conversational topic would come to a halt. After this happened several times, it became clear to me that I was doing something wrong. But for a long time, I didn't know what it was.

Finally, after listening carefully to many Japanese conversations, I discovered what my problem was. Even though I was speaking Japanese, I was handling the conversation in a Western way.

Japanese-style conversations develop quite differently from Western-style conversations. And the difference isn't only in the languages. I realized that just as I kept trying to hold Western-style conversations even when I was speaking Japanese, so my English students kept trying to hold Japanese-style conversations even when they were speaking English. We were unconsciously playing entirely different conversational ballgames.

A Western-style conversation between two people is like a game of tennis. If I introduce a topic, a conversational ball, I expect you to hit it back. If you agree with me, I don't expect you simply to agree and do nothing more. I expect you to add something—a reason for agreeing, another example, or an elaboration to carry the idea further. But I don't expect you always to agree. I am just as happy if you question me, or challenge me, or completely disagree with me. Whether you agree or disagree, your response will return the ball to me.

And then it is my turn again. I don't serve a new ball from my original starting line. I hit your ball back again from where it has bounced. I carry your idea further, or answer your questions or objections, or challenge or question you. And so the ball goes back and forth, with each of us doing our best to give it a new twist, an original spin, or a powerful smash.

And the more vigorous the action, the more interesting and exciting the game. Of course, if one of us gets angry, it spoils the conversation, just as it spoils a tennis game. But getting excited is not at all the same as getting angry. After all, we are not trying to hit each other. We are trying to hit the ball. So long as we attack only each other's opinions, and do not attack each other personally, we don't expect anyone to get hurt. A good conversation is supposed to be interesting and exciting.

If there are more than two people in the conversation, then it is like doubles in tennis, or like volleyball. There's no waiting in line. Whoever is nearest and quickest hits the ball, and if you step back, someone else will hit it. No one stops the game to give you a turn. You're responsible for taking your own turn.

But whether it's two players or a group, everyone does his best to keep the ball going, and no one person has the ball for very long.

A Japanese-style conversation, however, is not at all like tennis or volleyball. It's like bowling. You wait for your turn. And you always know your place in line. It depends on such things as whether you are older or younger, a close friend or a relative stranger to the previous speaker, in a senior or junior position, and so on.

When your turn comes, you step up to the starting line with your bowling ball, and carefully bowl it. Everyone else stands back and watches politely, murmuring encouragement. Everyone waits until the ball has reached the end of the alley, and watches to see if it knocks down all the pins, or only some of them, or none of them. There is a pause, while everyone registers your score.

Then, after everyone is sure that you have completely finished your turn, the next person in line steps up to the same starting line, with a different ball. He doesn't return your ball, and he does not begin from where your ball stopped. There is no back and forth at all. All the balls run parallel. And there is always a suitable pause between turns. There is no rush, no excitement, no scramble for the ball.

No wonder everyone looked startled when I took part in Japanese conversations. I paid no attention to whose turn it was, and kept snatching the ball halfway down the alley and throwing it back at the bowler. Of course the conversation died. I was playing the wrong game.

This explains why it is almost impossible to get a Western-style conversation or discussion going with English students in Japan. I used to think that the problem was their lack of English language ability. But I finally came to realize that the biggest problem is that they, too, are playing the wrong game.

Whenever I serve a volleyball, everyone just stands back and watches it fall, with occasional murmurs of encouragement. No one hits it back. Everyone waits until I call on someone to take a turn. And when that person speaks, he doesn't hit my ball back. He serves a new ball. Again, everyone just watches it fall.

So I call on someone else. This person does not refer to what the previous speaker had said. He also serves a new ball. Nobody seems to have paid any attention to what anyone else has said. Everyone begins again from the same starting line, and all the balls run parallel. There is never any back and forth. Everyone is trying to bowl with a volleyball.

And if I try a simpler conversation, with only two of us, then the other person tries to bowl with my tennis ball. No wonder foreign English teachers in Japan get discouraged.

Now that you know about the difference in the conversational ballgames, you may think that all your troubles are over. But if you have been trained all your life to play one game, it is no simple matter to switch to another, even if you know the rules. Knowing the rules is not at all the same thing as playing the game.

Even now, during a conversation in Japanese I will notice a startled reaction, and belatedly realize that once again I have rudely interrupted by instinctively trying to hit back the other person's bowling ball. It is no easier for me to "just listen" during a conversation than it is for my Japanese students to "just relax" when speaking with foreigners. Now I can truly sympathize with how hard they must find it to try to carry on a Western-style conversation.

If I have not yet learned to do conversational bowling in Japanese, at least I have figured out one thing that puzzled me for a long time. After his first trip to America, my husband complained that Americans asked him so many questions and made him talk so much at the dinner table that he never had a chance to eat. When I asked him why he couldn't talk and eat at the same time, he said that Japanese do not customarily think that dinner, especially on fairly formal occasions, is a suitable time for extended conversation.

Since Westerners think that conversation is an indispensable part of dining, and indeed would consider it impolite not to converse with one's dinner partner, I found this Japanese custom rather strange. Still, I could accept it as a cultural difference even though I didn't really understand it. But when my husband added, in explanation, that Japanese consider it extremely rude to talk with one's mouth full, I got confused. Talking with one's mouth full is certainly not an American custom. We think it very rude, too. Yet we still manage to talk a lot and eat at the same time. How do we do it?

For a long time, I couldn't explain it, and it bothered me. But after I discovered the conversational ballgames, I finally found the answer. Of course! In a Western-style conversation, you hit the ball, and while someone else is hitting it back, you take a bite, chew, and swallow. Then you hit the ball again, and then eat some more. The more people there are in the conversation, the more chances you have to eat. But even with only two of you talking, you still have plenty of chances to eat.

Maybe that's why polite conversation at the dinner table has never been a traditional part of Japanese etiquette. Your turn to talk would last so long without interruption that you'd never get a chance to eat.

For Consideration:

1. How do the conversational ballgames that Japanese and Americans play relate to their cultural characteristics? In other words, what in the culture of Japan leads them to bowling styled, and what in the culture of America leads to tennis styled conversations?

2. Write two short scripts (one an American styled tennis match and the other a Japanese styled bowling game) for a conversation between an American and a Japanese student who have been assigned to work on a term paper together and must decide on a topic. Which was harder to write? How did the Japanese approach yield a decision?

Excerpted from Sakamoto, N. M. (1995). Conversational ballgames. In R. Holton (Ed.), *Encountering Cultures* (pp. 60–63). Englewood Cliffs, NJ: Prentice-Hall.

for creating many, unplanned digital conversations (Engdahl, 2007). Communicating through some forms of social media is equivalent to inviting thousands of people into a conversation with you. Always keep your intended audience (and unintended audiences) in mind.

Conversational Spontaneity

conversational spontaneity—the degree to which a conversation unfolds in an informal and natural fashion

Face-to-face communication is characterized by **conversational spontaneity**—the degree to which a conversation unfolds in an informal and natural fashion. Face-to-face conversation is unscripted, informal, and free-flowing. Communication through social media, on the other hand, may lack this spontaneity. Although e-mails and blogs are somewhat interactive, the sender can carefully edit and craft each message before sending or posting it. Even social media outlets such as Twitter and Facebook—known for their characteristically informal, often spontaneous outbursts—have become nothing more than another marketing channel in the hands of certain individuals, companies, and institutions, whose ostensibly spontaneous digital conversations are often carefully scripted, artfully articulated, and meticulously managed. Although this approach can provide a coherent and calming message in a time of crisis, the message tends to be quite static, and oftentimes, free of emotion and social cues. If you saw your roommate's girlfriend kissing another man, you may want to address this delicate situation with your roommate. You may be uncomfortable with the lack of interactivity and spontaneity offered by social media. Although you may be able to carefully craft a message through e-mail or Facebook, try to have a face-to-face conversation with your roommate to provide a rich opportunity for an interactive and spontaneous conversation. Your roommate may appreciate that you cared enough about him to deliver the bad news face-to-face, rather than in an e-mail or text message.

INTER-ACT WITH SOCIAL MEDIA

When we use social media, it is not always clear to everyone which conversations are taking place with whom. Consider a recent Facebook status update that garnered over thirty comments. Or scan your Twitter feed and examine a series of posts pertaining to a single topic. Can you clearly follow the conversation flow? How might you evaluate each user's ability to respond appropriately to the comments of another?

Abruptness of Disengagement

Digital conversations often lack the clear beginnings and endings that characterize face-to-face conversations, such as "hello" and "see you later." Have you ever IM'd with someone only to have the person quickly type "brb" (be right back) or "gotta go, bye"? Or maybe your friend disappeared from your online list altogether without even saying goodbye. These abrupt endings can be frustrating because we often expect our digital conversational partners to follow the rules that typically apply to face-to-face conversations. Understanding that digital conversations can be terminated suddenly is one requirement for practicing effective conversations through social media. We know that the digital communication context is different from face-to-face settings, so we may consider abrupt endings acceptable for digital conversations. If you are IMing with a friend on Facebook, and you notice that the person has stopped responding to your messages, don't be frustrated. Although it can be easy to perceive your friend's lack of response as rude, he or she may have had to quickly step away from the computer, take a phone call, or may have lost an Internet connection altogether. If your friend goes

Does it bother you when someone you are talking with interrupts your conversation to answer a cell phone call, check for IMs and e-mails, or engage in other technology-mediated communication?

offline, try following up with an e-mail or text message. Chances are your friend meant no harm by not responding, but a follow-up message can ease any feelings of frustration you may have and clarify any misunderstandings.

Multiplicity of Conversations

Without a doubt, more than one face-to-face conversation can occur at any one time. Consider a class project group that is working on an upcoming assignment. In face-to-face settings, all members of the group recognize when multiple conversational topics are being discussed and who the participants in side conversations are. Digital conversations, however, do not always clearly specify which conversations are taking place with whom. For instance, while the group is meeting face-to-face, Melissa may briefly disengage from the group to take a quick phone call; Sean may exchange a few text messages with a few friends he plans to meet afterwards; Chrissy may use her laptop to reply to an e-mail from her mom; and Darren may announce that their professor just posted exam grades online. Although this can seem like a group meeting gone awry, participants often consider this behavior acceptable or even normal. Does it bother you when someone you are talking with in person interrupts your conversation to answer a phone call or send a text message? Although we can carry on many digital conversations while simultaneously talking with others in face-to-face settings, this behavior can be considered rude. If you must take a phone call, politely put your face-to-face conversation on hold. Quickly take your phone call, hang up, and then thank your conversational partner for his or her cooperation and patience. Knowing how to manage multiple conversations will improve your interpersonal communication competence. Similarly, you've likely tried to split your attention between a face-to-face conversation and texting with another friend. If you are having a face-to-face conversation with another person—a parent, a friend, or a professor—avoid trying to simultaneously text with another person. When we practice interpersonal communication in face-to-face or digital contexts, each person that we communicate with deserves our full attention. Avoiding the problem of "split attention" will lead others to perceive you as a competent communicator.

Managing Privacy

By their nature, some social media devices can compromise the privacy of our digital conversations. You likely have had the unpleasant experience of clearly overhearing another person's cell phone conversation. When we use social media in public places, it is easy to forget that other people are present and events are occurring that are not part of our conversation. So our private conversation can become public and available for others to experience. Likewise, aspects of your Facebook profile and your texted or tweeted conversations can be available for unintended audiences if your privacy settings are not appropriately managed. In an effort to update the mechanics behind the social network site, technicians at Facebook often alter how users can manage their privacy settings. If you are an active Facebook user, get in the habit of regularly checking your privacy settings to be sure the information

---

A QUESTION OF ETHICS ● What Would You Do?

Tonia is her Uncle Fred's only living relative, and he has been her favorite relative for as long as she can remember. About three years ago, Fred was diagnosed with lung cancer that eventually led to surgery and a round of radiation and chemotherapy. At that time, Fred made out his will, naming Tonia as his executor and giving her his medical power of attorney. Recently, he also signed a waiver so that his medical team would be able to disclose all his medical information to Tonia even though he has been feeling great.

Uncle Fred has worked hard all his life and has talked about, dreamed about, and saved for a trip to visit his mother's hometown in northern Italy. Last week he called Tonia very excited and told her that he had just finished making all his reservations and was scheduled to leave for Italy in two weeks. While Tonia was really happy for him, she wondered if his doctor had approved his trip.

Reluctant to rain on his parade, Tonia nonetheless phoned the doctor to see if Uncle Fred had told him about the trip. She was alarmed to learn that not only had Uncle Fred not mentioned the trip to his doctor

but also his latest follow-up CT scan showed that the cancer was growing aggressively. The doctor believed that Fred needed to cancel his trip and immediately begin another round of chemotherapy. When Tonia asked about the likelihood of the treatments bringing the cancer back into remission, the doctor said, "To be perfectly honest, there is only a 10 percent chance that the chemo will work. But without treatment, the cancer is sure to kill him in less than six months." Then the doctor implored Tonia to talk with her uncle and convince him to cancel his plans and begin treatment.

For Consideration:
1. Was it ethical for Tonia and her uncle's doctor to have this conversation?
2. Is it ethical for Tonia to try to convince her uncle to stay and have chemotherapy?
3. Should Tonia agree to talk with her uncle? If so, what ethical issues will she confront?
4. If she chooses to have this conversation with her uncle, how can Johannesen's guidelines for ethical dialog—authenticity, empathy, confirmation, presentness, equality, and supportiveness—help her create an effective conversation?

you want to share is available to others, while information you want to conceal is hidden. A new Facebook update can change how your private information is made available to your friends, your friends of friends, and strangers.

Summary

Conversations are interactive, extemporaneous, locally managed, and sequentially organized interchanges of thoughts and feelings between two or more people. Conversations vary in type, purpose, sequence, tone, participants, and setting.

Good communicators follow the general guidelines for conducting effective conversations, which include focusing on others, taking turns appropriately and avoiding interruptions, maintaining conversational coherence, practicing politeness, protecting privacy, and engaging in ethical dialog.

To improve conversation when you interact with someone for the first time, there are strategies for initiating, sustaining, and ending conversation. The strategies for initiation are making a comment, asking a ritual question, and introducing yourself. You can sustain conversation more effectively if you use free information, ask questions (both closed-ended and open-ended), seek high-interest topics, self-disclose in appropriate ways, and actively listen. Terminating conversation goes most smoothly if you pay attention to and use both verbal and nonverbal leave-taking cues, verbalize a desire to end the conversation, and conclude with a simple parting comment.

Many aspects of the traditional concept of conversation have changed as a result of technological innovation and proliferation, including awareness of audience, degree of conversational spontaneity, abruptness of disengagement, multiplicity of conversations, acceptance of interruptions, and notions of privacy. The effectiveness of digital conversation largely depends on the level of engagement or attention given to such interactions. Social presence is the perception that our conversational partners are near us in space and time. Mediated communication technologies vary in their capacity to enhance our feelings of social presence. Finally, it is also important to recognize that conversational styles vary with culture.

Chapter Resources

What You Should Be Able *to Explain:*

- A conversation
- The characteristics of conversation
- Six ways in which conversations vary
- Guidelines to be a more effective conversationalist
- Strategies to initiate, sustain, and close conversations effectively
- Issues in mediated conversations
- Cultural variations in conversation

What You Should Be Able *to Do:*

- Use effective turn-taking in a conversation
- Comfortably initiate a conversation with a stranger
- Skillfully sustain conversations
- Comfortably close conversations

Self-test questions based on these concepts are available on the companion Web site (www.oup.com/us/verderber) as part of Chapter 8 resources.

Key Words

Flashcards for all of these key terms are available on the *Inter-Act* Web site.

Authenticity, p. 237
Closed-ended questions, p. 240
Co-narration, p. 232
Confirmation, p. 237
Conversation, p. 227
Conversation purpose, p. 230
Conversation tone, p. 233
Conversational coherence, p. 236
Conversational spontaneity, p. 248
Ethical dialog, p. 237

Equality, p. 237
Extemporaneous, p. 227
Face-saving, p. 236
Formality, p. 233
Free information, p. 240
Gossip, p. 229
Leave-taking cues, p. 242
Local management, p. 228
Open-ended questions, p. 240
Politeness, p. 236

Presentness, p. 237
Ritual question, p. 238
Scripted, p. 232
Self-disclosure, p. 241
Sequential organization, p. 229
Small talk, p. 229
Social presence, p. 245
Supportiveness, p. 237
Talk time, p. 235
Turn-taking, p. 227

Apply Your Knowledge

The following activities challenge you to demonstrate your mastery of the concepts, theories, and frameworks in this chapter by using them to explain what is happening in a specific situation.

Inter-Action Dialogue: Conversations

Skills of effective conversation include focusing on the other, appropriately taking turns, maintaining conversational coherence, practicing politeness (especially, helping others save face), considering privacy needs, and engaging in ethical dialog. *Susan and Sarah are close friends who share the same religious background and the occasional frustration related to their families' beliefs.* The following is a transcript of their conversation.

8.1　Do a line-by-line analysis of this Inter-Action Dialogue and determine the type of conversation that is taking place. Look for the signs of effective conversation just mentioned. You can watch a video of this conversation on the *Inter-Act* Web site and use a form provided to write down your own analysis of the conversation.

DIALOGUE

Susan: So how are you and Bill getting along these days?

Sarah: Oh, not too well, Suze. I think we've got to end the relationship. There are so many issues between us that I just don't have the same feelings.

Susan: Yeah, you know, I could tell. Is there one specific thing that's a problem?

Sarah: Yes, and it's ironic because early on I didn't think it would be a problem, but it is. You know he's not Jewish, and since we've started talking about marriage, I've realized that it is a problem. While Bill's a great guy, our backgrounds and beliefs just don't mesh. I never realized how important my Jewishness was to me until I was faced with converting. And Bill feels similarly about the issue.

Susan: I think I'm kind of lucky, well, in the long run. Remember in high school, my parents wouldn't let me go out with anybody who wasn't Jewish? At the time I resented that, and we both thought they were reactionary, but now I'm kind of glad. At the time my parents said, "You never know what's going to come out of a high school relationship." Well, it never got that far, but it did force me to think about things.

Sarah: Yes, I remember that. You hated it. It's amazing to realize your parents can actually be right about something.

Susan: Right, it was annoying at the time, but at least it spared me the pain you and Bill are going through. It must be awful to be in love with someone you realize you don't want as a life partner.

Sarah: Exactly, but I'm glad that my parents didn't restrict my dating to Jewish guys. I've learned a lot by dating a variety of people, and I know that I've made this decision independently. Bill's a great guy, but for me to be me, I need to have a Jewish man for a partner—and Bill knows he can't be that. Making this choice has been hard, but it's helped me grow. I guess I understand myself better.

Susan: So where have you guys left it? Are you going to still see each other? Be friends?

Sarah: We hope so. But right now, it's too fresh. It hurts to see him, so we're trying to give each other some space. It will really be tough when I hear he's seeing someone else. But I'll get by.

Susan: Well, you know I'm here for you. And when you're ready there are some real hotties at Hillel. I'll be glad to introduce you.

Sarah: Thanks, Suze. So how's your new job?

Susan: Oh, it's great. I really like my boss, and I've gotten a new assignment that fits right in with my major. Plus my boss has been flexible in assigning my hours. I just wish that it wasn't so far away.

Sarah: I thought it was downtown.

Susan: It is, but it takes me over an hour because I have to change buses three times.

Sarah: Wow—are you at least able to study while you ride?

Susan: Not really. I get carsick.

Skill Practice

Skill practice activities give you the chance to rehearse a new skill by responding to hypothetical or real situations. Additional skill practice activities are available at the companion Web site.

Practice Initiating Conversation

For each of the following scenarios, come up with a way to initiate conversation using at least two of the three strategies described in this chapter (make a comment, ask a ritual question, or introduce yourself).

8.2   You've just moved to a new town. You love to swim and play racquetball, so you decide to join the nearest health club. Today, after finishing your first workout at the gym, you see someone in the locker room who looks like a regular.

Your Opening:

8.3   You are at the mall with your eight-year-old daughter. You are in Gap Kids, and she is whining because you don't want to purchase a frivolous item that isn't on sale. Another parent grins in your direction.

Your Opening:

8.4 You are a new employee at a company. Tonight is the mid-year company party at a downtown hotel. You're in a long line for drinks. The person in front of you is someone you've seen in the hallway at work but have never talked with.

Your Opening:

8.5 You're at a friend's Super Bowl party. You're getting settled on one of the couches and someone you don't know sits down on the loveseat opposite you.

Your Opening:

8.6 You're bored on the bus home from work, and your iPod (or iPhone) battery is dead. The person sitting next to you is staring off into space.

Your Opening:

8.7 You're walking your dog on a leash in the park. When you stop at a drinking fountain, your dog starts sniffing a dog whose owner is sitting on the bench next to the fountain.

Your Opening:

Communication Improvement Plan: Conversation

How would you like to improve your conversational skills as discussed in this chapter?

- Developing an other-centered focus
- Engaging in appropriate turn-taking
- Maintaining conversational coherence
- Practicing politeness
- Balancing appropriateness and efficiency
- Protecting privacy
- Engaging in ethical dialogue

8.8 Pick a skill, and write a communication improvement plan. You can find a communication improvement plan worksheet on our Web site at www.oup.com/us/verderber.

Inter-Act with Media

Television

Live with Regis and Kelly (2011). Regis Philbin, Kelly Ripa.

Live with Regis and Kelly was a television morning talk show hosted by Kelly Ripa and Regis Philbin (who recently retired from the popular show). Regis and Kelly typically bantered back-and-forth, hosted phone-in contests, and welcomed celebrity and non-celebrity guests. Central to the show's concept, the first twenty-two minutes were known as "host chat," an improvised conversation between Philbin and Ripa. During the very popular host chat segment, Philbin and Ripa would react to stories in the media and share stories about their recent evening out on the town. Their conversation featured a contrast between Philbin's argumentative and often pushy persona and Ripa's cheerful and positive outlook. After host chat, a viewer was called to participate in a trivia game and had the chance to win a lavish prize—often a vacation to a warm and sunny location. Following the contest, the show featured special segments and interviews with both celebrities and regular people with a story to tell. The final three minutes were devoted to the "Regis and Kelly's Inbox" segment when viewer mail was read.

IPC Concepts: Turn-taking, extemporaneous conversations, local management

To the Point:

> How would you evaluate Regis and Kelly's ability to use turn-taking during the *Live with Regis and Kelly* show?
> How might you characterize the structure and variation of their conversations on the show?

Cinema

Freedom Writers (2007). Richard LaGravenese (director). Hilary Swank, Imelda Staunton.

Dedicated new high school teacher Erin Gruwell (Swank) takes a job at Woodrow Wilson High School in Long Beach, California, far removed from her familiar hometown surroundings. The school used to be quite high achieving, but recently implemented an integration plan. Her students challenge her enthusiasm when she realizes that her students are all "at-risk" for failure. The students band together in racial groups; fights break out in the classroom; and eventually, many stop attending class. After finding a racist drawing made by one of her students, Gruwell uses it as a teachable moment about the Holocaust. She slowly begins to earn their trust and purchases notebooks so they can record diaries. In those powerful diaries, they describe their abusive experiences, instances when they saw their friends die, among many other experiences. Her students begin to show respect, learn, and share more personal information in conversations with her and other class members. Gruwell asks her students to compose their diaries in book form, which she compiles into *The Freedom Writers Diary*. In opposition to her department head's wishes, Gruwell convinces the superintendent to permit her to teach her students during their junior and senior years. The film ends with notations indicating that Gruwell successfully prepared many high school students for graduation so they could attend colleges and universities.

IPC Concepts: Scripted conversations, conversational tone, formality, protection of privacy, authenticity, presentness, equality.

To the Point:

> How might you explain the conversational tone of the interactions between Erin Gruwell and Margaret Campbell, her department head?
> During the interactions between Erin Gruwell and her students, how would you characterize Gruwell's ability to protect students' privacy while still being perceived by them as present, authentic, and equal in their many conversations?

What's on the Web

Find links and additional material, including self-quizzes, on the companion Web site at www.oup.com/us/verderber.

9

Supporting Others

"Hi, Maria," said Ben as he slid into the booth across from her. "How's it going?"

" Oh, Ben. I'm really depressed and scared. I couldn't make my rent this month, and I think I may have to take the kids and move home with my mom," Maria whispered as she began to cry softly.

"Wow, that's heavy," Ben replied. "Have you ever thought about leaving school for a while to regroup?"

"Yes, but if I do that I will lose my Pell grants and other loans, and without any job prospects, I count on those to live," Maria responded.

"Well, what about getting someone to move in and share the rent?" suggested Ben.

"Get serious, who's going to want to live in a small two-bedroom apartment with me and my kids?" Maria retorted as she dried her eyes.

"Hmmm. OK, well, it sounds like you've got no choice. Maybe moving home with your mom for a while isn't such a bad idea. I bet she will even help with the kids," Ben responded as he shrugged his shoulders.

"Right! Thanks for all the good advice! I don't know why I even bothered to tell you about this. I should have figured that you just wouldn't get it," Maria snapped as she stood up and strode away.

What you should be able *to* *explain* after you have studied this chapter:

- The concept of empathy
- Three approaches to empathy
- Ways to improve your capacity to empathize
- Social support
- The characteristics of effective and ineffective supporting
- Supporting positive feelings and experiences with celebratory messages
- Supporting negative feelings and experiences with comforting messages
- The four supportive interaction phases
- The five supportive message skills
- Gender and cultural similarities and differences in supporting
- The nature of effective digital empathy and support

What you should be able *to* *do* after you have studied this chapter:

- Use celebratory support messages to respond to others' positive feelings and experiences
- Use comforting messages to respond to others' negative feelings and experiences
- Clarify supportive intentions
- Buffer face threats
- Create other-centered messages
- Reframe information
- Give advice

Have you ever been in a situation similar to Ben's, where you tried to be helpful to someone only to have it blow up in your face? Why didn't Maria find Ben's responses helpful? What did she really want from Ben when she began the conversation? Most of us understand the importance of providing support for our friends and family members. But too often our attempts to help others are awkward, inappropriate, or not appreciated because, like Ben, we don't really understand how to comfort and support others. Research has linked effective messages of comfort and support with longer life, reduced incidence of disease, better recovery from illness, improved ability to cope with chronic illness, and better overall mental health (Albrecht & Goldsmith, 2003). For example, supportive communication has been shown to have a significant impact on cancer survival rates (Ahuja, 2007; Carpenter, 2006) and beneficial effects on cardiovascular, endocrine, and immune system health (Uchino, Cacioppo, & Kiecolt-Glaser, 1996). In addition, supportive communication can contribute to healthier relationships, with such benefits as marital satisfaction, healthy family interactions, strong friendships, and amicable work relationships

(Goldsmith, 2004). These are just a few of the reasons that make it important to become skillful at offering comfort and support.

In this chapter, you will study the supportive communication process and how to become more proficient at providing comfort, support, and advice. We begin by explaining the concept of empathy and describing how to increase your ability to empathize. Then we discuss supportive messages and the characteristics of effective and ineffective supporting. This is followed by a discussion of the four phases of supportive interaction. Next, we describe the five message skills that will enable you to provide effective support to others. Finally, we examine how giving and receiving support occurs, increasingly, in an online environment, as well as how gender and cultural differences and similarities play a role in supporting others.

Empathizing

The foundation of supporting others is **empathy**—the cognitive and affective process of perceiving the emotions others are feeling and then acting on our perception (Preston & de Waal, 2002). Scholars recognize that empathy is an important element in understanding and maintaining good interpersonal relationships (Omdahl, 1995). When you empathize, you attempt to understand or experience what your partner understands or experiences; in effect, you put yourself in the other person's shoes. It obviously requires effort to empathize with someone who is very different from you or with someone who is experiencing something that is out of your realm of experience. But your effective supporting and comforting begins with your ability to empathize with what another is experiencing. In this section, we discuss the three types of empathy and the steps you can take to improve your ability to empathize.

Empathy—the cognitive and affective process of perceiving the emotions others are feeling and then acting on our perception.

LEARN ABOUT YOURSELF　●　Empathy Tendencies

Take this short survey to learn something about yourself. Answer the questions honestly based on your first responses. There are no right or wrong answers. For each item, use the following scale and provide a number score to indicate how well the item describes you:

0	1	2	3	4
Does not describe me well				Describes me very well

_____ 1. Before criticizing people, I try to imagine how I would feel if I were in their place.

_____ 2. I sometimes try to understand my friends better by imagining how things look from their perspective.

_____ 3. I believe that there are two sides to every question, and I try to look at them both.

_____ 4. I find it easy to see things from another person's point of view.

_____ 5. I try to look at everybody's side of a disagreement before I make a decision.

_____ 6. When I'm upset at someone, I usually try to put myself in his or her shoes for a while.

_____ 7. When I see someone being taken advantage of, I feel protective of this person.

_____ 8. I often have tender, concerned feelings for people less fortunate than me.

_____ 9. I would describe myself as a pretty soft-hearted person.

_____ 10. Sometimes I feel sorry for other people when they are having problems.

_____ 11. Other people's misfortunes usually upset me a lot.

_____ 12. I am often quite touched by things that I see happen.

_____ 13. When I see someone who badly needs help in an emergency, I go to pieces.

_____ 14. I sometimes feel helpless when I am in the middle of a very emotional situation.

_____ 15. In emergency situations, I feel apprehensive and ill at ease.

_____ 16. Being in a tense emotional situation scares me.

_____ 17. When I see someone get hurt, it freaks me out.

_____ 18. I tend to lose control during emergencies.

Scoring the survey: This survey measures your tendencies to use each of the three types of empathy. Add your scores for Items 1 through 6. This indicates your tendency to use perspective taking when you empathize. Add your scores for items 7 through 12. This indicates your tendency to use sympathetic responsiveness when you empathize. Add your scores for items 13 through 18. This indicates your tendency to use empathic responsiveness when you empathize.

Adapted from Davis, M. H. (1980). A multidimensional approach to individual differences in empathy. *JSAS Catalog of Selected Documents in Psychology, 10,* 85.

Three Types of Empathy

Scholars who study empathy have identified three different ways that people empathize: perspective taking, empathic responsiveness, and sympathetic responsiveness (Weaver & Kirtley, 1995).

Perspective taking is empathizing by using everything we know about our partner and our partner's circumstances to help us understand how he or she is feeling. If we don't know our partner very well, we consider how most people would feel in this situation. For example, suppose that Jackson tells James that he is in really serious financial trouble. James, who has known Jackson since grade school, understands that he is very conservative and was raised by parents who were frugal and paid their bills on time. Because of what he knows about Jackson, James understands that he must be panicked about his accumulating debt.

Empathic responsiveness (which has also been called empathic distress) is personally experiencing an emotional response parallel to another person's actual or anticipated display of emotion (Omdahl, 1995; Stiff, Dillard, Somera, Kim, & Sleight, 1988). For instance, if James not only senses the stress and anxiety that Jackson is feeling but also feels stress and anxiety himself, we would say that James has experienced empathic responsiveness. Empathic responsiveness is most common when there is a close or intimate relationship between the person in need of support and the person called on to provide it. Because of a strong relational bond, you may identify more easily with the emotions of a close friend, family member, or intimate partner and experience those emotions along with the other person. Conversely, if someone you just met recently asks for your support or if what the person is experiencing is beyond your experience, it may be more difficult for you to experience empathic responsiveness. Some of us are predisposed to become emotional in stressful situations and to intensely experience the feelings that others are experiencing, so much so that empathic responsiveness is also called empathic distress, a debilitating state that causes you to focus on your own feelings rather than your partner's. Consequently, you become unable to support your partner because you are overcome with your own feelings.

Sympathetic responsiveness is empathizing by feeling concern, compassion, or sorrow for another person because he or she is in a distressing situation but not identifying with the specific emotion he or she is experiencing. Some scholars call this "emotional concern" (Stiff et al., 1988), while others use the term "sympathy" (Eisenberg & Fabes, 1990). Sympathetic responsiveness differs from the other two types of empathy in that you don't attempt to understand the feelings of another person. Rather than identifying with the emotions of the speaker, your response will be concern or compassion for that person. We may use sympathetic responsiveness when the person we are listening to is recounting an experience or an emotional response that is unimaginable to us. In our example, if James always pays his bills on time and can't imagine being in financial difficulty, he can empathize with Jackson through a sympathetic response. He understands that Jackson is stressed and worried, but instead of trying to

Perspective taking—empathizing by using everything we know about our partner and our partner's circumstances to help us understand how he or she is feeling.

Empathic responsiveness (also called empathic distress)—empathizing by personally experiencing an emotional response parallel to another person's actual or anticipated display of emotion.

Sympathetic responsiveness (also called emotional concern)—empathizing by feeling concern, compassion, or sorrow for another person because he or she is in a distressing situation but not identifying with the specific emotion he or she is experiencing.

OBSERVE AND ANALYZE

Empathizing Effectively

Describe the last time you effectively empathized with another person. Write a short summary of the episode. Be sure to cover the following: What was the person's emotional state? How did you recognize it? What were the nonverbal cues? Verbal cues? What type of relationship do you have with this person? How long have you known the person? How similar is this person to you? Have you ever had a real or vicarious experience similar to the one the person was reporting? Did you use empathic responsiveness, perspective taking, or sympathetic responsiveness? Why? What was the outcome of this communication episode?

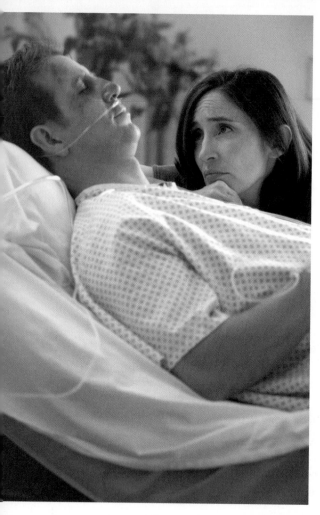

feel Jackson's emotions directly or imagining how he himself would feel in a similar situation, James instead feels concern and compassion for his friend Jackson.

Guidelines for Improving Empathy

While some people seem to have an inherent capacity to empathize, most of us need to improve our ability to empathize. As you can guess, successful empathizing demands active listening. In addition, the following three guidelines can help you improve your ability to empathize.

1. Pay attention to nonverbal and paralanguage cues. What people feel about what they are saying is usually conveyed in the nonverbal parts of the message. These cues are your best indication of what they are feeling. How well you empathize depends on how clearly you observe and read the nonverbal messages others send. Research studies have shown that when people concentrate, they can do well and are adept at recognizing such primary emotions as happiness, sadness, surprise, anger, and fear (greater than 90 percent accuracy) and are good at recognizing contempt, disgust, interest, determination, and bewilderment (80 to 90 percent accuracy; Leathers, 1997). The research also suggests that recognizing facial expressions is the key to perceiving emotion (Leathers, 1997). To improve your understanding of nonverbal messages, try mentally answering two questions when talking with others: "What emotions do I believe the person is experiencing right now?" and "What cues am I seeing to draw this conclusion?" Consciously raising these questions can help you focus your attention on the nonverbal aspects of messages, which convey most of the information regarding the person's emotional state. To ensure that you understand another's emotions accurately, use the skill of perception checking, which you learned about in Chapter 2.

2. Pay attention to the emotional content of the verbal message. Although most of the emotional message will be conveyed in the paralinguistic and nonverbal portions of a message, your partners will also provide cues about how they are feeling by the specific language that they use as well as their direct statements about their feelings. For example, when your friend tells you what his grandmother sent for his birthday, he might say, "She only sent me fifty bucks," or he might say, "She sent me fifty dollars, which is a lot since she is retired."

3. Use your observations to infer how and why your partner is feeling and thinking a certain way. Having observed the nonverbal, paralinguistic, and verbal aspects of the message, you should be able to understand your partner's emotional perspective on what she or he is saying. With this understanding, you will be better able to support your partner.

Supportive Messages

Social support is the process of providing emotional, informational, and instrumental resources to someone we perceive is in need of this aid (Burleson, 2010). Social support includes providing for both the tangible or physical needs and the intangible or psychological needs of others. **Supportive messages** are communications that provide intangible support for your partner, including emotional support, information, advice, and motivation. Figure 9.1 provides a list of typical support messages. Supportive communication signals care, concern, interest, compassion, and even love. Our voluntary relationships often grow from times when we have offered support. And we can develop or maintain our relationships by our supportive communication. When we are not supportive of our partners our relationships tend to decline.

Not all efforts to provide support are effective. Whether a particular message is perceived as supportive can depend on who delivers the message, what the context of the interaction is, what nonverbal communication accompanies the message, and how the message is worded (Goldsmith, 2004). For example, suppose Emily confides in someone else that she thinks she might be pregnant and her boyfriend doesn't know. The response, which on the surface seems straightforward and innocuous, is, "You'd better go talk to him." But is this actually

Social support—the process of providing emotional, informational, and instrumental resources to someone we perceive is in need of this aid.

Supportive messages—communications that provide intangible support for your partner, including emotional support, information, advice, and motivation.

TYPE OF SUPPORT	DESCRIPTION	EXAMPLE
Celebratory	Honoring achievements or transitions, wishing good luck, and expressing relief	*"Wow, congratulations on finishing that paper. It isn't even due for three days."* *"I'm so proud of how well you have adjusted to college."* *"I know you were worried about your sister. You must be relieved to know that the tumor wasn't cancerous."*
Comforting	Acknowledging everyday hurts and disappointments	*"I know how much you wanted to win that race, but your time still qualified you for the conference championships."*
Grief management	Supporting through bereavement and major losses	*"I know that you are shocked by your Dad's passing. Are you afraid of how your mom will manage without him?"* *"I can tell that you are devastated that Theo wants a divorce. Do you want to talk about it?"*
Esteem support	Helping process failures, rejections, and transgressions	*"It's OK to be disappointed about flunking that quiz. But it's not as though you studied a lot for it. I'm sure that with study you'll do fine on the test."* *"I know how much you wanted the lead in that play. Do you know why you weren't cast?"* *"You seem to feel really guilty and sorry for what you did. Do you know why you did this and what you can do to make amends?"*
Informational support (Advice)	Aiding in problem solving and decision making	*"Since you asked for my advice, I agree with your brother. I think it's time for you to get an attorney."*
Motivational support	Encouraging change in a problematic behavior	*"I know you are trying to quit smoking. That's hard to do, and I'm proud of you. How has it been going?"*

FIGURE 9.1 Types of Social Support Messages. Based on Burleson, 2010.

INTER-ACT WITH SOCIAL MEDIA

People frequently use Facebook as a forum for social support. Scan your Facebook newsfeed for friends who post supportive messages. Pay careful attention to the comments posted in response to a friend's support-seeking message. Evaluate the nature of the support communicated through Facebook in light of the characteristics of effective and ineffective support messages discussed in this chapter.

supportive? It depends. First, it depends on who delivers the message. This may be seen as caring and helpful advice if Emily would typically expect silence or a negative message from the person she has told. On the other hand, this may seem unsupportive if offered by a friend, parent, or other family member, whom Emily would expect to focus first on addressing her feelings, not on giving her advice. Second, the context of the interaction will influence the perception of support. If the comment occurred in the later stages of a lengthy conversation, Emily may see it as supportive. But if "You'd better go talk to him" is the first thing said or, even worse, is all that is said to her, Emily may view this as curt, unsupportive, and unwanted advice. Third, the nonverbal communication accompanying the response will determine how the message is viewed. As you can imagine, Emily would interpret a harsh tone of voice, avoidance of eye contact, or a disapproving facial expression as unsupportive, whereas she would interpret a soothing vocal delivery, direct and sympathetic eye contact, or a smile as supportive.

Research on supportive responses suggests that people who use sophisticated supporting strategies are perceived as more sensitive, concerned, and involved (Burleson & Samter, 1990; Kunkel & Burleson, 1999; Samter, Burleson, & Murphy, 1987). Sophisticated support messages show that you care about your partners and what happens to them, and they demonstrate that you empathize with your partners' feelings, whatever their direction or intensity (Burleson, 1994).

Characteristics of Effective and Ineffective Support Messages

Much research has been directed toward understanding what types of messages and message scripts are perceived as supportive and what types of messages and message scripts are perceived as unsupportive. In his research, Burleson (2003) identified a number of effective and ineffective types of supporting responses. Effective supporting responses do the following:

1. **Clearly state an aim to help and support the other:** "I'd like to help you. What can I do?" or "You know that I'm going to be here for you for as long as it takes."
2. **Express acceptance, love, and affection for the other:** "I love you and understand how upset (happy) this makes you," or "I understand that you just can't seem to accept this."
3. **Demonstrate care, concern, and interest in the other's situation:** "What are you planning to do now?" or "Tell me more," or "What happened then?"
4. **Indicate the availability to listen and support the other:** "If you need to talk more, please call," or "Sometimes it helps to have someone to listen, and I'd like to do that for you."

We can support others not only with our verbal messages but also by joining in celebrations of important milestones. How does attending someone's graduation show support?

5. **Declare a position as the other's ally:** "I'm with you on this," or "Well, I'm on your side—this isn't right."

6. **Acknowledge the other's feelings and situation as well as express sincere support:** "I'm so sorry to see you feeling so bad. I can see that you're devastated by what has happened," or "I can see that you're excited, and I am with you 100 percent. Way to go."

7. **Affirm the legitimacy of the other's feelings:** "With what has happened to you, you deserve to be angry," or "I can see why you're so happy. I'd feel exactly the same way if I were in your shoes."

8. **Encourage the other to elaborate on the story:** "Uh huh, yeah," or "I see. How did you feel about that?" or "Well, what happened before that? Can you elaborate?"

According to Burleson, ineffective supporting messages, on the other hand, do the following:

1. **Condemn and criticize the other's feelings and behaviors:** "I think you're wrong to be angry with Paul," or "That's dumb. Why do you feel like that?" or "I don't see what the big deal is. Anyone could have done that."

2. **Imply that the other's feelings are not warranted:** "You have no right to feel that way. After all, you've dumped men before," or "Don't you think you're being overdramatic? Why are you acting like you won the Nobel Prize. It was just an A on a Chem 101 lab report."

3. **Tell the other how to feel, or advise the other to ignore justifiable feelings about the situation:** "You should be really happy about this," or "Hey, you should just act as if you don't care."

4. **Take attention away from the other and focus on the self:** "I know exactly how you feel because when I . . ."

5. **Impose advice on a relative stranger:** "I know we've just met, but I know how to help you here."

© A.BACALL

"Of course I'm listening to your expression of spiritual suffering. Don't you see me making eye contact, striking an open posture, leaning towards you and nodding empathetically?"

Spotlight on Scholars

Read about research into comforting and supporting responses and the work of Brant Burleson at www.oup.com/us/verderber.

Sometimes we are called on to support our partners' positive experiences and feelings. At other times, we need to comfort our partners. Let's look more closely at these different support situations and the types of messages effective in each.

Supporting Positive Feelings: Celebratory Messages

We all like to treasure our successes and make the most of the good feelings that come from them. When good things happen to us, we like to share these with others. **Capitalization** is process of sharing our successes and leveraging the good feelings that come from them by telling others with the expectation that they will celebrate with us (Langston, 1994). When we share our successes, we don't want them belittled by listeners' inappropriate or insensitive responses. Rather, we disclose these events in the hope that our partner's response will magnify how good we

Capitalization—the process of sharing our successes and leveraging the good feelings that come from them by telling others with the expectation that they will celebrate with us.

Emotional Support

Recall the last time you received emotional support from a partner. Describe the situation. Did you feel better because of this conversation? Which characteristics of effective support and ineffective support were evident in the messages of your partner? Does this help explain how comforted you felt? Next, consider each of the characteristics again. Which of these do your messages often exhibit?

Celebratory messages—active-constructive feedback whose goal is to leverage your partner's positive feelings that stem from a happy event or accomplishment.

Comforting messages—active-constructive feedback whose goal is to alleviate or lessen the emotional distress felt by someone else.

are feeling about what has happened (Gable, Reis, Impett, & Asher, 2004). Responses to capitalization messages can be constructive or destructive and active or passive, constituting a total of four types: constructive-active, constructive-passive, destructive-active, and destructive-passive (Gable et al., 2004). Consider the following example:

> As Kendra hangs up the telephone, she does a little dance step and exclaims to Selena: *"That was the bank. He said that I've been approved for the loan. Can you believe it? I'm going to have my own pottery studio."*
>
> Selena: *"Do you really think you're up to making this thing work? I mean you have no business experience."*
>
> (Active-destructive: Rather than supporting Kendra's success, Selena's response forcefully undermines Kendra's good feelings about the accomplishment.)
>
> Selena: *"Do you want to watch a movie tonight?"*
>
> (Passive-destructive: Selena's response does not acknowledge the capitalization attempt.)
>
> Selena: *"That's nice."*
>
> (Passive-constructive: Selena smiles faintly as she acknowledges Kendra's news, but her response does not really reward Kendra with enthusiastic support for her feelings.)
>
> Selena: *"Wow! Way to go! In this economy, that's a terrific accomplishment. All the work you put into your business plan really paid off. You must be so excited. I'm proud of you."*
>
> (Active-constructive: Selena provides a supportive response that celebrates Kendra's accomplishment and acknowledges her feelings.)

Celebratory messages are active-constructive feedback whose goal is to leverage your partner's positive feelings that stem from a happy event or accomplishment. Research studies have found that when we try to capitalize on our successes, only celebratory messages from our partner help us continue to feel good about what has happened and to feel good about our relationship (Gable et al., 2004). Further studies have confirmed that when we see that a partner can be counted on to positively support us, we feel more intimacy, trust, and commitment (Gable, Gonzaga, & Strachman, 2006).

Supporting Negative Feelings: Comforting Messages

When a person who has had an unfortunate experience is in the midst of or is recalling unpleasant emotional reactions, supporting negative feelings provides much-needed comfort. Our responses to our partner's negative feelings in these situations can also be active or passive and constructive or destructive. **Comforting messages** are active constructive feedback whose goal is to alleviate or lessen the emotional distress felt by someone else (Burleson & Samter, 1985). By acknowledging the person's feelings and affirming the person's right to those feelings, you can help the person work through them. Responding to negative feelings can feel awkward and difficult. But when people are in pain or when they are feeling justifiably angry, they need to be comforted by effective supporting statements, a skill that we need to practice. An appropriate comforting statement in response to negative feelings demonstrates empathy, sensitivity, and a willingness to be actively involved if need be. Consider the following example:

> Bill: *My sister called today to tell me that Mom's biopsy came back positive. She's got cancer, and it's untreatable.*
>
> Dwight: *Bill, you must be in shock. I'm so sorry that this is happening. Is there anything I can do for you?*

Notice how Dwight begins by empathizing: "*Bill, you must be in shock.*" He continues with statements that show his sensitivity to the seriousness of the situation: "*I'm so sorry that this is happening.*" Finally, he shows that he wants to be involved: "*Is there anything I can do for you?*" He affirms his willingness to take time to talk about Bill's negative emotions and help if he can.

We offer the exchanges between Kendra and Selena and between Bill and Dwight as an introduction to supporting skills. Later in the chapter, we'll see that these are just two examples of how to provide support. Although we can attempt to support a person with a single supporting response, supporting someone usually involves a longer conversation or series of conversations. In the next section, we will describe the phases typical in these supportive interactions.

Supportive Interaction Phases

A **supportive interaction** is a conversation or series of conversations in which messages of support are offered to someone. Support may be offered numerous times in a single conversation, and supportive interaction may involve numerous conversations spanning days, weeks, or even months. Regardless of the length of the supportive interaction, the role of the supporter is to give emotional care to someone who is having ongoing difficulty mentally and emotionally adjusting to a change in circumstances. For example, people facing financial ruin or grieving the death of a loved one are unlikely to be comforted by only one message. Rather, they will likely need ongoing supportive interactions. Whether a distressed person is comforted in one conversation or requires many conversations, Barbee and Cunningham (1995) have identified four well-ordered phases through which supportive interactions progress: support activation, support provision, target reaction, and helper responses.

Supportive interaction—a conversation or series of conversations in which messages of support are offered to someone.

   1. Phase one: support activation. Supportive interactions begin when something happens to trigger an initial supportive response, such as the words or behaviors of the person needing support/comforting. Alternatively, a relational partner who perceives a need to support the other can trigger support activation. For example, if Brianne comes home, walks into the kitchen, and finds her mother slumped over the sink silently sobbing into her arm, she is likely to activate support by rushing over, putting her arms around her mom, and asking, "Mom, are you all right? What's happened?" Support, then, can be activated either by the person needing comfort or by the person offering comfort.

   2. Phase two: support provision. During the second phase of a supportive interaction, comforters enact active-constructive messages designed to support the partner by focusing on the emotions being displayed or on the problem that has been expressed. Once Brianne's mother shares that she is crying because she lost her job, Brianne may provide solace by saying, "I'm so sorry. I can understand why you're terrified about how we'll pay this month's rent." In this way, Brianne offers support for her mother's feelings.

3. Phase three: target reaction. Once a comforter has responded to the person needing support, that person will react to what the helper has said or done. This reaction will indicate how successful the helper's message was at comforting the partner. Brianne's mother may be somewhat soothed by Brianne's message and stop crying long enough to respond, "I'm not just worried about the rent. There's the car payment, and I just finished paying off the credit card bill. I don't know if I can face going into debt again."

4. Phase four: helper responses. The final step in supportive interactions consists of any further messages from the comforter or helper regarding what the partner has initially expressed. If the partner remains in need of comforting, the interaction will cycle back to a previous phase and continue until one of the partners changes the subject or ends the conversation. In our previous example, since Brianne's first message provided the needed support allowing her mother to regain some composure and disclose her fears about going into debt, the helper-responses phase may not be necessary. At this point, Brianne might refocus the discussion by suggesting solutions for the family's financial problems.

As you have probably experienced during your own supportive interactions, these conversations are not always smooth. There may be false starts, interruptions, topic changes, and other disruptions during the course of the interaction. And the messages themselves will vary from very brief nonverbal cues to short verbal messages to lengthy narratives complete with subplot digressions. Nonetheless, you will more effectively support others if the messages you use during phases two and four incorporate the supportive message skills presented next.

Supportive Message Skills

Five supportive message skills can help us form messages that provide active-constructive emotional support (Burleson, 2003). Three of these skills allow you to actively demonstrate your sensitivity to the emotional needs of your partner: clarifying supportive intentions, buffering face threats (through positive and negative facework), and using other-centered messages. The other two skills enable you to constructively help your partner with problem solving: framing information and giving advice. Occasionally, you may find that one of these skills will provide the necessary support, but you will more likely need a combination of them. Let's take a look at each of these individual skills in turn.

Clarifying Supportive Intentions

People who are experiencing emotional turmoil can have trouble reaching out to and fully trusting those whose support they seek. As a result, comfort givers may need to engage in clarifying supportive intentions. **Clarifying supportive intentions** means openly stating that one's goal is to help the person in need of support.

Clarifying supportive intentions— openly stating that one's goal in a supportive interaction is to help the person in need of support.

Often a prelude to using other support skills, these messages are vitally important because those in need of support may be in a vulnerable position and guarded about their emotions. Through clarifying supportive intentions, you let these people know that your motive is simply and solely to help them. You reassure them that someone is on their side, and you provide a context for their understanding of your comments. To clarify supportive intentions, follow these guidelines: (1) directly state your intentions by emphasizing your desire to help, (2) remind your partner of your commitment to your relationship (if necessary), (3) indicate that helping is your only motive, and (4) phrase your clarification in a way that reflects helpfulness. Let's look at an example of an exchange in which the helper makes it clear that his goal is to be supportive:

People who need to be comforted may feel vulnerable and may be hesitant about disclosing until you have given several reassurances of your supportive intentions. But how can you tell if someone just needs reassurance or if he or she wishes to maintain privacy?

> David, noticing Paul sitting in his cubicle with his head in his lap and his hands over his head, asks, *Paul, is everything OK?*
>
> Paul, sitting up with a miserable but defiant look on his face, replies. *Yeah, everything's fine. You sure don't want to hear about my problems.*
>
> David responds: *Paul, I do care. You've been working for me for five years. You're one of our best analysts. So if something's going on, I'd like to help, even if all I can do is listen.*

Will this statement be enough to convince Paul to open up? Maybe it will. But if not, David can restate and amplify his supportive intentions, hoping that another expression of his position will be effective:

> Paul: *Look, you've got a lot to do without listening to my sad story. I can take care of this myself, so just forget it.*
>
> David: *Paul, I do have lots to do, but I always have time to listen and help you. I don't want to pry. I just want to help.*

With his second response, David has clarified his supportive intentions, following all the guidelines described earlier. He directly states his desire to help: *"I'd like to help, even if all I can do is to listen,"* and *"I always have time to listen and to help you."* He reminds his partner of his commitment to the relationship: *"You've been working for me for five years. You're one of our best analysts."* He indicates that helping is his only motive: *"I don't want to pry. I just want to help."* And he phrases his clarification in a way that reflects helpfulness, using the word "help" several times.

People needing comfort can feel vulnerable and may not be comfortable disclosing until you have repeatedly reassured them of your supportive intentions. But you also need to be sensitive to your partner's right to privacy. Repeated statements of supportive intentions can become counterproductive if your partner feels coerced and ends up disclosing information that he or she would have just as soon withheld. Supporters need to be sensitive to the fine line that exists between encouraging someone to open up and invading that person's privacy to satisfy your own curiosity. Even if your only motive is to help the other person, there will be times when you should not pursue the matter. If Paul, for example, insists a third time that he'd rather not talk about it, David should respect his wishes, perhaps concluding with a statement like, "OK, I understand that you may not want to talk, but if you change your mind, feel free to drop by my office." In this way, he has provided emotional support without insisting on hearing the full details of Paul's situation.

Buffering Face Threats

When we try to support someone, we need to consider the effect that supportive responses may have on the self-image of the person receiving the support. Every person needs to "save face" or preserve a public self-image (Goffman, 1959; Brown & Levinson, 1987). Once you've clarified your intentions to provide support, you may discover that the very act of providing emotional support can be threatening to the face needs of your partner in two ways. First, providing emotional support in a distressing situation can threaten face needs if your partner is concerned with inclusion, respect, appreciation, and approval. For example, Leon's mother wants her son to respect her. So, she is likely to be embarrassed and ashamed when revealing to her son that she has a drinking problem. Second, providing emotional support can threaten people's face needs if they feel that our support may violate their freedom and privacy. In short, support messages carry an altruistic meaning that signals you want to help, but they also convey a potentially disturbing hidden meaning that says to another, "You are needy." As a result, those in need of support may try to save face by denying they actually need help. For example, if Marta tells Cindy that she'd like to help her, Cindy may say, "I can take care of this myself, so just forget it." Here Cindy is reacting to Marta's unintentional **face-threatening act (FTA)**—a statement that a person in need may interpret as a threat to his or her public self-image.

Face-threatening act (FTA)—a statement of support that a person in need may interpret as a threat to his or her public self-image.

SKILL BUILDERS ● Clarifying Supportive Intentions

SKILL	USE	PROCEDURE	EXAMPLE
Openly stating that your goal in the conversation is to help your partner	To let people in need of support know that someone is on their side and that your motive is simply and solely to help them, and to provide a context for their understanding of your comments	1. Directly state your intentions, emphasizing your desire to help. 2. Remind your partner about your ongoing relationship. 3. Indicate that helping is your only motive. 4. Phrase your clarification in a way that reflects helpfulness.	After listening to Sonja complain about flunking her geology midterm, her friend Deepak replies: "Sonja, you're a dear friend, and I'd like to help if you want me to. I did well enough on the midterm that I think I could be of help. Maybe we could meet once a week to go over the readings and class notes together."

Because supportive messages are also FTAs that can be interpreted as questioning another's respectability, approval, freedom, or privacy, comforters need to buffer or cushion the effect of their words with both positive and negative facework messages. **Facework** is messages that we send whose goals are to maintain or restore another person's sense of self-worth (Ting-Toomey & Chung, 2005). **Positive facework** messages affirm a person or a person's actions in a difficult situation to protect his or her respectability and public approval. **Negative facework** messages offer information, opinions, or advice that protect a person's freedom and privacy.

Positive facework messages (1) convey positive feelings about what your partner has said or done in the situation, (2) express admiration for your partner's courage or effort in the situation, (3) acknowledge the difficulty of the situation, and (4) affirm that your partner has the qualities and skills to endure or succeed. In the previous examples, David would be performing positive facework if he were to say to Paul (assuming Paul self-discloses that his wife has left him), "I know it's a terrible situation, but you are always amazing at pulling through in times of stress. And this is certainly not your fault, so hang in there." In Brianne's conversation with her mom, she could perform positive facework by acknowledging how difficult it must be to be fired, indicating how much she admires her mom's determination to stay out of debt, and affirming her belief that her mother is talented and resourceful enough to quickly find a new job.

Negative facework messages (1) ask for permission before making suggestions or giving advice, (2) verbally defer to the opinions and preferences of your partner, (3) use tentative language to hedge and qualify opinions and advice, and (4) offer suggestions indirectly by describing similar situations or hypothetical options. The first, yet most often overlooked, step when performing negative facework is

Facework—the messages that we send with the goal of maintaining or restoring another person's sense of self-worth.

Positive facework—messages that affirm a person or a person's actions in a difficult situation to protect his or her respectability and public approval.

Negative facework—messages that offer information, opinions, or advice that protect a person's freedom and privacy.

SKILL BUILDERS ● Positive Facework

SKILL	USE	PROCEDURE	EXAMPLE
Providing messages that affirm a person or a person's actions in a difficult situation	To protect the other person's respectability and public approval	1. Convey positive feelings about what your partner has said or done in the situation. 2. Express your admiration for your partner's courage or effort in the situation. 3. Acknowledge how difficult the situation is. 4. Express your belief that your partner has the qualities and skills to endure or succeed.	Having learned that Ken has suffered his brother's anger because of an intervention he initiated to help him, Anja says, "I really respect you for the way you have acted during this. It takes a lot of guts to hang in there like you've been doing, especially when you've been attacked for doing so. I know that you've got the skills to help you get through this."

to ask whether your partner wants to hear your opinions or advice before you offer such assistance. For example, you might say, "Would you like to hear my ideas on this?" At times, our partners are not interested in having us solve their problems but instead want someone with whom to commiserate. If you brazenly offer unsolicited opinions or advice, your efforts may be seen as FTAs by your partner that undermine the very support you are trying to provide. Second, even when your partner has indicated that he or she is receptive to hearing your opinions and advice, word your messages carefully. Your opinions and advice should be conveyed in a way that acknowledges that your partner is a competent decision maker who is free to accept or reject the advice. "This is just a suggestion; you are the one who has to make this decision" is a message that expresses deference to your partner's opinions and preferences. Third, your messages should use language that hedges and qualifies your opinions and advice, making it easier for your partner to disagree with what you have said. For instance, you might say, "I'm not sure that this will work or that you would want to proceed this way, but if I were in a situation like this, I might think about doing. . . ." Finally, your supportive messages will be less threatening if you offer suggestions indirectly by relating what others have done in similar situations or by offering hypothetical suggestions. For instance, you might say, "You know, when my friend Tom lost his job, he . . ." or "Maybe one option to try might be. . . ."

Facework needs to be adapted to each individual that you meet. In this chapter's **Diverse Voices** selection, the authors describe the difficulties in communication between disabled and nondisabled people. Much of what they say points to the need for facework to be personalized.

SKILL BUILDERS ● Negative Facework

SKILL	USE	PROCEDURE	EXAMPLE
Providing messages that offer information, opinions, or advice in a way that acknowledges that the other is a competent person.	To protect the other person's freedom and privacy	1. Ask for permission before making suggestions or giving advice. 2. Verbally defer to the opinions and preferences of your partner. 3. Use tentative language to hedge and qualify opinions and advice. 4. Offer suggestions indirectly by describing similar situations or hypothetical options.	Judy has learned that Gloriana has been badly hurt by rejection from a best friend. Judy says, "Would you like any advice on this?" Gloria says that she would, and Judy then offers suggestions: "These are just a few suggestions, and I think you should go with what you think is best. Now, I'm not sure that these are the only way to go, but I think...." After stating her opinions, Judy says, "Depending on what you want to accomplish, I can see a couple of ways that you might proceed...."

Using Other-Centered Messages

The **theory of conversationally induced reappraisals** suggests that people experience emotional stress when they believe that their current situation is at odds with their life goals and that to reduce emotional distress and move forward, people must make sense of what has happened to them. They do this with a comforter who helps them reevaluate their situation and determine how it relates to their goals (Burleson & Goldsmith, 1998). The role of the comforter is to use other-centered messages to create a supportive conversational environment in which the emotionally distressed person can talk through his or her situation and arrive at a solution. **Other-centered messages** are communications that focus on the needs of the person requiring support through active listening and expressions of compassion, understanding, and encouragement.

For many of us, other-centered messages are difficult to master. We may have been raised in families or come from cultures that have taught us not to dwell on the problems or pry into the business of others. Consequently, even when a friend or intimate broaches the subject, our gut reaction may be to change the topic or make light of the situation, both of which are destructive messages. In our rush to help another person, we may also inadvertently change the focus to ourselves. For instance, if Eric discloses that he came out to his sister and now she won't talk to him, his friend Stacy may switch topics to the new Lady Antebellum album in an effort to take Eric's mind off his troubles or perhaps to relieve her own discomfort at not knowing what to say. Regardless, her topic change was not supportive. It shifted attention from Eric and didn't allow him any space to work through his pain. Other-centered messages that focus on the person in need of support are especially important in these situations.

When creating other-centered messages, follow these guidelines:

1. **Ask questions that prompt your partner to elaborate on what happened:** *"Really, what happened then?"*
2. **Emphasize your willingness to listen to an extended story:** "You've got to tell me all about it, and don't worry about how long it takes. I want to hear the whole thing from start to finish."
3. **Use vocalized and nonverbal encouragement to communicate your continued interest without interrupting your partner as the account unfolds:** *"Uh huh." "Wow." "I see.";* head nodding, leaning forward, etc.
4. **Affirm, legitimize, and encourage exploration of the feelings expressed by your partner:** *"Yes, I can see that you're disappointed. Most people would be disappointed in this situation. Is this as difficult as when . . .?"*
5. **Demonstrate that you understand and connect with what has happened, but avoid shifting the focus to yourself:** *"I know that I felt angry when my sister did that to me. So what happened then?"*

For example, instead of changing the subject or as a follow-up to her initial misstep, Stacy might say:

"I'm sorry your sister wasn't able to accept what you told her. Why don't you tell me more about how you're feeling? I'm all ears and want to help you make sense out of this."

Theory of conversationally induced reappraisals—the premise that people experience emotional stress when they believe that their current situation is at odds with their life goals and that to reduce emotional distress and move forward, people use conversations to reconcile what has happened to them.

Other-centered messages—communications that focus on the needs of the person requiring support through active listening and expressions of compassion, understanding, and encouragement.

"Which Is My Good Leg?"

by Dawn O. Braithwaite and Charles A. Braithwaite

Jonathan is an articulate, intelligent, 35-year-old professional man who has used a wheelchair since he became a paraplegic when he was 20 years old. He recalls inviting a nondisabled woman out to dinner at a nice restaurant. When the waitperson came to take their order, she looked only at his date and asked, in a condescending tone, "And what would *he* like to eat for dinner?" At the end of the meal the waitperson presented Jonathan's date with the check and thanked her for her patronage.

Kim describes her recent experience at the airport: "A lot of people always come up and ask can they push my wheelchair. And I can do it myself. They are invading my space, concentration, doing what I wanted to do *on my own*.... And each time I said, "No, I'm doing fine!" People looked at me like I was strange, you know, crazy or something. One person started pushing my chair anyway. I said, [in an angry tone], "Don't touch the wheelchair." And then she just looked at me like I'd slapped her in the face."

Jeff, a nondisabled student, was working on a group project for class that included Helen, who uses a wheelchair. He related an incident that really embarrassed him. "I wasn't thinking and I said to the group, 'Let's run over to the student union and get some coffee.' I was mortified when I looked over at Helen and remembered that she can't walk. I felt like a real jerk." Helen later described the incident with Jeff, recalling:

> "At yesterday's meeting, Jeff said, 'Let's run over to the student union' and then he looked over at me and I thought he would die. It didn't bother me at all. In fact, I use that phrase myself. I felt bad that Jeff was so embarrassed but I didn't know what to say. Later in the group meeting I made it a point to say, 'I've got to be running along now.' I hope that Jeff noticed and felt OK about what he said."

Although it may seem hard for some of us to believe, these scenarios represent common experiences for many people with physical disabilities and are indicative of what often happens when people with disabilities and nondisabled others communicate.

For people with disabilities, personal control and independence are vitally important, and "maintenance of identity and self-worth are tied to the perceived ability to control the illness, minimize its intrusiveness, and be independent" (Lyons et. al., 1995, p. 134). This does not mean that people with disabilities deny their physical condition, but rather that they find ways to manage it, to obtain whatever help they need and to lead their lives. Although it is possible to identify and find accommodations for physical challenges associated with mobility, self-care, and employment, the two key life functions of social relationships and communication often present much more formidable challenges. It is often less difficult to detect and correct physical barriers than it is to deal with the insidious social barriers facing people with disabilities.

When people with disabilities begin relationships with nondisabled people, the challenges associated with forming any new relationship are often greater. For nondisabled people this may be due to lack of experience interacting with people who are disabled, which leads to high uncertainty about how to react with a person who is disabled. Nondisabled persons may be uncertain about what to say or how to act. They are afraid of saying or doing the wrong thing or of hurting the feelings of the person with the disability, much as Jeff with his group member Helen. As a result, nondisabled persons may feel self-conscious, and their actions may be constrained, self-controlled, and rigid. Their behavior, in turn, may appear as uninterested or unaccepting to the person who is disabled. The nondisabled person will need to figure out how to communicate appropriately and sometimes these communication attempts are not successful. At times their attempts to act in ways that are acceptable to a disabled person will be perceived as offensively patronizing disabled people with unwanted help or sympathy. Even when a nondisabled person tries to "say the right thing" and wants to communicate acceptance to the person with the disability, his or her nonverbal behavior may communicate rejection and avoidance instead. For example, people with disabilities have observed that many nondisabled persons may keep a greater physical distance, avoid eye contact, avoid mentioning the disability, or cut the conversation short. These nondisabled persons may be doing their best not to show their discomfort or not crowd the person with the disability. However, the outcome may be that the person with the disability perceives they do not want to interact. In this case, a person's disability becomes a handicap in the social environment as it can block the development of a relationship with a nondisabled person who finds the interaction too uncomfortable.

When nondisabled persons make the effort to overcome discomfort and stereotypes to interact with people from the disabled culture, they often find themselves with conflicting expectations. On the one hand, Americans are taught to "help the handicapped." At the same time, Americans conceptualize persons as "individuals" who "have rights" and "make their own choices" and thus are taught to treat all people equally. However, when nondisabled persons encounter a person with a disability, this model of personhood creates a real dilemma. How can you both help a person and treat that person equally? For example, should you help a person with a disability open a door or try to help him up if he falls? If you are working with a blind person, should you help her find a doorway or get her lunch at the cafeteria? These dilemmas often result in high uncertainty for nondisabled people, who often end up trying to give more help than people with disabilities want or need.

It should not be surprising to learn that most people with disabilities are well aware of the feelings and fears many nondisabled persons have. In fact, disabled people report that they believe that they can just "tell" who is uncomfortable around them, and they develop communication strategies to help them interact in these situations. For example, people with disabilities when meeting nondisabled persons will communicate in ways designed to get the discomfort "out of the way." They want the nondisabled person to treat them as a "person like anyone else," rather than focus solely on their disability. One man told the following story: "Now there were two girls about eight playing and I was in my shorts. And I played a game with them and said, 'Which is my good leg?' And that gets them to thinking. 'Well this one [he pats his artificial leg] is not nearly as old as the other one!'" Not only may disabled people use humor, but they may talk about topics they believe they have in common with the nondisabled person, such as cooking, sports, or music. They also plan ahead and develop strategies to help when they may need help from nondisabled persons and at times accept help they do not need because they understand that refusing help might increase the discomfort and uncertainty of the nondisabled person. In closing, we suggest the following practical proscriptions and prescriptions:

DON'T
- Avoid communication with people who are disabled simply because you are uncomfortable or unsure.
- Assume the people with disabilities cannot speak for themselves or do things for themselves.
- Force your help on people with disabilities.
- Use terms such as "handicapped," "physically challenged," "crippled," "victim," and the like, unless requested to do so by people with disabilities.
- Assume that a disability defines who a person is.

DO
- Remember that people with disabilities have experienced others' discomfort before and likely understand how you might be feeling.
- Assume that people with disabilities can do something unless they communicate otherwise.
- Let people with disabilities tell you if they want something, what they want, and when they want it. If a person with a disability refuses your help, don't go ahead and help anyway.
- Use terms such as "people with disabilities" rather than "disabled people." The goal is to stress the person first, before the disability.
- Treat people with disabilities as persons first, recognizing that you are not dealing with a disabled person but with a person who has a disability. This means actively seeking the humanity of the person with whom you are speaking and focusing on individual characteristics instead of superficial physical appearance. Without diminishing the significance of the person's disability, make a real effort to focus on all of the many other aspects of that person as you communicate.

For Consideration:
1. How does your need to maintain face affect your interactions with disabled people?
2. How does this article help you to better understand the face needs of disabled people? How can you use this to avoid face threatening acts and support the positive and negative face needs of disabled persons?

Excerpted and adapted from Braithwaite, D. O., & Braithwaite, C. A. (2012). "Which Is My Good Leg?": Cultural communication of persons with disabilities. In L. A. Samovar, R. E. Porter, & E. R. McDaniel (Eds.), *Intercultural Communication: A Reader* (13th ed.). Boston, MA: Wadsworth.

During Eric's elaboration, Stacy should indicate that she's listening by vocally and/or nonverbally signaling her encouragement, and when he seems finished, she might say:

"I see what you're saying and I empathize, believe me. While I'm not gay, I had to confront my parents with my anorexia. At first, they were in denial and wouldn't help me get help, but eventually they recognized that I wasn't healthy or happy and they made sure that I went to the best program. While you're in the opposite situation—you don't need help changing—can you cut your sister some slack?. She loves you but obviously was clueless about your sexuality. Let her have some space to reorient her thinking. I know that will be hard, but, just like my parents, she's in shock and with time may work through her feelings."

Framing information—providing support by offering information, observations, and opinions that enable the receiver to better understand or see her or his situation in a different light.

Framing Information

When people's emotions are running high, they are especially likely to perceive events in very limited ways. **Framing information** is providing support by offering information, observations, and opinions that enable the receiver

---

SKILL BUILDERS ● Other-Centered Messages

SKILL	USE	PROCEDURE	EXAMPLE
Focusing on the needs of the person in need of support through active listening and expressions of compassion, understanding, and encouragement	To help partners in their efforts to reevaluate an emotionally distressing event	1. Ask questions that prompt your partner to elaborate on what happened. 2. Emphasize your willingness to listen to an extended story. 3. Use vocalized encouragement and nonverbal encouragement to communicate your continued interest without interrupting your partner as the account unfolds. 4. Affirm, legitimize, and encourage exploration of the feelings expressed by your partner. 5. Demonstrate that you understand and connect with what has happened but avoid shifting the focus to you.	Angie begins to express what has happened to her. Allison says, "Really, what happened then?" As Angie utters one more sentence and then stops, Allison says, "Tell me all about it, and don't worry about how long it takes. I want to hear the whole thing from start to finish." During Angie's discussion, Allison encourages her, saying, "Go on...," "And then...?," and she nods her head, leans forward, and so on. To affirm, Allison says, "Yes, I can see that you're disappointed. Most people would be disappointed in this situation. Is this as difficult as when...?" Allison continues, adding, "I know that I felt angry when my sister did that to me. So what happened then?"

to better understand or see her or his situation in a different light. By sharing information, observations, and opinions, we often provide a different frame through which someone can see a situation—thus supplying a different, and perhaps less painful, way of interpreting what took place. Consider the following situation:

> After class, Travis announces to his roommate, Abe, *"Well, I'm flunking calculus. It doesn't matter how much I study or how many of the online problems I do; I just can't get it. This level of math is above me. I might as well just drop out of school before I flunk out completely. I can ask for a full-time schedule at work and not torture myself with school anymore."*

In this example, Travis has not only described his situation but has also interpreted it in a limited way to mean that he is not smart enough to handle college-level math courses. Yet there could be information that Travis doesn't have or hasn't thought about that would lead to other interpretations. For example, Abe might remind Travis that he has been putting in a lot of hours at his part-time job this term, a work schedule that may be interfering with his studies. Or Abe might tell Travis that he heard the calculus instructor likes to scare the class by grading hard initially but curving the grades at the end of the semester. In this way, Abe provides Travis with a new frame for understanding what has happened in light of alternative explanations. Interpretations other than the inability to understand math may account for Travis's poor grade.

Framing statements are supportive when they soothe your partner's feelings by helping him or her look at what has happened in ways that are less threatening to his or her self-esteem. To form framing messages (1) listen to how your

SKILL BUILDERS ● Framing Information

SKILL	USE	PROCEDURE	EXAMPLE
Offering information, observations, and opinions that enable the receiver to better understand or see his or her situation in a different light	To support others when you believe they have made interpretations based on incomplete information or have not considered other viable explanations	1. Listen to how your partner is interpreting events. 2. Notice information that your partner may be overlooking or overemphasizing in the interpretation. 3. Clearly present relevant, truthful information, observations, and opinions that enable your partner to develop a less ego-threatening explanation of what has happened.	Pam: "Katie must be really angry with me. Yesterday she walked right by me at the market and didn't even say 'Hi.'" Paula: "Are you sure she's angry? She hasn't said anything to me. And you know, when she's mad I usually hear about it. Maybe she just didn't see you."

partner is interpreting events, (2) notice information that your partner may be overlooking or overemphasizing in the interpretation, and (3) clearly present relevant, truthful information, observations, and opinions that enable your partner to reframe what has happened. Notice how the framing statements in the next two examples (Karla and Shelby, then Micah and Khalif) suggest less distressing interpretations of events.

> Karla: *"I'm just furious with Deon. All I said was, 'We've got to start saving money for a down payment or we'll never get a house.' And he didn't say a word. He just got angry and stomped out of the room."*
>
> Shelby: *"Yes, I can see what you mean, and I'd be frustrated, too. It's hard to work through issues when someone up and leaves. But perhaps Deon feels guilty about not being able to save. You know his dad. Deon was raised to believe that the measure of a man is his ability to provide for his family. So, when you said what you did, unintentionally, you may have hurt his male ego."*
>
> Micah: *"I just don't believe Magdalena anymore. We had my annual evaluation last week and she says my work is top-notch, but I haven't had a pay raise in over two years."*
>
> Khalif: *"I can see that you're discouraged. No one in my department has gotten a raise either. But have you forgotten that we're still under that salary freeze? At least Magdalena is continuing to do performance reviews, so you know where you stand and what you should be eligible for when the freeze is over."*

Giving Advice

Advice is a message or series of messages intended to help another person manage or solve a problem. Advice can comfort our partners when we offer it in a well-established supportive climate. Unfortunately, we often rush to provide advice before we really understand the problem or before we have developed a rapport that allows our partner to see the advice as helpful. In general, advice giving (and to a lesser extent, framing information) should occur after supportive intentions are understood, facework has been performed, and an other-centered focus has been sustained in an interaction. Only when we believe that our partners have had enough time to understand, explore, and make their own sense out of what has happened to them should we offer advice about unresolved issues.

Research has found that many of us offer advice as our first response to hearing another person's problem, although this may not be appropriate (Goldsmith, 2000). The same research also reports that requested advice is more likely to be positively received than unsolicited counsel. Someone who has not asked for advice may see it as interfering. In addition, our advice will be most helpful if our partners perceive that

Advice—a message or series of messages intended to help another person manage or solve a problem.

the advice can solve the problem and can be accomplished by them without too many drawbacks (Feng & Burleson, 2008; MacGeorge, Feng, Butler, & Budarz, 2004).

Scholars who study giving advice offer the following suggestions (Mac-George, Feng, & Thompson, 2008). First, don't assume that everyone who has a problem needs or wants advice. Sometimes nothing can be done about a problem, and sometimes partners do not want advice; rather, they want you to acknowledge their feelings, provide a sounding board, and help them reframe a situation. Second, offer advice only when you have some expertise with the problems facing your partner. If you have limited knowledge of or experience with a situation, it can be more helpful for you to ask questions that allow your partners to find their own solutions. Third, before offering a specific solution, carefully consider what your partners will think and how they will feel about your suggestion. Just because your solution will work or is what you would do, does not mean that it is the appropriate approach for your partners. Fourth, be careful about how you phrase your advice. Even those of us who claim that we like blunt honesty and value directness may be hypersensitive when emotionally distressed. So we might view your direct-advice messages as bossy, patronizing, or critical. Finally, remember that advice is a form of persuasion. You are trying to influence what your partners are going to do, and if followed, your advice could turn out to be good or bad. You need to consider and indicate the downside as well as the upside, the potential consequences for your partner if things don't go well.

SKILL BUILDERS ● Giving Advice

SKILL	USE	PROCEDURE	EXAMPLE
Presenting suggestions and proposals a partner could use to satisfactorily resolve a situation	To comfort our partners after a supportive climate has been established and our partners are unable to find their own solutions	1. Ask for permission to give advice. 2. Word the message as one of many suggestions that the recipient can consider. 3. Present any potential risks or costs associated with following the advice. 4. Indicate that you will not be offended should your partner choose to ignore your recommendation or look for another alternative.	After a friend has explained a difficult situation she faces, Felicia might say, "I have a suggestion if you'd like to hear it. As I see it, one way you could handle this is to talk to your co-worker about this issue. This is just one idea—you may come up with a different solution that's just as good. So think this one over, and do what you believe is best for you."

OBSERVE AND ANALYZE

Support on Social Media

Read at least fifteen postings of any online support group. Identify examples of empathic responsiveness, perspective taking, sympathetic responsiveness, clarifying supportive intentions, buffering face threats, other-centered messages, framing information, and giving advice. What conclusions can you draw about giving and receiving supportive messages online?

Keeping these recommendations in mind, you can skillfully give advice by following these procedures: (1) ask for permission to give advice, (2) word the message as one of many suggestions that the recipient can consider, (3) present any potential risks or costs associated with following the advice, and (4) indicate that you will not be offended should your partner choose to ignore your recommendation or look for another alternative. For instance, suppose Shawn is aware that his manager relies on him to help solve major problems that confront their work team. Yet on two occasions when positions that pay much more than Shawn's have opened up, his manager recommended others who are less qualified. When Shawn shares his frustration with his friend Marino, Marino responds by acknowledging Shawn's frustrations and posing questions to help him better understand the problem. Then he asks permission to give advice: "Shawn, we've helped each other a lot over the years. Are you interested in hearing my ideas about what you could do?" When Shawn nods, Marino continues: "I know you have many choices. You could get a different job. But if I were in your shoes, before I did anything radical, I would make a point of seeing my manager. I would tell him how much I appreciate his confidence in me. Then I'd tactfully describe my disappointment at not being promoted and ask him why he hasn't suggested me for these jobs." Keeping in mind the risks and mindful that his advice is not the only option, Marino adds: "Now this could irritate him, but it seems to me that if you don't let him know how you perceive this situation, you will begin to resent him and may begin to dislike your job." Finally, Marino indicates that he won't be offended if Shawn doesn't take his advice or pursues another option: "Still, it's your decision, and there are probably other ways to go about it. But I think my suggestion is worth thinking about."

Gender and Cultural Similarities and Differences in Supporting

According to popular belief, men and women value emotional support differently, the common assumption being that women expect, need, and provide more comfort than men. Yet a growing body of research indicates that both men and women of various ages place a high value on emotional support from their partners in a variety of relationships (Burleson, 2003). Studies also find that men and women have similar ideas about what messages are more or less effective at reducing emotional distress. Both men and women find that messages encouraging them to explore and elaborate on their feelings provide the most support. Although both men and women value other-centered support messages, research has found a major gender difference in that men are less likely to use other-centered messages when providing support. This suggests that we need to focus greater attention on enhancing men's abilities in the comforting realm (Kunkel & Burleson, 1999).

Research has also been directed toward understanding cultural differences in supportive situations. While studies have found some differences, Burleson

(2003) reports that for members of all cultural groups, solace strategies—especially other-centered messages—are the most sensitive and comforting ways to provide emotional support.

Using Social Media to Offer Empathy and Support

When we face stress or crises in our lives, we naturally turn to close friends and family with whom we have strong interpersonal relationships. Traditionally, we used face-to-face communication to seek and to offer support and comfort. Today, however, people who experience stress and crises are increasingly turning to social media as new avenues of support (Bambina, 2007). In some situations, providing support through digital communication has some advantages, such as increased social distance, increased presence of others, benefits for apprehensive individuals, ease of management, and opportunities for dealing with loss (Bambina, 2007; Walther & Parks, 2002).

Increased Social Distance

Digital support creates a social distance that frees some people to disclose problems that they would be uncomfortable talking about in face-to-face contexts. Through social media, people can even remain anonymous and receive comfort from a stranger. Although social media can bring us closer together, the increased social distance also created by technology allows individuals to participate in the support process from the comfort of their computer. Although she is friends with Carla, Jill may feel more comfortable disclosing her health diagnosis to everyone via Facebook because the social networking site offers a bit of social distance between her and her friends. Although Jill can find support in talking about her illness with others face-to-face, those rich interactions may lead Jill to cry and become even more upset. Oftentimes, we widely share information through social media to reach a large audience of people very quickly and distance ourselves from any potential outpouring of face-to-face support.

Increased Presence of Others

The number of individuals who participate in an online support group enhances opportunities to receive support from people who have experienced the same situation (Mirivel & Thombre, 2010). In Alcoholics Anonymous group meetings, members sit in a circle, share personal information, and receive support from others in the same room. Even though fellow group members may have experienced similar struggles with alcohol, the presence of others in the room may cause some participants to hesitate to disclose their experiences with alcohol use and sobriety. Now, anonymous online support groups exist that enable participants to actively send and receive empathic and supportive messages. While close friends and loved ones may try to put themselves in your situation, being able to chat with people who are in your exact situation can provide more meaningful comfort and support. Individuals who struggle with an eating disorder or a rare illness may turn to online support groups as the only way to find others who can truly empathize. In addition, the increased presence of others through social networking sites such as Facebook provides additional opportunities for a person to receive support from others. Consider a Facebook friend who frequently posts status messages that highlight life's latest misfortunes. How often have you read a status message from a friend who vents about difficult college classes, unhelpful professors, or struggles with landing a job? Those support-seeking status updates are often followed by a host of Facebook friends who comment and offer support, empathy, and comfort.

Benefits for Apprehensive Individuals

Individuals, who are apprehensive communicating in face-to-face settings, benefit greatly from receiving support through social media. Digital support can be particularly advantageous for people who are extremely introverted, shy, or prone to loneliness (Segrin, 1998). Individuals who experience anxiety when communicating face-to-face often turn to social media as outlets for empathy and support. If Jimmy has difficulty initiating relationships in face-to-face contexts, the relationships that he develops online may be his primary source of receiving supportive messages. However, the digital supportive messages that Jimmy receives through social media may be free of rich social cues that are often present in face-to-face interactions. In many ways, those cues may be what cause Jimmy to experience apprehension and uncomfortable feelings when he communicates with others in face-to-face settings. The sheer absence of these cues through social media may attract Jimmy to Facebook, texting, or e-mail as outlets for receiving support. If you are shy in face-to-face settings, know that you can receive support from others through social media. Your support providers will need to work hard to communicate their thoughts and feelings as they comfort you during your difficult time.

Ease of Management

Comforters, too, may more easily manage the sending of empathy and support through social media. When we digitally send support, we can carefully choose our words and craft the most effective and helpful messages possible. In face-to-face contexts, we have all served as the go-to support person for a particular friend experiencing stress or a life crisis. These repeated interactions require significant emotional energy to demonstrate to the support seeker that we care enough about him or her to offer adequate comfort. Unlike our face-to-face interactions, we can choose when to begin and end digital supportive interactions without the support seeker assuming that we are annoyed, frustrated, or bothered by his or her need for comfort. Even though we are able to carefully craft supportive messages through social media, we must give extra effort to communicating care and concern through those messages. Remember that certain forms of social media—such as texting—lack the social cues that are present in face-to-face interactions. When you offer digital support through social media, remember to choose your words wisely and position them alongside smiley faces and other emoticons that communicate empathy and warmth.

Memorializing Others through Digital Communication

The rapid development of social media has generated new ways to help others cope with the loss of a dear friend or loved one. Increasingly, one or more family members may honor their loved one by preparing a commemorative Web page that memorializes the life of the departed. Web sites such as Legacy.com, MyDeathSpace.com, and Memory-Of.com have been around for over a decade to facilitate the creation of interactive online memorials. An article in *The Boston Globe* described Shawn Kelley's "moving tribute" to his brother Michael, a National Guardsman killed in Afghanistan. The 60-second video featured a picture slideshow of Michael growing up while quiet classical music played softly and a voice-over recounted Michael's attributes and interests. Shawn reported that it made him feel good to be able to "talk" about his brother, and over a year later, he was still visiting the site to watch the video and to view the messages left by family members and friends (Plumb, 2006). In many ways, Facebook and other social networking sites have taken the form of "electronic grief counselor" (Stingl, 2007). How many Facebook memorial groups have you seen in recent months? Chances are you've seen quite a few. We use these groups to post messages to our deceased friends to cope with loss and offer others support.

Interactive memorial Web sites have become places where mourners can connect with other mourners, express condolences, and share stories about the deceased, activities that traditionally occurred at a funeral or memorial service. Communicating on social network memorial walls and groups reconnects the living with the deceased and helps us make sense of our lives without these friends and loved ones. Denise McGrath, a mother who created "R.I.P. Tony," a memorial Web page for her teenage son on MySpace, explained that it was "just a place for his friends to go" (Plumb, 2006). Today Legacy.com hosts permanent memorials for over two-thirds of the people who die in the United States and is visited by over 14 million users each month (Legacy.com, 2011). People can visit with their departed loved one and even leave messages directed to him or her. Sending such a digital message through a Web site or social networking site is called **transcorporeal communication**, "trans" indicating beyond and "corporeal" indicating the physical, material body (DeGroot, 2009).

When President John F. Kennedy was assassinated decades ago, citizens turned to television and radio and gathered together with family members to cope with the tragedy. Now, social media offers opportunities for grieving individuals to send and receive support related to the loss of their friends and loved ones. Although our methods of grieving and seeking support have changed over the years, one issue remains: We still need to connect and communicate with others as we grieve and offer comfort and support.

OBSERVE AND ANALYZE

Examining Facebook Memorial Groups

Think about the last Facebook memorial group you visited. Go to that Facebook page. Spend some time looking through and reflecting on the postings that others made to honor the deceased person. How would you describe the comments that people made on this page? Did you post on this page? If so, what motivated you to make a comment? Think about the relationship that you had with the deceased person. Write a short paragraph describing your relationship with the person. In another paragraph, describe the types of comments that people made on this page. In a final paragraph, explain how this Facebook page might have been used as an outlet for grieving individuals to seek empathy and support over the loss of the friend or loved one.

Transcorporeal communication—a process through which a living person sends a digital message to a deceased person through a Web site or social networking site.

Summary

Supporting others begins with being able to empathize. Empathizing is the cognitive and affective process of perceiving the emotions others are feeling and then acting on our perceptions. It is shown through empathic responsiveness, perspective taking, and sympathetic responsiveness. Empathizing requires taking the time to

A QUESTION OF ETHICS ● What Would You Do?

Kendra and Emma are roommates and have been best friends since grade school. For the past three years, Kendra had been dating Emma's older brother, Dominic. Dominic finished college recently and moved to Chicago, about an hour away from where Kendra and Emma go to school. This past weekend, Dominic invited Kendra to visit him. She even told Emma that she was sure he was going to ask her to marry him. Emma gently tried to discourage her from expecting that, but Kendra remained convinced that this was the purpose for the invitation.

Far from proposing, Dominic spent the weekend watching TV and picking fights with Kendra. By the end of the weekend, Kendra was miserable, hurt, and worried about their relationship. She decided to test him by remarking, "Well, it just seems like you aren't very glad to see me, so maybe we should just forget it and start seeing other people." She was dumbfounded when Dominic replied, "Well, if that's what you want, OK," turning his attention back to the football game on TV. In shock, Kendra quickly gathered her things and left.

By the time she got back to the apartment she shared with Emma, she was a mess. Crying and screaming, she called Dominic every name she could think of as she walked in the front door. When Emma raced into the room, Kendra exclaimed, "I can't believe you let me go up there and be so humiliated! What kind of a friend are you? You're just like your brother—mean." Stunned by Kendra's outburst, Emma asked, "Kendra, what are you talking about? What happened? Is Dominic OK?"

Kendra: "Oh sure, you worry about Dominic, but what about me? Sure, take your brother's side. I don't

know what else I should have expected from you. You were probably in on it. It's just not fair."

Emma: "Wait a minute, Kendra, in on what? What happened?"

Kendra: "Dominic broke up with me."

Emma: "He did? I can't believe it."

Kendra: "Well . . . no, but, yeah, well kind of . . ."

Emma: "Kendra, you're not making any sense. Did Dominic break up with you or not? Tell me. What happened?"

Kendra: "Well, he made it pretty clear that he didn't really want to be with me anymore."

Emma: "Kendra, did he or did he not break up with you?"

Kendra: "Well, he certainly didn't propose marriage."

Emma: "Is that what this is about? Kendra, what made you think he was ready to propose? He just finished school. He has a ton of college debt, and he's still looking for a job. He can't help it if you got it in your head that he was going to propose. But I can't believe that he broke up with you. So what really happened?"

Kendra: "Emma, I don't want to talk about it, especially not with you. Now would you please just leave me alone? Your family has done enough damage to me today."

With that, Kendra stomped into her bedroom and slammed and locked the door.

For Consideration:
1. What ethical principles were violated in this encounter?
2. Is it ethical for Kendra to expect Emma to support her if this means disowning her brother?
3. How can Emma support Kendra and not violate the ethical call to speak the truth?

empathize, observing and reading the nonverbal messages sent by others by asking questions and paraphrasing, and employing one of the three types of empathy.

Social support is the process of providing emotional, informational, and instrumental resources to someone we perceive in need of this aid. Supportive messages are communications that provide intangible support for your partner including emotional support, information, advice, and motivation. We can support people's positive feelings with celebratory messages or support their negative feelings with comforting messages. Effective comforting messages have different characteristics than ineffective ones. Although we can attempt to comfort a person with a single supportive comment, more often our support requires a longer conversation or series of conversations over days, months, or years. Regardless of their length, supportive interactions typically go through four phases. Research has identified five supportive message skills: clarifying supportive intentions, buffering face threats with positive and negative facework, using other-centered messages, framing information, and giving advice. Online therapy, support groups, and social networking sites may be effective vehicles for achieving and providing support. The desire to be comforted appears to be universal, with little substantial difference reported between men and women or across cultures.

People who experience stress and crises are increasingly turning to social media as new avenues of support. Digital support creates a social distance that frees some people to disclose problems that they would be uncomfortable talking about in face-to-face contexts. The number of individuals who participate in an online support group enhances opportunities to receive support from people who have experienced the same situation. Individuals who are apprehensive communicating in face-to-face settings benefit greatly from receiving support through social media.

Chapter Resources

What You Should Be Able *to Explain:*

- The concept of empathy
- Three approaches to empathy
- Ways to improve your capacity to empathize
- Social support
- The characteristics of effective supporting
- Supporting positive feelings and experiences with celebratory messages
- Supporting negative feelings and experiences with comforting messages
- The four supportive interaction phases
- The five supportive message skills
- Gender and cultural similarities and differences in supporting

What You Should Be Able *to Do:*

- Use celebratory support messages to respond to others' positive feelings and experiences
- Use comforting messages to respond to others' negative feelings and experiences
- Clarify supportive intentions
- Buffer face threats
- Create other-centered messages
- Reframe information
- Give advice

Self-test questions based on these concepts are available on the companion Web site (www.oup.com/us/verderber) as part of Chapter 9 resources.

Key Words

Flashcards for all of these key terms are available on the *Inter-Act* Web site.

Advice, p. 278
Capitalization, p. 265
Celebratory messages, p. 266
Clarifying supportive intentions, p. 268
Comforting messages, p. 266
Empathic responsiveness, p. 261
Empathy, p. 259

Face-threatening act (FTA) , p. 270
Facework, p. 271
Framing information, p. 276
Negative facework, p. 271
Other-centered møessages, p. 273
Perspective taking, p. 261
Positive facework, p. 271

Social support, p. 263
Supportive interaction, p. 267
Supportive messages, p. 263
Sympathetic responsiveness, p. 261
Theory of conversationally induced
    reappraisals, p. 273
Transcorporeal communication, p. 283

Apply Your Knowledge

The following activities challenge you to demonstrate your mastery of the concepts, theories, and frameworks in this chapter by using them to explain what is happening in a specific situation.

Inter-Action Dialogue: Supporting Others

9.1   Do a line-by-line analysis of this *Inter-Action Dialogue* and indicate where you see evidence of Rob using supportive messages. Be sure to note which specific skills and guidelines he follows as well as noting any challenges or problems you see in his supportive behavior. How is this conversation affected by the use of support messages? Also note the supportive interaction phases. You can watch a video of this conversation on the Inter-Act Web site and use a form provided to write down your own analysis of the conversation.

DIALOGUE

Rob and James, meeting after class, have the following exchange:

Rob: Hey man, what's up? You look rough.
James: Well, I'm not feeling very good. But I'll get by.
Rob: Well, tell me what's bothering you—maybe I can help. I've got the time.
James: Come on—you've got better things to do than to listen to my sad story.
Rob: (sitting down and leaning toward James) Hey, I know you can take care of it yourself, but I've got the time. So humor me, and spill it. What's got you so down?
James: It's my dad.
Rob: Uh huh.
James: You know I hardly ever see him, what with him living out West and all.
Rob: That's hard.
James: (lowering his voice and dropping his head) And, you know, I thought that now that my mom remarried and has a whole bunch of stepkids and grandkids to take care of that maybe I could go out to California to college and, you know, live with my dad.
Rob: Yeah, that's understandable. So, did you call him? What did he say?

James: Oh, I called him, and he said it was fine. Then he said we could share expenses. Share expenses? I can't even afford the bus ticket out there. And I was hoping he'd pay for college.

Rob: Ouch.

James: Rob, my dad's always had lots of money. Been living the good life. At least that's what he's been telling me all these years. He never sent the support money, but that's because he said he was building his business. My mom's always been putting him down, but I believed him. Now I don't know what to think. What a fool I was.

Rob: Hey, you're no fool. Why wouldn't you believe him? But it sounds like he's been lying to you, and now you're really disillusioned. Is that it?

James: Yeah, I guess. You know, I always thought that when I was a man, the two of us could, you know, get together. I love my mom. She's my hero. She raised me. But I was always proud of my dad with his business and all, and I just wanted to spend time with him. Get to know him.

Rob: I can relate. My dad died when I was young, but I'd sure like to have known him better. So have you told your mom about any of this?

James: No.

Rob: What do you think she'd say?

James: Oh, she'd probably just hug me and tell me to let it be.

Rob: Can you do that?

James: Maybe.

Rob: Do you want my advice?

James: Sure, why not.

Rob: Well, it's your decision, and I'm sure that there are other ways to handle it, but my advice is do what your mom says—let it go. If he wants to see you, let him call you. You've got a great family here.

James: Maybe you're right. I'm so tired of being let down. And my stepdad is a good guy. He's been taking me to the gym, and we play a little ball in the driveway. He's not my dad, but even with all the other kids around, at least he makes time to be with me. I guess getting close to my dad is just not meant to happen. And I guess I don't really need him. If he can't even help with college, then why would I want to leave here? I mean, I have great friends . . . right?

Rob: Right.

Skill Practice

Skill practice activities give you the chance to rehearse a new skill by responding to hypothetical or real situations. Additional skill practice activities are available at the companion Web site.

Supportive Interactions and Supportive Message Skills

For each of the following situations write a multiturn dialogue/script in which you demonstrate the four phases of supportive interactions and use at least four of the five skills of supportive messages. Use a two-column format. In the left hand column, write your dialogue. In the second column, identify each phase of the supportive interaction being enacted and which message skills are present in each of your turns.

9.2   Your best friend walks into the restaurant, flops down in the booth, and sighs, *"My manager is trying to fire me or get me to quit. He told me that my error rate was higher than average, so he wants me to drive all the way downtown to headquarters and take another ten hours of training on my own time."*

9.3   As you turn the corner at work, you spy your co-worker Janet leaning against the wall, silently sobbing into her hand.

9.4   Your sister (or brother) storms in the front door, throws her (or his) backpack on the floor, and stomps upstairs. You slowly follow.

9.5   As you are watching TV, your roommate bursts into the room exclaiming, *"I did it. I did it. I really did it! I got accepted to law school! Woohoo!"*

Communication Improvement Plan: Empathizing and Supporting

Would you like to improve your use of the following skills discussed in this chapter?

- Empathizing
- Celebratory support messages
- Comforting messages
- Clarifying supportive intentions
- Positive and negative facework
- Other-centered messages
- Framing information
- Giving advice

9.6   Pick a skill, and write a communication improvement plan. You can find a communication improvement plan worksheet on our Web site at www.oup.com/us/verderber.

Inter-Act with Media

Television

Family Guy, episode: "Stew-Roids" (2009)

Connie D'Amico comes to the decision that she needs a change from dating popular boys at school. She attempts to find the biggest loser and convert him to a popular and cool person. She settles on Chris Griffin after seeing him picking his nose and scratching himself. On their first date, Chris shares that he honestly likes Connie because she is nice and pretty. Connie is surprised by Chris's nice comments. Chris becomes very popular at school because he is now dating Connie. He begins to fit in with the popular athletes and other cool students.

Meg Griffin, Chris's the unpopular sister, who thought Chris's relationship with Connie would finally be her ticket into the cool kids clique, refuses to accept the relationship, while at a family dinner.

Later, Chris and Connie organize a party at the Griffins' home. Chris's unpopular sister, Meg, does not receive an invite. Meg is very upset and Lois Griffin, Meg's mother, tries to console her. Lois has a more noncaring personality toward Meg and will often show absolutely no emotion or interest in some very emotional situations. In this instance, Lois just gives up, gives Meg some pills, a book, and walks out of the room saying, "Whatever happens, happens."

IPC Concepts: Empathizing, empathic responsiveness, perspective taking

To the Point:

> How might Lois have better used empathic responsiveness to comfort Meg?
> How might you characterize Lois's overall approach to offering support to others?

Cinema

Divine Secrets of the Ya-Ya Sisterhood (2002). Callie Khouri (director). Sandra Bullock, Ellen Burstyn.

Sidda Walker (Bullock) and her mother Vivi (Burstyn) are in a mother-daughter struggle. Sidda is a very successful young playwright who mistakenly tells *Time* magazine about her childhood with an alcoholic and very abusive mother. When Vivi reads the *Time* article, she flies into a rage. She and Sidda pass nasty messages back and forth and soon stop speaking completely. The "Ya-Ya Sisterhood," a group made up of Vivi's lifelong friends who pledged in childhood to always support each other, enters the picture to support Sidda. This group of friends step in as mediators and determine that the best way to repair the relationship is to help Sidda better understand and empathize with her mother.

Vivi's friends allow Sidda into the "divine secrets" of the Ya-Ya Sisterhood. The Ya-Ya sisters do not excuse Vivi's self-centered behavior; they know her weaknesses. But by sharing stories from the past to help her better understand Vivi, the Ya-Ya sisters truly believe that Sidda can break this pattern and repair her relationship with her mother.

IPC Concepts: Empathizing, empathic responsiveness, perspective taking

To the Point:

> How might Sidda have learned more about the personal side of her mother's life?
> During the interactions between Sidda and Vivi, how would you characterize their ability to employ empathic responsiveness and perspective taking?

What's on the Web

Find links and additional material, including self-quizzes, on the companion Web site at www.oup.com/us/verderber.

10

Communicating Personal Information

Disclosure and Privacy

"Brian, I'm so upset! Kai just told me how happy she is that you and I might be moving in together this summer. I thought we agreed not to tell anyone until I get a chance to tell my parents. Did you tell Amber, and then Amber told Kai?"

"I'm sorry, Annie. I didn't mean to say anything to Amber, but she kept bugging me about being the fourth person in their apartment next year, and she's my sister, so I didn't want to leave her stranded. I told her that you and I might get a place, but she swore not to tell anybody."

"You know that if you tell Amber anything, she's going to tell Kai. She tells her everything—they're best friends. And anyway, Amber couldn't keep a secret if her life depended on it."

"I really trusted Amber to keep that information private. I mean we've kept each other's secrets all of our lives. I feel so bad. Forgive me?"

"Private? Once you tell *anyone* our private information, it isn't private! You and I had an agreement on this. Not only does

291

everyone know our private plans now, but I've got to see my parents tonight before my mom hears it from Kai's mom at church on Sunday. And yes, I forgive you, but you have to promise that you won't share our personal stuff with Amber. She may be your sister, but I'm the woman you say you're going to marry, and I don't want your family knowing all of our business. Your loyalty is supposed to be with me now."

What you should be able *to explain* after you have studied this chapter:

- The disclosure-privacy dialectic
- Communication privacy management (CPM) theory
- The five factors that influence disclosure-privacy rules
- How disclosure and privacy affect relationships
- Self-disclosure skills
- Privacy-keeping skills

- Personal feedback skills
- Important considerations for effective management of your digital personal information

What you should be able *to do* after you have studied this chapter:

- Own your thoughts and feelings by making "I" statements
- Describe behavior
- Describe your feelings
- Communicate personal boundaries
- Ask for personal feedback
- Offer praise
- Provide constructive criticism

When it comes to sharing personal information, we are constantly in a balancing act between disclosure and privacy. Sometimes you are the only one who knows your private information, and sometimes others whom you trust to maintain your confidentiality know your private information. When you disclose private information, the person you share it with then must decide whether to keep the information private or reveal it to others. As we saw with Brian and Annie, there can be misunderstandings or violated expectations about disclosure and privacy. A complex matter affected by many factors, the communication of personal information has an important impact on our relationships.

In this chapter we begin by discussing the dialectic of disclosure and privacy. Then we turn to the theory of communication privacy management (CPM) and the factors that affect people's disclosure and privacy rules. Next, we explain how disclosure and privacy affect relationships and the effects of technology on privacy boundaries. After that, we present skills for self-disclosure and privacy management. Finally, we describe how to give personal feedback, both praise and constructive criticism, and how to ask for feedback about ourselves.

The Disclosure-Privacy Dialectic

You will recall from Chapter 6 that in any relationship, both people may experience opposite pulls or dialectics. One of these dialectics is the tension between openness and closedness. This is also called the **disclosure-privacy dialectic**, the tension between sharing personal information and keeping personal information confidential. Let's take a closer look at the two parts of the dialectic.

Disclosure is revealing confidential or secret information. While it includes self-disclosure, sharing your own biographical data, personal ideas, and feelings, it is a larger concept that includes disclosing confidential information about others as well (Petronio, 2002). For example, suppose Jim tells Bella that he was a bed wetter until he was in the sixth grade and has never told anyone else about it for fear of being teased. Jim has engaged in self-disclosure to Bella because he has revealed information about himself. Later when Bella is in a conversation in which people are sharing their childhood secrets, she comments that Jim used to be a bed wetter. While Bella is making a disclosure, it is not self-disclosure because she is disclosing Jim's private information, not her own.

Privacy, the opposite of disclosure, is withholding confidential or secret information to enhance autonomy and/or minimize vulnerability (Margulis, 1977). The concept of privacy rests on the assumption that people own their personal information and have the right to control it by determining whether that information may be communicated to others (Petronio, 2002). Like Jim, you have personal information that you can choose to reveal to or conceal from others. Over time and as your relationship with another person develops, you and your partner will share sensitive information with each other. Then, either of you may choose to reveal that sensitive information to others outside the relationship or maintain it within the privacy of your relationship. If your partner has your permission to share an item of your personal information with others, or if you no longer care that others know an item of your personal information, then if your partner discloses it to others, it is unlikely to affect your relationship. If, however, you have not given your partner permission to disclose that information and/or if you still expect that information to be held privately within your relationship, then your partner disclosing it will likely damage trust and undermine your relationship. Therefore, when Jim hears that Bella has "outed" him as a former bed wetter, he may feel embarrassed, hurt, and violated because Bella has breached his privacy.

Because the disclosure-privacy dialectic occurs within an individual and within a relationship, tensions may occur because each person has different self-disclosure and privacy needs as well as different expectations about what should be held privately within and disclosed outside the relationship. To further complicate matters, these needs and expectations often vary over time. If Jim and Bella are both sixteen when Jim self-discloses his bed-wetting history, Jim may see this as a very risky disclosure and be much more sensitive should Bella breach his privacy. But he may be less

Disclosure-privacy dialectic— tension between sharing personal information and keeping personal information confidential.

Disclosure—revealing confidential or secret information.

Privacy—the opposite of disclosure, withholding confidential or secret information to enhance autonomy and/or minimize vulnerability.

OBSERVE AND ANALYZE

The Disclosure-Privacy Dialectic

Think about a recent encounter in which you consciously decided to disclose information that you would normally have kept private. What rule that you had previously followed did you violate to make this decision? What was the result of this disclosure? Did the benefits you received by making the disclosure outweigh the risks you took? In retrospect, if you had to do it over again, would you make the same decision about disclosure? Explain. Now consider a time when you decided to maintain your privacy by not disclosing something to your partner. What rule did you use to make this decision? What was the result of maintaining your privacy? What risks did you take by not disclosing, and what benefits did you receive? In retrospect, if you had to do it over again, would you make the same choice? Explain.

LEARN ABOUT YOURSELF ● Personal Disclosure

Take this short survey to learn something about yourself and your relationship with a specific partner, whom you should be thinking of when completing this survey. This is a test of your personal disclosure in a relationship. Answer the questions honestly based on your first response. There are no right or wrong answers. For each question, select one of the numbers to the left that best describes your own behavior or your views about your partner's behavior.

1 = Strongly agree

2 = Agree somewhat

3 = Neutral

4 = Disagree somewhat

5 = Strongly disagree

_____ 1. I often talk about my feelings.

_____ 2. I often reveal undesirable things about myself.

_____ 3. I like to show my innermost self.

_____ 4. I do not hesitate to disclose personal things about myself.

_____ 5. I feel safe sharing any personal information.

_____ 6. My partner shares personal information with me.

_____ 7. My partner reveals personal feelings to me.

_____ 8. I am completely sincere in revealing my own feelings.

_____ 9. My partner expresses personal beliefs and opinions.

_____ 10. I can be honest about anything.

Scoring the survey: Add all of your scores for the ten items. Your total score will range from 10 to 50. The lower (closer to 10) your score, the more you and your relational partner engage in personal disclosure. The higher (closer to 50) your score, the less you and your relational partner engage in personal disclosure.

Adapted from Derlega, V. J., Metts, S., Petronio, S., & Margulis, S. T. (1993). *Self-Disclosure*. Newbury Park, CA: Sage.

sensitive about Bella's disclosure years later when they are both thirty-five because Jim may no longer view this as ego threatening. In short, the revealing or withholding of personal information is a very complex. In the next sections we describe Privacy Management Theory, an explanation for our decision making about these issues. Then we examine the effects that privacy and disclosure have on our relationships. Finally we present specific skills you can use to effectively disclose and manage privacy.

Communication Privacy Management Theory

Communication privacy management—a theory that provides a framework for understanding the decision-making processes people use to manage disclosure and privacy.

Communication privacy management (CPM) theory is a framework for understanding the decision-making processes people use to manage disclosure and privacy. CPM was developed by Sandra Petronio, who is featured as this chapter's "Spotlight on Scholars," which you can read on the book's Web site at www.oup.com/us/verderber. CPM theory says that each of us has developed rules about privacy and disclosure to guide our behaviors as we make choices to disclose or conceal personal information about ourselves and about others. Over time, we

When you share private information you run the risk of your partner sharing it with others. Have you ever had someone disclose information you had shared but thought would be held in private? How did you handle this breach of confidentiality? What was the long-term effect on your relationship?

come to rely on the rules that we have developed in previous situations and relationships to guide our choices in new situations and relationships. These rules are designed to help us maximize the benefits of disclosure while minimizing risks (Petronio, 2002). As we develop a relationship, we negotiate rules with our partner about how the private information we have shared within the relationship will or will not be disclosed to others outside of the relationship, or we simply assume that our partner understands what rules apply (Petronio, 2002).

Spotlight on Scholars

Read about research into disclosure and the work of Sandra Petronio at www. oup.com/us/verderber.

Factors that Influence Disclosure and Privacy Rules

Why do people differ in the rules that they use to manage privacy and disclosure? Four factors influence our personal rules about disclosure and privacy: culture, gender, motivation, and context.

1. Culture. Our rules about privacy and disclosure are influenced by how our culture values privacy. In some cultures, a person's privacy is highly respected, and people who choose to disclose information generally regarded as confidential violate cultural norms. Members of these cultures are less likely to disclose personal information to anyone but close intimates. As you might expect, individualistic cultures value privacy more than collectivist cultures do. For instance, British and German people are less inclined to disclose and more likely to be protective of their privacy. The United States is an individualistic culture where privacy is also valued, yet it is also less formal than other individualistic cultures (Samovar & Porter, 2001, p. 82). As a result, Americans tend to disclose more about themselves than people from many other individualistic cultures, especially individualistic European cultures. For example, Sharon, who is English, was raised to place a high value on privacy. She came to the United States to attend college and was assigned Skyler as a dorm mate. Skyler, who was raised

What type of disclosures might you share at a large family gathering like this one? What disclosures would be inappropriate? How do your family's cultural norms about disclosure affect the answers you gave?

in the tell-all informal pop culture of the United States, tends to make Sharon very uncomfortable as she breezily chats about her dysfunctional family, her romantic relationships, and her religious beliefs. Because the rules that Sharon uses to manage privacy are very different from those guiding Skyler's behavior, her discomfort with Skyler's level of disclosure may be due in part to differences in cultural background. While most of us adopt attitudes toward privacy and disclosure that correspond to the norms of our culture, some of us rebel against cultural expectations and develop privacy and disclosure rules that are significantly different from the norms of our cultural group.

2. Gender. Men and women who strongly identify as masculine or feminine are likely to use rules for disclosure and privacy that correspond to sex role expectations (Snell, Belk, & Hawkins, 1986). The expectation for men throughout much of the world includes "strong and silent" and competitive characteristics. Consequently, men may keep their feelings to themselves and avoid disclosing private information that might be used against them in a competitive situation. For example, if Horst sees himself as very masculine or macho, he probably won't disclose that as a child he studied ballet, fearing that if he disclosed this event from his past, he would be ridiculed. The expectation for women throughout much of the world is that women are nurturing and sensitive. Therefore, women who identify with these characteristics are more likely to disclose personal information. For example, if Ashley considers herself very feminine, she may easily share her innermost feelings or disclose information about someone else as a way of strengthening her self-image and relationships with others. People whose identities are not strongly rooted in gender roles are less likely to ground their disclosure-privacy rules in gendered expectations.

3. Motivation. People differ in how eager they are to disclose to someone (Petronio, 2002). Motivation to disclose or to maintain privacy is influenced by our

Risks of Disclosure	Risks of Privacy	Benefits of Disclosure	Benefits of Privacy
loss of control	social isolation	building relationships	control
vulnerability	being misunderstood by others	coping with stress	independence
embarrassment		emotional or psychological relief	

FIGURE 10.1 Risks and Benefits of Disclosure and Maintaining Privacy

risk-benefit analysis. In **risk-benefit analysis**, we weigh what advantages we might gain by disclosing private information or maintaining private information against the dangers. Figure 10.1 lists the benefits and risks of both disclosure and privacy. Consider the following example: After getting in an accident at school and being arrested for DUI, Joe is given a severe warning with community service. He not only completes his community service, but also becomes a full-time volunteer. Should Joe confide his past to his new girlfriend, who lost her best friend to a drunk driver? On one hand, if Joe discloses, he risks losing his girlfriend, who may not be able to get past his drunk driving episode. On the other hand, he may benefit psychologically from coming clean and alleviate the guilt caused by hiding this from her. If Joe maintains his privacy, he benefits by controlling his image and saving face about the DUI. Yet maintaining privacy in this way runs the risk of promoting continued dishonesty in the relationship while not allowing his girlfriend to fully understand his commitment to this volunteer work.

4. Context. Privacy and disclosure rules, like other communication rules, are influenced by the circumstances in which people find themselves. For example, you may disclose private information to a therapist or counselor to help you cope with a difficult situation. Likewise, in times of crisis, you may need to adjust your need for privacy and open up to people to whom you would not normally disclose. Just as supportive communication improves one's mental and physical health, research also shows that disclosure during times of stress contributes to physical and mental health (Pennebaker, 1995; Tardy, 2000). Moreover, circumstances related to a relationship may influence you to disregard the privacy needs of another person. If, for example, Sal tells Greg that he's extremely depressed, Greg may tell one or two of Sal's close friends about this disclosure to help deal with this potentially dangerous situation.

Risk-benefit analysis—weighing what advantages we might gain by disclosing private information or maintaining private information against the dangers.

INTER-ACT WITH SOCIAL MEDIA

Some people have violated their own privacy by failing to make wise disclosure-privacy decisions when communicating with social media. What rules guide your disclosure versus privacy decisions on social networking sites, in blogs, in e-mails, and in public on your cell phone? How do these rules differ from each other and from your face-to-face disclosure-privacy rules?

Effects of Disclosure and Privacy on Relationships

Disclosure and privacy decisions impact relationships in many ways, but the three most important are those decisions that affect intimacy, expectations for reciprocity, and information co-ownership.

Effects on Intimacy

You will recall from our discussion of social penetration theory in Chapter 6 that over time, our relationships move from lesser to greater intimacy based on the increasing number of topics that we discuss with our partners and the depth of personal information we both disclose on those topics (Altman & Taylor, 1973). The preponderance of research evidence supports the premise of social penetration theory that through disclosure our relationships become more intimate. But research has also shown that the dialectical tension of openness-closedness explains why we cycle between periods of deep disclosure and attempts to reestablish privacy boundaries (Altman, 1993). Thus rather than moving in a straight line toward greater intimacy, our relationships cycle between disclosure and privacy. As you can imagine, this can create problems between you and your partner if one of you craves greater intimacy when the other needs more distance. In addition, research indicates that disclosure of personal information can at times actually hurt your relationships. If Joe, for example, decides to disclose his DUI to his girlfriend, for a time she may disengage from or even break off the relationship.

Focusing on privacy rather than disclosure, research shows that in some cases opting for privacy may preserve the intimacy and positive feelings in a relationship (Hendrick, 1981) and avoid conflict with our relational partners (Roloff & Ifert, 2000). Individuals may choose privacy over disclosure for many legitimate reasons, including protecting the other person's feelings, avoiding unnecessary conflict, being sensitive to the face needs of the other person, and protecting the relationship. People with life-threatening illnesses may not share this information with others because they don't want to be pitied or because they fear that a partner may abandon them. Similarly, people whose religious, social, political, or sexual orientations conflict with the value systems of others may choose to keep their orientations private (Petronio, 2002). In newer relationships, people may manage their privacy to control the pace at which the relationship is developing. If a casual dating relationship seems to be moving too quickly toward greater emotional attachment, the relational partners may, for a certain period of time, avoid communicating on topics such as the state of the relationship, expectations of each other in the relationship, prior romantic relationships, and extra-relationship activity (Knobloch & Carpenter-Theune, 2004).

Effects on Reciprocity

Reciprocity is the mutual disclosure of similarly sensitive information by both partners. In general, we expect reciprocity of disclosure in our relationships. For instance, if we disclose who our first love was, we expect our partner to share similar information. Mutual disclosure deepens our relationships. Earlier research argued that one person's disclosure in a relationship would typically be quickly reciprocated with a partner's parallel disclosure (Jourard, 1971). More recent research (Dindia, 1988, 2000), however, has found that sometimes there can be long time lags between when you disclose a particular type of information and when your partner

Reciprocity—the mutual disclosure of similarly sensitive information by both partners.

Scan your Facebook profile and assess the extent to which you self-disclose personal information to your Facebook friends. Evaluate your privacy settings to see what information you share with others. To what extent do you "co-own" your digital image with others? How is this image different from the image you present in face-to-face settings?

does. For example, after a fourth date, Kristoff may blurt out, "Natalie, I love you and I know that I'm going to marry you!" Natalie may not voice parallel feelings for many more months. Nevertheless, the two of them continue to see each other, building a common history and deepening their relationship by reciprocally disclosing other personal information.

Effects of Disclosure and Privacy on Information Co-ownership

A third way that decisions about disclosure and privacy affect relationships involves information co-ownership. **Information co-ownership** is the private information that each partner has shared with the other so that it is now jointly held. When you share your private information with your partner or your partner shares secret information with you, that information is now the "property" of you both. When you disclose secret information to your partner, you expect that your partner will respect your privacy and will not disclose this to others without your permission. Similarly, over the course of your relationship, you and your partner may share private experiences and make decisions that would typically be considered private, and each of you will expect the other to protect this type of information as well. Therefore, whether we actually honor the commitment to hold this information in confidence or share it with others can affect the relationship. For example, if a friend confides in you that she is adopted and asks you not to tell others, you and your friend have become the co-owners of that information. You risk damaging the trust and intimacy of that friendship if you reveal to others what your friend shared with you. Interestingly, families also co-own different types of private information and establish rules about communicating that information outside of the family. Some families may be very private about disclosing negative information about the family or its members. We are all familiar with the rule of not "airing dirty laundry in public." Taboo topics usually include personal, legal, or financial information, subjects that all family members are instructed to avoid discussing with nonfamily members (Afifi & Guerrero, 2000).

Information co-ownership—the private information that each partner has shared with the other so that it is now jointly held.

Self-Disclosure and Privacy Management Skills

Once we have decided to either disclose or maintain privacy with regard to a particular item of our personal information, we then need to either disclose or protect this information. If we are not skillful at disclosing the information or keeping it private, we can harm our relationships. In this section you will learn skills to form effective self-disclosure messages as well as skills to maintain your privacy effectively.

Self-Disclosure Skills

Messages that effectively self-disclose use the skills of owning, disclosing behavior, and disclosing feelings.

Owning

A basic skill of self-disclosure is **owning**, using "I" statements to credit yourself for your ideas and feelings. An "I" statement, any statement that uses a first-person pronoun such as *I, my, me,* or *mine,* helps the listener fully and accurately understand the nature of the message being self-disclosed. Instead of owning our feelings and opinions and honestly self-disclosing them as such, we often express our thoughts in impersonal or generalized language or attribute them to unknown or universal sources. Consider the following paired statements:

"Lots of boys wet the bed."   "I was a bed wetter."
"Everybody thinks Colin is unfair."   "Colin hurt my feelings with his
                                                criticism, which I perceived as unfair."

"Nobody likes to be laughed at."   "Being laughed at embarrasses me."
"Jon is a flirt."   "Jon has been flirting with me."

Being both accurate and honest in our self-disclosures requires taking responsibility for our own feelings and opinions. We all have a right to our reactions. If what you are self-disclosing is truly your opinion or an expression of how you really feel, let others know by taking responsibility for it.

Describing Behavior

When disclosing personal information, many of us have a strong impulse to form our messages based on generalized evaluative conclusions we have reached about that information. So rather than just providing a description of what we want our partner to know, we provide an evaluation of it. "I really messed up when I was in high school hanging around with gang bangers and generally acting like a tough guy." This message is both evaluative and vague. Rather than evaluating behavior, effective personal messages use **describing behavior**, the disclosure skill of accurately recounting specific behaviors without drawing conclusions about those behaviors. For the example above a message that describes behavior might be phrased, "My freshman year in high school I began partying with a local gang. My grades dropped, I was arrested for shoplifting, and I got kicked off the football team. So instead of going to college on an athletic scholarship, I'm working my way through community college."

SKILL BUILDERS ● Owning

SKILL	USE	PROCEDURE	EXAMPLE
Making an "I" statement rather than a generalization to identify yourself as the source of an idea or feeling	To help others understand that the feeling or opinion is yours	When an idea, opinion, or feeling is yours, say so.	Instead of saying, "Maury's is the best restaurant in town," say, "I believe Maury's is the best restaurant in town."

Describing behavior is also useful when we decide to share feedback with someone who is blind to how they are behaving. Consider the following situation: Miguel and Jorge are discussing the last game in the World Cup playoffs. After Jorge interrupts Miguel for the third time, Miguel could say either "You're so rude with your interruptions," or "Do you realize that you interrupted me three times before I had the chance to finish a sentence?" Which way would you feel better about receiving this information? The first message is evaluative, and most of us would be embarrassed and even defensive. The second message is an accurate description of the behavior. Since Jorge already knows that interrupting is not "good form," this feedback, describing the behavior but leaving the evaluation of it unspoken, is more sensitive to Jorge's face needs and is therefore likely to cause less embarrassment, defensiveness, or damage to their relationship.

Describing behavior may seem simple, but because it requires moving backward in the perceptual process, it can be difficult. We have to resist the temptation to base our description on our overall impression and step back to identify the specific stimuli on which it is based. Miguel may have the overall impression that Jorge's interruptions fit the pattern he associates with the word "rude." But to describe the actual specific behavior, he must go back, recall, and verbalize the specific actions that elicited this impression.

The following guidelines will help you describe behavior effectively: (1) identify the overall impression you are experiencing, (2) recall the specific behaviors that have led you to form this impression, and (3) form a message in which you report only what you have seen or heard without drawing a conclusion about these behaviors. The skill of describing behavior is useful when we want to disclose personal information about ourselves and also when we want to share our observations about someone else's behavior.

SKILL BUILDERS ● Describing Behavior

SKILL	USE	PROCEDURE	EXAMPLE
Accurately recounting the specific behaviors without drawing conclusions about those behaviors	To increase the accuracy of your self-disclosures and to provide descriptive rather than evaluative feedback to your partners	1. Identify the overall impression you are experiencing. 2. Recall the specific behaviors that led you to this impression. 3. Form a message in which you report only what you did, saw, heard, or experienced without drawing an evaluative conclusion about these behaviors.	Instead of saying, "She is such a snob," say, "She has walked by us three times now without speaking."

Disclosing Feelings

Because we are emotional beings, we share our feelings with our partners. Sometimes when our feelings overwhelm us, we can surprise, scare, offend, or hurt our partners with spontaneous, uncontrolled emotional outbursts. These types of "disclosures" may temporarily or permanently damage our relationship. At other times, we purposefully mask or withhold our true feelings, maintaining privacy over them while we enact a controlled social performance of what our culture or social group thinks is the correct way to feel in a particular situation. When Larissa breaks up with Michael, for example, his hurt may morph into anger resulting in a stream of verbal abuse. Or he may play it cool and mask his hurt, tossing off, "Well, babe, that's your loss. See ya." Yet the essence of intimate self-disclosure often involves sharing intense feelings with your partner, so how can you effectively do this?

Describing feelings is the disclosure skill of owning and explaining the precise emotions you are experiencing. Many times people think they are describing their feelings when they are actually acting emotionally out of control. "Who the hell asked you for your opinion?" is an outburst that displays a feeling but does not disclose your internal emotional state and will probably make your partner defensive. When used effectively, the skill of describing feelings increases the likelihood of having a positive interaction with someone rather than an argument, and it decreases the chances of provoking defensiveness. When we describe our feelings, we can teach other people how we would like them to treat us without making an overt demand. For example, when LeRoy carefully and quietly tells Tony that he is annoyed that Tony borrowed his iPod without asking, Tony, who didn't mean to offend LeRoy, is more likely both to respond without defensiveness and to ask LeRoy's permission the next time. When used effectively to show affection or approval, the skill of describing feelings can have beneficial effects on the relationship. For example, when Paul's nana tells him straightforwardly and without gushing how much she enjoys his e-mails, Paul is likely not only to have good feelings about his nana but also to write her more frequently.

Describing feelings is a difficult skill to master. Simply beginning a sentence with "I feel" doesn't guarantee that you will end up actually describing a feeling. In many cases statements that begin with "I feel . . ." actually end up evaluating, blaming, or scapegoating someone or something. Consider Jay's statement, "I feel like you insulted me when you said. . . ." While Jay may believe that he has described a feeling, he has actually practiced blaming. The key to describing feelings is describing your own feelings, not labeling the person who made you feel that way or making assumptions about that person's intentions. Stop and think—if a person says something that you perceive as insulting, how might you *feel?* Perhaps you feel hurt, rejected, betrayed, or embarrassed. If so, then the descriptive statement might be "I felt hurt (rejected, betrayed, or embarrassed) when you said. . . ." Suppose, for instance, that your brother screamed at you for something you did. If you said, "I feel that you're angry with me," your statement echoes what the other person said but does not describe your present feelings. To

Describing feelings—the disclosure skill of owning and explaining the precise emotions you are experiencing.

describe your feelings you might instead say, "When you talk to me in an angry tone of voice, I feel scared (hurt, pained, or distressed)." Many times we have trouble describing our feeling because we don't have an adequate vocabulary to capture the subtle differences between some feelings. Table 10.1, A Vocabulary of Emotions, lists over 200 words you can use to accurately describe what you are feeling.

Describing feelings is a three-step process: (1) identify what has triggered the feelings (a trigger is anything that causes a feeling or reaction), (2) identify the particular emotion you are experiencing accurately—this sounds easier than it sometimes is—use Table 10.1, A Vocabulary of Emotions, to help you name the specific emotion you are feeling, and (3) use an "I feel . . ." followed by naming the specific feeling. The following two examples describe feelings effectively:

> "Thank you for your compliment [trigger]; I [owning the feeling] feel gratified [specific feeling] that you noticed the effort I made."
>
> "When you criticize my cooking on days that I've worked as many hours as you have [trigger], I [owning the feeling] feel very resentful [specific feeling]."

If you are new to describing feelings, practice your skills by describing positive feelings: "You know, taking me to that movie really cheered me up," or "When you offered to help me with the housework, I really felt relieved." As you become more comfortable describing your positive feelings, you can try describing negative feelings attributable to environmental factors: "It's so cloudy that I feel gloomy," or "When we have a thunderstorm, I get really anxious." Finally, you can move to negative descriptions resulting from what people have said or done to you: "When you step in front of me like that, I really get annoyed," or "When you use a negative tone of voice while saying that what I did pleased you, I really feel confused."

SKILL BUILDERS ● Describing Feelings

SKILL	USE	PROCEDURE	EXAMPLE
Owning and explaining the precise emotions one is feeling or felt	To honestly self-disclose your emotions rather than displaying or masking them	1. Identify what has triggered the feeling. 2. Identify what you are feeling—think specifically. Am I feeling amused? pleased? happy? ecstatic? 3. Own the feeling by using an "I feel" statement followed by naming the specific feelings.	"Because I didn't get the job, I feel depressed and discouraged." "The way you stood up for me when I was being put down by Leah makes me feel very warm and loving toward you."

TABLE 10.1 A Vocabulary of Emotions

Words related to *angry*

agitated	exasperated	infuriated	outraged
annoyed	furious	irked	peeved
bitter	hostile	irritated	resentful
cranky	incensed	mad	riled
enraged	indignant	offended	steamed

Words related to *helpful*

agreeable	collegial	cordial	obliging
amiable	compassionate	gentle	supportive
beneficial	constructive	kind	useful
caring	cooperative	neighborly	warm

Words related to *loving*

adoring	aroused	fervent	passionate
affectionate	caring	gentle	sensitive
amorous	charming	heavenly	tender

Words related to *embarrassed*

abashed	disconcerted	humiliated	shamefaced
anxious	disgraced	jittery	sheepish
chagrined	distressed	overwhelmed	silly
confused	flustered	rattled	troubled
conspicuous	humbled	ridiculous	uncomfortable

Words related to *surprised*

astonished	confused	jolted	rattled
astounded	distracted	mystified	shocked
baffled	flustered	perplexed	startled
bewildered	jarred	puzzled	stunned

Words related to *fearful*

afraid	bullied	jumpy	terrified
agitated	cornered	nervous	threatened
alarmed	frightened	petrified	troubled
anxious	horrified	scared	uneasy
apprehensive	jittery	shaken	worried

Words related to *disgusted*

afflicted	nauseated	repelled	revolted
annoyed	outraged	repulsed	sickened

Words related to *hurt*

abused	dismal	mistreated	resentful
awful	dreadful	offended	rotten
cheated	forsaken	oppressed	scorned
deprived	hassled	pained	slighted
deserted	ignored	piqued	snubbed
desperate	isolated	rejected	wounded

Words related to *belittled*

betrayed	disparaged	incapable	underestimated
defeated	downgraded	inferior	undervalued
deflated	foolish	insulted	unfit
demeaned	helpless	persecuted	unworthy
diminished	inadequate	powerless	useless

Words related to *happy*

blissful	ecstatic	glad	merry
charmed	elated	gratified	pleased
cheerful	exultant	high	satisfied
contented	fantastic	joyous	thrilled
delighted	giddy	jubilant	tickled

Words related to *lonely*

abandoned	discarded	ignored	rejected
alone	empty	isolated	renounced
bored	excluded	jilted	scorned
deserted	forlorn	lonesome	slighted
desolate	forsaken	lost	snubbed

Words related to *sad*

blue	dour	low	morose
crestfallen	downcast	melancholy	pained
dejected	gloomy	mirthless	sorrowful
depressed	heavyhearted	miserable	troubled
dismal	joyless	moody	weary

Words related to *energetic*

animated	forceful	lively	sprightly
bold	frisky	peppy	spry
brisk	hardy	potent	vibrant
dynamic	inspired	robust	vigorous
eager	kinetic	spirited	vivacious

© Mike Baldwin / Cornered

It was like he could read my mind.

Protecting Privacy

Maintaining privacy during interpersonal interactions can be awkward, especially when others ask prying questions or making deep disclosures that seem to demand a matching revelation. Or you may encounter someone who asks you personal questions that you do not want to answer. In these cases, you want to respond in a way that maintains your privacy while minimizing damage to the relationship. You can use three strategies to protect your privacy when someone is pressing you to disclose something that you are not comfortable sharing: change the subject, mask feelings, and tell white lies. These can be used occasionally but may not be effective, and overreliance on them can damage your relationships. So you may find the two message skills of describing feelings and establishing boundaries more effective as your primary way to manage privacy. Let's look at each of these.

1. Change the subject. If you are being pressed to self-disclose something you don't choose to share, simply change the subject. Partners who are sensitive will recognize this as a signal that you don't want to self-disclose. For example, when Pat and Eric are leaving economics class, Pat says to Eric, "I got an 83 on the test. How about you?" If Eric doesn't want to share his grade, he might redirect the conversation by saying, "Hey, that's a B. Good going. Did you finish the homework for calculus?"

2. Mask feelings. When you have decided that sharing your feelings is too risky, you may choose to conceal the verbal or nonverbal cues that would ordinarily enable others to decipher the emotions you are feeling. Alternately, you can mask your feelings through deception by enacting cues that signal emotions other than those you are feeling. A "poker face" can mask feelings, a neutral look that is impossible to decipher and remains the same whether the player's cards are good or bad. Or you may, for instance, laugh along with the others when someone makes fun of you, a common display that can mask your feelings of betrayal and embarrassment. On occasion, masking your feelings can be an effective response. If we rely excessively on this strategy, however, we can experience interpersonal communication problems because we are turning our feelings inward and not revealing them to others. We also risk stunting the growth of our relationships, since our partners won't really know or understand us.

3. Respond with white lies. You probably know that telling a **white lie** is making a false or misleading statement to avoid telling a truth that would embarrass or hurt an individual or a relationship. For example, had Eric responded, when asked about his test grade, "I'm not sure. I got a few tests back this week" (even though he knew full well what his grade was), Eric is telling a white lie.

White lie—a false or misleading statement to avoid telling a truth that would embarrass or hurt an individual or a relationship.

Although lying is not effective as a long-term or frequent strategy, we all occasionally use white lies because they can avoid hurting someone's feelings, maintain healthy relationships, and help either you or a partner save face.

4. Describe your feelings. One direct and honest way to protect your privacy while minimizing damage to your relationship is to use the message skill of describing your feelings that we just discussed. When used to protect your private information, a general form of this message might be, "When you ask me about XZY, I feel (emotion) and (emotion) to talk about something I'd rather not talk about." So Eric might tell Pat, "When you ask about my test score I feel annoyed and pressured because I don't want to turn our friendship into a competition by comparing our test scores."

5. Communicate your personal boundaries. Personal boundaries mark the points that separate the parts of ourselves that we are comfortable sharing with a relationship partner from the parts of ourselves that we maintain as our private inner life (Amodeo, 2010). Boundaries protect us from the potential harm that can come from sharing too much. When you communicate boundaries you politely tell your partner your policy regarding disclosing a particular type of information or engaging in a particular behavior. To communicate a boundary (1) recognize why you are choosing not to share the information, (2) identify and be ready to verbalize the privacy policy that guides your decision, (3) preface your boundary statement with an apology or some other statement that helps your partner save face, and (4) form a brief "I" message that diplomatically informs the person that you want to maintain your privacy. For example, if Pat asks Eric about his test grade, instead of changing the subject or telling a white lie as in

Personal boundaries—the points that separate the parts of ourselves that we are comfortable sharing with a relationship partner from the parts of ourselves that we maintain as our private inner life.

SKILL BUILDERS ● Communicating a Personal Boundary

SKILL	USE	PROCEDURE	EXAMPLE
Politely tell someone your policy regarding disclosing a particular type of information or engaging in a particular behavior	To help others understand your policy about the privacy of certain information	1. Recognize why you are choosing not to share the information. 2. Identify your privacy policy that guides your decision. 3. Preface your boundary statement with an apology or some other statement that helps your partner save face. 4. Form a brief "I" message that diplomatically informs the person that you wish to keep that information private.	"Paul, I know that you are curious about how much money I make. And a lot of people are comfortable sharing that information, so forgive me, but I'm not. Don't take it personally. It's not you—I don't tell anyone what I make. That's just me. I hope you understand and are OK with it."

the earlier examples, Eric might reply, "I know that everyone's different, and I don't mean to be rude or to hurt your feelings, but it's my policy not to ask other people about their grades and not to discuss my own."

Personal Feedback Messages

So far in this chapter, we have focused our discussion on self-disclosure and privacy, what we choose to reveal about ourselves to others. But as you will recall, our relationships grow through both self-disclosure and feedback. So now let's look at **personal feedback**, disclosing information about others to them, and how it relates to issues of privacy in relationships.

Personal feedback—disclosing information about others to them.

An important part of any relationship is honest feedback from our partner that allows us to see ourselves from our partner's vantage point. At times feedback like this comes easily, but at other times we need to prompt our partners to share how they view us. For example, when Jake and Courtney return from a party with friends, Jake notices that Courtney is acting like she is upset with him. Wanting to clear the air, he might ask her if he has done something wrong. Asking for feedback is a way to prompt our partners to share their perceptions of our behavior.

Sometimes in our interactions and relationships, it is appropriate to comment on another person's behavior by giving personal feedback; at other times, it is better to keep our opinions to ourselves. We need to consider carefully whether, when, and how we give our partner feedback. For example, although a bartender in a state with dram shop laws (laws that hold bars liable for the actions of patrons who drink too much) has the legal responsibility to give patrons feedback when they have drunk too much, you may need to weigh whether it is your place to tell a friend that she has been drinking too much lately. Or if your partner is driving you crazy by texting you 200 times a day, you need to consider the consequences of telling him or her to stop. You may believe that your sister's new jeans make her look fat, but can you tell her this without hurting her feelings? As you can see from these examples, giving someone negative personal feedback can be a minefield for our relationships. But providing this type of information is part of an honest relationship and, when done well, can increase intimacy.

Not all personal feedback is negative. Indeed, positive feedback is also important to developing and sustaining healthy relationships. Yet some find it difficult to praise their partners at all, while others praise ineffectively and end up embarrassing their partners or themselves. As you can see, improving our skills in providing personal feedback about both positive behaviors and accomplishments and negative behaviors will have broad use and application.

In addition to the skill of describing behavior, there are three additional message skills we can use to help us ask for and give personal feedback. First, we can skillfully request feedback from our partner. Second, when we want to disclose positive observations about our partner's behavior and accomplishments, we can use the skill of praise. Third, when we decide that it is necessary and appropriate to provide negative feedback, we can use the skill of constructive criticism to tactfully and respectfully disclose our honest observations.

Asking for Personal Feedback

We grow as people and as relationship partners when we learn how we affect others. At times, our partners will be comfortable initiating personal feedback, but at other times, we can prompt our partners to disclose things they have observed about us. **Asking for personal feedback** is the disclosure skill of gaining self-knowledge by requesting your partner discloses observations about your behavior. Think of personal feedback as being in your best interest. No one likes to be criticized, and some people are embarrassed by praise, but through personal feedback we often learn and grow. When you receive a different appraisal from the one you expected, you have learned something about yourself that you did not previously know. Whether you will do anything about the feedback is up to you, but the feedback you have solicited allows you to consider aspects of your behavior that you might not have identified on your own. Before you ask, make sure that you are ready for an honest response. If you ask for feedback, don't expect others to lie to you just to make you feel better. If you don't want an honest response, don't ask the question. For example, if you ask a friend, "What do you think of my speaking skills?" expect an honest reply, even if it is negative, such as, "Well, you tend to ramble a bit." If others realize that when you request personal feedback, you are typically fishing for a compliment, honest appraisals will not be forthcoming in the future.

Follow these guidelines when asking for personal feedback:

1. Specify the kind of personal feedback you are seeking. Rather than asking general questions about ideas, feelings, or behaviors, ask specific questions. If you say, "Colleen, is there anything you don't like about my ideas?," she will likely not know how to respond. But if you say, "Colleen, do you think I've given

Asking for personal feedback—the disclosure skill of gaining self-knowledge by requesting that your partner disclose observations about your behavior.

SKILL BUILDERS ● Asking for Feedback

SKILL	USE	PROCEDURE	EXAMPLE
Asking others for their reaction to you or to your behavior	Helping you understand yourself and your effect on others	1. Specify the kind of personal feedback you are seeking.	Lucy asks, "Tim, when I talk with the boss, do I sound defensive?"
		2. Ask neutral questions.	Tim replies, "I think so—your voice gets sharp and you lose eye contact, which makes you look nervous."
		3. Try to avoid negative verbal or nonverbal reactions to the feedback.	"So you think that the tone of my voice and my eye contact make the boss perceive me as defensive?"
		4. Paraphrase what you hear.	"Yes."
		5. Show gratitude for the feedback you receive.	"Thanks, Tim. I've really got to work on this."

enough emphasis to the marketing possibilities?," you will encourage Colleen to speak openly about the specific issue.

2. Ask neutral questions. You can't expect honest personal feedback if you ask loaded questions that invite a particular answer. For example, if you say, "I did a great job on that. Didn't I?" or "I screwed that up, right?," the person you ask isn't given full rein to provide honest feedback.

3. Try to avoid negative verbal or nonverbal reactions to the feedback. Suppose you ask your roommate how he likes your rearrangement of the furniture. If, when he replies, "It's going to be harder for everyone to see the TV when we have people over to watch a DVD," you look angry or exclaim, "Well, if you can do it any better, you can move the furniture!," your roommate will quickly learn not to give you personal feedback in the future, even when you ask for it.

4. Paraphrase what you hear. By paraphrasing the personal feedback you receive, you ensure that you do not overgeneralize what you have heard. For example, if Joshua asks his classmate to comment on his presentation but boils down the specific comments he receives to simply "good" or "bad," he is not going to learn anything constructive from the feedback he requested.

5. Show gratitude for the feedback you receive. Regardless of how what you heard makes you feel, thank people for their feedback. No one likes to be asked to provide personal feedback and then be ignored or even snubbed for providing what was asked.

Praising

Too often, we do not acknowledge the positive things people say and do and accomplish. Yet people's self-concepts and, consequently, their behaviors are shaped by how others respond to them. So when we keep our positive impressions of our partners private, we deprive them of self-concept enhancing information that encourages them to repeat the behaviors we think are praiseworthy. **Praising** is the disclosure skill of describing the specific behaviors or accomplishments of our partners and their positive effects on others. Praise provides others with personal feedback affirming what they have said or done as commendable. Praise is not flattery aimed at manipulating others or currying their favor. Rather, it is a disclosure of their specific behaviors and accomplishments that we consider valuable or significant. For example, if a child who tends to be forgetful remembers to return the scissors he or she borrowed, that exact behavior should be praised

Praising—the disclosure skill of describing the specific behaviors or accomplishments of our partners and their positive effects on others.

so that it will be reinforced. Vague, generalized praise such as, "You're so wonderful. You're on top of everything" reinforces nothing, as it fails to identify the particular behavior or accomplishment. An effective praise message might simply state, "Thanks for putting the scissors back where they belong—I really appreciate that." This response acknowledges the accomplishment by describing the specific behavior and the positive feeling of gratitude that the behavior inspired. The following are two more examples of appropriate praising:

> **Behavior:** Sonya selected and bought a group wedding present for a friend. The gift is a big hit.
> **Praise:** "Sonya, the present you chose for Steve and Joella was really thoughtful. Not only did it fit our price range, but they really liked it."

> **Accomplishment:** Cole receives a letter inviting him to a reception at which he is to receive a scholarship award for academic accomplishments and community service work.
> **Praise:** "Congratulations, Cole. I'm so proud of you! It's really great to see that the effort you put into studying, as well as the time and energy you've devoted to the Second Harvest Food Program and Big Brothers, is being recognized and valued."

Praising doesn't cost us much but is usually highly valued. Not only does praising disclose information and acknowledge the worth of another person, but it can also deepen our relationships by increasing openness. The disclosure message skill of praising follows these guidelines: (1) Make note of the specific behavior or

SKILL BUILDERS ● Praising

SKILL	USE	PROCEDURE	EXAMPLE
Sincerely describing the specific positive behaviors or accomplishments of another and their positive effects on others	To help people see themselves positively	1. Make note of the specific behavior or accomplishment that you want to reinforce.	"Marge, that was an excellent writing job on the Miller story. Your descriptions were particularly vivid."
		2. Describe the specific behavior or accomplishment.	
		3. Describe the positive feelings or outcomes that you or others experience as a result of the behavior or accomplishment.	
		4. Phrase your response so that the level of praise appropriately reflects the significance of the behavior or accomplishment.	

accomplishment that you want to reinforce, (2) describe the specific behavior or accomplishment, (3) describe the positive feelings or outcomes that you or others experience as a result of the behavior or accomplishment, and (4) phrase your response so that the level of praise appropriately reflects the significance of the behavior or accomplishment.

Constructively Criticizing

Research on reinforcement theory has found that people learn faster and better through positive rewards such as praise, but there are still times when you will want to address behavior that has created problems. Unfortunately, most of us are far too quick to criticize others and in ways that are less than constructive. At times we overstep our bounds by trying to help others become better people when they aren't interested in hearing from us. Even when the time is right for disclosing negative feedback, we may not always do a good job of expressing it. Although research shows that constructive criticism can actually strengthen relationships and improve interactions in the long run, criticism not empathetically grounded or otherwise poorly communicated is likely to hurt relationships and lead to defensiveness (Tracy, Dusen, & Robinson, 1987).

Although the word "criticism" can mean "harshly judgmental," the skill of constructive criticism is not based on blaming or mean-spirited faultfinding. **Constructive criticizing** is the disclosure skill of diplomatically describing the specific negative behavior of your partner and its effects on others. The constructive criticism process begins by empathizing with the other person and by forecasting how she or he will react to the feedback. If we decide that keeping what we have observed to ourselves would be more damaging to our relationship or to our partner than disclosing it, we will want to disclose our observations. Then we should work to formulate a personal feedback message that accurately communicates our meaning while attending to the face needs of our partner. The following guidelines can help you effectively disclose constructive criticism:

1. Begin by asking your partner's permission to disclose negative feedback. Because personal feedback is a privacy/disclosure issue, you should always make sure that your partner is willing to hear your feedback. There are times when people have acted poorly, and they know it. They don't really need others to remind them. At other times, people may be overloaded with emotional issues and hearing any negative feedback would be counterproductive. So before you disclose negative feedback, you should seek your partner's permission and willingness to hear what you have to say. Most often your partner will agree to hear you out. But sometimes a partner may respond, "No," "Not now," "I already know what you're going to say, and I don't want to hear it," and so forth. In these cases, you should honor your partner by keeping your observations private.

2. Whenever possible, preface a negative statement with a positive one. One way to address your partner's face needs is to begin your comments by praising

---

Constructive criticizing—the disclosure skill of diplomatically describing the specific negative behavior of your partner and its effects on others.

some related behavior. Of course, common sense suggests that superficial praise followed by crushing criticism will be seen for what it is. But criticism prefaced with valid praise can reduce defensiveness. Suppose that Dan asks Ryan, "What did you think of my presentation of a fundraising plan for the fraternity?" Ryan, who has several reservations about what Dan is proposing, might begin his feedback by saying, "I think the idea of the guys doing spring cleanup work for a daily fee is really creative." Here the praise provided is relevant and balances the negative feedback that follows.

3. Describe the problematic behavior by following the guidelines for describing behavior that we discussed earlier. Describing behavior lays a foundation by identifying what behavior needs to change. In addition, describing the behavior indicates that you are focused on a particular behavior rather than on attacking the person or evaluating his or her general worth, which would result in losing face. Instead of saying, "It's not going to make us much money," as a constructive critic, Ryan might say, "Well, I think the idea of the guys doing spring cleanup work for a daily fee is really creative, but I think the plan to have us sell magazines could be a problem. The rowing team just did that last month and made only one-third of their goals. They found that college students don't have extra money for magazine subscriptions." This criticism does not attack Dan's self-esteem, and it tells him what specifically may need to change.

SKILL BUILDERS ● Constructively Criticizing

SKILL	USE	PROCEDURE	EXAMPLE
Diplomatically describing the specific negative behaviors or actions of another and the their effects on others	To help people see themselves as others see them	1. Begin by asking permission to disclose negative personal feedback.	Carol says, "Bob, I've noticed something about your behavior with Jenny. Would you like to hear it?"
		2. Whenever possible, preface negative statements with positive ones.	After Bob assures her that he would, Carol continues: "Although you seem really supportive of Jenny, there are times when Jenny starts to relate an experience and you interrupt her and finish telling the story. You did this a few times while Jenny was trying to talk about her trip to Colorado, and she looked a little hurt. She's pretty sensitive about being interrupted, so you might want to try to let her finish her stories the rest of this evening or she might get upset."
		3. Describe the person's behavior or action.	
		4. Be as specific as possible.	
		5. When appropriate, suggest how the person can change the behavior or action.	

OBSERVE AND ANALYZE

Constructively Criticizing

Think about the last time you criticized someone's behavior. Which, if any, of the guidelines for constructive criticism did you follow or violate? Did you describe the behavior or action accurately? Did you preface negative comments with positive ones? Did you provide specific details? If called for, did you offer advice on how the person might change his or her behaviors or actions? If you were to offer the same criticism again, what would you say differently?

4. Be as specific as possible. The more specifically you describe the behavior you are going to criticize, the more effectively a person will be able to understand what needs to change and how to change it. In our example, it would not have been helpful for Ryan to simply say, "Some of your ideas won't work." This assertion would have been so general that Dan would have had no idea what Ryan believed needed to change. Instead, Ryan provided specific comments about how college students don't usually have enough funds for magazine subscriptions, supported by an example about the rowing team's efforts.

5. When appropriate, suggest how the person can change the behavior or action. Since the focus of constructive criticism is helping, suggestions that might lead to positive change are important. In responding to Dan's request for feedback, for example, Ryan might also have added, "Maybe we could find out what school supplies or personal care products are most often purchased and sell those instead." By including a positive suggestion, you not only help the person but also show that your intentions are constructive.

THE SOCIAL MEDIA FACTOR

Digitally Managing Your Personal Information

The rapid development and frequent use of social media have transformed how we practice digital communication and manage our personal information. Distinctions between public and private information are now blurred, and features of certain social media devices allow others to alter our digital image, at times without our even realizing a change has occurred.

Blurred Public and Private Distinction

The attributes of social media and how we use those features have muddied the line between what we consider public versus private communication (Kleinman, 2007). Although it may be easy and convenient to make a cell phone call to a friend while we run our errands, we often fail to remember that others can easily hear our conversations. Over the course of a typical week, you no doubt overhear friends exchange personal information in public settings. How many times in the last few days have you overheard a person's "private" cell phone conversation? As you wait in line at a coffee shop, you may observe two women sitting at a table, one of whom is complaining loudly to her friend about her boyfriend's recent rude behavior. These occurrences have become even more common, however, thanks to social media—cell phones in particular—that allow people to carry on private conversations in public spaces. These people may not recognize that they are revealing private information to complete strangers as well as to the person on the other end of the phone. The next time you need to have a private cell phone conversation with a friend, ask if others are within earshot. If so, arrange the call for a time when you and your friend can both be alone.

Indeed, the rules for when and where we share private information have changed, and social media have also changed *what* information we view as private and public. Did you know someone who kept a paper diary growing up? Chances are they kept their personal thoughts under lock and key and tucked under a mattress or in a dresser drawer. You know that reading another person's diary is considered taboo because diaries protect the private information we ink to the pages. Today, however, digital diaries—often in the form of blogs—are purposely made accessible to friends, acquaintances, and thousands of strangers online. Although your digital diary entries can keep you connected to a broader community of users, lead to friendships and maybe romance, and provide an outlet for venting, some individuals remain unaware of the long-term threats to their private information (Bahrampour, 2007). Always remain aware that potential employers, enemies, or even identity thieves can monitor the writings, photos, videos, and other information that you post online. Consider the potential costs that accompany the rewards of disclosing private information through social media.

Fifteen-year-old Tavi Gevinson's popular fashion blog garnered national attention. In 2011, she founded Rookie Magazine, a Web site with content geared toward a female teenage audience. While personal blogging has become popular, there are risks inherent in keeping an online diary of your personal thoughts. Do you blog? If so, do you censor what you write with an eye toward the future?

Ability of Others to Alter Digital Presence

Have you ever accepted a person's Facebook friend request before you met the individual in person? If so, you probably scanned the person's Facebook profile and studied wall postings, status updates, photographs, and other personal information to develop an impression of what this individual would be like in face-to-face interactions. When we form impressions about others via social media, we are often concerned about the reliability of the self-presentations others put forward online.

Warranting theory posits that online information about the personal characteristics and behaviors of others will seem more credible when it cannot be easily manipulated by the person whom it describes (Walther & Parks, 2002; Walther, Van Der Heide, Hamel, & Shulman, 2009). In other words, we tend to view information that friends post to another's Facebook Web site as more credible and reflective of who they are than the information that the profile owner shares online (Walther et al., 2009). After all, Facebook allows us to strategically reveal how we appear on the social networking site, so the information that others post about us may more accurately depict our personality. Because Facebook and other social media such as blogs allow others to comment on our disclosures, tag us in their photographs and posts, and in a way merge our digital identity with theirs, our awareness of another's ability to alter our digital image is critical.

Warranting theory—proposes that you will place more credibility on information about the personal characteristics and behaviors of others when the online information cannot be easily manipulated by the person whom it describes.

Summary

As an interpersonal communicator, it is important to manage the dialectic tension between disclosure and privacy. Disclosure is revealing confidential or secret information. Privacy is withholding confidential or secret information to enhance autonomy and minimize vulnerability. Communication privacy management (CPM) theory provides a framework for understanding the decision-making processes people use to manage disclosure and privacy. CPM asserts that each of us has developed rules about privacy and disclosure to guide our behaviors as we make choices to disclose or conceal personal information about ourselves and about others. These rules are designed to maximize the benefits of disclosure while minimizing risks. The rules we use to guide our decisions about disclosure vary with our culture, gender, motivation, context, and risk-benefit analysis.

The three most important ways that disclosure and privacy affect relationships are in terms of intimacy, expectations for reciprocity, and information co-ownership. Skills for self-disclosure include owning, describing behavior, and describing feelings. Strategies for privacy management include changing the subject, masking feelings, and telling white lies, in addition to describing feelings and communicating boundaries. Skills for disclosing personal feedback include asking for feedback, describing behavior, praising, and constructively criticizing.

A QUESTION OF ETHICS ● What Would You Do?

Fifteen-year-old Craig frequently self-discloses personal information to his older brother Marshall. In the past few months, Craig has told Marshall about some parties he has attended where alcohol has been present. When Marshall has asked Craig if he has been drinking at these parties, Craig has assured him that he has not. Nonetheless, Craig has asked Marshall not to tell their parents about these alcohol-related parties. Marshall has agreed to maintain Craig's privacy because Craig has refrained from drinking and because he likes his brother and does not want to get him in trouble with their parents.

Yesterday, when the brothers were hanging out, Craig told a story about getting drunk at a party the weekend before. When Marshall looked surprised, Craig told him to chill, explaining that drinking beer is just a natural part of growing up and that they were safely at a friend's house where everyone slept over and no one drove while under the influence. He pleaded with Marshall not to say anything to their parents because they would worry and likely ground Craig. As their family was under some financial stress, Craig felt even more strongly that it would be inappropriate for Marshall to add to it by sharing Craig's recent behavior. Marshall reluctantly agreed.

The next morning, their mom stopped Marshall as he was leaving for class and asked, "Has Craig confided in you about what happened last weekend? I know that he went to a party and that John, the friend he spent the night with, got picked up for a DUI." Marshall looked at her and replied, "Don't worry, Mom. Do you need me to pick anything up at the store on my way home from class?" Then he grabbed his keys and quickly left.

For Consideration:
1. Since Marshall had agreed to keep Craig's secret, was it ethical for him to change the subject when his mom asked whether Craig had confided in him?
2. Was it ethical for Craig to ask Marshall not to tell their folks that he had been drinking?
3. It appears that Craig didn't tell Marshall the truth about what had happened over the weekend. Does the fact that Craig lied change your perception of Marshall's ethical obligations?
4. Suppose that instead of disclosing that he had been drinking, Craig had told Marshall that he was shooting heroin. Does that change the ethics of this situation? If so, why? If not, why not?
5. How do the motivational, contextual, and risk-benefit issues in the privacy-disclosure dialectic change when the issue is heroin vs. alcohol use?

The rapid development and frequent use of social media have transformed how we practice digital communication and manage our personal information. The attributes of social media and how we use those features have muddied the line between what we consider public versus private communication. Warranting theory posits that online information about the personal characteristics and behaviors of others will seem more credible when it cannot be easily manipulated by the person whom it describes.

Chapter Resources

What You Should Be Able *to Explain*:

- The disclosure-privacy dialectic
- Communication privacy management (CPM) theory
- The five factors that influence disclosure-privacy rules
- How disclosure and privacy affect relationships
- Self-disclosure skills
- Privacy-keeping skills
- Personal feedback skills

What You Should Be Able *to Do*:

- Own your thoughts and feelings by making "I" statements
- Describe behavior
- Describe your feelings
- Communicate personal boundaries
- Ask for personal feedback
- Offer praise
- Provide constructive criticism

Self-test questions based on these concepts are available on the companion Web site (www.oup.com/us/verderber) as part of Chapter 10 resources.

Key Words

Flashcards for all of these key terms are available on the *Inter-Act* Web site.

Asking for personal feedback, p. 309
Communication privacy management (CPM) theory, p. 294
Constructive criticizing, p. 312
Describing behavior, p. 300
Describing feelings, p. 302

Disclosure, p. 293
Disclosure-privacy dialectic, 293
Information co-ownership, p. 299
Owning, p. 300
Personal boundaries, p. 307
Personal feedback, p. 308

Praising, p. 310
Privacy, p. 293
Reciprocity, p. 298
Risk-benefit analysis, p. 297
Warranting theory, p. 315
White lie, p. 306

Apply Your Knowledge

The following activities challenge you to demonstrate your mastery of the concepts, theories, and frameworks in this chapter by using them to explain what is happening in a specific situation.

Inter-Action Dialogue: Disclosure

10.1 Relationships can move toward friendship and intimacy through appropriate disclosure and feedback. Effective self-disclosures own feelings and opinions and describe feelings. Giving effective feedback requires describing specific behaviors and their effect on others. When the effects are positive, praise statements can be provided; when the effects are negative, constructive criticism can be provided. Do a line-by-line analysis of this dialogue noticing the disclosure and privacy messages of each. You can watch a video of this conversation on the Inter-Act Web site and use a form provided to write down your own analysis of the conversation.

DIALOGUE

Maria and Mark have coffee after seeing a movie.

Maria: That was a great movie! The characters were so fascinating, and I loved the way we slowly learned about their childhood.

Mark: Yeah, I liked it too, but at times it hit a little too close to home.

Maria: Really? How do you mean?

Mark: Well, remember how as a little guy he spent so much time alone?

Maria: Yes, that made me feel kind of sad.

Mark: Oh? Well, my mom and dad both had full-time jobs, and my dad often worked a second one as well. So since I was an only child, and we didn't have any other family here, I spent a lot of time alone.

Maria: That must have been hard on you.

Mark: In a way, yes, but I think it helped me become independent, resourceful, and very competitive at games and sports.

Maria: Gee, I guess I understand independent, but why do you say being alone helped you to become resourceful?

Mark: Well, usually no one was home when I came home from school, and sometimes my mom had to work late, so I had to get my own supper.

Maria: How did that make you resourceful?

Mark: When there were leftovers, it wasn't too hard to reheat them, but when there weren't any, I'd have to scrounge around in the cupboards and fridge. I wasn't allowed to use the stove or oven—just the microwave—so I sometimes had to be really creative.

Maria: Really? What did you make?

Mark: I was a master of microwave black beans and rice. If you're lucky, I'll make them for you someday.

Maria: I think I'll pass. I ate enough beans and rice when I was growing up. My mom wanted us to identify with our heritage and made a big deal of cooking recipes from her childhood a couple of times a week. Unfortunately, she's not a good cook, so we got pretty sick of it. Today, my favorite take-out is Thai— now that's cuisine!

Mark: I've never had Thai food. What's so great about it?

Maria: Well, it's very spicy-hot, with lots of complex flavoring.

Mark: Does it have much MSG? I'm allergic to that.

Maria: I don't know. Hey, back to our previous topic. You said being alone also made you competitive. How?

Mark: Well, since I was alone and had no friends to play with, I'd work out ways to compete with myself.

Maria: Really, like what?

Mark: I'd play horse. You play basketball, don't you?

Maria: Sure. But what's horse?

Mark: Well, horse is usually played with two or more people. One person takes a shot. If he makes it, the other person has to attempt the same shot. If that person misses, he gets an "h." If he makes it, then he takes a shot, and his opponent now has to try to make it. The first one to get all five letters, h-o-r-s-e, loses.

Maria: So how did that make you competitive?

Mark: Well, I used to play against my alter ego. Only he was a left-hander! After a while, I was as good left-handed as I was right-handed. I think that's how I made first string on my high school basketball team. I'm not very fast, but I can shoot with either hand from about anywhere on the court.

Maria: I guess that spending a lot of time alone wasn't all bad.

Mark: No. In truth I learned to enjoy my own company, and I still like to be alone a lot. In fact, I have trouble enjoying hanging out or partying with lots of people. It kind of seems like a waste of time. I enjoy smaller groups or one-on-one time, but the party scene leaves me cold.

Maria: Yes, I've noticed that when we're with the group, you don't have much to say. I used to think you thought you were better than us, but I guess I understand why you act that way now. Still, you might want to think about being more vocal. You're really an interesting guy, and I think others in the group don't know how to take you.

Skill Practice

Skill practice activities give you the chance to rehearse a new skill by responding to hypothetical or real situations. Additional skill practice activities are available at the companion Web site.

Owning

Rephrase each of the following statements to own the opinions or feelings expressed.

10.2 Disowned: *"No one likes her."*

Owned:

10.3 Disowned: *"Most people think that sky diving is dangerous."*

Owned:

10.4 Disowned: *"He should win American Idol."*

Owned:

10.5 Disowned: *"People who drink feel out of control."*

Owned:

10.6 Disowned: *"Everyone texts while driving."*

Owned:

Describing Feelings / Communicating Boundaries

Each of the statements below expresses feelings. Write a message based on this statement that describes behavior or feelings, or when appropriate, communicates a boundary.

10.7 Expressed: *"I can't believe that you told that story without my permission!"*

Described:

10.8 Expressed: *"Growing up without a dad was hard. But it's really none of your business."*

Described:

10.9 Expressed: *"It's not fair for you to expect me to share our dorm room with your boyfriend."*

Described:

10.10 Expressed: *"All you've done this whole lunch is text. I don't know why I bothered to come!"*

Described:

10.11 Expressed: *"When I'm with her, it's just crazy. She takes my breath away."*

Described:

Describing Behavior

Assume that you have made each of the statements below. Rephrase each so that it describes the behavior(s) that might have led you to this generalization.

10.12 *"You're a really good friend."*

Described:

10.13 *"You're always picking on me."*

Described:

10.14 *"I can't believe that you stabbed me in the back."*

Described:

10.15 *"I like that shirt on you better than the ones you usually wear."*

Described:

10.16 *"One of the things I admire about you is that you are so thoughtful."*

Described:

Disclosing Personal Feedback

For each of the following situations, write an appropriate feedback message.

10.17 You have been driving to school with a fellow student whose name you got from the transportation office at school. You have known him for only three weeks. Everything about the situation is great (he's on time, your schedules match, and you enjoy your conversations), except he drives 10 to 15 miles per hour faster than the speed limit, and this scares you.

Feedback:

10.18   A good friend of yours has fallen into the habit of saying "like" and "you know" more than once every sentence. You know she has a good vocabulary and is a dean's list student, yet she comes across as uneducated. She is about to graduate and has begun on-campus job interviews, but every employer with whom she has spoken has rejected her. Disappointed, she asks why you think she is having such a hard time.

Feedback:

10.19   For financial reasons, you have returned home to live with your parents after being on your own for five years. While you appreciate your parents' willingness to take you in, you are embarrassed to be living at home. Your mother has begun to treat you the way she did when you were a child. Specifically, she doesn't respect your privacy. She routinely enters your room without knocking and opens your drawers under the guise of putting away your clean clothes. Yesterday you found her looking at your bank statement, which was in an envelope on your desk. You are becoming resentful of these intrusions.

Feedback:

10.20   Your professor in this class has asked you for feedback on his or her teaching style. Based on your experience in this class, write a message of praise and one of constructive criticism.

Feedback:

THE SOCIAL MEDIA FACTOR

Use factors related to social media to explain what is happening in a specific situation.

Shana was at a weekend party at Megan's home. While there, Megan wanted her to meet Patrick who was across the room talking with other friends. From one side of the room and over loud music, Megan yelled, "Hey, Patrick! You have to meet my friend, Shana." Patrick smiled, waved, and then resumed the conversation he was having with his friends. As the party continued, Shana and Patrick did not have an opportunity to speak. Shana noticed that Patrick had left. Disappointed, she went home, went to bed, and awoke the next morning to routinely check her Facebook page. She had a friend request from Patrick! She accepted it and began to browse his profile. She noticed that Patrick's profile was full of personal information. She also saw that his friends post quite frequently on this wall, tag him in photographs, and comment on his postings. A few days later, Shana and Patrick planned to meet for lunch. Although they are Facebook friends and have seen each other's profile, this will be their first face-to-face meeting since they briefly saw each other at the party.

10.21   Use warranting theory to explain what can happen in this situation.

10.22   How can social presence theory explain how Shana might feel about conversations she has had/will have with Patrick?

Communication Improvement Plan: Developing Relationships Through Disclosure and Feedback

Would you like to improve your disclosure or feedback skills, as discussed in this chapter?

- Owning
- Describing feelings
- Managing privacy
- Communicating a personal boundary
- Describing behavior
- Praising
- Constructively criticizing
- Asking for personal feedback

10.23   Choose the skill(s) you want to work on and write a communication improvement plan. You can find a communication improvement plan worksheet on our Web site at www.oup.com/us/verderber.

Inter-Act with Media

Television

The Office, episode: "Cocktails" (2007). Steve Carell, John Krasinski, Jenna Fischer, Melora Hardin, David Denman.

Michael (Carell) and his supervisor, Jan (Hardin), share with everyone their romantic relationship at a house party with corporate executives. During their initial introductions, Michael blurts out, "Jan and I are lovers." Jan and Michael proceed to argue throughout the course of the party. On the way home after the party, Jan claims that going public with their relationship was a mistake. Michael confesses his feelings by claiming that he wants "the house, the picket fence, the ketchup fights, the tickling, and the giggling."

A subplot of this episode also involves communicating personal information: Pam (Fischer), who was previously engaged to Roy (Denman), reveals that she and colleague Jim (Krasinski) kissed before she broke off their engagement. Roy becomes irate over this instance and eliminates any hope for a reunion.

IPC Concepts: Balancing self-disclosure and privacy, owning feelings or opinions, displaying and describing feelings, managing privacy, describing behavior

To the Point:

What do the examples reveal about the role of self-disclosure and privacy in relationships?

How would you characterize the couples' ability to manage personal information and own their feelings and opinions?

Cinema

Little Children (2007). Todd Field (director). Kate Winslet, Patrick Wilson, Jennifer Connelly.

Sarah (Winslet), a bored and drab housewife, spends her time with her three-year-old daughter, Lucy, at the park with other attractive mothers. While Sarah differs from these women in the way she looks, the women share one thing in common: they are fascinated with Brad (Wilson). Brad is an attractive father who regularly visits the park with his young son. None of the women actually verbally communicate with Brad; rather, they call him "the Prom King" and wonder why he is free during the daytime hours. After the mothers dare Sarah to ask Brad for his telephone number, he makes small talk but then tells her to "ask what the person who wears the pants in the family does."

He shares that he failed the bar exam on multiple occasions and that he should find something else to do with his life. Sarah comes to the realization that Brad is quite lonely since he disclosed personal information very quickly and easily.

IPC Concepts: Appropriate self-disclosure, managing privacy

To the Point:

> How would you characterize Brad's ability to manage his private information?
> How would you describe the appropriateness of Sarah's behavior when she solicited
>   private information from Brad?

What's on the Web

Find links and additional material, including self-quizzes, on the companion Web site at www.oup.com/us/verderber.

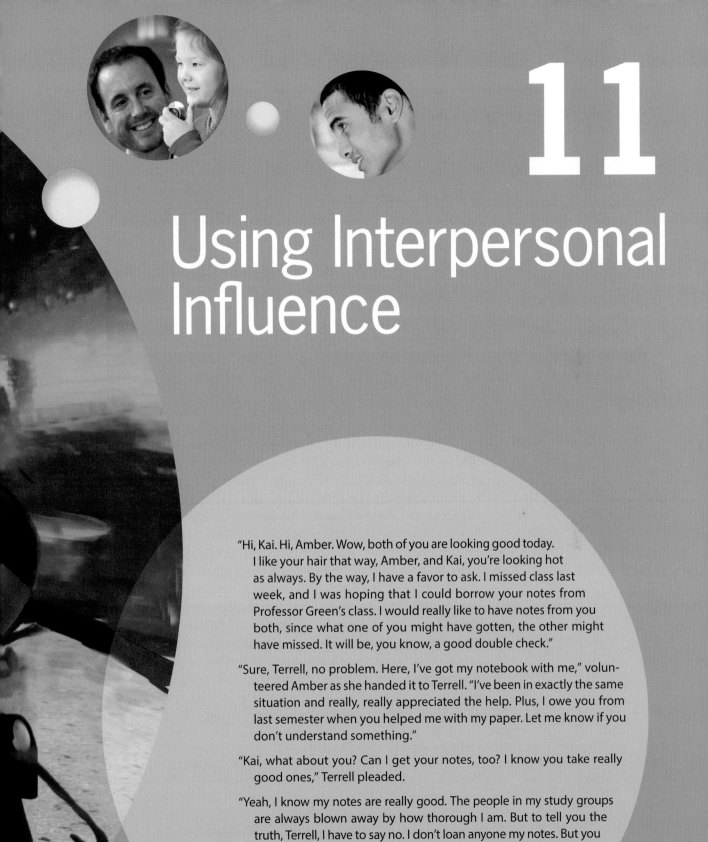

11

Using Interpersonal Influence

"Hi, Kai. Hi, Amber. Wow, both of you are looking good today. I like your hair that way, Amber, and Kai, you're looking hot as always. By the way, I have a favor to ask. I missed class last week, and I was hoping that I could borrow your notes from Professor Green's class. I would really like to have notes from you both, since what one of you might have gotten, the other might have missed. It will be, you know, a good double check."

"Sure, Terrell, no problem. Here, I've got my notebook with me," volunteered Amber as she handed it to Terrell. "I've been in exactly the same situation and really, really appreciated the help. Plus, I owe you from last semester when you helped me with my paper. Let me know if you don't understand something."

"Kai, what about you? Can I get your notes, too? I know you take really good ones," Terrell pleaded.

"Yeah, I know my notes are really good. The people in my study groups are always blown away by how thorough I am. But to tell you the truth, Terrell, I have to say no. I don't loan anyone my notes. But you know you're always welcome at the study group some of us have."

"Well, um," Terrell sputtered, "I uh, I . . ."

What you should be able *to explain* after you have studied this chapter:

- The concept of interpersonal influence
- The concept of interpersonal power
- Six principles of power
- Five types of power
- The concept of persuasion
- The two approaches to processing a persuasive message
- The six heuristics for automatically processing persuasive messages
- The three types of appeals analyzed when extensively processing persuasive messages
- What constitutes passive, aggressive, and assertive messages
- How to create assertive messages

What you should be able *to do* after you have studied this chapter:

- Make a complaint
- Make a personal request
- Refuse a request

Interpersonal influence—the act of changing the attitudes or behaviors of others.

I n this brief conversation, Terrell is trying to get Amber and Kai to lend him their class notes; in other words, he is trying to influence them. Amber quickly complies, while Kai refuses his request. Why was Terrell successful in influencing Amber, yet the same message was unsuccessful with Kai? This chapter explores **interpersonal influence**, the act of changing the attitudes or behaviors of others (Dillard, Anderson, & Knobloch, 2002). Interpersonal influence is a core element of our relationships because whenever we communicate, we intentionally or unintentionally influence each other (Parks, 2007). In addition to gaining assistance (Terrell's objective), the most common goals of interpersonal influence are to sway decisions, give advice, share activities, get permission, change attitudes, and alter relationships (Dillard & Marshall, 2003). All of these types of influence are part of everyday interactions and messages. This chapter explores what we currently know about interpersonal influence, including interpersonal power as the basis of influence, the processing of influence attempts, the types of effective persuasive messages, and forming messages that assert our rights and preferences without damaging our relationships.

Interpersonal Power

Power—the potential that you have to influence the attitudes, beliefs, and behaviors of someone else.

Power is the potential that you have to influence the attitudes, beliefs, and behaviors of someone else. Whether we are conscious of it or not, power dynamics are a part of all our relationships (Guerrero, Andersen, & Afifi, 2007). In some relationships, one person has relatively more power than the other, while in other relationships power is more equally distributed. And the way power is distributed between the people in relationships can change over time. Let's look at the five sources of power in relationships and the four principles that explain power dynamics.

Sources of Power

Research suggests that influence can stem from five distinct roots or sources of power (French & Raven, 1968; Hinken & Schriesheim, 1980).

1. Coercive power. **Coercive power** is the potential to influence rooted in our ability to physically or psychologically punish our partner. The playground bully and the abusive spouse clearly exemplify the use of coercive power. A playground bully may get his or her way by taunting another child psychologically or because he or she has demonstrated physical aggressiveness. Similarly, an abusive spouse may get his or her way because his or her partner fears further verbal or physical abuse. These are extreme examples of the direct use of coercive power. But this type of power may also be indirect, humorously illustrated in the old vaudeville joke, "Where does a gorilla sit when it enters the room? Anywhere it wants." Whether we use coercive power intentionally or unintentionally, if our partners perceive that we have the capacity to punish them in some way, they will be vulnerable to our attempts to influence them.

2. Reward power. **Reward power** is the potential to influence rooted in our ability to provide something our partner values and cannot easily get from someone else. Influence attempts based on reward power include the following statements: "I'll give you your allowance when you clean your room," and "If you don't tell Mom that I went to that party, you can use my iPad." Like coercive power, influence rooted in reward power may be direct, as in these two examples, or indirect. For example, you might agree to take your co-worker's shift on Friday night because you know that she belongs to a sorority that you would like to join. Your reward power depends on how much your partner values the rewards you control, how scarce they are, and how likely your partner believes you are to provide the rewards if they were to comply with an influence attempt. For example, suppose Maggie really wants to attend the sold-out Katy Perry concert and her brother Mitchell, who just broke up with his girlfriend, has an extra ticket. If Mitchell asks Maggie to take his turn picking up their younger brother after soccer practice, she may comply, hoping that Mitchell will reward her by taking her to the concert.

3. Legitimate power. **Legitimate power** is the potential to influence others rooted in the authority granted to a person who occupies a certain role. The power is called legitimate because it is officially bestowed and upheld by laws or rules that dictate how that power is used. Elected officials (regardless of whether you voted for them or agree with their election) are the most obvious example of legitimate power. Other people who hold a position of authority have legitimate power. For example, teachers have legitimate power with respect to their students, parents with their minor children, managers with employees, and nonelected government officials with citizens. If your instructor tells you that class attendance is mandatory, if your parents tell you that you have to get a summer job, if your manager suggests that you need to work overtime during inventory, or if you are speeding and a police car signals to pull you over, you comply because some authority you recognize and accept has given them the right to influence your behavior.

Coercive power—the potential to influence rooted in our ability to physically or psychologically punish our partner.

Reward power—the potential to influence rooted in our ability to provide something our partner values and cannot easily get from someone else.

Legitimate power—the potential to influence others rooted in the authority granted to a person who occupies a certain role.

In the doctor–patient relationship, the doctor is normally thought to have expert power. How is the availability of medical information on the Internet changing this?

Expert power—the ability to influence rooted in someone's subject-specific knowledge and competence.

4. Expert power. Expert power is the potential to influence rooted in someone's subject-specific knowledge and competence. For example, if you want to get a divorce and your friend is a family law attorney, she has the ability to influence your decisions about your divorce settlement because of her expertise. Since she doesn't have children and has little other experience with kids, however, she has little expert power over your child-rearing decisions. Class instructors can influence your thinking about what they are teaching because they usually have more subject-specific knowledge and expertise than you. Similarly, when a physician tells you to take a specific medication for your migraines, you are probably persuaded because your doctor has medical expertise and you do not. Even though someone may not actually be an expert, if we believe this person knows more than we do, she or he has the potential to influence us. For instance, when shopping for a water heater, sales associates can persuade us to buy a specific model. They may or may not be experts on water heaters. But if customers perceive them to be, then they have the potential to influence purchase decisions.

Referent power—the potential to influence rooted in liking, respect, or admiration.

5. Referent power. Referent power is the potential to influence rooted in liking, respect, or admiration. Let's face it. We want to be liked and to impress those we like, respect, or admire. As a result, we are susceptible to their influence attempts. If your best friend raves about an obscure art film showing at the local theater, you are likely to go see it, even though you've never heard of it and don't know any of the actors in it. Even when they don't try to exert influence, celebrities have this power because their fans admire them. For example, in an April 2011 interview with *GQ* magazine, Bruno Mars, commenting on his arrest for cocaine possession, echoed other celebrities when he said, "I'm not a role model, I'm a f****** musician." Nonetheless, he added, "I learned people are watching, so don't do nothing stupid" (Gratereaux, 2011). Most of us aren't celebrities, yet we still have referent power when someone likes us.

Principles of Power

Research has identified a number of basic principles of power dynamics (Guerrero et al., 2007).

1. Power is a perception, not a fact. While you may believe that you are powerful with the potential to influence your partner, if your partner doesn't perceive you as having power, you don't.

2. Power exists within a relationship. Power is not a personality trait or a behavior that you can learn and perform. Rather, the sources of power available to you are specific to each relationship and can change over time. For example, Joshua, who has taken a class on personal finance, may be perceived by his younger sister to be an expert on consumer credit, and she may take his advice when selecting a credit card. But Joshua is unlikely to be perceived as an expert in finance by his friend, who is a stockbroker.

3. Power is not inherently good or bad. In and of itself, power is neither good nor bad, but the use of power can lead to positive or negative outcomes for people or relationships. Whether the power dynamic in a relationship is healthy or sick will depend on the communication skills of both partners and the ethical use of power by the more powerful partner.

4. The person with greater power in a relationship can make and break the rules for the relationship. In families or in workplaces, parents or managers make and break the rules that children and employees must follow because they have more power. Likewise, in social groups, the more popular members may dictate how group members are expected to act and yet violate the very norms they have established.

Interpersonal Persuasion

Persuasion is using verbal messages designed to influence the attitudes and behaviors of others. We are using persuasion when we use words to directly attempt to influence. To understand how messages can influence, you first need to appreciate how we mentally process persuasive messages.

Processing Persuasive Messages: The Elaboration Likelihood Model (ELM)

Can you remember times when you carefully and thoughtfully listened to someone who was trying to convince you of something? Do you remember consciously thinking over what your partner had been saying, critically considering the basis of his or her appeal? Can you remember other times when you did what someone was advocating without really thinking much about it?

What determines how closely we listen to and how carefully we evaluate the hundreds of persuasive messages we hear each day? You'll recall from our

Persuasion—the use of verbal messages designed to influence the attitudes and behaviors of others.

Elaboration likelihood model (ELM) of persuasion—a theory that posits people will use either heuristics or more elaborate critical thinking skills when processing persuasive messages.

Peripheral route—automatically processing persuasive messages by using shortcut heuristics that save time and mental energy

Central route—consciously processing persuasive messages by critically evaluating the logic, credibility, and emotional appeals of the sender.

Spotlight on Scholars

Read about research into persuasion and the elaboration likelihood model (ELM) of Richard Petty at www.oup.com/us/verderber.

previous discussion of perception and listening, that we perceive and listen to messages in one of two ways. We can automatically process it using rules of thumb, or we can consciously process it using a slower deliberate approach. The **elaboration likelihood model (ELM) of persuasion** is a dual processing theory that holds that people will use either heuristics—mental shortcuts—or more elaborate critical thinking skills when processing persuasive messages (Petty & Cacioppo, 1996). The ELM posits that people use one of two routes to process persuasive messages. With the **peripheral route**, we automatically process the persuasive message, using shortcut heuristics that save us time and mental energy. With the **central route**, we consciously process the persuasive message, critically evaluating the logic, credibility, and emotional appeals of the sender. Obviously, the central route consumes more time and energy; rather than taking mental shortcuts, we carefully assess and mentally elaborate on the message to fully understand the basis on which our partner is trying to influence us.

According to the ELM, when the issue is vital to us, we are willing to expend the energy necessary for processing on the central route. When there is much at stake, we will pay attention to the speaker's arguments, evidence, and logic. We will carefully consider the speaker's credibility and use of various emotional appeals. But when the issue is less important to us, we will process the message on the peripheral route, using persuasive heuristics as shortcuts. For example, suppose that you are healthy and take a job at a company that offers several health care insurance options at a similar cost. If the friendly woman in human resources who is about your age mentions that she has Plan C and likes it, you may decide to bypass the pages and pages of information on all the plan options and immediately enroll in Plan C. But suppose you have a chronic illness that is expensive to treat. Because choosing an appropriate plan is much more important to you in this case, you will centrally process the information on each of the plans. You will carefully wade through all the material, evaluating each proposal to select the one that best meets your particular needs.

In addition, we are more likely to use extensive processing when we feel that we are capable of analyzing and understanding the information. Otherwise, we will use shortcuts and base our decisions on one or a limited number of factors that we do understand. For example, when Jason went shopping for an engagement ring, he didn't really know much about diamonds. So he went to a jewelry store recommended by a friend, told the attractive salesperson, who reminded him of his girlfriend, how much he could spend, and bought the first ring the salesperson showed him because she said it was the best one. On the other hand, Rob, a diamond cutter by trade, examined over 250 diamonds offered to him by various sales reps to find the perfect one, then cut it himself, and designed the setting before he proposed. Both men ended up spending about the same amount of money, but because Rob had expertise, he figured he was the best judge of a diamond's quality.

The ELM also suggests that when we form attitudes based on centrally processed persuasive messages, we are less likely to alter them than when we form attitudes based on peripherally processed persuasive messages. You can probably remember a time when you quickly agreed to something without really thinking it through. Later on after thinking about it or living with the consequences of your hasty decision, you regretted being swayed by the message and changed your mind. You also probably have some strongly held beliefs that are the result of carefully processing persuasive information. For example, many of us have religious beliefs we accept and whose tenets guide our behavior. Some of us have "inherited" our beliefs, accepting them because our parents, whom we admire and respect, passed them on to us. We have never bothered to really study the assumptions that underlie our beliefs. Others have come to their religious beliefs after periods of doubt and intense spiritual searching. According to the ELM, those who have engaged in the personal search are less likely to change their beliefs or to act contrary to them. But those of us who have inherited a set of religious principles can be easily swayed to think and act in ways inconsistent with the beliefs.

With the ELM in mind, let's look at the heuristics people use when automatically processing persuasive messages. Then we will discuss the factors that make messages persuasive when they are extensively processed.

Persuading Automatic Processors

When we are processing persuasive messages on the peripheral route, people can influence us by phrasing their requests in ways that trigger a particular heuristic. For example, most of us have been "programmed" to be helpful. Research has shown that people are more likely to comply with your request if you use the phrase "I need a favor," followed by a reason. Because we want to be helpful, we have been conditioned to respond favorably when someone asks for a favor. Research has also found that you increase the likelihood that someone will comply if you then disclose why you need the favor since we like to know why we are doing something (Bastardi & Shafir, 2000). So when we hear, "Can you do me a favor because . . ." we are likely to automatically comply with the request. There are six heuristics whose triggers can be woven into our persuasive messages (Cialdini, 2009).

1. Repay in kind. When you comply with someone's influence attempt because you believe that you are indebted to or obligated to him or her, you are operating from the **reciprocity heuristic**. We will believe or do what another person advocates as a way of paying back another person. This rule of thumb is deeply ingrained in the social contract of all cultures. If in the past someone has done something for you, you will feel obligated to reciprocate. For example, your brother loaned you his car last month when yours was in the shop. Today, when your brother says, "Hey, can I borrow your car? I don't want to put gas in mine," you may not really think about his driving record or whether his explanation is a good one. Instead, you may automatically answer, "Sure," as you toss him the keys. Notice that he didn't even have to remind you about your "debt." The need to reciprocate is so ingrained that we respond automatically to relieve the discomfort that being indebted causes. Therefore, if you want to be able to influence someone, give what you want to receive (Cialdini, 2001). Giving gifts

INTER-ACT WITH SOCIAL MEDIA

View the Web site of one of your favorite politicians. How does the politician use social media to interact with her or his followers? How would you evaluate the politician's use of interpersonal persuasion?

Reciprocity heuristic—being influenced by a perceived debt or obligation to someone else during peripheral processing of persuasive messages.

or doing favors for others obligate them to you. The more someone is indebted to you, the more likely she or he is to comply with your persuasive messages.

Social proof heuristic—being influenced by what others think or do during peripheral processing of persuasive messages.

2. Do what others do—follow the crowd. Being influenced by what others think or do is the **social proof heuristic** rule of thumb used during peripheral processing of persuasive messages. This following-the-crowd rule is especially powerful in social situations where we are unsure of how to act. The old sayings, "When in Rome, do as the Romans," and "there is safety in numbers," reflect the logic of this heuristic. Simon, for instance, is responding to the social proof heuristic when he asks the waiter if the bacon burgers are good, and the waiter replies, "Well, they're OK, but our pulled pork sandwich is the best seller," and Simon says, "Well, I don't usually eat pork, but I'll try it." The fact that the pork sandwich is a best seller is social proof that it is a good choice. Children and teens routinely try to influence their parents using the social proof message script, "Well, everyone is going, or doing it, or saying it," and so forth.

Liking heuristic—being influenced to believe or do what people we like advocate during peripheral processing of persuasive messages.

3. Do what your friends do. Being influenced to believe or do what people we like advocate is the **liking heuristic** rule of thumb used during peripheral processing of persuasive messages. When friends make a persuasive appeal, we are likely to comply with what they are saying just because we like them. Have you ever been on a diet yet agreed to buy overpriced candy bars from a friend at work whose child's school was selling them as a fundraiser? Did you want the candy bars? Probably not, but you didn't want to disappoint your friend, and you didn't want your friend to stop liking you. In 1936 Dale Carnegie published a book called *How to Win Friends and Influence People.* His recipe for influencing is simple: Be friendly. The book details ways to get others to like you, including smiling, calling others by name, listening, showing interest in what others are interested in, refraining from criticizing, and making other people feel important (Carnegie, 1936). People who like you are more likely to comply with your attempts to influence them.

Authority heuristic—being influenced by what knowledgeable professionals believe or advocate during peripheral processing of persuasive messages.

4. Do what the experts advise. Being influenced by what knowledgeable professionals believe or advocate is the **authority heuristic** rule of thumb used during peripheral processing of persuasive messages. You'll recall that one factor that encourages us to short-circuit how we process a persuasive message is our belief that the information is too difficult or complicated for us to understand. So when someone whom we recognize as an expert advocates that we adopt a particular idea or behavior, we may do so without critically evaluating the evidence. When the service rep at the local car dealership calls me to say that the mechanic thinks I need new brake pads, I may unquestioningly give them the go ahead to make this repair. Because I don't know anything about brake systems and I couldn't tell a brake pad that needed to be replaced from one that was OK, I automatically defer to the mechanic's authority.

Consistency heuristic—being influenced by our past active, voluntary, and public commitments during peripheral processing of persuasive messages.

5. Be consistent. Being influenced by our past active, voluntary, and public commitments is the **consistency heuristic** rule of thumb used during peripheral processing of persuasive messages. Because we like to believe that our behavior is consistent with our beliefs and principles, we can be influenced to comply with persuasive messages that are or appear to be consistent with our previously stated positions or actions. Zeke has volunteered for a local environmental watch group that has been taking monthly water samples from a local creek for the last two years. He was wearing his local group's T-shirt in the student center on campus when he was approached by someone he didn't know who commented that Zeke must be an environmentalist. When he nodded, the other student explained that he was raising money for the World Wildlife Fund. Without hesitating, Zeke reached in his pocket and gave the guy a twenty. Later he had to borrow money from a friend for bus fare home. Knowing what others are committed to can be used to influence them by linking our requests to their beliefs or past actions.

6. Get what is in short supply. Being influenced by the rarity or availability of something is the **scarcity heuristic** rule of thumb used during peripheral processing of persuasive messages. Believing scarce things to be more valuable, we can be influenced by how plentiful or rare something is portrayed to be. For example, suppose you call to schedule a physical. If the doctor's receptionist tells you that the only appointment available for the next month is on Tuesday at 10:00 a.m., and you have a breakfast meeting with your class project group scheduled at that time, what do you do? Without even thinking about it or checking your calendar, you may quickly accept the appointment time. Later you apologize to the group for having double-booked yourself, explaining, "It was the only appointment I could get." Buying into your scarcity appeal, your group agrees to move the meeting. Making appeals advocating what appears to be exclusive or less available can influence others. Anyone who shops on eBay is also subjected to a constant barrage of language declaring the scarcity or rarity of an item for sale, all for the purpose of boosting its potential auction price.

Scarcity heuristic—being influenced by the rarity or availability of something during peripheral processing of persuasive messages.

We use these six heuristics to automatically process and respond to persuasive messages because they are based on principles that generally hold true. For example, reciprocity is an ingrained social norm that enables humans to specialize their labor, share resources with others, and thus create a civilization. And as these heuristics are deeply ingrained, we automatically respond to appeals based on them. In most cases, this isn't a problem: The heuristic is appropriate for the situation, and the person with whom we are interacting has good intentions. But the automatic nature of heuristic use can allow people to take advantage of or manipulate us with persuasive appeals that directly or indirectly evoke these heuristics. The intentions of the person appealing to us determine whether these messages are ethical or unethical. For example, the parent who tells a child, "If you pick up your toys, I'll read you an extra bedtime story," is using the reciprocity heuristic, but since teaching a child to be responsible for clean-up and reading stories are both good for the child, the appeal is ethical. But if Sal tries to persuade Jan to have sex with him by saying, "Well, you gave that speech in class in support of friends-with-benefits relationships, so I know that you aren't a prude," he would be unethically pressuring Jan with the consistency principle. Unscrupulous use of these heuristics is not just unethical it is also shortsighted. Although people may comply with the immediate request, if the outcome is harmful to them, you lose their trust and their willingness to comply with your persuasive attempts in the future.

Persuading Extensive Processors

When an issue is important to us, we will take a central route to process the persuasive messages that we receive. As we analyze the message, we will evaluate (1) the quality of the reasoning, (2) the credibility of the speaker, and (3) the legitimacy of appeals to our emotions. Let's look at each of these.

1. Quality of the reasoning. Because people pride themselves on being rational—that is, they seldom believe or do anything without a reason—you increase the likelihood of persuading extensive processors if you can provide them with reasons rather than just claiming something. **Claims** are simple statements of belief or opinion. They don't answer the "why?" question. You can probably think of many times that you made a claim to which a person in effect responded, "I can't accept what you've said on face value—give me some reasons!" **Reasons** are statements that provide valid evidence, explanations, or justifications for a claim. They answer the question "why?" by providing information to back up your position. Let's look at a simple example to illustrate the relationship between claims and reasons. Suppose you're talking with a friend about movies. You might ask, "Have you seen *The King's Speech*?" If your friend says, "No," you might then make the claim, "It's great. You really need to see it." If your friend asks, "Why?" you might explain, "Well, first, it based on a true story of Queen Elizabeth's father, who had to become King of England during World War II even though he had a severe stutter. And the relationship between the king and his speech therapist is compelling." Your reasoning could be outlined as follows:

Claim: You need to see *The King's Speech*. (Why?)
Reason 1: Because it portrays the humanness of a real historical person.
Reason 2: Because it shows a special relationship between two men of unequal class and power.

Ethical communicators give good reasons to back up their claims so that their partners are able to weigh and evaluate for themselves the substance of the influence attempt. Having heard the reasons, they may accept or reject it based on how they evaluate the reasons. Now let's consider what makes a reason a good or effective reason.

- *Good reasons are relevant to the claim.* As you consider the reasons that you might provide to support a claim, you'll find that some are better than others because they relate more directly to the issue at hand. For example, the reasons just offered for seeing *The King's Speech*—"real person of historical significance" and "compelling relationship"—are relevant criteria that people likely look for in movies, unlike the reason, "it's only showing this week."
- *Good reasons are well supported by valid evidence.* You need to support your reasons with some type of **evidence**—facts, expert opinions, and relevant personal narratives that support the truth of a reason. Your friend may find those reasons relevant but still want additional information that justifies your position. As a result, you'll also need to provide specific support or evidence. In support of "real

Claims—simple statements of belief or opinion.

Reasons—statements that provide valid evidence, explanations, or justifications for a claim.

Evidence—facts, expert opinions, and personal narratives that support the truth of your reason.

person of historical significance," you could report that King George was required to give both public speeches and live broadcast speeches to rally the country during the bombing of London, and in support of "compelling relationship," you could summarize a particularly interesting conversation in the movie.

- *Good reasons are meaningful to the person you're trying to persuade.* There are times when you know something about your conversational partner that calls for you to give more weight to one particular reason than to another. Therefore, you also need to tailor your reasoning to make your assertions meaningful to the person you are trying to persuade. For instance, suppose the friend to whom you recommended *The King's Speech* also loves vintage cars. In this case, you might want to add as a third reason that the movie has some wonderful footage of the interiors of vintage cars.

   2. Source Credibility. Good reasons may be persuasive, but they are more powerful when presented by a credible source. **Credibility** is the extent to which your partner believes in your competence, trustworthiness, and likability. Automatic processors may mindlessly believe influence attempts by those claiming to be authorities, but extensive processors will critically examine your credibility. You may be able to recall times when no matter how logical the information appeared, you didn't believe it because you didn't trust the person presenting it. Whether your conversational partner has confidence in who you are as a person may determine whether your persuasive messages are effective. Three factors affect your credibility.

Credibility—the extent to which your partner believes in your competence, trustworthiness, and likability.

- *Competence* is the perception that you are credible because you are well qualified to provide accurate and reliable information. The more people perceive you as knowledgeable on a particular subject, the more likely they are to pay attention to your views on that subject. For

Competence—the perception that speakers are credible because they are well-qualified to provide accurate and reliable information.

example, if Reggie knows that his friend Gloriana has attended all of the meet-the-candidate sessions and has read candidate Web sites and party platforms, he will consider her competent, and her reasons may persuade him to vote for a particular candidate.

- **Trustworthiness** is the perception that you are competent because you are dependable, honest, and acting for the good of others. Your intentions or motives are particularly important in determining whether others will view you as trustworthy. For instance, if a sales clerk who is working on commission says to you, "Wow, you look terrific in those jeans," you may not give the opinion much weight. If your mom, however, looks at you and says, "Now those jeans really fit. They don't gap in the back at the waist, and they don't pull across your stomach," you are likely to accept her reasoning because you trust your mom to tell you the truth.

- **Likability** is the perception that you are credible because you are congenial, friendly, and warm. Automatic processors readily believe what those they like tell them, but extensive processors carefully assess the likability of speakers so that they don't succumb to scam artists and other unethical operators who cultivate likability to persuade others to do things not in their best interests.

Trustworthiness—the perception that speakers are credible because they are dependable, honest, and acting for the good of others.

Likability—the perception that speakers are credible because they are congenial, friendly, and warm.

You can become an expert in areas that you would like to have influence. You can also behave in ways that earn trust and work to cultivate pleasant relationships. By doing these things, you enhance your credibility and are ethical in your persuasive attempts.

3. Honest emotional appeals. The third component of persuasive messages, **emotional appeals**, are persuasive messages that influence others by evoking strong feelings in support of what the speaker is advocating. Messages from a credible source that provide good reasons are likely to influence others' attitudes and ideas. But when you're trying to influence others to *act*, you can increase the persuasiveness of your message by appealing to people's emotions (Jorgensen, 1998). Those who *believe* they should do something still may be reluctant to act on their belief without an additional appeal. For instance, Jonas may believe that

Emotional appeals—persuasive messages that influence others by evoking strong feelings in support of what the speaker is advocating.

"Everything's all screwed up. Nice job, people."

people should donate money to worthy causes, but he may not do so; Gwen may believe that people should exercise three times a week for forty-five minutes, but she may not do so. Often what motivates people to act on a belief is the degree of their emotional involvement. Appeals to negative emotions like fear, shame, anger, and sadness as well as appeals to positive emotions like happiness, joy, pride, relief, hope, and compassion nudge us from passive belief to overt action. When Jonas, for instance, is shown graphic photos of a town torn apart by a tornado, his feelings of compassion may prompt him to donate to the Red Cross.

The effectiveness of emotional appeals depends on the mood and attitude of the person you are persuading and the persuasive language being used. Suppose, for example, you are trying to convince your brother to loan you money to buy textbooks for the semester without waiting for your grant money to be released. In addition to your rational approach, you may want to include several appeals to his emotions using specific examples and experiences, such as, "I'm sure you remember how tough it is to understand the lectures when you haven't looked at the book," or "Mom will be on my back if I don't do well in this class," or "I know you want to be a nice guy and help your little brother here." Or even better, you may want to employ an emotional appeal that evokes stories from the past. For instance, instead of saying, "I thought you might be interested in going hiking and rock climbing with me tomorrow—it will be fun," you might say, "I thought you might be interested in going hiking and rock climbing with me. It will be like old times when we would spend the whole day at the gorge, just two brothers, bonding. Remember how much fun we had on our hike to Clear Creek Canyon?"

Asserting Rights and Expectations

So far our discussion of social influence has focused on general approaches to changing others' beliefs, attitudes, or behaviors through persuasion. Now we want to turn our attention to situations in which we need to influence others specifically, teaching them how to treat us by communicating our rights and expectations. These messages are riskier because they have the potential to damage our relationships and may require self-disclosure. In this section we describe three approaches to dealing with others who have violated our rights and expectations. Then we explain how to skillfully complain, make a request, or refuse a request, three common situations in which we need to persuade others. As we discuss each of these, we will provide general message scripts using communication skills you have already studied.

Approaches to Communicating Rights and Expectations

We can take three approaches when faced with a situation in which we feel someone has violated our rights or not met our expectations. We can behave passively, aggressively, or assertively. Let's look at each of these approaches and their interpersonal effectiveness.

The Passive Approach

The **passive approach** is concealing your feelings rather than voicing your rights and expectations to others. We may remain passive when someone violates our rights or expectations or comply with requests that are not in our best interests for several reasons. First, we may not believe that we have rights. Second, we may fear that if we complain or don't comply we will damage or lose our relationship. Third, we may lack self-esteem and consequently believe that we don't deserve to be treated well. Finally, we may be passive because we don't have the

Passive approach—concealing your feelings rather than voicing your rights and expectations to others.

LEARN ABOUT YOURSELF ● Assertiveness

Take this short survey to learn something about yourself. This is a test of your passive, assertive, and aggressive behaviors. Answer the questions based on your first response. There are no right or wrong answers. Just be honest in reporting your true behavior. For each question, select one of the numbers to the left that best describes your behavior.

1 = Strongly Agree
2 = Agree Somewhat
3 = Neutral
4 = Disagree Somewhat
5 = Strongly Disagree

_____ 1. I am aggressive in standing up for myself.
_____ 2. If a salesperson has gone to a lot of trouble to show me merchandise that I do not want to buy, I have no trouble saying "no."
_____ 3. If a close and respected relative were bothering me, I would keep my feelings to myself.
_____ 4. People do not take advantage of me.
_____ 5. If food in a restaurant is not satisfactory to me, I complain and insist on a refund.
_____ 6. I avoid asking questions for fear of sounding stupid.
_____ 7. I would rather make a scene than bottle up my emotions.
_____ 8. I am comfortable returning merchandise.
_____ 9. I find it difficult to ask friends to return money or objects they have borrowed from me.
_____ 10. If I hear that a person has been spreading false rumors about me, I confront that person and talk about it.
_____ 11. I can yell at others when I feel that I have been wronged.
_____ 12. I get anxious before making problem-solving business phone calls.

Scoring the survey: Add your scores for Items 3, 6, 9, and 12. Your score will range from 4 to 20. The lower (closer to 4) your score, the more you tend to engage in passive behavior.

Add your scores for Items 2, 4, 8, and 10. Your score will range from 4 to 20. The lower (closer to 4) your score, the more you tend to engage in assertiveness.

Add your scores for Items 1, 5, 7, and 11. Your score will range from 4 to 20. The lower (closer to 4) your score, the more you tend to engage in aggressive behavior.

Adapted from Rathus, S. (1973). A 30-item schedule for assessing assertive behavior. *Behavior Therapy, 4*, 398.

social skills needed to stand up for ourselves. Obviously, passive behavior is not influential, and those who use this method end up submitting to other people's demands, even when doing so is inconvenient, demeaning, or not in their best interests. For example, suppose that when Sergei uncrates the new plasma television he purchased at a local department store, he notices a deep scratch on the left side. If he is upset about the scratch but doesn't try to get the store to replace the expensive item, he is exhibiting passive behavior.

At times behaving passively is an appropriate response. If someone who is normally considerate of our rights and expectations inadvertently violates them, we may overlook the transgression and chalk it up to our friend having a bad day. In such cases we put our partner's needs ahead of our own, recognizing that what has occurred is not intentional and is unlikely to be repeated.

In most cases, however, passive behavior is ineffective because it fails to protect our interests and may also damage our relationships. Suppose that Alicia doesn't say anything to her ex-husband when he is late to pick up the children since it was the first time it had happened. Alicia's ex-husband may interpret her silence as indifference to the pick-up time. So the next time, he figures that he will just pick them up an hour later than the original agreement, which is more convenient for him. If Alicia chooses not to comment on his tardiness a second time, she will be teaching him that it is OK to pick the kids up an hour later, and this is likely to become a pattern as he doesn't see any problem with the new "arrangement."

Not only may passive behavior thwart our interests, but it may also damage our relationships because when we are passive, we are also private. When we don't share our honest reactions with our partner, we deprive them of the opportunity to meet our needs and to know us better. Marriages have dissolved because one partner was unable to voice his or her needs, protest violations of rights and expectations, or refuse the partner's requests. The sad thing in these cases is that partners may be totally unaware of their spouse's unhappiness. Although situations in which passive behavior is useful occur, in the long run, passive behavior is not in our own or our relationship's best interests.

The Aggressive Approach

Verbal aggression is sending messages that attack another person's self-esteem or express personal hostility for perceived violations of rights or expectations (Infante & Rancer, 1996). Verbally aggressive messages display our strong feelings, overstating our opinions in a manner that shows little regard for the situation or for the feelings, needs, or rights of others. Aggressive messages include name-calling, threatening, judging, or faultfinding. Suppose that after discovering the scratch on his new television set, Sergei storms back to the store, confronts the first salesperson he finds, and loudly demands his money back while accusing her of intentionally selling him damaged merchandise. Such aggressive behavior may or may not result in getting the damaged set replaced, but it will certainly damage his relationship with the salesperson. Even in a professional scenario, most receivers of aggressive messages are likely to feel hurt by them (Martin, Anderson, & Horvath, 1996).

INTER-ACT WITH SOCIAL MEDIA

Log in to your Facebook account and scan the messages available in your news feed. Pay attention to whether the message is a status update, a post to a friend's wall, or an exchange between two or more friends. How would you describe the tendency for passive, aggressive, and assertive approaches to using social media? Are your Facebook friends more inclined to use social media to communicate aggressive messages?

Verbal aggression—sending messages that attack another person's self-esteem or express personal hostility for perceived violations of rights or expectations.

Flaming—sending an aggressive message using social media.

Argumentativeness—defending our own ideas or attacking the reasoning of others while according them respect.

Passive-aggressive behavior—messages that indirectly express hostility.

Assertiveness—the skill of sending messages that declare and defend personal rights and expectations in a clear, direct, and honest manner while at the same time respecting the preferences and rights of others.

While Sergei may not care about his relationship with the salesperson, if he is prone to aggression as a means of communicating his rights and expectations, he will likely damage other more intimate relationships. Studies have found that verbal aggression leads to less satisfying relationships, family violence, and lower credibility, and it causes employees to lose respect and loyalty for managers (Hample, 2003). Today, certain textual, visual, and audio forms of online messages have the potential to harm others because they employ aggressive messages (Kleinman, 2007). **Flaming** is sending an aggressive message using social media.

Verbal aggression is different from **argumentativeness**, defending our own ideas or attacking the reasoning of others while according them respect. While research has found that argumentative messages can enhance relationships, verbally aggressive people underestimate how much their messages hurt their partner.

Verbally aggressive messages may be overtly hostile, but aggression may also be characterized by **passive-aggressive behavior**, exhibited in messages that indirectly express hostility. Examples of passive-aggressiveness include being stubborn, unresponsive, intentionally refusing to help, and not owning up to one's responsibilities. For example, after Sergei finishes ranting at the salesperson, she takes his information, appears to apologize, and promises Sergei that she will rectify the situation. But once Sergei leaves, she behaves passive-aggressively by calmly throwing his contact information in the wastebasket and doing nothing.

Passiveness, verbal aggression, and passive-aggressive behavior are far too common, and most of us have probably used these approaches at some point in time. But the third approach to communicating our rights, expectations, and refusals is more likely to achieve our short-term goals while enhancing or maintaining our relationships.

The Assertive Approach

Assertiveness is the skill of sending messages that declare and defend personal rights and expectations in a clear, direct, and honest manner while at the same time respecting the preferences and rights of others. Assertive messages allow us to stand up for ourselves rather than acting passively or aggressively.

In contrast to passive behavior and aggressive messages, which are self-oriented, assertive messages focus simultaneously on both our interests and those of others. Unlike the passive approach, assertiveness respects and expresses our own rights and dignity by verbalizing our honest thoughts, feelings, and preferences. Unlike the aggressive approach, assertiveness also respects the rights and dignity of others by avoiding hostile and inflammatory language and nonverbal behavior (Alberti & Emmons, 2001). The difference between an assertive approach and a passive or aggressive approach is not in how we think and feel but in how our feelings work in conjunction with the thoughts and feelings of others. To return to our example, if Sergei chooses an assertive approach to handling the problem of the damaged TV, he will still feel angry. But instead of either doing nothing and living with the damaged merchandise, or verbally assaulting the salesperson, Sergei might call the store, describe the condition of the TV to a customer service representative, share his feelings on discovering the scratch, and state what he would like to see happen now. He might request that the store exchange the damaged set for a new one, or he might ask for a refund. Sergei's assertive messages should accomplish his own goals without annoying or hurting anyone else.

It's important to recognize that you will not always achieve your goals by being assertive and that being assertive involves risks. For instance, some people, not knowing the difference between assertiveness and aggressiveness, may be inclined to view assertive messages as aggressive. Nonetheless, the potential benefits far outweigh the risks. If you have trouble taking the first step to being more assertive, try beginning with situations in which your potential for success is high (Alberti & Emmons, 2001). Remember, our behavior teaches people how to treat us. If we are passive, people will ignore our feelings because we have taught them that it's OK. If we are aggressive, we teach people to respond in kind. By contrast, if we are assertive, we can influence others to treat us as we would prefer to be treated.

Since assertiveness is concerned not only with your own needs but also with maintaining your relationship, assertive messages are most effective when they are well timed, when they ask for the minimal effective response from a partner, and when they are politely pursued if a partner does not immediately comply (Rakos, 2006). While you will want to be timely in asserting your rights and expectations, it's important for your partner to be prepared to hear you. Choosing a time and place that allow for discussion and privacy is critical. In addition, as you consider what you want your partner to do or not do, you will want to ask for as little as you can while still having your needs met or your rights respected. You need, therefore, to figure out the minimal effective response that will satisfy you. Finally, it may take a longer conversation or several conversations to persuade your partner. So be prepared to persist.

In the remainder of this chapter, we are going to explain the communication skills that are part of assertive message scripts and then describe how to apply these skills to three specific occasions: when we complain about how we are being treated, when we make a request, and when we refuse a request that someone has made of us.

Assertive Message Skills

Assertiveness is difficult for many of us because these particular message scripts combine a number of interpersonal communication skills, including the following:

1. **Owning.** The purpose of assertive messages is to directly and respectfully represent your position or needs, so your message should be owned and include "I" statements like "I think . . . ," "My opinion is . . . ," "I feel . . . ," and "I would like. . . ."
2. **Describing behaviors and feelings.** If we want others to honor our rights and expectations, then we should provide them with specific descriptive information to justify our requests. We do this by describing the feelings we have, as well as the behaviors and outcomes we desire.
3. **Doing positive and negative facework.** The goal of assertive messages is to influence others without damaging relationships. Messages should be

OBSERVE AND ANALYZE

Passive, Aggressive, and Assertive Behaviors

For the next day or two, observe people and their behaviors. Make notes of situations in which you believe people behaved in passive, aggressive, and assertive ways. Which ways seemed to help people achieve what they wanted? Which ways seemed to maintain or even improve their interpersonal relationships with others?

formed in ways that both meet the face needs of others and assert your rights and expectations.

4. **Using appropriate nonverbal behaviors.** As you know, nonverbal behavior conveys much of a message's emotional meaning. We can reflect our self-confidence and our respect for the other person by using steady eye contact, a calm and sincere facial expression, relaxed and involved posture, and appropriate paralanguage, including fluent speech, appropriate volume, intonation, and firmness (Rakos, 2006).

Let's see how we can combine these skills to form assertive messages for three common situations in which we need to assert our rights and expectations.

Making a Complaint

Complaint—a message telling someone that what is or has occurred is unacceptable because it has violated your rights or expectations.

A **complaint** is a message telling someone that you find what is happening or has occurred unacceptable because it has violated your rights or expectations. A good complaint script assumes that the violation was unintentional and that your partner will want to cooperate with you in correcting the problem. Let's look at an example of how to make an assertive complaint.

Tanisha is the only woman in a professional role in her department. Whenever her manager has an especially interesting and challenging job, he assigns it to one of the men in the department. Despite constantly good performance reviews, Tanisha is stuck with routine assignments that are not challenging her or preparing her for promotion. She could respond passively by saying nothing, continuing to be frustrated and believing that she is being discriminated against. Or she could storm into her manager's office and accuse him of discrimination. But, alternatively, Tanisha decides to assertively complain. She begins by asking her manager if they can meet to discuss work assignments. To begin the meeting, she might say something to this effect:

"I know it must be hard to balance work assignments. So I'm not sure you are aware that during the past three months, every time there was a really interesting or challenging job to be done, you gave it to Tom, Rex, or Jamal, while you have assigned me all of the routine tasks. To the best of my knowledge, you believe that Tom, Rex, Jamal and I are equally competent. You've never said anything to suggest that you thought less of my work. So I would expect that we would each get opportunities to work on the more challenging and less routine assignments. But when you give the all the work that I perceive as interesting to my colleagues and continue to give me only the routine stuff, I feel really frustrated and discouraged. Do you understand what I'm saying?"

Tanisha's message followed these guidelines for making effective complaints:

1. *Begin by doing facework.* Tanisha begins by using the skill of positive facework: "I know it must be hard to balance work assignments . . ." acknowledges that the manager has a difficult job.
2. *Describe what has happened that you believe violates your rights or expectations.* Tanisha continues by specifically describing how the manager has behaved without using any evaluative language: "during the last three months every time there was an interesting . . ."
3. *Explain why what has happened violates your rights or expectations:* Tanisha explains, "I would expect that . . ."
4. *Describe how you feel about what has happened.* Tanisha describes, "I get really frustrated and discouraged."
5. *Invite the person to comment on or paraphrase what you have said.* Tanisha concludes, "Do you understand . . .?"

SKILL BUILDERS ● Complaining

SKILL	USE	PROCEDURE	EXAMPLE
"Sending" or "communicating" messages that tell someone that you find what is or has occurred unacceptable because it has violated your rights or expectations	To assert your rights and expectations when they have been violated	1. Begin by doing facework. 2. Describe what has happened that you believe violates your rights or expectations. 3. Explain why what has happened violates your rights or expectations. 4. Describe how you feel about what has happened. 5. Ask the person to comment on or paraphrase what you have said.	Colin ordered his food over twenty minutes ago. The people at two tables seated after him have eaten and left. Colin decides to complain, saying "Excuse me. I can see that things are really busy, but I ordered my food about twenty minutes ago, and two tables of people who ordered after me have come and gone. I expected that our food would be served in order. I'm really annoyed. Do you understand my position?"

Making a Personal Request

We make simple requests all the time: "Could you stop on the way home and pick up my prescriptions?" "Will you tell your brother that dinner is ready?" "Would you take out the garbage on your way out?" We probably make dozens of these mundane requests every day without really thinking about them, but other requests can be harder for us to make. **Personal requests** are messages that direct others how to respect our rights or meet our expectations in particular situations. These messages teach others how to treat us. A good personal request script assumes that our partners are willing to change their current behavior if they understand that it is a problem and that we find it unacceptable. For example, Margarita has invited two of her best friends, Nicole and Ramon, to hang out at her residence hall suite for the evening and watch a movie. When they arrive, they introduce her to Nick, Ramona's friend from high school. Shortly after the movie begins, Nick lights a cigarette. Margarita hates the smell of smoke and doesn't want her clothes to reek. Also afraid that someone will complain, as smoking in dorms is banned, she makes the following request:

> "Nick, please put your cigarette out. You probably forgot that dorms are non-smoking areas. I could get kicked out. I don't want my place and clothes to smell. When you need to smoke, I'll pause the movie so you can go outside. Thanks for understanding."

Margarita's message followed these guidelines for making effective personal requests:

1. *Politely but directly describe what you want the other person to do.* "Nick, please put your cigarette out." In this statement, Margarita does not ask Nick to stop smoking, she directs him to. Asking a question gives the person a choice and implies that we will accept a refusal. Suppose Margarita had asked, "Will you please put out your cigarette?" and Nick had said, "No." Now what does she do?
2. *Do facework.* When Margarita says, "You probably forgot that . . ." she is providing a face-saving explanation for Nick's violation.
3. *Describe how the behavior violates your rights or expectations.* Margarita's message notes two violations. First, she has the right to expect her guests to do what is legal in her space. Second, she expects that guests in her space will not be the source of offensive odors.
4. *When possible, offer an alternative to your partners' unacceptable behavior that meets their needs while not violating your rights and expectations.* Margarita tells Nick where he can smoke and offers to accommodate his need by pausing the movie.
5. *Assume that your partners will comply with the personal request and thank them.* Margarita closes her message by thanking Nick for understanding.

Refusing a Request

People make requests of you every day. Some requests are simple and easy to comply with, but others are inconvenient, difficult, and at times not in line with your own values, beliefs, or interests. All of us can think of times we regretted

SKILL BUILDERS ● Making a Personal Request

SKILL	USE	PROCEDURE	EXAMPLE
"Sending" or "communicating" messages that teach people how to treat you by directing them how to behave	To direct others to change their behavior because they are violating your rights or expectations	1. Politely but directly describe what you want the other person to do. 2. Do facework. 3. Describe how the behavior violates your rights or expectations. 4. When possible, offer an alternative to your partners' unacceptable behavior, which meets their needs while not violating your rights and expectations. 5. Assume that your partners will comply with the personal request and thank them.	"Rahm, don't criticize me in front of your children. If you don't agree with what I am doing, please tell me later when we can talk it out. I know you don't mean to undermine my authority, but when you interrupt me and contradict what I have said, that's what happens. It's hard to be a stepparent, but I think it's important for both sets of kids to see us as a team. I know you understand. Thanks, honey."

having done what someone asked us to. Often we comply with these requests because we don't know how to turn them down in a way that will not damage our image or relationship. Not only do we end up agreeing to something we later regret, we may even resent the person who made the request. We comply with uncomfortable requests when we feel indebted to someone, when we like someone, when we don't want to disappoint someone, and when there is group pressure. Overcoming these powerful and often indirect pressures is challenging. But you can use the communication skills that you have studied to develop a general script for turning down requests in a way that serves your interests and maintains your relationships.

Let's look at an example of how Carl dealt with pressure from his friend Reece. Carl and Reece are next-door neighbors who have become friendly. One night Reece invites Carl to go clubbing with several friends who work as roadies for a touring rock band in town for the night. Carl initially hesitates, but after some waffling, he reluctantly agrees to go, even though he is in recovery and tries to avoid the whole club scene—something he is not yet comfortable sharing with Reece. When the bartender asks for their order, Reece replies, "We'll have beers all around. What have you got on tap?" Carl quickly corrects Reece, saying to the bartender, "Make mine a Coke." Reece then turns to Carl, raises his eyebrows, and loudly says, "Hey, bro, loosen up, forget the Coke, let me buy you a beer." Carl sighs then says, "Hey, man, thanks for the offer, but no beer for me. You guys go ahead, but I never drink when I'm driving. I appreciate you springing for the round, but make mine a Coke."

Notice that in turning down Reece's offer, Carl maintains privacy concerning his chemical dependency, offering a generalized statement as an explanation. He also doesn't judge Reece and his friends or insinuate that there is anything wrong with their drinking beer. Carl just politely refuses Reece's request, then offers another valid an alternative explanation with which he is comfortable.

Carl's message followed these guidelines for effectively refusing requests:

1. *If appropriate, thank people for what they are asking you to do.* Carl begins, "Hey man, thanks for the offer," later adding, "I appreciate you springing for the round."
2. *Directly own that you are not willing to agree to the request.* Carl turns down the offer, saying ". . . no beer for me."
3. *State a generalized reason or alternative explanation for your refusal, but don't feel obligated to disclose something that you want to remain private.* Carl states, "I never drink when I'm driving."
4. *When possible, offer an alternative to which you can agree.* Carl offers, ". . . make mine a Coke."

One assertive message may accomplish your goal, but at other times, your assertion may lead to a conflict. In the next chapter you will learn how to use assertive message skills in combination with other communication skills to effectively resolve interpersonal conflicts.

SKILL BUILDERS ● Refusing a Personal Request

SKILL	USE	PROCEDURE	EXAMPLE
Messages that decline to act or believe as others would like you to	To inform others that we don't want to do or think what they want us to	1. When appropriate, thank people for what they are asking you to do.	"Would you take my shift next Friday? I'd really appreciate it."
		2. Directly own that you are not willing to agree to the request.	"Thanks for offering it to me, but sorry, I already have plans. Check with Heather, though, when she comes in. I think she was interested in picking up a shift."
		3. State a generalized reason for your refusal, but don't feel obligated to disclose something that you wish to keep private.	
		4. When possible, identify an alternative to the request that you could agree to.	

Assertiveness in Cross-Cultural Relationships

Assertiveness, like other communication skills, is valued by some cultures more than others. As Samovar and Porter (2009) observe, "Communication problems arise when cultures that value assertiveness come in contact with cultures that value accord and harmony" (p. 292). The standard of assertiveness considered appropriate in the dominant American culture can seem inappropriate to people with other cultural frames of reference.

Asian cultures, for example, clearly differ from American culture regarding assertiveness. Asian cultures value harmony and so direct assertiveness can cause problems, as it can be perceived as leading to conflict and discord. Research has shown that Japanese, Malaysian, and Filipino adults are less likely to engage in assertiveness than their Western counterparts (Niikura, 1999). Likewise, research has demonstrated that Turkish adolescents are less likely to engage in assertiveness than Western adolescents (Mehmet, 2003). In contrast, men in Latin and Hispanic societies are frequently taught to exercise a form of self-expression that goes far beyond the guidelines presented here for assertiveness. In these societies, the concept of "machismo" often guides male behavior. Though not exactly aggressive, machismo is more focused on the self than on a balance between the self and the other.

Thus, when we practice assertiveness—as with any other skill—we need to be aware that no single standard of behavior ensures the achievement of our goals. Although what is labeled appropriate behavior varies across cultures, the results of passive and aggressive behavior seem universal. Passive behavior fails to communicate problems, generating resentment on the part of the person behaving passively toward others; aggressive behavior also fails to communicate problems effectively, creating fear and misunderstanding of the person exhibiting the aggressive behavior. When talking with people whose cultures, backgrounds, or lifestyles differ from your own, you may need to observe their behaviors and their responses to your statements before you can communicate with them in a persuasive manner.

Summary

Interpersonal influence is the act of changing the attitudes or behaviors of others. It is a core element of our interpersonal relationships because whenever we communicate we intentionally or unintentionally affect others. Power is the potential you have to influence someone else. There are five sources or roots of power that we may have with respect to our partner: coercive power, reward power, legitimate power, expert power, and referent power.

Research suggests that there are several principles of power: power is a perception not a fact; power exists within a relationship; power is not inherently good or bad; and the person with more power in a relationship can make and break the relationship rules.

Persuasion is the use of verbal messages designed to influence the attitudes and behaviors of others. The elaboration likelihood model is a theory that posits that people will use either heuristics or more elaborate critical thinking skills when processing persuasive messages. When we receive persuasive messages that we believe are important, or about which we feel knowledgable, we take the central route and extensively process them, evaluating the arguments, credibility, and emotional appeals of the sender. When we think the issues are unimportant, we process them peripherally, using heuristics that shortcut our need to think.

When we extensively process persuasive messages, we analyze the logic of the reasoning, the credibility of the source, and the honesty of the emotional appeal.

We can use social influence not only to change the general attitudes and behavior of others but also to teach others how to treat us by asserting our rights and expectations. We can take three approaches when we think our rights and expectations have been breached. We can behave passively, aggressively, or assertively.

A QUESTION OF ETHICS ● What Would You Do?

Cassie and Pete have been very lucky. They both have well-paying jobs that they dearly love. Having worked hard and saved money during college, they had enough money to buy a house two years after graduating. Their first home has needed a lot of remodeling, but Cassie and Pete have found that they enjoy working together and learning how to do various projects. So far they have refinished the floors, repaired some drywall, removed the old wallpaper, and repainted every room in the house. Now it is time to tackle the kitchen.

The current kitchen is a mess. The cabinets are scratched, and several doors are loose. The flooring is discolored and coming up in places, and the appliances are from the 1970s. The more they have discussed the kitchen, the more they have found that they disagree on what needs to be done. Pete wants them to tackle the project themselves and believes that they can make the kitchen serviceable by removing the current floor, putting down ceramic tile, painting the current cabinets, and buying new appliances, phasing in the purchases over several years. Cassie, who loves to cook, wants the kitchen to be the centerpiece of the home. She wants to hire a kitchen designer to plan and execute a complete kitchen remodel. Pete adamantly refuses to consider spending the twenty thousand dollars or more that this would take. Having stated his position, Pete considers the conversation over. During

their most recent discussion of the issue, Pete walked out of the room, turned on the TV, and refused to say any more on the matter.

Recently, Cassie decided to take a different approach, asking, "Pete, do you really love me?" to which he replied, "Of course, I love you. Do you really need to ask?"

"Well, I was wondering if for our anniversary, we could take a couple of weeks and go to Europe? It would be expensive, but it would be such a wonderful treat."

"Hey, that's a great idea," Pete replied. "I'll talk to a travel agent tomorrow."

"Well, are you sure?" Cassie asked. "I mean, it's going to cost a lot, since we already used up our frequent flier miles."

"Don't worry, babe. We've got the money in the bank, and you know I only live to make you happy."

"Really," Cassie pounced. "Then why can't we hire a designer and have the kitchen done first-class? You know I hate to travel, but I love to cook. Why are you willing to pay for an expensive trip but not pay for my dream kitchen?"

For Consideration:
1. What ethical issues do Cassie and Pete confront in this situation?
2. Analyze the conversation between Cassie and Pete. Is Cassie's approach an ethical use of interpersonal influence or a manipulative trap?

Assertive messages are based on scripts that include specific communication skills such as owning, doing facework, describing behavior and feelings, and using appropriate nonverbal behaviors.

The appropriateness and form of assertiveness varies with culture. While assertiveness is not valued in some cultures, it is valued in most Western cultures.

Chapter Resources

What You Should Be Able *to Explain:*

- The concept of interpersonal influence
- The concept of interpersonal power
- Six principles of power
- Five types of power
- The concept of persuasion
- The two approaches to processing a persuasive message
- The six heuristics for automatically processing persuasive messages
- The three types of appeals analyzed when extensively processing persuasive messages
- What constitutes passive, aggressive, and assertive messages
- How to create assertive messages

What You Should Be Able *to Do:*

- Make a complaint
- Make a personal request
- Refuse a request

Self-test questions based on these concepts are available on the companion Web site (www.oup.com/us/verderber) as part of Chapter 11 resources.

Key Words

Flashcards for all of these key terms are available on the *Inter-Act* Web site.

Argumentativeness, p. 340
Assertiveness, p. 340
Authority heuristic, p. 332
Central route, p. 330
Claims, p. 334
Coercive power, p. 327
Competence, p. 335
Complaint, p. 342
Consistency heuristic, p. 332
Credibility, p. 335
Elaboration likelihood model (ELM) of persuasion, p. 330

Emotional appeals, p. 336
Evidence, p. 334
Expert power, p. 328
Flaming, p. 340
Interpersonal influence, p. 326
Legitimate power, p. 327
Likability, p. 336
Liking heuristic, p. 332
Passive approach, p. 338
Passive-aggressive behavior, p. 340
Peripheral route, p. 330
Personal requests, p. 344

Persuasion, p. 329
Power, p. 326
Reasons, p. 334
Reciprocity heuristic, p. 331
Referent power, p. 328
Reward power, p. 327
Scarcity heuristic, p. 333
Social proof heuristic, p. 332
Trustworthiness, p. 336
Verbal aggression, p. 339

Apply Your Knowledge

The following activities challenge you to demonstrate your mastery of the concepts, theories, and frameworks in this chapter by using them to explain what is happening in a specific situation.

Inter-Action Dialogue: Interpersonal Influence

11.1 Interpersonal influence occurs when one person attempts to change another person's attitudes or behaviors. As you read the following dialogue, do a line-by-line analysis of this conversation and indicate where you see evidence of the participants exerting power, using heuristics to influence, or providing logical reasons, appeals to credibility, or appeals to emotion as well as instances of responding passively, aggressively, or assertively. You can watch a video of this conversation on the Inter-Act Web site and use a form provided to write down your own analysis of the conversation.

DIALOGUE

Paul's friend Hannah stops by his dorm to show him what she has done.

Hannah: Hey, Paul. Take a look at my term paper.

Paul: *(quickly reading the first page)* Wow, so far this looks great. You must have put a lot of time into it.

Hannah: No, but it should be good. I paid enough for it.

Paul: What?

Hannah: I got it off the Internet.

Paul: You mean you bought it from one of those term paper sites? Hannah, what's up? That's not like you—you're not a cheater.

Hannah: Listen—my life's crazy. I don't have time to write a stupid paper. And besides, everyone does it.

Paul: What's stupid about the assignment?

Hannah: I think the workload in this class is ridiculous. The professor acts as if this is the only class we've got. There are three exams, a team project, and this paper. What's the point?

Paul: Well, I think the professor assigned this paper for several reasons, to see whether students really know how to think about the material they have studied and to help us improve our writing.

Hannah: Come on, we learned how to write when we were in elementary school.

Paul: That's not what I meant. Sure, you can write a sentence or a paragraph, but can you really express your own ideas about this subject? What the professor is doing is putting us in a position where we can show not only our understanding of the material but also our ability to phrase our thoughts in a sophisticated manner. By writing a term paper, we have the chance to develop our own thinking about a topic. We can read a wide variety of sources and then make up our own minds and in our writing explain our thoughts. And the neat thing is, we'll get feedback about how we did.

Hannah: Yes, but you're not listening—I just don't have time.

Paul: So you believe the best way to deal with the situation is to cheat?

Hannah: Man, that's cold. But like I said, I'm not the only one doing this.

Paul: Are you saying that since some people cheat, it's OK for you to cheat? Like people take drugs or sleep around, so it's OK for you?

Hannah: No, don't be silly, but I told you I'm up to here in work. I've got no time.

Paul: Right. So remind me what you did last night.

Hannah: You know. I went to Sean's party. I deserve to have a little social life. I'm only twenty after all.

Paul: Sure, point well taken. So what did you do the night before?

Hannah: Well, I worked until 8:00. Then Mary and I grabbed a bite to eat and then went clubbing.

Paul: So, for two nights you chose to do no schoolwork, but you had time to socialize? And you're saying you're "up to here in work." Hannah, I'm just not buying it. Your workload is no different from mine. And I manage to get my work done. It's not perfect—like your Internet paper. But it's mine. So who do you hurt when you cheat? Besides your own character, you hurt me.

Hannah: Hey, chill. You've made your point. But what can I do now? The paper's due in two days and I haven't even begun.

Paul: Do you have to work tonight?

Hannah: No.

Paul: Well, then you still have time. It will be a couple of long, hard days, but I'll bring you coffee and food.

Hannah: What a friend. Well, OK, I guess you win.

Paul: Hey wait. Let's seal it by tearing up that bought paper.

Hannah: What! You mean I can't even borrow a few ideas from it?

Paul: Hannah!

Hannah: OK. OK. Just kidding.

Skill Practice

Skill practice activities give you the chance to rehearse a new skill by responding to hypothetical or real situations. Additional skill practice activities are available at the companion Web site.

Identifying Heuristic Triggers in Messages

For each of the following messages, identify the heuristic that the sender is using.

11.2 "Well, I've been selling cell phone plans for three years, and I think that Verizon is the way to go if you want to get a smart phone."

Heuristic:

11.3 "I don't know anyone who enjoyed that class. You don't want to take it."

Heuristic:

11.4 "I really want to see you, but I'm leaving tomorrow morning. Can we have dinner together tonight?"

Heuristic:

11.5 "I loved my Zumba exercise class. And we both like exercising to music. You just have to try it. I know you'll love it."

Heuristic:

11.6 "Hey, man. Can I borrow twenty bucks until payday? You know I'd loan it to you if the situation was reversed."

Heuristic:

11.7 "Last time we went out, you didn't mind the fact that Justin came with us. So is it OK if I ask him again?"

Heuristic:

Creating Persuasive Messages

For each of the following situations, develop a message script that uses logical reasoning, credibility, and valid emotional appeals.

11.8 You are going to run in the Relay for Life cancer fundraiser and want to convince your friend to support you with a $25 donation.

Message:

11.9 You are an environmental studies major at college and want to convince your parents to put solar panels on their roof.

Message:

11.10 Your best friend has put on a lot of weight. Because heart disease runs in his family, you're worried about him and want to convince him to stop eating a high-fat diet.

Message:

11.11 You want to study abroad next semester, but your parents, whose help you need to fund the trip, aren't on board. The tuition for the program is about the same as what it would be if you stayed at your college, but there are some additional expenses. You are hoping that a semester abroad will not only improve your language skills, but also give you a leg up on others in the job market when you graduate.

Message:

Assertiveness

For each of the following situations, write an assertive message. Indicate what type of assertion you are making: a complaint, a personal request, or a refusal.

11.12 The woman who works the next shift is consistently five to twenty minutes late, and you can't leave until she gets there, even though you are off the clock and not paid.

Type of Assertion:

Message:

11.13 For five years, you have been a vegan, the only one in your family. Your older sister has invited you to a family dinner to celebrate your mother's sixty-fifth birthday. You'd like to go, but in the past her menus haven't accommodated your diet.

Type of Assertion:

Message:

11.14 Three weeks ago, you took a test in your family communication course, which the instructor has still not graded. She has offered one excuse after another, promising that she will have them for the next class. You have a comprehensive final in this class next week. A few minutes ago, she came into class, again without the tests.

Type of Assertion:

Message:

11.15   As a committed Christian, you are offended when others swear using the name of God or Jesus. You have a new co-worker who swears frequently.

Type of Assertion:

Message:

11.16   At a restaurant, the steak you ordered rare arrives medium well.

Type of Assertion:

Message:

11.17   Your best friend from childhood is getting married in Aruba and has asked you to be in the wedding party. Your friend has indicated that you will have to pay your own expenses. You are struggling to pay your rent and tuition, and you have maxed out your credit cards. In addition, you think destination weddings are selfish because they require friends and family to take vacation time and spend a lot of money going somewhere they might not have chosen to go.

Type of Assertion:

Message:

11.18   You are living rent free with your mom, who has asked you to babysit for your niece so she can go shopping with your sister. After an exhausting week, you had planned to take a nap and then go out with friends.

Type of Assertion:

Message:

11.19   The woman who lives in the apartment next door stops by and asks you to turn your music down as it is disturbing her. It's the middle of the day, and you don't think your music is too loud.

Type of Assertion:

Message:

11.20   You are proud of your yard and spend a lot of time working in it. The people who recently moved in next door have two large dogs. Although they walk their dogs on leashes and pick up after them, you have noticed that both dogs urinate on one of your bushes, which is turning yellow, dropping leaves, and looking sickly.

Type of Assertion:

Message:

11.21   You're out with a group of guys, one of whom points at a man who has just walked into the club and says, "Well, there's one of Tinkerbell's helpers. Everyone else nervously laughs, but you can't even feign amusement.

Type of Assertion:

Message:

11.22   Your roommate is supposed to do the dishes on the nights you cook, and vice versa. You always clean up right away, but your roommate sometimes waits until the next day to take the dishes off the table. Or she stacks them by the sink without even cleaning them off. In the morning, you are the first one up, and it makes you sick to your stomach to walk into the kitchen and smell last night's dinner.

Type of Assertion:

Message:

Interpreting the Opening Dialogue

11.23 Revisit the dialogue at the opening of this chapter. Using the concepts you studied in this chapter, explain Kai and Amber's differing responses to Terrell's request.

Communication Improvement Plan: Influencing Ethically

Would you like to improve your use of the following skills discussed in this chapter?

- Making a complaint
- Making a personal request
- Refusing a request

11.24   Choose the skill(s) you want to work on, and write a communication improvement plan. You can find a communication improvement plan worksheet on our Web site at www.oup.com/us/verderber.

Inter-Act with Media

Television

The Simpsons, episode: "That 90s Show" (2008). Dan Castellaneta, Julie Kavner.

In this flashback episode, Marge and Homer are living together before being married. It is during Marge's college days at Springfield University. Marge's professor, Stefan August, hints that he is romantically interested in her, though she doesn't immediately notice. To soften his presence as an authority, Professor August tells Marge that he is her advisor and not her professor. The professor contends that Marge's romance with high school sweetheart Homer is holding her back. When Marge shares a thoughtful note from Homer in which he says, "I miss you," the professor picks it apart and suggests that because '"I" is the subject and "you," the object,' Homer is expressing his sense of ownership over Marge. Marge shares that Homer is the one who pays for her college tuition. Professor August reinforces his statement about Homer's "ownership" of her. Marge and Homer put their relationship on hold temporarily and, during this time, she dates Professor August. When she learns, however, that he is against marriage, she returns to her relationship with Homer.

IPC Concepts: Interpersonal influence, interpersonal power in relationships, legitimate power, appeals to emotion

To the Point:

> How would you characterize Professor August's ability to use interpersonal power in his relationship with Marge?
> How would you describe Professor August's ability to influence Marge, specifically her relationship with Homer?

Cinema

The King's Speech (2010). Tom Hooper (director). Colin Firth, Geoffrey Rush, Helena Bonham Carter.

As the film opens, Prince Albert, Duke of York (Firth) and heir to the throne of England, is viewed delivering a public speech at the British Empire Exhibition of 1925. He has a severe stutter and is not only visibly uncomfortable giving his speech, but also causes ripples of uneasiness to ebb through his audience. Determined to rid himself of this speech impediment, the duke experiments with several treatments until his wife (Bonham Carter) arranges for an appointment with Lionel Logue (Rush), an Australian speech therapist. In their first official meeting, Logue informs the duke that he will be calling him by his nickname, Bertie, which is a breach of royal etiquette. Bertie is offended and clearly reluctant to receive treatment from this unorthodox doctor, so Logue makes him a bet. He claims that the duke is already capable of reading perfectly at that very moment. To prove this point, Logue asks the duke to read a passage from Hamlet while wearing headphones playing loud music. Logue makes a vinyl recording of the experiment. After attempting the reading, the duke is puzzled and frustrated because the headphones made it impossible for him to hear his own speaking. Logue gives him the recording as a keepsake and the duke leaves even more convinced that he is a hopeless case.

However, while at home, Bertie plays Logue's recording and hears himself making an unbroken recitation of Shakespeare. Bertie returns to Logue's treatment where he speaks more freely about the pressures and anxieties of being in the royal family. Logue and the duke develop a strong interpersonal relationship.

IPC Concepts: Interpersonal influence, interpersonal power in relationships

To the Point:

> How would you characterize Logue's ability to influence Bertie?
> How would you describe the role of interpersonal power in their interpersonal relationship?

What's on the Web

Find links and additional material, including self-quizzes, on the companion Web site at www.oup.com/us/verderber.

12
Managing Conflict

"Good morning, class. I hope that all of you had a good weekend. Today I had promised that we would review for the test, but I think that it would be better if we just continued on and dove into discussing the new novel that you were to have read a quarter of for today."

"Hey, wait a minute. That's not fair. I don't know about anyone else, Professor Boren, but I was counting on the review to help me focus my study time," Terrell loudly protested as he looked around for others' support.

"I'm with Terrell, Professor Boren. I really need the review, and you promised!" added Maria.

"Well, how about this?" Professor Boren offered. "Why don't I make up a study sheet and post it on the class Web site? I'll even make a list of the topics that might be covered as essays."

"That would be really helpful. Thank you for going out of your way for us. How soon would it be convenient for you post it?" asked Kai.

"How about tomorrow afternoon?" Professor Boren answered.

"I had planned to study tonight," Louisa complained. "And I really wanted the chance to ask you some questions."

"I see your point, Louisa, so I'll tell you what. I'm willing to hold an extra office hour right after class to answer any questions you might have," Professor Boren responded, adding, "Kai, you look concerned. Is the new plan OK with you?"

"I can see that the rest of the class and you are fine with it, so I'm OK with it, too," Kai consented in a quiet voice, averting her eyes.

"Well," Professor Boren replied, breaking into a big smile. "Now that's settled, let's talk about the opening lines of this book."

What you should be able *to explain* after you have studied this chapter:

- The concept of interpersonal conflict
- The six types of conflict
- Five conflict styles
- Face negotiation theory
- Destructive conflict patterns

- How to skillfully initiate, respond to, and mediate conflict
- How to repair relationships damaged by conflict
- How to manage the dark side of ditigal communication

What you should be able *to do* after you have studied this chapter:

- Skillfully initiate a conflict
- Describe a conflict in terms of behavior, consequences, and feelings
- Skillfully respond to a conflict
- Mediate a conflict
- Apologize effectively

Interpersonal conflict—disagreement between two interdependent people who perceive that they have incompatible goals.

Sometimes in our relationships, we find ourselves in serious conflicts over core issues; at other times, our conflicts occur over mundane, day-to-day issues, such as the one that Professor Boren had with his class in the opening dialog. In either case, how we choose to deal with conflict will affect our relationships. **Interpersonal conflict** may be defined broadly as disagreement between two interdependent people who perceive that they have incompatible goals (Guerrero, Andersen, & Afifi, 2007, p. 307).

Conflict is neither good nor bad. Although it can damage people and relationships, it can also help expose important issues and develop learning, creativity, trust, and openness (Brake, Walker, & Walker, 1995). We may not like verbal conflict, yet in American culture it is viewed as a normal part of any relationship. In other cultures, especially in collectivist cultures, verbal conflict is viewed as dysfunctional to relationships and damaging to social face (Ting-Toomey, 2006). Whether conflict hurts or strengthens a relationship ultimately depends on how those involved deal with it. Since conflict is inevitable, it should be managed in ways that are both culturally and interpersonally appropriate so that you maintain the relationship while satisfying the goals of both you and your partner. Understanding conflict and developing conflict management skills will make you a more effective interpersonal communicator, able to deal with conflict episodes in your relationships.

In this chapter we begin by looking at the six types of interpersonal conflict. Next, we discuss the five communication styles that people use to manage conflict. Then we describe how face is negotiated during conflicts and the importance of this in collectivist cultures. With this understanding in mind, we describe destructive conflict patterns that damage relationships. Then we introduce guidelines for effective conflict management, including how to initiate, respond to, and mediate interpersonal conflicts. We end the chapter by discussing how to repair relationships that have been damaged by conflict.

Types of Interpersonal Conflict

Conflicts generally fall into one of the following six broad categories: pseudoconflict, fact conflict, value conflict, policy conflict, ego conflict, and metaconflict.

1. **Pseudoconflict.** A **pseudoconflict** is disagreement that is caused by a perceptual difference between partners and is easily resolved. Pseudoconflicts usually occur in three situations: when communication partners ascribe different meanings to words; when partners have goals or needs that appear to be incompatible; and when one partner badgers (teases, taunts, mocks) the other. Pseudoconflicts can be resolved through paraphrasing to elucidate word meaning, clarifying goals, and asserting boundaries for appropriate teasing.

   Pseudoconflict—disagreement that is caused by a perceptual difference between partners and is easily resolved.

2. **Fact Conflict.** Simple or **fact conflict** is disagreement caused by a dispute over the truth or accuracy of an item of information. These conflicts can be resolved by consulting an external source. If you find yourself in a fact conflict, suggest to your partner that together you consult a source that can verify what is true or accurate.

   Fact conflict—disagreement that is caused by a dispute over the truth or accuracy of an item of information.

3. **Value Conflict.** A **value conflict** is a disagreement caused by differences in partners' deep-seated moral beliefs. Conflict stemming from differences in value systems can be difficult to resolve, and at times we must simply be content to respect each other but agree to disagree.

   Value conflict—disagreement caused by differences in partners' deep-seated moral beliefs.

4. **Policy Conflict.** A **policy conflict** is a disagreement caused by differences over a preferred plan or course of action. Given that both culture and situation determine what is perceived to be an appropriate policy, this type of conflict is common in most relationships. Because policy conflicts are based on highly personal considerations, there is no "right" or "wrong" way to resolve them; the best policy depends on what both parties feel personally comfortable with and agree to.

   Policy conflict—disagreement caused by differences over a preferred plan or course of action.

Conflicts in which values or egos are at issue often escalate. How can we manage conflicts of these types?

Ego conflict—disagreement that results when both parties insist on being the "winner" of the argument to confirm their self-concept or self-esteem.

Metaconflict—disagreement over the process of communication itself during an argument.

5. **Ego Conflict.** An **ego conflict** is a disagreement that results when both parties insist on being the "winner" of the argument to confirm their self-concept or self-esteem. When both people already engaged in a conflict see it as a measure of who they are, what they know, how competent they are, or how much power they have, an ego conflict may accompany and complicate other types of conflict. Ego conflicts can develop when one or both partners to a conflict make personal, negative, judgmental statements prompting them to ignore the central disagreement to defend themselves.

6. **Metaconflict.** **Metaconflict** is a disagreement over the process of communication itself during an argument (Guerrero et al., 2007). It is conflict about the conflict. In a metaconflict, we may accuse our partner of pouting, nagging, name-calling, not listening, showing too much emotion, fighting unfairly, or a variety of other negative behaviors related to the conflict communication process. Once we introduce metaconflict into the conversation, we then have two conflict issues to address: the original area of incompatibility and the conflict process itself. Metaconflict complicates our interpersonal communication, making it more difficult to find a satisfactory resolution to our conflict.

Styles of Managing Interpersonal Conflict

Think about the last time you experienced a conflict. How did you react? Did you try to avoid it? Did you give in? Did you force the other person to accept your will? Did you compromise, getting part of what you wanted and giving the other person part of what he or she wanted? Or did the two of you find a solution with which you were both completely satisfied? These styles differ in the amount of cooperation and assertiveness the participants display. The extent to which we are willing to cooperate when managing a conflict depends on how important we believe the relationship and the issue are to us. We each have one or two styles of conflict that are our default way of behaving, but if we are mindful, we can use other styles when they are more appropriate. Let's take a closer look at five different

LEARN ABOUT YOURSELF ● Conflict Management

Take this short survey to learn something about yourself. This is a test of your conflict management style. Answer the questions honestly based on your first response. There are no right or wrong answers. For each of the following state-ments, select one of the numbers to the right that best describes your behavior:

_____ 1. I try to avoid conflicts whenever possible.

_____ 2. I will give up my own desires to end a conflict.

_____ 3. It is important to win an argument.

_____ 4. I am willing to compromise to solve a conflict.

_____ 5. It is important to discuss both people's point of view in a conflict.

_____ 6. I am stubborn in holding to my position in a conflict.

_____ 7. In conflicts, I give up some points in exchange for other points.

_____ 8. I try to avoid conflicts.

_____ 9. I give in to others during conflict.

_____ 10. It is important to regard conflicts as problems to be solved together.

_____ 11. I strongly assert my views in a conflict.

_____ 12. I withdraw from disagreements.

_____ 13. I try to find the middle-ground position in a conflict.

_____ 14. I will give in to the other person to end an argument.

_____ 15. I try to be cooperative and creative in finding a resolution to a conflict.

1 = Always
2 = Often
3 = Sometimes
4 = Rarely
5 = Never

Scoring the survey: Add your scores for Items 1, 8, and 12. Your score will range from 3 to 15. The lower (closer to 3) your score, the more you tend to use with-drawal as a conflict management style.

Add your scores for Items 2, 9, and 14. Your score will range from 3 to 15. The lower (closer to 3) your score, the more you tend to use the accommodating style of conflict management.

Add your scores for Items 3, 6, and 11. Your score will range from 3 to 15. The lower (closer to 3) your score, the more you tend to use the forcing style of conflict management.

Add your scores for Items 4, 7, and 13. Your score will range from 3 to 15. The lower (closer to 3) your score, the more you tend to use the compromising style of con-flict management.

Add your scores for Items 5, 10, and 15. Your score will range from 3 to 15. The lower (closer to 3) your score, the more you tend to use the collaborating style of conflict management.

TABLE 12.1 Styles of Conflict Management

Approach	Characteristics	Goal	Outlook
WITHDRAWING	Uncooperative Unassertive	To keep from dealing with conflict	"I don't want to talk about it."
ACCOMMODATING	Cooperative Unassertive	To keep from upsetting the other person	"Getting my way isn't as important as keeping the peace."
FORCING	Uncooperative Assertive	To get my way	"I'll get my way regardless of what I have to do."
COMPROMISING	Partially cooperative Partially assertive	To get partial satisfaction	"I'll get part of what I want and other people also have part of what they want."
COLLABORATING	Cooperative Assertive	To solve the problem together	"Let's talk this out and find the best solution for both of us."

styles: withdrawing, accommodating, forcing, compromising, and collaborating (Thomas, 1976). As you read through this section, you can refer to Table 12.1, which summarizes the characteristics, goals, and outlooks of each conflict management style.

Withdrawing

Certainly one of the easiest ways to deal with conflict is to withdraw. **Withdrawing** is resolving a conflict by physically or psychologically removing yourself from the conversation. This style is both uncooperative and unassertive because at least one person involved in the conflict refuses to talk about the issue at all. A person may withdraw physically by leaving the site or psychologically withdraw by ignoring what the other person is saying.

Withdrawing—resolving a conflict by physically or psychologically removing yourself from the conversation.

From an individual satisfaction standpoint, withdrawing creates a lose/lose situation because neither party to the conflict really accomplishes what he or she wants. Withdrawing from a conflict provides a temporary escape from a potentially uncomfortable situation, but in an ongoing relationship, the issue will come up again. Meanwhile, your partner experiences frustration on two levels: Not only does the conflict not get resolved, but also your partner feels ignored and slighted. Recurring withdrawal hurts relationships in at least two ways. First, conflict eventually resurfaces and is usually more difficult to resolve at that time (Roloff & Cloven, 1990). Second, withdrawal leads to "mulling behavior," stewing over issues and behaviors to the point where they become bigger than they actually are. This can generate enduring ill feelings about the relationship.

What motivates people to withdraw? What's lost as a result?

Although habitually withdrawing from a conflict can result in dissatisfying relationships, withdrawing may be an appropriate style in at least three circumstances. First, withdrawal can be appropriate when neither the relationship nor the issue is really important to you. Second, when an issue is unimportant to you but the relationship is important, you might simply choose to hide your objections to your partner's position and go along with what he or she says, which can have a positive effect on your relationship (Caughlin & Golish, 2002). Third, withdrawing permits a temporary disengagement allowing you to check your strong emotional reactions. If both an issue and a relationship are important to you, you may find that temporarily withdrawing from the argument allows you to calm down and renew the discussion at a later time when you are able to approach the issue with a clear head.

Accommodating

Accommodating is resolving a conflict by satisfying the other person's needs or accepting the other person's ideas while neglecting one's own needs or ideas. This approach is cooperative but unassertive. It preserves friendly relationships but fails to protect your personal rights. When we feel insecure with others, we may accommodate to ensure that we don't lose the relationship. Considered from an individual satisfaction standpoint, accommodating creates a lose/win situation. When you accommodate, you choose to lose while you give in to what your partner wants. From a relational satisfaction standpoint, habitual accommodation creates two problems. First, accommodation may lead to poor decision making because you do not voice important facts, arguments, and positions that might lead to a better decision. Second, habitual accommodation risks damaging your self-concept and making you resentful, which can undermine the very relationship you were hoping to maintain.

There are also situations, of course, in which accommodating is appropriate and effective. When an issue is not important to you but the relationship is, accommodating is the best style. It may also be useful to accommodate from time to time to build "social credits" or goodwill that you can draw on later.

Forcing

Forcing is resolving a conflict by satisfying your own needs or advancing your own ideas with no concern for the needs or ideas of the other person or for the relationship. Forcing is uncooperative but assertive. You are forcing when you coerce, manipulate, or verbally or physically threaten someone to get your way. If your partner accommodates, the conflict episode ends. If, however, your partner also responds by forcing, your

Accommodating—resolving a conflict by satisfying the other person's needs or accepting the other person's ideas while neglecting one's own needs or ideas.

Forcing—resolving a conflict by satisfying one's own needs or advancing one's own ideas with no concern for the needs or ideas of the other person or for the relationship.

conflict escalates. Forcing creates an "I win/you lose" situation. You may win the conflict episode and get your way, but at your partner's expense. From a relational satisfaction standpoint, any episode of forcing usually hurts a relationship, at least in the short term. If forcing is your preferred style, you are likely to have trouble maintaining relationships that are healthy for you and your partner.

There are circumstances when forcing is an effective means of resolving conflict that does not damage a relationship. In emergencies, when quick and decisive action must be taken to ensure safety or minimize harm, forcing is useful. Firefighters, paramedics, and police officers, for example, use this style during crises to ensure the safety of others.

Compromising

Compromising is resolving a conflict by bargaining so that each partner's needs or interests are partially satisfied. With this approach, both you and your partner give up part of what you really want or believe, or trade one thing you want or believe, to get something else. Compromising is an intermediate between assertiveness and cooperativeness: Both you and your partner have to be somewhat assertive and somewhat cooperative, and both of you end up partially satisfied. From an individual satisfaction standpoint, compromising creates neither a lose/lose nor a win/win situation because you both lose something even as you win something else. From a relational satisfaction standpoint, compromise may be seen as neutral to positive since each partner is satisfied to some extent. Compromising is appropriate when the issue is moderately important, when there are time constraints, and when attempts at forcing or collaborating have not been successful. Although compromising is a popular and at least partially satisfying conflict management style, significant problems can be associated with it. Of special concern is the possibility that you may trade away a better solution to reach a compromise.

Compromising—resolving a conflict by bargaining so that each partner's needs or interests are partially satisfied.

Collaborating

Collaborating is resolving a conflict by using problem solving to arrive at a solution that meets the needs and interests of both parties in the conflict. Treating your disagreement as a problem to be solved, you and your partner discuss the issues, describe your feelings, and identify the characteristics of an effective solution. Collaborating is assertive and cooperative, assertive because you both voice your concerns, cooperative because you both work together to find a resolution.

From an individual satisfaction standpoint, collaborating creates a win/win scenario because the needs of both partners are met completely. From a relational satisfaction standpoint, collaboration is positive because you both feel heard. You get to share ideas, weighing and considering information in a way that satisfies both of you individually and strengthens your relationship as a result.

Collaborating—resolving a conflict by using problem solving to arrive at a solution that meets the needs and interests of both parties in the conflict.

Using Problem Solving to Collaborate

Managing conflict through collaboration requires some of the communication skills we have discussed in earlier chapters. For example, you must use accurate and precise language to describe your ideas and feelings, and you must empathetically listen to your partner's ideas and feelings. In addition, you will need to

Joint problem solving is a collaborative activity. Can you think of a time when you solved a problem with the help of someone else?

follow five problem-solving steps: (1) define the problem: what's the issue being considered?; (2) analyze the problem: what are the causes and symptoms of the issue?; (3) develop mutually acceptable criteria for judging solutions: what goals will a good solution attain?; (4) generate solutions and alternative solutions: what do you think about this idea, and what is another approach you could take if that other idea doesn't work?; and (5) select the solution or solutions that best meet the criteria identified: what do you say we go with this solution and that one, too, since we both seem to agree that these are the most realistic ones?

Let's apply these five steps to a conflict example: Justina and Eduardo are a young couple whose financial situation is precarious. Justina is worried that they may have to declare bankruptcy. Eduardo thinks that things are difficult but that they can manage. Because this issue is important to them both and because they really love each other, they sit down to talk things over. They begin by listening to each other's position, defining and analyzing the problem. Justina describes the threat she has received from the landlord about possible eviction if the rent checks continue to be late, and she expresses her anxiety about not paying the other bills on time. Eduardo may remind her that money is tight because he recently took a pay cut to start a new job with more potential. From this baseline, they can work together, creating a list of guidelines or criteria for a solution acceptable to them both. Justina asks that the solution allow them to pay bills on time, whereas Eduardo wants any option they pursue to lower their monthly costs. Once they have agreed on these two criteria, Justina might propose that they save money by eating out only once a month and using Netflix rather than going to movies. Eduardo might suggest

INTER-ACT WITH SOCIAL MEDIA

Think about the last time you attempted to manage a conflict through social media. Did you use Facebook, Skype, text messaging, or another device? Think about those interactions and, if possible, examine the texts or Facebook postings. How would you characterize your conflict style when you communicate through social media? Do you tend to manage conflict differently through social media compared to face-to-face communication? Explain.

that they have a yard sale and use the proceeds as a cushion that would allow them to pay bills on time, replenishing it when they get their paychecks. Once they have a satisfying list of options that they can both live with, they can then complete the collaborative problem-solving process by selecting the solution or solutions on which they agree. They might decide to go with three of the four ideas they came up with, such as paying more than the minimum credit card balances, eating out only once a month but still going to the movies occasionally, and having the yard sale.

Collaboration is hard work. When you and your partner commit to trying, however, chances are that through discussion you can arrive at creative solutions that meet your needs while simultaneously strengthening your relationship. As stated earlier, no single conflict style is best; all five are useful in some settings. Developing behavioral flexibility will allow you not only to use your couple of default modes, but also to switch between styles. In so doing, you will be able to competently handle the situations you face. As we will see next, an effective conflict style also depends on cultural considerations.

Face Negotiation in Conflict

Face—how we want our partners and other who are present to view us, our public self-image.

Each conflict style affects both your partner's and your **face**, how we want our partners and others who are present to view us, our public self-image. In any interaction, either partner can grant face to the other or cause him or her to lose face. We can fight for our face or the face of others, or we can be presented with it as a gift (Augsburger, 1992). Thus, in addition to managing a resolution to a conflict, we are also negotiating issues of face. In fact, loss of face can be more damaging to relationships than ineffective conflict resolution of a particular issue. For example, when Cindy arrived fifteen minutes after the morning team meeting had already begun, her manager confronted her in front of everyone, threatening, "The next time you are late, I will write you up. " The humiliation of this direct and public verbal reprimand was exacerbated by the manager adding that since Cindy was on salary she was "stealing" from the company when she was late. As someone who prided herself on her honesty, Cindy was devastated and immediately considered applying for a transfer to a different department.

Cultural Differences in the Meaning of Face

Face in Western Hemisphere cultures—the public self-image that you claim for yourself in a social situation or relationship that generally corresponds to your private self-image.

Self-face orientation—the inclination to uphold and protect our self-image in our interactions with others.

To complicate matters, the concept of face has different meanings for different cultural groups. **Face in Western Hemisphere cultures** (that are individualist and low context in their orientations) is the public self-image that you claim for yourself in social situations and relationships that generally corresponds to your private self-image (Augsburger, 1992). With individualist values and independent self-concepts, people in these cultures tend to take a self-face orientation to conflict focusing on their "rights"(Ting-Toomey & Kurogi, 1998). A **self-face orientation** is the inclination to uphold and protect our self-image in our interactions with others. If Cindy, for example, has a self-face orientation to conflict, she may perceive her manager's tirade as a direct attack on her self-esteem, which she might protect with her own forcing response, exclaiming: "Well, you don't have to worry about me stealing anymore. I don't need this abuse. I quit."

Face in Eastern and Southern Hemisphere cultures (that are collectivist and high context in their orientation) includes the public self-images of others who may be affected by the situation or relationship as well as your own self-image (Augsburger, 1992). People from these cultures value the group and have interdependent self-concepts that result in an other- or mutual-face orientation. An **other-face orientation** is the inclination to uphold and protect the self-images of our partners and other people affected by the conflict even at the risk of our own face. A **mutual-face orientation** is the inclination to uphold and protect others' self-images as well as our own when interacting in a conflict setting. Both other-face and mutual-face orientation focus on our responsibilities to the group (Ting-Toomey & Kurogi, 1998). If Cindy is other-face oriented, she may apologize to the manager and group for her selfish behavior. If she has a mutual-face orientation, she will apologize but might provide her reason for being late as a way to save her own face.

Face Negotiation Theory

Face negotiation theory proposes that in conflict settings we prefer conflict styles consistent with our cultural frame and the resulting face orientations (Ting-Toomey & Kurogi, 1998, and Ting-Toomey & Chung, 2005). According to this theory, those of us from individualist cultures are likely to have a self-face orientation. We also approach conflict from a low-context perspective, creating messages that tend to be issue- not group- oriented. Collaborating or forcing is our default style, as these both serve our self-face interests and can resolve the issue in a way that we can agree on. When we collaborate, we may chafe at the time it takes to reach consensus, but we feel ownership and pride in a resolution that was not imposed on us. When we successfully force our will on others, we feel good about ourselves because we have stood up for our rights. Because the fact that we may have damaged the face of our partner doesn't really enter our consciousness, we can be surprised when our victory damages our relationships. Cindy's response to her manager's public reprimand, "Well, you don't have to worry about me stealing anymore. I don't need this abuse. I quit," was her way of protecting her face and asserting her rights. Recounting this incident later, she may even say, "Well, I showed him, he had no *right* to talk to me that way, especially in front of my colleagues." Her spur-of-the-moment resignation probably caught her manager totally off guard. Reflecting on what happened, he might not even consider that his tirade shredded Cindy's face needs. Instead, he may rationalize his behavior by concluding that Cindy was just a disgruntled employee.

On the other hand, those of us who come from a collectivist culture probably have an other- or mutual-face orientation. Approaching conflict from a high-context and often high-power distance orientation, we sometimes believe that our responsibilities to others supersede our own rights. Our default style to any conflict is avoiding. When conflict can't be avoided, we will accommodate with those of higher status, force with those of lower status, and compromise with

Face in Eastern and Southern Hemisphere cultures—the public self-images of others who may be affected by the situation or relationship as well as your own self-image.

Other-face orientation—the inclination to uphold and protect the self-images of our partners and other people affected by the conflict even at the risk of our own face.

Mutual-face orientation—the inclination to uphold and protect others' self-images as well as our own when interacting in a conflict setting.

Face negotiation theory—a theory positing that in conflict settings we prefer conflict styles consistent with our cultural frame and the resulting face orientations.

our peers. If an issue is important to the collective, we prefer collaborating, considering the time it takes to reach consensus a wise investment. If this is Cindy's cultural background, she is likely other-face oriented or mutual-face oriented. Believing her lateness had selfishly inconvenienced her peers and disappointed her manager; she would experience acute shame and embarrassment, feelings that would motivate her apologetic response. Although she might find her manager's remarks exceedingly harsh, she would blame herself for having caused him to act in this way. As her colleagues would consider his direct and public reprimand rude, she would shamefully perceive her tardiness to have caused both her and her manager to lose face. Consequently, she would accommodate, apologizing to the group and her manager, an act of self-deprecation that would help her regain face if these people share her cultural values.

Face Negotiation and Conflict Styles in American Co-cultural Groups

As part of a multiethnic society with a variety of co-cultural groups, Americans often encounter people whose conflict resolution style differs from their own. The more that members of an ethic group identify with their culture, the more likely they are to see conflict through their particular cultural lens. You can be more effective at resolving conflict with people who identify with a different ethnic group if you understand that they are working to resolve the conflict in what for them is the culturally appropriate way. With this understanding, you can attempt to align your behavior with theirs and work toward a win-win collaborative solution. Let's look at how people who subscribe to dominant American, African American, Asian American, and Latin American cultures approach conflict.

The dominant American culture has historically reflected White European values and orientations. Those of us who identify with the dominant American culture seek to achieve a solution to the conflict issues and are insensitive to processes that will maintain the relationship. Some of us also work hard to control our emotions during conflict and adopt an analytical, neutral tone in our conflict messages (Ting-Toomey, 1985, 1986).

African American conflict styles are influenced by both the collectivist and high-power distance values of African culture and the individualist values of the dominant American culture. Within the family or community, younger African Americans are likely to accommodate older or more respected family members, giving them their "propers." In other circumstances, the typical African American mode of conflict is assertive, forcing, and emotionally expressive, which stems from not only the ethnic cultural background, but also from reactions to our shared history of racism. Because of the long history of racism and oppression, African Americans are very sensitive to loss of face. As a result, doing both positive and negative facework is important when working through a conflict with African Americans who strongly identify with their co-culture. In addition, you should recognize that an upfront, animated style is a cultural norm, not a sign of aggression (Ting-Toomey & Chung, 2005).

Asian American conflict styles reflect the collectivist, high-context cultures of their ethnic heritage, influenced by Confucianism, a philosophy that values collective face-saving. Asian Americans who strongly identify with their co-culture are likely to use avoiding and accommodating styles of conflict management. With important issues, these Asian Americans may seek the help of a respected third party to mediate the conflict. Asian Americans who identify more with the dominant American culture favor collaborating for managing conflict (Ting-Toomey, Oetzel, & Yee-Jung, 2001).

Hispanic or Latino/a American values are collectivist with high-power distance, cultural norms that dictate an other-face orientation. When the conflict is of little or no importance, Latinos who identify with the co-culture will use avoidance and accommodation as their default strategies. When, however, the conflict is important and their partner is of equal or lower status, Latinos who identify with the co-culture are more likely to use an emotionally animated, forcing style than Latinos who do not strongly identify with the co-culture (Garcia, 1996; Ting-Toomey Oetzel, & Yee-Jung, 2001).

In conflict situations, people may behave in accord with their co-cultural norms, or they may not. Nevertheless, you will be more effective at resolving interpersonal conflict if you are mindful that your partner's orientation toward conflict and her or his expectations for facework may differ from your own.

Destructive Conflict Patterns

As we stated at the beginning of this chapter, conflict is a fact of life in any relationship. It can be beneficial, drawing you and your partners closer together, or it can damage or end your relationships. Conflict that seriously damages relationships usually follows the **principle of negative reciprocity**, the proposition that we repay negative treatment with negative treatment. Similarly, the **principle of positive reciprocity** is the proposition that we repay positive treatment with positive treatment. In a conflict conversation, it is easy to fall into a back-and-forth pattern of answering one partner's hurtful message with another, a spiraling vortex of negative reciprocity. When this occurs, the likelihood of successfully resolving the conflict decreases as the likelihood that our relationship will be damaged increases. Furthermore, conflicts that follow patterns of negative reciprocity damage our physical and mental well-being (Roloff & Reznik, 2008). Notice that what causes the damage is not a single message but rather the tendency to reciprocate a negative message in what becomes a pattern of interaction. A number of these patterns can occur when we disagree with our partners. Let's look at five of the most common: serial arguing, counterblaming, cross-complaining, demand-withdrawal, and mutual hostility.

Serial Arguing

Most of us have experienced **serial arguing**, a conflict pattern in which partners argue about the same issue two or more times (Roloff & Johnson, 2002). In serial arguing, both partners are focused on the issue but disagree about how it should

Principle of negative reciprocity—the proposition that we repay negative treatment with negative treatment.

Principle of positive reciprocity—the proposition that we repay positive treatment with positive treatment.

Serial arguing—a conflict pattern in which partners argue about the same issue two or more times.

be resolved, exchanging messages that either defend their position or attack their partner's. As these conversations end without resolving the differences between partners, the issue has to be reargued when it comes up again. For example, newlyweds Michaela and Brant have a reccurring argument about Brant's participation in three evening basketball leagues that he had been playing in before he knew Michaela. Since their engagement, she has been arguing with him, urging him to give up at least one league. About once a month as Brant prepares to leave for a game, Michaela initiates this argument by telling Brant that it is not normal for a married man to spend so many evenings away from home playing ball with the guys. The back-and-forth arguing usually ends in Michaela crying and Brant stomping out of their apartment, returning long after Michaela is in bed. As you can see, this pattern of conflict is unlikely to be resolved unless one or both partners do something to break the pattern.

Counterblaming

Counterblaming—a conflict pattern in which you blame your partner for what he or she has accused you of doing, shifting responsibility and leaving the original issue unresolved.

A second destructive conflict pattern, **counterblaming**, is a conflict pattern in which you blame your partner for being the cause of what he or she has accused you of doing, shifting responsibility and leaving the original issue unresolved. Instead of resolving an argument, counterblaming only escalates a back-and-forth series of attacks. For example, suppose that Nicole says to her sister Stacey, "I can't believe you just took my new black skirt and wore it without asking." Here Stacey should respond to the issue at hand (unauthorized borrowing) by defending herself: "But you said I could always borrow anything from you," or she might apologize for what she did: "I'm sorry, but I needed something nice to wear to work." If, however, Stacey replies, "Well, it's your own fault, I would not have had to borrow your skirt for work today if you had done the laundry like you promised," she is counterblaming. Nicole may either respond appropriately, "Stacey, the issue is not why you needed to borrow the skirt, but that you did it without asking me," or she may take the bait and also counterblame: "I couldn't do the laundry because you didn't buy any laundry detergent when you went shopping, as usual." And Stacey may reciprocate Nicole's negativity: "Well, duh, how can I know that we need detergent when you don't bother to put it on the shopping list?" Notice how a counterblaming exchange strays further and further away from the original issue.

Cross-complaining

Cross-complaining—a conflict pattern in which partners trade unrelated criticisms, leaving the initial issue unresolved.

Similar to counterblaming, **cross-complaining** is a conflict pattern in which partners trade *unrelated* criticisms, leaving the initial issue unresolved. For example, Mia, irritated by her roommate Sasha for not putting his dishes in the dishwasher, says to him, "Sasha, I really get annoyed when I come home at night and your breakfast dishes are still on the counter. Is it asking too much for you to rinse them off and put them in the dishwasher?" If Sasha's reply is, "Well, look who's talking, Miss-Can't-Put-the-Cap-on-the-Toothpaste," he is cross-complaining. At this point, the subject of the conversation will shift to the toothpaste cap, or Mia may offer a different cross-complaint.

Demand-Withdrawal

The demand-withdrawal pattern can become a recurring pattern of conflict communication in long-term relationships (Caughlin & Huston, 2006). **Demand-withdrawal** is a conflict pattern in which one partner consistently demands while the other consistently withdraws. Typically, the person in the demanding position tends to be the less powerful and dissatisfied partner in the relationship, whereas the person in the withdrawing position is more powerful and happy with the status quo (Sagrestano, Heavey, & Christensen, 2006). If one person constantly demands to resolve a conflict while the other consistently ignores those demands, the result is an unhealthy escalation with no chance of resolution. For instance, imagine that Angelina, who is concerned about her husband's weight, introduces the topic by saying, "Kevin, I don't want to hurt your feelings, but you really need to lose a few pounds. It's not good for your health to be overweight. It's all the pop you drink and the bedtime snacks." Kevin, acting as though he did not hear a word Angelina has said, looks up from the computer and says, "Hey, we could get a great deal on a digital camera on eBay." He has met her demand with a withdrawal. If she switches topics, the issue of Kevin's weight may become fodder for a serial argument pattern in the relationship. Angelina may escalate, however, responding, "Kevin, quit with the eBay stuff. I'm talking to you. You need to lose weight while you're still young and it's relatively easy." Kevin may also escalate his withdrawal by getting up and walking out of the room in an attempt to end this episode. Angelina may follow him out of the room, yelling at his back more arguments about the relationship of health to weight until he stomps into the bathroom and slams the door. Since the issue really hasn't been discussed, Angelina is likely to raise it again.

> **Demand-withdrawal**—a conflict pattern in which one partner consistently demands while the other consistently withdraws.

Mutual Hostility Pattern

Perhaps the conflict pattern most damaging to relationships and to partners' self-esteem is **mutual hostility**, a conflict pattern in which partners trade increasingly louder verbal abuse, including inappropriate, unrelated personal criticism, name-calling, swearing, and sarcasm. Sometimes called "fighting," the pattern begins when one person interjects a hostile comment into a conflict conversation, which the other partner matches with one of his or her own. The longer this pattern continues, the more likely the conversation is to degenerate into hateful and bitter messages that can permanently damage a relationship as well as the mental and physical health of both participants (Roloff & Reznik, 2008). Most of us find conflict episodes that deteriorate into exchanges of mutual hostilities painful and shameful. We are hurt by our partner's comments and ashamed of the verbal abuse we inflict. Learning how to avoid and break patterns of destructive conflict can make us feel better about ourselves and our partners, while maintaining our personal health and the health of our relationships. Although destructive patterns are hard to break, we can learn strategies and skills for more effective conflict conversations.

> **Mutual hostility**—a conflict pattern in which partners trade increasingly louder verbal abuse, including inappropriate, unrelated personal criticism, name-calling, swearing, and sarcasm.

Guidelines for Effective Conflict Management

This section begins by identifying several recommendations to help you break a negative reciprocity cycle. Then we will describe how you can use the message skills learned in earlier chapters to create collaborative conflict conversations. Finally, we will discuss how you can repair relationships damaged by conflict.

Breaking Patterns of Destructive Conflict

You will recall that conflict can spiral into destructive patterns of negative reciprocity. Several strategies exist for breaking these negative patterns, including the following guidelines (Roloff & Reznik, 2008).

1. Avoid Negative Start-ups. The best way to break the cycle is not to start it in the first place. You can accomplish this in two ways. First, if you have developed a negative pattern with someone, have a conversation in which you set **ground rules**, mutually agreed on rules for behavior during conflict episodes. Examples of ground rules include no name-calling, no profanity or swearing, no interrupting, no walking out, paraphrasing your partner's comments before adding your own thoughts, and so forth. Ground rules are effective because both you and your partner agree to abide by them, so give the other person permission to remind you if you break a ground rule.

A second way you can avoid negative start-ups is to allow for some time to pass after the trigger incident and before the discussion. For example, Sarah and Katie Beth are sisters who go to the same college 200 miles away from their home. They share a car and drive back and forth for long weekends and vacations. Sarah prefers to do the driving because it keeps her from getting carsick. Katie Beth understands this but thinks that Sarah drives too fast. The last few times the girls have driven home or back to school, they have ended up in a big argument. Last time it was so bad that they didn't speak for two weeks. Katie Beth, dreading the trip home at Thanksgiving, wants to avoid the demand-withdrawal pattern that characterizes their arguments during the trips. So three weeks before they are scheduled to leave for home, she calls Sarah and asks her to meet for coffee to discuss this issue and hopefully find a solution they both can live with. By removing the discussion from the actual trip, Katie is hoping that they can find a win-win solution.

2. Manage Anger. The negative reciprocity spiral is usually fueled by the anger of one or both participants. So, managing your own and your partner's hostility can help. In conflict we often express our anger in ways that make our partners defensive. To protect themselves, partners often respond with angry messages of their own or by withdrawing. Two approaches can break this cycle.

First, during a conflict conversation if you find your anger getting in the way of working cooperatively with your partner, take a break. Saying something like, "Excuse me, but I need to step back and get my emotions under control. I'd like to continue our conversation when I can be rational. So let's take a five- (or ten-, or twenty-, etc.) minute break while I regroup." Asking for breathing

Ground rules—mutually agreed on rules for behavior during conflict episodes.

room can give you time to calm down and allow your partner a much needed break as well.

Second, a better long-term solution is to develop skills for constructively expressing anger in a way that doesn't make your partner defensive. In a heated conversation, directly describing your anger ("I'm really angry") can cause someone to become defensive. You may, therefore, want to choose synonyms for anger that will not be perceived as threatening. For example, if you say, "I am really mad at you for missing our date," your partner may become defensive. But if you say, "I'm totally frustrated. I thought we had a date, and when you didn't show up, I missed the opportunity to go to the movies with my roommate," your partner may feel guilty and apologize or calmly explain what happened. Trying to help, the typical response to someone's frustration differs from the typical response to someone's anger.

3. De-escalate the conflict. A dysfunctional conflict conversation tends to escalate: voices become louder, silences longer, nonverbal behaviors more exaggerated, messages more hostile, and positions more entrenched. One way to break this destructive conflict pattern is to prevent it from intensifying. There are four ways to do this. First, if this is a serial argument or if you have a history of dysfunctional conflict, you need to identify what triggers antagonism. We all have buttons that others can push. By reflecting on previous difficult conversations, we may discover what escalates the conflict—then, not do it. Second, noticing that a conflict is intensifying, we can try to calm our partners and ourselves. Sometimes simply acknowledging your partner's feelings and apologizing can have this effect: "Hey, wow, I can see your getting upset. I'm sorry. I didn't mean to make you cry." At other times, taking a break from the conversation can help. Finally, injecting humor into the discussion can be an effective way to soothe and de-escalate, especially if that humor is self-directed or points out something about the conflict. If directed at your partner, however, it will increase, not decrease, the emotional pitch.

Creating a Collaborative Conflict Conversation

Collaboration is usually the most competent way to resolve interpersonal conflict. You can use the message skills you have learned to initiate, respond to, and mediate conflict. The following guidelines are based on work from several fields of study (Gordon, 1970; Adler, 1977; Whetten & Cameron, 2010).

Guidelines for Initiating a Collaborative Conflict Conversation

1. Mentally rehearse what you will say before confronting the other person. Initiating a collaborative conflict conversation requires us to be in control of our emotions. Yet, despite our good intentions to keep on track, our emotions can still get the better of us, and in the heat of the moment, we may say things we should not. We should, therefore, take a minute to practice, incorporating the guidelines listed here. Mentally rehearse a few statements you think will lead to productive conflict resolution.

OBSERVE AND ANALYZE

Breaking Destructive Conflict Patterns

Think of a recent conflict you experienced in which a destructive pattern developed. Analyze what happened using the concepts from this chapter. What type of conflict was it? What conflict management style did you adopt? What was the other person's style? What triggered the pattern of negative reciprocity that developed? How might you change what happened if you could redo this conflict episode?

2. Recognize and state ownership of the conflict. If a conflict is to be managed, it is important to acknowledge that you are angry, hurt, or frustrated about something that has occurred between you and your partner. Honestly own your ideas and feelings by using "I" statements. For example, suppose you are trying to study for a test in your most difficult course, and your neighbor's music is so loud that your walls are shaking to the point where you can't concentrate. You own your problem if you approach him, saying, "Hi. I'm trying to study for an exam."

3. Describe the conflict in terms of behavior (b), consequences (c), and feelings (f). Once you have owned the conflict as your problem, describe your perception of the issue to your partner using the b-c-f—behavior, consequences, and feelings—sequence: "When a specific **b**ehavior happens, specific **c**onsequences result, and I **f**eel (emotion)" (Gordon, 1971). Earlier you learned the message skills of describing behavior and describing feelings. Notice that the b-c-f sequence uses these skills. To return to our loud music example, you would follow up on your ownership of the problem, opening with the b-c-f sequence. You might say, "When I hear your music [**b**], I get distracted and can't concentrate on studying [**c**], and then I get frustrated and annoyed [**f**]." The behavior is playing loud music; the consequences are distraction and inability to concentrate; the feelings are frustration and annoyance. Note that all of the statements here are I-centered: "When I hear your music, I get distracted," rather than "When you play your music so loud, you distract me"; and "I get frustrated and annoyed," rather than, "You frustrate and annoy me."

4. Do not blame or ascribe motives. Since your goal is to resolve the issue without escalating the conflict, be careful not to accuse your partner of bad motives or distort what the other person has done. You want to focus on what is happening to you.

5. Keep it short. Since collaboration requires interaction, it is important that you quickly engage the other person in the conversation. Effective turn-taking

---

SKILL BUILDERS ● Behavior, Consequences, and Feelings (b-c-f) Sequence

SKILL	USE	PROCEDURE	EXAMPLE
Describing a conflict in terms of behavior, consequences, and feelings (b-c-f)	To help the other person understand the problem completely	1. Own the message, using "I" statements. 2. Describe the behavior that you see or hear. 3. Describe the consequences that result from the behavior. 4. Describe your feelings that result from the behavior.	Jason says, "I have a problem that I need your help with. When I tell you what I'm thinking and you don't respond (b), I start to think you don't care about me or what I think (c), and this causes me to get angry with you (f)."

rather than dominating the exchange during its early stages will foster a problem-solving climate.

6. Be sure the other person understands your position. Even when you take the greatest care when briefly describing your needs, others may get the general drift of the message but underestimate the seriousness of the problem, or they may not understand you at all. The best way to check understanding is to ask your partners to tell you what they believe you have said. Their paraphrase should alert you to whether you need to follow up with additional explanation.

7. Phrase your preferred solution to focus on common ground. Once you have been understood and you have listened to your partner's position, suggest how you believe the issue can be resolved so that both of you benefit. If your solution is tied to a shared value, common interest, or shared constraint, your partner will see it as a viable solution. Returning to our example, you might say, "I think we both have had times when even little things got in the way of our being able to study. I realize I'm asking you for a favor, but I hope you can help me out by turning down your music for a couple of hours."

Guidelines for Responding to a Conflict that Invites Collaboration

Creating a collaborative climate is less difficult when responding to conflict that has been appropriately initiated. Your most difficult task as a responder is to take an ineffectively initiated conflict and turn it into a productive, problem-solving discussion. The following guidelines will help you respond effectively in these situations.

1. Put your shields up. Follow the example of the captains of the *Starship Enterprise,* when under attack, "Shields up!" When someone is overly aggressive in initiating a conflict, you must learn to raise your mental shields. This improves your capacity to listen and respond effectively rather than becoming defensive or counterattacking. One method for achieving this is to remember that the other person should be the one to own the problem, not you. In all likelihood, the anger being vented toward you is caused by accumulated frustration, only part of which directly relates to the current conflict. So put those shields up, take your time responding, and while you are doing so, think of your options for turning the attack into a problem-solving opportunity.

2. Respond empathetically with genuine interest and concern. A person who initiates a conflict, even with a bold order like, "Turn down that damn music!" will be watching you closely to see how you react. If you make light of the other person's concerns, become defensive, or counterattack, you will undermine the opportunity to solve the problem through cooperation. Even if you disagree with the complaint, you should demonstrate respect by being attentive and empathetic. Sometimes you can do this by allowing the other person to vent while you listen. Only when the other person has calmed down, can problem solving begin. In our music example, the neighbor responding to your request to turn down the volume might first say, "I can see you're upset. Let's talk about this."

3. Ask questions to clarify issues and paraphrase your understanding of the problem. Since most people are unaware of the b-c-f sequence, you may want to paraphrase in a way that captures your understanding of the b-c-f issues or ask questions to elicit this information. For instance, let's suppose that you not only berate your neighbor, saying, "Turn down that damn music! Quit being such a jerk to others," but also ascribe motives to the behavior, saying, "You must enjoy deliberately disrupting everyone!" If information is missing, as with this initiating statement, then the neighbor could ask questions to fill in the missing information, such as "I'm not sure what you're upset about. Are you studying right now? Is that the issue?" Then, having all the information needed, the neighbor could paraphrase following the b-c-f framework: "OK, so I take it you are upset (f) because my music is loud (b), and that's interrupting your ability to study (c). Is that right?" Verifying that the paraphrase is correct and that nothing else needs to been mentioned is also helpful. Sometimes people will initiate a conflict episode about a relatively minor issue without indicating what really needs to be considered.

4. Find common ground by agreeing with some aspect of the complaint. Regardless of how effective or ineffective the conflict initiation, once you have gotten to the stage of clarifying the issue, seek common ground. This does not mean giving in to the other person or pretending to agree. Using your skills of supportiveness, however, you can look for points on which you both can agree. Adler (1977) affirms that you can agree with a message without accepting all of its implications. You can agree with part of it. You can agree with it in principle. You can agree with the initiator's perceptions of the situation. You can agree with the person's feelings. For instance, the neighbor can agree in part ("I know it's hard to study for a tough exam"), agree in principle ("I know it's good to have a quiet place to study"), agree with the initiator's perception ("I can see that you're having trouble studying with loud music in the background"), or agree with the person's feelings ("I can see that you're frustrated and annoyed")—all of which can occur without agreeing with the initiator's conclusions or solutions. By agreeing to some aspect of the complaint, you create common ground for a problem-solving discussion.

5. Ask the initiator to suggest solutions. Once you are sure that the two of you have agreed on what the issue is, the final step is to ask the initiator for ways to handle the conflict. In response to the loud music conflict, the initiator's solutions may be to turn the music down or turn it off completely. Since the initiator has probably spent time thinking about what needs to be done, your request for a solution signals a willingness to listen and cooperate. You may find that one of the suggestions seems reasonable to you (e.g., using earphones instead of turning it off). If none of the suggestions are reasonable, you may be able to craft an alternative that builds on one of the ideas presented: "I'd be happy to turn the volume down, but most people are done with their exams, so you might also think about working in the designated quiet area if someone else starts playing music loud." In any case, asking for suggestions communicates your trust in the other person, strengthening the collaborative climate.

Guidelines for Mediating a Conflict Conversation

In collectivist cultures, it is common to have a trusted and respected person mediate conflicts, and in individualist cultures, the help of a mediator is sometimes sought. A **mediator** is a neutral and impartial guide who structures an interaction so that conflicting parties can find a mutually acceptable solution to an issue (Cupach & Canary, 1997). Working as a mediator, you can help friends and family repair relationships and communicate more positively by observing the following guidelines (Cupach & Canary, 1997; Whetten & Cameron, 2010).

1. Make sure that all people involved in the conflict agree to work with you. If one or both parties do not really want your help, you are unlikely to be able to do much good. You may be able to clarify this by saying, "I'm willing to help you work on this, but only if both of you want me to." If everyone does not agree to your serving as a mediator, bow out gracefully.

2. Establish ground rules. As the mediator, you are in a good position to have participants form ground rules that you can use later to return the conflict to a constructive conversation. You might begin this process by naming one ground rule you would like everyone to adhere to.

3. Probe until you identify the real conflict. Often people seem to be arguing about one thing when the true source of conflict has not been stated. Use clarifying questions, paraphrasing, and perception checking to probe the issue.

4. Remain neutral. Any perception of favoritism will test the patience of one of the parties and destroy the opportunity for successful mediation. Even if you believe one partner's position is stronger, you need to keep your opinions to yourself.

5. Keep the discussion focused on resolving the issue. If the conversation seems to drift to other issues than the conflict to be resolved, get the subject back on track with redirecting comments like, "I think we've gotten off topic. Let's get back to the issue."

6. Encourage equal talk time. It is important for the mediator to control the conversation in a way that gives both parties an equal chance to be heard As mediator, you can do this by directing questions to the more reticent or withdrawn party and by reminding the more assertive partner of ground rules.

7. Establish an action plan and follow-up procedure. Once a solution has been agreed on in principle, the participants can work out the details unassisted.

Mediator—a neutral and impartial guide who structures an interaction so that conflicting parties can find a mutually acceptable solution to an issue.

Spotlight on Scholars

Read more about research into appropriate and effective conflict management and the work of Daniel J. Canary at www.oup.com/us/verderber.

Mediating a conflict takes skill, as Leonard on *The Big Bang Theory* learned when he attempted to mediate a conflict between Sheldon and Penny that began during a paintball game.

The Power of Wastah in Lebanese Speech

by Mahboub Hashem

Mahboub Hashem is full professor and chair of the Mass Communication Department at American University of Sharjah, U.A.E. His research interests are the effects of mass media on society and intercultural interpersonal communication.

"Do you have any wastah?" This was the only question that many of my Lebanese friends and relatives asked me when I applied for one of the Chair of Administrative Affairs positions at the Lebanese University [some years ago]. I replied that I ranked among the top five in the competency exam and they needed to hire at least ten people, so why would I need a wastah? They simply shrugged and warned, "Wait and you'll see."

To make the story short, I was passed over and more than 10 other people were hired. Every one of those who were hired had some type of wastah. I was hired three years later only after I had acquired strong wastah, which included several influential individuals, among them Suleiman Frangieh, the President of Lebanon at that time....

By examining the wastah phenomenon in Lebanon and how it is practiced, one may be able to shed some light on this very important communicative behavior not only in Lebanon but also in the rest of the Middle East. This essay addresses the power of wastah (i.e., mediation), considered to be one of the most important communication patterns in the Lebanese cultural system....

Wastah has been the way of life in Lebanon since before it became a republic. The term wastah means many things to many Lebanese people, including clout, connections, networking, recommendations, a "go-between" for two parties with different interests, and a type of contraception to prevent pregnancy.

Wastah can be used within various contexts, such as family, clan, government organizations, neighbors, villages, and nations. It is usually necessary to get a job, a wife, a date, a passport, a visa, a car, or any other commodity. It can also resolve conflicts, facilitate government decisions, or solve bureaucratic problems. For instance, I once had to wait three hours until I could find an influential person to help me pay the annual tag fee for my car. The common perception in the Arab world, particularly in Lebanon, is that "one does not do for oneself what might better be done by a friend or a friend's friend."

But taking the essential final step of making sure that the parties have an action plan with clearly agreed to responsibilities is part of effective mediating. The plan should specify what each party is to do and how results will be measured and monitored.

Forgiveness: Repairing Relationships Damaged by Conflict

At times, no matter how hard you try you will be unable to resolve a conflict so that it successfully meets the needs of both parties. Some conflicts are extremely deep and complex, and they cannot be managed using only the communication skills you have studied thus far (Sillars & Weisberg, 1987). These conflicts usually stem from one partner deeply hurting the other partner and damaging the offended partner's ability to continue trusting the transgressor. Examples include

How Does the Process of Wastah Work?

Wastah is mostly used to find jobs for relatives or close friends and to solve conflicts. The extended family acts as an employment agency by searching for a wasit to help get a job, preferably one with high social status in the family. The wasit is supposed to be well "wired up," an insider who can make things happen (Hall, 1984). He must also be able to use the language of persuasion . . . with the elite of the religious and political groups of the nation.

In conflict situations, the wasit's job is to conciliate rather than to judge. Conciliation is intended to lead disputants toward a compromise through mutual concessions, as well as to reestablish their relationship on the basis of mutual respect. The wasit tries to talk to each disputant separately, then brings them together to reach a possible compromise that presumes to save face for everyone involved and their extended families.

Lebanese people prefer mediators from the same family or business, depending on the type and context of the conflict. . . . [T]he role of a wasit is to create a supportive climate of communication wherein conflicting parties can modify their behaviors. When a conflict is between members from two different clans, however, a wasit on each side tries to prevail over his or her own clan members. These mediators then come together to conciliate.

For instance, when a conflict occurred between my father and a man named Tony Ayoub, one elderly person from the Hashem clan and another one from the Ayoub clan came together to mediate and negotiate a possible settlement. Then each of the two met with their clan member to discuss the results of their meeting(s) and what the two believed to be a fair solution. After several private meetings between the two mediators, my father and Tony were asked to personally participate in the final one to announce the settlement of the problem. The common ground among mediators of different families is the mutual desire to keep the government out of the clans' affairs as much as possible. Hence, mediators seem better qualified than government agencies to resolve certain conflicts. . . .

The knowledge of these styles and how they are used in various cultures promotes more awareness and understanding of ourselves and others and can consequently lead to more effective intercultural relationships.

For Consideration:

1. How is the role of a wasit similar to or different from the role of a mediator?
2. Does having two wasits negotiate a resolution to a conflict rather than the people who are directly involved in the conflict make sense? If so, why do you think this? If not, same question.
3. How comfortable would you be using a wasit to resolve an important conflict you had with someone else?
4. What characteristics would you want a wasit who represented you in a conflict to have?

Excerpted from Hashem, M. (2012). The power of Wastah in Lebanese speech. In A. González, M. Houston, & V. Chen (Eds.), *Our Voices* (5th ed., pp. 176–180). New York: Oxford University Press.

---

lying, stealing, infidelity, and other violations of relationship trust. In addition, our behavior during a mundane conflict can get out of line and hurt our partners. To repair the damage done to the relationship, partners need to seek and bestow forgiveness. **Forgiveness** is a communication process that allows you and your partner to overcome the damage done to your relationship because of a transgression (Lulofs & Cahn, 2000). Scholars suggest that forgiveness has seven steps (Waldron & Kelley, 2008).

Forgiveness—a communication process that allows you and your partner to overcome the damage done to your relationship because of a transgression.

1. **Confession.** The process of forgiveness begins when the offending partner acknowledges the wrong that has been done and accepts responsibility for it: "Mom, I know I shouldn't have taken that money from your purse. It's my fault."

2. **Venting.** To forgive, offended partners may need to verbally and nonverbally express their negative emotions. The partner seeking

forgiveness should listen to and affirm the other partner's feelings. When your mom says, "I am so angry with you. I needed that money to pay our utility bill, and I was so embarrassed when I got to the head of the line and didn't have the money," You could respond, "I know, mom, that must have been humiliating."

3. **Understanding.** During this phase of forgiveness, partners explore what motivated the transgression: "Son, what were you thinking?" "Oh, mom, I wanted a new CD. I didn't have the money, and I knew if I asked you, you'd refuse. So I just took it."

4. **Apologize.** An **apology** is a direct verbal message that acknowledges responsibility, expresses regret or remorse, and directly requests forgiveness. Although some people have religious values that do not require an apology to precede forgiveness, most of us need an apology before we can forgive: "Mom, I'm so sorry I took the money from your purse. Please forgive me."

5. **Forgive.** Forgiving explicitly or implicitly communicates to our partners that we absolve them from the consequences or penalties we have a right to impose. Sometimes forgiveness is direct, and the offended person will say, "I forgive you." In other cases, forgiveness is implied as offended partners choose not to punish the transgressing partner and continue the relationships as if nothing happened.

6. **Set conditions.** When a partner's behavior has violated an explicit or implicit rule of the relationship, part of forgiveness is to re-establish the rule or set new rules. The forgiveness may be unconditional, or it may be contingent on the offending partner recommitting and honoring the relationship rules: "I forgive you, but if it ever happens again, I won't ever let you stay here alone again." "Don't worry, mom. I'm not a thief. I've learned my lesson."

7. **Monitor.** To forgive is not to forget. Partners should monitor the relationship as they move past the incident. Have the transgressing partners really changed their behavior? Has the offended partner really

Apology—a direct verbal message that acknowledges responsibility, expresses regret or remorse, and directly requests forgiveness.

SKILL BUILDERS ● Apologizing

SKILL	USE	PROCEDURE	EXAMPLE
A direct request for forgiveness	To repair a relationship that your behavior has damaged	1. Directly acknowledge your transgression by owning what you did. 2. Express regret or remorse for your behavior and its effect on your partner. 3. Directly request that your partner forgive you.	"I did lie about where I was Friday night. I was out with another girl. I am so sorry that I lied, and I'm really sorry that I hurt you and destroyed your trust in me. Can you forgive me?"

recovered from the hurt inflicted? Since the purpose of forgiveness is to mend a relationship, partners should watch for signs that trust has been restored in the relationship.

THE SOCIAL MEDIA FACTOR

Managing the Dark Side of Digital Communication

Among the most prevalent questions addressed in digital communication research is the extent to which Internet use fosters undesirable outcomes such as depression, loneliness, and reduced face-to-face social interaction (Caplan, 2003; Kim, LaRose, & Peng, 2009; Tokunaga & Rains, 2010; Whang, Lee, & Chang, 2003). While social media can help us form and maintain relationships, they can also create relationship problems including compulsive use, inappropriate self disclosure, and conflict-related behaviors such as flaming, cyberbullying, and cyberstalking.

Compulsive and Excessive Internet Use

Problematic Internet use is a syndrome characterized by cognitive and behavioral symptoms with potentially negative social, academic, and professional consequences (Caplan, 2007). More specifically, this syndrome may involve **compulsive Internet use**, resulting from a person's inability to control, reduce, or stop utilizing the Internet, or **excessive Internet use**, characterized by a user's feeling that he or she spends too much time online or even loses track of time while online (Caplan, 2002).

If Karl cannot resist responding in the middle of the night to a new e-mail message alert on his smartphone, he is likely engaging in compulsive Internet use. While cramming for a midterm, Suzy may become distracted by what is happening on Facebook. Although determined to study for her exam, she decides to quickly peek at her newsfeed. Subsequently, Suzy feels compelled to browse Facebook, chat with her friends, and post on her and others' wall. She then may tweet: "Really need to study for my midterm . . . Facebook is just soooo distracting." Thinking she took only a fifteen-minute break, Suzy notices that nearly two hours have passed. If this situation occurs on a regular basis, she is most likely engaging in excessive Internet use. If you find yourself using social media in a compulsive or excessive way, you may need to take action to improve your behavior. Consider the following recommendations:

1. Disable your smartphone's ability to push e-mail messages to you. If you feel attached to your iPhone or Blackberry, chances are it is set to automatically push or download e-mails to your phone, alerting you to incoming messages. Rather than being constantly disturbed in this way, you should reset your smartphone to have you manually check for new e-mails, which you can do when you have free time. All too often our compelling need to respond to an insignificant e-mail can interrupt special family gatherings or other important activities.

Problematic Internet use—a syndrome characterized by cognitive and behavioral symptoms that can result in negative social, academic, and professional consequences.

Compulsive Internet use—a person's inability to control, reduce, or stop utilizing the Internet.

Excessive Internet use—the degree to which a person feels that he or she spends an extreme amount of time online or even loses track of time while online.

2. Leave your social media devices behind when you plan to study. Students report being distracted by social media when they try to study for exams. If you often find yourself in this situation, silence your cell phone or turn it off altogether. Try leaving your laptop behind when you plan to study. If your class notes are on your laptop, print them and study from the hard copy. Revising notes with a pen or pencil may even increase your recall of information. Research indicates that students who take notes this way increase their learning and achievement (Titsworth & Kiewra, 2004).

3. Ask your friends to help you. If your face-to-face conversations are constantly interrupted because you cannot resist responding to a text or an e-mail, ask your friends to help you improve your behavior. If you check your iPhone for new e-mails during a face-to-face conversation with a friend, your friend should quickly bring your dependence on social media to your attention. Although your college friend may tolerate and even understand this practice of interrupting a face-to-face conversation, your unsympathetic manager may not.

4. Seek professional help if necessary. Research indicates that compulsive and excessive use of social media is a growing problem that may in many cases require professional help. If you are tied to social media and simultaneously feel lonely, depressed, and withdrawn from face-to-face interactions, you may need to seek professional assistance. If you notice a friend in a similar situation, encourage that person to seek help. Social media enhance interpersonal communication in numerous ways, but they also have a dark side.

Inappropriate Self-Disclosure

Self-disclosure is one of the most powerful communication practices we have for strengthening a relationship. It can backfire, however, if we share too much too soon or reveal information the other person finds inappropriate. Social media can accelerate the rate and depth of our self-disclosure. The convenience, reach, and mobility of social media have fostered inappropriate self-disclosures. Some people feel compelled to send sexually explicit text messages or photographs to others, a practice called **sexting**. In a recent in-depth examination of the sexting phenomenon, *MTV* and *The Associated Press* (2009) found that 30 percent of teenagers reported involvement in some type of naked sexting, one in ten having shared a naked image of themselves with another person, and 55 percent having passed the sext on to more than one person. In the age of social media, inappropriate self-disclosures need not be verbal. Think twice before you send a sext, and if you receive a sext, delete it immediately. Don't let digital communication compromise your identity or the identity of a friend. The recent launch of video-conference Web sites such as Chatroulette and Omegle has enabled people to behave in ways they otherwise would not. These sorts of Web sites randomly pair strangers so they can engage in video, audio, and text-based conversations with people from around the world. At any time during the chat session, either stranger can end the current chat by requesting another random connection. The sites permit users to behave anonymously if they choose—they can easily hide their faces from the webcam or turn it off completely. Research found that one in eight randomized pairings resulted in inappropriate disclosures, including nudity. Users were also more likely

Sexting—the act of sending sexually explicit messages or photographs, primarily between smartphones via text messaging.

to encounter other users holding signs requesting female nudity than actually see female nudity (Moore, 2010). The **Social Identity Model of Deindividuation Effects** (SIDE Model) helps explain the expression of inappropriate self-disclosures through social media, positing that the characteristics of the social media device, such as anonymity, often influence behavior (Spears & Lea, 1992). Here the anonymous nature of these randomized Web sites enables users (more often males than females) to behave in ways that are more closely aligned with *social* identities—behaviors common on the Web site—rather than *personal* identities, or how the person behaves in other contexts. Although the anonymous nature of these Web sites may tempt you to behave in ways you normally would not, always remember that social media's reach and replicability can place inappropriate disclosures in the hands of many unintended recipients.

Social identity model of deindividuation effects—describes the extent to which individuals identify and behave in accordance with social rather than personal identities.

Flaming

We have long been able to engage in anonymous communication. Before caller ID, prank phone calls were common, and you can still send an anonymous letter to a newspaper editor or assume a persona in your blog. The anonymity of digital communication has, however, increased the capacity for heated and often unproductive exchanges through social media—in blogs, e-mails, and through social networking sites. Social media have provided a vast space for flaming—digital communication that is deliberately hostile, aggressive, or insulting and usually intended to provoke anger.

Flame wars—erupt when friendly and productive digital discussions give way to insults and aggression.

Flame wars erupt when friendly and productive digital discussions give way to insults and aggression. This behavior is common in online group interactions where hostility escalates and draws in more participants. Others may urge participants to move the discussion to another venue or ignore the aggression, and eventually, the discussion fizzles out as people lose interest. But what if you find yourself actively participating in a flame war? In an online discussion group about household pets, imagine that you come across a post (an obvious flame) that reads "All kittens on the planet should be buried up to their necks at lawn-mowing time." If you're a cat lover, you may be inclined to immediately respond, fanning the fire, so to speak. People tempted to participate in a flame war should pause, take a deep breath, and consider the following recommendations:

1. *Respond privately.* Craft an e-mail that expresses your frustration with the poster's message. Direct your words at the content of the flame, not the flamer's character.
2. *Ignore the flame entirely.* Although your first impulse may be to privately or publicly respond to the poster, try to bear in mind that many flamers are new to digital communication and may simply lack basic social etiquette. Others who post offensive flames may be crying out for attention. A return flame could be just what the poster wants, and in all likelihood, your response won't change the person's behavior or position.
3. *Ask an authority to intervene.* In cases of flagrant flaming, you may consider sending a message to the flamer's system administrator.

THE SOCIAL MEDIA FACTOR

OBSERVE AND ANALYZE

Examining Online Flame Wars

Think about the last time you were involved in a flame war online. Was it in an online discussion group, a blog, or Facebook? If the comments are still available, go to that location. Spend some time looking through and reflecting on the postings made by you and others. How would you describe the comments that people made on this page? How active were you in the flame war? What motivated you to comment? Write a short paragraph describing your interaction in the flame war. In another paragraph, describe what you might do differently if given the opportunity.

Or you may report the flamer to the online group's moderator. Save this for extreme cases of repeatedly abusive flames.

Cyber Stalking and Cyberbullying

Social media have also created an arena for aggressive behaviors such as cyberbullying and cyber stalking.

Cyberbullying—abusive attacks that are carried out through social media.

Cyberbullying involves abusive verbal attacks carried out through social media. Social networking sites offer an open forum for bullies who demean or threaten people without risk of retaliation. Among teens and preteens, and even college students, the problem has serious consequences, as evidenced by the recent suicide of 13-year-old Megan Meier. Moments after receiving a MySpace message that said "the world would be a better place without you" from Josh Evans, a boy she connected with through the social network, Megan hanged herself with a belt. In the months before Josh viciously turned on her, she had been flirting with him. In their later exchanges, however, Josh said that he had heard she was a terrible friend to others and that he was no longer interested in being her friend. Other teenagers, also linked to Josh's profile, joined in the attack, sending Megan cruel messages. In the aftermath of her suicide, it was revealed that Josh Evans did not really exist: the mother of one of Megan's former friends had developed the fake profile and pretended to be Josh Evans, using social media to bully Megan (Maag, 2007).

The suicide of Rutgers University student Tyler Clementi in 2010 was also the tragic result of cyberbullying through social media. Tyler had complained to university officials that his roommate, Dharun Ravi, was spying on his sexual encounters with men. After essentially outing Tyler on Twitter, Dharun surreptitiously videostreamed his roommate with another man over the Internet from a webcam in their dorm room. Dharun subsequently engaged in another attempt to record Tyler in a similar situation, inviting his Twitter followers to watch. When Tyler found out soon after, he posted the following status update to his Facebook page: "Jumping off the gw bridge sorry." Having told no one about his despair and leaving no clues to his decision other than the Facebook status update, Clementi is thought to have made the one-hour drive from Rutgers to the George Washington Bridge, leaving his car, wallet, and cell phone on a side road before leaping to his death (CBS News, 2011). In 2012 Ravi was convicted on 15 charges including invasion of privacy and intimidation. The stories of Tyler and Megan both illustrate the disturbing consequences of the dark side of digital communication.

If you find that you are a victim of cyberbullying, immediately defriend and block the cyberbully. If you notice that this behavior is being directed toward a friend, encourage that person to block the cyberbully. Victims of cyberbullies might find it especially helpful to temporarily avoid social media for a few weeks or simply change and disguise their user names so it is extremely difficult for cyberbullies to identify the target of their negative behavior.

Cyber stalking—occurs when an individual repeatedly uses social media to stalk or harass others.

Cyber stalking occurs when an individual repeatedly uses social media to shadow or harass others. Individuals who engage in this dark-side behavior often make threats or false accusations against another person or constantly view and access a person's Facebook profile. Cyber stalker behavior includes grooming minors for sexual exploitation. Cyber stalkers may also digitally gather information and then use that information to harass another person in a face-to-face setting. Those who constantly watch what their friends are up to on Facebook are sometimes called "Facebook creepers." If you frequently monitor the Facebook profiles

A QUESTION OF ETHICS ● What Would You Do?

Kiara and Dion, a young African American couple, have been shopping at the outlet mall. After loading their purchases into the trunk of the car, they decide to move the car to a parking space closer to the next group of shops. As Kiara is backing out, she glances in the rearview mirror and cries, "She's going to hit us!" Kiara honks her horn, but the other vehicle, an SUV, continues backing up and bangs into Kiara's rear bumper. Kiara and Dion immediately hop out of the car to check out the damage.

Their hair covered by scarves, three conservatively dressed Arab women, who appear to be daughter, mother, and grandmother, slowly exit the SUV. Dion shouts, "What's wrong with you! Don't you know how to drive? Are you blind? Couldn't you see us or hear the horn?" Kiara tells Dion to shut up and turns to the driver, a young woman about her own age, and says, "Good grief! Just give me your information!" Rima, the other driver, turns to Dion and politely responds that she hadn't seen them or heard the horn. Then she tells the other two women to get back into the car. Finally, she turns to Kiara and explains that she needs to call her husband, hastily retreating into the SUV and pulling her cell phone out of her purse as she closes the door.

Kiara explodes, banging on Rima's window and shouting, "@#$^&$$ that. Why do you need to talk to your husband? He wasn't here! He doesn't have anything to do with this! Get back out here, now!" At this point, the second woman, apparently Rima's mother, cracks her window and quietly asks Kiara not to yell, to no avail. After a few moments, Rima rolls down her window and asks Kiara to speak with Rima's husband, who is on the phone. Kiara yells that she has no intention of speaking to anyone and again demands that Rima produce her license and insurance information. Rima replies that she is going to call the police and rolls up the window. The three women sit in the SUV until a police car arrives.

After talking with Kiara and Dion, the responding officer explains to Rima that police don't intervene in traffic accidents on private property if there are no injuries unless there is a problem with the parties exchanging information. Rima's grandmother interrupts to insist that Kiara's behavior had been profane, rude, and threatening. She demands that the officer make Kiara apologize for the affront to their dignity. The police officer replies that Kiara's behavior might have been aggressive, but her demand had been legal and was actually the proper procedure at the scene of this type of accident. Rima apologizes to the officer, adding that she had never had an accident before and had called her husband to find out what she should do. Because she was frightened by Kiara and Dion's intimidating behavior and because Kiara had refused to speak to him, Rima's husband had told her to call the police. So she obeyed. Had Kiara remained calm and been understanding, the officer would not have been inconvenienced.

For Consideration:

1. Given what you have learned about cultural difference in conflict situations, was it ethical for each person in this situation to use the conflict style chosen? Justify your answer.
2. Are there ethical principles that transcend culture as human universals?

of your friends to maintain an interpersonal connection, you are not necessarily engaging in cyber stalking if there is no malicious intent. If, however, Paul regularly monitors his ex-girlfriend's Facebook page to find out when she changes her relationship status to "In a Relationship," and then attacks her with rude, hurtful, and aggressive Facebook messages, Paul is not just a cyber stalker but also a cyberbully. If you learn that you are the victim of a cyber stalker, defriend and block the person immediately.

Summary

Interpersonal conflict is disagreement between two interdependent people who perceive that they have incompatible goals. Even in good relationships, conflicts are inevitable.

There are six types of interpersonal conflict: pseudoconflicts, fact conflicts, value conflicts, policy conflicts, ego conflicts, and metaconflicts. We manage conflict by withdrawing, accommodating, forcing, compromising, or collaborating, each of which can be effective in certain circumstances. During a conflict we are concerned not only with resolving the issue but also with face needs. The concept of face differs between Western and Eastern/Southern Hemisphere cultures. People from Western Hemisphere cultures tend to have a self-face orientation, whereas people from Eastern and Southern Hemisphere cultures tend to have other- or mutual-face orientations. In America, ethnic and other cocultural groups differ in their face orientations and conflict styles, which can complicate conflict resolution. Destructive patterns of conflict stem from negative reciprocity and include serial arguing, counterblaming, cross-complaining, demand-withdrawal, and mutual hostility. Several strategies can help you break these patterns. You can use the communication message skills you have learned to initiate, respond to, and mediate conflicts so that they are more likely to be resolved by win-win solutions. If conflict has damaged a relationship, however, we can attempt to repair it by seeking and granting forgiveness, for which apologizing is usually a prerequisite.

Problematic Internet use is a syndrome characterized by cognitive and behavioral symptoms with potentially negative social, academic, and professional consequences. The syndrome may involve compulsive Internet use or excessive Internet use, characterized by a user's inability to control their use of the Internet or the feeling that he or she spends too much time online. Such behavior can be checked by disabling the automatic pushing of text messages to your smartphone, leaving social media devices behind when it's time to study, or asking your friends to help you reduce overuse of the Internet.

The anonymity of digital communication has, however, increased the capacity for heated and often unproductive exchanges through social media—in blogs, e-mails, and through social networking sites. People tempted to participate in a flame war should pause, take a deep breath, and consider the consequences.

The convenience, reach, and mobility of social media have fostered inappropriate self-disclosures, including sexting. The Social Identity Model of Deindividuation Effects (SIDE Model) helps explain the expression of inappropriate self-disclosures through social media, positing that the characteristics of the social media device, such as anonymity, often influence behavior

Cyber stalking occurs when an individual repeatedly uses social media to stalk or harass others. Cyberbullying involves abusive attacks carried out through social media. Victims of cyberbullies might find it especially helpful to temporarily avoid social media for a few weeks or simply change and disguise their user names so it is extremely difficult for cyberbullies to identify the target of their negative behavior.

Chapter Resources

What You Should Be Able *to Explain:*

- The concept of interpersonal conflict
- The six types of conflict
- Five conflict styles
- Face negotiation theory
- The destructive conflict patterns
- How to skillfully initiate, respond to, and mediate conflict
- How to repair relationships damaged by conflict
- How to manage the dark side of digital communication

What You Should Be Able *to Do:*

- Initiate a conflict
- Use behavior-consequence-feelings messages
- Respond to a conflict
- Mediate a conflict
- Apologize

Self-test questions based on these concepts are available on the companion Web site (www.oup.com/us/verderber) as part of Chapter 12 resources.

Key Words

Flashcards for all of these key terms are available on the *Inter-Act* Web site.

Accommodating, p. 363
Apology, p. 380
Collaborating, p. 364
Compromising, p. 364
Compulsive Internet use, p. 381
Counterblaming, p. 370
Cross-complaining, p. 370
Cyberbullying, p. 384
Cyber stalking, p. 384
Demand-withdrawal, p. 371
Ego conflict, p. 360
Excessive Internet use, p. 381
Face, p. 366
Face in Eastern and Southern Hemisphere cultures, p. 367

Face in Western Hemisphere cultures, p. 366
Face negotiation theory, p. 367
Fact conflict, p. 359
Flame wars, p. 383
Forcing, p. 363
Forgiveness, p. 379
Ground rules, p. 372
Interpersonal conflict, p. 358
Mediator, p. 377
Metaconflict, p. 360
Mutual hostility, p. 371
Mutual-face orientation, p. 367
Other-face orientation, p. 367
Policy conflict, p. 359

Principle of negative reciprocity, p. 369
Principle of positive reciprocity, p. 369
Problematic Internet use, p. 381
Pseudoconflict, p. 359
Self-face orientation, p. 366
Serial arguing, p. 369
Sexting, p. 382
Social identity model of deindividuation effects (SIDE), p. 383
Value conflict, p. 359
Withdrawing, p. 362

Apply Your Knowledge

The following activities challenge you to demonstrate your mastery of the concepts, theories, and frameworks in this chapter by using them to explain what is happening in a specific situation.

Interpreting the Opening Dialogue

12.1 Revisit the opening dialogue, using what you have learned in this chapter to explain each person's reaction to Professor Boren's decision to forego the review for the exam. What type of conflict was this? What style of conflict did each person appear to be using? What led you to these conclusions?

Inter-Action Dialogue: Interpersonal Conflict

12.2 Interpersonal influence occurs when one person attempts to change another person's attitudes or behaviors. As you read the following dialogue, do a line-by-line analysis of this conversation and indicate where you see evidence of the participants showing types of conflict, styles of managing conflict, and skills that promote successful conflict management. You can watch a video of this conversation on the Inter-Act Web site and use a form provided to write down your own analysis of the conversation.

DIALOGUE

Brian and Matt share an apartment. Matt is consistently late in paying his share of expenses. Brian has tolerated this for over six months, but he has finally had enough and decides to confront Matt.

Brian: Matt, I need to talk with you.

Matt: What's up?

Brian: Well, I have a problem. When I got home from class today, I tried to call my mom, and guess what? The phone's been disconnected.

Matt: You're kidding.

Brian: No, I'm not. And when I went next door and called the phone company, you know what they said?

Matt: I can guess.

Brian: They said the bill hadn't been paid and that this was the fourth month in a row that it was over two weeks late.

Matt: Look man, I can explain.

Brian: Like you explained not paying the utility bill on time last month? We were just lucky that it was a cool week and that we didn't fry without air conditioning. The candlelit dinner was charming and all that, but I really resented having to go to the library to study for my test. Matt, I just can't go on like this. I mean, I gave you my share of the phone bill three weeks ago. I always give you my half of the utility bill the day it arrives. And I'm sick and tired of having to nag you for your share of the rent. For the last four months I've had to cover your share by taking money out of what I am saving to buy Angie's engagement ring. I know that you eventually pay me back, but I lose the interest, and it's just not fair.

Matt: Gosh, I didn't know that you were so upset. I mean it's not like I don't pay. I always make good, don't I?

Brian: Yes, so far that's true, but every month it's later and later before you pay me back. And I'm not a lending agency. Why do you expect me to loan you money each month? We work at the same place, make the same money, and we've both got the same expenses. If I can come up with the rent and other expenses on time, you can too.

Matt: Listen, I apologize about the phone bill. I thought I'd mailed it. So, I'll check it out with the phone company tomorrow morning. And the utility bill was just a mistake. I lost the bill and didn't realize it hadn't been paid. I know that I've not always had the money for the rent when you asked, but you usually ask me for it a week or more before it's due. You are really good at saving ahead, but I'm not. You say we have the same expenses, but that's not true. I have a car loan and you don't. And since I got that ticket last year, my car insurance has skyrocketed. Some months I'm living really close to the edge. I know it's no excuse, but I want you to understand that I'm not just some deadbeat who's trying to leech off of you.

Brian: Matt, I'm sorry that I said we have similar expenses. You're right. Yours are higher. And if I understood you correctly, our problems with the utility company and the phone company weren't caused by you not having the money but were because somehow the bills just slipped through the cracks?

Matt: Yeah. I'm never very organized, but right now things are chaos. Between work, school, and the stuff that's going on with my family, I don't know if I'm coming or going.

Brian: Well, I can understand that you are under a lot of pressure. And I hope you can understand that when you don't pay bills on time, it's not just you that suffers. Angie and I want to buy a house before we get married, so I'm really careful about paying bills on time so that I have a good credit rating. That's why I ask you for the rent so early. When you forget to pay the utility and phone bills, not only do we lose service, but since both of our names are on the bill, we both take a hit in our credit ratings. A poor credit rating will make it harder for me to get a loan. And it also will make it harder for you to get credit later. I know that you wouldn't intentionally do anything to hurt me, but the fact is, you have.

Matt: Whoa, I never really thought about it this way. Gee, I'm sorry.

Brian: Apology accepted. So how can we work this out?

Matt: Well, you seem to have thought more about it than I have. Do you have any ideas?

Brian: Yeah, as a matter of fact, a couple of alternatives come to mind. One, we could agree on a date each month to sit down and pay the bills together. That way, I'd know that the bills had been written and sent, and you could control my tendency to bug you for your half of the rent before it really needs to be sent. Or, with each paycheck, we could each put a certain amount into a joint account. Then when the bills come in I would just write the checks out of that account, and you wouldn't have to bother with it at all.

Matt: Maybe we could do a combination of those things.

Brian: What do you mean?

Matt: Well, I don't want to totally turn control over to you. I mean, I really need to learn how to be responsible for getting stuff done on time. But I'm really jammed for time right now. So how about if we set the date for paying the bills but also set up the joint account? That way, if something comes up, and I don't have the time to sit down with you and pay the bills, you can still get them done on time. But when I do have time, we can do it together. I think I can probably learn some good budgeting habits from you.

Brian: That's fine as long as you put in your share each pay period. I actually enjoy managing my personal finances, and I'd be glad to show you what I do. It may not work for you, but you might get some ideas that you can adapt to your style. In any case, I'm glad we talked. I was getting close to the breaking point with you, and now I'm feeling like things are going to be OK. So when can we get together for our bill-paying date and when should we set up the joint account?

Skill Practice

Skill practice activities give you the chance to rehearse a new skill by responding to hypothetical or real situations. Additional skill practice activities are available at the companion Web site.

Identifying Types of Conflict

Label the following conflicts as S (pseudoconflict), F (fact conflict), V (value conflict), P (policy conflict), E (ego conflict) or M (metaconflict). Then explain why you categorized each as you did.

12.3   Joe wants to live with Mary, but Mary wants the two of them to get married.

12.4   Stan believes that because he is an insurance salesman, Jerry should not dispute his position on annuities.

12.5   George defends his failure to present an anniversary gift to Agnes by asserting that their anniversary is not today, May 8, but May 18.

12.6   Martin calls to announce that he is bringing the boss home for dinner. His wife replies, "That will be impossible. The house is too messy to be seen, and I have nothing good enough in the fridge to serve guests."

12.7   Jane says, "Harry, pick up your clothes. I'm not your maid!" Harry replies, "I thought we agreed that it's your job to take care of the house. I take care of the yard."

12.8   When Jill and Vince argue about their finances, Vince gets agitated, raising his voice and essentially drowning Jill out. She responds by criticizing him for being domineering.

Answers: 12.3 V; 12.4 E; 12.5 F; 12.6 S; 12.7 P; 12.8 M

Initiating a Conflict

For each situation below prepare a message that would effectively initiate a conflict.

12.9 Situation: *You observe your longtime romantic partner flirting with another person. Your partner's arm is around this person's waist, and they are laughing and periodically whispering in each other's ear.*

Initiating Message:

12.10 Situation: *Your roommate borrows your iPod and returns it late last night. You put it on your desk without really looking at it. This morning when you grab it to listen to at the gym, you notice that the display is cracked. You are certain it was not this way before your roommate borrowed it.*

Initiating Message:

12.11 Situation: *Halfway through your shift, your manager calls you into the office to inform you that someone has called in sick and that you will have to stay until closing. You have a test tomorrow and need to study.*

Initiating Message:

Responding to a Conflict

For each situation below, prepare a response that would move the conflict toward a collaboration.

12.12 Initiating Message: *"I saw you yesterday, and boy were you enjoying yourself. So I hope you really had fun because it's over between you and me. You can't cheat on me and expect me to take it."*

Your Response:

12.13 Initiating Message: *"I can't believe that you broke my iPod and then didn't have the guts to tell me."*

Your Response:

12.14 Initiating Message: *"There's no way I'm staying late again to close the store. You never even consider the fact that some of us have other things to do besides cover for you."*

Your Response:

Apologizing

For each of the following situations, create an effective apology message.

12.15 Situation: *Your longtime romantic partner caught you flirting with someone else.*

Your apology:

12.16 Situation: *You borrowed your roommate's iPod and returned it without telling your roommate that you had accidently dropped it, cracking the display.*

Your apology:

12.17   Situation: *You told your best employee to stay until closing tonight because someone else could not make it to work. Although you didn't intend to anger your employee, you are afraid that this person is upset enough to quit.*

Your apology:

Communication Improvement Plan: Conflict Management

Would you like to improve the following aspects of your conflict resolving behaviors, as discussed in this chapter?

- Initiating conflict
- Responding to conflict
- Mediating the conflicts of others
- Apologizing

12.18   Pick an aspect, and write a communication improvement plan. You can find a communication improvement plan worksheet on our Web site at www.oup.com/us/verderber.

Inter-Act with Media

Television

Teen Mom 2 (2011). Jenelle Evans, Chelsea Houska, Kailyn Lowry, Leah Simms.

Teen Mom 2 depicts the lives of four young girls as they make their way through their first year of being a mother. The show also focuses on themes of their evolving relationships between family, friends, and boys. It highlights the struggles teenage mothers experience as they strive to raise their children.

In the course of the program, Chelsea and her baby Aubree move out of her father's house while she is trying to finish high school. She begins spending time with her ex-boyfriend Adam, Aubree's father. Chelsea's friends are not happy with this decision. Chelsea wants to give Adam another chance, so she lets Adam move in with them so Aubree can experience a normal family life. Adam moves in, but Chelsea tries to hide the situation from her father who is assisting Chelsea with her finances. Chelsea tries to shift her focus back to school, while Chelsea's father continues to put pressure on Adam to find a job. Conflict between Chelsea and Adam starts to rise. Chelsea is annoyed because Adam does not come home until the wee hours of the morning and, as a result, he does not help with Aubree. Chelsea and Adam eventually break up. Afterward, Chelsea and her friends decide to celebrate both her birthday and her breakup with Adam by taking a road trip to a Lady Gaga concert.

IPC Concepts: Interpersonal conflict, types of interpersonal conflict, conflict management styles, mediation

To the Point:

How would you describe the type of interpersonal conflict experienced by Chelsea, her father, Megan, and Adam?

How would you characterize Chelsea's role as a mediator in the conflict experienced between Adam and Chelsea's roommate, Megan?

Cinema

The Break-Up (2006). Peyton Reed (director). Jennifer Aniston, Vince Vaughn.

Couple Gary Grobowski (Vaughn) and Brooke Meyers (Aniston) are pushed to the boiling point after their latest argument. Brooke feels unappreciated and criticizes Gary's immaturity and unwillingness to work on improving their relationship. Gary is quite frustrated by Brooke's controlling attitude and wants more space. They break up but neither person is willing to move out of the condo that they share, so they agree to live as roommates and they begin acting out to annoy each other.

When their real estate agent sells the condo, Gary and Brooke have two weeks to move out. Brooke invites Gary to a concert hoping he will perceive it as one last attempt to repair their damaged relationship. Gary misses the concert, which breaks Brooke's heart. Brooke now realizes she does not love Gary. Gary attempts to win her back by cleaning the condo and preparing a fancy meal for her as a surprise, but Brooke admits that she no longer loves him. The two agree to part ways for good.

Gary begins to throw himself into his job and Brooke travels the world. She eventually comes back to Chicago. They happen to meet again on the street. After awkward yet friendly small talk, they walk their separate ways. Each person looks back and they share a smile.

IPC Concepts: Interpersonal conflict, types of interpersonal conflict, conflict management styles

To the Point:

> How would you describe the type of interpersonal conflict experienced by Gary and Brooke?
> How would you characterize the conflict management styles exhibited by Gary and Brooke?

What's on the Web

Find links and additional material, including self-quizzes, on the companion Web site at www.oup.com/us/verderber.

Communicating in Intimate Relationships

Families, Friendships, Marriages, and Other Life Partnerships

"Hello?"

"Hey, Brian. Have you talked to Mom today?"

"No, Amber. But then I'm not glued to her hip like you are. I'm not sure why you bothered to come here for school. You haven't exactly cut the apron strings."

"Give it up. I don't talk to her every day, though we do text a lot."

"So, why did you ask if I'd talked to her? Is something wrong?"

"I think you need to call her. Now."

"Why? What's going on? Tell me."

"Just call Mom," Amber sobs, breaking down. "You need to hear it from her."

"Amber, you're scaring me. What's going on?"

"She left him."

"What? Left who?"

"What do you mean 'Left who'? Dad. Dad. Dad, stupid! After twenty-seven years, she's left dad. Now call her," Amber yells and then abruptly hangs up.

What you should be able *to explain* after you have studied this chapter:

- The characteristics of intimate conversations
- The characteristics of intimate relationships
- The primary dimensions of parental communication
- The types of attachment and their implications for relationships
- Three parenting styles and their effects on children
- The strengths and challenges of intergenerational family communication
- How communication between siblings changes over the life span

- Three ways to improve family communication
- Communication skills especially important in friendships
- How men's and women's friendships differ
- The factors that define long-term romantic partnerships
- The types of long-term couple relationships
- The characteristics of successful long-term relationships
- How to deal with the dark side of intimate relationships
- Media multiplexity theory
- Social Information Processing theory

What you should be able *to do* after you have studied this chapter:

- Understand the health of family and intimate relationships
- Identify techniques for reducing relational uncertainty with intimates
- Know some of the pitfalls of using social media with family and intimates

People, it seems, are designed to be in relationships. But our relationships don't always work out. We acquire an understanding of the importance of relationships early on when we bond with our parents and family members. As we grow into maturity, most of us develop intimate relationships with a few people whom we expect will stand by us regardless of the circumstances, sharing in our joy and comforting us without judgment in our times of need. We think of these relationships as our safe harbor, people who will be there for us after we take risks and fail. You may have a large number of friends and acquaintances, but if you are lucky, you also have a handful of intimate relationships: people who really know you and to whom you entrust your innermost secrets. These relationships may be romantic or platonic, same sex or opposite sex. They may cross age, gender, racial, and ethnic lines but are all defined by the key characteristic of intimacy.

In this chapter we will explore the role that communication plays in intimate relationships, including families, platonic friendships, and long-lasting romantic relationships. We begin this chapter by exploring the concept of intimacy, what makes interactions and relationships intimate. The remainder of the chapter is devoted to understanding three types of intimate relationships: family, friendship, and romantic relationships. Our discussion will explain how communication can foster intimacy in and personal growth for the people involved in these types of relationships. We will also discuss two difficulties that can arise in intimate relationships and suggest how these might be handled.

The Nature of Intimacy

In Chapter 1 we defined intimacy as the degree of emotional closeness, acceptance, and disclosure in a relationship. This definition, which describes intimacy by how we might measure it, allows us to talk about how levels of intimacy vary from one type of relationship to another. Now we want to look more closely at intimacy. In so doing, we will see that intimacy is both a characteristic of conversations and a characteristic of relationships (Reis & Shaver, 1988). We can have an intimate conversation with someone with whom we do not necessarily have an intimate relationship. We can also have a relationship that others suppose is intimate without it really being so. Consider the

---

LEARN ABOUT YOURSELF ● Respect for Partner

Take this short survey to learn something about yourself and your feelings about a partner in an intimate relationship. Answer the questions honestly based on your first response. There are no right or wrong answers. For each statement, select one of the numbers to the right that best describes your feelings.

_____ 1. My partner is trustworthy.

_____ 2. My partner fosters a relationship of mutual care.

_____ 3. My partner shows interest in me.

_____ 4. My partner is sensitive and considerate of my feelings.

_____ 5. My partner provides unconditional love.

_____ 6. My partner is open and receptive.

_____ 7. My partner is honest and truthful.

_____ 8. My partner fosters good two-way communication.

_____ 9. My partner is committed to me.

_____ 10. My partner is understanding and empathic.

1 = Always
2 = Often
3 = Sometimes
4 = Rarely
5 = Never

This is a test of your level of respect for a partner.

Scoring the survey: Add the scores together for all ten questions. The score will range from 10 to 50.

The lower your score (closer to 10), the more you feel respect for your relationship partner. The higher your score (closer to 50), the less respect you feel for your relationship partner.

Adapted from Frei, J. R., & Shaver, P. R. (2002). Respect in close relationships: Prototype definition, self-report assessment, and initial correlates. *Personal Relationships, 9,* 121–139.

stranger on the airplane who discloses some deep problem, and you respond with supportive messages and then reciprocate by revealing a personal problem for which you receive this person's support. Once the flight is over, you go your separate ways, having had an intimate conversation. But if you never see the person again, you don't really have a relationship, let alone an intimate one. Moreover, most of us have known people we thought were intimate partners who ended the relationship explaining, "We just drifted apart." Thus, to understand the nature of intimacy we need to understand what constitutes an intimate interaction and what constitutes an intimate relationship.

Intimacy Is an Interaction Pattern

In one sense, intimacy is an *interaction pattern.* That is, intimacy is not just a self-disclosing or supportive message that you might send. Both your messages and your partner's responses make a conversation an intimate interaction (Reis, 1998). Intimacy resides in the "inter-act" between you. Suppose that walking across campus to their next class, Clarissa discloses to a casual friend, "I have a problem, and I just have to tell someone. I saw two people cheating on the midterm in the class we're headed to. It really shocked and disappointed me. Since we have an honor code, I'm thinking of telling our instructor." In disclosing this, she is not just making a statement, she is looking for some type of support. If her friend holds up her hand, palm out, and responds, "Stop. I don't want to hear about it," she is rebuffing Clarissa's bid to begin an intimate interaction. Therefore, even though Clarissa disclosed, this was not an intimate interaction. Let's look at what actually makes a conversation intimate.

Characteristics of Intimate Conversations

In Chapter 8 you learned about conversations, with an emphasis on casual conversations: those that occur at a party, at a relaxed gathering with friends, or at the dinner table with your mom when you both recount the events of your day. An intimate conversation differs from these casual conversations. Emotional disclosures, mutual understanding, and warm feelings in both verbal messages and nonverbal cues characterize an intimate conversation.

You'll recall from our earlier discussion of self-disclosure that we can disclose simple facts about ourselves, or we can make more personal and emotional disclosures. Both types are important in a relationship, but it is emotional disclosures that characterize intimate conversations. **Emotional disclosures** reveal sensitive, private, and personally risky information, signaling to our partners the desire for intimacy (Morton, 1978). Disclosing our emotions, our feelings of inadequacy, our screw-ups and failings, and our deepest fears lets our partners know us at a deeper level. Your best friend and you may have had a series of intimate conversations in which you shared painful stories of growing up with your alcoholic father. She was there attentively listening. She encouraged you to continue by prompting you with questions and short responses like "oh my" and "you poor thing." You felt comforted and supported in your disclosure. You felt that she really understood you. Then, she kept your confidence. In a different

Emotional disclosures—disclosures that reveal sensitive, private, and personally risky information, signaling to our partners the desire for intimacy.

conversation, she shared with you the news that her fiancée had broken off their engagement. You asked her about her feelings and reflected back that you understood what she had said. In this way, you helped her better understand herself and how she wanted to handle the situation. As this example demonstrates, in a single conversation, both partners may or may not reciprocate emotional disclosures. Only one person may disclose while the other one provides support for the disclosure.

Intimate interactions are also characterized by **mutual understanding**; partners comprehending what the other is saying from both their own and their partner's point of view (Stern, 1993). In an intimate conversation, partners mentally swing back and forth between understanding what is being said from their own point of view and from their partner's (Levine, 1997). For example, you and your older sister may have had an intimate talk as teenagers when she risked your mother's rage by explaining the facts of life to you at an early age, confiding in you in detail about her boyfriend's kissing expertise. As you giggled appropriately, you may have entertained two thoughts at once: "Yuck" (your point of view) and "Well, her boyfriend really seems to make her happy" (your sister's point of view). As you probably have experienced, mutual understanding occurs when we connect with our partner through empathy while still retaining our independent perceptions.

The third characteristic of intimate conversations is **warm feelings**, the positive feelings you have about yourself and your partner during and immediately after an interaction, including happiness, excitement, yearning, peace, gratitude, contentment, desire, and love. Warm feelings are not to be confused with physical attraction or lust, which are physical and not interpersonal feelings. Rather, warm feelings occur during and after an intimate conversation as the result of the closeness mutually created by the quality of the interaction. So although you may have thought that your sister's graphic recounting of a passionate kiss with her boyfriend was yucky, you may also have felt happy because she thought enough about you to share this.

The verbal and nonverbal messages you and your partner exchange in intimate conversations signal your closeness and reduce the distance between you. Your verbal messages attempt to reduce the psychological distance between you by using open-ended questions, humor, emotional self-disclosures, inclusive pronouns (we, us, ours), praise, quick and frequent responses that encourage the partner who is speaking, and short messages that signal attentiveness and engagement ("uh huh," "wow," "go on," etc.). Your nonverbal behaviors attempt to reduce the physical distance between you, including a high level of mutual gaze, close personal space, proximity, forward body leaning, smiling, touching, and prolonged body contact (Mehrabian, 1971).

Characteristics of Intimate Relationships

An **intimate relationship** is a relationship in which partners share regular intimate interactions, feel affection for each other, trust each other, and are cohesive (Prager, 1997). Regular intimate conversations are the glue in an intimate

---

INTER-ACT WITH SOCIAL MEDIA

It can be challenging to convey warm feelings in a digital conversation compared to a face-to-face interaction. Sometimes our words are not enough. Scan your Facebook posts, text messages, and e-mails. How do you tend to communicate emotion and warm feelings through social media?

Mutual understanding—partners comprehending what the other person is saying from both their own and their partner's point of view.

Warm feelings—the positive feelings you have about yourself and your partner during and immediately after an interaction.

Intimate relationship—a relationship in which partners share regular intimate interactions, feel affection for each other, trust each other, and are cohesive.

relationship. But one intimate conversation does not an intimate relationship make; an intimate relationship requires regular intimate interactions. When these cease, close partners may lose their connection and start drifting apart.

Intimate relationships are characterized by mutual affection, the feelings of attraction, liking, and love that you feel for your partner. Mutual affection, developing from the warm feelings we experience during intimate conversations, is often conveyed through our nonverbal behavior. Childhood friends Sonia and Chas, for example, continue to meet at least once a week to share the joys and problems they are experiencing in their lives. When they see each other, they usually hug, sit close, and often hold hands. When Chas began dating Destiny, he had to explain that while he and Sonia were best friends, there wasn't any chemistry between them and their touching was just an outgrowth of their platonic affection.

Partners in intimate relationships also trust each other. When you trust your partner, you feel secure in the belief that you can depend on your partner to be there for you, helping and not doing anything to intentionally harm you. We earn our partner's trust over time by doing what we say we will do and by not revealing our partner's confidences. Chas and Destiny trust each other because over the years they both have kept each other's secrets and have made personal sacrifices to keep promises to each other.

Finally, partners in intimate relationships are cohesive. **Cohesiveness** is a sense of togetherness that we develop from sharing time, activities, and relationships with others, and creating a shared identity. Intimates spend time together, even when they are separated by physical distance. Before e-mail and texting, intimate partners who were separated spent time together by writing letters. Thanks to technology, today you can talk together on Skype or iChat. People text and tweet what they are doing as a way of spending time and sharing activities with their absent partners. As we develop an intimate relationship, we merge our social networks, becoming acquainted with and then close to our partner's families and friends. We may "friend" our partner's siblings on Facebook. Some couples become a cohesive unit with a joint identity that others may recognize. Acknowledging and playing up their distinct couple identity, the press has dubbed Brad Pitt and Angelina Jolie, for example, both celebrities in their own right, "Brangelina." With this introduction to intimate conversations and intimate relationships in mind, let's now turn our attention to understanding communication processes in three types of close relationships: families, friendships, and marriages or other long-term romantic relationships.

Cohesiveness—a sense of togetherness developed from sharing time, activities, and relationships with others, and creating a shared identity.

Families

A **family** is a network "of people who share their lives over long periods of time bound by ties of marriage, blood, or commitment, legal or otherwise, who consider themselves a family, and who share a significant history and anticipated future of functioning in a family relationship" (Galvin, Bylund, & Brommel, 2003, p. 5). As this definition suggests, families are not always made up of two opposite-sex married parents living with one or more of their children. In 2008 married couples represented just 48 percent of American households (Pew Research Center, 2010). Furthermore, although the term "family" is often interpreted as including children, approximately 5 percent of married couples experience infertility. And more and more couples are electing to remain "childfree," but they still consider themselves a family. Figure 13.1 describes both traditional family structures and other common family configurations. This chapter's "Diverse Voices" article, "Performing Commitment" by Jacqueline Taylor, describes a nontraditional but increasingly common family structure and explains how

Family—a network of people who share their lives over long periods of time bound by ties of marriage, blood, or commitment, legal or otherwise, who consider themselves a family, and who share a significant history and anticipated future of functioning in a family relationship.

- Traditional family: Family consisting of two opposite-sex parents who are married and living with one or more children from the union of those two parents.
- Single-parent family: Family in which one parent lives with the children; the other is not present in the home and may or may not be actively parenting the children.
- Shared-custody family: Family in which the parents have divorced; the children live alternately with each parent.
- Blended family: Family consisting of two adults and one or more children, some of whom were born to those parents in previous relationships.
- Common-law family: Family consisting of unmarried opposite-sex partners living with the children of their union.
- Gay and lesbian family: Family in which same-sex partners are raising children.
- Extended family: Family consisting of multiple generations of related people living together.
- Communal family: Family of unmarried people related by nongenetic factors who participate in a cooperative living arrangement.

FIGURE 13.1 Common Family Structures

Performing Commitment

by Jacqueline Taylor

Families are structured in different ways. In this excerpt, the author describes how mundane daily activities as well as rituals and public ceremonies serve as performances of commitment in her family.

For over 13 years I have created family within the context of my commitment to Carol, my partner and longtime companion. The law says we are not a couple, but two single women. No church or state has blessed or ratified our union. Although our property and our finances are by this time as entwined as our hearts and lives, the state does not apply its joint-property laws to us or give us the right to inherit from each other in the absence of a will. I cannot include her on the family insurance benefits my university offers. The only place we can purchase a family membership is at the women's bookstore.

Eight years ago we became mothers together, with the adoption of our first daughter, Lucy. One year later we adopted Grace. The law recognized us not as one family, but as two—two single mothers living in the same house with our two adopted children. No blood ties unite any of the four of us. We are a family not because but in spite of the social and legal structures that refuse to name us so. Because our status as a family has been ignored or denied by the laws and customs of our society, our existence as a family can never be taken for granted but must be constantly created and recreated. That our family differs in some significant ways from conventional notions of what constitutes a family means that our creation of family must simultaneously affirm and critique familial structures....

The process of knitting ourselves into a family has taken years and has been characterized more by daily and, yes, mundane performances of commitment than by rituals and ceremonies. Yet we have also participated in public rituals that have helped us to construct ourselves.

The arrival of our babies was greeted by four different showers thrown by friends. Each of our workplaces and two sets of friends organized parties. The various communities we participate in have worked hard to fill the gap between what the law and convention define as family and what our experience reveals. The four of us create our own rituals, as well....

Carol reminds me that the most important performance of commitment is the daily care and love we give to our daughters. Parents communicate commitment every day through the constant and repetitive tasks that children's survival depends on—changing diapers, wiping up spills, kissing "owies"—and later on, supervising homework, chauffeuring to sports and music lessons, listening to their stories. For heterosexual families perhaps this is enough. But we gay and lesbian (and adoptive) families create family outside the context of the social and legal structures that allow traditional families to take themselves for granted, and so we must do more.

Thus, we have learned to use language consciously, carefully, and repetitively to define ourselves to each other and our social world. "Family" we say, over and over. "Thank you for carrying that package. You are helping our family." "This party is just for our family." "In our family, we don't hit."

Our family doesn't fit anybody's mold. But we are a family, held together by ties of love, loyalty, commitment, and daily life. Because our family does not conform to traditional definitions of family, the performances that connect us to the social fabric and to one another take on even greater importance. Through the anniversaries, ceremonies, rituals, and holidays that mark our years and the repeated mundane actions of commitment that mark our days, we perform the bonds that make us kin.... [F]amily is a group of people who live together and love each other, bound by their shared commitment to the health, growth, and welfare of all.

For Consideration:

1. How does this article support the definition of family given in the chapter?
2. How might the changing legal landscape with regard to same-sex marriage affect premises of this article? Will married gay and lesbian couples no longer feel the need to engage in unique ritual behaviors?

Excerpted from Taylor, J. (2002). Performing commitment. In J. N. Martin, T. K. Nakayama, & L. A. Flores (Eds.), *Readings in Intercultural Communication* (pp. 310–318). New York: McGraw-Hill.

Taylor's family uses communication to reinforce their ties. In this section we will explore communication in families, focusing in turn on communication between parents and children, grandparents and grandchildren, and siblings. We will conclude the section with some recommendations for improving communication in families.

Parent-Child Communication

Many scholars agree that there are two fundamental dimensions of parents' communication with their children: nurturing and controlling (LePoire, 2006). One type of communication is **nurturing parental communication**, parental messages that encourage a child's physical, social, emotional, and intellectual development. Support, praise, displays of affection, and meeting children's needs send nurturing messages. Another type of communication is **controlling parental communication**, parental messages that attempt to influence or regulate a child's behavior. Commanding, negotiation, persuasion, and discipline send controlling messages. Many parental messages are simultaneously nurturing and controlling. For example, a mother who is teaching her preschooler how to hold a pencil correctly is controlling the child's behavior (how the fingers wrap around the pencil) as she nurtures the child's capacity to draw and write. Good parenting requires a balance of nurturing and controlling messages that are adapted to the individual child and that change as the child grows, moving from one stage of development to the next. Let's take a closer look at the effects of nurturing and control on children and their ability to form and maintain healthy relationships.

Developing Attachment Style

Parent-child communication strongly influences the way children understand and carry out relationships with others. Right from birth, infants need caregivers to act as secure bases of comfort and safety. In other words, they need nurturing behavior. Depending on how consistently and appropriately caregivers respond to their needs for nurturance, infants develop different **working models of attachment**, mental models of whether others are trustworthy and whether they (the infants) are worthy of others' care (Bowlby, 1982). Infants whose caregivers consistently meet their needs for nurturing develop a **secure attachment**, the belief that they are worthy of care and that others can be trusted to provide it. So, by feeding 10-week-old Juanita when she's hungry, changing her diaper, and holding her tenderly and often throughout the day, Juanita's mother not only keeps her physically healthy but also helps her develop a positive sense of herself and her relationships with others. Unfortunately, when caregivers provide inconsistent nurturing by meeting an infant's needs only from time to time, infants become highly attentive to the behavior of the caregiver and anxious about whether or not their need will be met. These infants develop an **anxious-ambivalent attachment**, the belief that they are not worthy of care and that others cannot be trusted. Infants whose needs are consistently ignored may die. If they survive this abusive treatment, however, they may develop an **avoidant attachment**, the belief that they are worthy of care but others are untrustworthy. Infants with

Nurturing parental communication—parental messages that encourage a child's physical, social, emotional, and intellectual development.

Controlling parental communication—parental messages that attempt to influence or regulate a child's behavior.

Working models of attachment—infants' mental models of whether others are trustworthy and whether they are worthy of others' care.

Secure attachment—infants' perception that they are worthy of care and that others can be trusted to provide it.

Anxious-ambivalent attachment—infants' perception that they are unworthy of care and others are untrustworthy.

Avoidant attachment—infants' perception that they are worthy of care and caregivers are untrustworthy.

this attachment style grow up to depend on themselves rather than seek aid or comfort from others.

Attachment styles—perceptions of self-worth and trust in others.

Secure attachment style—an adult attachment style characterized by high self-worth and trust in others.

Dismissive attachment style—an adult attachment style characterized by high self-worth but lack of trust in others.

Preoccupied attachment style—an adult attachment style characterized by low self-worth and high trust in others.

Fearful attachment style—an adult attachment style characterized by low self-worth and lack of trust in others.

As infants grow into childhood and young adulthood, working models of attachment evolve into **attachment styles**, adult perceptions of self-worth and trust in others. These attachment styles are similar to infant attachment models but reflect the behavior of adults rather than children (Bartholomew & Horowitz, 1991). Similar to infants with a secure attachment, adults with a **secure attachment style** have high self-worth and trust others. Similar to the infant avoidant attachment style, the adult **dismissive attachment style** is characterized by high self-worth but lack of trust in others. People with this attachment style are self-reliant and independent, but because of their inability to trust others, they can have difficulty sustaining close relationships. Adults with an attachment style similar to the anxious-ambivalent infants are said to have a **preoccupied attachment style**, which combines low self-worth with high trust in others. People with this style are preoccupied with their relationships; that is, they are excessively focused on how relational partners are thinking about and acting toward them. If you know people who are constantly concerned about the state of their romantic relationships or friendships and who tend to base their opinions of themselves on how they are being treated by others, they may have a preoccupied attachment style. A fourth adult style, known as the **fearful attachment style**, involves the combination of low self-worth and low trust in others. This is similar to the anxious-ambivalent style in infants. Fortunately, this style seems to be relatively rare.

Adult attachment styles are especially important because of their influence on romantic relationships. Your attachment style can affect many different aspects of your communication with your romantic partner, including self-disclosure, emotional expression, relational maintenance behaviors, and supportive communication (Guerrero, Andersen, & Afifi, 2011). For example, if Sheila has a secure attachment style, she will tend to disclose to her boyfriend at a relatively high but appropriate level, directly and effectively express her feelings to him, demonstrate her commitment to the relationship, and offer sensitive comfort when he is upset. Given these communication tendencies, it is not surprising that adults with secure attachment styles tend to be more satisfied with their romantic relationships than adults with other styles. This is especially true when "secures" are in relationships with other secures. Table 13.1 provides additional detail about communication behaviors associated with different attachment styles.

The model of attachment you develop in infancy can directly engender your adult attachment style, but it doesn't necessarily have to. Our relationships with our parents and other caregivers as well as our perceptions of these relationships can change throughout childhood and adolescence, revising the way we see ourselves and others (Le Poire, Shepard, & Duggan, 1999). An infant with a secure attachment might develop a preoccupied style in young adulthood if, for example, a bitter divorce causes either or both parents to become unreliable nurturers or caregivers during his adolescence. Or an abused or neglected child with an avoidant attachment might be adopted by a nurturing family who eventually instill in him the belief that others will be there for him when he needs help. The

TABLE 13.1 Attachment Styles and Communication Preferences

	Secure	Preoccupied	Fearful	Dismissive
Conflict Behavior	Most compromising and adept with problem solving	Demanding, exhibits dominating behavior, nagging, whining	Accommodating, responds passively	Withdrawing, less accommodating, more interrupting
Maintenance Behavior	Highest level of maintenance	High level of maintenance	Relatively low level of maintenance	Less maintenance overall, especially less romance and assurances
Emotional Expression	Readily expresses emotion in a direct, prosocial manner	Expresses negative emotions using aggression or passive aggression	Inhibits the expression of negative emotions	Experiences and expresses emotions (negative and positive) the least
Self-disclosure	High levels of appropriate disclosure, able to elicit disclosure from others	High levels of disclosure that is sometimes inappropriate or indiscriminate	Low levels of disclosure especially with strangers or acquaintances	Low levels of disclosure
Nonverbal Intimacy	Relatively high levels of facial and vocal pleasantness, laughter, touch, and smiling	Mix of positive and negative nonverbal cues, depending on the situation	Relatively low levels of facial and vocal pleasantness, expressiveness, and smiling	Relatively low levels of facial and vocal pleasantness, expressiveness, and smiling
Social Skill	Assertive, responsive to others, able to provide effective care and comfort	Overly sensitive, difficulty controlling emotional expression	Trouble expressing self and being assertive, exhibits anxiety cues such as lack of fluency and long pauses before responding	Trouble expressing self and comforting others

From Guerrero, Andersen, & Afifi, 2011, p. 171, used with permission.

critical point is that parents' nurturing behavior communicates messages to children about their self-worth and the trustworthiness of others. The early messages of caregivers can have an enduring effect, beneficial or detrimental, on a person's ability to form satisfying relationships with others.

Providing Discipline

Just as the nurturance parents provide, or fail to provide, influences their children's lives, so do their efforts to discipline or control their children's behavior. There are three primary styles of parenting that differ in their approaches to discipline and to nurturance (Baumrind, 1971). A **permissive parenting style** involves moderate to high levels of nurturing but little control over children's behavior. Permissive parents set few rules, make few demands, and typically give in to whatever the child wants. On those few occasions when they try to get children to do something or to stop misbehaving, they generally employ coercive strategies such as guilt ("Don't hit Carl. You don't want mommy to get a bad headache, do you?") or diversion ("Stop hitting Carl. Here's a candy bar."). The

Permissive parenting style—a parenting style involving moderate to high levels of nurturing but little control.

Authoritarian parenting style—a parenting style involving high levels of control behavior but low levels of nurturing.

Authoritative parenting style—a parenting style involving firm control balanced by ample nurturing.

authoritarian parenting style combines high levels of control with low levels of nurturing. Authoritarian parents value order and tradition; demand respect and obedience; and use punishment (sometimes severe) to enforce their will ("If you hit Carl again, you're getting a spanking and going to your room for the rest of the day."). They are generally unresponsive to children's efforts to reason or negotiate, even when those efforts are logical and polite. An authoritarian parent might say, "It doesn't matter what you want. I'm your dad, and you'll do what I say." Authoritarian parents also express little affection, empathy, or support for their children. Finally, the **authoritative parenting style** is characterized by firm control balanced with ample nurturing. Authoritative parents set clear and high standards for their children, but they indicate *why* certain behaviors are better or worse with facts and reasoning, such as, "When you hit Carl, it hurts. He won't want to play with you if you keep hurting him." They are also respectful of children's efforts to reason and negotiate, and whenever possible, reward positive behavior rather than punish negative behavior. For example, an authoritative parent might say, "I'm proud of you for not hitting Carl when he frustrated you again. We'll read an extra book at bedtime tonight."

These parenting styles matter because they affect how children grow up and live their lives. Compared to children with authoritative parents, children raised by authoritarian or permissive parents have lower self-esteem and self-confidence, perform less well at school, and have lower career aspirations. Children with authoritarian parents also have more difficulty getting along with their peers and experience more conflict with their parents than children with authoritative parents (LePoire, 2006). As you can see, the authoritative style of parenting has clear advantages. Our style of parenting is expressed in the messages we direct at our children. So, when talking to their children, parents need to send messages that consistently nurture and communicate an authoritative discipline.

Modeling Communication Skills

Parental communication also affects children by providing a working model of communication. For example, parents are often mortified to hear their toddlers who are beginning to talk innocently repeat profanity they've heard at home. And parental influence on children's communication extends well beyond specific words or phrases. Parents serve as role models for virtually every aspect of communication, regardless of whether they want or intend to. Modeling behavior is especially important in teaching children how to manage conflict. Young children react in various ways when they believe they have been wronged. As they will scream, cry, hit, scratch, and bite as ways of asserting their own desires, they must be directly coached to employ more appropriate ways of resolving their differences with others. ("Carson, we don't bite our friends. If you would like Kristen to move so you can see the garbage truck, say, 'Kristen, please move over.'")

Direct teaching is not, however, the only way that parents shape conflict behavior, especially as children get older. Parents who use destructive conflict strategies with each other such as counterblaming and cross-complaining (discussed in Chapter 12) teach their children that this is how to handle conflict.

Although it is possible for some children and adolescents to deliberately reject their parents' example, children may still adopt aspects of their harmful conflict behaviors. For example, research shows that teenagers whose parents use hostile conflict behavior, such as rudeness, criticism, sarcasm, insults, and expressions of anger, are significantly more likely to use these behaviors in conflict in their own marriages and to be unhappy in these marriages (Whitton et al., 2008).

Fortunately, parents who exhibit collaboration by describing their feelings, calmly discussing options, and supporting each other even during their disagreements not only protect their own relationships but also model for their children how loving people work through conflict. Parents have a similar impact on their children's comforting skills. If Courtney observes her parents listening attentively to each other's problems, providing sensitive comfort and measured advice to each other, she will be more likely to practice the same behavior when she interacts with siblings, friends, and other people in her life. If, however, she is exposed to her parents reacting insensitively to each other's distress, she will learn to behave similarly, with similar consequences for her relationships.

Communication in Other Types of Family Relationships

Of course, parent-child relationships are not the only relationships within families. With more than one child, there are sibling relationships. The extended family includes relationships with grandparents, aunts, uncles, and cousins. In many family configurations, there are "steps" and "halfs," and in less traditional families, there are relationships for which there are currently no set terms. Some of these may even involve **fictive kin**, people who are considered family members even through there are no genetic or marital ties. Each of these relationships creates its own communication opportunities, rewards, and challenges.

Fictive kin—people who are considered family members even though there is no genetic or marital tie.

Intergenerational relationships, for example, can be rewarding because they allow older family members to transmit cultural and family values, enabling younger family members to carry on family traditions. Still, elderly and younger family members may find it difficult to communicate with each other because of their different interests and values, the geographic distance between them, the fast pace of contemporary life, and societal stereotypes of youth and the elderly (Ryan, Pearce, Anas, & Norris, 2004). One of the most frequently reported communication problems between younger and older family members is how young adults speak to their elders. Gould (2004) found that when younger family members speak to elder ones, they often **overaccommodate**, excessively adapting their communication style to the perceived needs or desires of the older person. The younger family members inappropriately restrict topics, oversimplify their speech, talk too loudly, and repeat their remarks. Unless they are cognitively impaired, older family members recognize and resent this style of communication as limiting and patronizing and are consequently less satisfied with these interactions and relationships. Younger family members can improve communication by accommodating no more than necessary. For example, speak loudly to your great-aunt Bertha if she isn't wearing her hearing aid but in normal tones to your grandfather whose hearing is unimpaired.

Overaccommodate—excessively adapting one's communication style to the perceived needs or desires of the other person.

Recognition and support help family members feel valuable and help them get over difficult times they face. Recall an incident in your own life when a family member gave you support. How did that behavior affect your relationship?

Often lasting from infancy to old age, sibling relationships can span more time than any other family relationship (Segrin & Flora, 2005). Although the sibling relationship is typically created through sharing at least one parent, the nature of the relationship at any given time depends on the quantity and quality of communication that occurs. Throughout childhood, siblings provide a training ground for many kinds of communication behavior, including affection and comforting but also persuasion and conflict. In young childhood, siblings are often playmates and competitors, or if there is a sufficient age difference, one sibling may act as caregiver for another. In early and middle adulthood, as siblings leave their family of origin and establish families of their own, the amount of contact between them and the intimacy of their relationship may vary. Siblings' spouses and children can bring them closer together or, equally likely, create greater separation. As siblings establish their adult identities, the conflicts and rivalries from childhood may either persist or fade. Nevertheless, most siblings make some effort to maintain their relationships by engaging in self-disclosure, assuring one another of their continued relationship, and sharing tasks such as babysitting, caring for elderly parents, and hosting family events. Siblings use communication instrumentally to get things done and to maintain the relationship. In later life, elderly siblings typically provide each other with companionship, practical help, and emotional support, which often take the form of reminiscing about the childhood they shared. Late-life siblings often find ways to resolve conflicts or rivalries that characterized their earlier relationships. With siblings, it is easy to see how communication constitutes the relationship, serves as an instrument for accomplishing things, and indexes intimacy (see Chapter 6 for a review of these functions of communication in relationships).

Guidelines for Improving Family Communication

Countless books and articles have been written on communicating in families. Although their recommendations vary, most would likely support the following guidelines for improving communication in the family.

1. Create opportunities for intimate communication. Many people spend very little time each day actually communicating in an intimate way with other family members. To sustain positive relationships with other family members, time needs to be set aside for talk that involves more than requests, orders, or mundane planning. One good time for families to talk is during the evening meal, and the benefits of these family dinners can be profound. A series of studies conducted by the National Center on Addiction and Substance found that the more dinners teens share with family, the higher the quality of their relationships with their parents and the lower their likelihood of using drugs (Feinstein, 2010).

What clues suggest that this family enjoys each other's company?

Unfortunately, many families allow work and activity schedules to prevent them from sitting down together, or they let mediated forms of communication (television, Facebook, texting, etc.) replace meaningful face-to-face interaction with each other. Families who do not regularly share meals should consider scheduling these each week, assigning chores that family members do together, participating in hobbies or sports as a family, or having family "play dates." Whatever the means, families can improve their relationships by ensuring that they have time to interact in meaningful ways.

2. Respect individual interests and accomplishments. Family relationships benefit from individual members treating each other as important. Chapters 7 and 8 discuss the importance of listening to, understanding, and supporting others, skills that certainly should be applied to family relationships. Yet family communication can be marked by apathy when it comes to the interests and accomplishments of individual members. Sometimes individuals are overly concerned with differentiating themselves from other family members, such as children not wanting to be too much like their "uncool" parents, siblings asserting their individuality in relation to their brothers and sisters, or even parents viewing themselves as too sophisticated to be fully engaged with the "juvenile" pursuits of their children. When dad rolls a 300 game in his bowling league, little Mark gets a 100 percent on a spelling test, or Therese's mini-skirt gets selected for the 4-H fashion show, these accomplishments need to be celebrated within the family.

3. Recognize and adapt to change. Family members know each other so well that they may be quick to predict how a particular relation will think, feel, or act in various circumstances. These predictions will not always be accurate, however, because people change over time, gradual transformations that family members are often the last to recognize. Even as children grow and change in seemingly obvious ways, their brothers and sisters, and especially their parents, continue to see them as they once were, not as they are or are becoming. Recognizing and adapting to change seems especially difficult in families as children become teens and strive to achieve independence. At the same time, their parents may be experiencing changes associated with midlife transition. They may continue to interact with their children in a habitual way and justify this behavior by asserting that children must earn the right to be treated like adults. Yet teenagers who are treated like children will probably rebel or act out, whereas those treated as adults are likely to reason and discuss. Recall our discussion in Chapter 2 of how social perceptions are not always accurate. This is the case even with the perceptions of family members who claim to know each other like the back of their hand. As a result, the skill of perception checking is as important with family members as with strangers. Dating information and indexing generalizations, discussed in Chapter 4, are also important skills for family members to master.

Friendships

As the saying goes, "Friends are the family we choose for ourselves." Regardless of how much people enjoy and value their familial relationships, they also value their friendships, especially their close friendships. As discussed in Chapter 6, friendships are voluntary, platonic relationships characterized by equality and reciprocity. In other words, friends usually have relatively equal influence over each other and enjoy a pattern of equitable give-and-take that includes activities, resources, and communication (Samter, 2003).

Friendships are most likely to form between people who have the opportunity for frequent contact, who have similar demographic characteristics such as age, gender, and education, and who engage in the same kinds of activities. If you think about it, most of your friends are probably people you live near, work with, or do something with, such as attending the same religious services, taking your children to the same practice, or pursuing the same hobby. Because they are founded in contact and similarity, friendships are vulnerable to changes in life circumstances and often fade if friends are unable to see one another regularly or embark on very different life paths. If you've gone away to college and have high school friends who stayed in your hometown, you may have seen some of these friendships weaken. Close friendships, however, are more likely to be sustained over time and distance. With cell phones, e-mail, texting, and social networking sites such as Facebook, friends motivated to stay in contact now have many means to do so.

Communication plays a significant role in the formation and maintenance of friendships. Five groups of communication skills appear especially important for friendships: initiation, responsiveness, self-disclosure, emotional support, and conflict management (Samter, 2003). As noted, each of these skills is discussed in more detail in a prior chapter.

• **Initiation.** Friendships begin and are maintained when you or your partner makes the first move to get in touch with the other or start a conversation. Competent initiations are smooth, relaxed, and enjoyable. We may laugh at the idea of rehearsed pick-up lines, yet friendships are unlikely to develop if neither partner is adept at beginning enjoyable conversations. (See Chapter 8 for a discussion of initiating conversations.)

• **Responsiveness.** Friends are sensitive and aware of their partners. Listening and responding skills help you focus on your friends' needs and react appropriately. It is difficult to form and maintain friendships with others who focus only on themselves, and for this reason, responsiveness is a key friendship competency. (See Chapter 7 for material on effective listening.)

• **Self-disclosure.** Because friends share personal information and feelings with each other, a friendship is unlikely to form if people discuss only abstract ideas or surface issues. The skill of self-disclosure—describing feelings and behaviors—is, therefore, important to maintaining friendships. (Self-disclosure skills are discussed in Chapter 8.)

• **Emotional support.** People expect their friends to comfort and support them. Thus, empathizing, comforting, and praising are important ways to provide the emotional confirmation your friends need. (Emotional support skills are explored in Chapter 8.)

• **Conflict management.** Friends will inevitably disagree about ideas or behaviors. Maintaining your friendships depends on how you handle these disagreements. The skills of collaboration and constructive criticism—both of which are types of conflict management—can help your friendship weather and even benefit from periods of disagreement. (Conflict management skills are described in Chapter 12.)

Gender Differences in Same-Sex Friendships

If you've noticed that friendships between women are conducted somewhat differently than those between men, you're not alone. Research indicates that men's friendships usually focus on shared activities (playing basketball, working on

Male friendship usually focuses on activities, and men regard practical help, mutual assistance, and companionship as benchmarks of caring.

Men's and Women's Friendships

Interview two men and two women about their close friendships, using the following questions:

1. What makes a friendship a close friendship?

2. When you think about your closest friendships with other men or women, what are those relationships like?

3. When you spend time with your closest friends, what do you do? What do you talk about?

Compare the responses of your male and female interviewees. How well do they reflect what you have learned about typical friendships between men and between women? How different are their responses? Do you see any evidence that women's friendships are more intimate?

Covert intimacy—delivering messages that use mild insults, competition, or put-downs to signal closeness, trust, and equality.

cars, or playing video games, for example) and the exchange of goods and practical assistance (loaning tools or helping each other move, for example). Men's conversations tend to take place during their shared activities and tend to center on their present activities, politics, work, current events, or sex rather than on disclosing thoughts or feelings, or exploring relationships. Women's friendships also incorporate plenty of shared activity, but women are more likely than men to spend time "just talking," self-disclosing, and emotionally supporting each other. These gender differences should not be exaggerated as claims that men never just talk and women never do anything but just talk. These varied tendencies seem to persist, however, even as gender roles in society become more flexible.

One interpretation of these differences between men's and women's friendship behavior is that men's same-sex friendships are not as intimate as those of women. It does seem that men may lack or choose not to make full use of their self-disclosure and emotional support skills in their friendships with other men. Remember that intimate conversations were defined earlier in the chapter as those involving emotional disclosure, mutual understanding, and warm feelings. By this definition, men's conversations with their male friends seem deficient, at least in the area of emotional disclosure. Indeed, studies have found that men rate their friendships as less close or intimate than women rate their friendships. Men also commonly report that their friendships with women are closer and more meaningful than their friendships with other men (Fehr, 1996).

Yet some argue that this research inappropriately judges men's friendships by feminine standards. Julia Wood argues that men create an "alternate path" to intimacy through their shared activities and favors, claiming that "covert intimacy" substitutes for the lack of self-disclosure and emotional support in men's friendships. **Covert intimacy** is delivering messages that use mild insults, competition, or put-downs to signal closeness, trust, and equality (Wood, 2010). With an acquaintance, these behaviors would signal distance, distrust, and even hostility, but in the context of a well-established male friendship, these messages usually convey affection. For example, Nick might playfully say to Alex, his childhood friend and now roommate, "Hey, idiot. Hasn't that girlfriend of yours realized yet that she can do better than you?" Alex might respond, "At least I have a girlfriend, loser. When are you going to stop creeping around the girls' dorm?" Such covert intimacy perhaps offers male friends a masculine way of communicating that they care about each other.

Marriage and Long-Term Romantic Relationships

Extensive research has been directed at understanding intimacy in long-term, committed romantic relationships, including marriages and other life partnerships. Satisfaction in good relationships of these types may be greater than in any other type of intimate relationship. In a survey of more than two thousand married Americans, J. D. Bloch (1980) found that 40 percent of all respondents considered their spouses their best friends. In a different study of married people, 88 percent of married men and 78 percent of married women named their spouses as the people closest to them (Fischer & Narus, 1981, p. 449).

Studies comparing heterosexual and homosexual life partners find no significant differences on any measures of relationship satisfaction. The few studies of committed relationships that have included older gay men and lesbians have found that relationships lasting twenty years or more are not uncommon. Research shows that most lesbians and gay men want long-term committed relationships and are successful at creating them (Peplau, 1993).

Factors Defining Long-Term Relationships

Mary Anne Fitzpatrick, a leading scholar of marriage, has identified three factors that define long-term relationships: independence, ideology, and communication (Fitzpatrick, 1988; Fitzpatrick & Badzinski, 1994).

1. **Independence.** First, couples can be defined on the basis of their independence, the extent to which the partners share their feelings with each other. Some couples are independent, less reliant on their partners for emotional sharing and support. Other couples are interdependent, depending primarily on their partners for comfort, expressions of love, and fun.

2. **Ideology.** The second factor that defines long-term relationships is ideology, the extent to which the partners adhere to long-established belief systems. Some couples adhere strongly to traditional belief systems and values, for example, believing in traditional sex roles, traditional rules about the institution of marriage, sexual fidelity, and the like. Some couples, on the other hand, are open to alternative belief systems, including unorthodox sex-role relationships or unconventional long-term living arrangements.

3. **Communication.** The third factor that defines long-term relationships is one that Fitzpatrick originally called "conflict avoidance" but now calls "communication." This dimension measures the extent to which couples avoid or engage in conflict as they interact.

Types of Couple Relationships

One important insight about marriages and other long-term romantic relationships is that patterns of communication vary, establishing different ways of relating that can result in successful, long-term partnerships. In other words, you don't have to recreate your parents' marriage to be satisfied in your own. Based on

How does a traditional marriage differ from an independent one?

how relationships vary on the three dimensions of independence, ideology, and communication, Fitzpatrick identifies three basic types of couples: traditional, independent, and separate (Fitzpatrick, 1988; Fitzpatrick & Badzinski, 1994).

Traditional couples—couples who share a traditional ideology about their long-term relationships, are interdependent, and engage in conflict.

1. Traditional couples. These couples share a traditional ideology about their long-term relationships, are interdependent, and engage in conflict. Both partners follow the values accepted by their parents and grandparents. They place more emphasis on stability than spontaneity, and they almost always choose marriage and its traditional customs over alternative living arrangements. For example, the wife is likely to take her husband's last name, and neither would tolerate infidelity. Traditional couples are interdependent, meeting many of their intimacy needs within the relationship. They are likely to face their conflicts rather than avoid them.

Independent couples—couples who share an independent or unorthodox ideology, are interdependent, and engage in conflict.

2. Independent couples. These couples share an ideology that is independent and not defined by tradition. Partners may believe, for example, that their relationship should not constrain their individual freedoms. They may not share physical space, even living in different cities, without either partner feeling abandoned or lonely. They may keep separate schedules, one partner working days and the other nights, without feeling relationship stress. Like traditional couples, independent couples are interdependent in some ways but develop unconventional methods for meeting their emotional and intimacy needs. Also like traditional couples, independents engage in rather than avoid conflict.

Separate couples—couples who share a traditional ideology but are independent and avoid conflict.

3. Separate couples. These couples are similar to traditional couples in that they embrace traditional ideology but dissimilar in that they are independent and avoid conflict. For example, they adhere to customary sex roles and prefer marriage to other living arrangements. They differ, however, from both traditional and independent couples in that they are emotionally distant, relying on other relationships to satisfy their emotional needs, and they prefer to avoid conflict. Many couples in arranged marriages fit this type.

Two-thirds of the married couples Fitzpatrick studied agreed about their relationship types, yet a third disagreed. In these cases, the wife most frequently classified herself as a "traditional," and the husband more frequently saw himself as a "separate." Fitzpatrick called these types of couples "separate-traditionals." In these relationships, both the husband and wife accept the traditional institution of marriage, but the wife views marriage as an interdependent relationship in which conflict should be expressed, whereas the husband views marriage as a more emotionally distant relationship in which conflict should be avoided.

Examining these couple types and focusing on the actual conversations of couples, Fitzpatrick and her research associates, as well as other scholars, have been able to understand how different couple types handle conflict, deal with persuasive messages, display power and control, engage in casual conversation, and discuss the issues and themes important to a long-term relationship. Fitzpatrick has concluded that no couple type is necessarily better than another; rather, each type has its strengths and weaknesses. Her work is featured in the "Spotlight on Scholars" on the Web site.

Spotlight on Scholars

Read more about research couple types and communication and the work of Mary Anne Fitzpatrick at www.oup.com/us/verderber.

Characteristics of Successful Long-Term Relationships

What is the secret to a long and happy intimate romantic relationship? In an effort to answer what many consider to be the most important question about long-term relationships, researchers have identified three common characteristics of married couples who have stayed together for more than fifty years (Dickson, 1995).

1. **Mutual respect.** The first characteristic of successful long-term relationships is mutual respect. This exists when partners in the long-term relationship treat each other with dignity and value each other for what and who they are. The survey in the Learn About Yourself Box at the beginning of this chapter measured your respect for one of your partners.

2. **Presence of a shared plan or life vision.** The second characteristic of maintaining long-term relationships is the presence of a shared plan or life vision. In some relationships, this is consciously negotiated; in others, it just seems to happen. The important point is that both partners agree on their long-term goals—and, of course, that they see each other in those long-term plans. These partners talk about "we" and "us" rather than "I" or "me."

3. **Comfortable level of closeness.** The third characteristic of healthy long-term relationships is a comfortable level of closeness, enjoyed by partners who spend a mutually satisfying amount of time with each other. This does not mean that longtime partners need to be together all the time. Some partners desire constant companionship; others are content with less. As previously noted, traditional couples typically spend considerable time with each other, while independent couples may not. Both partners should continue to know each other, employing whatever level of closeness works for them. Many couples drift apart over time—that is, they quit seeking each other's company or come to prefer the company of different people. To counter this, couples must make an effort to remain close. Several communication strategies that help maintain the connection between partners are discussed in the next section.

Positive Communication for Stronger Romantic Relationships

The prior chapters in this textbook have presented many communication skills relevant to marriage and other long-term partnerships. If you are married or in a long-term relationship, for instance, you probably already recognize the importance of listening, providing emotional support, and managing conflict. In this section, we discuss some additional methods for improving your romantic relationships, all of which can be grouped under the heading of "positive communication," or communication that enhances positive feelings in your relationship. Positive communication is extremely important to couples, affirms John Gottman, a scholar who has spent much of his career studying conflict in marriages. His research has found that happiness in marriage requires a ratio of approximately five positive behaviors for every one negative behavior (Gottman, Gottman, & DeClaire, 2007). Most people, no matter how happy their relationship or skilled their communication, will sometimes act insensitively, complaining harshly, making demands, displaying frustration or anger, neglecting something important, or offending their partners in some other way. Negative behaviors tend to have a stronger, more enduring impact on how couples feel about each other, so partner satisfaction can only be cultivated in a decidedly positive relationship climate. Here are some brief tips for increasing the positivity in your relationship:

1. Show your affection. Couples dealing with the stress and busyness of everyday life often neglect to display the affection they feel toward their partners. Affectionate communication is behavior that portrays feelings of fondness and positive regard for another (Floyd, 2006). When you choose to kiss, gently touch, or smile at your significant other, recount a story you know will be enjoyed, share a private joke, comment on something positive the other person has done, or just say, "Hey . . . I love you! And I like you, too!" you are adding funds to what Gottman has called your "emotional bank account." More good news: affectionate communication is not only good for your partner and your relationship; it's also good for your health. In one study, one group of people in married and cohabiting (living-together) relationships were told to kiss more over a 6-week period, while another group received no instructions. At the end of the six weeks, the kissing group reported less stress and more relational satisfaction—and had healthier cholesterol levels (Floyd & Riforgiate, 2008).

2. Use symbols and rituals to display your commitment. As intimacy develops in a relationship, partners usually choose symbols and create rituals that display their connection, uniqueness, and commitment. For example, many couples wear jewelry that commemorates and publicizes their relationship (e.g., promise, engagement, or wedding rings), and most partners celebrate significant events in their relationship, such as the anniversaries of their marriage, their meeting, their first date, and so forth. Justine and Silvia, who actually met as children in a nursery playgroup, make time for a weekly coffee "date" after dropping their children off at playschool. Sonia wears the ring that Eduardo gave her when they became engaged, and they now celebrate "monthiversaries" of their engagement by going out to dinner. People who have been together for longer may come to feel that such symbols and rituals are less important, even optional, but these remain important, positive forms of communication regardless of how long a relationship has lasted. Couples benefit from regular reminders of their unique bond with each other.

3. Talk about sex. The key distinction between romantic and platonic relationships is that people in romantic relationships act on their sexual feelings toward each other. Extensive research indicates that in marriages and other long-term romantic relationships, sexual satisfaction is closely connected with love, relationship satisfaction, and commitment to the relationship (Sprecher, Christopher, & Cate, 2006). This finding is not terribly surprising, since good sex is both physically and emotionally rewarding, and when you associate these benefits with your partner, you tend to feel great about the relationship. This research also shows that couples can improve their sexual satisfaction by talking about sex, specifically, the sexual behaviors they like and dislike. To enhance positive feelings in your relationship, it's important to talk with your partner about what you enjoy doing. For example, Evan might say to Tina, "I really like it when we experiment with different positions. It makes me feel like we're just falling in love again." You should also discuss what needs to be changed to make you both happier. Raquel might tell Oscar, "Hey, I know you're trying to make it great for me, but for whatever reason, playing with my ears just doesn't do much for me. If you nibbled on my neck, though. . . ." The skills for effective praise and criticism discussed in Chapter 8 are highly relevant to sexual communication.

The Dark Side of Intimacy

Intimacy in relationships with family, friends, and romantic partners is difficult to achieve and maintain, and a number of ills can arise that will damage or destroy the health of any of these relationships. In this final section, we describe two potential obstacles on the road to relational intimacy—relational uncertainty and possessiveness, the latter behavior exemplifying the dark side of intimacy. As we noted in the first chapter, the dark side involves inappropriate and/or unethical interpersonal communication. After describing these problems, we discuss how improved communication can help address these concerns in intimate relationships.

Relational Uncertainty

Relational uncertainty is a feeling of doubt about the nature of a relationship. It may stem from three sources: an absence of clarity about the nature of the relationship, a tension between closeness and separation, and concern about the future.

Relational uncertainty—a feeling of doubt about the nature of a relationship.

    1. Absence of clarity about the nature of the relationship. A first source of relational uncertainty is an absence of clarity between partners about whether the relationship is platonic or romantic. Aspects of both may be occurring simultaneously, confusing one or both parties about the nature of the relationship. Because both partners rarely want to move from casual dating to a serious romantic attachment at the exact same time, this type of relational uncertainty is most prevalent as the relationship progresses from one stage to another (Knobloch & Solomon, 2002).

    2. Tension between closeness and separation. A second source of relational uncertainty stems from a dialectical tension in which partners desire closeness one day and separateness the next. You will recall from the discussion of relational dialectics in Chapter 6 that competing tensions often pull people back and forth in their relationship needs. These variations can occur both within and between individuals.

    3. Concern about the future. A third source of relational uncertainty arises from concern about the future of a relationship, stemming from perceived distancing, unresolved conflicts, or life changes. At times, people in committed relationships begin to notice and become concerned about signs that the relationship has become more distant, with less sharing or less time spent on mutually enjoyable activities. At other times, partners may worry about unresolved (or irresolvable) conflicts, such as differences in money management philosophies or religious beliefs. At still other times, normal life transitions give rise to concerns about the future. When a daughter marries, for instance, her mother may experience relational uncertainty about the future as their relationship develops new boundaries, or best friends may not know how their relationship will change as they prepare to leave for different colleges.

The best way to deal with relational uncertainty is to consciously acknowledge it to yourself and discuss your feelings of uncertainty with your partner. Such openness may be difficult, but communicating directly about our feelings can help reduce uncertainty and sustain the relationship. For example, imagine that Dana and Jamie have been close friends their whole lives. Recently, Jamie has not been returning Dana's calls or responding to e-mails. They have not found the time to get together socially in months either. Dana misses her close friendship with Jamie and feels uncertain about whether they will remain close friends. To help lessen the uncertainty, Dana might ask Jamie directly, "Do you think that our friendship is drifting apart? It seems to me that we haven't gotten together in about six months, and we seldom talk by phone or e-mail. I wonder what the future holds for our friendship." Jamie may clarify by responding, "Hey, I feel bad about not being able to get together or even talk once in a while. I am swamped at work right now, and I'm in the middle of trying to finish building the deck on my house before the weather turns cold. I don't want you to think that I'm blowing off our friendship. I hope that whatever happens in our separate lives, we can count on each other as friends."

Possessiveness

Possessiveness—the desire to control another person to ensure that he or she is one's exclusive partner.

Possessiveness is the desire to control another person to ensure that he or she is one's exclusive partner. Possessive behaviors can range from mild to severe, holding a partner's hand at a party to communicate to others that your partner "belongs" to you, for example, or physically or psychologically intimidating partners into compliance with your "ownership" of them. Possessiveness is caused by **jealousy**, an intense suspicion that your partner values, likes, or loves someone more than you. It can occur in a variety of intimate relationships. Sibling rivalries are a form of jealousy that stems from children vying for parental attention and affection. Either parent may also succumb to jealousy if the children appear to favor mom over dad or vice versa, or parents may become jealous of the relationships that their older children develop with other adults. Jealousy can trouble platonic same-sex friendships if friends perceive that their partners are spending more time with others, and, of course, romantic relationships and life partnerships are also susceptible to jealousy. Like other feelings, jealousy is inherently neither good nor bad. It can provoke appropriate concern when there is a legitimate threat to your relationship, and it can motivate you to talk with

Jealousy—an intense suspicion that your partner values, likes, or loves someone more than you.

"Hello, remember me?" How do jealousy and possessiveness affect relationships?

your partner about your feelings. But jealousy can also be a destructive force that may ruin your relationship if it becomes extreme possessiveness (Pelusi, 2006). According to one study, 57 percent of respondents cited a former friend's jealous feelings or critical attitude toward the respondent's other relationships as a "moderate to very important" reason for the breakup of their relationship (Marsh, 1988, p. 27).

Open, honest communication in the form of simple conversations between partners can reduce feelings of jealousy, prevent misunderstandings, and discourage possessive behaviors. If, for example, at a party Paul notices that his fiancée, Jocelyn, is spending most of the evening engrossed in conversation with a very handsome man whom Paul does not know, he may feel jealous. To prevent these feelings from deteriorating into possessiveness, he may politely interrupt the conversation, ask Jocelyn to dance, and confess his jealousy, diplomatically admitting, "Honey, I don't know who that guy is and what you're talking about with him, but I do know that I am feeling jealous." In doing so, he may learn that the mystery man is actually an old friend of her brother, who recently lost his wife in an accident.

Giving your partner feedback and describing his or her possessive behaviors in a tactful and sensitive way may discourage unreasonable jealousy. For instance, if Sarella and Cary have been seeing each other for several months and are getting serious, but Janette, Sarella's best friend and roommate, has begun to erase Cary's voice mail, Sarella may need to speak with Janette about this. She might broach the subject by saying, "Janette, during the past week I know that Cary has left three messages on the answering machine that weren't there when I got home. Can you help me understand what's happening?" This nonthreatening description may encourage Janette to confess her possessive feelings, opening the door to an extended conversation that deepens their understanding of and appreciation for the importance of their friendship.

These candid conversations can alleviate jealousy and possessive behaviors by building and restoring trust before the relationship is permanently damaged. Unfortunately, jealousy and possessiveness can in some instances become psychopathic, leading to stalking and harassment. If you find one of your intimates crossing the line, moving from possessiveness to stalking, and if conversations have not helped, it may be time for you to distance yourself from the relationship and even seek help from law enforcement if this person persists.

THE SOCIAL MEDIA FACTOR

Using Digital Communication Skills to Improve Relationships

The convenience, reach, and mobility of social media have altered how we practice interpersonal relationships with others. Texting, Facebook, Skype, and other services enable us to keep in constant contact with friends, rapidly respond to their messages, and ultimately strengthen our interpersonal connections.

Digital Communication Skills in Personal Relationships

One of the most important benefits of social media is the ability to easily maintain our interpersonal relationships. Even though we may regularly see many of our Facebook friends in face-to-face settings, we still use social media to strengthen those connections. Most relationships are characterized by **media multiplexity**— meaning that we carry out those relationships through more than one form of social media and that those in closer relationships use more forms of social media (Haythornthwaite, 2005). Media multiplexity theory explains the presence of strong and weak social ties in an individual's relational network. **Strong ties** include relationships such as those with friends, romantic partners, and family members. These relationships exhibit behavior that reflects heightened emotion, interdependence, intimacy, and high levels of closeness. In contrast, **weak ties** are casual contacts that are more loosely connected to an individual's social network and are not characterized by intimacy (Haythornthwaite, 2005). According to media multiplexity theory, the number of different social media that friends use is strongly associated with whether a tie is weak or strong. Specifically, strong ties use several forms of social media, but weak ties use only one or two social media. Think about your best friend. You likely use many forms of social media to maintain this strong tie. You may interact on Facebook, text regularly, talk on the phone, and maybe even Skype several times a week. Now, think about a weak tie, perhaps an acquaintance from a large college class. If you are Facebook friends, you may comment on a wall post every now and then, but you probably rarely, if ever, talk on the phone, text, and Skype. Social media are important devices that enhance our strong social ties and give us the opportunity to maintain our weak social ties. Scan your Facebook friends list and identify your weak ties. Reach out to those people to strengthen your interpersonal connection.

Media multiplexity theory—explains that we carry out those relationships through more than one form of social media, and those in closer relationships use more forms of social media.

Strong ties—include relationships such as those with friends, romantic partners, and family members. These relationships exhibit behavior that reflects heightened emotion, interdependence, intimacy, and high levels of closeness.

Weak ties—are casual contacts that are more loosely connected to an individual's social network and are not characterized by intimacy.

Although people in close relationships use social networking sites to communicate with each other, most relationships maintained primarily through Facebook are actually weak. In fact, students report that, of their entire friend network on Facebook, only about one-third of those individuals are "real" friends (Baron, 2008; Ellison, Steinfeld, & Lampe, 2009). Even though social networking sites allow users to exchange synchronous and asynchronous messages, a vast majority of friends never seem to do this. The success of Facebook and other social networking sites as relationship maintenance tools comes from their wide but selective reach. Although you may keep in closer contact with strong ties, you can communicate with multiple weak ties simultaneously. Shelby can share the news of her engagement to all friends in a tweet or status update. Or she can choose who can receive the message in wall posts. If you are a frequent Facebook user, you probably share photos on a regular basis. Even though all your Facebook friends may not comment on your newly posted photos, simply having access to one another's updates on Facebook may facilitate some sense of interpersonal connection (Humphreys, 2007).

Initiating Relationships

Social networking sites are also used to establish new relationships. Social networks are home to many **latent ties**—potential relationships within a social circle that are present but have not been activated, such as those with friends of friends on Facebook (Haythornthwaite, 2002). In addition, people may also explicitly seek new relational partners online through dating sites such as eHarmony.com and Match.com. Matchmaking is not new to social media, however. Ask your grandparents. Newspapers and magazines have always featured classified ads for people seeking romantic connections.

Even if not expressly looking for them, people might form new relationships online for many reasons. Regardless of the form of social media used to initiate the relationship, people are intrinsically motivated to reduce their uncertainty (or anxiety) about others and find similarities with them. Joseph Walther (1992) proposed **Social Information Processing** (SIP) theory to explain how relationships evolve online. His theory posits that our need to reduce uncertainty will encourage us to adapt our language and behaviors in online settings to reveal our own personal information and actively seek similar information from others. The longer the interaction or the higher the expectation of future interaction, the more likely social information processing will continue (Walther, 1994). SIP suggests that online interpersonal relationship development might require more time to develop than traditional face-to-face relationships. Once established, however, online relationships will demonstrate the same relational dimensions and qualities as face-to-face relationships. Consider Melissa and Matt, who met at a party, and Joe and Chrissy, who met online through Match.com. According to SIP theory, even though Joe and Chrissy met online, over time their relationship will possess the same qualities of closeness and connection as Melissa and Matt, who met face-to-face.

INTER-ACT WITH SOCIAL MEDIA

Do you use social media to keep in touch with your parents or family members? If so, take a moment to review the digital messages that you exchange with them. Do you use one social media outlet more frequently than others to remain connected with certain individuals? How do you think social media influence the attachment you feel with your parent or loved one?

Latent ties—potential relationships within a social circle that are present, but have not been activated.

Social information processing theory—explains that because we feel a need to reduce uncertainty, in online settings we will likely adapt our language and behaviors to reveal our own personal information and actively seek similar information from others.

Hyperpersonal communication— suggests that digital interactions can become hyperpersonal because the context affords message senders a host of communicative advantages over traditional face-to-face interactions.

Online relationship development has certain benefits, yet these interactions also present potential challenges. **Hyperpersonal communication** theory suggests that digital interactions can become intense and overly intimate because the context affords message senders a host of communicative advantages over traditional face-to-face interactions (Walther, 1996). In a hyperpersonal message, the sender takes advantage of the greater opportunity to strategically develop and edit his presentation of self, compared to ordinary face-to-face conversations. If Andy is seeking a romantic relationship through eHarmony.com, he may post personal pictures from a time when he was thinner and regularly working out at the gym. In other words, hyperpersonal users are able to select their messages for optimized presentation to others. Hyperpersonal users must always remember to practice digital communication ethically and avoid intentionally deceiving other people. Although the advantages of social media can present a host of opportunities for digital communication, many ethical principles of face-to-face communication are still applicable toward communication in digital contexts.

A QUESTION OF ETHICS ● What Would You Do?

Jackie and Michael had been dating for a year and were talking about marriage when Michael's company transferred him to Columbus for six months. Two months into their separation, Jackie visited Michael's new city and had a chance to meet his co-workers at a party, including Veronica, a beautiful woman a few years younger than herself. Michael had talked to Jackie about all his new colleagues, including Veronica, but she had had no idea how attractive she was. As the evening went on, Jackie could sense that Michael and Veronica were forming a special friendship. She couldn't help but feel a twinge of jealousy for this woman who got to spend time with her boyfriend. Nevertheless, Michael seemed completely attentive to Jackie, and they had a wonderful visit.

A couple of weeks later, while on a business trip to Columbus, Gwen, an acquaintance of Jackie's, happened to see Michael and Veronica having dinner together at a restaurant. The day after her return, Gwen ran into Jackie at the grocery store and casually remarked that she had seen Michael with Veronica. When Jackie commented that Michael and Veronica were co-workers, Gwen hesitantly replied, "Well, they

certainly seem to have a close working relationship." Jackie blanched. Trying to soothe her, Gwen said, "I'm sure there's an explanation for everything. I mean there could be lots of reasons for him to be holding her hand. I'm sorry I said anything." But Jackie did not feel better.

Later that evening when Michael called, Jackie immediately confronted him by asking sarcastically, "So, how's Veronica?"

When Michael replied, "What do you mean?" Jackie went on, "Don't give me any of your innocent 'what do I mean' stuff—you were seen and you know it!"

"Oh, Gwen," said Michael. "So you'll take the word of some nosy, troublemaker and judge me before you find out the real situation? If that's all the trust you have in me, then I'm not sure. . . ."

"Oh, sure, defend yourself by blaming Gwen. But she did see you. You're right about one thing, this is about trust."

For Consideration:
1. What ethical issues are involved in this situation?
2. What could/should Jackie have said to her friend Gwen and to Michael?
3. How could/should Michael have responded?

Summary

Intimacy is both an interaction pattern and a quality of relationships. The characteristics of intimate conversations are emotional disclosures, mutual understanding, and warm feelings. An intimate relationship is a relationship in which partners share regular intimate interactions, feel affection for each other, trust each other, and are cohesive. Three types of intimate relationships are family relationships, friendships, and long-term romantic relationships, which include marriages and other life partnerships.

A family is a network "of people who share their lives over long periods of time bound by ties of marriage, blood, or commitment, legal or otherwise, who consider themselves a family, and who share a significant history and anticipated future of functioning in a family relationship" (Galvin et al., 2003, p. 5). There are two fundamental dimensions of parents' communication with their children: nurturing and controlling. Depending on their caregivers' behavior, infants acquire secure, anxious-ambivalent, or avoidant models of attachment. Evolving from infant models, adult attachment includes secure, dismissive, preoccupied, and fearful styles. Parenting includes permissive, authoritarian, and authoritative styles. Parents influence their children's communication skills through modeling. Intergenerational communication brings both opportunities and challenges, and communication in a sibling relationship changes over its life span. Family communication and relationships can be improved by creating opportunities for intimate communication, respecting individual interests and accomplishments, and recognizing and adapting to change.

Friendships are voluntary, platonic relationships characterized by equality and reciprocity. Friendships are most likely to form between people who have frequent contact, similar demographic traits, and engage in the same activities. Five groups of communication skills are especially important for friendships: initiation, responsiveness, self-disclosure, emotional support, and conflict management. Men's and women's same-sex friendships differ: men's relationships are more activity-focused, whereas women are more likely to engage in " just talking," self-disclosure, and emotional support. Although men's same-sex friendships may appear less intimate than women's, men may express their feelings of closeness through covert intimacy.

Strong and enduring intimacy often occurs in long-term relationships like marriages and other life partnerships. Defined by three dimensions—independence, ideology, and communication—long-term couples generally fit into three types—traditional, independent, and separate. Regardless of type, however, mutual respect, a comfortable level of closeness, and the presence of a plan or life vision characterize successful long-term relationships.

Relational uncertainty and possessiveness are two potential problems in intimate relationships. The best way to reduce relational uncertainty is to acknowledge it and discuss it with your partner. To reduce feelings of jealousy, engage in open, honest communications about your feelings. To curb a partner's possessiveness that often stems from jealousy, provide feedback and describe the possessive behaviors.

Chapter Resources

What You Should Be Able *to Explain:*

- The characteristics of intimate conversations
- The characteristics of intimate relationships
- The primary dimensions of parental communication
- The types of attachment and their implications for relationships
- Three parenting styles and their effects on children
- The strengths and challenges of intergenerational family communication
- How communication between siblings changes over the life span
- Three ways to improve family communication
- Communication skills are especially important in friendships
- How men's and women's friendships differ
- The factors that define long-term romantic partnerships
- The types of long-term couple relationships

- The characteristics of successful long-term relationships
- How to deal with the dark side of intimate relationships
- Media multiplexity theory
- Social Information Processing theory

What You Should Be Able *to Do:*

- Ascertain the health of family and intimate relationships
- Use techniques to reduce relational uncertainty with intimates
- Apply best practices to digital communications with family and intimates.

Self-test questions based on these concepts are available on the companion Web site (www.oup.com/us/verderber) as part of Chapter 13 resources.

Key Words

Flashcards for all of these key terms are available on the *Inter-Act* Web site.

Anxious-ambivalent attachment, p. 403
Attachment styles, p. 404
Authoritarian parenting style, p. 406
Authoritative parenting style, p. 406
Avoidant attachment, p. 403
Cohesiveness, p. 401
Controlling parental communication, p. 403
Covert intimacy, p. 412
Dismissive attachment style, p. 404
Emotional disclosures, p. 398
Family, p. 401
Fearful attachment style, p. 404

Fictive kin, p. 407
Hyperpersonal communication, p. 422
Independent couples, p. 414
Intimate relationship, p. 399
Jealousy, p. 418
Latent ties, p. 421
Media multiplexity theory, p. 420
Mutual understanding, p. 399
Nurturing parental communication, p. 403
Overaccommodate, p. 407
Permissive parenting style, p. 405
Possessiveness, p. 418

Preoccupied attachment style, p. 404
Relational uncertainty, p. 417
Secure attachment style, p. 404
Secure attachment, p. 403
Separate couples, p. 414
Social Information Processing (SIP), p. 421
Strong ties, p. 420
Traditional couples, p. 414
Warm feelings, p. 399
Weak ties, p. 420
Working models of attachment, p. 403

Apply Your Knowledge

The following activities challenge you to demonstrate your mastery of the concepts, theories, and frameworks in this chapter by using them to explain what is happening in a specific situation.

Improving Communication Among Family and Intimates

Assume that you write a personal advice column for an online newspaper. Respond to each of the letters asking for advice. In each response, preface your advice by explaining to the writer what you see happening, using the concepts and theories you have studied in this chapter.

13.1 Dear Doc. Comm,

I am a 21-year-old woman and have been dating a really fantastic man. He owns his own business and is very successful. Not only that, but he is really good looking with a fantastic body—in other words, a real catch. I think he likes me as much as I like him, but the problem is that while I am very open with him, he doesn't tell me much about his life. Whenever I ask about his family or other relationships he's had, he either politely changes the subject or ends the conversation, claiming to suddenly remember something that needs to be done at work. Is this normal for guys, or should I be concerned?

Signed,
Hanging in Helena

13.2 Dear Doc. Comm,

I am a 75-year-old man who has been forced to move in with my married daughter and her family. While I am grateful to her and her husband for taking me in, I am thoroughly disgusted by how my grandchildren behave. First, they seem to run the show. Both my daughter and her husband dote on the children. The kids who are 5, 8, and 13 are allowed to do whatever they want. There is no set bedtime, no study time, and no household chores. The house is a complete disaster as the kids leave stuff all over, and neither my daughter nor her husband (who both work long hours) has the energy to pick anything up. Yesterday, the 8-year-old came into my room when I wasn't there and broke the remote control to my TV. I lost my cool, grabbed him by the arm, and dragged him out of my room, kicking and screaming. My daughter, hearing the commotion, came running and proceeded to fuss over the boy as though I had hurt him. Then she turned to me and said, "We don't believe in touching our children in anger. If you do this again, you will have to leave." I can't afford to live on my own, but I don't think I should have to put up with my grandchildren destroying my property. What can I do now?

Signed,
Grandpa in the Dog House

13.3 Dear Doc. Comm,

I am heartbroken. I just learned that my husband of twenty-five years is having an online affair with a woman in Hartford, CT (We live in Dallas, TX). Not only has he been corresponding with her for months, but it also appears that they have been sexting and she has sent him nude pictures of herself. When I confronted him with my discovery (which really happened accidently as he forgot to shut down his e-mail and log out of his account on our home computer), he told me that it was "nothing to worry about. Everyone does this from time to time, and it was just a little online fun." I want to believe him. Is it normal for people to carry on with someone online? Should I just get over this? I thought we had a good marriage, but now I wonder. What do you advise?

Signed,
Devastated in Dallas

Understanding Digital Media Concepts

Read the following and then answer the questions below to explain what is happening in this situation.

> *Eddie attends a college in a different state, about 16 hours from his hometown. He only goes home for holidays. Midway through his first year, Eddie begins to realize how difficult it is to remain in touch with his friends from high school. It seems that they rarely communicate anymore. About once a month, Eddie posts a comment on the Facebook pages of his high school friends. He sees his college friends almost every day. Even though they see each other so often, they still text many times a day, talk on the phone, exchange e-mails, and interact on Facebook. Before Eddie comments on his roommate's Facebook status message, he notices that his roommate is Facebook friends with Caroline, a woman in Eddie's large biology class. He never talked to Caroline before, but he thinks she is attractive. He would like to get to know her more. Eddie sends Caroline a Facebook friend request and hopes for the best.*

13.4   Use media multiplexity theory to explain what is happening in this situation.

13.5   How might social information processing theory explain how things might evolve with Eddie and Caroline's relationship?

Communication Improvement Plan: Intimate Relationships

Would you like to improve your use of the following aspects of intimate relationship communication discussed in this chapter?

- Communication in families
- Communication in friendships
- Communication in marriages or long-term romantic relationships

13.6   Choose one specific relationship that you would like to improve. Then using the interpersonal communication skills you have studied in the course, write a communication improvement plan. You can find a communication improvement plan worksheet on our Web site at www.oup.com/us/verderber.

Inter-Act with Media

Television

Little People, Big World. (2010)

The show revolves around the daily family life of the Roloffs, led by parents Matt and Amy, who are both dwarfs (little people) and their four children. It is moving to learn about the struggles that Matt, Amy, and their son Zach face living in a world where everything is built for people over four feet tall. Zach must attempt to relate to his average-height twin, who is nearly two feet taller than he is. The parents, Matt and Amy, communicate about important family decisions when Matt is an idealistic dreamer and Amy is a logical planner. Through all of the sports practices and mishaps around their Oregon farm, viewers watch the Roloffs navigate communication in their family through openness, affection, discipline, humor, and sarcasm. Matt and Amy reveal that they are highly invested in teaching their children family customs and traditions, beliefs and values, and the communication skills to face life's challenges. They want their children to feel loved and secure so that they achieve success both professionally and personally.

IPC Concepts: Parent-child communication, attachment style, discipline, modeling communication skills

To the Point:

> How would you describe the communication between members of the Roloff family? How would you characterize the parents' ability to prepare their children for life in a "big" world?

Cinema

Lars and the Real Girl. (2007). Craig Gillespie (director). Ryan Gosling, Emily Mortimer, Paul Schneider, Kelly Garner, Patricia Clarkson.

Lars (Gosling) is a shy man who lives in the garage, which is owned by his brother (Schneider) and sister-in-law (Mortimer). Lars has acquaintances at work, but is extremely socially anxious. This prevents him from establishing strong emotional and physical connections with other people. At one point, Lars goes on the Internet to purchase "Bianca," a very lifelike sex doll. He begins a relationship with her. A physician (Clarkson) claims that Lars needs to own this delusion to work through the social phobia that prevents him from strongly bonding with other people. Throughout the course of the film, Gus, Karin, and the town citizens treat Lars and "Bianca" as being in an actual relationship. People begin to treat Bianca as a real live woman. This leads to Gus deepening his communication with Lars. Through his relationship with a fake "Bianca," Lars takes small steps toward developing authentic interpersonal relationships with others.

IPC Concepts: Family relationships, family communication and self-concept formation, improving family communication, problems associated with intimacy

To the Point:

> How would you describe Lars's self-concept and its relationship to his communication competence?
> How would you characterize Lars's ability to interact effectively with members of his family?

What's on the Web

Find links and additional material, including self-quizzes, on the companion Web site at www.oup.com/us/verderber.

14

Communicating in the Workplace

"Hi, Maria. I heard you started your new job. How's it going?" asked Amber sliding into the seat next to Maria.

"It's OK. The hiring process was really weird. At first, I didn't hear from them, so I called. And as it turns out, I wasn't being considered because my résumé didn't come through well. You had to apply over the Internet and I didn't understand about the format. Anyway, since the deadline hadn't passed, once I called, they let me resubmit in the proper format. I thought maybe they were just doing that because I'm a minority and I "count." I really didn't expect to get an interview, let alone the job. But they called and asked me to interview. So I prepped like crazy. I knew everything about the company, including last quarter's earnings and the projections for the next year. That really impressed them," Maria replied, adding, as she shrugged her shoulders and sighed, "But I'm not sure if it was worth all the time and effort. I think I'm going to quit before I get fired."

"Fired? Why would you get fired? You've just begun," Amber exclaimed.

"Well, there's this man named Sam who has a lot of influence with our manager, and he's been hitting on me. I tried to let him know that I wasn't interested, but he kept it up. So I reported him to human resources. Since then, my manager has been watching me like a hawk and has been hypercritical of my work. Carlos, that's my manager, was supposed to train me on the order entry system, but since I reported Sam, he says he just can't find time. And half of my job requires me to use that system, so I've been trying to figure it out myself. But I mess up sometimes, and then Carlos gets on my case. And Sam has begun sending me these creepy voice and text messages. I don't even know how he got my cell number. It's really a bad situation, and I can't wait around to get fired and have to explain that whenever I apply for a job."

"Wow, that's so not fair. I can see why you'd want out. But I thought you really needed the job, and in this economy it's tough to find work. Are you sure there's nothing you can do to salvage the situation?" Amber asked supportively.

What you should be able *to* explain after you have studied this chapter:

- The role of communication in the hiring process
- How to prepare an electronic résumé
- How to write an effective cover e-mail
- How to interview for a job
- Effective communication in manager-employee relationships
- Effective communication in co-worker relationships
- Effective communication with customers/clients
- The effects of diversity in the workplace
- How to handle the dark side of workplace communication
- Guidelines for developing digital communication skills in professional relationships

What you should be able *to* do after you have studied this chapter:

- Develop job leads
- Prepare an e-résumé
- Prepare an e-mail cover letter
- Interview for a job

Most adults spend about half of their waking hours on the job. Thus, many of the relationships we maintain are with work colleagues. These relationships differ from friendships and family relationships because, for the most part, they serve different purposes and are not voluntary. Apart from deciding to take a specific job, you usually don't choose the people you work with or for. Yet the relationships you establish and maintain at work are important to your career success and to your general life satisfaction. In fact, the longer you work for one organization the more likely you are to have colleagues who are also friends and, in some cases, intimate friends. In this chapter we will look at communicating in the workplace. You can't have workplace relationships until you have a job. So we begin by explaining how to present yourself during the hiring process, including how to find job openings and prepare electronic résumés and e-mail cover letters, as well as how to prepare for, conduct yourself during, and follow-up a job interview. Next, we identify effective communication practices in managerial, co-worker, and client relationships. Then, we describe how diversity affects workplace relationships. Finally, we discuss how to handle dark-side communication issues like the one confronting Maria at her job.

Finding a Job

Did you know that in the past fifty years, the average number of years a person continues to work with the same organization has dropped from 23½ years to 3½ years (Taylor & Hardy, 2004)? Not only that, but between 15 and 20 million Americans will find themselves changing jobs each year (Bashara, 2006). As

we continue to recover from the Great Recession, competition for jobs is fierce. This means that we spend more time seeking employment than ever before. Throughout this book, we have discussed the role communication plays in how you present yourself to others and how this affects their perceptions of you. It is, therefore, not surprising that the way you present yourself during the hiring process is key to getting a job. You may have an excellent background and all the skills required to be successful in the job, but if you are ineffective at communicating this and presenting yourself as an acceptable employee and co-worker, then you will probably be under- or unemployed. In this section we want to describe how to find job openings, how to prepare an electronic résumé and e-mail cover letter, and how to interview for a job.

Locating Job Openings

At this point in your life, you have probably been through the hiring process at least once and know how stressful it can be. You also know that simply finding out about job openings can be difficult. Let's briefly review three ways you can learn about potential jobs.

1. Campus Career Center. All reputable colleges and universities have student career centers that actively court local and national employers to come to campus to recruit students. Your tuition dollars pay for this service, so it's the first place you should check. You will find job postings probably online as well as at the center in addition to a list of employers holding on-campus interviews. But more importantly, you will find the professionals in these offices offer a variety of services, from helping you polish your résumé to offering mock interviews with feedback on your performance.

2. Online Job Posting Sites. There are literally hundreds of job search Web sites. These range from national giants (e.g., CareerBuilder.com, Monster.com, and HotJobs.com) to government sites (e.g., USAJOBS.gov as well as state, county, and city specific sites) to specialty sites (e.g., CollegeJobBank.com, a site dedicated to recent college graduates) to regional sites (e.g., CraigsList.org) to local online classified ads associated with the local newspaper to company-specific sites. Some sites allow you to post your résumé online and will deliver it to employers if your credentials fit their needs. Although most employers will comb national, specialty, regional, and local sites, they find that it is easier to find acceptable candidates through their own sites (Light, 2011). You can improve your chances of landing an interview if you apply on the company's own Web site.

3. Networking. Networking is developing or using established relationships to gain career information and insight, including access to the **hidden job market**, jobs that are never advertised because employers hire people already known to them. It has been estimated that the majority of jobs are filled this way (Betty, 2010). Your network consists of the people you know, as well as the people known to the people you know. To uncover the hidden job market in your field and geographic area, you need to do two things.

Networking—developing or using established relationships to gain career information and insight, including access to the hidden job market.

Hidden job market—jobs that are never advertised because employers hire people already known to them.

First, reach out to the people you know and tell them you are in the job market. Your family, friends, classmates, softball teammates, barber, insurance broker, bank teller, college professors, and so forth are all part of your network, and you should let them know when you are looking for a job. Don't assume they know your résumé, so be prepared to provide them with a 60-second verbal highlight reel of your qualifications and the type of job you are seeking. Ask the people you contact if they know of any openings in your field, and ask them to keep their ears open and pass on anything they hear that might be of interest to you.

Second, grow your network. Attend networking events in your area, such as those hosted by your local Chamber of Commerce, and meetings of your high school and college alumni associations. Join professional (e.g., Women in Communication, the American Marketing Association) and civic organizations (e.g., Kiwanis Club, International Rotary Club). Volunteer to work for a nonprofit or community group using the skills you would like to develop. Use online networking tools such as LinkedIn, Facebook, and Twitter. The key to effective networking is remembering that it involves relationships: you need to be able to provide something for your partners through whom you hope to find job openings. You can read much more about effective networking techniques in career development books and at online job search Web sites.

Résumés and Cover Letters

Because interviewing is time consuming, most organizations do not interview all the people who apply for a job. Rather, they use a variety of screening devices to identify candidates who best meet their technical qualifications. Chief among these screening devices is evaluating the qualifications you present on your résumé and in the accompanying cover letter. A **résumé** is a summary document outlining your work history, educational background, skills, and accomplishments. A **cover letter** is a short, well-written e-mail or letter expressing your interest in a particular position. The goal of your résumé and cover letter is to sell you and get an interview (Farr, 2008). Today, you typically send these to the employer online, and then you bring hard copies of your résumé to the interview. Let's look at how you should tailor your résumé.

1. Craft your résumé for a particular position. Your résumé should highlight your qualifications for *a particular job*. To do so, you need to know something about the job requirements and the company and tweak your standard résumé to indicate how your skills and accomplishments have prepared you for this position. For most companies, you can find a wealth of information by doing a Google search and by visiting the company's own Web site. Career center advisors at your college or university can also assist you with your research.

2. Highlight your skills and experiences. There are two basic types of résumés. Both begin by supplying basic demographic information (name, address, e-mail, phone number, educational background, career objective or personal statement). A **chronological résumé** lists your job positions and accomplishments

Résumé—a summary sheet outlining your work history, educational background, skills, and accomplishments.

Cover letter—a short, well-written letter or e-mail expressing your interest in a particular position.

Chronological résumé—a format that lists your job positions and accomplishments in reverse chronological order.

Elisa C. Vardin
2326 Tower Place   (513) 861-2497
Cincinnati, OH 45220   ECVardin@yahoo.com

Professional Objective:
An entry-level market research position where I can use my quantitative training to create and analyze marketing data and use my organizing, writing and public speaking skills to communicate technical findings to decision makers.

Educational Background:
University of Cincinnati, Cincinnati, OH, B.A.

June 2001. Major: Applied Mathematics, Minor: Marketing. GPA 3.36. Dean's List.

Work and Other Relevant Experience:
Marketing Solutions, Inc., Cincinnati, OH. Summer 2011.

Intern, market research.

Provided administrative support to market research team. Created a new method for tracking internal project workflow. Designed surveys, analyzed data, and contributed to client reports.

McMicken College of Arts and Sciences, U.C. Student Ambassador. 2008-2011.

Chair, Activities Committee 2010-11.

Responsible for planning social events and scheduling over 6,000 student visits. Gave over 45 presentations to groups.

Strategic Planning Committee, Summit Country Day School, Cincinnati, OH. Fall 2006–2007.

One of two student committee members.

Worked with the board of directors to develop the first strategic plan for a new, independent, day school (pre-K to 12) with over a thousand students.

AYF National Leadership Conference, Miniwanca Conference Center, Shelby, MI. Summer 2005–2006.

Participant in conference sponsored by American Youth Foundation.

Technical Skills and Training:
MINITAB, SAS, SPSS, MatLab. MATHSTAT, Microsoft Office. Survant, Mentor. Coursework in Statistics, regression analysis, math stats, non parametric stats, applied complex analysis, marketing research.

FIGURE 14.1 Sample Chronological Resume

Functional résumé—a format that categorizes and lists relevant skills and experiences rather than chronologically listing your work history.

in reverse chronological order. This type of résumé is the most common and preferred by most hiring managers, since they are used to seeing these. They are appropriate if you have held jobs in the past related to the position you seek. The second type of résumé, a **functional résumé**, categorizes and lists your skills and experiences related to the job in question. Rather than organizing around a chronological work history, a functional résumé uses three or four key terms to categorize your skills and accomplishments. You may find a functional résumé a better way to highlight your skills and accomplishments if you are changing careers, have a gap in your work history, or have very limited paid work experience

Elisa C. Vardin
2326 Tower Place   **(513) 861-2497**
Cincinnati, OH 45220   **ECVardin@yahoo.com**

Professional Objective:
Entry-level market research position allowing me to use my quantitative training to create and analyze market data and apply my organizing, writing, and public speaking skills to communicate technical findings to clients.

Educational Background:
University of Cincinnati, Cincinnati, OH, B.A. June 2011.

Major: Applied Mathematics, Minor: Marketing. GPA 3.36. Dean's List.

Relevant Coursework: Multivariate Stats, Regression Analysis, Math Stats, Non Parametric Stats, Applied Complex Analysis, Marketing Research.

Technical Skills: MINITAB, SPSS, SAS, MatLab, MATHSTAT, MicroSoft Office

Professional Skills:

Statistical Analysis
• Proficient with various statistical software packages used to analyze marketing research data.
• Hands-on experience cleaning market research data sets
• Analyzed complex statistical output from a multi-site marketing research study on time and on budget.

Organizing/Leadership Skills
• Created and coordinated a schedule for over 6,000 client visits.
• Participated in strategic planning process for an independent private school.
• Graduated from two-year national leadership development program

Communication Skills
• Presented over 45, 10–30 minute presentations using PowerPoint
• Drafted market research report and PowerPoint presentation for client
• Completed coursework in public speaking, persuasion, and technical writing

Experience:
Marketing Solutions, Inc., Cincinnati, OH. Summer 2011.
Intern

McMicken College of Arts and Sciences, U.C. Student Ambassador. 2008-2011
Chair, Activities Committee 2010-11

Strategic Planning Committee, Summit Country Day School, Cincinnati, OH. Fall 2006–2007.
Student Representative. Strategic Planning Committee

National Leadership Conference, American Youth Foundation. Summer 2005–2006.
Invited participant.

FIGURE 14.2 Sample Functional Résumé

but have acquired job-related skills and accomplishments in other ways. Figure 14.1 and Figure 14.2 illustrate a chronological and a functional résumé for the same college graduate. You can find up-to-date advice about the specifics of preparing each type of résumé online at many job search Web sites. Be sure to have someone knowledgeable review your résumé. Again, your campus career center probably offers this service.

3. Format for the online application process. Because you will apply for most jobs online, it is important that your résumé can be submitted in several formats allowing you to meet the requirements of the company or online job

TABLE 14.1 Résumé Formats for Online Distribution

Type	Use	File Extention	Advantages	Disadvantages
Formatted	—print résumés or e-mail attachments	.doc .wpd .wps .rtf	—visually attractive	—vulnerable to viruses —inconsistencies in formatting from computer to computer
Text	—posting to job boards —conversion to scannable résumé	.txt	—key-word searchable —consistent formatting from computer to computer —not vulnerable to viruses	—not visually appealing
Rich Text	—when sending résumé as an attachment —when employer's format preference is not known	.rtf	—résumé attachment compatible with all platforms and word processing programs —retains formatting well —less vulnerable to viruses	none
Portable Document	—when retaining identical formatting and pagination —when employers request it	.pdf	—invulnerable to viruses or tampering —compatible across computer systems	—difficult to key-word search —expensive software required for revisions by others
Web Based	—passive job searching —posting to a Web site	.html .htm	—employer can find your résumé —available 24/7	—need a host site

Adapted from Hanson, K. (2011). Your e-resume's file format aligns with its delivery method. Retrieved from Quintessential Careers.com: <http://www.quintcareers.com/e-resume_format.html>

INTER-ACT WITH SOCIAL MEDIA

The digital persona that you present through social media can positively or negatively impact a potential employer's perception of your professional competency. Take a moment to assess the image you portray through social media. Look at your Facebook, MySpace, blog, and other platforms. Is the digital image that you present consistent with your performance as a professional? When reviewing your presence on social media, what conclusions might a potential employer draw? Ask a few friends to evaluate your social media image as well.

search site. There are a variety of formats for online résumés. Table 14.1 describes and compares each of these.

4. Craft a cover e-mail or letter. When you e-mail your résumé to a prospective employer your message should serve as a cover letter. Most of us use e-mail to write short informal messages, but when we submit our résumé to an employer, our e-mail message needs to be a carefully considered and well-written communication. The cover e-mail should be short, no longer than four paragraphs highlighting your job-related skills and experiences with key words that appeared in the job posting. Many employers use software programs that scan e-mails and résumés for job-relevant key words. Using these in your cover letter will increase the likelihood that someone will actually look at your credentials. It is critical that both your cover e-mail and your résumé appear professional throughout and be error free. Run these documents through a grammar and spell check, carefully proofreading for errors that these programs don't catch. After drafting and proofing the e-mail message in a word processing program, paste it in your e-mail, and don't forget to also attach your résumé. Figure 14.3 provides a sample cover e-mail.

Dear Mr. Jones:

I am applying for the position of Research Assistant at Acme Marketing Research Associates. Professor Robert Carl at the University of Cincinnati suggested that I might be a good fit for your company.

I have prepared myself for a career in market research. I am an applied mathematics major at the University of Cincinnati with a minor in marketing. I have worked hard to develop a comprehensive background in statistics and have gained hands-on familiarity with key statistical packages used in market research. In addition to these technical qualifications, I have also developed my organizational, leadership, and communication skills though a variety of paid and volunteer positions.

I am excited by the prospect of beginning my career at AMRA because you are known for your cutting-edge market research programs as well as high ethical standards. I look forward to having the opportunity to speak with you. I have attached my résumé in both .txt and .rtf formats for your consideration. I look forward to hearing from you about the next steps I can take to become a member of your market research team.

Sincerely,

Elisa C. Vardin

FIGURE 14.3 Sample Cover Letter E-mail

Interviewing

An **interview** is a structured conversation with the goal of exchanging information needed for decision-making. A **job interview** is a conversation or a series of conversations between a job candidate and representatives of the hiring organization that allows you both to assess whether there is a good fit. Successful interviewing is a process that requires pre-interviewing preparation, effective interview performance, and interview follow-up.

Prepare for the Interview

While your résumé and cover letter can make you an attractive candidate for an employer, most employers use an interview as part of the hiring process. So, effective interview preparation can help you perform well during this important interaction. There are several things you should do to prepare for an interview.

Interview—a structured conversation with the goal of exchanging information needed for decision making.

Job interview—a conversation or set of conversations between a job candidate and representatives of the hiring organization that allows both to assess whether there is a good fit.

How can you prepare to successfully present yourself in an interview?

Many companies use social media to promote their image and interact with customers and clients. Identify a company or organization where you would like to work. Scan its corporate Web site to see if the organization uses social media to interact with customers and clients. As you prepare for a job interview with this company, what can you learn about the company based on its use of social media? What questions would you have for the person or persons whom you will meet during your interview?

1. Learn about the company. If you haven't done extensive research on the position and company in preparation for updating or writing your résumé and cover letter, do it before the interview. Be sure you know the company's products and services, its areas of operation, ownership structure, and its financial health. Nothing puts you in a worse light than coming to an interview without knowing this basic information.

2. Come prepared with questions and answers. The employment interview should be a two-way street: you size up the company as the interviewer sizes you up. You should prepare and identify specific questions to ask the interviewer: "Can you describe a typical work day for the person in this position?" or "What is the biggest challenge in this job?"; "Why is this position open?" "What happened to the person who used to have this job?"; and so forth. You should also spend time anticipating the kinds of questions you will be asked and thinking about how you can answer them truthfully while at the same time presenting yourself in a positive light. If, for example, you were fired from your last job because of tardiness, how can you disclose this yet turn it into a positive?

3. Rehearse the interview. Several days before the interview, spend time reviewing the job requirements and determining how your knowledge, skills, and experiences meet those requirements. Create and practice a sixty-second "commercial" selling you to the interviewer. Practice answering questions commonly asked in interviews, such as those listed in Figure 14.4. You can find many others at job search Web sites.

4. Dress appropriately and conservatively. Because job seeking is self-presentation, you will want your physical appearance to suggest that you fit in with the organization. As a sign of respect, you want to be dressed somewhat more formally than the people who already work in the organization doing the type

School

How did you select the school you attended?

How did you determine your major?

What extracurricular activities did you engage in at school?

In what ways does your transcript reflect your ability?

How were you able to help with your college expenses?

Personal

What are your hobbies? How did you become interested in them?

Give an example of how you work under pressure.

At what age did you begin supporting yourself?

What causes you to lose your temper?

What are your major strengths? Weaknesses?

Give an example of when you were a leader and what happened.

What do you do to stay in good physical condition?

What was the last non-school-assigned book that you read? Tell me about it.

Who has had the greatest influence on your life?

What have you done that shows your creativity?

Position

What kind of position are you looking for?

What do you know about the company?

Under what conditions would you be willing to relocate?

Why do you think you would like to work for us?

What do you hope to accomplish?

What qualifications do you have that would make you beneficial to us?

How do you feel about traveling?

In what part of the country would you like to settle?

With what kinds of people do you enjoy interacting?

What do you regard as an equitable salary for a person with your qualifications?

What new skills would you like to learn?

What are your career goals?

How would you proceed if you were in charge of hiring?

What are your most important criteria for determining whether you will accept a position?

FIGURE 14.4 Commonly Asked Interview Questions

of work that you are interested in. A good way to gauge this is to stand outside the organization's facility at quitting time and watch the people as they leave. Notice how they are dressed. Then choose clothing one notch up. Your goal is to make the best impression you can. In general, men should wear freshly-ironed, collared shirts and chino or dress slacks. They should have a recent haircut and be clean-shaven (or have facial hair well groomed). Women can wear skirts or pants, but in all cases, clothing should be modest, with no cleavage visible. Choose skirts long enough to maintain your modesty without needing constant readjustment while sitting. In some cases, men and women will want to wear a suit. In general, both men and women are wise to wear a suit-like jacket.

Not only does a jacket pull your outfit together with a professional look, it also hides a multitude of body flaws. Makeup should be unnoticeable. Hair should be clean and worn away from the face. Very long hair should be worn up or pulled back. In addition, jewelry and other decorative body adornments should be kept to a minimum. Remove excessive body art jewelry and if possible cover tattoos. Remember that while your goal is to stand out from other candidates during the interview, you don't want to be remembered for an inappropriate physical self-presentation.

5. Plan to arrive early. The interview is the organization's first exposure to your work habits. Therefore, you don't want to be late. To find out how long it will take you to travel to the interview, make a dry run several days before. Leave for the actual interview in plenty of time, anticipating how long it will take if you should miss your train or bus, for example, or encounter more traffic than usual. Plan on arriving at the office of your interviewer ten to fifteen minutes before your appointment, as you may be asked to fill out paperwork prior to the actual interview. An early arrival signals respect and interest while giving you a chance to catch your breath and get the lay of the land.

6. Bring interview materials. Bring extra hard copies of your résumé and reference list, a pen and pad for taking notes, as well as the list of questions you plan to ask. You may also want to bring a portfolio of your work product, including hard copies of research reports you have written, PowerPoint presentations you have prepared, artwork you have created, and so forth.

Interview Well

Although the interview itself can be a stressful experience, several guidelines can help you put your best foot forward.

1. Listen actively. When we are anxious, we sometimes have trouble listening carefully. As a result, you will need to work on attending to, understanding, and retaining what is asked of you. Remember that the interviewer will be aware of your nonverbal behaviors, so be sure to make and keep eye contact as you listen, sitting forward to show your interest. Avoid slouching, refrain from fidgeting, and so on.

2. Think before responding. If you have prepared for the interview, you should be able to answer the questions smoothly. If you are initially stumped by a question, don't dive in and just wing it. Take a moment to consider how you can answer the question in a way that portrays your skills and experiences in the best light. "Tell me about yourself" is not an invitation to give the interviewer your life history. You should be prepared with concise and thoughtful answers to this and other stock questions.

3. Provide specific examples that highlight your qualifications. You don't want to exaggerate your experiences, yet an interview is no place for modesty. Rather than discussing your skills in the abstract, provide concrete examples. Recount specific instances that demonstrate past achievements. The interviewer wants to get to know you through dialog, so as you answer questions, give plenty of free information that directs the conversation to your areas of strength.

4. Be enthusiastic. If you come across as bored or uninterested, the interviewer is likely to conclude that you would be an unmotivated employee. Show that you genuinely want the job.

5. Ask questions. As the interview is winding down, be sure to ask the questions you prepared that have not already been answered. You may also want to ask how well the interviewer believes your qualifications match the position, and then elaborate on how you are qualified, if necessary.

6. Avoid discussing salary and benefits. You should not ask about the salary and benefits offered with the job in your initial interview. In all likelihood, the interviewer will volunteer this information, but if not, wait until you are approached with a job offer and then discuss salary and benefits. If possible parry questions that try to pin you down about your salary expectations. Why? Because answering that question is a no-win situation for you. You may relegate yourself to a salary lower than you deserve, or you may request a salary higher than the company is willing to pay. So you might say something like, "What do you normally pay someone with my qualifications in this position?" or "I would like to defer talking about salary until we know we are a match." As benefits are also typically not negotiable, this discussion should also wait until you receive an offer.

7. As the interview ends, thank the interviewer and restate your interest in the position. Be attentive to cues that the interview is coming to an end. Don't extend the conversation or overstay your welcome. But as you prepare to leave, be sure to thank the interviewer and indicate your continuing interest in the position.

Interview Follow-up

When the interview is complete, you should take important follow-up steps.

1. Send a thank-you note. It is appropriate to write a short note thanking the interviewer for the experience and re-expressing your interest in the job. You can send the thank-you note immediately after the interview by e-mail, but if the decision is not imminent, you may also want to send a traditional hand-written letter by ground mail as well. The thank-you note should express your gratitude to the interviewer for her or his time and reaffirm your interest in the job. You may also want to highlight qualifications that were not well covered in the interview or clarify anything you think you mishandled. If there was more than one interviewer, you should write separate, individualized notes to each person. You may want to help them remember you by referencing something the two of you have in common or something memorable that you discussed.

2. Self-assess your performance. Take time to critique your performance. How well did you do? What can you do better next time?

3. Contact the interviewer for feedback. If you don't get the job, you might call the interviewer and ask for feedback. Be sure to be polite and to indicate that you are calling simply to get some feedback to improve your interviewing skills. Actively listen, using questions and paraphrases to clarify what the interviewer says. Be sure to thank the interviewer for helping you.

Interviewing

Recall a recent job interview. Describe the ways in which the experience was difficult for you. Suppose you were to engage in that same interview again. Which of the guidelines presented in the text would be most helpful for you?

Communicating in Workplace Relationships

Good communication skills are universally recognized as essential for successful interactions with colleagues at work (Whetten & Cameron, 2005). You will need to use your interpersonal communication skills to develop and maintain healthy relationships with others at work, including your managers, co-workers, customers or clients, and work teams.

Communicating in Managerial Relationships

Managerial relationships develop over time and are maintained through the communication and interaction of a manager with an employee. To develop the type of relationship you would like to have with your manager, you need to understand how these relationships develop. Although a wide variety of educational and training programs are dedicated to helping current and future managers communicate with their employees, few programs exist to help employees communicate more effectively with their managers. Here we will limit our discussion to how you can use your communication skills to improve your relationship with your manager.

Understanding Manager-Employee Relationships

Because no two employees are alike, co-workers who report to the same manager will each have different relationships. The Vertical Dyadic Exchange Model explains how these relationships develop (Graen, 1976). The model begins with the premise that managers usually have more work to get done than they have people to do it. Thus, they look for employees willing to do more than what is normally expected of someone in their job.

Those individuals who do go above and beyond become more valuable to the manager, who comes to depend on them. These employees develop richer relationships with their managers. They spend more time interacting with the boss and receive more challenging developmental assignments. They may be asked to accompany him or her to meetings and events not normally open to people at their level in the organization, and they get more feedback on and public recognition for their performance. Since we have an inherent need to make these fair exchanges, managers reciprocate in a variety of ways. Although the compensation may be financial (e.g., bonuses), it is more likely to take the form of choice developmental task assignments, better office space, public praise (e.g., employee-of-the-month awards), access to information not usually shared with employees at that level, and closer interpersonal relationships with their managers. Employees often describe these as **mentoring relationships**, relationships with a more experienced person designed to helped mentees develop career skills and expertise beyond what would normally be learned on the job. These skills in turn make them more valuable to the organization as a whole and help them advance in their careers.

At the other end of the spectrum are a small number of individuals whose performance does not meet standards and also a larger number of employees who perform their jobs acceptably but not exceptionally well. These people don't

Mentoring relationship—a relationship with a more experienced person designed to helped mentees develop career skills and expertise beyond what would normally be learned on the job.

volunteer or happily take on extra assignments, although they competently perform the work for which they are paid. When given opportunities to do this special type of work, they may decline, or if they accept, they may get it done late or not well. If they do their own jobs well, they will get good but not the best evaluations. They may get modest pay raises, but performing the routine work of their group, they are unlikely to be promoted. They will have less contact with their managers, and they are less likely to have an accurate perception of how these people view them. They are also more likely to be dissatisfied with their job. Thus, the relationships that managers and employees develop exist on a continuum. At one end, some employees have close mentoring, almost peer relationships with their manager. At the opposite, employees have cursory or even contentious relationships (Graen & Uhl-Bien, 1995).

Guidelines for Effectively Communicating with Your Manager

To foster a close relationship with your manager, you need to ask yourself, "How can I make my manager's job easier?"; "What can I volunteer to do that isn't already expected of someone in my job?"; and most importantly, "What communication skills can I use to develop a close working relationship?" The following guidelines can help you relate to and communicate with your manager.

1. Identify how you can help your manager. To establish a high-quality relationship with your manager, you must begin by assessing the skills and expertise you possess that may be of value in helping your manager accomplish the work that falls outside the formal role prescriptions of your job. These skills may be those that are in short supply in your work unit or those that your manager lacks. For instance, suppose your manager has a big presentation to give and needs to have a terrific PowerPoint to use with it. If you know your manager isn't very adept with presentation software, but you are a PowerPoint maven, you have a skill that is valuable to your manager.

2. Volunteer for specific assignments. Once you are aware of what skills and expertise you can bring to an exchange relationship, you need to communicate your willingness to perform extra assignments that require your talents and knowledge. For example, suppose your manager comments, "I'm dreading working on the presentation I have to give next week. I know what I want to say, but it's going to take me forever to get the PowerPoint done and I really don't have the time." As a savvy employee, instead of just commiserating, you might directly volunteer for the job. "Barb, I took a PowerPoint class at the local high school last year. I love doing PowerPoints, and I'm good at it. Can I do this for you?"

3. Clarify assignments. Managers aren't perfect communicators. Sometimes when you are asked to do something or in the midst of doing it, you will realize that you are not sure of what the assignment really calls for you to do. In these situations, you need to ask for clarification. You can do this by *asking questions, paraphrasing* what you understand the assignment to be, and *checking your perceptions* of your manager's nonverbal messages. So if your manager accepts your

OBSERVE AND ANALYZE

Vertical Dyadic Exchange Model in Action

Interview someone who manages employees. Describe the Vertical Dyadic Exchange. Then ask the manager to describe how this model fits with his or her experiences. Use questioning to probe for details and examples. Then write a brief report describing this manager's experience and what you learned.

offer to prepare the PowerPoint and hands you a copy of the written report on which the presentation is to be based, you will still need to clarify details about the presentation itself. Questions like, "How much time do you have to make the presentation?," "How many slides were you wanting to show?," and "Is there specific information you want depicted?," can help you plan your work. Then you can use paraphrasing to check your understanding of the assignment. "OK, you're giving a 5-minute recap of this report to the executive committee, and you'd like twenty colored slides to accompany what you are going to say. There should be a title slide and one or two slides to review your recommendations. Then there should be slides that explain the process you used to come up with the recommendations, but the bulk of the slides will detail how you plan to implement the new program. And you'd like to see a draft of the presentation tomorrow afternoon. At this point, is there anything else I should know?"

4. Ask for feedback. In Chapter 10 you learned the skill of *asking for feedback.* Too often, employees believe that no news is good news, so they wait until formal performance reviews to hear feedback from their managers. Formal summary feedback may be helpful, but because it is based on your performance over a long period, it may not be specific enough to help you identify and correct performance problems that are affecting the quality of your current work. And it certainly doesn't allow you to make mid-course corrections during a task. If you want to develop a good working relationship with your manager, you need timely feedback about how well your work is meeting your manager's expectations. You need to ask for feedback in real time. For example, after giving your manager the draft of the PowerPoint slides, you might directly ask, "In what ways is this what you expected?" "What's not working?" "What changes do I need to make to the slides so that they will work better for you?" By frequently asking directly for feedback, you learn about how your manager views your work product, and you also learn about your manager. You also give yourself a chance to improve your work during the process rather than having to live with the consequences of your mistakes. Feedback from your manager should inform you about and allow you to internalize your manager's expectations. It's important that you don't become defensive when the feedback is negative. Remember your goal is to improve, not to debate.

5. Adapt to your manager's communication preferences. Managers differ in how they prefer to interact with their employees. Some like to manage by walking around and stopping by your work area to briefly chat, assign work, and give on-the-spot feedback. Other managers won't seek you out but have an open-door policy and welcome employees who stop by when they have questions or need help. Still other managers prefer to communicate by phone or e-mail. Some managers want to see things in writing to have time to think before interacting. Others are comfortable with information that is communicated orally and like to respond in the moment. So you need to observe how your manager prefers to communicate and then adapt to this style.

6. Develop a mentoring relationship. Mentors can help you understand your organization, your profession, and your job. They can give you feedback on work issues, and because they have more experience, they can share their stories as examples of what to do and what not to do. Your manager may or may not be the best person to be your mentor. But unless you have an incompetent manager or a contentious relationship with her or him, you should begin your search by sharing that you would like to have a mentor. Your manager may volunteer, may refer you to a company-wide mentoring program, or recommend you to a peer manager. By letting your manager know that you would like to be mentored, you communicate that you are interested in improving your work-related competencies and that you are open to developmental feedback.

Once you have identified a mentor, you will want to meet with this person and tell them what you expect to get out of the relationship. Be specific. Do you want help improving your performance on specific job tasks? Do you want someone who can help you understand how the office politics work? Do you want someone who can provide career advice? Once you have agreed to begin the relationship, set up a regular schedule with specific goals for each meeting. You need to be prepared to be open with your mentor, honestly sharing problems, weaknesses, and fears. Then you need to be nondefensive when your mentor gives you constructive feedback. As your relationship develops, you and your mentor may begin to discuss personal as well as work issues. This is fine as long as you are comfortable sharing, but be ready to politely define a boundary if you feel the conversation is becoming too personal.

Communicating in Co-worker Relationships

Co-workers are peers who are at the same level in an organization's hierarchy and have no formal authority over each other. They may be other members of your work group, team, or department. They may be in other departments. They may or may not report to your manager. But a co-worker must have some type of job-related interaction with you. Co-workers influence both the quality of our job performance and our job satisfaction (Jablin & Krone, 1994). Therefore, don't take co-worker relationships for granted; they are just as important as employee-manager relationships. Let's look at the types of co-worker relationships that you may develop at work and then look at several guidelines to help you manage these relationships. Finally we'll discuss romantic relationships between co-workers.

Informational relationships—work-based peer relationships in which the interaction and conversation is solely devoted to work topics.

Types of Co-worker Relationships

There are three types of co-worker or peer relationships (Kram & Isabella, 1985; Odden & Sias, 1997). **Informational relationships** are work-based peer relationships in which interaction and conversation are devoted solely to work topics. In informational relationships you talk about and share task information,

What kinds of communication skills are recognized as essential for successful interaction with colleagues at work?

Collegial relationships—work-based peer relationships that have developed into friendships so that co-workers share career strategies and provide job feedback.

Special relationships—work-based peer relationships that have developed into "best-friend" intimate relationships.

job-related experiences, and career information. **Collegial relationships** are work-based peer relationships that have developed into context-based friendships. We often refer to these people as our work friends. These colleagues share career strategies and provide job feedback. They also provide a limited type of work-related social support. You may also talk about family or other romantic relationships but maintain boundaries and don't discuss private personal information. These are the people you may go to lunch with, sit next to at meetings, and so forth. Although you are friends at work, you spend little or limited time together outside of work. **Special relationships** are work-based peer relationships that have developed into "best-friend," intimate relationships that extend beyond the workplace. Not only do these friends interact at work, but they merge their social lives outside of the work context. Partners in these relationships bond, and their topics of conversation include both career and family. They share organizational information and provide social support on the job, but they also talk about personal issues, trusting that their partner will maintain the privacy of co-owned information.

Guidelines for Communicating in Co-worker Relationships

Like other relationships, your co-worker relationships are developed through your communication experiences. The following guidelines can help you in interactions with your co-workers.

1. Use positive nonverbal cues that make it easy for someone to approach you. Work is hard enough without having to deal with grumpy, sarcastic, or irritable peers. Effective co-worker communication begins when we adopt nonverbal behaviors that put others at ease and make them feel welcomed. A pleasant smile, head nod, and open body posture all communicate that you would enjoy talking with your co-worker.

2. Share information freely. Believing that knowledge is power, some people hoard what they know, intentionally misleading or withholding important information. This hurts the quality of work as it alienates co-workers. While you should not share information imparted to you in confidence, you should share ordinary work information with all who ask and be proactive in sharing with co-workers who need this information to perform better. Doing so builds credits with peers who will likely reciprocate.

3. Resolve conflict through collaboration. Because everyone in an organization benefits when the best solution is found for problems, you should work to resolve conflicts using collaboration, skills you learned in Chapter 12.

4. Talk in person. Limit your use of e-mail. The best way to communicate with someone is still face-to-face or over the phone.

5. Demonstrate respect. Your peers will be more likely to share information and feedback with you if you demonstrate that you respect them by attentively listening to their points of view and by demonstrating that you understand and appreciate their perspective on a work issue even if you disagree.

6. Don't gossip. Destructive gossip wastes time in the workplace. If you hear it, don't pass it on. If you hear it and you think the concerns are valid, suggest that the person passing this on to you talk instead with the person who is the topic of the gossip. Or you can talk with this person yourself and, using the guidelines for giving feedback, provide them with constructive advice. If the gossip is not valid, politely correct the person who is gossiping. As a rule of thumb, you should always support a person who is not present and is being talked about. Doing so sends the message to others that you can be relied on to have their backs as well.

7. Be a good team member. Today, much of the work that goes on inside organizations occurs in teams (Eisenberg & Goodall, 2004). A **workplace team** is a formally established group with a clear purpose and appropriate structure in which members know each other's roles and work together to achieve goals (Conrad & Poole, 2005). Good team members meet their obligations to the team by performing **task roles**, communication behaviors that help a team focus on the issue under discussion, and **maintenance roles**, communication behaviors that improve interactions among team members. They come to meetings prepared and share in task roles such as initiating a discussion of issues, offering and soliciting information and opinions during discussion, analyzing what is said, and orienting the group to keep the discussion moving on track. They also share in maintenance roles that foster a positive work climate. These include ensuring that everyone has a chance to speak, verbally encouraging and supporting others, relieving group tension, and managing group conflict. They work hard to remain focused and avoid multitasking and other distractions like text messaging. After team meetings, they review their notes and incorporate their assignments into their work priorities and calendars so that they complete their commitments on time.

Romantic Relationships at Work

Organizational romance is sexual or romantic involvement between people who work for the same organization. Since co-workers have much in common and are in frequent contact, it is no surprise that some become attracted to each other. In addition, employees who spend long hours at work may have little free time in which to meet partners elsewhere. The issue of organizational romance is a controversial one, however. Some people believe in separating workplace from personal relationships completely, while others see the workplace as a good environment for developing social and romantic relationships. Most organizations allow co-workers to date but forbid romantic relationships between supervisors and their subordinates because of the inherent conflict of interest in such relationships (Berryman-Fink, 1997).

Factors to consider when deciding whether to date a work colleague include company policies on romantic relationships, potential reactions from co-workers and managers, the possible effects of interoffice dating on your career, and the possibility that the relationship could end badly, making it difficult for former partners to work together. Of these factors, workplace employees who agree to become romantically involved should be most careful about reviewing and following their workplace policy about organizational romance. If the policy allows co-workers to date, then the partners should agree on standards for appropriate

Workplace team—a formally established group with a clear purpose and appropriate structure in which members know each other's roles and work together to achieve goals.

Task roles—communication behaviors that help a team focus on the issue under discussion.

Maintenance roles—communication behaviors that improve interactions among team members.

Organizational romance—sexual or romantic involvement between people who work for the same organization.

verbal and nonverbal communication with each other while at work, and they should continue to self-monitor their communications to maintain professionalism in the workplace at all times.

Communicating in Customer, Client, and Vendor Relationships

Some of us spend most of our workday communicating with other members of our organization, while others spend most of their time communicating with people who are not members of their organization. There are two types of outside relationships. **Customers and clients** are the people, groups, or organizations that use our organization's goods or services. **Vendors** are the people, groups, or organizations that supply our organization with necessary raw materials or other goods and services. **Boundary spanning** is the process of communicating with people outside of our organization in a mutually beneficial relationship. Jobs with heavy boundary-spanning responsibilities include inside and outside sales representatives, store clerks, customer service representatives, service technicians, delivery people, social workers, public accountants, lawyers, buyers, purchasing agents, dispatchers, caregivers, medical staff (such as technicians, nurses, orderlies, etc.), and, of course, teachers. You may notice that although the educational requirements for these positions may vary, for the most part, these are entry-level jobs. So organizations should be training new hires to effectively manage their boundary relationships. When boundary spanners are well trained, the organization benefits by having happy customers, clients, and suppliers. But how often have you called a customer service hotline only to be greeted by someone who not only doesn't communicate respect but also gives you incorrect information or can't answer your questions? In many cases, this occurs because they have not had formal training in the communication skills that are key to their success. When you are in a boundary-spanning position, it is important to recognize that the people you talk to see you as your organization and how you treat them will affect their future decisions about doing business or working with your organization.

Guidelines for Communicating in Boundary-Spanning Relationships

Communicating with customers, clients, and vendors can be stressful because while you are responsible for interacting with these important people, you probably have little or no control over the policies you have to follow and communicate. The following guidelines can help you be more effective in these relationships.

   1. Listen to understand. In most cases, your boundary-spanning conversations will center on how you can fulfill the other's expectations. Sometimes these conversations will occur before you do business; at other times, the conversations will occur after expectations have not been met. In either case, the key to a successful interaction is listening to understand. This means not only *paraphrasing* what you have heard but also *asking questions to clarify* what needs to be done. Assuming that we understand what someone else needs can create problems. For example, when Karen informed a sales clerk, "I need to return

---

Customers and clients—the people, groups, or other organizations that use an organization's goods or services.

Vendors—the people, groups, or organizations that supply an organization with its raw materials or other goods and services.

Boundary spanning—the process of communicating with people outside of our organization in a mutually beneficial relationship.

this blouse," the clerk glared at her and asked caustically, "Did you not read our sign—Exchanges provided with receipt. Absolutely no returns?" Karen actually wanted to exchange the blouse for another size, but instead of *asking a question to clarify* these intentions, the clerk publicly humiliated her. Consequently, the store lost Karen as a customer and probably several others whom she told about the incident.

2. Demonstrate empathy and provide comfort. When you are boundary spanning with clients or customers who are having problems, you need to empathize and offer emotional support, even when you can't solve their problem. For example, as Cassie was complaining about her new printer, the tech support responded empathetically with short *perception checking* and *supportive* comments like, "Wow, I can see that you're really frustrated. I would be, too." Then the tech apologized for not being able to answer her questions but identified people who could: "I'm so sorry. I'd really like to help, but I don't know anything about your printer. If you can tell me your printer brand, though, I can give you the number of your printer's tech support. Sorry." Although the tech couldn't solve the problem, the empathy and support that Cassie received made her a walking advertisement for her computer company.

3. When turning down a request, honestly explain the reasoning behind a company policy as well as the limitations of your authority. People are more willing to accept an unfavorable outcome if they realize the policy has a rational basis, which is explained to them before a problem arises. Many discount chains give cashiers a script to use as they ring up sales: "We cannot accept returns and keep our prices low, so be sure to check the merchandise before you leave." In addition, you should clearly state the boundaries of your authority in representing your organization: "I wish I could refund your money, but without a receipt the only thing I can do is make an exchange."

Communicating in a Diverse Workplace

Today's workplace reflects the increasing diversity of our country as women and men of various races, ethnicities, sexual orientations, ages, socioeconomic status, political persuasions, religious traditions, and countries come together to work side by side. This means that success in the workplace depends increasingly on your ability to understand and communicate with people who differ from you. You may face various challenges at work stemming from the diversity of our workforce, including negotiating differences in culture-based work style, gendered communication, and intergenerational work values and practices. Let's take a brief look at each of these.

Culture-Based Work Style

How we approach our work depends on our culture, much like communication in other settings. In addition to the cultural differences that we have already discussed, some cultures value work over relationships, while others value relationships over work. Moreover, some cultures value a sequential approach to large

Results-oriented culture—a culture that prioritizes results over building relationships at work.

Relationship-oriented culture—a culture that prioritizes building relationships at work over results.

Sequential task-completion culture—a culture that believes that large or complex tasks should be broken down into separate parts and completed one part at a time and in order.

Holistic task-completion culture—a culture that believes in tackling large and complex tasks in their entirety.

tasks, while others favor a holistic approach. When we go to work, we bring these cultural preferences with us, and when our co-workers are from other cultures, culture-based work style differences can cause conflict (Varner & Beamer, 1995).

A **results-oriented culture** is likely to be individualistic and, like the dominant culture of the United States, prioritizes results over building relationships at work; whereas a **relationship-oriented culture** is likely to be collectivist, like those of Japan, Spain, and Mexico, and prioritizes building relationships at work over results (Varner & Beamer, 1995). Employees from results-oriented cultures see little need to spend time establishing or maintaining relationships, preferring to get right down to business. They view time as precious, and their ultimate goal is to get the job done. Getting to know customers or business associates on a personal level before doing business with them is not considered necessary. In fact, anything believed to distract from the professional objective would be seen as annoying or counterproductive. In contrast, employees from relationship-oriented cultures see the quality of their personal relationships with customers and business associates as the primary business concern. People from these cultures prefer not to conduct business until they have established or refreshed a personal relationship.

A second culture-based work style difference is the way people prefer to approach large or complex tasks. A **sequential task-completion culture** is a culture that believes that large or complex tasks should be broken down into separate parts and completed one part at a time and in order; that is, Step A is finished before beginning Step B and so on until the task is completed. In contrast, a **holistic task-completion culture** is a culture that believes in tackling large and complex tasks in their entirety. Rather than completing one part of the task before beginning work on another, holistic task-completion cultures advocate simultaneously working on all parts of the task; that is, working on one part, then another, then back to the first, in an iterative fashion. As you can imagine, when teammates from sequential task-completion cultures work with those from holistic cultures, problems arise. For example, suppose that department store assistant managers Greg (a typical Canadian sequential task completer) and Chun-Hae (a typical Korean holistic task completer) have been asked by their boss to work together to develop a plan for displaying the store's new fall merchandise. Chun-Hae would be inclined to look at the whole problem at once, talking for a few minutes about what to put where, then bouncing around her ideas about how to physically handle the moving process, then describing how possibly to involve the sales associates in the plan, and finally returning to discussing new ideas about what to put where. Although another holistic task completer would be comfortable with this approach, Greg is likely to become confused and frustrated, wishing Chun-Hae would focus on one issue, work through it, make decisions, and then move on to the next topic. Likewise, if Greg initiates the discussion and tries to hold Chun-Hae to his step-by-step process, she is likely to become annoyed and bored.

Effective business communication depends on awareness of and sensitivity to cultural differences in work styles without assuming some approaches are better

The Group: A Japanese Context

by Delores Cathcart and Robert Cathcart

Team roles and decision-making styles are greatly influenced by culture. In this excerpt, the authors describe how interdependence leads to a climate of agreement and decision making based on consensus in Japanese groups.

One of Japan's most prominent national characteristics is the individual's sense of the group. Loyalty to the group and a willingness to submit to its demands are key virtues in Japanese society. This dependency and the interdependency of all members of a group is reinforced by the concept of *on*. A Japanese is expected to feel indebtedness to those others in the group who provide security, care, and support. This indebtedness creates obligation and when combined with dependency is called *on*. *On* functions as a means of linking all persons in the group in an unending chain because obligation is never satisfied, but continues throughout life. *On* is fostered by a system known as the *oyabun–kobun* relationship. Traditionally the *oyabun* is a father, boss, or patron who protects and provides for a son, employee, or student in return for his or her service and loyalty. This is not a one-way dependency. Each boss or group leader recognizes his own dependency on those below. Without their undivided loyalty he or she could not function. *Oyabun* are also acutely aware of this double dimension because of having had to serve a long period of *kobun* on the way up the hierarchy to the position at the top. All had *oyabun* who protected and assisted them, much like a father, and now each must do the same for their *kobun*. *Oyabun* have one or more *kobun* whom they look after much as if they were children. The more loyal and devoted the "children," the more successful the "father."

This relationship is useful in modern life where large companies assume the role of superfamily and become involved in every aspect of their workers' lives. Bosses are *oyabun* and employees are *kobun*....

This uniquely Japanese way of viewing relationships creates a distinctive style of decision-making known as *consensus decision*. The Japanese devotion to consensus building seems difficult for most Westerners to grasp but loses some of its mystery when looked at as a solution to representing every member of the group. In a system that operates on *oyabun–kobun* relationships nothing is decided without concern for how the outcome will affect all. Ideas and plans are circulated up and down the company hierarchy until everyone has had a chance to react. This reactive process is not to exert pressure but to make certain that all matters affecting the particular groups and the company are taken into consideration. Much time is spent assessing the mood of everyone involved and only after all the ramifications of how the decision will affect each group can there be a quiet assent. A group within the company may approve a decision that is not directly in its interest (or even causes it difficulties) because its members know they are not ignored, their feelings have been expressed, and they can be assured that what is good for the company will ultimately be good for them. For this reason consensus decisions cannot be hurried along without chancing a slight or oversight that will cause future problems.

The process of consensus building in order to make decisions is a time-consuming one, not only because everyone must be considered, but also because the Japanese avoid verbalizing objections or doubts in order to preserve group harmony. The advice, often found in American group literature, that group communication should be characterized by open and candid statements expressing individual personal feelings, wishes, and dislikes, is the antithesis of the Japanese consensus process. No opposing speeches are made to argue alternate ideas; no conferences are held to debate issues. Instead, the process of assessing the feelings and mood of each work group proceeds slowly until there exists a climate of agreement. This process is possible because of the tight relationships that allow bosses and workers to know each other intimately and to know the group so well that needs and desires are easy to assess.

For Consideration:

1. How is the Japanese system of *oyabun–kobun* relationships similar and different from the old paternal (old boy's network) American model of business?

2. Do you think the Japanese style of decision making would be effective where you work or have worked?

Excerpted from Cathcart, D., and Cathcart, R. (1997). The group: A Japanese context. In L. A. Samovar & R. E. Porter (Eds.), *Intercultural Communication: A Reader* (8th ed., pp. 329–339). Belmont, CA: Wadsworth. Reprinted by permission of the authors.

than others. It is also important to realize that a person from a particular culture may or may not communicate in the style typical of that culture, so you should not assume that, for instance, all Americans are results-oriented and sequential or that all Koreans are relationship-oriented and holistic. A strategy for dealing with cultural differences is to acknowledge and communicate about respective cultural styles. Parties working across cultural boundaries may benefit from talking about preferred ways of doing business and negotiating an agreement between the business partners. As workplaces become more culturally diverse, employees need to be flexible with their natural work style and learn alternate styles. For another example of how cultural styles vary, see this chapter's "Diverse Voices" box in which Delores Cathcart and Robert Cathcart describe how Japanese workers work differently in groups than many of us in the United States.

Gendered Linguistic Style in the Workplace

Linguistic style—the patterned way in which you use language to communicate.

Your **linguistic style** is the patterned way in which you use language to communicate. Because of the different ways that they were socialized, most men and women have different linguistic styles, patterns they also, not surprisingly, use at work. How we talk can have profound effects on not only how we are perceived but also how we perceive others, as we use our own style to help us interpret the pragmatic and sociolinguistic meaning of others messages. Specifically, we tend to value those who talk like we do. In most organizations, where men are over-represented in more powerful positions, women can be at a disadvantage not because they are less competent at performing their jobs but because their communication style unconsciously encourages the male managerial decision makers to view them as less competent. Some scholars believe that this is a major reason why women encounter the **glass ceiling**, an invisible yet real barrier that prevents deserving employees from advancing. Let's take a closer look at how the communication styles of men and women differ in linguistic usage, attention to social dynamics, conversational rituals, and communicating authority and how these differences play out at work (Tannen, 1995).

Glass ceiling—an invisible yet real barrier that prevents deserving employees from advancing.

Women and men tend to differ in how they use language to communicate their meanings. It is critical to note that although extensive evidence supports the existence of different linguistic styles, this does not mean that all women or any particular woman has a feminine style or that all men and or any particular man has a masculine style. Women can and do develop masculine linguistic styles, and men can and do develop feminine linguistic styles. Nevertheless, understanding these can help us as we try to separate a person's communication style from their actual performance in the workplace.

A feminine linguistic style uses indirect language when giving orders to an employee. A female manager might give an assignment by saying, "Could you get me the budget report needed by the V.P. by noon on Friday?" Whereas, her male peer manager might say, "You need to prepare an expected-to-realize year-to-date budget update for me and have it on my desk by tomorrow at 10:00." Men tend to use indirect language, however, to acknowledge a mistake or problem: "There was a problem in estimating our telecommunications budget needs, and I will make sure this doesn't happen again." A woman, on the other hand, would likely acknowledge the mistake was hers and apologize: "I made a mistake when I estimated our telecommunications budget needs. I am so sorry." Women and men also differ in their personal pronoun use. Women tend to use inclusive first-person plural pronouns (we, our, ours) and men first-person singular and third-person pronouns (I, he, she, they). She says, "In our department we've done a good job and are actually below our anticipated budget," whereas he says, "I've really been watching the budget like a hawk, so I'm happy to report that my department is below my anticipated budget." What is the effect of these differences? Managers predominantly of one gender could perceive a different gendered style inaccurately. A female manager may view her male employees as too direct and self-serving, while a male manager may view his female employees as unable to exercise authority, incapable of assuming leadership, and not particularly competent.

Men and women also are sensitive to different language dynamics. Men tend to be attuned to the power dynamic communicated by how something is said. When speaking, they try to maintain a one-up position and avoid more tentative, one-down messages; they prefer to make assertive statements rather than ask questions. Women, on the other hand, tend to be attuned to the relationship or rapport dynamic in an interaction, forming messages that save face or buffer the face threats of others. When speaking to an assistant, for example, he says, "Get John on the phone," while she says, "Would you please get John on the phone for me. Thanks." "His speak" asserts his right to command and his more powerful status. "Her speak" attends to her assistant's face needs, putting her legitimate demand in the form of a request rather than simply ordering her subordinate to do her bidding.

A number of conversational rituals also differ in gendered ways that affect workplace perceptions, including the use of apology, giving and understanding feedback, giving compliments, and the use of ritual argument. First, women use an apology as a ritual way of comforting. When she says, "I'm so sorry that you missed the deadline," she is not apologizing for causing you to miss the deadline but rather expressing empathic sorrow. Men, however, who view an apology as a one-down power position, generally don't offer this kind of support.

Second, women begin giving feedback by praising something positive, then communicating constructive criticism. The criticism will likely be duly noted by other women but possibly missed by male employees, who are attuned to the praise. Male managers who do not use this ritual, providing direct criticism without acknowledging positive aspects of a performance, are likely to hurt the morale of female employees.

Third, female conversations are marked by a ritual exchange of compliments. A woman who praises the way you managed the work team meeting expects you to compliment her in return. If you don't, she might prime you by asking a question that invites a compliment: "What did you think of my argument about reducing costs by using temps?" A man may not recognize this question as part of a ritual compliment exchange, providing instead honest feedback that points out the flaws in her proposal.

He Speak–She Speak

At the *Inter-Act* Web site, download two copies of the He Speak–She Speak observation sheet. For one week, unobtrusively observe and take notes on the linguistic style of one male and one female co-worker. Then analyze what you have recorded. To what extent did the man demonstrate a masculine linguistic style and to what extent did the woman use a feminine linguistic style? How did colleagues and managers react to these people and their particular communication style?

Fourth, men may vigorously argue as a ritual, not because they are fundamentally opposed to another's assertions but as a way of testing the strengths and weaknesses of various positions and options. What looks adversarial is really cooperative, and no damage is done to their relationship. Heated arguments between women, however, typically mean that they are, indeed, opposed to another's position or adamant about their own. Such arguments are considered a breach of the relationship that will require repair through a forgiveness process.

The final gendered difference in linguistic style involves perceptions of confidence and authority. Men are more likely to seek out and spend time with upper managers, seizing the opportunity, for instance, to sit with top managers at luncheons or other social occasions and spotlight their recent accomplishments. Women, on the other hand, are likely to consider this behavior overly forward, even intrusive. Socialized to be self-effacing, they are less likely to talk up their achievements with upper managers even when given the chance. Consequently, male upper managers tend to view male employees as more accomplished than the women.

At this point in the evolution of our workplaces, men are disproportionately represented in the ranks of upper management, a situation that puts women at a disadvantage because of their linguistic style. Regrettably, little can be done to alter this situation—other than being aware of these differences and their consequences. Women, for example, who adopt a masculine style are generally seen negatively and labeled "pushy," "bitchy," or "ball-busting." Men, however, can also suffer if they violate traditional expectations for gendered communication. Men who employ a feminine linguistic style may be seen as even more indecisive and overly sensitive than women (who are expected to be this way).

Intergenerational Communication Issues

There is no mandatory retirement age in many countries including the United States. As a result, age range in an organizations workforce may span four decades. As a result, the possibility of age-based misunderstandings occurring in the workplace has increased. Scholars have found that older and younger employees tend to differ in their views of authority, approach to rules, priorities regarding work versus leisure, and competence with technology (Zemke, Raines, & Filipczak, 2000).

In general, people sixty or older tend to have greater respect for authority. They grew up in a time when our culture valued greater power distance. The frequent use of formal titles and other deferential behavior demonstrated respect for more powerful figures whose authority was not questioned. In contrast, people under the age of thirty tend to be more skeptical of and less formal when dealing with authority figures. They grew up in an era of greater equality in a society that commonly challenged the status quo. Consequently, they are more likely to question their managers, openly disagree with their decisions, and call them and co-workers by their first names.

Older individuals tend to adhere more strictly to company rules and expect others to do the same, believing that employers have the right to make the rules and that employees have the responsibility to follow those rules as a condition of employment. They may even find company regulations reassuring because they promote predictability. Many younger co-workers, however, may see rules as suggestions to be followed or not, depending on one's own analysis of a situation. Having been raised with situational ethics, younger people may believe that extenuating circumstances call for flexibility, thus allowing them to ignore or bend the rules. Such differences in perspective may cause us to judge one another, thereby impeding team cohesiveness at work.

For many older individuals, work always takes priority over family and leisure. In fact, many older Americans consider a strong work ethic one of a person's most respectable personality traits. In contrast, many individuals under thirty, who have not yet experienced the challenges of providing for a family or have seen the toll that work has taken on their parents, may place a higher priority on leisure. Co-workers of different ages also differ regarding their use of and competence with technology. For many older employees, the challenges of learning to use new technology can cause anxiety. For younger people who are digital natives, adapting to ever-changing technology is expected and relatively effortless.

It is important to keep in mind that there is no right or wrong set of generational values. Nevertheless, generational differences in values and behaviors can create enormous challenges for workplace communication. The more we understand and are sensitive to age-related differences in workplace behavior, the more we can communicate with flexibility across the age gap. The interpersonal skills of assertiveness, questioning, perception checking, describing behavior, and owning feelings may also prove useful in preventing or managing intergenerational communication conflicts at work.

How can you communicate effectively across generational differences at work?

The Dark Side of Workplace Communication

While most exchanges at work are task related or intended to foster positive working relationships, two types of communication can damage people, their workplace relationships, and their performance: aggression and sexual harassment.

Aggression at Work

Workplace aggression is any counterproductive behavior at work intended to hurt someone else (Rai, 2002). Aggression can be active or passive, verbal or physical, direct or indirect (Baron & Neuman, 1996). When Joe, for example, chooses to ignore an e-mail from Thom that asks for a copy of last quarter's sales figures by tomorrow, Joe's behavior is passive, verbal, direct aggression: passive because he has hurt Thom's ability to do his job by avoiding responding to his request, verbal because he is not providing the report, direct because his behavior

Workplace aggression—any counterproductive behavior at work intended to hurt someone.

is aimed squarely at hurting Thom. Workplace aggression also varies in whether it is verbal, behavioral, or physical.

Verbal aggression—sending verbal messages intended to hurt someone.

Verbal aggression is sending verbal messages intended to hurt someone. It includes incivility, rudeness, teasing, brushing people off, name-calling, and verbal fighting. Gossiping, spreading rumors, and slandering others at work are also forms of verbal aggression. Verbal aggression can occur face-to-face, over the phone, or through electronic means like flaming e-mails, text messages, and so forth. Some verbal aggression stems from the inability to be assertive and resorting instead to a verbally aggressive message when frustrated, angry, or defensive. If you are the target of verbal aggression, you should respond assertively. Suppose you are trying to explain to a co-worker that as a result of his incomplete research, you were unable to submit a report on time. His response is verbally intimidating: "Oh, you're just such a perfectionist. Nothing anyone does is ever good enough for you. Well, you can just shove it because you're not my boss, and I don't have to listen to this s***." Using your interpersonal assertiveness skills, you might respond: "I know it must be hard to hear that the research was insufficient, but I haven't done anything to deserve this outburst, and I am really disappointed in you. Do you understand why I would feel this way?" Then listen. Sometimes a verbally aggressive person is overwrought about issues unrelated to the immediate situation. Once you have identified the real area of conflict, you can use a collaborative approach to solve the problem.

Behavioral aggression—nonverbal acts intended to hurt someone.

Behavioral aggression is nonverbal acts intended to hurt someone. It includes brushing people off, shunning, withholding resources, and sabotaging others' work products. For example, at the quarterly management meeting, when people were told to break into groups to discuss next quarter's goals, Maddie purposefully turned her back on Karin, who was waving and walking toward her. This was behavioral aggression. It would have been honest and not aggressive for Maddie to simply set a boundary, politely telling Karin that she didn't wish to work with her on this task. When you feel that someone is being behaviorally aggressive, you can use your assertiveness skills to teach the other person how you expect to be treated.

Physical aggression—nonverbal acts of violence against another person with the intent to do bodily harm.

Physical aggression is nonverbal acts of violence against another person with the intent to do bodily harm. It includes gross violations of personal space (getting in your face), pushing, hitting, threatening with a weapon, and so forth. If you experience or witness physical aggression in your workplace, you should report it to your manager (unless the manager is the violent person) and to human resources. Even if the person who behaved this way seems contrite and promises to never do it again, you need to report the behavior. When you do this, be careful to describe the exact sequence of events without evaluating the cause or attributing motives, of which you may not be aware.

Bullying—the habitual use of aggression or the repeated use of aggression against one target individual.

In some instances, aggression is an aberration. It happens only once. But at other times, the behavior is a repeated pattern. **Bullying** includes both the habitual use of aggression and the repeated use of aggression against one target individual. When we talk about bullies, however, we generally mean people who are habitually aggressive with most others; and when we talk about bullying, we generally mean aggression against a specific target person. Although we normally think of bullies and bullying as a schoolyard phenomenon, studies have suggested that bullying is widespread in workplaces. One study found that 13 percent of their national sample reported being victims of weekly aggression at work (Schat, Frone, & Kelloway, 2006). You can often short-circuit a bully before you become a victim by asserting yourself at the first incident of aggression. Bullies target victims who don't fight back. It helps to remind yourself that there is nothing wrong with you; it is the bully's behavior that is inappropriate. If the aggression continues, you should keep a journal detailing each incident. Record each act of aggression, indicating the date, place, and specific chronology of behavior, and report the incidents to your manager or human resource officer.

Sexual Harassment

Sexual harassment is unwanted verbal or physical sexual behavior that interferes with work performance. More specifically, according to the U.S. Equal Employment Opportunity Commission (EEOC), "sexual harassment is a form of sex discrimination that violates Title VII of the Civil Rights Act of 1964," which includes "unwelcome sexual advances, requests for sexual favors, and other verbal or physical conduct of a sexual nature when this conduct explicitly or implicitly affects an individual's employment, unreasonably interferes with an individual's work performance, or creates an intimidating, hostile, or offensive work environment." According to the EEOC, the sexual harasser may be a woman or a man, the victim's supervisor, an agent of the employer, a supervisor in another area, a co-worker, or a nonemployee, and the harasser's conduct must be unwelcome. Sexual harassment may be a direct sexual advance or an indirect result of other's behaviors. The victim may or may not be of the opposite sex. Finally, sexual harassment may or may not have resulted in economic injury or employment termination of the victim.

> **Sexual harassment**—unwanted verbal or physical sexual behavior that interferes with work performance.

Prevention is the best way to eliminate sexual harassment in the workplace. Employers create a safe working environment by clearly communicating to employees that sexual harassment will not be tolerated. They should hand out a policy statement that defines and gives examples of sexual harassment, provide training that helps employees both identify and avoid sexual harassment, establish an effective complaint or grievance process, and take immediate and appropriate action when an employee complains.

If you perceive that you are the target of sexual harassment in the workplace or if you are experiencing a hostile work environment because of another's inappropriate sexual behavior, two principal communication strategies are useful. First, begin by directly informing the harasser that his or her conduct is unwelcome and must stop. You should privately document the first incident of harassment. Date, sign, and keep it for possible future use. It may also be wise to e-mail a copy to yourself so that the date you recorded the incident can't later be called into question. Second, decide whether to use the employer complaint mechanism or grievance system available to you. If you perceive the first instance of sexual harassment to be extremely offensive or serious, immediately make a formal complaint. On the other hand, if you consider the first instance to be only mildly offensive, you may want to refrain from making a formal complaint, trusting that the behavior will not continue. If the offensive behavior does continue after you have communicated to the harasser that his or her conduct is unwelcome, you should inform the harasser of your intention to file a formal complaint and then follow through using the appropriate channels. Once a formal complaint has been made at work, it is the organization's responsibility to investigate and provide resolution. If your complaints are dismissed, if you are retaliated against, or if you are dismissed from your job, contact the EEOC for their advice.

THE SOCIAL MEDIA FACTOR

Digital Communication Skills in Professional Relationships

Professionals spend more than half their waking hours engaged in some activity related to their occupation. Social media allow us to remain in touch with our profession when we are "out of the office." Because of the tremendous reach, mobility, and interactivity of social media, we are technically available anywhere, anytime, blurring the line between our personal and professional lives (Kleinman, 2007). Relationships with professional colleagues may comprise the bulk of our interpersonal relationships. Being an effective communicator with your colleagues and supervisors can lead to promotions and other important career opportunities (Whetten & Cameron, 2005). Therefore, by learning how to take advantage of opportunities provided by social media and understanding how to avoid drawbacks of new technologies, you can better position yourself for

professional success. Social media can influence potential professional relationships long before you actually start a full-time position. It is important to understand how you can develop professional relationships through social media while simultaneously serving as an effective manager of your online identity. You must also become familiar with guidelines for digital communication etiquette.

Enabling Digital Communication between Colleagues

Workplace communication is a two-way street: managers must effectively communicate with employees, and employees must effectively communicate with managers. Today, many of those interactions can be carried out through social media. Since you may always be connected to the office through your mobile phone, you are just one call, text, or e-mail away. If you tend to respond quickly to texts and e-mail messages, your manager will likely develop an expectation that you will respond right away—even when you are out of the office. Try turning on an automated "out of office" reply on your e-mail account. Then, when your manager sends you an e-mail when you are out of the office, she will receive an automatically generated e-mail explaining that you are unable to respond to messages. If employees are required to use social media to facilitate their work performance, they must digitally communicate and manage digital conversations in ways that a manager perceives as effective and ethical. If you are exchanging e-mail messages with a manager or colleague, always remain aware of your audience. If you raise a sensitive workplace issue, you may notice only after having sent the e-mail that your boss was inadvertently copied, which could leave you with some uncomfortable explaining to do. Additionally, consider the often frowned on use of company e-mail for personal or social exchanges with noncolleagues and the use of e-mail to discuss sensitive company issues that the company would not want made public. This is especially important for people who work in government institutions, whose e-mails might be readily requisitioned through the Freedom of Information Act.

Social media permit us to manage multiple conversations while on the job. When you are browsing Facebook at your desk, your computer may ding with a new e-mail, your iPhone may alert you to an incoming text message, and your Skype program may ring with an incoming video call. As you learn to manage multiple conversations at work, remember that each person deserves your full attention. Client relationships, profits, and your job may be on the line. If you struggle managing many conversations through social media, try limiting the number of gadgets you use while in the office. Decide that you will only check Facebook when you are at home or on lunch. When you are on lunch, do not answer your phone—let your voicemail take the call. These strategies will move you toward becoming an effective digital communicator in the workplace.

Implications for Privacy in Professional Relationships

Many companies have strict guidelines that prohibit the use of social networking sites on company computers. If your employer does allow employees to use Facebook while at work, proceed with caution. Think twice before accepting a colleague's friend request. Are you willing to invite your colleagues into the personal side of your life on Facebook? Scan your Facebook page for any potentially incriminating photos that may lead a co-worker to draw inaccurate perceptions about your professionalism. If you regularly use Twitter, be careful what you tweet to your followers. If you say some not-so-nice things about a colleague, that brief message could make its way into the hands of your supervisor. You don't want to lose a potential raise or promotion over 140 rude and hastily typed characters. Since tweets display a prominent time stamp (e.g., ten minutes ago, two hours ago), you may also want to restrict your posts to after work hours in case somebody else is monitoring your Twitter messages. A current or prospective employer might not appreciate the fact that you were tweeting during working hours. If you approach social media with discretion, you may have to explain to your colleague why you declined her Facebook friend request. Make sure you have an answer when she inquires. You might say, "I've been using Facebook to reconnect with my high school friends, but I would be more than happy to connect with you on LinkedIn." By offering a professional network alternative to Facebook, you indicate that you are still willing to use social media to establish an interpersonal connection with others in the workplace. Remember to present a professional image to the world as you prepare to graduate from college and begin your job search. Many companies use Google and other Web sites to learn more about applicants' backgrounds. No company will want to hire a person featured online in outrageous party pictures. What would these pictures say about a potential employee's level of professionalism? If you have not done so already, immediately begin preparing your digital image for the job search. Increase your Facebook privacy settings, remove any questionable photos from your Web page, and think twice about posting an outlandish comment to a friend's Facebook page. Any unprofessional photo or comment from the past can return to haunt you. Begin to regularly Google your name and versions of it. You need to be familiar with what appears in the list of search results. When you look at the list of search results, count the number of personal hits relating to aspects of your non-work life and the number of professional hits relating to aspects of your career life. For example, when Dylan Googled his name, he found six professional hits, items pertaining to his work as a writer for the university's newspaper. He also discovered two personal hits, questionable photos from a recent fraternity social event. He quickly e-mailed the fraternity's webmaster and asked him to remove the pictures from the Web site. Consider the ratio of professional-to-personal hits when scanning search results. You always want more professional items appearing in a search. If you find yourself in the unfortunate situation of having a preponderance of personal items in an online search, work to repair that image immediately.

Digital Communication Etiquette in Your Profession

Social media have drastically changed how colleagues interact in professional settings. Numerous devices exist to enhance communication among team members, especially when those groups may not have the opportunity to meet face-to-face. Social media such as e-mailing, instant messaging, Skype, blogs, podcasts, and wikis, used individually or in combination, allow team members to communicate easily, regularly, and inexpensively as they seek to accomplish professional goals.

Appropriately integrating social media into your professional relationships with colleagues and clients is an essential skill. Let's consider professional guidelines for using social media in the workplace.

1. Match your purpose with the social media device. If your team is preparing and revising an executive summary of your committee's work, it would be inefficient to e-mail a draft to the team for each member to comment on and separately e-mail those revisions back to the team leader. Instead, consider using a wiki where users can collaboratively add and edit content. Once authorized to participate, all team members can post changes, and previous versions of the material are stored. A wiki is a powerful social media tool that allows each team member to work when and where it's convenient yet still collaborate in creating a report.

A QUESTION OF ETHICS ● What Would You Do?

Ken shifted in his chair as Ms. Goldsmith, his interviewer, looked over his résumé.

"I have to tell you that you have considerably more experience than the average applicant we usually get coming straight out of college," Ms. Goldsmith said. "Let's see, you've managed a hardware store, been a bookkeeper for a chain of three restaurants, and were the number one salesman for six straight months at a cell phone store."

"That's right," Ken said. "My family has always stressed the value of hard work, so I have worked a full-time job every summer since I entered junior high school, right through my last year of college. During the school year, I usually worked four to six hours a day after class."

"Very impressive," Ms. Goldsmith said. "And still you managed to get excellent grades and do a considerable amount of volunteer work in your spare time. What's your secret?"

"Secret?" said Ken nervously. "There's no secret—just a lot of hard work."

"Yes, I see that," said Ms. Goldsmith. "What I mean is that there are only 24 hours in a day and you obviously had a lot on your plate each day, especially for someone so young. How did you manage to do it?"

Ken thought for a moment before answering, "I only need five hours of sleep a day." He could feel Ms. Goldsmith's eyes scrutinizing his face. He hadn't

exactly lied on his résumé—just exaggerated a little bit. He had, in fact, helped his father run the family hardware store for a number of years. From time to time, he had helped his aunt keep track of her restaurant's receipts. He had also spent one summer selling cell phones for his cousin. Of course, his family always required him to do his schoolwork first before they let him help at the store, so Ken often had little time to help at all, but there was no reason Ms. Goldsmith needed to know that.

"And you can provide references for these jobs?" Ms. Goldsmith asked.

"I have them with me right here," said Ken, pulling a typed page from his briefcase and handing it across the desk.

For Consideration:

1. Are the exaggerated claims Ken made in his résumé ethical? Do the ethics of his actions change at all if he has references (family members) who will vouch for his claims?

2. Many people justify exaggerating or even lying on their résumés by claiming that everybody does it, so if they don't do it too, they will be handicapping themselves in a competitive job market. If the consequences of acting ethically diminish your professional prospects, are you justified in bending the rules? Explain your answer. If you think bending the rules is acceptable in such circumstances, how far can you bend them before the behavior becomes unacceptable?

2. Respond to ideas, not to people. Ideas and not personalities should animate workplace conversations. It is inappropriate for team members to discredit Jimmy's opinion and position on an issue because his Facebook profile features many pictures of his nights on the town with friends. Although Jimmy may have made a bad choice by using social media to bring aspects of his personal life into the workplace, Jimmy deserves to have his ideas critiqued and not his personal choices.

3. Use social media to add value to a conversation. Enter any digital discussion with the goal of enhancing the interaction. Remember that social media provide users with an opportunity to hide behind a device. Consequently, users are more likely to say or do things that they would not say or do in person. Before posting a message on a blog or raising an issue in a virtual meeting through Skype, ask yourself: How is this providing value to the conversation? To the company? If, for example, you are frustrated with your employer's inability to offer a raise, do not vent those frustrations through social media.

4. Respond appropriately and efficiently. Timely responses to e-mails and other messages are appreciated. Although the burden of responding to multiple e-mails can be great, try to give each message the attention that it deserves. Since e-mailing and text messaging tend to be lean in terms of social cues, eliminating typographical errors, communicating emotion, and conveying your feelings are important. Take the time to adequately address these issues in each message. Do not put off responding to a colleague, who may be waiting on you for approval or insight. You do not want to be a dam in a conversation flow.

5. Give praise where appropriate. Share good news about yourself through Facebook or Twitter, but do not go overboard. Self-promotion is generally okay as long as it is not excessive. Social media are even more effective when you praise others and give them a moment in the spotlight. If Jenny surpassed her sales quota for the month, tweet it to the entire company, if appropriate. Here you can use social media's reach to congratulate a colleague and quickly share her good news with others.

Summary

Effective workplace communication begins with how you present yourself during the hiring process through your résumé, which may be organized chronologically or functionally, and your interviewing skills. The first pieces of your work that a potential employer sees, your résumé and accompanying cover letter, should be prepared with care. A résumé should be tailored to highlight your skills and experiences relevant to the particular position for which you are applying. A job interview is a conversation or set of conversations between a job candidate and representatives of the hiring organization, allowing both to assess whether there is a good fit. To interview effectively, you need to prepare, present yourself as an acceptable candidate, and follow up after the interview.

Important relationships at work include those with your manager, co-workers, and customers and clients. Guidelines for effectively communicating with your manager include identifying how you can help your manager, volunteering for specific assignments, clarifying assignments, asking for feedback, adapting to your manager's communication preferences, and developing a mentoring relationship. Co-workers, organizational peers at the same level in the organization's hierarchy with no formal authority over each other, have three types of relationships: informational, collegial, and special. One type of a special relationship is an organizational romance. To improve your co-worker relationships, use positive nonverbal cues that make it easy for someone to approach you, share information freely, resolve conflicts through collaboration, talk in person, demonstrate respect, don't gossip, and be a good team member. A third important workplace relationship is with customers and clients. You can effectively communicate with customers and clients by listening to understand; by demonstrating empathy and providing comfort; and by honestly explaining, when turning down a request, the reason for the policy as well as the limitations of your authority. Diversity in the workforce means that we are interacting with people of different cultures, genders, and generations, a situation that requires varied and flexible approaches to communication in the workplace. Sometimes at work we experience and have to respond to the dark-side communication behaviors of aggression and sexual harassment.

Social media allow us to remain in touch with our profession when we are "out of the office." Learning how to take advantage of opportunities provided by social media and understanding how to avoid drawbacks of new technologies can better position you for professional success. If employees are required to use social media to facilitate their work performance, they must digitally communicate and manage digital conversations in ways that a manager perceives as effective and ethical. Appropriately integrating social media into your professional relationships with colleagues and clients is an essential skill that can be improved by following certain rules of digital communication etiquette.

Chapter Resources

What You Should Be Able *to Explain:*

- The role of communication in the hiring process
- How to prepare an electronic résumé
- How to write an effective cover e-mail
- How to interview for a job
- Effective communication in manager-employee relationships
- Effective communication in co-worker relationships
- Effective communication with customers/clients
- The effects of diversity in the workplace
- How to handle the dark side of workplace communication

What You Should Be Able *to Do:*

- Develop job leads
- Prepare an e-résumé
- Prepare an e-mail cover letter
- Interview for a job

Self-test questions based on these concepts are available on the companion Web site (www.oup.com/us/verderber) as part of Chapter 13 resources.

Key Words

Flashcards for all of these key terms are available on the *Inter-Act* Web site.

Behavioral aggression, p. 456
Boundary spanning, p. 448
Bullying, p. 456
Chronological résumé, p. 433
Collegial relationships, p. 446
Cover letter, p. 433
Customers and clients, p. 448
Functional résumé, p. 434
Glass ceiling, p. 452
Hidden job market, p. 432
Holistic task-completion culture, p. 450

Informational relationships, p. 445
Interview, p. 437
Job interview, p. 437
Linguistic style, p. 452
Maintenance roles, p. 447
Mentoring relationship, p. 442
Networking, p. 432
Organizational romance, p. 447
Physical aggression, p. 456
Relationship-oriented culture, p. 450
Results-oriented culture, p. 450

Résumé, p. 433
Sequential task-completion culture,
    p. 450
Sexual harassment, p. 457
Special relationships, p. 446
Task roles, p. 447
Vendors, p. 448
Verbal aggression, p. 456
Workplace aggression, p. 455
Workplace team, p. 447

Apply Your Knowledge

The following activities challenge you to demonstrate your mastery of the concepts, theories, and frameworks in this chapter by using them to explain what is happening in a specific situation.

Interpreting the Opening Dialogue

14.1   Revisit the opening dialogue. Then using what you have learned in this chapter, explain Maria's situation. What would you advise her to do next?

14.2   Imagine a more pleasant and productive workplace environment for Maria. In this "bright-side" scenario, Maria respects and even admires her manager, Carlos, who has always treated her ethically and appropriately. She enjoys her part-time job immensely, gets along well with her co-workers, and hopes to advance in this company. Advise Maria on how she could pursue a mentoring relationship that would help her achieve this goal.

Skill Practice

Skill practice activities give you the chance to rehearse a new skill by responding to hypothetical or real situations. Additional skill practice activities are available at the companion Web site.

Testing the Job Market

Go online to Monster.com or CareerBuilder.com. Identify a job opening in your field or a field you are considering.

14.3   Research the target organization and answer these questions: What does the organization do? What is its mission? Where is it headquartered? What goods/ services does it provide? If it is a for-profit organization, is it making money? How does the job you are applying for fit into what this organization does? Who is the CEO of this organization? What if any national, regional, or local awards or recognitions has this organization received recently? What is the "big news" in the last six months for this organization?

14.4 Prepare your résumé tailored to this position in the format in which the organization prefers to receive it.

14.5 Write a cover e-mail to send with your résumé for this position.

Communication Improvement Plan: Workplace Communication

Would you like to improve the following aspects of your work relationships?

- Networking
- Résumé and cover letter development
- Relationship with your manager
- Relationship with your co-worker(s)
- Relationships with your customers/clients/vendors?
- Dealing with aggression
- Dealing with sexual harassment

14.6 Pick an aspect, then using the interpersonal communication skills you have studied in the course, write a communication improvement plan. You can find a communication improvement plan worksheet on our Web site at www.oup.com/us/verderber.

Inter-Act with Media

Television

Family Guy, episode: "Peter-assment" (2010)

During a stint as a paparazzo, Peter films the town's mayor and local television personalities. Annoyed, Ollie Williams, the TV weatherman, breaks Peter's video camera and his glasses. The next day, Peter goes to his regular job wearing contacts. His typically gruff boss, Angela, takes a romantic interest in him because he is no longer wearing glasses. She intentionally drops pencils on the floor and asks Peter to bend over and pick them up. She orders him to wear short shorts and skimpy shirts at work. Peter complies with her demand to visit her at home but refuses to have sex with her. Angela then fires him, after which Peter spends some time at the local bar, where he watches an old movie starring Robert Mitchum, who gives him a pep talk on how to be a "real man" circa 1950s. He returns to Angela's home to confront her, only to discover that she is attempting to kill herself. Angela shares with Peter that no man has been romantically attracted to her in ten years. With this information in mind, Peter sets up Angela on a blind date with his "friend." The "friend" is actually Peter in a disguise. During their sexual encounter at the conclusion of the date, Angela recognizes Peter and offers him his job back.

IPC Concepts: Sexual harassment, workplace aggression, bullying

To the Point:

How would you characterize Peter's feelings throughout this incident?
After Angela rehires Peter, what future challenges do you perceive that they will face?

Cinema

Quite Contrary (2005). Nello DeBlasio (director). Shannon McManus, Andra Whitt, Hugh Hill.

Mary (McManus) is anxious to make a positive impression during her job interview. From the very beginning, however, fate appears to be her worst enemy. Planning ahead, she requests a wake-up call from her hotel. The wake-up call is made late, so Mary has to quickly shower and dress for her interview. She repeatedly tries to find a taxi with no luck. Eventually, she throws in the towel and walks to the job interview. While waiting for an elevator in the lobby, she notices that it is completely full with an endless number of employees who are trying to get to work on time. She decides to take the stairs. Despite these frustrating setbacks, she makes it to the office on time for her interview.

Although Mary was eager to make a very strong positive impression, the office staff appeared quite determined to make a negative impression. The receptionist (Whitt) babbles profanity over the phone with a strange smile. Workers are seen in heated arguments. Finally, once the interview actually begins, Mr. Brown (Hill), the interviewer, spews off on personal and irrelevant negative tangents that alarm Mary. Throughout the course of the entire interview experience, not one person allows Mary to speak a single word. When she finally gets the opportunity to speak, she starts to make an impression of her own.

IPC Concepts: Job interview, workplace aggression

To the Point:

How would you encourage Mary to better prepare for her job interview?
Based on her job-interview experience, what conclusions might Mary draw about this job's workplace environment?

What's on the Web

Find links and additional material, including self-quizzes, on the companion Web site at www.oup.com/us/verderber.

Glossary

Abusive relationship a relationship in which the interactions are physically, mentally, or emotionally harmful to one or both partners.

Accommodating resolving a conflict by satisfying the other person's needs or accepting the other person's ideas while neglecting one's own needs or ideas.

Acoustic space the area over which your voice or other sounds can be comfortably heard.

Acquaintances people we know by name and talk to when the opportunity arises but with whom our interactions are limited.

Action-oriented listening style the personal listening style that prefers to focus on the point that the speaker is trying to make with a message.

Active listening the skillful, intentional, deliberate, conscious process of attending to, understanding, remembering, critically evaluating, and responding to messages that we hear.

Advice a message or series of messages intended to help another person manage or solve a problem.

Affection need our desire to love and be loved.

Anxious-ambivalent attachment infants' perception that they are unworthy of care and others are untrustworthy.

Apology a direct verbal message that acknowledges responsibility, expresses regret or remorse, and directly requests forgiveness.

Appropriate messages messages that conform to the social, relational, and ethical expectations of the situation.

Argumentativeness defending our own ideas or attacking the reasoning of others while according them respect.

Artifacts the objects we use to adorn our territory.

Asking for personal feedback the disclosure skill of gaining self-knowledge by requesting your partner disclose observations about your behavior.

Assertiveness the skill of sending messages that declare and defend personal rights and expectations in a clear, direct, and honest manner while at the same time respecting the preferences and rights of others.

Asynchronous delays that occur in communication; each interactant must take turns being the sender and receiver of a message.

Attachment styles perceptions of self-worth and trust in others.

Attending the process of willfully striving to perceive selected sounds that are being heard.

Attributions reasons we give for others' and our own behavior.

Authenticity communicating information and feelings that are relevant and legitimate to the subject at hand directly, honestly, and straightforwardly.

Authoritarian parenting style a parenting style involving high levels of control behavior but low levels of nurturing.

Authoritative parenting style a parenting style involving firm control balanced by ample nurturing.

Authority heuristic being influenced by what knowledgeable professionals believe or advocate during peripheral processing of persuasive messages.

Automatic processing a fast, top-down, subconscious approach to perceiving that draws on previous experience to make sense out of what we are now encountering.

Autonomy the desire to act and make decisions independent of your relationship partner.

Avoidant attachment infants' perception that they are worthy of care but caregivers are untrustworthy.

Back-channel cues verbal and nonverbal signals that indicate you are listening and attempting to understand the message.

Behavioral aggression nonverbal acts intended to hurt someone.

Behavioral flexibility the capacity to react in a variety of ways to the same or similar situations.

Body language the intentional or unintentional movement of various body parts that sends nonverbal messages.

Body orientation your position in relation to another person.

Boundary spanning the process of communicating with people outside of our organization in a mutually beneficial relationship.

Breadth a dimension of relationships that gauges the variety of conversational topics and activities that partners share, as well as the number of contexts in which they interact.

Bullying the habitual use of aggression or the repeated use of aggression against one target individual.

Canned plan your "mental library" of scripts that you draw on when you create certain types of messages that also informs how you understand what others say to you.

Capitalization the process of sharing our successes and leveraging the good feelings that come from them by telling others with the expectation that they will celebrate with us.

Celebratory messages active-constructive feedback whose goal is to leverage your partner's positive feelings that stem from a happy event or accomplishment.

Central route consciously processing persuasive messages by critically evaluating the logic, credibility, and emotional appeals of the sender.

Chronemics the study of how perception of time differs between individuals and cultures.

Chronological résumé a format that lists your job positions and accomplishments in reverse chronological order.

Claims simple statements of belief or opinion.

Clarifying question a response designed to get further information or to remove uncertainty from information already received.

Clarifying supportive intentions openly stating that one's goal in a

supportive interaction is to help the person in need of support.

Closed-ended questions questions that can be answered with "yes," "no," or a few words.

Closedness the desire to maintain privacy.

Co-cultures cultures that exist side by side with the dominant culture and are comprised of smaller numbers of people who hold common values, attitudes, beliefs, and orientations that differ from those of the dominant culture.

Codeswitch to alter linguistic and nonverbal patterns to conform to the dominant or co-culture depending on the topics or co-participants in a conversation.

Coercive power the potential to influence rooted in our ability to physically or psychologically punish our partner.

Cohesiveness a sense of togetherness developed from sharing time, activities, and relationships with others, and creating a shared identity.

Collaborating resolving a conflict by using problem solving to arrive at a solution that meets the needs and interests of both parties in the conflict.

Collectivist culture a culture that values community, collaboration, shared interests, harmony, the public good, and avoiding embarrassment.

Collegial relationships work-based peer relationships that have developed into friendships so that co-workers share career strategies and provide job feedback.

Comforting messages active-constructive feedback whose goal is to alleviate or lessen the emotional distress felt by someone else.

Commitment a dimension of relationships that gauges how dedicated or loyal partners are to each other.

Communication code change a dimension of relationships that gauges how much partners have developed scripts that are exclusive to their relationship.

Communication competence another person's perception that your messages are both effective and appropriate in a given relationship.

Communication privacy management (CPM) theory a theory that provides a framework for understanding the decision-making processes people use to manage disclosure and privacy.

Communication setting the background conditions surrounding an interaction including the physical, social, historical, psychological, and cultural contexts that influences the understandings in a communication encounter.

Communication skills generic messages, scripts, or canned plans that you have mastered which increase the change that you will have an effective and appropriate interaction.

Communication skill scripts mental texts that include micro communication skills and usually require a series of messages to reach the communication goal.

Competence the perception that speakers are credible because they are well-qualified to provide accurate and reliable information.

Complaint a message telling someone that what is or has occurred is unacceptable because it has violated your rights or expectations.

Compromising resolving a conflict by bargaining so that each partner's needs or interests are partially satisfied.

Compulsive Internet use a person's inability to control, reduce, or stop utilizing the Internet.

Co-narration Specific type of conversational sequencing in which people finish each other's sentences because they have intimate knowledge of the topic and each other's style.

Concrete language words that describe something that can be sensed.

Confirmation expressing a warm affirmation of others as unique persons without necessarily approving of their behaviors or views.

Connection the desire to link your actions and decisions with those of your relationship partner.

Connotation the feelings or evaluations we personally associate with a word.

Conscious processing a slow, deliberative approach to perceiving during which we examine and think about the stimuli.

Consistency heuristic being influenced by our past active, voluntary, and public commitments during peripheral processing of persuasive messages.

Constitutive function the communi-cation messages exchanged in a relationship form the relationship.

Constructive criticizing the disclosure skill of diplomatically describing the specific negative behavior of your partner and its effects on others.

Content paraphrase a feedback message that conveys your understanding of the denotative meaning of a verbal message.

Content-oriented listening style the personal listening style that prefers to focus on the facts and evidence in a message.

Control extent to which each person has power or is "in charge" in the relationship.

Controlling parental communication parental messages that attempt to influence or regulate a child's behavior.

Control need our desire to influence the events and people around us and to be influenced by others.

Conversation an interactive, extemporaneous, locally managed, and sequentially organized interchange of thoughts and feelings between two or more people.

Conversation purpose what the conversation is intended to do.

Conversation tone emotional and relational quality, or how it feels "inside" the interaction.

Conversational coherence the extent to which the comments made by one person relate to those made previously by others in a conversation.

Conversational maxims specific rules that cooperating partners count on others to follow.

Conversational spontaneity the degree to which a conversation evolves in an informal and natural fashion.

Cooperative principle the pragmatic principle that states that conversational partners are able to understand what the other means to do with their verbal messages because they assume that their partners are collaborating by sharing verbal messages in line with the shared purpose of the conversation.

Counterblaming a conflict pattern in which you blame your partner for what he or she has accused you of doing, shifting responsibility and leaving the original issue unresolved.

Cover letter a short, well-written letter or e-mail expressing your interest in a particular position.

Covert intimacy delivering messages that use mild insults, competition, or put-downs to signal closeness, trust, and equality.

Credibility the extent to which your partner believes in your competence, trustworthiness, and likability.

Critically evaluating the process of determining how truthful, authentic, or believable you judge the message and the speaker to be.

Cross-complaining a conflict pattern in which partners trade unrelated criticisms, leaving the initial issue unresolved.

Cultural context the set of beliefs, values, and attitudes that define the specific culture that participants belong to that influence the understandings in a communication encounter.

Cultural identity that part of your self-image that is based on the cultural group or groups with which you most closely associate and align yourself.

Culture the system of shared values, beliefs, attitudes, and orientations learned through communication that guide what is considered to be appropriate thought and behavior in a particular segment of the population.

Culture shock the psychological discomfort you experience when you must interact in a new culture.

Customers and clients the people, groups, or other organizations that use an organization's goods or services.

Cyberbullying abusive attacks that are carried out through social media.

Cyber stalking occurs when an individual repeatedly uses social media to stalk or harass others.

Dark-Side messages those messages that are not ethical and/or appropriate.

Dating information the communication skill that improves the semantic accuracy of verbal messages by pointing out when the information in a message was true.

Decoding the process of interpreting the messages we receive from others.

Demand-withdrawal a conflict pattern in which one partner consistently demands while the other consistently withdraws.

Denotation the direct, explicit meaning of a word found in a written dictionary of the language community.

Depth a dimension of relationships that gauges how intimate the partners have become though disclosing personal and private information.

Describing behavior the disclosure skill of accurately recounting the specific behaviors of others without drawing conclusions about those behaviors.

Describing feelings the disclosure skill of owning and explaining the precise emotions you are experiencing.

Dialect a form of a more general language spoken by a specific culture or co-culture that, while differing from the general language, shares enough commonality that most people who belong to a particular language community can understand it.

Digital communication the electronic transmission of digitally encoded information. We use social media to express, interpret, and coordinate messages to create shared meaning, meet social goals, manage personal identity, and carry out our relationships.

Digital communication apprehension nervousness associated with communicating through social media.

Digital communication literacy the ability to critically attend to, analyze, evaluate, and express digital messages.

Digital self-disclosure a tendency to reveal and conceal private information in digital settings versus other contexts.

Digital social connection a tendency to use social media to maintain connection with others.

Direct verbal style message language that openly states the speaker's intention and message content that is straightforward and unambiguous.

Disclosure revealing confidential or secret information.

Discrimination acting differently toward a person based on prejudice.

Dismissive attachment style an adult attachment style characterized by high self-worth but lack of trust in others.

Dispositional attribution attributing behavior to some cause that is under the control of the person.

Diversity variations between and among people.

Dominant culture the learned system of values, beliefs, attitudes, and orientations held by the majority of people in a society.

Effective messages messages achieve the goals that you and your partner have for the interaction.

Ego conflict disagreement that results when both parties insist on being the "winner" of the argument to confirm their self-concept or self-esteem.

Elaboration likelihood model of persuasion (ELM) a theory that posits people will use either heuristics or more elaborate critical thinking skills when processing persuasive messages.

Emblems gestures that substitute completely for words.

Emoticons typed or graphic symbols that convey facial expressions in online messages.

Emotional appeals persuasive messages that influence others by evoking strong feelings in support of what the speaker is advocating.

Emotional intelligence the ability to monitor your own and others' emotions and to use this information to guide your communications.

Empathy demonstrating an understanding of another person's point of view without giving up one's own position or sense of self.

Emotional disclosure disclosures that reveal sensitive, private, and personally risky information, signaling to our partners the desire for intimacy.

Empathic responsiveness (also called empathic distress) empathizing by personally experiencing an emotional response parallel to another person's actual or anticipated display of emotion.

Encoding the process of choosing the words, sentences, and nonverbal behaviors to form a message.

Equality treating conversational partners as peers, regardless of the status differences that separate them from other participants.

Ethical dialog a conversation characterized by authenticity, empathy, confirmation, presentness, equality, and supportiveness.

Ethics a set of moral principles that may be held by a society, a group, or an individual.

Ethnicity a classification of people based on shared national characteristics such as country of birth, geographic origin, language, religion, ancestral customs, and tradition.

Ethnocentrism the belief that one's own culture is superior to that of others.

Ethnorelativism the point of view allows you to see the value in other cultural perspectives.

Evidence facts, expert opinions, and personal narratives that support the truth of your reason.

Excessive Internet use the degree to which a person feels that he or she spends an extreme amount of time online or even loses track of time while online.

Expectations things we notice because we are accustomed to noticing them.

Expert power the ability to influence rooted in someone's subject-specific knowledge and competence.

Extemporaneous uttered in the spur of the moment without lengthy preplanning.

External noises sights, sounds, and other stimuli that draw people's attention away from intended meaning.

Eye contact using eye focus to signal attention, respect, emotional reactions, or dominance.

Face how we want our partners and others who are present to view us, our public self-image.

Face in Eastern and Southern Hemisphere cultures the public self-images of others who may be affected by the situation or relationship as well as your own self-image.

Face in Western Hemisphere cultures the public self-image that you claim for yourself in a social situation or relationship that generally corresponds to your private self-image.

Face negotiation theory a theory positing that in conflict settings we prefer conflict styles consistent with our cultural frame and the resulting face orientations.

Face-saving helping others to preserve their self-image or self-respect.

Face-threatening act (FTA) a statement of support that a person in need may interpret as a threat to his or her public self-image.

Facework the messages that we send with the goal of maintaining or restoring another person's sense of self-worth.

Facial expression arranging facial muscles to communicate emotion or provide feedback.

Fact conflict disagreement that is caused by a dispute over the truth or accuracy of an item of information.

Facts statements whose accuracy can be verified or proven.

Family a network of people who share their lives over long periods of time bound by ties of marriage, blood, or commitment, legal or otherwise, who consider themselves a family, and who share a significant history and anticipated future of functioning in a family relationship.

Fearful attachment style an adult attachment style characterized by low self-worth and lack of trust in others.

Feedback a message that is in response to a previous message indicating whether and how the original message was understood.

Feelings paraphrase a feedback message that conveys one's understanding of the emotional meaning behind a speaker's verbal message.

Feminine culture a culture in which people regardless of sex can

assume a variety of roles depending on the circumstances and their own choices.

Fictive kin people who are considered family members even though there is no genetic or marital tie.

Filtering messages the tendency to attend to messages that reinforce what we already think of ourselves and to downplay or not register messages that contradict this image.

Flame wars erupt when friendly and productive digital discussions give way to insults and aggression.

Flaming digital communication that is deliberately hostile, aggressive, or insulting and usually intended to provoke anger.

Forced consistency the perceptual bias in which we inaccurately interpret different perceptions of another person so that our interpretation of what we see remains consistent.

Forcing resolving a conflict by satisfying one's own needs or advancing one's own ideas with no concern for the needs or ideas of the other person or for the relationship.

Forgiveness a communication that allows you and your partner to overcome the damage done to your relationship because of a transgression.

Formality degree to which a conversation follows scripted norms, rules, and procedures.

Framing information providing support by offering information, observations, and opinions that enable the receiver to better understand or see her or his situation in a different light.

Free information information volunteered during conversation rather than specifically required or requested.

Friends people with whom we have voluntary personal relationships characterized by equality, mutual involvement, reciprocal liking, self-disclosure, and reciprocal social support.

Functional résumé a format that categorizes and lists relevant skills and experiences rather than chronologically listing your work history.

Fundamental attribution error the tendency to overattribute others' negative behavior to their disposition and overattribute our own negative behavior to the situation.

Gesture using hand, arm, and finger movement to replace, complement, and augment a verbal message.

Glass ceiling an invisible yet real barrier that prevents deserving employees from advancing.

Go viral messages that reach enormous audiences by "infecting" viewers and users with the message.

Good relationship a relationship in which the interactions are satisfying and healthy for those involved.

Gossip discussion of people who are not present for the conversation.

Ground rules mutually agreed on rules for behavior during conflict episodes.

Halo effect a perceptual bias that occurs when we misperceive that a person has a whole set of related personality traits when only one trait has actually been observed.

Heuristics rules of thumb for how something is to be viewed based on our past experience with similar stimuli.

Hidden job market jobs that are never advertised because employers hire people already known to them.

High power-distance culture a culture in which both high- and low-

power holders accept the unequal distribution of power.

High uncertainty-avoidance culture a culture characterized as having a low tolerance for and a high need to control unpredictable people, relationships, or events.

High-context culture a culture in which much of the real meaning of a message is indirect and can only be accurately decoded by referring to unwritten cultural rules and subtle nonverbal behavior.

Historical context the background provided by previous communication episodes between the participants that influences understandings in the current communication encounter.

Holistic task-completion culture a culture that believes in tackling large and complex tasks in their entirety.

Hyperpersonal communication suggests that digital interactions can become hyperpersonal because the context affords message senders a host of communicative advantages over traditional face-to-face interactions.

Idiolect our personal symbolic system that includes our active vocabularies, our pronunciation of words, and our grammar and syntax when talking or writing.

Idioms expressions used by members of a language or speech community whose meaning differs from the usual meanings associated with that combination of words.

Impersonal relationship a relationship in which one person relates to another merely because the other fills a role that satisfies an immediate need.

Implicit personality theory a belief that two or more personal traits or characteristics go together.

Inclusion need our desire to be in the company of other people.

Independent self-perception self-perception in which people view their traits and abilities as internal and universally applicable to all situations.

Indexical Function embedded in the communication messages that are exchanged in a relationship are measures of who is in control, how much partners trust each other, and the level of intimacy in the relationship.

Indexing generalizations the communication skill that improves the semantic meaning of a verbal message by acknowledging that individual instances may differ from the truth statement of our message.

Indirect verbal style message language that masks the speaker's true intentions and roundabout, vague message content whose real meaning is embedded in the social or cultural context.

Individualistic culture a culture that values personal rights and responsibilities, privacy, voicing one's opinion, freedom, innovation, and self-expression.

Inferences claims or assertions based on the facts presented.

Information co-ownership the private information that each partner has shared with the other so that it is now jointly held.

Informational relationships work-based peer relationships in which the interaction and conversation is solely devoted to work topics.

Instrumental function the communication messages exchanged in a relationship are the means through which we accomplish our personal and our relationship goals.

Interaction coordination the activity which participants in a conversation take in order to adjust their behavior to that of their partner.

Interactivity the ability of a communication tool to facilitate social interaction between groups or individuals.

Intercultural communication interactions that occur between people whose cultures are so different that the communication between them is altered.

Intercultural competence the effective and appropriate behavior and communication in intercultural situations.

Interdependence a dimension of relationships that gauges the extent to which partners rely on each other to meet their needs.

Interdependent self-perception self-perception in which people perceive their traits, abilities, and personality within the context of their relationships.

Interests things that prompt our curiosity but are not essential to sustain us biologically or psychologically.

Internal noises thoughts and feelings that interfere with interpreting meaning.

Interpersonal communication the complex process through which people express, interpret, and coordinate messages to create shared meaning, meet social goals, manage personal identity, and carry out their relationships.

Interpersonal conflict disagreement between two interdependent people who perceive that they have incompatible goals.

Interpersonal influence the act of changing the attitudes or behaviors of others.

Interpersonal needs theory the premise that all of us have inclusion,

affection, and control needs that we try to meet through our relationships, although our need for each of these varies in degree from person to person.

Interpersonal trust a dimension of relationships that gauges the extent to which partners believe that they know what to expect from the relationship, know how they are supposed to act, and know that they want to act according to expectations.

Interview a structured conversation with the goal of exchanging information needed for decision making.

Intimacy the degree of emotional closeness, acceptance, and disclosure in a relationship.

Intimate relationship a relationship in which partners share regular intimate interactions, feel affection for each other, trust each other, and are cohesive.

Intimates or close friends those few people with whom we share a high degree of interdependence, commitment, disclosure, affection, understanding, and trust.

Intonation the variety, melody, or inflection of a person's voice.

Involuntary relationship a relationship in which we have no choice about the other people with whom we interact.

Jargon technical terminology whose meaning is understood by only a select group of people in a specialized speech community based on shared activities or interests.

Job interview a conversation or set of conversations between a job candidate and representatives of the hiring organization that allows both to assess whether there is a good fit.

Johari window a visual framework for understanding how self-disclosure

and feedback work together in a relationship.

Kinesics the study of body language.

Language a symbolic system used by people to communicate verbal or written messages.

Language community all people who can speak or understand a particular language.

Latent ties potential relationships within a social circle that are present, but have not been activated.

Leave-taking cues nonverbal behaviors that indicate someone wants to end the conversation.

Legitimate power the potential to influence others rooted in the authority granted to a person who occupies a certain role.

Lexicon the collection of words and expressions in a language.

Likability the perception that speakers are credible because they are congenial, friendly, and warm.

Liking heuristic being influenced to believe or do what people we like advocate during peripheral processing of persuasive messages.

Linguistic sensitivity using language that respects others while avoiding language that offends.

Linguistic style the patterned way in which you use language to communicate

Listening the process of receiving, constructing meaning from, and responding to spoken and/or nonverbal messages.

Listening apprehension the anxiety we feel about listening that interferes with our ability to be effective listeners.

Listening style your favored but usually unconscious approach to attending to your partner's messages.

Local management the way that conversational partners produce and monitor every aspect of the conversational give-and-take.

Low power-distance culture a culture in which members prefer power to be more equally distributed.

Low uncertainty-avoidance culture a culture that tolerates uncertainty and is less driven to control unpredictable people, relationships, or events.

Low-context culture a culture in which message meanings are usually encoded in the verbal part of the message.

Maintenance roles communication behaviors that improve interactions among team members.

Masculine culture a culture in which men are expected to adhere to traditional sex roles.

Meaning the significance that the sender (speaker) and the receiver (listener) each attach to a message.

Media multiplexity theory explains that we carry out those relationships through more than one form of social media, and those in closer relationships use more forms of social media.

Media richness theory describes communication channels by the amount of verbal and nonverbal information that can be exchanged through a particular channel.

Mediator a neutral and impartial guide who structures an interaction so that conflicting parties can find a mutually acceptable solution to an issue.

Mentoring relationship a relationship with a more experienced person designed to helped mentees develop career skills and expertise beyond what would normally be learned on the job.

Message a performance that uses words, sentences, and/or nonverbal behaviors to convey the thoughts, feeling, and intentions of the speaker.

Message interpretation the activities that those listening to the message take to understand what the speaker intends.

Message production the actions that you take when you send a message.

Metaconflict disagreement over the process of communication itself during an argument.

Micro communication skills learned message templates that have a specific interaction purpose.

Mindfulness the process of drawing novel distinctions.

Miscommunication misinterpretations associated with deriving meaning from a digital message.

Mnemonic device a learning technique that associates a special word or short statement with new and longer information.

Mobility extent to which social media are portable or stationary.

Monochronic a time orientation that views time as being small, even units that occur sequentially.

Mutual hostility a conflict pattern in which partners trade increasingly louder verbal abuse, including inappropriate, unrelated personal criticism, name-calling, swearing, and sarcasm.

Mutual-face orientation the inclination to uphold and protect others' self-images as well as our own when interacting in a conflict setting.

Mutual understanding partners comprehending what the other person is saying from both their own and their partner's point of view.

Needs things we consciously or unconsciously feel we require to sustain us biologically or psychologically.

Negative facework messages that offer information, opinions, or advice that protect a person's freedom and privacy.

Networking developing or using established relationships to gain career information and insight, including access to the hidden job market.

Neutralization the strategy of dealing with dialectical tensions by compromising between the desires of those in the relationship.

Noise any stimulus that interferes with shared meaning.

Nonverbal communication all human communication events that transcend spoken or written words.

Novelty the desire for originality, freshness, and uniqueness in your partner's behavior or in your relationship.

Nurturing parental communication parental messages that encourage a child's physical, social, emotional, and intellectual development.

Olfactory cues messages sent through smells and scents.

Online communication attitude a collection of cognitive and affective orientations that may foster or inhibit a person's tendency to engage in digital communication.

Open-ended questions questions that require answers with more elaboration and explanation.

Openness the desire to share intimate ideas and feelings with your relationship partner.

Organizational romance sexual or romantic involvement between people who work for the same organization.

Other-centered messages communications that focus on the needs of the person requiring support through active listening and expressions of compassion, understanding, and encouragement.

Other-face orientation the inclination to uphold and protect the self-images of our partners and other people affected by the conflict even at the risk of our own face.

Overaccommodate excessively adapting one's communication style to the perceived needs or desires of the other person.

Owning (also known as crediting yourself) the disclosure skill of making "I" statements that identify the speaker as the source of a particular idea, experience, or feeling.

Paralanguage using the voice to convey meaning.

Paraphrase an attempt to verify your understanding of a message by putting it into your own words and sharing it with the speaker.

Passive approach concealing your feelings rather than voicing your rights and expectations to others.

Passive listening the effortless, thoughtless, and habitual process of receiving the messages we hear.

Passive-aggressive behavior messages that indirectly express hostility.

Pattern recognition the organization of stimuli into easily recognizable patterns or systems of interrelated parts.

People-oriented listening style the personal listening style that prefers to focus on what a message tells us about our conversational partners and their feelings.

Perception the process of attending to, organizing, and interpreting the information that we receive through our senses.

Perception check sharing your perception of another's behavior to see if your interpretation is accurate.

Peripheral route automatically processing persuasive messages by using shortcut heuristics that save time and mental energy.

Permissive parenting style a parenting style involving moderate to high levels of nurturing but little control.

Personal boundaries the points that separate the parts of ourselves that we are comfortable sharing with a relationship partner from the parts of ourselves that we maintain as our private inner life.

Personal feedback disclosing information about others to them.

Personal identity the traits and characteristics that taken as a whole distinguish you from other people.

Personal relationship a relationship in which people care about each other, share at least some personal information with each other, and meet at least some of each other's interpersonal needs.

Personal requests messages that direct others how to respect our rights or meet our expectations in particular situations.

Personal space the area that surrounds a person, moves with that person, and changes with the situation as well as moment to moment.

Persuasion the use of verbal messages designed to influence the attitudes and behaviors of others.

Phonology the sounds used to pronounce words.

Physical aggression nonverbal acts of violence against another person with the intent to do bodily harm.

Physical context the place where the participants exchange messages that influences understandings in a communication encounter.

Pitch the rate of vibration of your vocal cords.

Platonic relationship a relationship in which partners are not sexually attracted to each other or choose not to act on their sexual attraction.

Policy conflict disagreement caused by differences over a preferred plan or course of action.

Politeness relating to others in ways that meet their needs to be appreciated and respected.

Polychronic a time orientation that views time as a continuous flow.

Positive facework messages that affirm a person or a person's actions in a difficult situation to protect his or her respectability and public approval.

Possessiveness the desire to control another person to ensure that he or she is one's exclusive partner.

Posture the position and movement of the whole body.

Power the potential that you have to influence the attitudes, beliefs, and behaviors of someone else.

Power distance the extent to which members of a culture expect and accept that power will be unequally shared.

Pragmatic meaning meaning of a verbal message that arises from understanding the practical consequences of an utterance.

Praising the disclosure skill of describing the specific behaviors or accomplishments of our partners and their positive effects on others.

Precise words words that identify a smaller grouping within a larger category.

Predictability the desire for consistency, reliability, and dependability in your partner's behavior or in your relationship.

Predicted outcome value theory the premise that in our early conversations with potential relationship partners, we gather information to predict whether the benefits of future interactions will outweigh the costs.

Prejudice stereotyping a person based on the characteristics of a group to which the person belongs without regard to how the person may vary from the group characteristics.

Preoccupied attachment style an adult attachment style characterized by low self-worth and high trust in others.

Presentness the willingness to become fully involved with another person by taking time, avoiding distractions, being responsive, and risking attachment.

Primacy effect the tendency to remember information that we heard first over what we heard in the middle.

Principle of negative reciprocity the proposition that we repay negative treatment with negative treatment.

Principle of positive reciprocity the proposition that we repay positive treatment with positive treatment.

Privacy the opposite of disclosure, withholding confidential or secret information to enhance autonomy and/or minimize vulnerability.

Probing questions questions that search for more information or try to resolve perceived inconsistencies in a message.

Problematic Internet use a syndrome characterized by cognitive and behavioral symptoms that can result in negative social, academic, and professional consequences.

Process a systematic series of actions that lead to an outcome.

Projection the perceptual bias that occurs when we incorrectly think someone who is like us in one respect will share other characteristics and attitudes.

Proxemics the study of space.

Pseudoconflict disagreement that is caused by a perceptual difference between partners and is easily resolved.

Psychological context the moods and feelings each person brings to an interpersonal encounter that influences the understandings in the communication encounter.

Quality the sound of a person's voice.

Rate the speed at which a person speaks.

Reasons statements that provide valid evidence, explanations, or justifications for a claim.

Recency effect the tendency to remember information that we heard last over what we heard in the middle.

Reciprocity the mutual exchange of information characterized by similar levels of disclosure by both partners.

Reciprocity heuristic being influenced by a perceived debt or obligation to someone else during peripheral processing of persuasive messages.

Referent power the potential to influence rooted in liking, respect, or admiration.

Reframing the strategy of dealing with dialectical tensions by changing perceptions about the level of tension.

Relational dialectics the conflicting pulls that exist in relationships as well as within each individual in a relationship.

Relational uncertainty a feeling of doubt about the nature of a relationship.

Relationship a set of expectations two people have for each other based on their pattern of interaction.

Relationship costs negative outcomes to a relationship, including the time and energy we spend developing a relationship and the negative experiences that may arise like hurt feelings, conflict episodes, jealousy, etc.

Relationship-oriented culture a culture that prioritizes building relationships at work over results.

Relationship rewards positive outcomes to a relationship, including having basic relationship needs for affection, control, and inclusion met.

Relationship transformation continuing to interact and influence a partner through a different type of relationship after one type of relationship has ended.

Religion a system of beliefs, rituals, and ethics based on a common perception of the sacred or holy.

Remembering the process of moving information from short-term memory to long-term memory.

Responding the process of providing feedback to your partner's message.

Results-oriented culture a culture that prioritizes results over building relationships at work.

Résumé a summary sheet outlining your work history, educational background, skills, and accomplishments.

Reward power the potential to influence rooted in our ability to provide something our partner values and cannot easily get from someone else.

Risk-benefit analysis weighing what advantages we might gain by disclosing private information or maintaining private information against the dangers.

Ritual question a question about the other person or the situation that is easy to answer and doesn't pry into personal matters.

Romantic relationship relationships in which partners act on their mutual sexual attraction to each other.

Scarcity heuristic being influenced by the rarity or availability of something during peripheral processing of persuasive messages.

Script text that instructs you what to say and do in a specific situation.

Scripted highly routinized.

Secure attachment infants' perception that they are worthy of care and that others can be trusted to provide it.

Secure attachment style an adult attachment style characterized by high self-worth and trust in others.

Selective perception distortion that arises from paying attention only to what we expect to see or hear and from ignoring what we don't expect.

Self-concept your perception of your competencies and personality traits.

Self-disclosure verbally sharing personal ideas and feelings with others.

Self-esteem your evaluation of your perceived competence and personal worthiness.

Self-face orientation the inclination to uphold and protect our self-image in our interactions with others.

Self-fulfilling prophecies events that happen as the result of being foretold, expected, or talked about.

Self-perception the overall view people have of themselves.

Self-talk communicating with yourself through your thoughts.

Semantic meaning meaning of a verbal message derived from the language itself.

Semantic noises distractions aroused by the words that the speaker uses that interfere with meaning.

Sequential organization the identifiable beginnings (openings), middles (bodies), and ends (closings) of conversations.

Sequential task-completion culture a culture that believes that large or complex tasks should be broken down into separate parts and completed one part at a time and in order.

Serial arguing a conflict pattern in which partners argue about the same issue two or more times.

Sexting the act of sending sexually explicit messages or photographs, primarily between smartphones, via text messaging.

Sexual harassment unwanted verbal or physical sexual behavior that interferes with work performance.

Shared meaning this occurs when the receiver's interpretation of the message is similar to what the speaker thought, felt, and intended.

Shared social networks a dimension of relationships that gauges how much the partners' interactions and relationships with other people overlap.

Simplicity the reduction of very complex stimuli to easily recognizable forms.

Situational attribution the perception that the cause of the behavior is some situation outside the control of the person.

Slang the informal vocabulary developed and used by particular co-cultural groups in a society.

Small talk a type of conversation focused on inconsequential topics such as the weather, uncontroversial news topics, harmless facts, and predictions.

Social class a level in the power hierarchy of a society whose membership is based on income, education, occupation, and social habits.

Social context the type of relationship that may already exist between the participants that influences understandings in the current communication encounter.

Social cues verbal and nonverbal features of a message that offer more information about the context, meaning, and the identities of the involved parties.

Social exchange theory the premise that we continue to develop a relationship as long as we feel that its rewards outweigh its costs and we perceive that what we get from a particular relationship is more than we would be able to get if we invested elsewhere.

Social identity model of deindividuation effects describes the extent to which individuals identify and behave in accordance with social rather than personal identities.

Social information processing theory explains that because we feel a need to reduce uncertainty, in online settings we will likely adapt our language and behaviors to reveal our own personal information and actively seek similar information from others.

Social media highly accessible technologies that facilitate communication and interaction.

Social network a group of individuals who are connected by friendship, family ties, common interests, beliefs, or knowledge.

Social network the structure of your relationships.

Social penetration theory the premise that self-disclosure is integral to all stages of relationships, but the nature and type of self-disclosure changes over time as people move from being strangers to being intimates.

Social perception the set of processes by which people perceive themselves and others.

Social presence theory explains that, through social media, available social cues permit us to perceive the intimacy of the conversation and the degree of closeness we feel with our conversational partner.

Social proof heuristic being influenced by what others think or do during peripheral processing of persuasive messages.

Social support the process of providing emotional, informational, and instrumental resources to someone we perceive is in need of this aid.

Sociolinguistic meaning the meaning of a verbal message that varies according to the language norms and expectations of a particular cultural or co-cultural group.

Special relationships work-based peer relationships that have developed into "best-friend" intimate relationships.

Specific language language in an utterance that uses concrete and precise words, as well as details and examples, combining them in accord with the rules of grammar and syntax for that language.

Speech act the action that the speaker takes by uttering a verbal message that implies how the listener should respond.

Speech community the members of a larger language community who speak a common dialect with a particular style and observe common linguistic norms or scripts.

Stereotyping applying the beliefs you have about the characteristics of a group to an individual whom you identify as a member of that group.

Strong ties include relationships such as those with friends, romantic partners, and family members. These relationships exhibit behavior that reflects heightened emotion, interdependence, intimacy, and high levels of closeness.

Supportive interaction a conversation or series of conversations in which messages of support are offered to someone.

Supportive messages communications that provide intangible support for your partner including emotional support, information, advice, and motivation.

Supportiveness encouraging your partners to continue talking by acknowledging your appreciation of what they are saying.

Sympathetic responsiveness (also called emotional concern) empathizing by feeling concern, compassion, or sorrow for another person because he or she is in a distressing situation but not identifying with the specific emotion he or she is experiencing.

Synchronous communication that occurs in real time; each interactant is simultaneously a sender and a receiver.

Syntax and grammar the rules for combining word to form sentences and into larger units of expression.

Talk time the share of time participants each have in a conversation.

Task roles communication behaviors that help a team focus on the issue under discussion.

Temporal selection the strategy of dealing with dialectical tensions by choosing one side of a dialectical opposition while ignoring the other for a period of time.

Temporal structure the time it takes to send and receive messages or the time that elapses during a communication interaction.

Territory the space over which we claim ownership.

Theory of conversationally induced reappraisals the premise that people experience emotional stress when they believe that their current situation is at odds with their life goals and that to reduce emotional distress and move forward, people must make sense of what has happened to them.

Time-oriented listening style the personal listening style that prefers brief and swift conversations.

Topical segmentation the strategy of dealing with dialectical tensions by choosing certain areas in which to satisfy one side of a dialectical tension while choosing other areas to satisfy the opposite side.

Touch putting part of the body in contact with something or someone.

Transcorporeal communication a process through which a living person sends a digital message to a deceased person through a Web site or social networking site.

Trust the extent to which partners in a relationship rely on, depend on, and have faith that their partner will not intentionally do anything to harm them.

Trustworthiness the perception that speakers are credible because they are dependable, honest, and acting for the good of others.

Turning point any event or occurrence that marks a relationship's transition from one stage to another.

Turn-taking alternating between speaking and listening in an interaction.

Uncertainty avoidance the extent to which the people in a culture look for ways to predict what is going to happen as a way of dealing with the anxiety caused by uncertain situations or relationships.

Uncertainty reduction theory a way to explain how individuals monitor their social environments to know more about themselves and others.

Understanding accurately decoding a message so you comprehend the semantic, pragmatic, and sociolinguistic meaning of a message.

Understanding and predictability a dimension of relationships that gauges how well partners understand and can predict each other's behaviors.

Utterance a complete unit of talk that is bounded by the speaker's silence.

Value conflict disagreement caused by differences in partners' deep-seated moral beliefs.

Values the commonly accepted preference for some states of affairs over others.

Vendors the people, groups, or organizations that supply an organization with its raw materials or other goods and services.

Verbal aggression sending messages that attack another person's self-esteem or express personal hostility for perceived violations of rights or expectations.

Vocal interferences extraneous sounds or words that interrupt fluent speech.

Volume the loudness of a person's vocal tone.

Voluntary relationship a relationship in which we freely choose the people with whom we interact.

Warm feelings the positive feelings you have about yourself and your partner during and immediately after an interaction.

Warranting theory proposes that you will place more credibility on information about the personal characteristics and behaviors of others when the online information cannot be easily manipulated by the person whom it describes.

Weak ties are casual contacts that are more loosely connected to an individual's social network and are not characterized by intimacy.

White lie a false or misleading statement to avoid telling a truth that would embarrass or hurt an individual or a relationship.

Withdrawing resolving a conflict by physically or psychologically removing yourself from the conversation.

Words the arbitrarily chosen symbols used by a language or speech community to name or signify things.

Working models of attachment infants' mental models of whether others are trustworthy and whether they are worthy of others' care.

Workplace aggression any counterproductive behavior at work intended to hurt someone.

Workplace team a formally established group with a clear purpose and appropriate structure in which members know each other's roles and work together to achieve goals.

References

Chapter 1

Anderson, P. (2000). Cues of culture: The basis of intercultural differences in nonverbal communication. In L. A. Samovar & R. E. Porter (Eds.), *Intercultural Communication: A Reader* (9th ed., pp. 258–266). Belmont, CA: Wadsworth.

Baym, N. K. (2010). *Personal Connections in the Digital Age.* Malden, MA: Polity Press.

Berger, C. R. (1997). *Planning Strategic Interaction: Attaining Goals through Communicative Action.* Mahwah, NJ: Lawrence Erlbaum. 26.

Berger, C. R. (2002). Goals and knowledge structures in social interaction. In M. L. Knapp & J. A. Daly (Eds.). *Handbook of Interpersonal Communication* (pp. 181–212). Thousand Oaks, CA: Sage.

Burgoon, J. K. (1998). It takes two to tango: Interpersonal adaptation and implications for relationship communication. In J. S. Trent (Ed.), *Communication: Views from the Helm for the 21st Century* (pp. 53–59). Boston: Allyn & Bacon.

Burleson, B. R. (2010). The nature of interpersonal communication: a message-centered approach. In *The Handbook of Communication Science, 2nd Ed* (pp. 145–163). C. R. Berger, M. E. Roloff, & D. R. Roskos-Ewoldsen, (Eds.). Thousand Oaks, CA: Sage.

Daft, R. L., & Lengel, R. H. (1984). Information richness: A new approach to managerial behavior and organizational design. *Research in Organizational Behavior, 6,* 191–233.

Littlejohn, S. W., & Foss, K. A. (2008). *Theories of Human Communication* (9th ed., p. 194). Belmont, CA: Thomson Wadsworth.

Millar, F. E., & Rogers, L. E. (1987). Relational dimensions of interpersonal dynamics. In M. E. Roloff & G. R. Millar (Eds.), *Interpersonal Processes: New Directions in Communication Research* (pp. 117–139). Newbury Park, CA: Sage.

Salovey, P., & Meyer J. D. (1990). Emotional intelligence. *Imagination, Cognition, and Personality, 9,* 185–211.

Spitzberg, B. H. (2000). A model of intercultural communication and competence. In L. A. Samovar & R. E. Porter (Eds.), *Intercultural Communication: A Reader* (9th ed., pp. 375–387). Belmont, CA: Wadsworth.

Spitzberg, B. H., & Cupach, W. R. (2007). Disentangling the dark side of interpersonal communication. In B. H. Spitzberg & W. R. Cupach (Eds.), *The Dark Side of Interpersonal Communication* (2nd ed., pp. 3–29). Mahwah, NJ: Lawrence Erlbaum.

Terkel, S. N. & Duval, R. S. (Eds.) (1999). *Encyclopedia of Ethics* (p. 122). New York: Facts on File.

Chapter 2

Aron, A., Mashek, D. J., & Aron, E. N. (2004). Closeness as including other in the self. In D. J. Mashek & A. Aron (Eds.), *Handbook of Closeness and Intimacy* (pp. 27–41). Mahwah, NJ: Lawrence Erlbaum.

Baron, R. A., & Burn, D. (2003). *Social Psychology* (10th ed.). Boston: Allyn & Bacon.

Baumeister, R. (2005). *The Cultural Animal.* New York: Oxford University Press.

Benet-Martínez, V., & Haritatos, J. (2005). Bicultural identity integration (BII): Components and psychological antecedents. *Journal of Personality, 73,* 1015–1050.

Berger, C. R., & Bradac, J. J. (1982). *Language and Social Knowledge: Uncertainty in Interpersonal Relations.* London: Arnold.

Campbell, J. D. (1990). Self-esteem and clarity of the self-concept. *Journal of Personality and Social Psychology, 59,* 538.

Centi, P. J. (1981). *Up with the Positive: Out with the Negative.* Englewood Cliffs, NJ: Prentice Hall.

Chen, G. M., & Starosta, W. J. (1998). *Foundations of Intercultural Communication.* Boston: Allyn & Bacon.

Demo, D. H. (1987). Family relations and the self-esteem of adolescents and their parents. *Journal of Marriage and the Family, 49,* 705–715.

Downey, G., Freitas, A. L., Michaelis, B., & Khouri, H. (2004). The self-fulfilling prophecy in close relationships: Rejection sensitivity and rejection by romantic partners. In H. T. Reis & C. E. Rusbult (Eds.), *Close Relationships* (pp. 435–455). New York: Psychology Press.

Engdahl, S. (Ed.). (2007). *Online Social Networking.* New York: Thomson Gale.

Guerrero, L. K., Andersen, P. A., & Afifi, W. A. (2007). *Close Encounters: Communication in Relationships* (2nd Ed.). Thousand Oaks, CA: Sage.

Hattie, J. (1992). *Self-Concept.* Hillsdale, NJ: Lawrence Erlbaum.

Hollman, T. D. (1972). Employment interviewers' errors in processing positive and negative information. *Journal of Psychology, 56,* 130–134.

Hinduja, S., & Patchin, J. W. (2009). *Bullying Beyond the School Yard: Preventing and Responding to Cyber*

Bullying (p. 14). Thousand Oaks, CA: Corwin Press.

Jones, M. (2002). *Social Psychology of Prejudice*. Upper Saddle River, NJ: Prentice Hall.

Leary, M. R. (2002). When selves collide: The nature of the self and the dynamics of interpersonal relationships. In A. Tesser, D. A. Stapel, & J. V. Wood (Eds.), *Self and Motivation: Emerging Psychological Perspectives* (pp. 119–145). Washington, DC: American Psychological Association.

Ledbetter, A. M. (2009). Measuring online communication attitude: Instrument development and validation. *Communication Monographs, 76*, 463–486.

Littlejohn, S. W. & Foss, K. A. (2005). *Theories of Human Communication* (8th ed.). Belmont, CA: Thomson Wadsworth.

Markus, H. R. & Kitayama, S. (1991). Culture and the self: Implications for cognition, emotion, and motivation. *Psychological Review, 98*, 224–253.

Miller, G. R., & Steinberg, M. (1975). *Between People: A New Analysis of Interpersonal Communication*. Chicago: SRA.

Mruk, C. (2006). *Self-Esteem: Research, Theory, and Practice* (3rd ed.). New York: Springer.

Niedenthal, P. M., Halberstadt, J. B., Margolin, J., & Innes-Ker, A. H. (2000). Emotional state and the detection of change in facial expressions of emotion. *European Journal of Social Psychology, 30*, 211–222.

Raynor, S. G. (2001). Aspects of the self as learner: Perception, concept, and esteem. In R. J. Riding & S. G. Raynor (Eds.), *Self-Perception: International Perspectives on Individual Differences* (Vol. 2, p. 42). Westport, CT: Ablex.

Sampson, E. E. (1999). *Dealing with Differences: An Introduction to the Social Psychology of Prejudice*. Fort Worth, TX: Harcourt Brace.

Shedletsky, L. J., & Aitken, J. E. (2004). *Human Communication on the Internet*. New York: Pearson Education.

Weiten, W. (2002). *Psychology: Themes and Variations* (5th ed.). Belmont, CA: Thomson Wadsworth.

Willis, J., & Todorov, A. (2006). First impressions: Making up your mind after a 100 Ms exposure to face. *Psychological Science, 17,* 592–598.

Chapter 3

Andersen, P. A., Hecht, M. L., Hoobler, G. D., & Smallwood, M. (2003). Nonverbal communication across cultures. In W. B. Gudykunst (Ed.), *Cross-Cultural and Intercultural Communication* (pp. 73–90). Thousand Oaks, CA: Sage.

Bonvillain, N. (2003). *Language, Culture and Communication: The Meaning of Messages* (4th ed.). Upper Saddle River, NJ: Prentice Hall.

Carlo-Casellas, J. R. (2002, January 14). *Marketing to US Hispanic population requires analysis of cultures, National Underwriter Life and Health.* Farmington Hills, MI: The National Underwriter Company, p. 9. Retrieved November 17, 2008, from http://www.highbeam.com/doc/1G1-81892605.

Chen, G. M., & Starosta, W. J. (1998). *Foundations of Intercultural Communication*. Boston: Allyn & Bacon.

Chuang, R. (2004). An examination of Taoist and Buddhist perspectives on interpersonal conflict, emotions and adversities. In F. E. Jandt (Ed.), *Intercultural Communication: A Global Reader* (pp. 38–50). Thousand Oaks, CA: Sage.

Deardorff, D. K. (2006). The identification and assessment of intercultural competence. *Journal of Studies in International Education, 10,* 241–266.

Ellis, D. G. (1999). *Crafting Society: Ethnicity, Class and Communication Theory*. Mahwah, NJ: Lawrence Erlbaum.

European Commission. (2001). *Report Number 55*. The EuroBarometer Public Opinion in the European Union Report. Retrieved from http://ec.europa.eu/public_opinion/archives/eb/eb55/eb55_en.pdf

Fasold, R. (1984). *The sociolinguistics of society*. Oxford: Blackwell.

Hall, E. T. (1976). *Beyond Culture*. New York: Anchor/Doubleday.

Haviland, W. A. (1993). *Cultural Anthropology*. Fort Worth, TX: Harcourt, Brace, Jovanovich.

Hofstede, G. (1980). *Culture's Consequences*. Beverly Hills, CA: Sage.

Hofstede, G. (1997). *Cultures and Organizations: Software of the Mind*. New York: McGraw Hill.

Hofstede, G. (1998). (Ed.). *Masculinity and Femininity: The Taboo Dimension of National Cultures*. Thousand Oaks, CA: Sage.

Hofstede, G. (2000). The cultural relativity of the quality of life concept. In G. R. Weaver (Ed.), *Cultural Communication and Conflict: Readings in Intercultural Relations*. Boston: Allyn & Bacon.

Jandt, F. E. (2001). *Intercultural Communication: An Introduction* (3rd ed.). Thousand Oaks, CA: Sage.

Klyukanov, I. E. (2005). *Principles of Intercultural Communication*. New York: Pearson.

Kottak, C. (2012). *Anthropology: The Exploration of Human Diversity* (14th ed.) New York: McGraw-Hill.

Luckmann, J. (1999). *Transcultural Communication in Nursing*. New York: Delmar.

McComb, C. (2001). *About One in Four Americans Can Hold a Conversation in a Second Language*. Retrieved from Gallup News Service Web site. http://www.gallup.com/poll/1825/about-one-four-americans-can-hold-conversation-second-language.aspx

Neuliep, J. W. (2006). *Intercultural Communication: A Contextual Approach* (3rd ed.). Thousand Oaks, CA: Sage.

Prensky, M. (2001). *Digital Natives, Digital Immigrants. On the Horizon*

(Vol. 9, No. 5). West Yorkshire, England: MCB University Press. Retrieved from http://www.marcprensky.com/writing/Prensky%20-%20Digital%20Natives,%20Digital%20Immigrants%20-%20Part1.pdf

Rogers, E. M., Hart, W. B., & Miike, Y. (2002). Edward T. Hall and the History of Intercultural Communication: The United States and Japan. *Keio Communication Review, 24,* 3–26. Retrieved from http://www.mediacom.keio.ac.jp/publication/pdf2002/review24/2.pdf

Samovar, L. A., Porter, R. E., & McDaniel, E. R. (2010). *Communication between Cultures* (7th ed.). Belmont, CA: Thomson Wadsworth.

Smedley, A., & Smedley, B. D. (2005). Race as biology is fiction, racism as a social problem is real: Anthropological and historical perspectives on the social construction of race." *American Psychologist, 60*(1), 16–26.

Ting-Toomey, S., Yee-Jung, K., Shapiro, R., Garcia, W., Wright, T., & Oetzel, J. G. (2000). Cultural/ethnic identity salience and conflict styles. *International Journal of Intercultural Relations, 23,* 47–81.

Wood, J. T. (2007). *Gendered Lives: Communication, Gender, and Culture* (7th ed.). Belmont, CA: Wadsworth.

Zemke, R., Raines, C., & Filipczak, B. (2000). *Generations at Work.* New York: AMACOM.

Chapter 4

Aronoff, M., & Rees-Miller, J. (Eds.). (2001). *The Handbook of Linguistics.* Oxford: Blackwell.

Burke, K. (1968). *Language as Symbolic Action.* Berkeley, CA: University of California Press.

Chaika, E. (2007). *Language: The Social Mirror* (4th ed.). Boston: Heinle ELT/Cengage.

Cvetkovic, L. (2009, February 21). *Serbian, Croatian, Bosnian, or Montanegren, or "Just our language."* Retrieved from the Radio Free Europe/Radio Liberty Web site. http://www.rferl.org/content/Serbian_Croatian_Bosnian_or_Montenegrin_Many_In_Balkans_Just_Call_It_Our_Language_/1497105.html.

Freed, A. F. (2003). Reflections on language and gender research. In J. Holmes & M. Meyers (Eds.), *The Handbook of Language and Gender* (pp. 699–721). Malden, MA: Blackwell Publishing.

Grice, H. P. (1975). Logic and conversation. In P. Cole & J. L. Morgan (Eds.), *Syntax and Semantics: Volume 3. Speech Acts.* New York: Academic Press.

Guj riots a national shame, not IPL going abroad: PC. (2009, March 23). *The Financial Express.* Retrieved from http://www.expressindia.com

Higginbotham, J. (2006) Languages and Idiolects: Their Language and Ours. In E. Lepore & B. C. Smith (Eds.), *The Oxford Handbook of Philosophy of Language* (pp. 140–150). Oxford: Oxford University Press.

Hindustan Times. (2009, March 23). Don't care for Nano or No-No: Mamata. Retrieved from http://www.hindustantimes.com

Kachru, B. B. (1986). *The Alchemy of English: The Spread, Functions, and Models of Non-Native Englishes.* Oxford: Pergamon Press.

Kachru, B. B. (1986). *The Other Tongue: English Across Cultures.* Urbana: University of Illinois Press.

Korta, K., & Perry, J. (2008). Pragmatics. In E. N. Zalta (Ed.), *The Stanford Encyclopedia of Philosophy* (Fall 2008 Edition). Retrieved from http://plato.stanford.edu/archives/fall2008/entries/pragmatics/

Langer, E. J., & Moldoveanu, M. (2000). The Construct of Mindfulness. *Journal of Social Issues, 56,* 1–9.

Lewis, M. P. (Ed.). (2009). *Ethnologue: Languages of the World* (16th ed.) Dallas, TX: SIL International. Retrieved from http://www.ethnologue.com/

O'Grady, W., Archibald, J., Aronoff, M., & Rees-Miller, J. (2001). *Contemporary Linguistics* (4th ed.). Boston: Bedford/St. Martin's.

Patrolling intensified in sea, on shores in Tamil Nadu. (2009, March 23). *Press Trust of India.* Retrieved from http://www.ptinews.com

Saeed, J. I. (2003). *Semantics* (2nd ed.). Malden, MA: Blackwell Publishing.

Stewart, L. P., Cooper, P. J., Stewart, A. D., & Friedley, S. A. (2003). *Communication and Gender* (4th ed.). Boston: Allyn & Bacon.

Ting-Toomey, S., & Chung, L. C. (2005). *Understanding Intercultural Communication.* New York: Oxford University Press.

Wiltshire, C., & Moon, R. (2003). Phonetic stress in Indian English vs. American English. *World Englishes, 22*(3), 291–303.

Wright, R. (2010). *Chinese Language Facts.* Retrieved from http://www.languagehelpers.com/languagefacts/chinese.html

Zardari is 5th biggest loser in world: Foreign policy magazine. (2009, March 23). *NDTV.* Retrieved from http://www.ndtv.com

Chapter 5

Axtell, R. E. (1998). *Gestures: The Do's and Taboos of Body Language Around the World* (rev. ed.). New York: Wiley.

Burgoon, J. K. (1994). Nonverbal signals. In M. L. Knapp & G. R. Miller (Eds.), *Handbook of Interpersonal Communication* (2nd ed., pp. 229–285). Thousand Oaks, CA: Sage.

Burgoon, J. K., Buller, D. B., & Woodall, W. G. (1996). *Nonverbal Communication: The Unspoken Dialogue* (2nd ed.). New York: Harper & Row.

Cegala, D. J., & Sillars, A. L. (1989). Further examination of nonverbal manifestations of interaction involvement. *Communication Reports, 2,* 45. New York: Routledge.

Chen, G. M, & Starosta, W. J. (1998). *Foundations of Intercultural Communication.* Color blindness and equal opportunity. Boston: Allyn & Bacon.

DiTomaso, N., Parks-Yancy, R., and Post, C. (2003). White views of civil rights: Color blindness and equal opportunity. A. W. Doane & E. Bonilla-Silva (Eds.), *Whiteout: The Continuing Significance of Racism.* NY: Routledge.

Ekman, P. (2003). *Emotions revealed: Recognizing Faces and Feelings to Improve Communication and Emotional Life.* New York: Times Books.

Furlow, F. B. (1996). The smell of love. *Psychology Today, 29* (Mar/Apr), 38–45.

Gudykunst, W. B., & Kim, Y. Y. (1997). *Communicating with Strangers: An Approach to Intercultural Communication* (3rd ed.). Boston: Allyn & Bacon.

Hall, E. T. (1969). *The Hidden Dimension.* Garden City, NY: Doubleday.

Henley, N. M. (1977). *Body Politics: Power, Sex and Nonverbal Communication.* Englewood Cliffs, NJ: Prentice-Hall.

Johnson, K. R. (2004). Black kinesics: Some non-verbal communication patterns in the black culture, In R. L. Jackson (Ed.), *African-American Communication and Identities* (pp. 39–46). Thousand Oaks, CA: Sage.

Kleinman, S. (2007). Displacing Place: Mobile Communication in the Twenty-First Century. New York: Peter Lang.

Knapp, M. L., & Hall, J. A. (2006). *Nonverbal Communication in Human Interaction* (6th ed.). Belmont, CA: Wadsworth/ Thomson Learning.

Martin, J. N., & Nakayama, T. K. (2006). *Intercultural Communication in Contexts* (4th ed.). New York: McGraw Hill.

Mehrabian, A. (1972). *Nonverbal Communication.* Chicago: Aldine.

Patterson, M. L. (1994). Strategic functions of nonverbal exchange. In J. A. Daly (Ed.), *Strategic Interpersonal Communication* (pp. 273–293). Hillsdale, NJ: Erlbaum.

Pearson, J. C., West, R. L., & Turner, L. H. (1995). *Gender and Communication* (3rd ed.). Dubuque, Iowa: Brown & Benchmark.

Samovar, L. A., Porter, R. E., & McDaniel, E. R. (2007). *Communication Between Cultures* (6th ed.). Belmont, CA: Thompson/Wadsworth.

Walther, J. B., & Parks, M. R. (2002). Cues filtered out, cues filtered in: Computer-mediated communication and relationships. In M. C. Knapp & J. A. Daly (Eds.), *Handbook of Interpersonal Communication* (pp. 529–563). Thousand Oaks, CA: Sage.

Wood, J. T. (2007). *Gendered Lives: Communication, Gender, and Culture* (7th ed.). Belmont, CA: Wadsworth.

Chapter 6

Altman, I. & Taylor, D. (1973). *Social penetration: The development of interpersonal relationships.* New York, NY: Holt.

Aron, A., Aron, E. N., Tudor, M., & Nelson, G. (2004). Close relationships as including other in the self. In H. T. Reis & C. E. Rusbult (Eds.), *Close Relationships* (pp. 365–379). New York: Psychology Press.

Baron, N. S. (1998). Letters by phone or speech by other means: The linguistics of email. *Language and Communication, 18,* 133–170.

Baxter, L. (1982). Strategies for ending relationships: Two studies. *Western Journal of Speech Communication, 46,* 223–241.

Baxter, L. A., & Bullis, C. (1993). Turning points in developing romantic relationships. In S. Petronio, J. K. Alberts, M. L. Hecht, & J. Buley (Eds.), *Contemporary Perspectives on Interpersonal Communication* (pp. 358–374). Chicago: Brown and Benchmark.

Baxter, L. A., & Erbert, L. A. (1999). Perceptions of dialectical contradictions in turning points of development in heterosexual romantic relationships. *Journal of Social and Personal Relationships, 16,* 547–569.

Baxter, L. A., & Montgomery, B. M. (1996). *Relating: Dialogues & Dialectics.* New York: Guilford Press.

Baxter, L. A., & West, L. (2003). Couple perceptions of their similarities and differences: A dialectical perspective. *Journal of Social and Personal Relationships, 20,* 491–514.

Berger, C. R., Calabrese, R. J. (1975). Some Exploration in Initial Interaction and Beyond: Toward a Developmental Theory of Communication. *Human Communication Research, 1,* 99–112.

Boon, S. D. (1994). Dispelling doubt and uncertainty: Trust in romantic relationships. In S. Duck (Ed.), *Dynamics of relationships* (pp. 86–111). Thousand Oaks, CA: Sage.

Canary, D. J., Stafford, L., & Semic, B. A. (2002). A panel study of he association between maintenance characteristics and relational characteristics. *Journal of Marriage and Family, 64,* 395–406.

Canary, J. C., & Dainton, M. (2002). Preface. In J. C. Canary & M. Dainton, (Eds.), *Maintaining Relationships Through Communication: Relational, Contextual and Cultural Variations* (pp. xiii–xv.). Mahwah, NJ: Erlbaum.

Carnevale, P., & Probst, T. M. (1997). Conflict on the internet. In S. Kiesler (Ed.), *Culture of the internet* (pp. 233–255). Mahwah, NJ: Erlbaum.

Cupach, C. R., & Metts, S. (1986). Accounts of relational dissolution: A comparison of marital and nonmarital relationships.

Communication Monographs, 53, 319–321.

Dindia, K. & Baxter, L. (1987). Strategies for maintaining and repairing marital relationships. *Journal of Social and Personal Relationships, 4,* 143–158.

Duck, S. (1987). How to lose friends without influencing people. In M. E. Roloff & G. R. Miller (Eds.), *Interpersonal Processes: New Directions in Communication Research* (pp. 278–298). Beverly Hills, CA: Sage.

Duck, S. (2007). *Human Relationships* (4th ed.). Thousand Oaks, CA: Sage.

Duck, S. W. (1982). A Topography of Relationship Disengagement and Dissolution. In S. W. Duck. (Ed.), *Personal Relationships 4: Dissolving Personal Relationships.* London: Academic Press.

Duck, S., & Gilmour, R. (Eds.). (1981). *Personal Relationships.* London: Academic Press.

Fehr, B. (1996). *Friendship Processes.* Newbury Park, CA: Sage.

Fehr, B. (2008). Friendship Formation. In S. Sprecher, A. Wenzel, & J. Harvey (Eds.). *Handbook of Relationship Initiation,* New York, NY: Psychology Press.

Gladwell. M. (2000). *The tipping point: How little things make big differences.* New York, NY: Brown, Little, & Co.

Knapp, M. L. & Vangelisti, A. L. (2005). *Interpersonal Communication and Human Relationships* (5th ed.). Boston: Allyn & Bacon.

Knapp, M. L. & Vangelisti (2011). A. L. Relationship Decline. In K. M. Galvin *Making Connections, 5th Ed.* (pp. 273–278). New York: Oxford University Press.

Knobloch, L. K. & Miller, L. E. (2008). Uncertainty and Relationship Initiation. In S. Sprecher, A. Wenzel, & J. Harvey (Eds.). *Handbook of Relationship Initiation,* New York, NY: Psychology Press.

LaFollette, H. (1996). *Personal Relationships: Love, Identity,* *and Morality.* Cambridge, MA: Blackwell.

Littlejohn, S. W. & Foss, K. A. (2005). *Theories of Human Communication* (8th ed.). Belmont, CA: Thomson Wadsworth.

Luft, J. (1970). *Group Processes: An Introduction to Group Dynamics.* Palo Alto, CA: Mayfield.

McDowell, S. W. (2001). The Development of Online and Offline Romantic Relationships: A Turning Point Study. Unpublished Master's Thesis. University of Washington.

McKenna, K. Y. A., & Bargh, J. A. (1998). Coming out in the age of the internet: Identity "demarginalization" from virtual group participation. *Journal of Personality & Social Psychology, 74,* 681–694.

Millar, F. E., & Rogers, E. (1976). A relational approach to interpersonal communication. In G. R. Miller (Ed.), *Explorations in interpersonal communication,* (pp. 87–103). Beverly Hills, CA: Sage.

Moore, D. W. (2003, Jan. 3). Family, health most important aspects of life. Gallup Pool Tuesday Briefing, pp. 19–20.

O'Sullivan, P. B., Hunt, S., & Lippert, L. (2004). Mediated immediacy: A language of affiliation in a technological age. *Journal of Language and Social Psychology, 23,* 464–490.

Parks, M. R. (2007). *Personal Relationships and Personal Networks.* Mahwah, NJ: Lawrence Erlbaum Associates.

Pearce, W. B. (1974). Trust in interpersonal Communication. *Communication Monographs.* 41:3. 236–244.

Rodin, M. J. (1982), Non-engagement, failure to engage, and disengagement. In S. Duck (Ed.), *Dissolving Personal Relationships,* London: Academic Press.

Schutz, W. (1966). *The Interpersonal Underworld.* Palo Alto, CA: Science & Behavior Books.

Sunnafrank, M. Predicted outcome value and uncertainty reduction theories, A test of competing perspectives. *Human Communication Research, 17,* 76–103.

Taylor, D. A., & Altman, I. (1987). Communication in interpersonal relationships: Social penetration theory. In M. E. Roloff & G. R. Miller (Eds.), *Interpersonal Processes: New Directions in Communication Research* (pp. 257–277). Beverly Hills, CA: Sage.

Thibaut, J. W., & Kelley, H. H. (1986). *The Social Psychology of Groups* (2nd ed.). New Brunswick, NJ: Transaction Books.

Wood, J. T. (2000). Dialectical theory. In K. M. Galvin & P. J. Cooper (Eds.), *Making Connections: Readings in Relational Communication* (pp. 132–138). Los Angeles: Roxbury Publishing Company.

Wood, J. T., & Inman, C. C. (1993). In a different mode: Masculine styles of communicating closeness. *Journal of Applied Communication Research, 21,* 279–295.

Chapter 7

Bostrom, R. N. (2006). The process of listening. In O. Hargie (Ed.), *Handbook of Communicaiton Skills* (3rd ed., pp. 267–291). New York: Routledge.

Brownell, J. (2006). *Listening: Attitudes, Principles, and Skills* (3rd ed.). Boston, MA: Allyn & Bacon.

Ellinor, L., & Gerard, G. (1998). *Dialogue: Rediscover the Transforming Power of Conversation.* New York: Wiley.

Estes, W. K. (1989). Learning theory. In A. Lesgold & R. Glaser (Eds.), *Foundations for a Psychology of Education* (pp. 1–49). Hillsdale, NJ: Erlbaum.

Halone, K. K. & Pecchioni, L. L. (2001). Relational listening: A grounded theoretical model. *Communication Reports, 14,* 5.

Harris, J. A. (2003). Learning to listen across cultural divides. *Listening Professional, 2,* 4–21.

Kanalley, C. (2011, March 10). Charlie Sheen not dead, but virus spreads on Facebook. *The Huffington Post.*

Kiewitz, C., Weaver, J. B., Brosius, H. B., & Weimann, G. (1997). Cultural differences in listening style preferences. *International Journal of Public Opinion Research, 9,* 233–247.

O'Shaughnessey, Brian. (2003). Active Attending or a Theory of Mental Action. *Consciousness and the World, 29,* 379–407.

Pew Internet and American Life Project. (2001). Teenage life online: The rise of the instant message generation and the Internet's impact on friendships and family relationships. www.pewinternet.org.

Pew Internet and American Life Project. (2010). Teens, cell phones and texting: Text messaging becomes centerpiece communication. www.pewinternet.org.

Purdy, M. (1996). What is listening? In M. Purdy & D. Borisoff (Eds.), *Listening in Everyday Life: A Personal and Professional Approach* (2nd ed., pp. 1–20). New York: University Press of America.

Salisbury, J. R. & Chen, G. M. (2007). An examination of the relationship between conversational sensitivity and listening styles. *Intercultural Communication Studies.* XVI:1, 251–262.

Sargent, S. L. & Weaver, J. B. (2007). The Listening Styles Profile. In *Handbook of Research on Electronic Surveys and Measurements* (pp. 335–338). R. A. Reynolds, R. Woods, and J. D. Baker (Eds.). Hershey, PA: Idea Group References.

Steil, L. K., Barker, L. L., & Watson, K. W. (1983). *Effective Listening.* Reading, MA: Addison-Wesley.

Ward, C. C., & Tracey, T. J. G. (2004). Relation of shyness with aspects of online relational involvement. *Journal of Social and Personal Relationships, 21,* 611–623.

Watson, K. W., Barker, L. L., & Weaver, J. B., III (1995). The listening styles profile (LSP-16): Development and validation of an instrument to assess four listening styles. *International Journal of Listening, 9,* 1–13.

Weaver, III, J. B. & Kirtley, M. D. Listening styles and empathy. *The Southern Communication Journal.* 1995; 60(2):131–140.

Wheeless, L. R. (1975). An investigation of receiver apprehension and social context dimensions of communication apprehension. *The Speech Teacher, 24,* 261–268.

Wolvin, A. D., & Coakley, C. G. (1992). *Listening.* Dubuque, IA: Wm. C. Brown.

Chapter 8

Brown, P., & Levinson, S. (1987). *Politeness: Some Universals in Language Usage.* Cambridge, UK: Cambridge University Press.

Duck, S. (2007). *Human Relationships* (4th ed.). Thousand Oaks, CA: Sage.

Engdahl, S. (Ed.) (2007). *Online Social Networking.* New York: Thompson Gale.

Fraley, B., & Aron, A. (2004). The effect of a shared humorous experience on closeness in initial encounters. *Personal Relationships, 11,* 61–78.

Gabor, D. (2001). *How to start a conversation and make friends.* New York: Simon & Schuster.

Garner, A. (1997). *Conversationally Speaking* (3rd ed.). Los Angeles: Lowell House.

Goldsmith, D. J. & Baxter, L. A. (2006). Constituting relationships in talk: A taxonomy of speech events in social and personal relationships. *Human Communication Research, 23,* 87–114.

Gudykunst, W. B., & Matsumoto, Y. (1996). Cross-cultural variability of communication in personal relationships. In W. B. Gudykunst, S. Ting-Toomey, & T. Nishida (Eds.), *Communication in Personal Relationships Across Cultures* (pp. 19–56). Thousand Oaks, CA: Sage.

Johannesen, R. L, Valde, K. S., & Whedbee, K. E. (2008). *Ethics in Human Communication* (6th ed.). Long Grove, IL.: Waveland Press.

Kennedy, C. W., & Camden, C. T. (1983). A new look at interruptions. *Western Journal of Speech Communication, 47,* 55.

Littlejohn, S. & Foss, K. A. (2005). *Theories of Human Communication* (8th ed.). Belmont, CA: Thomson Wadsworth

Lovink, G. (2008). *Zero Comments: Blogging and Critical Internet Culture.* New York: Routledge.

McLaughlin, M. L. (1984). *Conversation: How Talk Is Organized.* Newbury Park, CA: Sage.

Nofsinger, R. E. (1991). *Everyday Conversation.* Thousand Oaks, CA: Sage.

Sakamoto, N. M. (1995). Conversational ballgames. In R. Holton (Ed.), *Encountering Cultures* (pp. 60–63). Englewood Cliffs, NJ: Prentice-Hall.

Sawyer, R. K. (2001). *Creating Conversations: Improvisation in Everyday Discourse.* Cresskill, NJ: Hampton Press.

Shedletsky, L. J. & Aitken, J. E. (2004*). Human Communication on the Internet.* New York: Pearson Education.

Short, J., Williams, E., & Christie, B. (1976). *The Social Psychology of Telecommunications.* Chichester, UK: Wiley.

Chapter 9

Ahuja, N. (2007). Hopelessness and social support as predictors of physical status for breast cancer patients coping with recurrence. Columbus, OH: Ohio State University Knowledge Bank.

Albrecht, T. L. & Goldsmith, D. J. (2003). Social support, social networks and health. In T. L. Thompson, A. M. Dorsey, K. I. Miller, & B. R. Parrott (Eds.). *Handbook of Health Communication* (pp. 263–284). Mahwah, NJ: Erlbaum.

Bambina, A. (2007). *Online Social Support*. Youngstown, NY: Cambria Press.

Barbee, A. P., & Cunningham, M. R. (1995). An experimental approach to social support communication: Interactive coping in close relationships. In B. R. Burleson (Ed.), *Communication Yearbook 18* (pp. 381–413). Thousand Oaks, CA: Sage.

Burleson, B. R. (1994). Comforting messages: Significance, approaches, and effects. In B. R. Burleson, T. L. Albrecht, & I. G. Sarason (Eds.), *Communication of Social Support: Messages, Interactions, Relationships, and Community* (pp. 3–28). Thousand Oaks, CA: Sage.

Burleson, B. R. (2003). Emotional support skills. In J. O. Green & B. R. Burleson (Eds.), *Handbook of Communication and Social Interaction Skills* (pp. 551–594). Mahwah, NJ: Erlbaum.

Burleson, B. R., & Goldsmith, D. J. (1998). How the comforting process works: Alleviating emotional distress through conversationally induced reappraisals. In P. A. Andersen & L. K. Guerrero (Eds.), *Handbook of Communication and Emotion: Research, Theory, Applications, and Contexts* (pp. 248–280). San Diego, CA: Academic Press.

Burleson, B. R., & MacGeorge, E. L. (2002). Supportive communication. In M. L. Knapp, J. A. Daly, & G. R. Miller (Eds.), *Handbook of Interpersonal Communication* (3rd ed., pp. 374–424). Thousand Oaks, CA: Sage.

Burleson, B. R., & Samter, W. (1990). Effects of cognitive complexity on the perceived importance of communication skills in friends. *Communication Research, 17,* 165–182.

Burleson, B. R. (2010). Explaining cultural variations in responses to social support and influence. *NRC Workshop on Unifying Social Frameworks.* August 2010. Washington, DC.

Burleson, B. R., & Samter, W. (1985). Consistencies in theoretical and naïve evaluations of comforting messages. *Communication Monographs, 52,* 103–123.

Carpenter, K. (2006). The stress-buffering effect of social support in gynecological cancer survivors. Columbus, OH: Ohio State University.

Cunningham, M. R., & Barbee, A. P. (2000). Social support. In C. Hendrick & S. S. Hendrick (Eds.), *Close Relationships: A Sourcebook* (pp. 272–285). Thousand Oaks, CA: Sage.

DeGroot, J. M. (2009). *Reconnecting with the dead via Facebook: Examining Transcorporeal Communication as a way to maintain relationships,* (Doctoral dissertation, Ohio University, 2009). ProQuest Digital Dissertations, AAT 3371475.

Eisenberg, N., & Fabes, R. A. (1990). Empathy: Conceptualization, measurement, and relation to prosocial behavior. *Motivation and Emotion, 14,* 131–149.

Gable, S. L., Reis, H. T., Impett, E., & Asher, E. R. (2004). What do you do when things go right? The intrapersonal and interpersonal benefits of sharing positive events. *Journal of Personality and Social Psychology, 87,* 228–245.

Gable, S. L. Gonzaga, G. C., & Strachman, A. (2006). Will you be there for me when things go right? Supportive responses to positive event disclosures. *Journal of Personality and Social Psychology.* 91-5, 904–917.

Goldsmith, D. J. (2000). Soliciting advice: The role of sequential placement in mitigating face threat. *Communication Monographs, 67,* 1–19.

Goldsmith, D. J. (2004). Communicating Social Support. Cambridge, UK: Cambridge University Press.

Heller, K. & Rook, K. S. (2001). Distinguishing the theoretical functions of social ties: Implications for supportiveness interventions.

In B. Saranson & S. Duck (Eds.) *Personal Relationships: Implications for Clinical and Community Psychology* (pp. 119–139). Chichester, England: Wiley.

Jerome, L. W., DeLeon, P. H., James, L. C., Folen, R., Earles, J., & Gedney, J. J. (2000). The coming age of telecommunications in psychological research and practice. *American Psychologist, 55,* 407–421.

Kunkel, A. W., & Burleson, B. R. (1999). Assessing explanations for sex differences in emotional support: A test of the different cultures and skill specialization accounts. *Human Communication Research, 25* (March), 307–340.

Langston, C. A. (1994). Capitalizing on and coping with daily-life events: Expressive responses to positive events. *Journal of Personality and Social Psychology, 67,* 1112–1125.

Leathers, D. G. (1997). *Successful Nonverbal Communication: Principles and Applications* (3rd ed.). Boston: Allyn & Bacon.

Legacy.com. (2011). About Legacy.com, Inc. http://legacy.com/NS/About

Lyons, R. F., Sullivan, M. H. L., Ritvo, P. G. & Coyne, J. C. (1995). *Relationships in chronic illness and disability.* Thousand Oaks, CA: Sage.

MacGeorge, E. L., Feng, B., Butler, G. L., & Budarz, S. K. (2004). Understanding advice in supportive Interactions: Beyond the facework and message evaluation paradigm. *Human Communication Research, 30*(1), 42–70.

MacGeorge, E. L., Feng, B. & Thompson, E. R. Good and bad advice: How to advise more effectively. In M. T. Motley (Ed.), *Studies in Applied Interpersonal Communication* (pp. 553–575). Los Angeles, CA: Sage.

Mirivel, J. C., & Thombre, A. (2010). Surviving online: An analysis of how burn survivors recover from life crises. *Southern Communication Journal, 75,* 232–254.

Net generation grieves with Facebook posting (http://www.newobserver.com/102/story/521293.html)

Omdahl, B. L. (1995). *Cognitive Appraisal, Emotion, and Empathy.* Mahwah, NJ: Erlbaum.

Plumb, T. (2006, August 31). Websites offer mourning for youths online. *The Boston Globe.*

Preston, S. D., & de Waal, D. B. M. (2002). Empathy: Its ultimate and proximate bases. *Behavioral and Brain Sciences, 25,* 1–72.

Samter, W., Burleson, B. R., & Murphy, L. B. (1987). Comforting conversations: The effects of strategy type of evaluations on messages and message producers. *Southern Speech Communication Journal, 52,* 263–284.

Segrin, C. (1998). Disrupted interpersonal relationships and mental health problems. In B. H. Spitzberg & W. H. Cupach (Eds.), *The dark side of close relationships* (pp. 327–365). Mahwah, NJ: Erlbaum.

St. John, W. (2006). Rituals of grief go online. *New York Times,* April 27, 2006.

Stiff, J. B., Dillard, J. P., Somera, L., Kim, H., & Sleight, C. (1988). Empathy, communication, and prosocial behavior. *Communication Monographs, 55,* 198–213.

Stingl, J. (2007, February 20). Grief finds expression electronically. *Milwaukee Journal Sentinel.*

Ting-Toomey, S. & Chung, L. C. (2005) *Understanding Intercultural Communication.* New York: Oxford University Press.

Uchino, B. N., Cacioppo, J. T. & Kiecolt-Glaser (1996). The relationship between social support and physiological processes: A review with emphasis on understanding mechanisms and implications for health. *Psychological Bulletin, 119,* 488–531.

Walther, J. B., & Parks, M. R. (2002). Cues filtered out, cues filtered in: Computer-mediated communication and close relationships. In M. L. Knapp &

J. A. Daly (Eds.), *Handbook of interpersonal communication* (3rd ed., pp. 529–563). Thousand Oaks, CA: Sage.

Weaver, III, J. B., & Kirtley, M. B. (1995). Listening styles and empathy. *Southern Communication Journal 60,* 131–140.

Chapter 10

Afifi, W. A. & Geuerrero, L. K. (2000). Motivations underlying topic avoidance in close relationships. In Petronio, S. (Ed.) *Balancing the Secrets of Private Disclosures* (pp. 165–179). Mahwah, NJ: Lawrence Erlbaum.

Altman, I. (1993). Dialectics, physical environments, and personal relationships. *Communication Monographs, 60,* 26–34.

Altman, I., & Taylor, D. A. (1973). *Social Penetration: The Development of Interpersonal Relationships.* New York: Holt, Rinehart & Winston.

Amodeo, J. (2010). Forward. In *Boundaries in relationships: Knowing, protecting, and enjoying the self* (pp. xvii–xix). By Charles L. Whitfield. Deerfield Beach, FL: Health Communications, Inc.

Bahrampour, T. (2007). What used to be private thoughts are now made public. In Engdahl, S. (Ed.) *Online Social Networking* (pp. 185–189). Farmington Hills, MI: Thomson Gale.

Dindia, K. (1988). A comparison of several statistical tests of reciprocity of self-disclosure. *Communication Research, 15,* 726–752.

Dindia, K. (2000). Sex differences in self-disclosure, reciprocity of self-disclosure, and self-disclosure and liking.: Three meta-analyses reviewed. In S. Petronio (Ed.) *Balancing the Secrets of Private Disclosures* (pp. 21–36). Mahwah, NJ: Lawrence Erlbaum.

Dindia, K., & Allen, M. (1992). Sex differences in self-disclosure: A meta-analysis. *Psychological Bulletin, 112,* 106–128.

Hendrick, S. S. (1981). Self-disclosure and marital satisfaction. *Journal of*

Personality and Social Psychology, 40, 1150–1159.

Jourard, S. M.(1971). *The Transparent Self.* New York: Van Nostrand Reinhold.

Kleinman, S. (2007*). Displacing Place: Mobile Communication in the Twenty-First Century.* New York: Peter Lang.

Knobloch, L. K., & Carpenter-Theune, K. E. (2004). Topic avoidance in developing romantic relationships: Association with intimacy. and relational uncertainty. *Communication Research, 31,* 173–205.

Lovink, G. (2008). *Zero Comments: Blogging and Critical Internet Culture.* New York: Routledge.

Margulis, Stephen T. (1977). Concepts of privacy: Current status and next steps. *Journal of Social Issues.* 33 (3) pp. 5–21.

Pennebaker, J. W.(1995). Emotion, disclosure, and health: An overview. In J. W. Pennebaker (Ed.) *Emotion, Disclosure and Health* (pp. 3–10). Washington, DC: American Psychologial Association.

Petronio, S. (2002). *Boundaries of Privacy: Dialectics of Disclosure.* Albany: State University of New York Press.

Roloff, M. E., & Ifert, D. E., (2000). Conflict management through avoidance: Withholding complaints, suppressing arguments and declaring topics taboo. In S. Petronio (Ed.) *Balancing the Secrets of Private Disclosures* (pp. 151–163). Mahwah, NJ: Lawrence Erlbaum.

Samovar, L. A., & Porter, R. E. (2001). *Communication Between Cultures* (4th ed.). Belmont, CA: Wadsworth.

Snell, W. E., Belk, S. S., & Hawkins, R. C. II (1986). The masculine and feminine self-disclosure scale: The politics of masculine and feminine self-presentation. *Sex Roles, 15,* 249–267.

Tardy, C. H. (2000). Self-disclosure and health: Revisiting Sidney Jourard's hypothesis. In S. Petronio (Ed.) *Balancing the Secrets of Private*

Disclosures (pp. 111–122). Mahwah, NJ: Lawrence Erlbaum.

Tracy, K., Dusen, D. V., & Robinson, S. (1987). "Good" and "bad" criticism. *Journal of Communication, 37,* 46–59.

Walther, J. B., & Parks, M. R. (2002). Cues filtered out, cues filtered in: Computer-mediated communication and close relationships. In M. L. Knapp & J. A. Daly (Eds.), *Handbook of interpersonal communication* (3rd ed., pp. 529–563). Thousand Oaks, CA: Sage.

Walther, J. B., Van Der Heide, B., Hamel, L., & Shulman, H. (2009). Self-generated versus other-generated statements and impressions in computer-mediated communication: A test of warranting theory using Facebook. *Communication Research, 36,* 229–253.

Chapter 11

Alberti, R. E., & Emmons, M. L. (2001). *Your Perfect Right: Assertiveness and Equality in Your life and Relationships* (8th ed.). San Atascadero, CA: Impact Publishers.

Bastardi, A., & Shafir, E. (2000). Nonconsequential reasoning and its consequences. *Current Directions in Psychological Science, 9,* 216–219.

Carnegie, D. (1936). *How to Win Friends and Influence People.* New York, NY: Simon & Schuster, Inc.

Cialdini, R. B. (2001). Harnessing the science of persuasion. *The Harvard Business Review.* October 2001. 70–80.

Cialdini, R. B. (2009). *Influence Science and Practice, 5th Ed.* Boston: Pearson Education, Inc.

Dillard, J. P., & Marshall, L. J. (2003). Persuasion as a social skill. In J. O. Greene & B. R. Burleson (Eds.), *Handbook of Communication and Social Interaction Skills* (pp. 479–513). Mahwah, NJ: Erlbaum.

Dillard, J. P., Anderson, J. W., & Knobloch, L. K. (2002). Interpersonal Influence. In M. L. Knapp & J. A. Daly, (Eds.), *Handbook of Interpersonal Communication* (3rd ed., pp. 425–474). Thousand Oaks, CA: Sage.

Eskin, M. (2003). Self-reported assertiveness in Swedish and Turkish adolescents: A cross-cultural comparison. *Scandanavian Journal of Psychology, 44,* 7–12.

French, Jr., J. R. P., & Raven, B. (1968). The bases of social power. In D. Cartwright & A. Zander (Eds.), *Group Dynamics* (3rd ed., pp. 259–269). New York: Harper & Row.

Gratereaux, A. (March 23, 2011). I'm not gonna preach I'm a role model. *Fox New Latino.* Accessed online May 17, 2011 at http://latino.foxnews.com/latino/entertainment/2011/03/23/bruno-mars-cocaine-bust-im-gonna-preach-im-a-role-model/

Guerrero, L. K., Andersen, P. A. & Afifi, W. A. (2007). Close Encounters: Communication in Relationships (2nd Ed.). Thousand Oaks, CA: Sage.

Hample. D. (2003) Arguing Skill. In J. O. Greene & B. R. Burleson (Eds.) *Handbook of Communication and Social Interaction Skills.* Mahwah, NJ: Erlbaum.

Hinken, T. R., & Schriesheim, C. A. (1980). Development and application of new scales to measure the French and Raven (1959) Bases of Social Power. *Journal of Applied Psychology, 74,* 561–567.

Infante, D. A. & Rancer, A. S. (1996). Argumentativeness and verbal aggression: A review of recent theory and research. In B. R. Burleson (Ed.), *Communication yearbook, 19* (pp. 319–351). Thousand Oaks, CA: Sage.

Jorgensen, P. E. (1998). Affect, persuasion, and communication process. In P. A. Anderson & L. K. Guerrero (Eds.), *Handbook of Communication and Emotion: Research, Theory, Applications, and Contexts* (pp. 403–422). San Diego, CA: Academic Press.

Kleinman, S. (2007). Displacing Place: Mobile Communication in the Twenty-First Century. New York: Peter Lang.

Martin, M. M., Anderson, C. M., & Horvath, C. L. (1996). Feelings about verbal aggression: Justifications for sending and hurt from receiving verbally aggressive messages. *Communication Research Reports, 13*(1), 19–26.

Niikura, R. (1999). The psychological process underlying Japanese assertive behavior: Comparison of Japanese with Americans, Malaysians, and Filipinos. *International Journal of Intercultural Relations, 23,* 47–76.

Parks, M. R. (2007). *Personal Relationships and Personal Networks.* Mahwah, NJ: Lawrence Erlbaum.

Petty, R. E. DeSteno, D., & Rucker, D. (2001). The role of affect in persuasion and attitude change. In J. Forgas (Ed.), *Handbook of Affect and Social Cognition* (pp. 212–233). Mahwah, NJ: Erlbaum.

Petty, R. E., & Cacioppo, T. T. (1996). Attitudes and persuasion: Classic and contemporary approaches. Boulder, CO: Westview Press.

Petty, R. E., Wheeler, S. C., & Bitzer, G. Y. (2000). Attitude functions and persuasion: An elaboration likelihood approach to matched versus mismatched messages. In G. R. Maio & J. M. Olson (Eds.), *Why We Evaluate: Functions of Attitudes* (pp. 133–162). Mahwah, NJ: Erlbaum.

Rakos, R. F. (2006). Asserting and confronting. In O. Hargie (Ed.) *The Handbook of Communication Skills, 3rd. Ed.* New York: Routledge.

Samovar, L. A., & Porter, R. E. (2001). *Communication Between Cultures* (4th ed.). Belmont, CA: Wadsworth.

Chapter 12

Adler, R. B. (1977*). Confidence in Communication: A Guide to Assertive and Social Skills.* New York: Holt, Rinehart, & Winston.

Augsburger, D. W. (1992). *Conflict Mediation Across Cultures: Pathways and Patterns.* Louisville, KY: Westminister/John Knox Press.

Brake, T., Walker, D. M., & Walker, T. (1995). *Doing business internationally: The guide to cross-cultural success*. New York: Irwin.

Canary, D. J. & Lakey, S. G. (2006). Managing conflict in a competent manner: A mindful look at events that matter. In J. G. Oetzel & S. Ting-Toomey (Eds.) *The SAGE Handbook of Conflict Communication: Integrating Theory, Research, and Practice* (pp. 185–210). Thousand Oaks, CA: Sage Publications.

Canary, D. J. (2003). *Maintaining Relationships through Communication: Relational, Contextual, and Cultural Variations*. Mahwah, NJ: Erlbaum.

Caplan, S. E. (2002). Problematic Internet use and psychosocial well-being: Development of a theory-based cognitive-behavioral measure. *Computers in Human Behavior, 18,* 533–575.

Caplan, S. E. (2003). Preference for online social interaction: A theory of problematic Internet use and psychosocial well-being. *Communication Research, 30,* 625–648.

Caplan, S. E. (2007). Relations among loneliness, social anxiety, and problematic Internet use. *CyberPsychology & Behavior, 10,* 234–242.

Caughlin J. P. & Golish, T. D. (2002). An analysis of the association between topic avoidance and dissatisfaction: Comparing perceptual and interpersonal explanations. *Communication Monographs, 69,* 275–295.

Caughlin, J. P. & Huston, T. L. (2006). Demand/withdraw patterns in marital relationships: An individual differences perspective. In R. M. Dailey & B. A. LePoire (Eds.) *Applied Interpersonal Communication Matters: Family, Health, & Community Relations* (pp. 11–38). New York: Peter Lang.

CBS News. (2011, March 23). Tyler Clementi's parents want tougher charges. Retrieved May 2, 2011 from http://www.cbsnews.com

Cloven, D. H., & Roloff, M. E. (1991). Sense-making activities and interpersonal conflict: Communicative cures for the mulling blues. *Western Journal of Speech Communication, 55,* 134–158.

Cupach, W. R., & Canary, D. J. (1997). *Competence in Interpersonal Conflict*. New York: McGraw-Hill.

Garcia, W. R. (1996). Respecto: A Mexican base for interpersonal relationships. In W. Gudykunst, S. Ting-Toomey, T. Nishida (Eds.) *Communication In Personal Relationships Across Cultures*. Thousand Oaks, CA: Sage.

Gordon, T. (1970). *Parent Effectiveness Training*. New York: Peter H. Wyden.

Gordon, T. (1971). *The Basic Modules of the Instructor Outline for Effectiveness Training Courses*. Pasadena, CA: Effectiveness Training Associates.

Guerrero, L. K., Andersen, P. A., & Afifi, W. A. (2007) *Close Encounters: Communication in Relationships* (2nd ed.). Thousand Oaks, CA: Sage.

Kim, J., LaRose, R., & Peng, W. (2009). Loneliness as the cause and the effect of problematic Internet use: The relationship between Internet use and psychological well-being. *CyberPsychology & Behavior, 12,* 451–455.

Lulofs, R. S., & Cahn, D. D. (2000). *Conflict: From Theory to Action* (2nd ed.). Boston: Allyn & Bacon.

Maag, C. (2007, November 28). A hoax turned fatal draws anger but no charges. *The New York Times*.

Martin, J. N., & Nakayama, T. K. (1997). *Intercultural Communication in Contexts*. Mountain View, CA: Mayfield.

Moore, R. J. (2010, March 16). Chatroulette is 89 percent male, 47 percent American, and 13 percent perverts. *TechCrunch*. Retrieved May 2, 2011 from http://techcrunch.com/2010/03/16/chatroulette-stats-male-perverts

MTV and The Associated Press (2009, September 23). The *MTV-Associated Press* poll digital abuse survey. http://www.athinline.org/MTV-AP_Digital_Abuse_Study_Full.pdf

Putnam, L. L. (2006). Definitions and approaches to conflict and communication. . In J. G. Oetzel & S. Ting-Toomey (Eds.) *The SAGE Handbook of Conflict Communication: Integrating Theory, Research, and Practice* (pp. 1–32). Thousand Oaks, CA: Sage Publications.

Roloff, M. E. & Miller, C. W. (2006). Social cognition approaches to understanding interpersonal conflict and communication. In J. G. Oetzel & S. Ting-Toomey (Eds.) *The SAGE Handbook of Conflict Communication: Integrating Theory, Research, and Practice* (pp. 97–128). Thousand Oaks, CA: Sage Publications.

Roloff, M. E., & Cloven, D. H. (1990). The chilling effect in interpersonal relationships: The reluctance to speak one's mind. In D. D. Cahn (Ed.), *Intimates in Conflict: A Communication Perspective* (pp. 49–76). Hillsdale, NJ: Erlbaum.

Roloff, M. E. & Johnson, K. L. (2002). Serial arguing over the relational life course: antecedents and consequences. In A. L. Vangelisti, H. T. Reis, and M. Fitzpatrick, *Stability and Change in Relationships* (pp. 107–128). Cambridge, UK: Cambridge University Press.

Roloff, M. E. & Reznik, R. M. (2008). Communication during serial arguments: Connections with individuals mental and physical health. In M. T. Motley (Ed.). *Studies in Applied Communication* (pp. 97–119). Thousand Oaks, CA: Sage.

Samovar, L. A., & Porter, R. E. (2009). *Communication Between Cultures* (7th ed.). Boston, MA: Wadsworth/Cengage.

Sangrestano, L. M., Heavey, C. L., & Christensen, A. (2006). Individual differences versus social structural approaches to explaining demand-withdraw and social influence behaviors. In K. Dindia & D. J.

Canary (Eds.), *Sex Differences and Similarities in Communication* (2nd ed., pp. 378–395). Mahwah, NJ: Lawrence Erlbaum.

Sillars, A. L., & Weisberg, J. (1987). Conflict as a social skill. In M. E. Roloff & G. R. Miller (Eds.), *Interpersonal Processes: New Directions in Communication Research* (pp. 140–171). Beverly Hills, CA: Sage.

Spears, R., & Lea, M. (1992). Social influence and the influence of the "social" in computer-mediated communication. In M. Lea (ed.) *Contexts of computer-mediated communication* (pp. 30–65). Hemel Hempstead: Harvester Wheatsheaf.

Thomas, K. W. (1976). Conflict and Conflict Management. In M. D. Dunnette (Ed.), *Handbook of Industrial and Organizational Psychology* (pp. 889–935). Chicago, IL: Rand-McNally.

Ting-Toomey, S. & Chung L. C. (2005). *Understanding Intercultural Communication.* New York, NY: Oxford University Press. 274–281.

Ting-Toomey, S. (1985). Toward a theory of conflict and culture. In W. Gudykunst, L, Stewart, & Ting-Toomey (Eds.), *Communication, Culture, and Organizational Processes.* Beverly Hills, CA: Sage.

Ting-Toomey, S. (1986). Conflict communication styles: A face negotiation theory. In Y. Y. Kim & W. Gudykunst (Eds.) *Theories of Intercultural Communication.* Newbury Park, CA: Sage.

Ting-Toomey, S. (2006). Managing intercultural conflicts effectively. In L. A. Samovar & R. E. Porter (Eds.), *Intercultural Communication: A Reader* (11th ed., pp. 366–377). Belmont, CA: Wadsworth.

Ting-Toomey, S., & Kurogi, A. (1998). Facework competence in intercultural conflict: An updated face negotiation theory. *International Journal of Intercultural Relations, 22,*187–225.

Ting-Toomey, S., Oetzel, J., & Yee-Jung, K. (2001) Self-construal

types and conflict management styles. *Communication Reports, 14,* 87–104.

Titsworth, B. S., & Kiewra, K. A. (2004). Organizational lecture cues and student notetaking as facilitators of student learning. *Contemporary Educational Psychology, 29,* 447–461.

Tokunaga, R. S., & Rains, S. A. (2010). An evaluation of two characterizations of the relationships between problematic Internet use, time spent using the Internet, and psychosocial problems. *Human Communication Research, 36,* 512–545.

Waldron, V. R. & Kelley, D. L. *Communicating Forgiveness* Thousand Oaks, CA: Sage.

Whang, L. S.-M., Lee, S., & Chang, G. (2003). Internet over-users' psychological profiles: A behavior sampling analysis on Internet addiction. *CyberPsychology & Behavior, 6,* 143–150.

Whetten, D. A., & Cameron, K. S. (2010). *Developing Management Skills* (8th ed.). Upper Saddle River, NJ: Prentice Hall.

Chapter 13

Baron, N. S. (2008). *Always on: Language in an online and mobile world.* New York: Oxford University Press.

Bartholomew, K., & Horowitz, L. M. (1991). Attachment styles among young adults: A test of a four-category model. *Journal of Personality and Social Psychology, 61,* 226–244.

Baumrind, D. (1971). Current patterns of parental authority. *Developmental Psychology Monographs, 4,* 99–102.

Bloch, J. D. (1980). *Friendship.* New York: Macmillan.

Bowlby, J. (1982). *Attachment and Loss: Vol. 1* (2nd ed.). New York: Basic Books.

Dickson, F. C. (1995). The best is yet to be: Research on long-lasting marriages. In J. T. Wood & S. Duck (Eds.), *Under-Studied Relationships: Off the Beaten Track*

(pp. 22–50). Thousand Oaks, CA: Sage.

Fehr, B. (1996). *Friendship Processes.* Thousand Oaks, CA: Sage.

Feinstein, Emily. *The Importance of Family Dinners, VI.* The National Center on Addiction and Substance Abuse at Columbia University. (September, 2010). Available online: http://www.casacolumbia. org/upload/2010/20100922family dinners6.pdf

Fischer, J. L., & Narus, Jr., L. R., (1981). Sex roles and intimacy in same-sex and other-sex relationships. *Psychology of Women Quarterly, 5,* 444–455.

Fitzpatrick, M. A. (1988). *Between Husbands and Wives: Communication in Marriage.* Beverly Hills, CA: Sage.

Fitzpatrick, M. A. (2006). Epilogue: The future of family communication theory and research. In L. H. Turner & R. L. West (Eds.) *The Family Communication Sourcebook* (p. 491). Thousand Oaks, CA: Sage.

Fitzpatrick, M. A., & Badzinski, D. M. (1994). All in the family: Interpersonal communication in kin relationships. In M. L. Knapp & G. R. Miller (Eds.), *Handbook of Interpersonal Communication* (2nd ed., pp. 726–771). Thousand Oaks, CA: Sage.

Fitzpatrick, M. A., & Bochner, A. (1981). Perspectives on self and other: Male-female differences in perceptions of communication behavior. *Sex Roles, 7,* 523–535.

Fitzpatrick, M. A., & Caughlin, J. (2003). Interpersonal communication in family relationships. In M. Knapp & J. Daly (Eds.), *Handbook of Interpersonal Communication* (pp. 726–778). Thousand Oaks, CA: Sage.

Fitzpatrick, M. A., & Koerner, A. (2002). A theory of family communication. *Communication Theory, 12*(1), 70–91.

Fitzpatrick, M. A., & Ritchie, L. D. (1994). Communication schemata within the family: Multiple perspectives on family interaction. *Human Communication Research, 20,* 275–301.

Floyd, K. (2006). *Communicating Affection: Interpersonal behavior and social context.* New York: Cambridge University Press.

Floyd, K., & Riforgiate, S. (2008). Affectionate communication received from spouses predicts stress hormone levels in healthy adults. *Communication Monographs, 75,* 353–370.

Frei, J. R., and Shaver, P. R. (2002). Respect in close relationships: Prototype definition, self-report assessment, and initial correlates. *Personal Relationships, 9,* 121–139.

Galvin, K. M., Bylund, C. L., & Brommel, B. J. (2003). *Family communication: Cohesion and change* (6th ed.). New York: Allyn & Bacon.

Gould, O. (2004). Telling stories and getting acquainted: How age matters. In M. W. Pratt & B. H. Fiese (Eds.), *Family Stories and the Lifecourse* (pp. 327–351). Mahwah, NJ: Erlbaum.

Guerrero, L. K., Andersen, P. A., & Afifi, W. A. (2011). *Close encounters: Communication in relationships* (3rd ed.). Los Angeles, CA: Sage.

Haythornthwaite, C. (2002). Strong, weak, and latent ties and the impact of new media. *Information Society, 18,* 385–401.

Haythornthwaite, C. (2005). Social networks and Internet connectivity effects. *Information, Communication & Society, 8,* 125–147.

Humphreys, L. (2007). Mobile social networks and social practice: A case study of Dodgeball. *Journal of Computer-Mediated Communication, 13*(1).

Knobloch, L. K., & Solomon, D. H. (2002). Information seeking beyond initial interaction: Negotiating relational uncertainty within close relationships. *Human Communication Research, 28,* 243–257.

Le Poire, B. A., Shepard, C., & Duggan, A. (1999). Nonverbal involvement, expressiveness, and pleasantness as predicted by parental and partner attachment style. *Communication Monographs, 66,* 293–311.

LePoire, B. A. (2006). *Family communication: Nurturing and control in a changing world.* Thousand Oaks, CA: Sage.

Levine, P. A. (1997). *Walking the Tiger: Healing Trauma.* Berkeley, CA: North Atlantic Books.

Marsh, P. (Ed.). (1988). *Eye to Eye: How People Interact.* Topsfield, MA: Salem House.

Mehrabian, A. (1981) *Silent Messages: Implicit communication of emotions and attitudes.* Belmont, CA: Wadsworth Publishing.

Morton, T. L. (1978). Intimacy and reciprocity of exchange: A comparison of spouses and strangers. *Journal of Personality and Social Psychology, 36,* 72–81.

Pelusi, Nando. Jealousy: A Voice of Possessiveness Past. *Psychology Today,* July 6, 2006: 34–35.

Peplau, L. A. (1993). Lesbian and gay relationships. In L. D. Garnets & D. C. Kimmel (Eds.) *Psychological Perspectives on Lesbian and Gay Male Experiences* (pp. 395–419). New York: Columbia University Press.

Prager, K. J. (November, 1997) Intimacy-Oriented Couple Therapy. Workshop presented at the Annual Meeting, Association for the Advancement of Behavior Therapy, Miami, FL.

Reis, H. T. (1998). Gender differences in intimacy and related behaviors: Context and process. In D. J. Canary & K. Dindia (Eds.), *Sex Differences and Similarities in Communication: Critical Essays and Empirical Investigations of Sex and Gender in Interaction* (pp. 203–231). Mahwah, NJ: Erlbaum.

Reis, H. T., & Shaver, P. (1988). Intimacy as an interpersonal process. In S. Duck (Ed.), *Handbook of personal relationships* (pp. 367–389). Chichester, England: Wiley.

Ryan, E. B., Pearce, K. A., Anas, A. P., & Norris, J. E. (2004). Writing a connection: Intergenerational communication through stories. In M. W. Pratt & B. H. Fiese (Eds.), *Family Stories and the Lifecourse* (pp. 375–398). Mahwah, NJ: Erlbaum.

Samter, W. (2003). Friendship interaction skills across the life span. In J. O. Greene & B. R. Burleson (Eds.), *Handbook of communication and social interaction skills* (pp. 637–684). Mahwah, NJ: Erlbaum.

Segrin, C. & Flora, J. (2005). *Family communication.* Mahwah, NJ: Erlbaum.

Sprecher, S., Christopher, F. S., & Cate, R. (2006). Sexuality in close relationships. In A. Vangelisti & D. Perlman (Eds.), *The Cambridge Handbook of Personal Relationships* (pp. 463–482). Cambridge University Press, New York.

Stern, D. N. (1993). The role of feelings for an interpersonal self. In U. Neisser (Ed.), *The Perceived Self: Ecological and Interpersonal Sources of Self Knowledge.* New York, NY: Cambridge University Press.

Walther, J. B. (1992). Interpersonal effects in computer-mediated interaction. *Communication Research, 19,* 52–90.

Walther, J. B. (1994). Anticipated ongoing interaction versus channel effects on relational communication in computer-mediated interaction. *Human Communication Research, 20,* 473–501.

Walther, J. B. (1996). Computer-mediated communication: Impersonal, interpersonal, and hyperpersonal interaction. *Communication Research, 23,* 3–43.

Werner, C. M., Altman, I., Brown, B. B., & Ginat, J. (1993). Celebrations in personal relationships: A transactional/dialectical perspective. In S. Duck (Ed.), *Social Context and Relationships* (pp. 109–138). Newbury Park, CA: Sage.

Whitton, S. W., Waldinger, R. J., Shultz, M. S., Allen, J. P., Crowell,

J. A., & Hauser, S. T. (2008). Prospective associations from family-of-origin interactions to adult marital interactions and relationship adjustment. *Journal of Family Psychology, 22,* 274–286.

Wood, J. T. (2010). *Gendered Lives: Communication, Gender and Culture* (9th ed.). Belmont, CA: Wadsworth.

Chapter 14

Baron, R. A. & Neuman, J. H. (1996). Workplace violence and workplace aggression: evidence of their relative frequency and potential causes. *Aggressive Behavior* 22: 161–173.

Berryman-Fink, C. (1997). Gender issues, management style, mobility and harassment. In P. Y. Byers (Ed.), *Organizational Communication: Theory and Behavior* (pp. 259–283). Boston: Allyn & Bacon.

Beatty, K. (2010, July, 1) The Math Behind the Networking Claim. Accessed online at: http://blog.jobfully.com/2010/07/the-math-behind-the-networking-claim/

Conrad, C., & Poole, M. S. (2005). *Strategic Organizational Communication in a Global Economy.* Belmont, CA: Thompson Wadsworth.

Eisenberg, E. M., & Goodall, H. L. (2004). *Organizational Communication: Balancing Creativity and Constraint.* New York: Bedford St. Martin's.

Farr, M. J. (2008). *The Quick Resume and Cover Letter Book: Write and Use An Effective Resume in Only One Day.* Indianapolis: JIST Publishing

Graen, G. (1976). Role making processes within complex organizations. In M. D. Dunette (Ed.), *Handbook of Industrial and Organizational Psychology* (pp. 1201–1245). Chicago: Rand McNally.

Graen, G. B. & Uhl-Bien. M. (1995). Relationship-based approach to leadership: Development of leader-member exchange (LMX) theory over 25 years: Applying a multi-level multi-domain perspective. *Leadership Quarterly, 6*(2). 219–242.

Jablin, F. M., & Krone, K. J. (1994). Task/work relationships: A life-span perspective. In M. L. Knapp & G. R. Miller (Eds.), *Handbook of Interpersonal Communication* (2nd ed., pp. 621–675). Thousand Oaks, CA: Sage.

Kleinman, S. (2007). *Displacing Place: Mobile Communication in the Twenty-First Century.* New York: Peter Lang.

Kram, K. E. & Isabella, L. A. (1985). Mentoring alternatives: the role of peer relationships in career development. *Academy of Management Journal, 28*(1), 110–132.

Larson, C. E., & LaFasto, F. M. J. (1989). *Team Work: What Must Go Right / What Can Go Wrong.* Newbury Park, CA: Sage.

Lee, J., & Jablin, F. M. (1995). Maintenance communication in superior-subordinate work relationships. *Human Communication Research, 22,* 220–257.

Light, J. (2011, April, 4). For job seekers, company sites beat online job boards, social media. *The Wall Street Journal.* Accessed online at: http://online.wsj.com/article/SB10001424052748703806304576236731318345282.html?KEYWORDS=JOE+LIGHT

Odden, C. M. & Sias, P. M. (1997). Peer communication relationships, psychological climate, and gender. *Communication Quarterly, 45,* 153–166.

Potoker, E. S. (2005). *Managing Diverse Working Styles: The Leadership Competitive Advantage.* Mason, OH: South Western Publishing.

Rai, S. (2002). Preventing workplace aggression and violence—A role for occupational therapy. *Journal of Prevention, Assessment, and Rehabilitation, 18,* 15–22.

Schat, A. C. H., Frone, M. R., & Kelloway, E. K. (2006). Prevalence of workplace aggression in the U. S. workforce: Findings from a national study. In E. K. Kelloway, J. Barling, and J. Hurrell (Eds.), *Handbook of workplace violence* (pp. 47–89). Thousand Oaks, CA: Sage.

Sias, P. M., & Jablin, F. M. (1995). Differential superior-subordinate relations, perceptions of fairness, and coworker communication. *Human Communication Research, 22,* 5–38.

Stewart, C. J., & Cash, W. B. (2008). *Interviewing: Principles and Practices* (12th ed.). Boston: McGraw Hill Higher Education.

Tannen, D. (1995). The power of talk: Who gets heard and why. *Harvard Business Review, 75*(5), 138–148.

Taylor, J. & Hardy, J. (2004). *Monster Careers: How to Land the Job of Your Life.* New York: Penguin.

Varner, I., & Beamer, L. (1995). *Inter-cultural Communication in the Global Workplace.* Chicago: Irwin.

Whetten, D. A., & Cameron, K. S. (2005). *Developing Management Skills* (6th ed.). Upper Saddle River, NJ: Prentice Hall.

Whetten, D. A., & Cameron, K. S. (2005). *Developing management skills* (6th ed.). Upper Saddle River, NJ: Prentice Hall.

Zemke, R., Raines, C., & Filipczak, B. (2000). *Generations at Work.* New York: AMACOM.

Photo Credits

Index

Note: images are indicated by an italic page number; tables are indicated by an italic *t;* and figures are indicated by an italic *f.*